AFRICA
NINTH EDITION

Dr. F. Jeffress Ramsay

OTHER BOOKS IN THE GLOBAL STUDIES SERIES
- China
- Europe
- India and South Asia
- Japan and the Pacific Rim
- Latin America
- The Middle East
- Russia, the Eurasian Republics, and
  Central/Eastern Europe

McGraw-Hill/Dushkin Company
530 Old Whitfield Street, Guilford, Connecticut 06437
Visit us on the Internet—*http://www.dushkin.com*

STAFF

Ian A. Nielsen	Publisher
Brenda S. Filley	Director of Production
Lisa M. Clyde	Developmental Editor
Roberta Monaco	Editor
Charles Vitelli	Designer
Robin Zarnetske	Permissions Coordinator
Joseph Offredi	Permissions Assistant
Lisa Holmes-Doebrick	Administrative Coordinator
Laura Levine	Graphics
Michael Campbell	Graphics/Cover Design
Tom Goddard	Graphics
Eldis Lima	Graphics
Nancy Norton	Graphics
Juliana Arbo	Typesetting Supervisor
Larry Killian	Copier Coordinator

Cataloging in Publication Data
Main Entry under title: Global Studies: Africa. 9th ed.
    1. Africa—History—1960–. I. Title: Africa. II. Ramsay, F. Jeffress, *comp.*
ISBN 0–07–243371–X   960.3   91–71258

Ninth Edition

Printed in the United States of America   1234567890BAHBAH54321   Printed on Recycled Paper

AFRICA

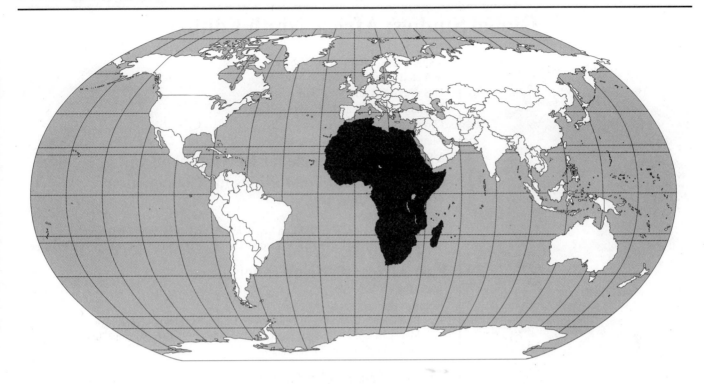

AUTHOR/EDITOR

Dr. F. Jeffress Ramsay

Dr. F. Jeffress ("Jeff") Ramsay, the author/editor of *Global Studies: Africa,* obtained his Ph.D. in African history from Boston University. He has extensive experience in both secondary and tertiary education in the United States and in Botswana, where he is currently the principal of Legae Academy in Gaborone. Dr. Ramsay writes regularly for Botswana newspapers as well as popular and academic periodicals; he is the chairperson of the Botswana Media Consultative Council; and he has been involved in the development of regional museums. A recent recipient of Botswana's Presidential Order of Honour for his varied contributions to the country, Dr. Ramsay is a Botswana citizen.

Along with Barry Morton and Themba Mgadla, Dr. Ramsay is the coauthor of *Building a Nation, a History of Botswana from 1800–1910* (Longman Botswana, 1996); he is the coeditor with Fred Morton of *Birth of Botswana, a History of the Bechuanaland Protectorate from 1910–1966* (Longman Botswana, 1987); he coauthored *A Historical Dictionary of Botswana* (Scarecrow Press, 3rd ed., 1997), with Barry Morton and Fred Morton; he collaborated with Barry Morton on *The Making of a President, Sir Ketumile Masire's Early Years* (Pula Publishing, 1996) and on *Comrade Fish, Memories of a Freedom Fighter on the Botswana Underground* (Pula Publishing, 2000); and, along with Lucey Clarke, he coauthored *New Three Year I. C. Social Studies Revision Notes* (Tasalls, 1997).

SERIES CONSULTANT
H. Thomas Collins
PROJECT LINKS
George Washington University

Contents

Global Studies: Africa, Ninth Edition

Africa   Page 9

North Africa   Page 83

Southern Africa   Page 94

West Africa   Page 128

Using Global Studies: Africa

THE GLOBAL STUDIES SERIES

The Global Studies series was created to help readers acquire a basic knowledge and understanding of the regions and countries in the world. Each volume provides a foundation of information—geographic, cultural, economic, political, historical, artistic, and religious—that will allow readers to better assess the current and future problems within these countries and regions and to comprehend how events there might affect their own well-being. In short, these volumes present the background information necessary to respond to the realities of our global age.

Each of the volumes in the Global Studies series is crafted under the careful direction of an author/editor—an expert in the area under study. The author/editors teach and conduct research and have traveled extensively through the regions about which they are writing.

In this *Global Studies: Africa* edition, the author/editor has written an introductory essay on the continent as a whole, several regional essays, and country reports for each of the countries included.

MAJOR FEATURES OF
THE GLOBAL STUDIES SERIES

The Global Studies volumes are organized to provide concise information on the regions and countries within those areas under study. The major sections and features of the books are described here.

Regional Essays

For *Global Studies: Africa,* the author/editor has written several essays focusing on the religious, cultural, sociopolitical, and economic differences and similarities of the countries and peoples in the various regions of Africa. Regional maps accompany the essays.

Country Reports

Concise reports are written for each of the countries within the region under study. These reports are the heart of each Global Studies volume. *Global Studies: Africa, Ninth Edition,* contains 48 country reports.

The country reports are composed of five standard elements. Each report contains a detailed map visually positioning the country among its neighboring states; a summary of statistical information; a current essay providing important historical, geographical, political, cultural, and economic information; a historical timeline, offering a convenient visual survey of a few key historical events; and four "graphic indicators," with summary statements about the country in terms of development, freedom, health/welfare, and achievements.

A Note on the Statistical Reports

The statistical information provided for each country has been drawn from a wide range of sources. (The most frequently referenced are listed on page 234.) Every effort has been made to provide the most current and accurate information available. However, sometimes the information cited by these sources differs to some extent; and, all too often, the most current information available for some countries is somewhat dated. Aside from these occasional difficulties, the statistical summary of each country is generally quite complete and up to date. Care should be taken, however, in using these statistics (or, for that matter, any published statistics) in making hard comparisons among countries. We have also provided comparable statistics for the United States and Canada, which can be found on pages viii and ix.

World Press Articles

Within each Global Studies volume is reprinted a number of articles carefully selected by our editorial staff and the author/editor from a broad range of international periodicals and newspapers. The articles have been chosen for currency, interest, and their differing perspectives on the subject countries. There are 14 articles in *Global Studies: Africa, Ninth Edition.*

The articles section is preceded by an annotated table of contents as well as a topic guide. The annotated table of contents offers a brief summary of each article, while the topic guide indicates the main theme(s) of each article. Thus, readers desiring to focus on articles dealing with a particular theme, say, the environment, may refer to the topic guide to find those articles.

WWW Sites

An extensive annotated list of selected World Wide Web sites can be found on the facing page (vii) in this edition of *Global Studies: Africa.* In addition, the URL addresses for country-specific Web sites are provided on the statistics page of most countries. All of the Web site addresses were correct and operational at press time. Instructors and students alike are urged to refer to those sites often to enhance their understanding of the region and to keep up with current events.

Glossary, Bibliography, Index

At the back of each Global Studies volume, readers will find a glossary of terms and abbreviations, which provides a quick reference to the specialized vocabulary of the area under study and to the standard abbreviations used throughout the volume.

Following the glossary is a bibliography, which lists general works, national histories, and current-events publications and periodicals that provide regular coverage on Africa.

The index at the end of the volume is an accurate reference to the contents of the volume. Readers seeking specific information and citations should consult this standard index.

Currency and Usefulness

Global Studies: Africa, like the other Global Studies volumes, is intended to provide the most current and useful information available necessary to understand the events that are shaping the cultures of the region today.

This volume is revised on a regular basis. The statistics are updated, regional essays and country reports revised, and world press articles replaced. In order to accomplish this task, we turn to our author/editor, our advisory boards, and—hopefully—to you, the users of this volume. Your comments are more than welcome. If you have an idea that you think will make the next edition more useful, an article or bit of information that will make it more current, or a general comment on its organization, content, or features that you would like to share with us, please send it in for serious consideration.

Selected World Wide Web Sites for Africa

All of these Web sites are hot-linked through the *Global Studies* homepage:
http://www.dushkin.com/globalstudies/ **(just click on a book).**

Some Web sites are continually changing their structure and content, so the information listed may not always be available.

GENERAL SITES

BBC World Service—*http://www.bbc.co.uk/worldservice/ index.htm*—The BBC, one of the world's most successful radio networks, provides the latest news from around the world, including from almost all of the African countries.

CNN Online Page—*http://www.cnn.com*—The U.S. 24-hour video news channel provides news that is updated every few hours. Text, pictures, and film are available along with good external links.

C-SPAN ONLINE—*http://www.c-span.org*—Access C-SPAN International on the Web for International Programming Highlights and archived C-SPAN programs.

International Network Information Center at University of Texas—*http://inic.utexas.edu*—This gateway has pointers to international sites, including Africa, as well as African Studies Resources.

I-Trade International Trade Resources & Data Exchange—*http:// www.i-trade.com*—Monthly exchange-rate data, U.S. Global Trade Outlook, and recent World Fact Book statistical demographic and geographic data for 180-plus countries can be found on this Web site.

Penn Library: Resources by Subject—*http://www.library.upenn. edu/resources/subject/subject.html*—This vast site is rich in links to information about African studies, including demography and population.

Political Science RESOURCES—*http://www.psr.keele.ac.uk*—A dynamic gateway to sources available via European addresses, it provides a list of country names.

ReliefWeb—*http://www.reliefweb.int*—The UN's Department of Humanitarian Affairs clearinghouse for international humanitarian emergencies presents daily news updates, including Reuters, VOA, PANA.

Social Science Information Gateway (SOSIG)—*http://sosig.esrc. bris. ac.uk*—The Economic and Social Research Council (ESRC) project catalogs 22 subjects and lists developing countries' URL addresses.

Speech and Transcript Center—*http://gwis2.circ.gwu.edu/ ~gprice/speech.htm*—This Web site is the repository of transcripts of every kind, from radio and television, to speeches by world government leaders, to the proceedings of groups such as the United Nations, NATO, and the World Bank.

United Nations System—*http://www.unsystem.org*—The official Web site for the United Nations system of organizations can be found here. Everything is listed alphabetically, and examples include UNICC and the Food and Agriculture Organization.

UN Development Programme (UNDP)—*http://www. undp.org*—Publications and current information on world poverty, Mission Statement, UN Development Fund for Women, and more are available on this Web site. Be sure to see Poverty Clock.

UN Environmental Programme (UNEP)—*http://www. unep.org*—This UNEP official site provides information on UN environmental programs, products, services, and events. A search engine is also available.

U.S. Agency for International Development (USAID)—*http://www.usaid.gov/region/afr*—The U.S. policy regarding assistance to African countries is presented at this site.

U.S. Central Intelligence Agency (CIA)—*http://www. odci.gov*—This site includes publications of the CIA, such as the World Fact Book, Factbook on Intelligence, Handbook of International Economic Statistics, and CIA maps.

U.S. Department of State—*http://www.state.gov/countries/*—Organized alphabetically, data on human rights issues, international organizations, and country reports as well as other data are available here.

World Bank Group—*http://www.worldbank.org*—News (press releases, summary of new projects, speeches), publications, topics in development, and reports on countries and regions can be accessed on this Web site. Links to other financial organizations are also provided.

World Health Organization (WHO)—*http://www.who.ch*—Maintained by WHO's headquarters in Geneva, Switzerland, this site uses the Excite search engine to conduct keyword searches.

World Trade Organization (WTO)—*http://www.wto.org*—WTO's Web site topics include information on world trade systems, data on textiles, intellectual property rights, legal frameworks, trade and environmental policies, recent agreements, and other issues.

AFRICAN SITES

Africa News Web Site: Crisis in the Great Lakes Region—*http:// www.africanews.org/specials/greatlakes.html*—African News Web Site on Great Lakes (Rwanda, Burundi, Zaire, and Kenya, Tanzania, Uganda) can be found here with frequent updates and good links to other sites. It is possible to order e-mail crisis updates here.

African Policy Information Center (APIC)—*http://www.africapolicy. org*—Developed by the Washington Office on Africa to widen policy debate in the United States on African issues, this Web site includes special topic briefs, regular reports, and documents on African politics.

Africa: South of the Sahara—*http://www-sul.stanford.edu/depts/ ssrg/africa/guide.html*—On this site, Topics and Regions link headings will lead to a wealth of information.

African Studies WWW (U.Penn)—*http://www.sas.upenn.edu/ African_Studies/AS.html*—This Web site provides facts about each African country, which includes news, statistics, and links to other Web sites.

Library of Congress Country Studies—*http://lcweb2.loc.gov/ frd/cs/cshome.html#toc/*—Of the 71 countries that are covered in the continuing series of books available at this Web site, at least a dozen of them are in Africa.

South African Government Index—*http://www.polity.org.za/ gnuindex.html*—This official site includes links to government agencies, data on structures of government, and links to detailed documents.

Weekly Mail & Guardian (Johannesburg)—*http://www.mg.co.za/mg/*—This free electronic daily South African newspaper includes archived back issues as well as links to other related sites on Africa.

Most individual country report pages have additional Web sites.

The United States (United States of America)

GEOGRAPHY

Area in Square Miles (Kilometers):
3,618,770 (9,578,626) (slightly larger than China)

Capital (Population): Washington, D.C. (567,100)

Environmental Concerns: air pollution resulting in acid rain; water pollution from runoff of pesticides and fertilizers; desertification; habitat loss; other concerns

Geographical Features: vast central plain, mountains in the west; hills and low mountains in the east; rugged mountains and broad river valleys in Alaska; volcanic topography in Hawaii

Climate: mostly temperate; wide regional variations

PEOPLE

Population

Total: 270,312,000

Annual Growth Rate: 0.87%

Rural/Urban Population Ratio: 24/76

Major Languages: predominantly English; a sizable Spanish-speaking minority; many others

Ethnic Makeup: 83% white; 12% black; 5% Asian, Amerindian, and others

Religions: 56% Protestant; 28% Roman Catholic; 2% Jewish; 14% others or no affiliation

Health

Life Expectancy at Birth: 73 years (male); 80 years (female)

Infant Mortality Rate (Ratio): 6.44/1,000

Average Caloric Intake: 138% of FAO minimum

Physicians Available (Ratio): 1/381

Education

Adult Literacy Rate: 97.9% (official) (estimates vary widely)

Compulsory (Ages): 7–16; free

COMMUNICATION

Telephones: 1 per 1.6 people

Daily Newspaper Circulation: 228 per 1,000 people; approximately 63,000,000 circulation

Televisions: 1 per 1.2 people

TRANSPORTATION

Highways in Miles (Kilometers): 3,906,960 (6,261,154)

Railroads in Miles (Kilometers): 149,161 (240,000)

Usable Airfields: 13,387

Motor Vehicles in Use: 200,500,000

GOVERNMENT

Type: federal republic

Independence Date: July 4, 1776 (from Britain)

Head of State: President George W. Bush

Political Parties: Democratic Party; Republican Party; others of minor political significance

Suffrage: universal at 18

MILITARY

Military Expenditures (% of GDP): 3.8%

Current Disputes: none

ECONOMY

Per Capita Income/GDP: $30,200/$8.08 trillion

GDP Growth Rate: 3.8%

Inflation Rate: 2%

Unemployment Rate: 4.9%

Labor Force: 136,300,000

Natural Resources: metallic and non-metallic minerals; petroleum; natural gas; timber

Agriculture: food grains; feed crops; oil-bearing crops; livestock; dairy products

Industry: diversified in both capital- and consumer-goods industries

Exports: $625.1 billion (primary partners Canada, Western Europe, Japan, Mexico)

Imports: $822 billion (primary partners Canada, Western Europe, Japan, Mexico)

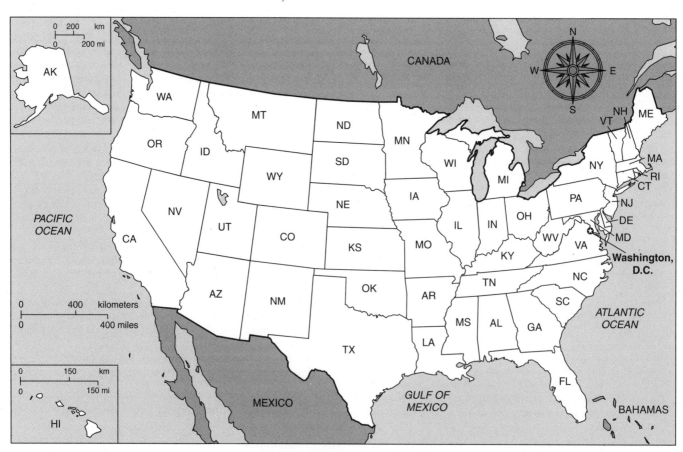

Canada

GEOGRAPHY

Area in Square Miles (Kilometers):
3,850,790 (9,976,140) (slightly larger than the United States)

Capital (Population): Ottawa (1,000,000)

Environmental Concerns: air pollution and resulting acid rain severely affecting lakes and damaging forests; water pollution

Geographical Features: permafrost in the north; mountains in the west; central plains

Climate: from temperate in south to subarctic and arctic in north

PEOPLE

Population

Total: 30,676,000

Annual Growth Rate: 1.09%

Rural/Urban Population Ratio: 23/77

Major Languages: both English and French are official

Ethnic Makeup: 40% British Isles origin; 27% French origin; 20% other European; 1.5% indigenous Indian and Eskimo; 11.5% others, mostly Asian

Religions: 46% Roman Catholic; 16% United Church; 10% Anglican; 28% others

Health

Life Expectancy at Birth: 76 years (male); 83 years (female)

Infant Mortality Rate (Ratio): 5.59/1,000

Average Caloric Intake: 127% of FAO minimum

Physicians Available (Ratio): 1/464

Education

Adult Literacy Rate: 97%

Compulsory (Ages): primary school

COMMUNICATION

Telephones: 1 per 1.7 people

Daily Newspaper Circulation: 189 per 1,000 people

Televisions: 1 per 1.5 people

TRANSPORTATION

Highways in Miles (Kilometers): 637,104 (1,021,000)

Railroads in Miles (Kilometers): 48,764 (78,148)

Usable Airfields: 1,139

Motor Vehicles in Use: 16,700,000

GOVERNMENT

Type: confederation with parliamentary democracy

Independence Date: July 1, 1867 (from Britain)

Head of State/Government: Queen Elizabeth II; Prime Minister Jean Chrétien

Political Parties: Progressive Conservative Party; Liberal Party; New Democratic Party; Reform Party; Bloc Québécois

Suffrage: universal at 18

MILITARY

Military Expenditures (% of GDP): 1.53%

Current Disputes: none

ECONOMY

Currency ($U.S. Equivalent): 1.53 Canadian dollars = $1

Per Capita Income/GDP: $21,700/$658 billion

GDP Growth Rate: 3.5%

Inflation Rate: 1.8%

Unemployment Rate: 8.6%

Labor Force: 15,300,000

Natural Resources: petroleum; coal; natural gas; fish and other wildlife; minerals; cement; forestry products

Agriculture: grains; livestock; dairy products; potatoes; hogs; poultry and eggs; tobacco

Industry: oil production and refining; natural-gas development; fish products; wood and paper products; chemicals; transportation equipment

Exports: $208.6 billion (primary partners United States, Japan, Britain)

Imports: $194.4 billion (primary partners United States, Japan, Britain)

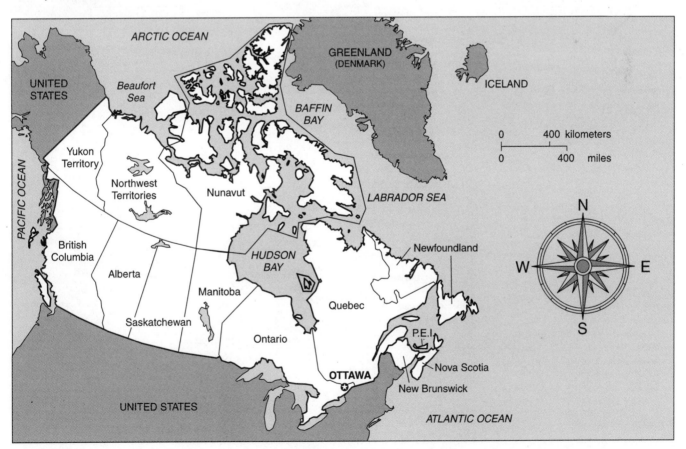

This map is provided to give you a graphic picture of where the countries of the world are located, the relationships they have with their region and neighbors, and their positions relative to economic and political power blocs. We have focused on certain areas to illustrate these crowded regions more clearly.

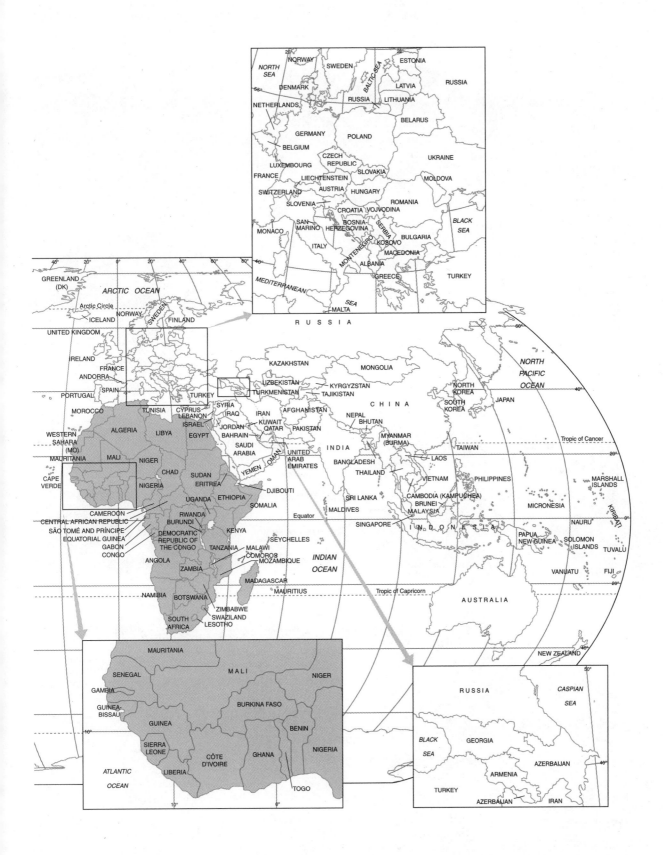

Africa

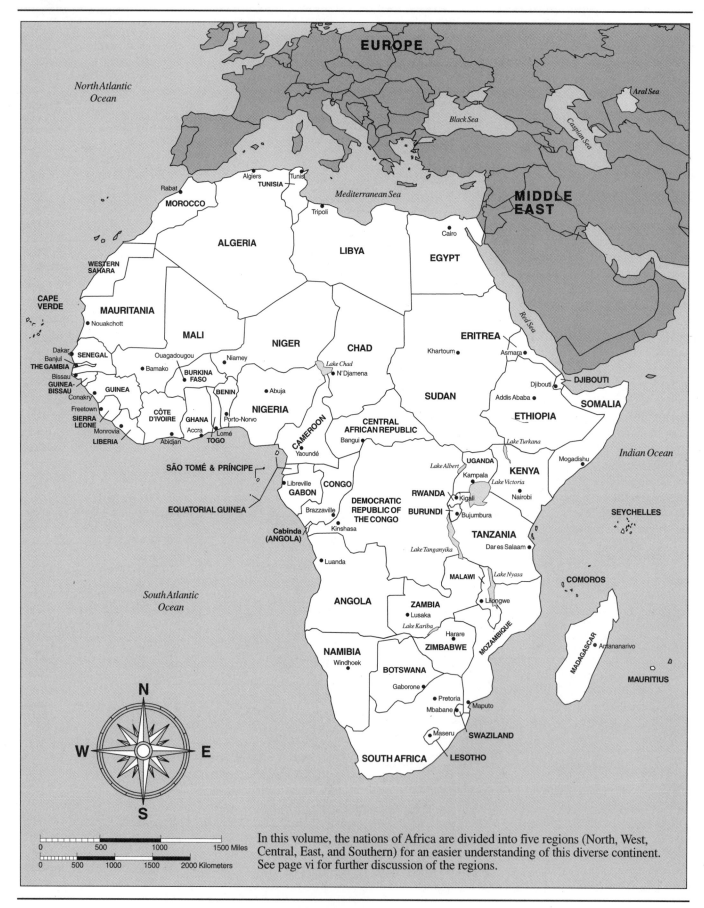

In this volume, the nations of Africa are divided into five regions (North, West, Central, East, and Southern) for an easier understanding of this diverse continent. See page vi for further discussion of the regions.

Africa: The Struggle for Development

Seventeen African nations gained their independence in 1960, liberating most of the continent from colonial rule. The times were electric. In country after country, the flags of Great Britain, Belgium, France, and the United Nations were replaced by the banners of new states, whose leaders offered idealistic promises to remake the continent and thus the world. Hopes were high, and the most ambitious of goals seemed obtainable. Even non-Africans spoke of the resource-rich continent as being on the verge of a developmental takeoff. Some of the old, racist myths about Africa were at last being questioned.

Yet today, four decades after the great freedom year, conditions throughout Africa are sobering rather than euphoric. For most Africans, independence has been more of a desperate struggle for survival rather than an exhilarating path to development. Now Africa is often described in the global media as a "continent in crisis," a "region in turmoil," "on a precipice," and "suffering"—phrases that echo the sensationalist writings of nineteenth-century missionaries eager to convince others of the continent's need for "salvation." But the modern headlines are far more accurate than the mission tracts of yesteryear. Today, millions of Africans are indeed seeking some form of salvation—but now from the grinding poverty, pestilence, and, in many areas, wars that afflict their lives. Perhaps this hunger is why contemporary African evangelists are so much more successful in swelling their congregations than were their counterparts in the past. It is certainly not for lack of competition; Africa is a continent of many, often overlapping, faiths. In addition to Islam and other spiritual paths, Africans have embraced a myriad of secular ideologies: Marxism, African socialism, people's capitalism, structural adjustment, pan-Africanism, authenticity, nonracialism, the one-party state, and the multiparty state. The list is endless, but salvation seems ever more distant.

Africa's current circumstances are indeed difficult, yet it is also true that the years have brought progress as well as problems. The goals so optimistically pronounced at independence have, for the most part, not been abandoned. Even when the states have faltered, the societies that they encompass have remained dynamic and adaptable to shifting opportunities. The support of strong families continues to allow most Africans to overcome enormous adversity. There are starving children in Africa today, but there are also many more in school uniforms studying to make their dreams a reality.

A DIVERSE CONTINENT

Africa, which is almost four times the size of the United States (excluding Alaska), ranks just below Asia as the world's biggest continent. Well over one quarter of the membership of the United Nations consists of African states—more than 50 in all. Such facts are worth noting, for even well-educated outsiders often lose sight of Africa's continental scope when they discuss its problems and prospects.

Not only is the African continent vast but, archaeology tells us, it was also the cradle of human civilization. It should therefore not be surprising that the 900 million or so contemporary Africans maintain extraordinarily diverse ways of life. They speak more than 1,000 languages and live their lives according to a rich variety of household arrangements, kinship systems, and religious beliefs. The art and music styles of the continent are as varied as its people.

Given its diversity, it is not easy to generalize about Africa. For each statement, there is an exception. However, one aspect that is constant to all African societies is that they have always been changing, albeit in modern times at an ever-increasing rate. Cities have grown and people have moved back and forth between village and town, giving rise to new social groups, institutions, occupations, religions, and forms of communication that have made their mark in the countryside as well as in the urban centers. All Africans, whether they be urban computer programmers or hunter-gatherers living in the remote corners of the Kalahari Desert, have taken on new practices, interests, and burdens, yet they have retained their African identity. Uniquely African institutions, values, and histories underlie contemporary lifestyles throughout the continent.

Memories of past civilizations are a source of pride and community. The medieval Mali and Ghana empires, the glory of Pharaonic Egypt, the Fulani caliphate of northern Nigeria, the knights of Kanem and Bornu, the Great Zimbabwe, and the Kingdom of the Kongo, among others, are all remembered. The past is connected to the present through the generations and by ties to the land. In a continent where the majority of people are still farmers, land remains "the mother that never dies." It is valued for its fruits and because it is the place to which the ancestors came and were buried.

The art of personal relationships continues to be important. People typically live in large families. Children are considered precious, and large families are still desired for social as well as economic reasons. Elders are an important part of a household; nursing homes and retirement communities generally do not exist. People are not supposed to be loners. "I am because we are" remains a valued precept. In this age of nation-states, the "we" may refer to one's ethnic community, while obligations to one's extended family often take precedence over other loyalties.

Most Africans believe in a spiritual as well as a material world. The continent contains a rich variety of indigenous belief systems, which often coexist with the larger religions of Islam and various Christian sects. Many families believe that their lives are influenced by their ancestors. Africans from all walks of life will seek the services of professional "traditional" healers to explain an illness or suggest remedies for such things as sterility or bad fortune. But this pattern of behavior does not preclude one from turning to scientific medicine; all African governments face strong popular demands for better access to modern health-care facilities.

WOULD YOU BELIEVE?

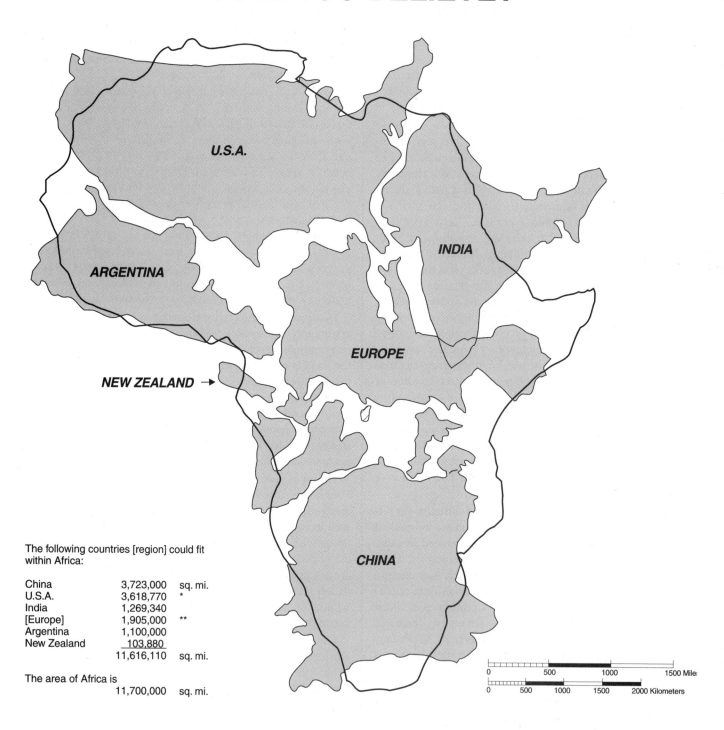

U.S.A.

ARGENTINA

INDIA

EUROPE

NEW ZEALAND →

CHINA

The following countries [region] could fit
within Africa:

China	3,723,000	sq. mi.
U.S.A.	3,618,770	*
India	1,269,340	
[Europe]	1,905,000	**
Argentina	1,100,000	
New Zealand	103,880	
	11,616,110	sq. mi.

The area of Africa is
	11,700,000	sq. mi.

Source of data: *The 1997 Information Please Almanac and 1997 World
Almanac and Book of Facts.*
* Total, land and water, 50 states
** *1997 Information Please Almanac.* Includes Iceland. Excludes the former
European Soviet Union and European Turkey.

Islam has long been a strong force in Africa. Today that religion rivals Christianity as the fastest-growing faith on the continent. The followers of both religions often adapt their faiths to accommodate local traditions and values. Some people also join new religious movements and churches, such as the Brotherhood of the Cross and Star in Nigeria or the Church of Simon Kimbangu in the former Zaire, that link Christian and indigenous beliefs with new ideas and rituals. Like other institutions in the towns and cities, the churches and mosques provide their followers with social networks.

Local art, like local religion, often reflects the influence of the changing world. An airplane is featured on a Nigerian gelede mask, the Apollo space mission inspires a Burkinabe carver, and a Ndebele dance wand is a beaded electric pole.

THE TROUBLED PRESENT

Some of the crises in Africa today threaten its peoples' traditional resiliency. The facts are grim: In material terms, the average African is poorer today than at independence, and it is predicted that poverty will only increase in the immediate future. Drought conditions in recent decades have led to food shortages across the continent. In the 1980s, widespread famine occurred in 22 African nations; the Food and Agriculture Organization (FAO) of the United Nations estimated that 70 percent of all Africans did not have enough to eat. An outpouring of assistance and relief efforts at the time saved as many as 35 million lives. Overall per capita food production in Africa dropped by 12 percent between 1961 and 1995. One factor in the decline has been the tendency of agricultural planners to ignore the fact that up to 70 percent of Africa's food crops are grown by women. It has also been estimated that up to 40 percent of the continent's food crops go uneaten as a result of inadequate transport and storage facilities. Although agricultural production rose modestly in the 1990s, the food crisis continues. In 1994, large parts of East Africa, in particular, faced the prospect of renewed hunger. Other areas have become dependent on outside food aid. Marginal advances in agricultural production, through better incentives to farmers, have often been counterbalanced by declining commodity prices on world markets, explosive population growth, and recurring drought and locust infestations. Problems of climate irregularity, and obtaining and transporting needed goods and supplies require continued assistance and long-range planning. Wood, the average person's source of energy, grows scarcer every year, and most governments have had to contend with the rising cost of imported fuels.

Armed conflicts have devastated portions of Africa. The current carnage in Angola, Djibouti, Liberia, Sierra Leone, Somalia, Sudan, and the former Zaire (now called the Democratic Republic of the Congo), due to internal strife encouraged to greater or lesser degrees by outside forces, places them in a distinct class of suffering—a class that until recently (and that may yet again) also included Chad, Eritrea, Ethio-pia, Mozambique, and Uganda. More than 2 million people have died in these countries over the past decade, while millions more have become refugees. Except for scattered enclaves, normal economic activities have been greatly disrupted or ceased altogether.

Almost all African governments are deeply in debt. In 1991, the foreign debt owed by all the sub-Saharan African countries except South Africa stood at about $175 billion. Although it is smaller in its absolute amount than that of Latin America, as a percentage of its economic output, the continent's debt is the highest in the world and is rising swiftly. The combined gross national product (GNP) for the same countries, whose total populations are in excess of 500 million, was less than $150 billion, a figure that represents only 1.2 percent of the global GNP and is about equal to the GNP of Belgium, a country of 10 million people. In Zambia, an extreme example, the per capita foreign debt theoretically owed by each of its citizens is nearly $1,000, while its annual per capita income is well below that.

A factor that helps to account for Africa's relative poverty is the low level of industrial output of all but a few of its countries. The decline of many commodity prices on the world market has further reduced national incomes. As a result, the foreign exchange needed to import food, machinery, fuel, and other goods is very limited in most African countries. In 1987, the continent's economy grew by only 0.8 percent, far below its population growth rate of about 3.2 percent. In the same year, cereal production declined 8 percent and overall agricultural production grew by only 0.5 percent. There has been some modest improvement in subsequent years. But more recent estimates put the continent's economic growth rate at 1.5 percent—still the world's lowest and far below that of the population growth rate.

In order to obtain money to meet debts and pay for their running expenses, many African governments have been obliged to accept the stringent terms of global lending agencies, most notably the World Bank and the International Monetary Fund (IMF). These lending terms have led to great hardship, especially in the urban areas, through austerity measures such as the abandonment of price controls on basic foodstuffs and the freezing of wages. Many African governments and experts are questioning both the justice and practicality of these terms.

But perhaps the greatest challenge facing Africa today is in the area of health. The HIV/AIDS pandemic has spread at an alarming rate over the past two decades, already claiming millions of lives and threatening millions more. Southern Africa has been especially hard hit in recent years, with more than one in five adults said to be HIV-positive in a number of countries. As a result, estimates of life expectancy have been declining dramatically. Botswana is a notable example. By the early 1990s, average overall life expectancy in the nation had risen to about 65 years, due to sustained public investment in providing universal access to primary health care. But

MEASURING MISERY

United Nations Human Development Index, 1998*

Country	Rank	Country	Rank
Seychelles	53	Democratic Republic of Congo	152
Mauritius	71	Zambia	153
South Africa	103	Côte d'Ivoire	154
Cape Verde	105	Senegal	155
Swaziland	112	Tanzania	156
Namibia	115	Benin	157
Botswana	122	Uganda	158
Gabon	123	Eritrea	159
Lesotho	127	Angola	160
Ghana	129	Gambia	161
Zimbabwe	130	Guinea	162
Equatorial Guinea	131	Malawi	163
São Tomé & Príncipe	132	Mali	165
Cameroon	134	Central African Republic	166
Comoros	137	Chad	167
Kenya	138	Mozambique	168
Congo	139	Guinea-Bissau	169
Madagascar	141	Burundi	170
Sudan	143	Ethiopia	171
Togo	145	Burkina Faso	172
Mauritania	147	Niger	173
Djibouti	149	Sierra Leone	174
Nigeria	151		

*Standings among 174 countries, with the ranking 174 indicating the lowest development.

Source: UNDP, *Human Development Report 2000*. See also http://www.undp.og/hdr2000/english/book/back1.pdf.

recent United Nations (UN) figures suggest that average life expectancy in Botswana could drop to only 31 years in the next few years. Put another way, unless the pandemic can be brought under control, it has been estimated that AIDS will eventually claim the lives of one out of every two Batswana (as the people of Botswana are known) born in the new millennium. The battle against AIDS in Africa has been complicated by the existence of a number of strains of the HIV virus, of which the most virulent is currently concentrated in Southern Africa. The spread of HIV/AIDS has contributed to the resurgence of diseases such as tuberculosis. Mortality due to malaria—Africa's traditional scourge—has also been rising in many areas, as has cholera. Diseases afflicting livestock, such as rinderpest and foot-and-mouth disease, have also been making a comeback in certain regions.

THE EVOLUTION OF AFRICA'S ECONOMIES

Africa has seldom been rich, although it has vast resources, and some rulers and other elites have become very wealthy. In earlier centuries, the slave trade greatly contributed to limiting economic development in many African regions. During the period of European exploration and colonialism, Africa's involvement in the world economy greatly increased with the emergence of new forms of "legitimate" commerce. But colonial-era policies and practices assured that this development was of little long-term benefit to most of the continent's peoples.

During the 70 or so years of European colonial rule over most of Africa, its nations' economies were shaped to the advantage of the imperialists. Cash crops such as cocoa, coffee, and rubber began to be grown for the European market. Some African farmers benefited from these crops, but the cash-crop economy also involved large foreign-run plantations. It also encouraged the trends toward use of migrant labor and the decline in food production. Many people became dependent for their livelihood on the forces of the world market, which, like the weather, were beyond their immediate control.

Mining also increased during colonial times, again for the benefit of the colonial rulers. The ores were extracted from African soil by European companies. African labor was employed, but the machinery came from abroad. The copper, diamonds, gold, iron ore, and uranium were shipped overseas to be processed and marketed in the Western economies. Upon independence, African governments received a varying percentage of the take through taxation and consortium agreements. But mining remained an enclave industry, sometimes described as a "state within a state" because such industries were run by outsiders who established communities that used imported machinery and technicians and exported the products to industrialized countries.

Inflationary conditions in other parts of the world have had adverse effects on Africa. The raw materials that Africans export today often receive low prices on the world market, while the manufactured goods that African countries import are expensive. Local African industries lack spare parts and machinery, and farmers frequently cannot afford to transport crops to market. As a result, the whole economy slows down. Thus, Africa, because of the policies of former colonial powers and current independent governments, is tied into the world economy in ways that do not always serve its peoples' best interests.

THE PROBLEMS OF GOVERNANCE

Outside forces are not the only cause of Africa's current crises. In general, Africa has been a misgoverned continent. After independence, the idealism that characterized various nationalist movements, with their promises of popular self-determination, gave way in most states to cynical authoritarian regimes. By 1989, only Botswana, Mauritius, soon-to-be-independent Namibia, and, arguably, The Gambia and Senegal could reasonably claim that their governments were elected in genuinely free and fair elections.

During the 1980s, the government of Robert Mugabe in Zimbabwe, in Southern Africa, undoubtedly enjoyed majority support, but political life in the country was already seriously marred by violence and intimidation aimed at the Mugabe regime's potential opposition. Past multiparty contests in the North African nations of Egypt, Morocco, and Tunisia, as well as in the West African state of Liberia, had

THE AIDS PANDEMIC

Perhaps the greatest challenge currently facing Africa is the spread of HIV/AIDS. The statistics are chilling. According to the United Nations, of the 36 million people worldwide living with the HIV virus, some 24 million live in sub-Saharan Africa. Of the 5.3 million new infections estimated for the year 2000, 3.8 million were in Africa. AIDS is already the leading cause of death on the continent. In all, 2.4 million AIDS-related deaths were recorded for Africa in 2000, representing about 80 percent of the worldwide total.

AIDS-related fatalities have also resulted in a rapidly growing number of "AIDS orphans." According to Kingsley Amoako, executive secretary of the Economic Commission for Africa, more than 12 million children have been orphaned in Africa due to AIDS (out of the global estimate of just over 13 million). Speaking at a gathering of African leaders in November 2000, Amoako noted that, "Within the next 10 years, it is projected that there will be 40 million AIDS orphans in Africa. . . . The AIDS pandemic is undermining social and economic structures and reversing the fragile gains made since independence . . . in parts of Africa, AIDS is killing one in every three adults, making orphans out of every tenth child and decimating entire communities."

The worst-hit parts of the continent in recent years have been East and Southern Africa, with some countries having infection rates of more than a fifth of their adult populations. According to published figures, the most affected countries are Botswana, South Africa, and Zimbabwe, where it is currently estimated that one in every two people under age 15 could die from the disease.

Inevitably, the spread of HIV/AIDS is having a devastating impact on economic and social development. For example, it is estimated that in the next decade, South Africa's gross domestic product will be 17 percent lower than it would have been without the pandemic.

Amid the gloom there is, nonetheless, grounds for hope that the scourge can ultimately be overcome. According to a UN report issued at the end of 2000, some parts of the continent are finally seeing a decrease in new HIV cases. The report notes that this has resulted in a modest overall decrease in the total number of new HIV cases in Africa as a whole. The decrease has been partially attributed to the gradual success of prevention programs, especially in the East African countries.

Africa's ability to fight HIV/AIDS is compromised by its debt burden and the high cost of HIV/AIDS treatment drugs. One of the most outspoken figures on the relationship between disease and debt on the continent has been Botswana's president, Festus Mogae. In a direct appeal to the wealthier nations, he observed:

> Your wealth in recent years increased by trillions and therefore what we owe is peanuts. It will not affect anybody, not the balance sheets of banks or anybody. It's just a matter of principle. You are insisting on repayment as a matter of principle, but it has no financial consequences for anybody else except the debtor. For him it's a lot of money. . . . Pharmaceutical companies have come forward and offered us discounts. Some of these discounts are very generous but are still more than our faint means can allow us to afford, and therefore we are still not able to take full advantage of the offer. . . . We are saying the rest of the world, including and especially the United States and the rest of the G-7, at the governmental level should do something to make it possible for us to access these treatments that are currently available.

been manipulated to assure that the ruling establishments remained unchallenged. Elsewhere, the continent was divided between military and/or one-party regimes, which often combined the seemingly contradictory characteristics of weakness and absolutism at the top. While a few of the one-party states, most notably Tanzania, then offered people genuine, if limited, choices of leadership, most were, to a greater or lesser degree, simply vehicles of personal rule.

But since 1990 there has been a democratic reawakening in Africa, which has toppled the political status quo in some areas and threatened its survival throughout the continent. Whereas in 1989 some 35 nations were governed as single-party states, by 1994 there were none, though Swaziland and Uganda were experimenting with no-party systems. In a number of countries—Benin, Cape Verde, Central African Republic, Congo, Madagascar, Mali, Malawi, Niger, São Tomé and Príncipe, Senegal, South Africa, and Zambia—ruling parties were decisively rejected in multiparty elections, while elections in other areas led to a greater sharing of power between the old regimes and their formerly suppressed oppositions.

In many countries, the democratic transformation is still ongoing and remains fragile. There have been accusations of manipulation and voting fraud in a growing number of countries in the past decade; while in Algeria, The Gambia, Niger, Nigeria, and Sierra Leone, the seeming will of the electorates has been overridden by military coups.

A fragile democracy has since been restored to Nigeria, Africa's most populous state, while military rule in Sierra Leone has given way to an ongoing attempt to restore a democratic consensus through UN–sanctioned intervention by international peacekeeping forces. In The Gambia, where three decades of multiparty democracy were ended through a military coup, there have also been elections. But their legitimacy has been questioned.

Events in Benin have most closely paralleled the recent changes of Central/Eastern Europe. Benin's military-based, Marxist-Leninist regime of Mathieu Kérékou was pressured into relinquishing power to a transitional civilian government made up of technocrats and former dissidents. (Television broadcasts of this "civilian coup" enjoyed large audiences in neighboring countries.) In several other countries, such as Equatorial Guinea, Gabon, and Togo, mounting opposition has resulted in the semblance without the substance of free elections by long-ruling military autocrats. In the Democratic Republic of the Congo, attempts to establish a framework for reform through a multiparty consultative conference were overshadowed by the almost complete collapse of state structures. A victory by externally backed rebels in 1997 was followed by renewed civil war and foreign intervention. Continued conflict in the country has contributed to the further destabilization of neighboring states. Many people fear that these countries may soon experience turmoil similar to that which has engulfed Ethiopia, Liberia, Rwanda, Somalia, and Uganda, where military autocrats have been overthrown by armed rebels.

Why did most postcolonial African governments, until recently, take on autocratic forms? And why are these forms now being so widely challenged? There are no definitive answers to either of these questions. One common explanation for authoritarianism in Africa has been the weakness of the states themselves. Most African governments have faced the difficult task of maintaining national unity with diverse, ethnically divided citizenries. Although the states of Africa may overlay and overlap historic kingdoms, most are products of colonialism. Their boundaries were fashioned during the late-nineteenth-century European partition of the continent, which divided and joined ethnic groups by lines drawn in Europe. The successful leaders of African independence movements worked within the colonial boundaries; and when they joined together in the Organization of African Unity (OAU), they agreed to respect the territorial status quo.

While the need to stem interethnic and regional conflict has been one justification for placing limits on popular self-determination, another explanation can be found in the administrative systems that the nationalist leaderships inherited. All the European colonies in Africa functioned essentially as police states. Not only were various forms of opposition curtailed, but intrusive security establishments were created to watch over and control the indigenous populations. Although headed by Europeans, most colonial security services employed local staff members who were prepared to assume leadership roles at independence. A wave of military coups swept across West Africa during the 1960s; elsewhere, aspiring dictators like Life President Ngwazi Hastings Banda of Malawi were quick to appreciate the value of the inherited instruments of control.

Africa's economic difficulties have also frequently been cited as contributing to its political underdevelopment. On one hand, Nigeria's last civilian government, for example,

was certainly undermined in part by the economic crisis that engulfed it due to falling oil revenues. On the other hand, in a pattern reminiscent of recent changes in Latin America, current economic difficulties resulting in high rates of inflation and indebtedness seem to be tempting some African militaries, such as Benin's, to return to the barracks and allow civilian politicians to assume responsibility for the implementation of inevitably harsh austerity programs.

External powers have long sustained African dictatorships through their grants of military and economic aid—and, on occasion, direct intervention. For example, a local attempt in 1964 to restore constitutional rule in Gabon was thwarted by French paratroopers, while Joseph Desiré Mobutu's kleptocratic hold over Zaire relied from the very beginning on overt and covert assistance from the United States and other Western states. The former Soviet bloc and China also helped in the past to support their share of unsavory African allies, in places like Ethiopia, Equatorial Guinea, and Burundi. But the end of the Cold War has led to a reduced desire on the part of outside powers to prop up their unpopular African allies. At the same time, the major international lending agencies have increasingly concerned themselves with the perceived need to adjust the political as well as economic structures of debtor nations. This new emphasis is justified in part by the alleged linkage between political unaccountability and economic corruption and mismanagement.

The ongoing decline of socialism on the continent is also having a significant political effect. Some regimes have professed a Marxist orientation, while others have felt that a special African socialism could be built on the communal and cooperative traditions of their societies. In countries such as Guinea-Bissau and Mozambique, a revolutionary socialist orientation was introduced at the grassroots level during the struggles for independence, within areas liberated from colonialism. The various socialist governments have not been free of personality cults, nor from corruption and oppressive measures. And many governments that have eschewed the socialist label have, nonetheless, developed public corporations and central-planning methods similar to those governments that openly profess Marxism. In recent years, virtually all of Africa's governments, partly in line with IMF and World Bank requirements but also because of the inefficiency and losses of many of their public corporations, have placed greater emphasis on private-sector development.

REASONS FOR OPTIMISM

Although the problems facing African countries have grown since independence, so have the continent's collective achievements. The number of people who can read and write in local languages as well as in English, French, or Portuguese has increased enormously. More people can peruse newspapers, follow instructions for fertilizers, and read the labels on medicine bottles. Professionals trained in modern technology who, for example, plan electrification schemes, organize large office

Children are deeply treasured in the African cultural heritage.

staffs, or develop medical facilities are more available because of the large number of African universities that have developed since the end of colonialism. Health care has also expanded and improved in most areas. Outside of the areas that have been ravaged by war, life expectancy has generally increased and infant mortality rates have declined.

The problems besetting Africa have caused deep pessimism in some quarters, with a few observers going so far as to question whether the postcolonial division of the continent into multiethnic states is viable. But the states themselves have proved to be surprisingly resilient. Central authority has reemerged in such traumatized, once seemingly ungovernable countries as Uganda, Mozambique, and most recently Liberia. Despite the terrible wars that are still being waged in a few nations, mostly in the form of civil wars, postwar African governments have been notably successful in avoiding armed conflict with one another (although this fact is currently being severely tested by external interventions in the Civil War in the Democratic Republic of the Congo). Of special significance is South Africa's recent transformation into a nonracial democracy, which has been accompanied by its emergence as the leading member of the Southern African Development Community and has brought an end to its previous policy of regional destabilization.

Another positive development is the increasing attention that African governments and intra-African agencies are giving to women, as was exemplified in a global population summit held in Cairo, Egypt, in 1994. The pivotal role of women in agriculture and other activities is increasingly being recognized and supported. In many countries, prenatal and hospital care for mothers and their babies have increased, conditions for women workers in factories have improved, and new cooperatives for women's activities have been developed. Women are also playing a more prominent role in the political life of many African countries.

The advances that have been made in Africa are important ones, but they could be undercut by continued economic decline. Africa needs debt relief and outside aid just to maintain the gains that have been made. Yet as an African proverb observes, "Someone else's legs will do you no good in traveling." Africa, as the individual country reports in this volume observe, is a continent of many and varied resources. There are mineral riches and a vast agricultural potential. However, the continent's people, the youths who make up more than half the population and the elders whose wisdom is revered, are its greatest resource. The rest of the world, which has benefited from the continent's material resources, can also learn from the social strengths of African families and communities.

Central Africa

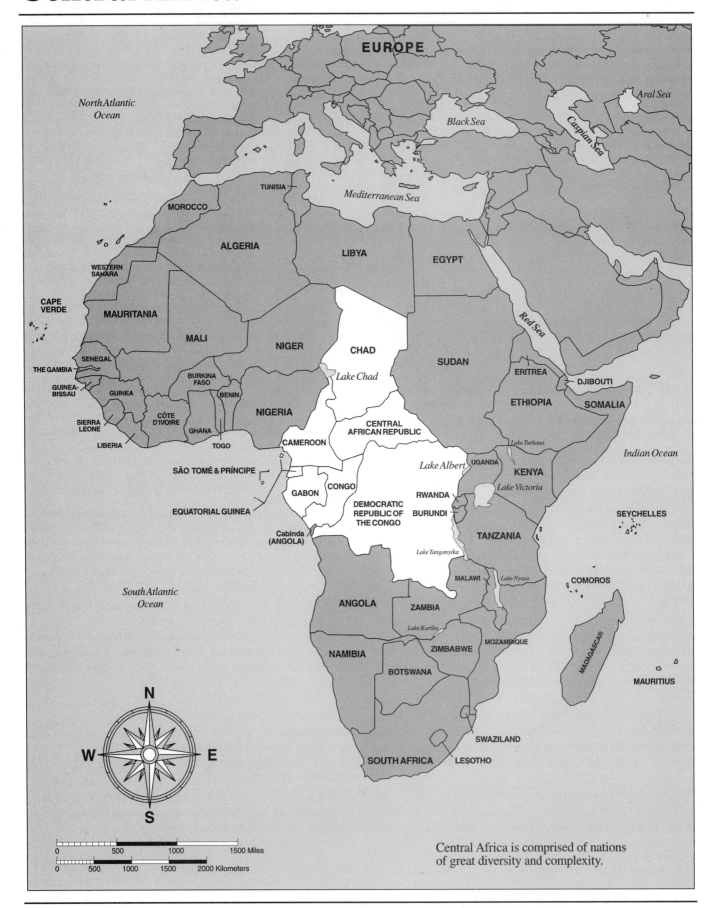

EUROPE

North Atlantic
Ocean

Aral Sea

Black Sea

Caspian Sea

TUNISIA

Mediterranean Sea

MOROCCO

ALGERIA

LIBYA

EGYPT

WESTERN
SAHARA

Red Sea

CAPE
VERDE

MAURITANIA

MALI

NIGER

CHAD

SUDAN

ERITREA

Lake Chad

DJIBOUTI

THE GAMBIA

SENEGAL

BURKINA
FASO

ETHIOPIA

SOMALIA

GUINEA-
BISSAU

GUINEA

BENIN

SIERRA
LEONE

CÔTE
D'IVOIRE

GHANA

NIGERIA

CENTRAL
AFRICAN REPUBLIC

Lake Turkana

LIBERIA

TOGO

CAMEROON

Indian Ocean

SÃO TOMÉ & PRÍNCIPE

Lake Albert

UGANDA

KENYA

GABON

CONGO

Lake Victoria

EQUATORIAL GUINEA

DEMOCRATIC
REPUBLIC OF
THE CONGO

RWANDA

BURUNDI

SEYCHELLES

Cabinda
(ANGOLA)

TANZANIA

Lake Tanganyika

South Atlantic
Ocean

MALAWI

Lake Nyasa

COMOROS

ANGOLA

ZAMBIA

Lake Kariba

MOZAMBIQUE

MADAGASCAR

NAMIBIA

ZIMBABWE

MAURITIUS

BOTSWANA

SWAZILAND

SOUTH AFRICA

LESOTHO

N
W   E
S

0   500   1000   1500 Miles
0   500   1000   1500   2000 Kilometers

Central Africa is comprised of nations
of great diversity and complexity.

Central Africa: Possibilities for Cooperation

The Central African region, as defined in this book, brings together countries that have not shared a common past; nor do they necessarily seem destined for a common future. Cameroon, Chad, Central African Republic, Congo, the Democratic Republic of the Congo (the D.R.C., or Congo-Kinshasa, formerly known as Zaire), Equatorial Guinea, Gabon, and São Tomé and Príncipe are not always grouped together as one region. Indeed, users of this volume who are familiar with the continent may also associate the label "Central Africa" with such states as Angola and Zambia rather than with some of the states mentioned here. Geographically, Chad is more closely associated with the Sahelian nations of West Africa than with the heavily forested regions of Central Africa to its south. Similarly, the southern part of Democratic Republic of Congo has long-standing cultural and economic links with Angola and Zambia, which in this text are associated with the states of Southern Africa, largely because of their political involvements.

Yet the eight countries that are designated here as belonging to Central Africa have much in common. French is a predominant language in all the states except Equatorial Guinea and São Tomé and Príncipe. All except São Tomé and Príncipe and the Democratic Republic of Congo share a common currency, the CFA franc. And while Chad's current economic prospects appear to be exceptionally poor, the natural wealth found throughout the rest of Central Africa makes the region as a whole one of enormous potential. Finally, in the postcolonial era, all the Central African governments have made some progress in realizing their developmental possibilities through greater regional cooperation.

The countries of Central Africa incorporate a variety of peoples and cultures, resources, environments, systems of government, and national goals. Most of the modern nations overlay both societies that were village-based and localized, and societies that were once part of extensive state formations. Islam has had little influence in the region, except in Chad and northern Cameroon. In most areas, Christianity coexists with indigenous systems of belief. Sophisticated wooden sculptures are one of the cultural achievements associated with most Central African societies. To many people, the carvings are only material manifestations of the spiritual potential of complex local cosmologies. However, the art forms are myriad and distinctive, and their diversity is as striking as the common features that they share.

The postcolonial governments of Central Africa have ranged from outwardly conservative regimes (in Gabon and the Democratic Republic of Congo) to self-proclaimed revolutionary Marxist-Leninist orders (in Congo and São Tomé and Príncipe). More fundamentally, all of the states in the region have in the past fallen under the control of unelected autocracies, whose continued existence has been dependent on the coercive capacities of military forces—sometimes external ones. But the authoritarian status quo has been challenged in recent years. In Central African Republic, Congo,

(United Nations photo)

In Africa, cooperative work groups such as the one pictured above often take on jobs that would be done by machinery in industrialized countries.

and São Tomé and Príncipe, democratic openings have resulted in the peaceful election of new governments. However, the elected government in Congo has since been overthrown by forces loyal to its former dictator. Elsewhere in the region, opposition parties have been legalized but otherwise have made limited progress.

GEOGRAPHIC DISTINCTIVENESS

All the states of the Central African region except Chad encompass equatorial rain forests. Citizens who live in these regions must cope with a climate that is hot and moist while facing the challenges of utilizing (and in some cases, unfortunately, clearing) the resources of the great forests. The problems of living in these areas account, in part, for the relatively low, albeit growing, population densities of most of the states. The difficulty of establishing roads and railroads impedes communication and thus economic development. The peoples of the rain-forest areas tend to cluster along riverbanks and existing rail lines. In modern times, largely because of the extensive development of minerals, many inhabitants have moved to the cities, accounting for a comparatively high urban population in all the states.

Central Africa's rivers have long been its lifelines. The watershed in Cameroon between the Niger and Congo (or Zaire) Rivers provides a natural divide between the West and Central African regions. The Congo River is the largest in the region, but the Oubangi, Chari, Ogooue, and other rivers are important also for the communication and trading opportunities they offer. The rivers flow to the Atlantic Ocean, a fact that has encouraged the orientation of Central Africa's external trade toward Europe and the Americas.

Many of the countries of the region have similar sources of wealth. The rivers are capable of generating enormous amounts of hydropower. The rain forests are also rich in lumber, which is a major export of most of the countries. Other forest products, such as rubber and palm oil, are widely marketed.

Extensive lumbering and clearing activities for agriculture, have created worldwide concern about the depletion of the rain forests. As a result, in recent years there have been some organized boycotts in Europe of the region's hardwood exports, although far more trees are felled to process plywood.

As one might expect, Central Africa as a whole is one of the areas least affected by the drought conditions that peri-

(Credit: UN photo)

Regional cooperation will be necessary to utilize the natural resources of Central African countries without ruining their precious but fragile environment. Environmentalists warn that the Central African forests are rapidly being destroyed.

(WFP photo by F. Mattioli)

Central Africa is generally not affected by drought, but Chad, Central African Republic, and certain parts of Cameroon have all faced food shortages due to the lack of rain. In these countries, care must be taken to maximize food supplies. These women are winnowing sesame seeds near the town of N'Djamena in Chad to ensure a "seed bank" for the next planting season.

odically plague Africa. Nevertheless, serious drought is a well-known visitor in Chad, Central African Republic, and the northern regions of Cameroon, where it contributes to local food shortages. Savanna lands are found in some parts lying to the north and the south of the forests. Whereas rain forests have often inhibited travel, the savannas have long been transitional areas, great avenues of migration linking the regions of Africa, while providing agricultural and pastoral opportunities for their residents.

The Central African countries share other resources besides the products of the rain forest. Cameroon, Congo, and Gabon derive considerable revenues from their petroleum reserves. Other important minerals include diamonds, copper, gold, manganese, and uranium. The processes involved in the exploitation of these commodities, as well as the demand for them in the world market, are issues of common concern among the producing nations. Many of the states also share an interest in exported cash crops such as coffee, cocoa, and

cotton, whose international prices are subject to sharp fluctuations. The similarity of their environments and products provides an economic incentive for Central African cooperation.

LINKS TO FRANCE

Many of the different ethnic groups in Central Africa overlap national boundaries. Examples include the Fang, who are found in Cameroon, Equatorial Guinea, and Gabon; the Bateke of Congo and Gabon; and the BaKongo, who are concentrated in Angola as well as in Congo and the Democratic Republic of the Congo. Such cross-border ethnic ties are less important as sources of regional unity than the European colonial systems that the countries inherited. While Equatorial Guinea was controlled by Spain, São Tomé and Príncipe by Portugal, and the D.R.C. by Belgium, the predominant external power in the region remains France. Central African Republic, Chad, Congo, and Gabon were all once part of

French Equatorial Africa. Most of Cameroon was also governed by the French, who were awarded the bulk of the former German colony of the Kamerun as a "trust territory" in the aftermath of World War I. French administration provided the five states with similar colonial experiences.

Early colonial development in the former French colonies and the Democratic Republic of the Congo was affected by European "concessions" companies, institutions that were sold extensive rights (often 99-year leases granting political as well as economic powers) to exploit such local products as ivory and rubber. At the beginning of the twentieth century, just 41 companies controlled 70 percent of all of the territory of contemporary Central African Republic, Congo, and Gabon. Mining operations as well as large plantations were established that often relied on forced labor. Individual production by Africans was also encouraged, often through coercion rather than economic incentives. While the colonial companies encouraged production and trade, they did little to aid the growth of infrastructure or long-term development. Only in the D.R.C. was industry promoted to any great extent.

In general, French colonial rule, along with that of the Belgians, Portuguese, and Spanish and the activities of the companies, offered few opportunities for Africans to gain training and education. There was also little encouragement of local entrepreneurship. An important exception to this pattern was the policies pursued by Felix Eboue, a black man from French Guiana (in South America) who served as a senior administrator in the Free French administration of French Equatorial Africa during the 1940s. Eboue increased opportunities for the urban elite in Central African Republic, Congo, and Gabon. He also played an important role in the Brazzaville Conference of 1944, which, recognizing the part that the people of the French colonies had played in World War II, abolished forced labor and granted citizenship to all. Yet political progress toward self-government was uneven. Because of the lack of local labor development, there were too few people at independence who were qualified to shoulder the bureaucratic and administrative tasks of the regimes that took power. People who could handle the economic institutions for the countries' benefit were equally scarce. And in any case, the nations' economies remained for the most part securely in outside—largely French—hands.

The Spanish on the Equatorial Guinea island of Fernando Po, and the Portuguese of São Tomé and Príncipe, also profited from their exploitation of forced labor. Political opportu-

(World Bank photo by Ivan Albert Andrews)

This palm-oil processing mill was financed by the World Bank as part of a development project in Cameroon.

nities in these territories were even more limited than on the African mainland. Neither country gained independence until fairly recently: Equatorial Guinea in 1968, São Tomé and Príncipe in 1975.

In the years since independence, most of the countries of Central Africa have been influenced, pressured, and supported by France and the other former colonial powers. French firms in Central African Republic, Congo, and Gabon continue to dominate the exploitation of local resources. Most of these companies are only slightly encumbered by the regulations of the independent states in which they operate, and all are geared toward European markets and needs. Financial institutions are generally branches of French institutions, and all the former French colonies as well as Equatorial Guinea are members of the Central African Franc (CFA) Zone. French expatriates occupy senior positions in local civil-service establishments and in companies; many more of them are resident in the region today than was true 30 years ago. In addition, French troops are stationed in Central African Republic, Chad, and Gabon, regimes that owe their very existence to past French military interventions. Besides being a major trading partner, France has contributed significantly to the budgets of its former possessions, especially the poorer states of Central African Republic and Chad.

Despite having been under Belgian rule, the Democratic Republic of the Congo is an active member of the Francophonic bloc in Africa. In 1977, French troops put down a rebellion in southeastern Zaire (as the D.R.C. was then known). Zaire, in turn, sent its troops to serve beside those of France in Chad and Togo. Since playing a role in the 1979 coup that brought the current regime to power, France has also had a predominant influence in Equatorial Guinea.

REGIONAL COOPERATION AND CONFLICT
Although many Africans in Central Africa recognize that closer links among their countries would be beneficial, there have been fewer initiatives toward political unity or economic integration in this region than in East, West, or Southern Africa. In the years before independence, Barthelemy Boganda, of what is now Central African Republic, espoused and publicized the idea of a "United States of Latin Africa," which was to include Angola and Zaire as well as the territories of French Equatorial Africa, but he was frustrated by Paris as well as by local politicians. When France offered independence to its colonies in 1960, soon after Boganda's death, the possibility of forming a federation was discussed. But Gabon, which was wealthier than the other countries, declined to participate. Central African Republic, Chad, and Congo drafted an agreement that would have created a federal legislature and executive branch governing all three countries, but local jealousies defeated this plan.

There have been some formal efforts at economic integration among the former French states. The Customs and Economic Union of the Central African States (UDEAC) was established in 1964, but its membership has been unstable. Chad and Central African Republic withdrew to join Zaire in an alternate organization. (Central African Republic later returned, bringing the number of members to six.) The East and Central African states together planned an "Economic Community" in 1967, but it never materialized.

In the 1980s there were efforts to make greater progress toward economic cooperation. Urged on by the United Nations Economic Commission for Africa, and with the stimulus of the Lagos Plan of Action, representatives of Central African states met in 1982 to prepare for a new economic grouping. In 1983, all the Central African states as well as Rwanda and Burundi in East Africa signed a treaty establishing the Economic Community of Central African States (ECCA). ECCA's goals were broader than those of UDEAC. Members hoped that the union would stimulate industrial activity, increase markets, and reduce the dependence on France and other countries for trade and capital. But with dues often unpaid and meetings postponed, ECCA has so far failed to meet its potential.

Hopes that the Central African states could work collectively toward a brighter future have been further compromised by the spread in recent years of extreme political instability and brutal and far-reaching armed conflicts both within and between states in the region. This is particularly true of the ongoing civil war in the region's biggest state, the Democratic Republic of the Congo; this war has not only divided the region but has involved states as far afield as Libya, Nigeria, and South Africa.

In the mid-1990s, there was a growing optimism that democratization might enable the region to become a center of a continental renaissance. This view was greatly boosted by the fall of the corrupt, authoritarian regime of Mobutu Sese Seko, which led to the nominal transformation of Zaire into the Democratic Republic of the Congo. But in subsequent years, such hopes have been largely dashed by a resurgence of dictatorship and kleptocracy built on a foundation of divide and misrule. With Mobutu's successor Laurent Kabila clinging on to power through external backers and implicit appeals for genocide against ethnic groups perceived as his enemies, the chances of Boganda's vision becoming a reality have never appeared more remote.

Cameroon (Republic of Cameroon)

GEOGRAPHY

Area in Square Miles (Kilometers):
183,568 (475,400) (about the size of California)

Capital (Population): Yaoundé (1,119,000)

Environmental Concerns:
deforestation; overgrazing; desertification; poaching; overfishing; water-borne disease

Geographical Features: diverse, with coastal plain in southwest, dissected plain in center, mountains in west, and plains in north

Climate: from tropical to semiarid

PEOPLE

Population

Total: 15,422,000

Annual Growth Rate: 2.47%

Rural/Urban Population Ratio: 54/46

Major Languages: English; French; Fulde; Ewondo; Duala; Bamelke; Bassa; Bali; others

Ethnic Makeup: 31% Cameroonian Highlander; 19% Equatorial Bantu; 11% Kirdi; 10% Fulani; 29% others

Religions: 40% indigenous beliefs; 40% Christian; 20% Muslim

Health

Life Expectancy at Birth: 54 years (male); 56 years (female)

Infant Mortality Rate (Ratio): 70.8/1,000

Physicians Available (Ratio): 1/11,848

Education

Adult Literacy Rate: 63.4%

Compulsory (Ages): 6–12; free

COMMUNICATION

Telephones: 75,200 main lines

Televisions: 72 per 1,000 people

Internet Service Providers: na

TRANSPORTATION

Highways in Miles (Kilometers): 20,580 (34,300)

Railroads in Miles (Kilometers): 693 (1,111)

Usable Airfields: 50

Motor Vehicles in Use: 153,000

GOVERNMENT

Type: unitary republic

Independence Date: January 1, 1960 (from UN trusteeship under French administration)

Head of State/Government: President Paul Biya; Prime Minister Peter Mafany Musonge

Political Parties: Cameroon Liberation and Development Movement; National Union for Democracy and Progress; Social Democratic Front; Cameroonian Democratic Union; Union of Cameroonian Populations; others

Suffrage: universal at 21

MILITARY

Military Expenditures (% of GDP): 1.4%

Current Disputes: various border conflicts, especially with Nigeria

ECONOMY

Currency ($ U.S. Equivalent): 529.43 CFA francs = $1

Per Capita Income/GDP: $2,000/$31.5 billion

GDP Growth Rate: 5.2%

Inflation Rate: 2.1%

Unemployment Rate: 30%

Natural Resources: petroleum; timber; bauxite; iron ore; hydropower potential

Agriculture: coffee; cocoa; cotton; rubber; bananas; oilseed; grain; roots; livestock; timber

Industry: petroleum production and refining; food processing; light consumer goods; textiles; lumber

Exports: $2 billion (primary partners Italy, Spain, France)

Imports: $1.5 billion (primary partners France, Nigeria, United States)

http://www.sas.upenn.edu/African_Studies/Country_Specific/Cameroon.html
http://www.cameroon.net/
http://www.telp.com/cameroon/home.htm

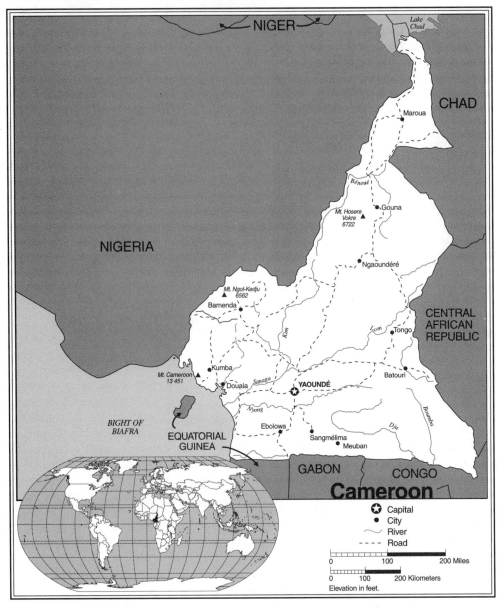

CAMEROON

Over the past decade, Cameroonians have been united by at least two things: support for their world-class national soccer team, the Indomitable Lions, and condemnation of neighboring Nigeria over a long-simmering border dispute. Politically, however, Cameroonians have remained deeply divided, notwithstanding incumbent President Paul Biya's claim of victory with 92 percent of the vote in the October 1998 elections. The poll, which was boycotted by the largest opposition parties, was a followup to the controversial elections of March 1992, which ended a quarter-century of one-party rule by Biya's Cameroon People's Democratic Party (CPDM). Although the CPDM relinquished its monopoly of power, it retained control of the government. With a plurality of 88 out of 180 seats, the CPDM was able to form a coalition government with the Movement for the Defense of Democracy, which won six seats. Two other parties, the National Union for Democracy and Progress (UNDP) and the Union of Cameroonian Populations (UPC), divided most of the remaining seats.

Like the 1998 elections, the legitimacy of the 1992 poll was compromised by the boycott of most of the opposition parties—most notably including the Social Democratic Front (SDF), the Democratic Union (CDU), and a faction of the UPC—boycotted the polls, allowing the CPDM to win numerous constituencies by default. The situation was aggravated in October 1992 when the CPDM's Paul Biya was declared the victor in a snap election accompanied by opposition allegations of vote-rigging. In March 1993, most of the opposition parties formed a new coalition. Under pressure from better-coordinated opposition, Biya agreed in June 1993 to revise the Constitution. But subsequent progress has been slow, and Cameroon's politics remains in turmoil.

Cameroon's fractious politics is a reflection of its diversity. In geographical terms, the land is divided between the tropical forests in the south, the drier savanna of the north-central region, and the mountainous country along its western border, which forms a natural division between West and Central Africa. In terms of religion, the country has many Christians, Muslims, and followers of indigenous belief systems. More than a dozen major languages, with numerous dialects, are spoken. The languages of southern Cameroon are linguistically classified as Bantu. The "Bantu line" that runs across the country, roughly following the course of the Sanaga River, forms a boundary between the Bantu languages of Central, East, and Southern Africa and the non-Bantu tongues of North and West Africa. Many scholars believe that the roots of the Bantu language tree are buried in Cameroonian soil. Cameroon is also unique among the continental African states in sharing two European languages, English and French, as its official mediums. This circumstance is a product of the country's unique colonial heritage.

Three European powers have ruled over Cameroon. The Germans were the first. From 1884 to 1916, they laid the foundation of much of the country's communications infrastructure and, primarily through the establishment of European-run plantations, export agriculture. During World War I, the area was divided between the British and French, who subsequently ruled their respective zones as League of Nations (later the United Nations) mandates. French "Cameroun" included the eastern four fifths of the former German colony, while British "Cameroons" consisted of two narrow strips of territory that were administered as part of its Nigerian territory.

In the 1950s, Cameroonians in both the British and French zones began to agitate for unity and independence. At the core of their nationalist vision was the "Kamerun Idea," a belief that the period of German rule had given rise to a pan-Cameroonian identity. The largest and most radical of the nationalist movements in the French zone was the Union of the Cameroonian People, which turned to armed struggle. Between 1955 and 1963, when most of the UPC guerrillas were defeated, some 10,000 to 15,000 people

(United Nations photo by Shaw McCutcheon)

Cameroon has experienced political unrest in recent years as various factions have moved to establish a stable form of government. At the heart of the political turmoil is the need to raise the living standards of the population through an increase in agricultural production. These farmers with their cattle herds are one part of this movement.

The establishment of the German Kamerun Protectorate
1884

The partition of Cameroon; separate British and French mandates are established under the League of Nations
1916

The UPC (formed in 1948) is outlawed for launching revolts in the cities
1955

The Independent Cameroon Republic is established with Ahmadou Ahidjo as the first president
1960

The Cameroon Federal Republic reunites French Cameroon with British Cameroon after a UN-supervised referendum
1961

The new Constitution creates a unitary state
1972

Ahidjo resigns and is replaced by Paul Biya; Lake Nyos releases lethal volcanic gases, killing an estimated 2,000 people
1980s

Nationwide agitation for a restoration of multiparty democracy; Biya retains the presidency in disputed elections
1990s

2000s

New clashes on the Bakassi Peninsula as the border dispute goes before the International Court of Justice

were killed. Most of the victims belonged to the Bamileke and Bassa ethnic groups of southwestern Cameroon, which continues to be the core area of UPC support. (Some sources refer to the Bamileke uprising as the Bamileke Rebellion.)

To counter the UPC revolt, the French adopted a dual policy of repression against the guerrillas' supporters and the devolution of political power to local non-UPC politicians. Most of these "moderate" leaders, who enjoyed core followings in both the heavily Christianized southeast and the Muslim north, coalesced as the Cameroonian Union, whose leader was Ahmadou Ahidjo, a northerner. In pre-independence elections, Ahidjo's party won just 51 out of the 100 seats. Ahidjo thus led a divided, war-torn state to independence in 1960.

In 1961, the southern section of British Cameroon voted to join Ahidjo's republic. The northern section opted to remain part of Nigeria. The principal party in the south was the Kamerun National Democratic Party, whose leader, John Foncha, became the vice president of the Cameroon republic, while Ahidjo served as president. The former British and French zones initially maintained their separate local parliaments, but the increasingly authoritarian Ahidjo pushed for a unified form of government. In 1966, all of Cameroon's legal political groups were dissolved into Ahidjo's new Cameroon National Union (CNU), creating a de facto one-party state. Trade unions and other mass organizations were also brought under CNU control. In 1972, Ahidjo proposed the abolition of the federation and the creation of a constitution for a unified Cameroon. This was approved by a suspiciously lopsided vote of 3,217,058 to 158.

In 1982, Ahidjo, believing that his health was graver than was actually the case, suddenly resigned. His handpicked successor was Paul Biya. To the surprise of many, the heretofore self-effacing Biya quickly proved to be his own man. He brought young technocrats into the ministries and initially called for a more open and democratic society. But as he pressed forward, Biya came into increasing conflict with Ahidjo, who tried to reassert his authority as CNU chairman. The ensuing power struggle took on overtones of an ethnic conflict between Biya's largely southern Christian supporters and Ahidjo's core following of northern Muslims. In 1983, Ahidjo lost and went into exile. The next year, he was tried and convicted, in absentia, for allegedly plotting Biya's overthrow.

In April 1984, only two months after the conviction, Ahidjo's supporters in the Presidential Guard attempted to overthrow Biya. The revolt was put down, but up to 1,000 people were killed. In the coup's aftermath, Biya combined repression with attempts to restructure the ruling apparatus. In 1985, the CNU was overhauled as the Cameroon People's Democratic Movement. However, President Biya became increasingly reliant on the support of his own Beti group.

An upsurge of prodemocracy agitation began in 1990. In March, the Social Democratic Front was formed in Bamenda, the main town of the Anglophonic west, over government objections. In May, as many as 40,000 people from the vicinity of Bamenda, out of a total population of about 100,000, attended an SDF rally. Government troops opened fire on school children returning from the demonstration. This action led to a wave of unrest, which spread to the capital city of Yaoundé. The government media tried to portray the SDF as a subversive movement of "English speakers," but it attracted significant support in Francophonic areas. Dozens of additional opposition groups, including the UNDP (which is loyal to the now deceased Ahidjo's legacy) and the long-underground UPC, joined forces with the SDF in calling for a transition government, a new constitution, and multiparty elections.

Throughout much of 1991, Cameroon's already depressed economy was further crippled by opposition mass action, dubbed the Ghost Town campaign. A series of concessions by Biya culminated in a November agreement between Biya and most of the opposition (the SDF being among the holdouts) to formulate a new constitution and prepare for elections. In this context, the government's decision to hold early elections (on March 1) was rejected by most of its opponents, although some reluctantly participated. The CPDM's subsequent failure to gain a majority of the vote, despite the partial opposition boycott and the CPDM's control of the election process, left the government weak.

DEVELOPMENT

The Cameroon Development Corporation coordinates more than half of the agricultural exports and, after the government, employs the most people. Cocoa and coffee comprise more than 50% of Cameroon's exports. Lower prices for these commodities in recent years have reduced the country's income.

FREEDOM

While Cameroon's human-rights record has improved since its return to multipartyism, political detentions and harassment continue. Amnesty International has drawn attention to the alleged starvation of detainees at the notorious Tchollire prison. Furthermore, the nation's vibrant free press has become a prime target of repression, with several editors arrested in 1998.

HEALTH/WELFARE

The overall literacy rate in Cameroon, about 63%, is among the highest in Africa. There exists, however, great disparity in regional figures as well as between males and females. In addition to public schools, the government devotes a large proportion of its budget to subsidizing private schools.

ACHIEVEMENTS

The strong showing by Cameroon's national soccer team, the Indomitable Lions, in the 1990 and 1994 World Cup competitions is a source of pride for sports fans throughout Africa. Their success, along with the record numbers of medals won by African athletes in the 1988 and 1992 Olympics, is symbolic of the continent's coming of age in international sports competitions.

Central African Republic

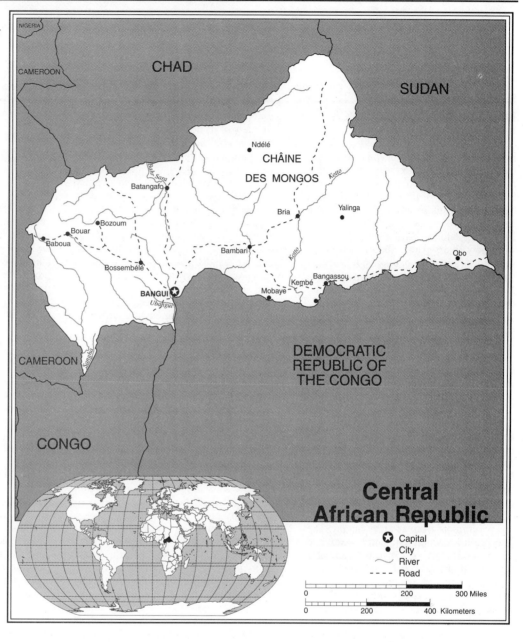

Central
African Republic

- ✪ Capital
- ● City
- ∿ River
- - - - Road

GEOGRAPHY

Area in Square Miles (Kilometers):
240,324 (662,436) (about the size of Texas)
Capital (Population): Bangui (553,000)
Environmental Concerns: poaching; desertification; deforestation
Geographical Features: vast, flat to rolling, monotonous plateau; scattered hills in the northeast and southwest; landlocked
Climate: tropical

PEOPLE

Population
Total: 3,513,000
Annual Growth Rate: 1.77%
Rural/Urban Population Ratio: 60/40
Major Languages: French; Songo; Arabic; Hunsa; Swahili
Ethnic Makeup: 34% Baya; 27% Banda; 21% Mandja; 10% Sara; 8% others
Religions: 25% indigenous beliefs; 25% Protestant; 25% Roman Catholic; 15% Muslim; 10% others

Health
Life Expectancy at Birth: 42 years (male); 46 years (female)
Infant Mortality Rate (Ratio): 106.7/1,000
Physicians Available (Ratio): 1/18,660

Education
Adult Literacy Rate: 60%
Compulsory (Ages): 6–14

COMMUNICATION
Telephones: 9,600 main lines
Televisions: 5 per 1,000 people
Internet Service Providers: na

TRANSPORTATION
Highways in Miles (Kilometers): 14,286 (23,810)
Railroads in Miles (Kilometers): none
Usable Airfields: 52
Motor Vehicles in Use: 20,000

GOVERNMENT
Type: republic
Independence Date: August 13, 1960 (from France)
Head of State/Government: President Ange-Félix Patassé; Prime Minister Anicet Georges Dologuele

Political Parties: Movement for the Liberation of the Central African People; Central African Democratic Assembly; Movement for Democracy and Development; others
Suffrage: universal at 21

MILITARY
Military Expenditures (% of GDP): 2.2%
Current Disputes: internal strife

ECONOMY
Currency ($ U.S. Equivalent): 529.43 CFA francs = $1
Per Capita Income/GDP: $1,700/$5.8 billion
GDP Growth Rate: 5%
Inflation Rate: 2.6%

Unemployment Rate: 6% (1993)
Natural Resources: diamonds; uranium; timber; gold; petroleum; hydropower
Agriculture: cotton; coffee; tobacco; manioc; millet; corn; bananas; timber
Industry: diamond mining; sawmills; breweries; textiles; footwear; assembly of bicycles and motorcycles
Exports: $195 million (primary partners Belgium-Luxembourg, Côte d'Ivoire, Spain)
Imports: $170 million (primary partners France, Côte d'Ivoire, Cameroon)

http://www.sas.upenn.edu/
African_Studies/Country_Specific/
Cent-A-R.html
http://www.emulateme.com/car.htm

Separate French administration of the Oubangui-Chàri colony is established
1904

Gold and diamonds are discovered
1912–1913

Barthelemy Boganda sets up MESAN, which gains wide support
1949

Boganda dies; David Dacko, his successor, becomes president at independence
1960

Jean-Bedel Bokassa takes power after the first general strike
1966

Bokassa declares himself emperor
1976

Bokassa is involved in the massacre of schoolchildren; Dacko is returned as head of state
1979

André Kolingba takes power from Dacko
1981

Ange-Félix Patassé wins the presidency; Patassé requires French intervention to overcome an army mutiny
1990s

2000s

The government has taken steps to reduce street crime

FRENCH EQUATORIAL AFRICA

In 1959, as Central African Republic (C.A.R.) moved toward independence, Barthelemy Boganda, a former priest and the leader of the territory's nationalist movement, did not share the euphoria exhibited by many of his colleagues. To him, the French path to independence was a trap. Where there once had been a united French Equatorial Africa (A.E.F.), there were now five separate states, each struggling toward its own nationhood. Boganda had led the struggle to transform the territory into a true Central African Republic. But in 1958, French president Charles de Gaulle overruled all objections in forcing the breakup of the A.E.F. Boganda believed that, thus balkanized, the Central African states would each be too weak to achieve true independence, but he still hoped that A.E.F. reunification might prove possible after independence.

CENTRAL AFRICAN REPUBLIC

In recent years, the government of C.A.R. president Ange-Félix Patassé, elected in 1993 and reelected in 1998, has struggled to bring political and financial stability to the poor, landlocked country, following three decades of military dictatorship. In April 1996, the French military rescued the government from an army mutiny. The intervention, which left three dead and 238 wounded, was resented by many as a sign of France's continuing control of C.A.R.s destiny. A national-reconciliation agreement was signed in March 1998 allowing UN peacekeepers to oversee elections and the training of a new army.

Although it gained its independence four decades ago, France's political, economic, and military presence in C.A.R. has remained pervasive. At the same time, the country's natural resources—as well as French largess—have been dissipated. Yet with diamonds, timber, and a resilient peasantry, the country is better endowed than many of its neighbors. C.A.R.'s population has traditionally been divided between the so-called river peoples and savanna peoples, but most are united by the Songo language. What the country has lacked is a leadership committed to national development rather than to internationally sanctioned waste.

In 1941, Boganda founded the Popular Movement for the Social Evolution of Black Africa (MESAN). While Boganda was a pragmatist willing to use moderate means in his struggle, his vision was radical, for he hoped to unite French, Belgian, and Portuguese territories into an independent republic. His movement succeeded in gaining a local following among the peasantry as well as intellectuals. In 1958, Boganda led the territory to self-government, but he died in a mysterious plane crash just before independence.

Boganda's successors have failed to live up to his stature. At independence, the country was led by David Dacko, a nephew of Boganda's, who succeeded to the leadership of MESAN but also cultivated the political support of local French settlers who had seen Boganda as an agitator. Dacko's MESAN became the vehicle of the wealthy elite.

A general strike in December 1965 was followed by a military coup on New Year's Eve, which put Dacko's cousin, Army Commander Jean-Bedel Bokassa, in power. Dacko's overthrow was justified by the need to launch political and economic reforms. But more likely motives for the coup were French concern about Dacko's growing ties with China and Bokassa's own budding megalomania.

The country suffered greatly under Bokassa's eccentric rule. He was often portrayed, alongside Idi Amin of Uganda, as an archetype of African leadership at its worst. It was more the sensational nature of his brutality—such as public torture and dismemberment of prisoners—rather than its scale that captured headlines. In 1972, he made himself president-for-life. Unsatisfied with this position, in 1976 he proclaimed himself emperor, in the image of his hero Napoleon Bonaparte. The $22 million spent on his coronation ceremony, which attracted widespread coverage in the global media, was underwritten by the French government.

In 1979, reports surfaced that Bokassa himself had participated in the beating to death of schoolchildren who had protested his decree that they purchase new uniforms bearing his portrait. The French government finally decided that its ally had become a liability. While Bokassa was away on a state visit to Libya, French paratroopers returned Dacko to power. In 1981, Dacko was once more toppled, in a coup that installed prime minister General André Kolingba. In 1985, Kolingba's provisional military regime was transformed into a one-party state. But in 1991, under a combination of local and French pressure, he agreed to the legalization of opposition parties.

Pressure for multiparty politics had increased as the government sank deeper into debt, despite financial intervention on the part of France, the World Bank, and the International Monetary Fund. Landlocked C.A.R.'s economy has long been constrained by high transport costs. But a perhaps greater burden has been the smuggling of its diamonds and other resources, including poached ivory, by officials who are high up in the government.

DEVELOPMENT

C.A.R.'s timber industry has suffered from corruption and environmentally destructive forms of exploitation. However, the nation has considerable forestry potential, with dozens of commercially viable and renewable species of trees.

FREEDOM

Despite its return to democracy, C.A.R.'s human-rights record remains poor. Its security forces are linked to summary executions and torture. Other human-rights abuses include harsh prison conditions, arbitrary arrest, detention without trial, and restrictions on freedom of assembly. President Patassé granted amnesty to former senior officials of the Kolingba regime and mutineers.

HEALTH/WELFARE

The literacy rate is low in Central African Republic—60%. Teacher training is currently being emphasized, especially for primary-school teachers. Poaching has diminished C.A.R.'s reputation as one of the world's last great wildlife refuges.

ACHIEVEMENTS

Despite recurrent drought, a poor infrastructure, and inefficient official marketing, the farmers of Central African Republic have generally been able to meet most of the nation's basic food needs.

Chad (Republic of Chad)

GEOGRAPHY

Area in Square Miles (Kilometers):
496,000 (1,284,634) (about 3
times the size of California)
Capital (Population):
N'Djamena (826,000)
Environmental Concerns: soil and
water pollution; desertification;
insufficient potable water;
waste disposal
Geographical Features: broad,
arid plains in the center;
desert in the north; mountains
in the northwest; lowlands in
the south; landlocked
Climate: tropical in the south;
desert in the north

PEOPLE

Population

Total: 8,425,000
Annual Growth Rate: 3.31%
Rural/Urban Population Ratio:
77/23
Major Languages: French;
Arabic; Sara; Sango; others
Ethnic Makeup: 200 distinct
groups
Religions: 50% Muslim; 25%
Christian; 25% indigenous
beliefs

Health

Life Expectancy at Birth: 49
years (male); 53 years (female)
Infant Mortality Rate (Ratio):
96.6/1,000
Physicians Available (Ratio):
1/27,765

Education

Adult Literacy Rate: 48%
Compulsory (Ages): 6 –14

COMMUNICATION

Telephones: 8,600 main lines
Televisions: 8 per 1,000 people
Internet Service Providers: 1 (1999)

TRANSPORTATION

Highways in Miles (Kilometers): 19,620
(32,700)
Railroads in Miles (Kilometers): none
Usable Airfields: 49
Motor Vehicles in Use: 24,000

GOVERNMENT

Type: republic
Independence Date: August 11, 1960
(from France)
Head of State/Government: President
Idriss Déby; Prime Minister Nagdum
Yamassoum

Political Parties: Patriotic Salvation
Movement; National Union for
Development and Renewal; many others
Suffrage: universal at 18

MILITARY

Military Expenditures (% of GDP): 3.5%
Current Disputes: civil war; border
conflicts

ECONOMY

Currency ($ U.S. Equivalent): 529.43
CFA francs = $1
Per Capita Income/GDP: $1,000/$7.6
billion
GDP Growth Rate: 0.6%

Inflation Rate: 12%
Natural Resources: petroleum; uranium;
natron; kaolin; fish
Agriculture: subsistence crops; cotton;
cattle; fish; sugar
Industry: livestock products; breweries;
natron; soap; textiles; cigarettes;
construction materials
Exports: $288 million (primary partners
Portugal, Germany, Thailand)
Imports: $359 million (primary partners
France, Nigeria, Cameroon)

 http://www.sas.upenn.edu/
African_Studies/Country_Specific/
Chad.html

CHAD

With the announcement of parliamentary election results in March 1997, Chad completed its transition to unified civilian rule under the firm guidance of its President Idriss Déby. A former regional warlord who seized power in 1990, Déby emerged in June 1996 with 67 percent of the vote as the second-round winner of the country's first genuinely contested presidential elections since its independence in 1960. The result can be interpreted as an endorsement of his government's gradual progress in rebuilding Chad's state structures, which had all but collapsed in the 1980s, when the country was referred to as "the Lebanon of Africa." While his success in defeating, marginalizing, and/or reconciling with rival armed factions has restored a semblance of statehood to Chad, Déby presides over a bankrupt government whose control over much of the countryside remains tenuous. His opting for a unitary rather than a federal state, which is favored by most southerners, is also divisive.

CIVIL WAR

Chad's conflicts are partially rooted in the country's ethnic and religious divisions. It has been common for outsiders to portray the struggle as being between Arab-oriented Muslim northerners and black Christian southerners, but Chad's regional and ethnic allegiances are much more complex. Geographically, the country is better divided into three zones: the northern Sahara, a middle Sahel region, and the southern savanna. Within each of these ecological areas live peoples who speak different languages and engage in a variety of economic activities. Wider ethno-regional and religious loyalties have emerged as a result of the Civil War, but such aggregates have tended to be fragile, and their allegiances shifting.

At Chad's independence, France turned over power to François Tombalbaye, a Sara-speaking Christian southerner. Tombalbaye ruled with a combination of repression, ethnic favoritism, and incompetence, which quickly alienated his regime from broad sectors of the population. A northern-

based coalition of armed groups, the National Liberation Front, or Frolinat, launched an increasingly successful insurgency. The intervention of French troops on Tombalbaye's behalf failed to stem the rebellion. In 1975, the army, tired of the war and upset by the president's increasingly conspicuous brutality, overthrew Tombalbaye and established a military regime, headed by Felix Malloum.

Malloum's government was also unable to defeat Frolinat; so, in 1978, it agreed to share power with the largest of the Frolinat groups, the Armed Forces of the North (FAN), led by Hissène Habré. This agreement broke down in 1979, resulting in fighting in N'Djamena. FAN came out ahead, while Malloum's men withdrew to the south. The triumph of the "northerners" immediately led to further fighting among various factions—some allied to Habré, others loyal to his main rival within the Frolinat, Goukkouni Oueddie. Earlier Habré had split from Oueddie, whom he accused of indifference toward Libya's unilateral annexation in 1976 of

(United Nations photo by John Isaac)

Thousands upon thousands of Chadians have died as a result of the Chadian Civil War. Compounding the civil strife in the 1980s was severe drought, which caused a great deal of internal migration. Migrating families such as that shown above became the rule rather than the exception.

Independence is
achieved under
President
François
Tombalbaye
1960

Revolt breaks out
among peasant
groups;
FROLINAT
is formed
1965–1966

Establishment of
a Transitional
Government of
National Unity
(GUNT) with
Hissène Habré
and Goukkouni
Oueddie
1978

Habré seizes
power and
reunites the
country in a
U.S.–supported
war against Libya
1980s

Habré is
overthrown by
Idriss Déby; Déby
promises to create
a multiparty
democracy, but
conditions remain
anarchic
1990s

2000s

Outbreaks of fighting
between government
security forces and armed
insurgents

Chad's northern provinces
bordering Libya remain
heavily landmined

the Aouzou Strip, along Chad's northern frontier. At the time, Libya was the principal foreign backer of Frolinat.

In 1980, shortly after the last French forces withdrew from Chad, the Libyan Army invaded the country, at the invitation of Oueddie. Oueddie was then proclaimed the leader in a "Transitional Government of National Unity" (GUNT), which was established in N'Djamena. Nigeria and other neighboring states, joined by France and the United States, pressed for the withdrawal of the Libyan forces. This pressure grew in 1981 after Libyan leader Muammar al-Qadhafi announced the merger of Chad and Libya. Following a period of intense multinational negotiations, the Libyan military presence was reduced at Oueddie's request.

The removal of the Libyan forces from most of Chad was accompanied by revived fighting between GUNT and FAN, with the latter receiving substantial U.S. support, via Egypt and Sudan. A peacekeeping force assembled by the Organization of African Unity proved ineffectual. The collapse of GUNT in 1982 led to a second major Libyan invasion. The Libyan offensive was countered by the return of French forces, assisted by Zairian troops and by smaller contingents from several other Francophonic African countries. Between 1983 and 1987, the country was virtually partitioned along the 16th Parallel, with Habré's French-backed, FAN-led coalition in the south and the Libyan-backed remnants of GUNT in the north.

A political and military breakthrough occurred in 1987. Habré's efforts to unite the country led to a reconciliation with Malloum's followers and with elements within GUNT. Oueddie himself was apparently placed under house arrest in Libya. Emboldened, Habré launched a major offensive north of the 16th Parallel

that rolled back the better-equipped Libyan forces, who by now included a substantial number of Lebanese mercenaries. A factor in the Libyan defeat was U.S.-supplied Stinger missiles, which allowed Habré's forces to neutralize Libya's powerful air force (Habré's government lacked significant air power of its own). A cease-fire was declared after the Libyans had been driven out of all of northern Chad with the exception of a portion of the disputed Aouzou Strip.

In 1988, Qadhafi announced that he would recognize the Habré government and pay compensation to Chad. The announcement was welcomed—with some skepticism—by Chadian and other African leaders, although no mention was made of the conflicting claims to the Aouzou Strip.

The long-running struggle for Chad took another turn in November 1990, with the sudden collapse of Habré's regime in the face of a three-week offensive by guerrillas loyal to his former army commander, Idriss Déby. Despite substantial Libyan (and Sudanese) backing for his seizure of power, Déby had the support of France, Nigeria, and the United States (Habré had supported Iraq's annexation of Kuwait). A 1,200-man French force began assisting Déby against rebels loyal to Habré and other faction leaders.

Between January and April 1993, Déby's hand was strengthened by the successful holding of a "National Convention," in which a number of formerly hostile groups agreed to cooperate with the government in drawing up a new constitution. In April 1994, his government was further boosted by Qadhafi's unexpected decision to withdraw his troops from the Aouzou Strip, leaving Chad in undisputed control of the territory. The move followed an International Court of Justice ruling in Chad's favor.

A BETTER FUTURE?

The long, drawn-out conflict in Chad has led to immense suffering. Up to a half a million people—the equivalent of 10 percent of the total population—have been killed in the fighting.

Even if peace could be restored, the overall prospects for national development are bleak. The country has potential mineral wealth, but its geographic isolation and current world prices are disincentives to investors. Local food self-sufficiency should be obtainable despite the possibility of recurrent drought, but geography limits the potential of export crops. Chad thus appears to be an extreme case of the more general African need for a radical transformation of prevailing regional and global economic interrelationships. Had outside powers devoted half the resources to Chad's development over the past decades as they have provided to its civil conflicts, perhaps the country's future would appear brighter.

DEVELOPMENT

Chad has potential petroleum and mineral wealth that would greatly help the economy if stable central government can be created. Deposits of chromium, tungsten, titanium, gold, uranium, and tin as well as oil are known to exist. Roads are in poor condition and are dangerous.

FREEDOM

Despite some modest improvement, Chad's human-rights record remains poor. Its security forces are linked to torture, extra-judicial killings, beatings, disappearances, and rape. A recent Amnesty International report on Chad was entitled "Hope Betrayed." Antigovernment rebel forces are also accused of atrocities. The judiciary is not independent.

HEALTH/WELFARE

In 1992, there were reports of catastrophic famine in the countryside. Limited human services were provided by external aid agencies. Medicines are in short supply or unavailable.

ACHIEVEMENTS

In precolonial times, the town of Kanem was a leading regional center of commerce and culture. Since independence in 1960, perhaps Chad's major achievement has been the resiliency of its people under the harshest of circumstances. The holding of truly contested elections is also a significant accomplishment.

Congo (Republic of the Congo; Congo-Brazzaville)

GEOGRAPHY
Area in Square Miles (Kilometers):
132,000 (342,000) (about the size of Montana)
Capital (Population): Brazzaville (1,004,000)
Environmental Concerns: air and water pollution; deforestation
Geographical Features: coastal plain; southern basin; central plateau; northern basin
Climate: tropical; particularly enervating climate astride the equator

PEOPLE

Population
Total: 2,831,000
Annual Growth Rate: 2.23%
Rural/Urban Population Ratio: 41/59
Major Languages: French; Lingala; Kikongo; Teke; Sangha; M'Bochi; others
Ethnic Makeup: 48% BaKongo; 20% Sangha; 17% Teke; 15% others
Religions: 50% Christian; 48% indigenous beliefs; 2% Muslim

Health
Life Expectancy at Birth: 44 years (male); 50 years (female)
Infant Mortality Rate (Ratio): 101.5/1,000
Physicians Available (Ratio): 1/3,873

Education
Adult Literacy Rate: 75%
Compulsory (Ages): 6–16

COMMUNICATION
Telephones: 22,000 main lines
Televisions: 17 per 1,000 people
Internet Service Providers: na

TRANSPORTATION
Highways in Miles (Kilometers): 7,680 (12,800)
Railroads in Miles (Kilometers): 494 (797)
Usable Airfields: 36
Motor Vehicles in Use: 37,000

GOVERNMENT
Type: republic
Independence Date: August 15, 1960 (from France)
Head of State/Government: President Denis Sassou-Nguesso is both head of state and head of government
Political Parties: Congolese Labor Party; Pan-African Union for Social Development; Congolese Movement for Democracy and Integral Development; many others
Suffrage: universal at 18

MILITARY
Military Expenditures (% of GDP): 3.8%
Current Disputes: civil conflicts; boundary issue with Democratic Republic of Congo

ECONOMY
Currency ($ U.S. Equivalent): 529.43 CFA francs = $1
Per Capita Income/GDP: $1,530/$4.15 billion
GDP Growth Rate: 5%
Inflation Rate: 4%
Natural Resources: timber; potash; lead; zinc; uranium; petroleum; natural gas; copper; phosphates
Agriculture: cassava; cocoa; coffee; sugarcane; rice; peanuts; vegetables; forest products
Industry: processing of agricultural and forestry goods; cement; brewing; petroleum
Exports: $1.7 billion (primary partners United States, Belgium-Luxembourg, Germany)
Imports: $770 million (primary partners France, United States, Belgium)

http://www.sas.upenn.edu/
African_Studies/Country_Specific/
Congo.html

Map

CAMEROON

CENTRAL AFRICAN REPUBLIC

EQ. GUINEA

Souanké

Impfondo

Sangha

Oubangui

Ubangi

GABON

Makoua

Owando

Likouala

Okoyo

Gamboma

Congo

Djambala

DEMOCRATIC REPUBLIC OF THE CONGO

Mossendjo

Inoni

Kouilou

Loubomo

Madingou

BRAZZAVILLE

Pointe-Noire

ATLANTIC OCEAN

ANGOLA

Congo

⭐ Capital
● City
∼ River
--- Road

| 0 | 15 | 30 | | 60 Miles |
| 0 | 15 | 30 | 60 | 90 Kilometers |

A TIME OF TRANSITION

In October 1997, rebel forces loyal to the former Congolese dictator General Denis Sassou-Nguesso seized control of the capital city of Brazzaville, effectively ending the four-month-long revolt against the government of Pascal Lissouba, which had been reelected in 1995. The return to power of Sassou-Nguesso, who had won only 17 percent of the vote in 1995, would not have been possible without the intervention in his favor of Angolan government forces, whose overt violation of Congolese sovereignty attracted little international comment. The Angolans were apparently motivated by allegations that Lissouba was supportive of UNITA rebels in their own country. With Brazzaville and much of the countryside in ruins, militias loyal to Lissouba and other political rivals active in some areas, and the economy in a state of near collapse, the return of Sassou-Nguesso does not bode well for the future of this once relatively prosperous nation.

The overthrow of Lissouba is all the more unfortunate in that his government had seemed to have been making progress in negotiating an end to the violence among the political factions that has plagued the country for the past decade. A 1995 agreement was supposed to lead to the disarmament of party militias. But instead, efforts to assure the disarmament of Sassou-Nguesso's men set off the revolt in June 1997. Previously, in November 1993, large sections of Brazzaville had been a battleground between troops loyal to the elected Pan-African Union of Social Democracy (UPADS) government of President Lissouba and the so-called Ninjas—armed supporters of opposition leader Bernard Kolelas's Union for the Renewal of Democracy (URD). After several weeks of fighting, peace was finally restored, with the intervention of an Organization of African Unity mediator. The crisis underscored the continuing fragility of Congo's difficult political transition into a multiparty democracy.

Sassou-Nguesso had previously ruled Congo as the head of a self-proclaimed, Marxist-Leninist one-party state. But in 1990, the ruling Congolese Workers Party (PCT) agreed to abandon both its past ideology and its monopoly of power. In 1991, a four-month-long "National Conference" met to pave the way for a new constitutional order. An interim government headed by Andre Milongo was appointed pending elections, while Sassou-Nguesso was stripped of all but ceremonial power. In the face of coup attempts by elements of the old order and a deteriorating economy, legislative and executive elections were finally held in the second half of 1992, resulting in Lissouba's election and a divided National Assembly.

A new National Assembly election in 1993 resulted in a decisive UPADS victory over a URD–PCT alliance, but the losers rejected the results for five months. With the economy experiencing a prolonged depression, political tensions remained high.

(United Nations photo by Sean Sprague)

Since Congo achieved its independence in 1960, it has made enormous educational strides. Almost all children in the country now attend school, which has had a tremendous effect on helping to realize the potential of the country's natural resources.

Middle Congo becomes part of French Equatorial Africa
1910

Conference establishes French Union; Felix Eboue establishes positive policies for African advancement
1944

Independence is achieved, with Abbe Fulbert Youlou as the first president
1960

A general strike brings the army and a more radical government (National Revolutionary Movement) to power
1963

A new military government under Marien Ngouabi takes over; the Congolese Workers' Party is formed
1968–1969

Ngouabi is assassinated; Colonel Yhombi-Opango rules
1977

Denis Sassou-Nguesso becomes president
1979

Pascal Lissouba is elected president; former dictator Sassou-Nguesso seizes power
1990s

2000s

Congo tries to recover from the civil conflict of the late 1990s

Security problems remain despite the peace process

CONGO

The Republic of the Congo takes its name from the river that forms its southeastern border with the Democratic Republic of Congo (formerly Zaire). Because Zaire prior to 1971 also called itself the Congo, the two countries are sometimes confused. Close historical and ethnic ties do in fact exist between the nations. The BaKongo are the largest ethnolinguistic group in Congo and western former Zaire as well as in northern Angola. During the fifteenth and sixteenth centuries, this group was united under the powerful kingdom of the Kongo, which ruled over much of Central Africa while establishing commercial and diplomatic ties with Europe. But the kingdom had virtually disappeared by the late nineteenth century, when the territory along the northwest bank of the Congo River—the modern republic—was annexed by France, while the southeast bank—Zaire—was placed under the rule of King Leopold of Belgium.

Despite the establishment of this political division, cultural ties between Congo and the former Zaire, the former French and Belgian Congos, remained strong. Brazzaville sits across the river from the Zairian capital of Kinshasha. The metropolitan region formed by these two centers has, through such figures as the late Congolese artist Franco, given rise to *soukous,* a musical style that is now popular in such places as Tokyo and Paris as well as throughout much of Africa.

ECONOMIC DEVELOPMENT

Brazzaville, which today houses well over a third of Congo's population, was established during the colonial era as the administrative headquarters of French Equatorial Africa, a vast territory that included the modern states of Chad, Central African Republic, Gabon, and Congo. As a result, the city expanded, and the area around it developed as an imperial crossroads. The Congolese paid a heavy price for this growth. Thousands died while working under brutal conditions to build the Congo-Ocean Railroad, which linked Brazzaville with Pointe-Noire on the coast. Many more suffered as forced laborers for foreign concessionaires during the early decades of the twentieth century.

While the economies of many African states stagnated or declined during the 1970s and 1980s, Congo generally experienced growth, a result of its oil wealth. Hydrocarbons account for 90 percent of the total value of the nation's exports. But the danger of this dependence has been apparent since 1986, when falling oil prices led to a sharp decline in gross domestic product. An even greater threat to the nation's economic health is its mounting debt. As a result of heavy borrowing during the oil-boom years, by 1989 the total debt was estimated to be 50 percent greater than the value of the country's annual economic output. The annual cost of servicing the debt was almost equal to domestic expenditure.

The debt led to International Monetary Fund pressure on Congo's rulers to introduce austerity measures as part of a Structural Adjustment Program (SAP). The PCT regime and its interim successor were willing to move away from the country's emphasis on central planning toward a greater reliance on market economics. But after an initial round of severe budgetary cutbacks, both administrations found it difficult to reduce their spending further on such things as food subsidies and state-sector employment.

With more than half of Congo's population now urbanized, there has been deep concern about the social and political consequences of introducing harsher austerity measures. Many urbanites are already either unemployed or underemployed; even those with steady formal-sector jobs have already been squeezed by wages that fail to keep up with the inflation rate. The country's powerful trade unions, which are hostile to SAP, have been in the forefront of the democratization process.

Although most Congolese are facing tough times in the short run, the economy's long-term prospects remain hopeful. Besides oil, the country is endowed with a wide variety of mineral reserves. Timber has long been a major industry. And after years of neglect, the agricultural sector is growing. The goal of a return to food self-sufficiency appears achievable. Cocoa, coffee, tobacco, and sugarcane are major cash crops, while palm-oil estates are being rehabilitated.

The small but well-established Congolese manufacturing sector also has much potential. Congo's urbanized population is relatively skilled, thanks to the enormous educational strides that have been made since independence. Almost all children in Congo now attend school. Prior to the devastation that occurred during the 1997 revolt, the infrastructure serving Brazzaville and Pointe-Noire, coupled with the previous government's emphasis on private-sector growth, was potentially attractive to outside investors.

DEVELOPMENT

Congo's Niari Valley has become the nation's leading agricultural area, due to its rich alluvial soils. The government has been encouraging food-processing plants to locate in the region.

FREEDOM

Until 1990, political opposition groups, along with Jehovah's Witnesses and certain other religious sects, were vigorously suppressed. The new Constitution provides for basic freedoms of association, belief, and speech.

HEALTH/WELFARE

Almost all Congolese between ages 6 and 16 currently attend school. Adult-literacy programs have also proved successful, giving the country one of the highest literacy rates in Africa. However, 30% of Congolese children under age 5 are reported to suffer from chronic malnutrition.

ACHIEVEMENTS

There are a number of Congolese poets and novelists who combine their creative efforts with teaching and public service. Tchicaya U'Tam'si, who died in 1988, wrote poetry and novels and worked for many years for UNESCO.

Democratic Republic of the Congo
(Congo-Kinshasa; formerly Zaire)

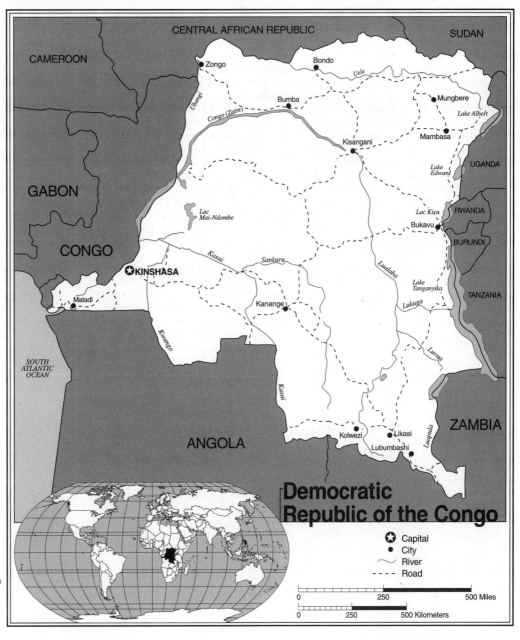

GEOGRAPHY

Area in Square Miles (Kilometers):
905,063 (2,300,000) (¼ the
size of the United States)
Capital (Population): Kinshasa
(4,241,000)
Environmental Concerns:
poaching; water pollution;
deforestation; soil erosion
Geographical Features: the vast
central basin is a low-lying
plateau; mountains in the east
Climate: equatorial

PEOPLE

Population
Total: 51,965,000
Annual Growth Rate: 3.19%
Rural/Urban Population Ratio:
71/29
Major Languages: French;
Lingala; Kingwana; others
Ethnic Makeup: Bantu majority;
more than 200 African groups
Religions: 70% Christian; 20%
indigenous beliefs; 10% Muslim

Health
Life Expectancy at Birth: 47
years (male); 51 years (female)
Infant Mortality Rate (Ratio):
101.6/1,000
Physicians Available (Ratio):
1/15,584

Education
Adult Literacy Rate: 77.3%
Compulsory (Ages): 6–12

COMMUNICATION
Telephones: 21,000 main lines
Daily Newspaper Circulation:
3 per 1,000 people
Internet Service Provider: 1 (1999)

TRANSPORTATION
Highways in Miles (Kilometers):
97,340 (157,000)
Railroads in Miles (Kilometers):
3,206 (5,138)
Usable Airfields: 232
Motor Vehicles in Use: 530,000

GOVERNMENT
Type: dictatorship; presumably undergoing
a transition to representative government
Independence Date: June 30, 1960
(from Belgium)
Head of State/Government: President
Laurent Kabila is both head of state
and head of government
Political Parties: Popular Movement of
the Revolution; Democratic Social
Christian Party; others
Suffrage: universal and compulsory at 18

MILITARY
Military Expenditures (% of GDP): 4.6%
Current Disputes: civil war; boundary
issue with Congo

ECONOMY
Currency ($ U.S. Equivalent): 3,275 new
Zaires = $1
Per Capita Income/GDP: $710/$35.7 billion
GDP Growth Rate: 1%
Labor Force: 14,510,000
Natural Resources: cobalt; copper;
cadmium; petroleum; zinc; diamonds;
manganese; tin; gold; silver; bauxite;
iron ore; coal; hydropower; timber; others

Agriculture: coffee; palm oil; rubber; tea;
manioc; bananas; root crops; corn;
fruits; sugarcane; wood products
Industry: mineral mining and processing;
consumer products; cement; diamonds
Exports: $530 million (primary partners
Belgium, United States, South Africa)
Imports: $460 million (primary partners
South Africa, Belgium, Nigeria)

 http://www.sas.upenn.edu/
African_Studies/Country_Specific/
DR_Congo.html

DEMOCRATIC REPUBLIC OF THE CONGO (Congo–Kinshasa) (Zaire)

In recent years, countries throughout Central, East, and Southern Africa have been drawn into the ongoing civil war in the Democratic Republic of the Congo (D.R.C., formerly known as Zaire and sometimes referred to as Congo-Kinshasa). The uprising began in August 1998, when rebels calling themselves the Congolese Assembly for Democracy, heavily backed by Rwandan and Ugandan military units, advanced rapidly from the east. This occured shortly after the then–15-month-old Congolese regime of Laurent Kabila called for the removal of foreign forces from the country. Early rebel hopes of a quick victory were frustrated by the intervention of Angolan, Namibian, and Zimbabwean forces. While neither side appears able to achieve victory, UN/OAU–backed mediation efforts under the chairmanship of former Botswanan president Sir Ketumile Masire have faltered. Meanwhile, the rebels have themselves become divided, with Rwandan and Ugandan forces at times turning on each other. As the D.R.C. has once more become a battlefield for external interests, the optimism that followed upon the 1997 overthrow of Mobutu Sese Seko, under whom the country had suffered three decades of corrupt authoritarian rule, has all but evaporated.

Laurent Kabila came to power as the leader of the Alliance of Democratic Forces for the Liberation of Congo-Zaire, a rebel movement that was itself heavily dependent on external support, especially from Rwanda, Uganda, and Zimbabwe. In the final months of 1996, Kabila's forces seized control of eastern Zaire, and they arrived in Kinshasa in May 1997. Once in power, Kabila changed the name of the country from Zaire, an identity that had been imposed by Mobutu in 1971, to its former title: Democratic Republic of the Congo.

Hopes that the new government would bring an end to the chronic corruption and mismanagement that have long plagued the country, or lead to an opening for democracy and improved human rights, soon proved misplaced. A leading Mobutu opponent, Etienne Tshisekedi wa Mulumba, was assaulted by Kabila's men within days of their victory. Tshisekedi remains the head of a nonviolent opposition coalition, the Union for Democracy and Social Progress, that is calling for a transition to democracy through a negotiated government of national unity. So far, this plea has been ignored by outside powers as well as the warring factions.

Meanwhile, the country's already decayed social and economic infrastructure continues to disintegrate. The informal sector now dominates the local economy. In the process, national unity is being challenged by the reemergence of secessionist tendencies in the mineral-rich provinces of Katanga (Shaba) and Kasai. Western and eastern former Zaire has been inundated by an influx of some 2 million refugees from the killing fields of Rwanda and Burundi. A vast country of potentially great wealth, the D.R.C.'s fate will ultimately affect the future of neighboring states as well as its own citizens.

Geographically, the D.R.C. is the hub of Africa. Located at Africa's center, it encompasses the entire Congo, or Zaire, River Basin, whose waters are the potential source of 13 percent of the world's hydroelectric power. This immense area, about one quarter the size of the United States, encompasses a variety of land forms. It contains good agricultural possibilities and a wide range of natural resources, some of which have been intensively exploited for decades.

The D.R.C. links Africa from west to east. Its very narrow coastline faces the Atlantic. Eastern former Zaire has long been influenced by forces from the East African coast, however. In the mid-nineteenth century, Swahili, Arab, and Nyamwezi traders from Tanzania established their hegemony over much of southeastern Zaire, pillaging the countryside for ivory and slaves. While the slave trade has left bitter memories, the Swahili language has spread to become a lingua franca throughout the eastern third of the country.

The nearly 52 million people of the Democratic Republic of the Congo belong to more than 200 different ethnic groups, speak some 700 languages and dialects, and have varied lifestyles. Boundaries established in the late nineteenth century hemmed in portions of the Azande, Konga, Chokwe, and Songye peoples, yet they maintain contact with their kin in other countries.

Many important precolonial states were centered here, including the Luba, Kuba, and Lunda kingdoms, the latter of which, in earlier centuries, exploited the salt and copper of southeastern Zaire. The kingdom of Kongo, located at the mouth of the Congo River, flourished during the fifteenth and sixteenth centuries, establishing important diplomatic and commercial

(United Nations photo by Caracciolo/Banoun)

The Democratic Republic of the Congo is the geographical hub of Africa. On the west, the Congo (or Zaire) River Basin empties into the South Atlantic, where a small fishing industry exists.

(AP photo by Michel Euler)

In the mid-1990s, these refugee children lined up for medical treatment at a field hospital near Goma, in eastern Democratic Republic of the Congo (then called Zaire). Most of the refugees in the region were from Rwanda.

relations with Portugal. The elaborate political systems of these kingdoms are an important heritage for the Democratic Republic of the Congo.

LEOPOLD'S GENOCIDE
The European impact, like the Swahili and Arab influences from the east, had deeply destructive results. The Congo Basin was explored and exploited by private individuals before it came under Belgian domination. King Leopold of Belgium, as a private citizen, sponsored H. M. Stanley's expeditions to explore the basin. In 1879, Leopold used Stanley's "treaties" as a justification for setting up the "Congo Independent State" over the whole region. This state was actually a private proprietary colony. To turn a profit on his vast enterprise, Leopold acted under the assumption that the people and resources in the territory were his personal property. His commercial agents and various concessionaires, to whom he leased portions of his colony, began to brutally coerce the local African population into providing ivory, wild rubber, and other commodities. The armed militias sent out to collect quotas of rubber and other goods committed numerous atrocities against the people, including destroying whole villages.

No one knows for sure how many Africans perished in Congo Independent State as a result of the brutalities of Leopold's agents. Some critics estimate that the territory's population was reduced by 10 million people over a period of 20

years. Many were starved to death as forced laborers. Others were massacred in order to induce survivors to produce more rubber. Women and children were suffocated in "hostage houses" while their men did their masters' bidding. Thousands fled to neighboring territories.

For years the Congo regime was able to keep information of its crimes from leaking overseas, but eventually reports from missionaries and others did emerge. Public outrage was stirred by accounts such as E. D. Morel's *Red Rubber* and Mark Twain's caustic *King Leopold's Soliloquy,* as well as gruesome pictures of men, women, and children whose hands had been severed by troops (who were expected to produce the hands for their officers as evidence of their diligence). Joseph Conrad's fictionalized account of his experiences, *The Heart of Darkness,* became a popular literary classic. Finally even the European imperialists, during an era when their racial arrogance was at its height, could no longer stomach Leopold, called by some "the king with ten million murders on his soul."

During the years of Belgian rule, 1908 to 1960, foreign domination was less genocidal, but a tradition of abuse had nevertheless been established. The colonial authorities still used armed forces for "pacification" campaigns, tax collection, and labor recruitment. Local collaborators were turned into chiefs and given arbitrary powers that they would not have had under indigenous political systems. Conces-

sionary companies continued to use force to recruit labor for their plantations and mines. The colonial regime encouraged the work of Catholic missionaries. Health facilities as well as a paternalistic system of education were developed. A strong elementary-school system was part of the colonial program, but the Belgians never instituted a major secondary-school system, and there was no institution of higher learning. By independence, only 16 Congolese had been able to earn university degrees, all but two in non-Belgian institutions. A small group of high-school–educated Congolese, known as *évolués* ("evolved ones"), served the needs of an administration that never intended nor planned for Zaire's independence.

In the 1950s, the Congolese, especially townspeople, were affected by the independence movements that were emerging throughout Africa. The Belgians began to recognize the need to prepare for a different future. Small initiatives were allowed; in 1955, nationalist associations were first permitted, and a 30-year timetable for independence was proposed. This sparked heated debate. Some évolués agreed with the Belgians' proposal. Others, including the members of the Alliance of the Ba-Kongo (ABAKO), an ethnic association in Kinshasa, and the National Congolese Movement (MNC), led by Prime Minister Patrice Lumumba, rejected it.

A serious clash at an ABAKO demonstration in 1959 resulted in some 50 deaths. In the face of mounting unrest, further encouraged by the imminent independence of French Congo (the Republic of the Congo), the Belgians conceded a rapid transition to independence. A constitutional conference in January 1960 established a federal-government system for the future independent state. But there was no real preparation for this far-reaching political change.

THE CONGO CRISIS

Democratic Republic of the Congo became independent on June 30, 1960, under the leadership of President Joseph Kasavubu and Prime Minister Patrice Lumumba. Within a week, an army mutiny had stimulated widespread disorder. The scars of Congo's uniquely bitter colonial experience showed. Unlike in Africa's other postcolonial states, hatred of the white former masters turned to violence in Congo, resulting in the hurried flight of the majority of its large European community. Ethnic and regional bloodshed took a much greater toll among the African population. The wealthy Katanga Province (now Shaba) and South Kasai seceded.

Lumumba called upon the United Nations for assistance, and troops came from a variety of countries to serve in the UN force. Later, as a result of a dispute with President Kasavubu, Lumumba sought Soviet aid. Congo could have become a Cold War battlefield, but the army, under Lumumba's former confidant, Joseph Desiré Mobutu, intervened. Lumumba was arrested and turned over to the Katanga rebels; he was later assassinated. Western interests and, in particular, the U.S. Central Intelligence Agency (CIA) played a substantial if not fully revealed role in the downfall of the idealistic Lumumba and the rise of his cynical successor, Mobutu. Rebellions by Lumumbists in the northeast and Katanga secessionists, supported by foreign mercenaries, continued through 1967.

MOBUTUISM

Mobutu seized full power in 1965, ousting Kasavubu in a military coup. With ruthless energy, he eliminated the rival political factions within the central government and crushed the regional rebellions. Mobutu banned party politics. In 1971, he established the Second Republic as a one-party state in which all power was centralized around the "Founding President." Every citizen, at birth, was legally expected to be a disciplined member of Mobutu's Popular Revolutionary Movement (MPR). With the exception of some religious organizations, virtually all social institutions were to function as MPR organs. The official ideology of the MPR republic became "Mobutuism"— the words, deeds,

and decrees of "the Guide" Mobutu. All citizens were required to sing his praises daily at the workplace, at schools, and at social gatherings. In hymns and prayers, the name Mobutu was often substituted for that of Jesus. A principal slogan of Mobutuism was "authenticity." Supposedly this meant a rejection of European values and norms for African ones.

But it was Mobutu alone who defined what was authentic. He added to his own name the title *Sese Seko* ("the All Powerful") while declaring all European personal names illegal. He also established a national dress code; ties were outlawed, men were expected to wear his abacost suit, and women were obliged to wear the *paigne,* or wrapper. (The former Zaire was perhaps the only place in the world where the necktie was a symbol of political resistance.) The name of the country was changed from Congo to *Zaire,* a word derived from the sixteenth-century Portuguese mispronunciation of the (Ki)Kongo word for "river."

Outside of Zaire, some took Mobutu's protestations of authenticity at face value, while a few other African dictators, such as Togo's Gnassingbé Eyadéma, emulated aspects of his fascist methodology. But the majority of Zairians grew to loathe his "cultural revolution."

Authenticity was briefly accompanied by a program of nationalization. Union Minière and other corporations were placed under government control. In 1973 and 1974, plantations, commercial institutions, and other businesses were also taken over, in what was called a "radicalizing of the Zairian Revolution."

But the expropriated businesses simply enriched a small elite. In many cases, Mobutu gave them away to his cronies, who often simply sold off the assets. Consequently, the economy suffered. Industries and businesses were mismanaged or ravaged. Some individuals became extraordinarily wealthy, while the population as a whole became progressively poorer with each passing year. Mobutu allegedly became the wealthiest person in all of Africa, with a fortune estimated in excess of $5 billion (about equal to Zaire's national debt), most of which was invested and spent outside of Africa. He and his relatives owned mansions all over the world.

Until his last year in power, no opposition to Mobutu was allowed. Those critical of the regime faced imprisonment, torture, or death. The Roman Catholic Church and the Kimbanguist Church of Jesus Christ Upon This Earth were the only institutions able to speak out. Strikes were not allowed. In 1977 and 1978, new revolts in the Shaba Province were crushed by U.S.-backed Moroccan, French, and Belgian

military interventions. Thus in 1997, rebels under Laurent Kabila ousted the ailing Mobutu and renamed the country the Democratic Republic of the Congo.

ECONOMIC DISASTER

The country's economic potential was developed by and for the Belgians, but by 1960, that development had gone further than in most other African colonial territories. It started with a good economic base, but the chaos of the early 1960s brought development to a standstill, and the Mobutu years were marked by regression. Development projects have been initiated, but often without careful planning. World economic conditions, including falling copper and cobalt prices, have contributed to Zaire's difficulties.

But the main obstacle to any sort of economic progress was the rampant corruption of Mobutu and those around him. The governing system in Zaire was characterized as a kleptocracy (rule by thieves). A well-organized system of graft transferred wealth from ordinary citizens to officials and other elites. With Mobutu stealing billions and those closest to him stealing millions, the entire society operated on an invisible tax system; for example, citizens had to bribe nurses for medical care, bureaucrats for documents, principals for school admission, and police to stay out of jail. For most civil servants, who are paid little or nothing, accepting bribes was a necessary activity. This fundamental fact also applied to most soldiers, who thus survived by living off the civilian population. The U.S. military learned this lesson first-hand when it conducted joint military exercises with former Zairian paratroopers. When a number of American troops' parachutes got caught in trees, the soldiers were robbed of their possessions by former Zairian troops, who then deserted into the forest.

Ordinary people suffered. By 1990, real wages of urban workers in former Zaire were only 2 percent of what they were in 1960. Rural incomes had also deteriorated. The official 1990 price paid to coffee farmers, for example, was only one fifth of what it was in 1954 under the exploitive Belgian regime. The situation has worsened since, due to periods of hyperinflation.

Much of the state's coffee and other cash crops have long been smuggled, more often than not through the connivance of senior government officials. Thus, although the country's agriculture has great economic potential, the returns from this sector continue to shrink. Despite its immense size and plentiful rainfall, it must import about 60 percent of its food requirements. Rural people move to the city or, for lack of employment, move

Leopold sets up the Congo Independent State as his private kingdom
1879

Congo becomes a Belgian colony
1906

Congo gains independence; civil war begins; a UN force is involved; Patrice Lumumba is murdered
1960

Joseph Desiré Mobutu takes command in a bloodless coup
1965

The name of the state is changed to Zaire
1971

Central authority crumbles; millions of Rwandan and Burundian refugees flood into Zaire; Mobutu is overthrown
1990s

2000s

Civil war continues

Laurent Kabila clings to power

back to the country and take up subsistence agriculture, rather than cash-crop farming, in order to ensure their own survival. The deterioration of roads and bridges has led to the decline of all trade.

In 1983, the government adopted International Monetary Fund austerity measures, but this only cut public expenditures. It had no effect on the endemic corruption, nor did it increase taxes on the rich. Under Mobutu's regime, more than 30 percent of former Zaire's budget went for debt servicing.

In June 1997, Kabila announced short-term economic priorities, including job creation, road and hospital rebuilding, and a national fuel-supply pipeline. But it was unclear where the money would come from to implement these plans.

U.S. SUPPORT FOR MOBUTU

Mobutu's regime was able to sidestep its financial crises and maintain power through the support of foreign powers, especially Belgium, France, Germany, and the United States. A U.S. intelligence report prepared in the mid-1950s concluded that the then–Belgian Congo was indeed the hub of Africa and thus vital to America's strategic interests. U.S. policy was thus the first to promote and then to perpetuate Mobutu as a pro-Western source of stability in the region. Mobutu himself skillfully cultivated this image.

Mobutu collaborated with the United States in opposing the Marxist-oriented Popular Movement for the Liberation of Angola. By so doing, he not only set himself up as an important Cold War ally but also was able to pursue regional objectives of his own. The National Front for the Liberation of Angola, long championed by the CIA as a counterforce to the MPLA,

was led by an in-law of Mobutu, Holden Roberto. Mobutu also long coveted Angola's oil-rich enclave of Cabinda and thus sought CIA and South African assistance for the "independence" movement there. In recent years, millions of U.S. dollars were spent upgrading the airstrip at Kamina in Shaba Province, used by the CIA to supply the guerrillas of the National Union for the Total Independence of Angola, another faction opposed to the MPLA government. In 1989, Mobutu attempted to set himself up as a mediator between the government and the UNITA rebels, but even the latter grew to distrust him.

The United States had long known of Mobutu's human-rights violations and of the oppression and corruption that characterized his regime; high-level defectors as well as victims had publicized its abuses. Since 1987, Mobutu responded with heavily financed public-relations efforts aimed at lobbying U.S. legislators. U.S. support for Mobutu continued, but the eventual collapse of his authority led Washington belatedly to search for alternatives.

Mobutu also allied himself with other conservative forces in Africa and the Middle East. Moroccan troops came to his aid during the revolts in Shaba Province in 1977 and 1978. For his part, Mobutu was a leading African supporter of Morocco's stand with regard to the Western Sahara dispute. Under his rule the country was also an active member of the Francophonic African bloc. In 1983, Mobutu dispatched 2,000 Zairian troops to Chad in support of the government of Hissène Habré, then under attack from Libya, while in 1986, his men again joined French forces in propping up the Eyadéma regime in Togo. He also maintained and strengthened his ties with South Africa (today, the former Zaire

imports almost half its food from that state). In 1982, he renewed the diplomatic ties with Israel that had been broken after the Arab–Israeli War of 1973. Israelis subsequently joined French and Belgians as senior advisers and trainers working within the former Zairian Army. In 1990, the outbreak of violent unrest in Kinshasha once more led to the intervention of French and Belgian troops.

Despite Mobutu's cultivation of foreign assistance to prop up his dictatorship, internal opposition grew. In 1990, he tried to head off his critics both at home and abroad by promising to set up a new Third Republic, based on multiparty democracy. Despite this step, repression intensified.

In October 1996, while Mobutu was in Europe recovering from cancer surgery, rebel troops under the leadership of Laurent Kabila seized their first major town, Uvira. Thousands of Rwandan Hutu refugees were forced to flee back to Rwanda. When Mobutu returned home in April 1997, he declared a nationwide state of emergency. Kabila's supporters then closed down Kinshasa as part of the campaign to oust Mobutu. Following negotiations with South Africa's Mandela, Mobutu left Kinshasa and went into exile.

DEVELOPMENT

Western aid and development assistance were drastically reduced in 1992, but new aid was pledged in 1994 as a reward for Mobutu's cooperation in dealing with the Rwandan conflict. An agreement was signed with Egypt for the long-term development of Zaire's hydroelectric power.

FREEDOM

The regime in the Democratic Republic of the Congo has shown little respect for human rights. One Amnesty International report concluded that all political prisoners are tortured. Death squads are active.

HEALTH/WELFARE

In 1978, more than 5 million students were registered for primary schools and 35,000 for college. However, the level of education has since declined. Many teachers were laid off in the 1980s, though nonexistent "ghost teachers" remained on the payroll. The few innovative educational programs that do manage to exist are outside of the state system.

ACHIEVEMENTS

Kinshasha has been called the dance-music capital of Africa. The most popular sound is souskous, or "Congo rumba." The grand old man of the style is Rochereau Tabu Ley. Other artists, like Papa Wemba, Pablo Lubidika, and Sandoka, have joined him in spreading its rhythms internationally.

Equatorial Guinea (Republic of Equatorial Guinea)

GEOGRAPHY
Area in Square Miles (Kilometers):
10,820 (28,023) (about the size of Maryland)
Capital (Population): Malabo (58,000)
Environmental Concerns: desertification
Geographical Features: coastal plains rise to interior hills; volcanic islands
Climate: tropical

PEOPLE

Population
Total: 475,000
Annual Growth Rate: 2.47%
Rural/Urban Population Ratio: 57/43
Major Languages: Spanish; French; Bubi; Fang; Ibo
Ethnic Makeup: primarily Biokor, Rio Muni; fewer than 1,000 Europeans
Religions: nominally Christian, predominantly Roman Catholic; indigenous beliefs

Health
Life Expectancy at Birth: 52 years (male); 56 years (female)
Infant Mortality Rate (Ratio): 94.8/1,000
Physicians Available (Ratio): 1/3,532

Education
Adult Literacy Rate: 78.5%
Compulsory (Ages): 6–11; free

COMMUNICATION
Telephones: 5,400 main lines
Televisions: 88 per 1,000 people
Internet Service Providers: na

TRANSPORTATION
Highways in Miles (Kilometers): 1,786 (2,880)
Railroads in Miles (Kilometers): none
Usable Airfields: 3
Motor Vehicles in Use: 7,600

GOVERNMENT
Type: republic
Independence Date: October 12, 1968 (from Spain)
Head of State/Government: President (Brigadier General) Teodoro Obiang Nguema Mbasogo; Prime Minister Serafin Seriche Dougan
Political Parties: Democratic Party for Equatorial Guinea; Progressive Democratic Alliance; Popular Action of Equatorial

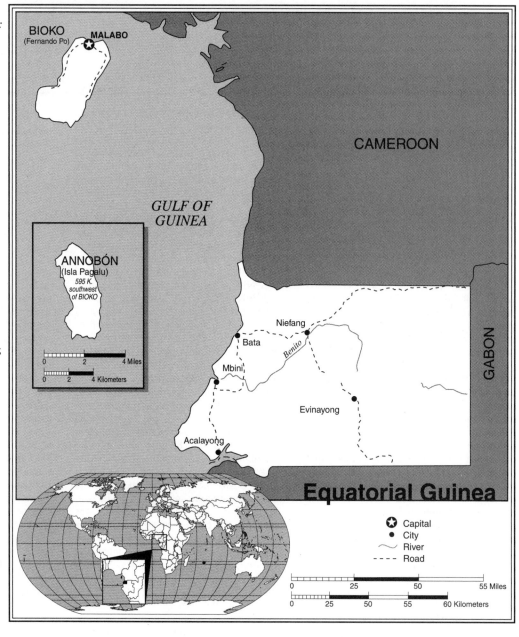

Guinea; Convergence Party for Social Democracy; others
Suffrage: universal at 18

MILITARY
Military Expenditures (% of GDP): 0.6%
Current Disputes: maritime boundary disputes with Cameroon, Gabon, and Nigeria

ECONOMY
Currency ($ U.S. Equivalent): 529.43 CFA francs = $1
Per Capita Income/GDP: $2,000/$960 million
GDP Growth Rate: 15%
Inflation Rate: 6%
Unemployment Rate: 30%
Natural Resources: timber; petroleum; gold; manganese; uranium
Agriculture: cocoa; coffee; timber; rice; yams; cassava; bananas; palm oil; livestock
Industry: fishing; sawmilling; petroleum; natural gas
Exports: $555 million (primary partners United States, Spain, China)
Imports: $300 million (primary partners United States, France, Spain)

 http://www.sas.upenn.edu/ African_Studies/E-Guinea.html

Europeans explore modern Equatorial Guinea
1500s

The Dutch establish slave-trading stations
1641

Spain claims the area of Equatorial Guinea; de facto control is not completed until 1926
1778

The League of Nations investigates charges of slavery on Fernando Po
1930

The murder of nationalist leader Acacio Mane leads to the founding of political parties
1958

Local autonomy is granted
1963

Independence; Macias Nguema begins his reign
1968

A coup ends the dictatorial regime of Macias Nguema; Teodoro Obiang Nguema Mbasogo becomes the new ruler
1979

A shift to multipartyism is accompanied by wave of political detentions; Obiang Nguema Mbasogo claims electoral victory
1990s

2000s

The exploitation of large oil reserves boosts the economy

EQUATORIAL GUINEA

Few countries have been more consistently misruled than Equatorial Guinea. Having been traumatized during its first decade of independence by the sadistic Macias Nguema (1968–1979), the country continues to decay under his nephew and former security chief, Obiang Nguema Mbasogo. In 1992, Obiang officially transformed his regime into a multiparty democracy. But this gesture has been widely dismissed as a thinly disguised sham for the benefit of the French, Spanish, and Americans who provide assistance to his regime. And in the end, the move may have backfired. As a result of the government's failure to honor its commitments under a March 1993 multiparty national election, all the significant opposition groups boycotted the November 1993 election, describing it as a farce. Subsequent opposition attempts to come to an accommodation with the government were set back in April 1995, when the leader of the Party of Progress, Severo Moto, was arrested. (He was later released as a result of international pressure.) In February 1996, Obiang Nguema Mbasogo claimed 97.85 percent of the vote in a new presidential poll.

Equatorial Guinea's current suffering contrasts with the mood of optimism that characterized the country when it gained its independence from Spain in 1968. Confidence was then buoyed by a strong and growing gross domestic product, potential mineral riches, and exceptionally good soil.

The republic is comprised of two small islands, Fernando Po (now officially known as Bioko) and Annobón, and the larger and more populous coastal enclave of Rio Muni. Before the two islands and the enclave were united, during the 1800s, as Spain's only colony in sub-Saharan Africa, all three areas were victimized by their intense involvement in the slave trade.

Spain's major colonial concern was the prosperity of the large cocoa and coffee plantations that were established on the islands, particularly on Fernando Po. Because of resistance from the local Bubi, labor for these estates was imported from elsewhere in West Africa. Coercive recruitment and poor working conditions led to frequent charges of slavery.

Despite early evidence of its potential riches, Rio Muni was largely neglected by the Spanish, who did not occupy its interior until 1926. In the 1930s and 1940s, much of the enclave was under the political control of the Elar-ayong, a nationalist movement that sought to unite the Fang, Rio Muni's principal ethnic group, against both the Spanish and the French rulers in neighboring Cameroon and Gabon. The territory has remained one of the world's least developed areas.

In 1968, then–fascist-ruled Spain entrusted local power to Macias Nguema, who had risen through the ranks of the security service. Under his increasingly deranged misrule, virtually all public and private enterprise collapsed; indeed, between 1974 and 1979, the country had no budget. One third of the nation's population went into exile; tens of thousands of others were either murdered or allowed to die of disease and starvation. Many of the survivors were put to forced labor, and the rest were left to subsist off the land. Killings were carried out by boys conscripted between the ages of seven and 14.

Although no community in Equatorial Guinea was left unscarred by Macias's tyranny, the greatest disruption occurred on the islands. By 1976, the entire resident-alien population had left, along with most surviving members of the educated class. On Annobón, the government blocked all international efforts to stem a severe cholera epidemic in 1973. The near-total depopulation of the island was completed in 1976, when all able-bodied men on Annobón, along with another 20,000 from Rio Muni, were drafted for forced labor on Fernando Po.

If Equatorial Guinea's first decade of independence was hell, the years since have at best been purgatory. No sector of the economy is free of corruption. Uncontrolled—and in theory illegal—logging is destroying Rio Muni's environment, while in Malabo, the police routinely engage in theft. Food is imported and malnutrition commonplace. It has been reported that the remaining population of Annobón is being systematically starved while Obiang Nguema Mbasogo collects huge payments from international companies that use the island as a toxic-waste dump.

At least one fifth of the Equato-Guinean population continue to live in exile, mostly in Cameroon and Gabon. This community has fostered a number of opposition groups. The government relies financially on French and Spanish aid. But Madrid's commitment has been strained by criticism from the Spanish press, which has been virtually alone in publicizing Equatorial Guinea's continued suffering.

DEVELOPMENT

The exploitation of oil and gas by U.S., French, and Spanish companies should soon greatly increase government revenues. The U.S. company Walter International recently finished work on a gas-separation plant.

FREEDOM

In September 1998, Amnesty International cautiously welcomed a decree by President Obiang Nguema Mbasogo commuting the death sentences of 15 political opponents, including 4 exiles judged in absentia, who had been convicted in a summary trial the previous June. The reprieves were considered a vindication of those arguing for the continued need to put international pressure on the regime.

HEALTH

At independence, Equatorial Guinea had one of the best doctor-to-population ratios in Africa, but Macias's rule left it with one of the lowest. Health care is gradually reviving, however, with major assistance coming from public and private sources.

ACHIEVEMENTS

At independence, 90% of all children attended school, but the schools were closed under Macias. Since 1979, primary education has revived and now incorporates most children. Major assistance currently comes from the World Bank and from Spanish missionaries.

Gabon (Gabonese Republic)

GEOGRAPHY

Area in Square Miles (Kilometers):
102,317 (264,180) (about the
size of Colorado)
Capital (Population): Libreville
(363,000)
Environmental Concerns:
deforestation; poaching
Geographical Features: narrow
coastal plain; hilly interior;
savanna in the east and south
Climate: tropical

PEOPLE

Population
Total: 1,208,500
Annual Growth Rate: 1.08%
Rural/Urban Population Ratio:
49/51
Major Languages: French; Fang;
Myene; Eshira; Bopounou;
Bateke; Bandjabi
Ethnic Makeup: about 95%
African, including Eshira,
Fang, Bapounou, and Bateke;
5% European
Religions: 55%–75% Christian;
less than 1% Muslim; remainder
indigenous beliefs

Health
Life Expectancy at Birth: 49
years (male); 51 years (female)
Infant Mortality Rate (Ratio):
96.3/1,000
Physicians Available (Ratio):
1/2,337

Education
Adult Literacy Rate: 63.2%
Compulsory (Ages): 6–16

COMMUNICATION
Telephones: 1 per 41 people
Televisions: 1 per 26 people
Internet Service Provider: 1 (1999)

TRANSPORTATION
Highways in Miles (Kilometers):
4,650 (7,500)
Railroads in Miles (Kilometers): 402 (649)
Usable Airfields: 61
Motor Vehicles in Use: 33,000

GOVERNMENT
Type: republic; multiparty presidential regime
Independence Date: August 17, 1960
(from France)
Head of State/Government: President El
Hadj Omar Bongo; Prime Minister
Jean-Francois Ntoutoume-Emane
Political Parties: Gabonese Democratic
Party; Gabonese Party for Progress;
others
Suffrage: universal at 21

MILITARY
Military Expenditures (% of GDP): 1.6%
Current Disputes: maritime boundary
dispute with Equatorial Guinea

ECONOMY
Currency ($ U.S. Equivalent): 529.43
CFA francs = $1
Per Capita Income/GDP: $6,500/$7.9 billion
GDP Growth Rate: 1.7%
Inflation Rate: 2.9%
Unemployment Rate: 21%
Natural Resources: petroleum; iron ore;
manganese; uranium; gold; timber;
hydropower
Agriculture: cocoa; coffee; palm oil

Industry: petroleum; lumber; mining;
chemicals; ship repair; food processing;
cement; textiles
Exports: 2.4 billion (primary partners
United States, China, France)
Imports: $1.2 billion (primary partners
France, United States, Cameroon)

http://www.sas.upenn.edu/
African_Studies/Country_Specific/
Gabon.html
http://www.presidence-gabon.com/
index-a.html

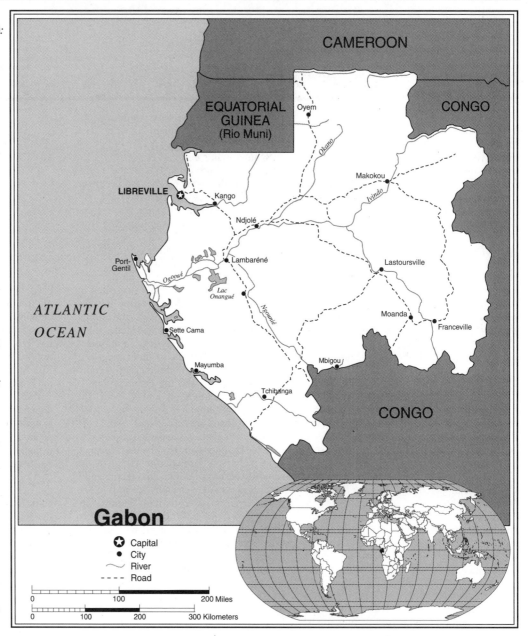

Libreville is
founded by the
French as a
settlement for
freed slaves
1849

Gabon becomes
a colony within
French
Equatorial Africa
1910

The Free French
in Brazzaville
seize Gabon
from the
pro-Vichy
government
1940

Independence is
gained; Leon
M'ba becomes
president
1960

Omar Bongo
becomes
Gabon's second
president after
M'ba's death
1967

The Gabonese
Democratic Party
(PDG) becomes
the only party of
the state
1968

Bongo agrees to
multiparty
elections but
seeks to put
limits on the
opposition; riots
in Port-Gentil
1990s

2000s

The PDG retains power

GABON

Since independence, Gabon has achieved one of the highest per capita gross domestic products in Africa, due to exploitation of the country's natural riches, especially its oil. But there is a wide gap between such statistical wealth and the real poverty that still shapes the lives of most Gabonese.

At the top of the local governing elite is President Omar Bongo, whose main palace, built at a reported cost of $300 million, symbolizes his penchant for grandeur. Shortly after taking office, in 1967, Bongo institutionalized his personal rule as the head of a one-party state. Until recently, his Democratic Party of Gabon (PDG) held a legal monopoly of power. But, although the PDG's Constitution restricted the presidency to the "Founder President," it has been Gabon's former colonial master, France, not the ruling party's by-laws, that has upheld the Bongo regime.

The French colonial presence in Gabon dates back to 1843. Between 1898 and 1930, many Gabonese were subject to long periods of forced labor, cutting timber for French concessions companies. World War II coincided with a period of political liberalization in the territory under the Free French government of Felix Emboue, a black man born in French Guiana. Educated Gabonese were promoted for the first time to important positions in the local administration. In the 1950s, two major political parties emerged to compete in local politics: the Social Democratic Union of Gabon (UDSG), led by Jean-Hilaire Aubame; and the Gabonese Democratic Bloc (BDG) of Indjenjet Gondjout and Leon M'ba.

In the 1957 elections, the UDSG received 60 percent of the popular vote but gained only 19 seats in the 40-seat Assembly. Leon M'ba, who had the support of French logging interests, was elected leader by 21 BDG and independent depu-

ties. As a result, it was M'ba who was at the helm when Gabon gained its independence, in 1960. This birth coincided with M'ba's declaration giving himself emergency powers, provoking a period of prolonged constitutional crisis.

In January 1964, M'ba dissolved the Assembly over its members' continued refusal to accept a one-party state under his leadership. In February, the president himself was forced to resign by a group of army officers. Power was transferred to a civilian "Provisional Government," headed by Aubame, which also included BDG politicians such as Gondjout and several prominent, unaffiliated citizens. However, no sooner had the Provisional Government been installed than Gabon was invaded by French troops. Local military units were massacred in the surprise attack, which returned M'ba to office. Upon his death, M'ba was succeeded by his hand-picked successor, Omar Bongo.

It has been suggested that France's 1964 invasion was motivated primarily by a desire to maintain absolute control over Gabon's uranium deposits, which were vital to France's nuclear weapons program. Many Gabonese have believed that their country has remained a de facto French possession. France has maintained its military presence, and the Gabonese Army is outgunned by the Presidential Guard, mainly officered by Moroccan and French mercenaries. France dominates Gabon's resource-rich economy.

Gabon's status quo has been challenged by its increasingly urbanized population. Although Bongo was able to co-opt or exile many of the figures who had once opposed M'ba, a new generation of opposition has emerged both at home and in exile. The leading opposition group for the past decade has been the underground Movement for National Recovery (MORENA). In 1989, Bongo began talks with some ele-

ments within MORENA, which led to a division within its ranks. But the breakup of MORENA failed to stem the emergence of new groups calling for a return to multiparty democracy.

Demonstrations and strikes at the beginning of 1990 led to the legalization of opposition parties. But the murder of a prominent opposition leader in May led to serious rioting at Port-Gentil, Gabon's second city. In response, France sent troops to the area. Multiparty elections for the National Assembly, in September–October 1990, resulted in a narrow victory for the PDG, amid allegations of widespread fraud. In 1992, most opposition groups united as the Coordination of Democratic Opposition. Bongo's victory claim in the December 1993 presidential election was widely disbelieved. In September 1994, he agreed to the formation of a coalition "Transitional Government" and the drafting of a new Constitution, which was approved by 96 percent of the voters in July 1995.

In December 1996, the PDG won a sweeping victory in parliamentary elections. This was followed up in December 1998 by a landslide reelection victory for Bongo. Although opposition politicians claimed that the results had been rigged, independent observers credit the PDG with success in retaining the support rural base while co-opting potential opponents into its fold.

DEVELOPMENT

The Trans-Gabonais Railway is one of the largest construction projects in Africa. Work began in 1974 and, after some delays, most of the line is now complete. The railway has opened up much of Gabon's interior to commercial development.

FREEDOM

Since 1967 Bongo has maintained power through a combination of repression and the deft use of patronage. The current transition to a multiparty process, however, has led to an improvement in human rights.

HEALTH/WELFARE

The government claims to have instituted universal, compulsory education for Gabonese up to age 16. Independent observers doubt the government's claim but concur that major progress has been made in education. Health services have also expanded greatly.

ACHIEVEMENTS

Gabon will soon have a second private television station, funded by a French cable station. Profits will be used to fund films that will be shown on other African stations. Gabon's first private station is funded by Swiss and Gabonese capital.

São Tomé and Príncipe
(Democratic Republic of São Tomé and Príncipe)

GEOGRAPHY

Area in Square Miles (Kilometers):
387 (1,001) (about 5 times the
size of Washington, D.C.)
Capital (Population): São Tomé
(43,000)
Environmental Concerns:
deforestation; soil erosion; soil
exhaustion
Geographical Features: volcanic;
mountainous
Climate: tropical

PEOPLE

Population
Total: 160,000
Annual Growth Rate: 3.1%
Rural/Urban Population Ratio: 56/44
Major Languages: Portuguese;
Fang; Kriolu
Ethnic Makeup: Portuguese-African
mixture; African minority
Religions: 80% Christian;
20% others

Health
Life Expectancy at Birth: 64 years
(male); 67 years (female)
Infant Mortality Rate (Ratio):
50.4/1,000
Physicians Available (Ratio): 1/1,881

Education
Adult Literacy Rate: 73%
Compulsory (Ages): for 4 years
between ages 7–14

COMMUNICATION

Telephones: 3,100 main lines
Televisions: 154 per 1,000 people
Internet Service Providers: na

TRANSPORTATION

Highways in Miles (Kilometers): 198
(320)
Railroads in Miles (Kilometers): none
Usable Airfields: 2

GOVERNMENT

Type: republic
Independence Date: July 12, 1975
(from Portugal)
Head of State/Government: President
Miguel Trovoada; Prime Minister
Guilherma Posser da Costa
Political Parties: Party for Democratic
Convergence-Group of Reflection;
Movement for the Liberation of São
Tomé and Príncipe–Social Democratic
Party; Christian Democratic Front;
Democratic Opposition Coalition; others
Suffrage: universal at 18

São Tomé
and Príncipe

⭐ Capital
● City
〜 River
--- Road

MILITARY

Military Expenditures (% of GDP): 1.5%
Current Disputes: none

ECONOMY

Currency ($ U.S. Equivalent): 130 dobras = $1
Per Capita Income/GDP: $1,100/$169 million
GDP Growth Rate: 1.5%
Inflation Rate: 10.5%
Unemployment Rate: 50%
Natural Resources: fish; hydropower
Agriculture: cacao; coconut palms; coffee;
bananas; palm kernels; copra

Industry: light construction; textiles; soap;
beer; fish processing; timber
Exports: $4.9 million (primary partners
the Netherlands, Germany, Portugal)
Imports: $19.5 million (primary partners
Portugal, France, Angola)

http://www.state.gov/www.background
_notes/sao_tome_0397_bgn.html
http://www.emulateme.com/
saotome.htm
http://www.sas.upenn.edu/
African_Studies/Country_Specific/
Sao_Tome.html

| The Portuguese settle São Tomé and Príncipe **1500s** | Slavery is abolished, but forced labor continues **1876** | The Portuguese massacre hundreds of islanders **1953** | Factions within the liberation movement unite to form the MLSTP in Gabon **1972** | Independence **1975** | Manuel Pinto da Costa deposes and exiles Miguel Trovoada, the premier and former number-two man in the MLSTP **1979** | Economic and political liberalization; multiparty elections **1990s** |

2000s

Trovoada maintains an uneasy hold on power

SÃO TOMÉ AND PRÍNCIPE

In August 1995, soldiers in the small island-nation of São Tomé and Príncipe briefly deposed Miguel Trovoada, the country's first democratically elected president. The coup quickly collapsed, however, in the face of domestic and international opposition. While the country's new democracy survived, it remains vulnerable to a weak economy, which shows little prospect of significant improvement anytime soon.

The islands held their first multiparty elections in January 1991. The elections resulted in the defeat of the former ruling party, the Liberation Movement of São Tomé and Príncipe–Social Democratic Party (MLSTP–PSD), by Trovoada's Party for Democratic Convergence–Group of Reflection (PDC–GR). Subsequent elections in December 1992, however, reversed the PDC–GR advantage in Parliament, leading to an uneasy division of power. This division was reinforced with Trovoada's reelection in 1996, followed by an even greater MLSTP–PSD parliamentary victory in 1998.

São Tomé and Príncipe gained its independence in 1975, after a half-millennium of Portuguese rule. During the colonial era, economic life centered around the interests of a few thousand Portuguese settlers, particularly a handful of large-plantation owners who controlled more than 80 percent of the land. After independence, most of the Portuguese fled, taking their skills and capital and leaving the economy in disarray. But production on the plantations has since been revived.

The Portuguese began the first permanent settlement of São Tomé and Príncipe in the late 1400s. Through slave labor, the islands developed rapidly as one of the world's leading exporters of sugar. Only a small fraction of the profits from this boom were consumed locally; and high mortality rates, caused by brutal working conditions, led to an almost insatiable demand for more slaves. Profits from sugar declined after the mid-1500s due to competition from Brazil and the Caribbean. A period of prolonged depression set in.

In the early 1800s, a second economic boom swept the islands, when they became leading exporters of coffee, and, more important, cocoa. (São Tomé and Príncipe's position in the world market has since declined, yet these two cash crops, along with copra, have continued to be economic mainstays.) Although slavery was officially abolished during the nineteenth century, forced labor was maintained by the Portuguese into modern times. Involuntary contract workers, known as *servicais*, were imported to labor on the islands' plantations, which had notoriously high mortality rates. Sporadic labor unrest and occasional incidents of international outrage led to some improvement in working conditions, but fundamental reforms came about only after independence. A historical turning point for the islands was the Batepa Massacre in 1953, when several hundred African laborers were killed following local resistance to labor conditions.

Between 1975 and 1991, São Tomé and Príncipe was ruled by the MLSTP–PSD, which had emerged in exile as the island's leading anticolonial movement, as a one-party state initially committed to Marxist-Leninism. But in 1990, a new policy of *abertura*, or political and economic "opening," resulted in the legalization of opposition parties and the introduction of direct elections with secret balloting. Press restrictions were also lifted, and the nation's security police were purged. The democratization process was welcomed by previously exiled opposition groups, most of which united as the PDC–GR. The changed political climate has also been reflected in the establishment of an independent labor movement. Previously, strikes were forbidden.

The move toward multiparty politics was accompanied by an evolution to a market economy. Since 1985, a "Free Trade Zone" has been established, state farms have been privatized, and private capital has been attracted to build up a tourist industry. These moves have been accompanied by a major expansion of Western loans and assistance to the islands—an inflow of capital that now accounts for nearly half of the gross domestic product.

The government has also focused its development efforts on fishing. In 1978, a 200-mile maritime zone was declared over the tuna-rich waters around the islands. The state-owned fishing company, Empesca, is upgrading the local fleet, which still consists mostly of canoes using old-fashioned nets. The influx of aid and investment has resulted in several years of sustained economic growth.

The current inhabitants of São Tomé and Príncipe are primarily of mixed African and European descent. During the colonial period, the society was stratified along racial lines. At the top were the Europeans—mostly Portuguese. Just below them were the *mesticos* or *filhos da terra*, the mixed-blood descendants of slaves. Descendants of slaves who arrived later were known as *forros*. Contract workers were labeled as *servicais*, while their children became known as *tongas*. Still another group was the *angolares*, who reportedly were the descendants of shipwrecked slaves. All of these colonial categories were used to divide and rule the local population; the distinctions have begun to diminish, however, as an important sociological factor on the islands.

DEVELOPMENT

Local food production has been significantly boosted by a French-funded plan. Japan is assisting in fishery development. There is concern that tourist fishermen may adversely affect the local fishing industry.

FREEDOM

Before 1987, human rights were circumscribed in São Tomé and Príncipe. Gradual liberalization has now given way to a commitment to political pluralism. The current government has a good record of respect for human rights. Major problems are an inefficient judicial system, harsh prison conditions, and acts of police brutality. Outdated labor practices on the plantations limit worker rights.

HEALTH/WELFARE

Since independence, the government has had enormous progress in expanding health care and education. The Sãotoméan infant mortality rate is now among the lowest in Africa, and average life expectancy is among the highest. About 65% of the population between 6 and 19 years of age now attend school.

ACHIEVEMENTS

São Tomé and Príncipe shares in a rich Luso-African artistic tradition. The country is particularly renowned for poets such as Jose de Almeida and Francisco Tenreiro, who were among the first to express in the Portuguese language the experiences and pride of Africans.

East Africa

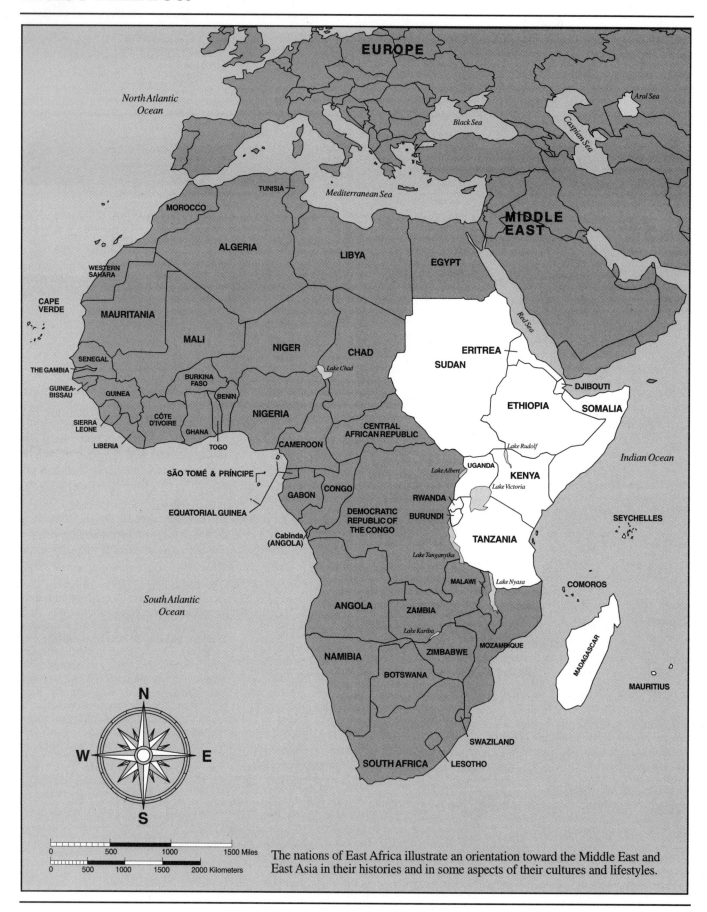

The nations of East Africa illustrate an orientation toward the Middle East and East Asia in their histories and in some aspects of their cultures and lifestyles.

East Africa: A Mixed Inheritance

The vast East African region, ranging from Sudan in the north to Tanzania and the Indian Ocean islands in the south, is an area of great diversity. Although the islands are the homes of distinctive civilizations with ties to Asia, their interactions with the African mainland give their inclusion here validity. Ecological features such as the Great Rift Valley, the prevalence of cattle-herding lifestyles, and long-standing participation in the Indian Ocean trading networks are some of the region's unifying aspects.

CATTLE-HERDING SOCIETIES

A long-horned cow would be an appropriate symbol for East Africa. Most of the region's rural inhabitants, who make up the majority of people from the Horn, to Lake Malawi, to Madagascar, value cattle for their social as well as economic importance. The Nuer of Sudan, the Somalis near the Red Sea (who, like many other peoples of the Horn, herd camels as well as cattle, goats, and sheep), and the Maasai of Tanzania and Kenya are among the pastoral peoples whose herds are their livelihoods. Farming communities such as the Kikuyu of Kenya, the Baganda of Uganda, and the Malagasey of Madagascar also prize cattle.

Much of the East African landmass is well suited for herding. Whereas the rain forests of West and Central Africa are generally infested with tsetse flies, whose bite is fatal to livestock, most of East Africa is made up of belts of tropical and temperate savanna, which are ideal for grazing. Thus pastoralism has long been predominant in the savanna zones of West and Southern, as well as East, Africa. Tropical rain forests are found in East Africa only on the east coast of Madagascar and scattered along the mainland's coast. Much of the East African interior is dominated by the Great Rift Valley, which stretches from the Red Sea as far south as Malawi. This geological formation is characterized by mountains as well as valleys, and it features the region's great lakes, such as Lake Albert, Lake Tanganyika, and Lake Malawi.

People have been moving into and through the East African region since the existence of humankind; indeed, most of the earliest human fossils have been unearthed in this region. Today, almost all the mainland inhabitants speak languages that belong to either the Bantu or Nilotic linguistic families. There has been much historical speculation about the past migration of these peoples, but recent research indicates that both linguistic groups have probably been established in the area for a long time, although oral traditions and other forms of historical evidence indicate locally important shifts in settlement patterns into the contemporary period. Iron working and, in at least a few cases, small-scale steel production have been a part of the regional economy for more than 2,000 years. Long-distance trade and the production of various crafts have also existed since ancient times.

The inhabitants of the region have had to confront insufficient and unreliable rainfall. Drought and famine in the Horn and in areas of Kenya and Tanzania have in recent years changed lifestyles and dislocated many people.

ISLAMIC INFLUENCE

Many of the areas of East Africa have been influenced—since at least as far back as Roman times and perhaps much further—by the Middle East and other parts of Asia. Over the past thousand years, most parts of East Africa, including the Christian highlands of Ethiopia and the inland interlake states such as Buganda, Burundi, and Rwanda, became familiar to the Muslim Arab traders of the Swahili and Red Sea coasts and the Sudanese interior. Somalia, Djibouti, and Sudan, which border the Red Sea and are close to the Arabian Peninsula, have been the countries most influenced by Arab Islamic culture. Mogadishu, the capital of Somalia, began as an Islamic trading post in the tenth century A.D. The Islamic faith, its various sects or brotherhoods, the Koran, and the Shari'a (the Islamic legal code) are predominant throughout the Horn, except in the Ethiopian and Eritrean highlands and southern Sudan. In recent years, many Somalis, Sudanese, and others have migrated to the oil-rich states of Arabia to work.

Farther south, in the communities and cultures on the perimeters of the east coast, Arabs and local Bantu-speaking Africans combined, from as early as the ninth century, but especially during the 1200s to 1400s, to form the culture and the language that we now call Swahili. In the first half of the nineteenth century, Seyyid Said, the sultan of Oman, transferred his capital to Zanzibar, in recognition of the outpost's economic importance. Motivated by the rapid expansion of trade in ivory and slaves, many Arab–Swahili traders began to establish themselves and build settlements as far inland as the forests of eastern Democratic Republic of the Congo. As a result, some of the noncoastal peoples also adopted Islam, while Swahili developed into a regional lingua franca.

The whole region from the Horn to Tanzania continued to be affected by the slave trade through much of the nineteenth century. Slaves were sent north from Uganda and southern Sudan to Egypt and the Middle East, and from Ethiopia across the Red Sea. Others were taken to the coast by Arab, Swahili, or African traders, either to work on the plantations in Zanzibar or to be transported to the Persian Gulf and the Indian Ocean islands.

In the late 1800s and early 1900s, South Asian laborers from what was then British India were brought in by the British to build the East African railroad. South Asian traders already resided in Zanzibar; others now came and settled in Kenya and Tanzania, becoming shopkeepers and bankers in inland centers, such as Kampala and Nairobi, as well as on the coast, in Mombasa and Dar es Salaam or in smaller stops along the railroad. South Asian laborers were also sent in large numbers to work on the sugar plantations of Mauritius; their descendants there now make up about two thirds of that island's population.

The subregions of East Africa include the following: the countries of the Horn, East Africa proper, and the islands. The *Horn* includes Djibouti, Ethiopia, Eritrea, Somalia, and Sudan, which are associated here with one another not so much because of a common heritage or on account of any compatibility of their governments (indeed, they are often hostile to one another), but because of the movements of peoples across borders in recent times. *East Africa proper* is comprised of Kenya, Tanzania, and Uganda, which do have underlying cultural ties and a history of economic relations, in which Rwanda and Burundi have also shared. The Indian Ocean *islands* include the Comoros, Madagascar, Mauritius, and Seychelles, which, notwithstanding the expanses of ocean that separate them, have certain cultural aspects and current interests in common.

THE HORN

Ethiopia traditionally has had a distinct, semi-isolated history that has separated the nation from its neighbors. This early Christian civilization, which was periodically united by a strong dynasty but at other times was disunited, was centered in the highlands of the interior, surrounded by often hostile lowland peoples. Before the nineteenth century, it was in infrequent contact with other Christian societies. In the 1800s, however, a series of strong rulers reunified the highlands and went on to conquer surrounding peoples such as the Afar, Oromo, and Somali. In the process, the state expanded to its current boundaries. While the empire's expansion helped it to preserve its independence during Africa's colonial partition, sectarian and ethnic divisions—a legacy of the imperial state-building process—now threaten to tear the polity apart.

Ethiopia and the other contemporary nations of the Horn have been influenced by outside powers, whose interests in the region have been primarily rooted in its strategic location. In the nineteenth century, both Britain and France became interested in the Horn, because the Red Sea was the link between their countries and the markets of Asia. This was especially true after the completion of the Suez Canal in 1869. Both of the imperial powers occupied ports on the Red Sea at the time. They then began to compete over the upper Nile in modern Sudan. In the 1890s, French forces, led by Captain Jean Baptiste Marchand, literally raced from the present-day area of Congo to reach the center of Sudan before the arrival of a larger British expeditionary force, which had invaded the region from Egypt. Ultimately, the British were able to consolidate their control over the entire Sudan.

Italian ambitions in the Horn were initially encouraged by the British, in order to counter the French. Italy's defeat by the Ethiopians at the Battle of Adowa in 1896 did not deter its efforts to dominate the coastal areas of Eritrea and southeastern Somalia. Later, under Benito Mussolini, Italy briefly (1936–1942) occupied Ethiopia itself.

During the Cold War, great-power competition for control of the Red Sea and the Gulf of Aden, which are strategically located near the oil fields of the Middle East as well as along

(WHO photo)

East African peoples, especially along the coast, blend heritages from Asia, the Middle East, and Africa.

the Suez shipping routes, continued between the United States and the Soviet Union. Local events sometimes led to shifts in alignments. Before 1977, for instance, the United States was closely allied with Ethiopia, and the Soviet Union with Somalia. However, in 1977–1978, Ethiopia, having come under a self-proclaimed Marxist-Leninist government, allied itself with the Soviet Union, receiving in return the support of Cuban troops and billions of dollars' worth of Socialist-bloc military aid, on loan, for use in its battles against Eritrean and Somali rebels. The latter group, living in Ethiopia's Ogaden region, were seeking to become part of a greater Somalia. In this irredentist adventure, they had the direct support of invading Somalia troops. Although the United States refused to counter the Soviets by in turn backing the irredentists, it subsequently established relations with the Somali government at a level that allowed it virtually to take over the former Soviet military facility at Berbera.

Discord and Drought

The countries of the Horn, unlike the other states in the region, are politically alienated from one another. There is thus little prospect of an effective regional community emerging among them in the foreseeable future. Although the end of the Cold War has reduced the interest of external powers, local animosities continue to wreak havoc in the region. The Horn continues to be bound together and torn apart by millions of refugees fleeing armed conflicts in all of the states.

Ethiopia, Somalia, and Sudan have suffered under especially vicious authoritarian regimes that resorted to the mass murder of dissident segments of their populations. Although the old regimes have been overthrown in Ethiopia and Somalia, peace has yet to come to either society. Having gained its independence only in 1993, Eritrea, Africa's newest nation, has struggled to overcome the devastating legacy of its 30-year liberation struggle against Ethiopia. Eritrea's well-being has been further compromised by reverses in a border war with Ethiopia. Recent battlefield victories against the Eritreans have revived the passions of some Ethiopians who have never fully accepted Eritrea's succession. The stability of neighboring Djibouti, once a regional enclave of calm, has also been compromised in recent years by sometimes violent internal political conflicts.

The horrible effects of these wars have been magnified by recurrent droughts. Hundreds of thousands of people have starved to death in the past decade, while many more have survived only because of international aid efforts.

Ethiopians leave their homes for Djibouti, Somalia, and Sudan for relief from war and famine. Sudanese and Somalis flee to Ethiopia for the same reasons. Today, every country harbors not only refugees but also dissidents from neighboring lands and has a citizenry related to those who live in adjoining countries. Peoples such as the Afar minority in Djibouti often seek support from their kin in Eritrea and Ethiopia. Many Somali guerrilla groups have used Ethiopia

(United Nations photo by Ray Witlin)

In the drought-affected areas of East Africa, people must devote considerable time and energy to the search for water.

as a base, while Somali factions have continued to give aid and comfort to Ethiopia's rebellious Ogaden population. Ethiopian factions allegedly continue to assist southern rebels against the government of Sudan, which had long supported the Tigray and Eritrean rebel movements of northern Ethiopia.

At times, the states of the region have reached agreements among themselves to curb their interference in one another's affairs. But they have made almost no progress in the more fundamental task of establishing internal peace, thus assuring that the region's violent downward spiral continues.

THE SOUTHERN STATES OF EAST AFRICA

The peoples of Kenya, Tanzania, and Uganda as well as Burundi and Rwanda have underlying connections rooted in the past. The kingdoms of the Lakes Region of Uganda, Rwanda, and Burundi, though they have been politically superseded in the postcolonial era, have left their legacies. For example, myths about a heroic dynasty of rulers, the Chwezi, who ruled over an early Ugandan-based kingdom, are widespread. Archaeological evidence attests to the actual existence of the Chwezi, probably in the sixteenth century. Peoples in western Kenya and Tanzania, who have lived under less centralized systems of governance but nonetheless have rituals similar to those of the Ugandan kingdoms, also share the traditions of the Chwezi dynasty, which have become associated with a spirit cult.

The precolonial kingdoms of Rwanda and Burundi, both of which came under German and, later, Belgian control during the colonial era, were socially divided between a ruling warrior class, the Tutsis, and a much larger peasant class, the Hutus. Although both states are now independent republics, their societies remain bitterly divided along these ethnoclass lines. In Rwanda, the feudal hegemony of the Tutsis was overthrown in a bloody civil conflict in 1959, which led to the flight of many Tutsis. But in 1994, the sons of these Tutsi exiles came to power, after elements in the former Hutu-dominated regime organized a genocidal campaign against all Tutsis. In the belief that the Tutsis were back on top, millions of Hutus then fled the country. In Burundi, Tutsi rule was maintained for decades through a repressive police state, which in 1972 and 1988 resorted to the mass murder of Hutus. Elections in 1993 resulted in the country's first Hutu president at the head of a government that included members of both groups, but he was murdered by the predominantly Tutsi army. Since then, the country has been teetering on the brink of yet another catastrophe, as some of its politicians try to promote reconciliation.

Kenya and Uganda were taken over by the British in the late nineteenth century, while Tanzania, originally conquered by Germany, became a British colony after World War I. In Kenya, the British encouraged the growth of a settler community. Although never much more than 1 percent of the colony's resident population, the British settlers were given the best agricultural lands in the rich highlands

region around Nairobi; and throughout most of the colonial era, they were allowed to exert a political and economic hegemony over the local Africans. The settler populations in Tanzania and Uganda were smaller and less powerful. While the settler presence in Kenya led to land alienation and consequent immiseration for many Africans, it also fostered a fair amount of colonial investment in infrastructure. As a result, Kenya had a relatively sophisticated economy at the time of its independence, a fact that was to complicate proposals for its economic integration with Tanzania and Uganda.

In the 1950s, the British established the East African Common Services Organization to promote greater economic cooperation among its Kenyan, Tanganyikan (Tanzanian), and Ugandan territories. By the early 1960s, the links among the states were so close that President Julius Nyerere of Tanzania

(United Nations photo by Milton Grant)

Of the millions of refugees who have been displaced by civil wars in Ethiopia, Somalia, and Sudan, fully 60 percent are children.

proposed that his country delay its independence until Kenya also gained its freedom, in hopes that the two countries would then join together. This did not occur.

In 1967, the Common Services Organization was transformed by its three (now independent) members into a full-fledged "common market," known as the East African Community (EAC). The EAC collectively managed the railway system, development of harbors, and international air, postal, and telecommunication facilities. It also maintained a common currency, development bank, and other economic, cultural, and scientific services. Peoples moved freely across the borders of the three EAC states. However, the EAC soon began to unravel, as conflicts over its operations grew. It finally collapsed in 1977. The countries disputed the benefits of the association, which seemed to have been garnered primarily by Kenya. The ideologies and personalities of its leaders at the time—Nyerere, Jomo Kenyatta of Kenya, and Idi Amin of Uganda—differed greatly. Relations between Kenya and Tanzania deteriorated to the point that the border between them was closed for several years.

In 1983, Kenya, Tanzania, and Uganda agreed on the division of the assets of the old Community; Kenya experienced the largest losses. Tanzania and Kenya opened their borders and began rebuilding their relationship. The economic strains that all three countries currently face in their dealings with the world economy make clear the value of the defunct EAC. But political factors continue to complicate the quest for greater regional cooperation. Kenyatta was succeeded by his vice president, Daniel arap Moi, whose regime over the past decade has become increasingly repressive in the face of mounting opposition. Uganda still suffers from years of warfare and instability, the legacies of the brutal regimes of Amin and Milton Obote, whose second administration was overthrown in a coup in 1985. Uganda's current president, Yoweri Museveni, maintains an uneasy control over a country still plagued by violence. Although the governments of Kenya, Rwanda, Sudan, Tanzania, and the former Zaire pledged in 1986 to prevent exiles from using asylum to destabilize their homelands, tensions in the region have continued. Relations between Uganda and Kenya have been strained over allegations that each has harbored the other's dissidents.

A number of joint projects may contribute to the rebirth of some form of East African community. A "Preferential Trade Area" of 19 East and Southern African nations was established in 1981. Burundi, Rwanda, Tanzania, and Uganda are sharing in the construction of a hydroelectric project on the Kagera River. Uganda has established cooperative military links with both Kenya and Tanzania. The governments of Burundi, Rwanda, Tanzania, and the Democratic Republic of the Congo have met to discuss security, trade, and cultural exchange in the region. Rwanda and Burundi are members of the Economic Community of Central African States (ECCA),

but their economic ties with East African states have led the UN Economic Commission on Africa, as well as other multinational organizations, to include them in the East African regional groupings.

There has been much talk of improving regional relations. "Think East Africa," *The Standard* of Kenya wrote, commenting on the cultural links that existed in the area before colonialism. Salim Salim, a Tanzanian statesman, noted, "You can choose a friend, but you cannot choose a brother. . . . In this case Kenyans and Ugandans are our brothers."

THE ISLANDS

The Comoros, Madagascar, Mauritius, and Seychelles each have their own unique characteristics. They all have some important traits in common. All four island nations have been strongly influenced historically by contacts with Asia as well as with mainland Africa and Europe. Madagascar and the Comoros have populations that originated in Indonesia and the Middle East as well as in Africa; the Malagasey language is related to Indonesian Malay. The citizens of Mauritius and Seychelles are of European as well as African and Asian origin.

All four island groups have also been influenced by France. Mauritius and Seychelles were not permanently inhabited until the 1770s, when French settlers arrived with their African slaves. The British subsequently took control of these two island groups and, during the 1830s, abolished slavery. Thereafter the British encouraged migration from South Asia and, to a lesser extent, from China to make up for labor shortages on the islands' plantations. Local French-based creoles remain the major languages on the islands.

In 1978, all the islands, along with opposition groups from the French possession of Réunion, formed the Indian Ocean Commission. Originally a body with a socialist orientation, the commission campaigned for the independence of Réunion and the return of the island of Diego Garcia by Britain to Mauritius, as well as the dismantling of the U.S. naval base located there. By the end of the 1980s, however, the export-oriented growth of Mauritius and the continuing prosperity of Seychelles' tourist-based economy were helping to push all nations toward a greater emphasis on market economics in their multilateral, as well as internal, policy initiatives. Madagascar and the Comoros have recently offered investment incentives for Mauritius-based private firms. Mauritians have also played prominent roles in the development of tourism in the Comoros.

In addition to their growing economic ties, the Comoros and Mauritius, and to a somewhat lesser extent, Madagascar and Seychelles, have created linkages with South Africa. In 1995, Mauritius followed South Africa's lead to become the 12th member of the Southern African Development Community (SADC).

Burundi (Republic of Burundi)

GEOGRAPHY
Area in Square Miles (Kilometers):
10,759 (27,834) (about the size of Maryland)
Capital (Population): Bujumbura (300,000)
Environmental Concerns: soil erosion; deforestation; habitat loss
Geographical Features: hilly and mountainous, dropping to a plateau in the east; some plains; landlocked
Climate: tropical to temperate; temperature varies with altitude

PEOPLE

Population
Total: 6,055,000
Annual Growth Rate: 3.15%
Rural/Urban Population Ratio: 92/8
Major Languages: Kirundi; French; Swahili; others
Ethnic Makeup: 85% Hutu; 14% Tutsi; 1% Twa and others
Religions: 67% Christian; 23% indigenous beliefs; 10% Muslim

Health
Life Expectancy at Birth: 45 years (male); 47 years (female)
Infant Mortality Rate (Ratio): 71.5/1,000
Physicians Available (Ratio): 1/31,777

Education
Adult Literacy Rate: 35.3%
Compulsory (Ages): 7–13; free

COMMUNICATION
Telephones: 16,000 main lines
Televisions: 7 per 1,000 people
Internet Service Providers: na

TRANSPORTATION
Highways in Miles (Kilometers): 8,688 (14,480)
Railroads in Miles (Kilometers): none
Usable Airfields: 4
Motor Vehicles in Use: 20,000

GOVERNMENT
Type: republic
Independence Date: July 1, 1962 (from UN trusteeship under Belgian administration)
Head of State/Government: President (General) Pierre Buyoyo is both head of state and head of government
Political Parties: Union for National Progress; Socialist Party of Burundi; others
Suffrage: universal for adults

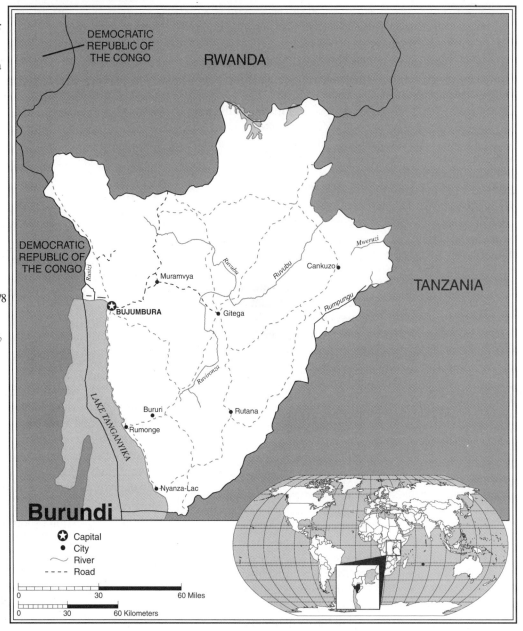

MILITARY
Military Expenditures (% of GDP): 2.6%
Current Disputes: severe interethnic conflict

ECONOMY
Currency ($ U.S. Equivalent): 248.5 Burundi francs = $1
Per Capita Income/GDP: $730/$4.2 billion
GDP Growth Rate: –1%
Inflation Rate: 26%
Labor Force: 1,900,000
Natural Resources: nickel; uranium; rare earth oxides; peat; cobalt; copper; platinum; vanadium; arable land; hydropower
Agriculture: coffee; cotton; tea; corn; sorghum; sweet potatoes; bananas; manioc; livestock
Industry: light consumer goods; assembly of imported components; public-works construction; food processing
Exports: $56 million (primary partners European countries)
Imports: $108 million (primary partners European countries)

http://www.sas.upenn.edu/
African_Studies/Country_Specific/
Burundi.html

BURUNDI

Through the tireless mediation efforts of former South African president Nelson Mandela, Burundi edged toward national reconciliation in 2000. But the small, beautiful, and crowded country remains deeply divided, with many among the governing ethnic-Tutsi elite opposed to any settlement that would bring to power the country's ethnic-Hutu majority. Since the 1993 murder of Melchior Ndadye, a Hutu who had been the country's only democratically elected president, more than 200,000 Burundians are believed to have perished in interethnic violence. Another 350,000 ethnic Hutus have been resettled in concentration camps. The current tragedy has deeper roots. In 1972 and again in 1988, tens of thousands of people, mostly Hutus, perished in genocidal attacks. In more recent years, the situation has been further complicated by the escalation of conflict between Tutsis and Hutus in the neighboring states of Rwanda and the Democratic Republic of the Congo.

In the past, the violence was initiated by members of the Tutsi governing elite seeking to maintain their privileged status through brutal military control. Today, the army's hold on the countryside is being increasingly challenged by an armed movement, Forces for the Defense of Democracy (FDD), which is spreading counterterror in the name of the country's Hutu majority. What *has* remained the same over the years is the general indifference of the outside world to Burundi's horrific record of genocide.

The successful holding of democratic elections in July 1993 gave rise to cautious optimism about the dawning of a new era of national reconciliation in Burundi. Ndadye was a Hutu who formed an interethnic coalition government of national unity. His death, followed by the April 1994 assassination of his successor, Cyprien Ntaryamira, sparked a wave of "ethnic cleansing." The capital city, Bujumbura, has been emptied of its Hutu majority, while ordinary Tutsis have had to abandon much of the countryside. In July 1996, the army overthrew what was left of civilian authority under President Sylveste Ntibantunganya, a Hutu, bringing back to power the Tutsi general Pierre Buyoyo, who had ruled the country from 1987 to 1993.

A DIVIDED SOCIETY

Burundi's population is ethnosocially divided into three distinctive groups. At the bottom of the social hierarchy are the Twas, commonly stereotyped as "pygmies." Believed to be the earliest inhabitants of the country, today the Twas account for only about 1 percent of the population. The largest group, constituting 85 percent of the population, are the Hutus, most of whom subsist as farmers. The dominant group are the Tutsis, who comprise some 14 percent of the population. Among the Tutsis, who are subdivided into clans, status has long been associated with cattle-keeping. Leading Tutsis continue to form an aristocratic ruling class over the whole of Burundi society. Until 1966, the leader of Burundi's Tutsi aristocracy was the *Mwami,* or king.

The Burundi kingdom goes back at least as far as the sixteenth century. By the late 1800s, when the kingdom was incorporated into German East Africa, the Tutsis had subordinated the Hutus, who became clients of local Tutsi aristocrats, herding their cattle and rendering other services. The Germans and subsequently the Belgians, who assumed paramount authority over the kingdom after World War I, were content to rule through Burundi's established social hierarchy. But many Hutus as well as Tutsis were educated by Christian missionaries.

In the late 1950s, Prince Louis Rwagazore, a Tutsi, tried to accommodate Hutu as well as Tutsi aspirations by establishing a nationalist reform movement known as the Union for National Progress (UPRONA). Rwagazore was assassinated before independence, but UPRONA led the country to independence in 1962, with King Mwambutsa IV retaining considerable power as head of state. The Tutsi elite remained dominant, but the UPRONA cabinets contained representation from the two major groups. This attempt to balance the interests of the Tutsis and Hutus broke down in 1965, when Hutu politicians within both UPRONA and the rival People's Party won 80 percent of the vote and the majority of the seats in both houses of the bicameral Legislature. In response, the king abolished the Legislature before it could convene. A group of Hutu army officers then attempted to overthrow the government. Mwambutsa fled the country, but the revolt was crushed in a countercoup by Tutsi officers, led by Michel Micombero.

In the aftermath of the uprising, Micombero took power amid a campaign of reprisals in which, it is believed, some 5,000 Hutus were killed. He deposed Mwambutsa's son, Ntare V, from the kingship and set up a "Government of Public Safety," which set about purging Hutu members from the government and the

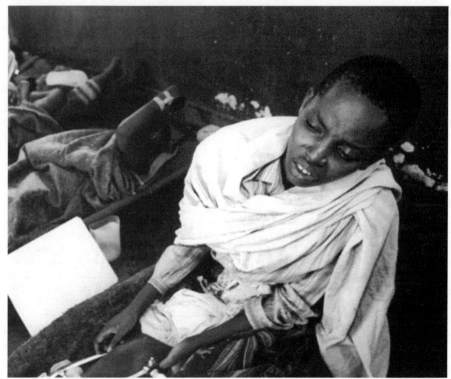

(AP photo by Jean-Marc Bosju)

Interethnic violence between the Hutus and Tutsis in Burundi in 1972, in 1988, and beginning again in the mid–1990s, has generated horrible genocides and left the population wounded, displaced, and in chaos. The urgent need for medical assistance has far outstripped the available resources.

Mwami Ntare Rugaamba expands the boundaries of the Nkoma kingdom
1795

The area is mandated to Belgium by the League of Nations after the Germans lose World War I
1919

Prince Louis Rwagazore leads a nationalist movement and founds UPRONA
1958–1961

Rwagazore is assassinated; independence is achieved
1961

A failed coup results in purges of Hutus in the government and army; Michel Micombero seizes power
1965–1966

Government forces massacre 200,000 Hutus
1972

Jean-Baptiste Bagaza comes to power in a military coup
1976

Bagaza is overthrown in a military coup led by Pierre Buyoyo
1987

Buyoyo loses in multiparty elections; Melchior Ndadye becomes Burundi's first Hutu president Buyoyo regains power in a military coup
1990s

2000s

Ethnic violence continues

Unrest in neighboring states complicates the situation in Burundi

Nelson Mandela mediates for national reconciliation

army. The political struggle involved interclan competition among the Tutsis as well as the maintenance of their hegemony over the Hutus.

Under Micombero, Burundi continued to be afflicted with interethnic violence, occasional coup attempts, and pro-monarchist agitation. A major purge of influential Hutus was carried out in 1969. In 1972, Ntare V was lured to Uganda by Idi Amin, who turned him over to Micombero. Ntare was placed under arrest upon his arrival and was subsequently murdered by his guards.

A declaration of martial law then set off another explosion of violence. In response to an alleged uprising involving the deaths of up to 2,000 Tutsis, government supporters began to massacre large numbers of Hutus. Educated Hutus were especially targeted in a two-month campaign of selective genocide, which is generally estimated to have claimed 200,000 victims (estimates range from 80,000 to 500,000 deaths for the entire period, with additional atrocities being reported through 1973). More than 100,000 Hutus fled to Uganda, Rwanda, Zaire, and Tanzania. Among the governments of the world, only Tanzania and Rwanda showed any deep concern for the course of events. China, France, and Libya used the crisis to significantly upgrade their military aid to the Burundi regime.

In 1974, Micombero formally transformed Burundi into a single-party state under UPRONA. Although Micombero was replaced two years later in a military coup by Colonel Jean-Baptiste Bagaza, power remained effectively in the hands of members of the Tutsi elite who controlled UPRONA, the civil service, and the army. In 1985, Bagaza widened existing state persecution of Seventh Day Adventists and Jehovah's Witnesses to include the Roman Catholic Church, to which a majority of Burundi's population belong, suspecting it of fostering seditious—that is,

pro-Hutu—sympathies. (The overthrow of Bagaza by Pierre Buyoyo, in a 1987 military coup, led to a lifting of the anti-Catholic campaign.)

Ethnic violence erupted again in 1988. Apparently some Tutsis were killed by Hutus in northern Burundi, in response to rumors of another massacre of Hutus. In retaliation, the army massacred between 5,000 and 25,000 Hutus. Another 60,000 Hutus took temporary refuge in Rwanda, while more than 100,000 were left homeless. In 1991, the revolutionary Party for the Liberation of the Hutu People, or Palipehutu, launched its own attacks on Tutsi soldiers and civilians, leading to further killing on all sides.

LAND ISSUES
Burundi is one of the poorest countries in the world, despite its rich volcanic soils and generous international development assistance (it has consistently been one of the highest per capita aid recipients on the African continent). In addition to the dislocations caused by cycles of interethnic violence, the nation's development prospects are seriously compromised by geographic isolation and population pressure on the land. About 25 percent of Burundi's land is under cultivation—generally by individual farmers trying to subsist on plots of no more than three acres. Another 60 percent of the country is devoted to pasture for mostly Tutsi livestock. Hutu farmers continue to be tied by patron–client relationships to Tutsi overlords. In recent years, the government has tied its rural development efforts to an unpopular villagization scheme.

This issue has complicated ongoing attempts to reach some kind of accommodation between the Tutsi elite and Hutu masses. Having cautiously increased Hutu participation in his government, while reserving ultimate power in the hands of the all-Tutsi Military Committee of National Salvation, Buyoyo agreed to the res-

toration of multiparty politics in 1991. A new Constitution was approved in March 1992; it allowed competition between approved, ethnically balanced, parties. In the resulting July 1993 election, Buyoyo's UPRONA was defeated by the Front for Democracy in Burundi (FRODEBU). FRODEBU's Ndadaye was sworn in as Burundi's first Hutu leader at the head of a joint FRODEBU–UPRONA government. His subsequent assassination by Tutsi hardliners in the military set off a new wave of interethnic killings. The firm stand against the coup by Buyoyo and the Tutsi/UPRONA prime minister, Sylvie Kinigi, helped to calm the situation, but attempts to make a fresh start collapsed when a plane carrying Ntaraymira and his Rwandan counterpart was shot down over Rwanda. The latest coup followed UPRONA's withdrawal from the government following the massacre of more than 300 Tutsis by FDD, who by September 1996 were attempting to besiege the capital.

During a four-week period from late October to November 1996, the Tutsi-led Burundian military massacred at least 1,000 civilians. The government forces fought with Hutu rebels, as some 50,000 Hutus returned from camps that had been closed in Zaire (present-day Democratic Republic of the Congo). The Tutsi-dominated military set up more than a dozen "protection zones" for Hutu civilians while soldiers continued battling Hutu rebels. Strife continued as an estimated 200,000 Burundians were living in refugee camps in Tanzania.

DEVELOPMENT

Burundi's sources of wealth are limited. There is no active development of mineral resources, although sources of nickel have been located and may be mined soon. There is little industry, and the coffee industry, which contributes 75% to 90% of export earnings, has declined.

FREEDOM

Beset by ongoing genocide, there is currently no genuine freedom in Burundi, for either its ethnic majority or minority populations.
People continue to flee the country by the tens of thousands.

HEALTH/WELFARE

Much of the educational system has been in private hands, especially the Roman Catholic Church. Burundi lost many educated and trained people during the Hutu massacres in the 1970s and 1980s.

ACHIEVEMENTS

Burundians were briefly united in July 1996 by the victory of their countryman Venuste Niyongabo in the men's 5,000-meter race at the Atlanta Summer Olympic Games. He dedicated his gold medal (the first for a Burundi citizen) to the hope of national reconciliation.

Comoros (Federal Islamic Republic of the Comoros)

GEOGRAPHY

Area in Square Miles (Kilometers):
838 (2,171) (about 12 times
the size of Washington, D.C.)
Capital (Population): Moroni
(30,000)
Environmental Concerns:
soil degradation and erosion;
deforestation
Geographical Features: volcanic
islands; interiors vary from
steep mountains to low hills
Climate: tropical marine

PEOPLE

Population
Total: 578,500
Annual Growth Rate: 3.05%
Rural/Urban Population Ratio:
69/31
Major Languages: Arabic;
French; Comoran
Ethnic Makeup: Antalote; Cafre;
Makoa; Oimatsaha; Sakalava
Religions: 98% Sunni Muslim;
2% Roman Catholic

Health
Life Expectancy at Birth: 58
years (male); 62 years (female)
Infant Mortality Rate (Ratio):
86.3/1,000
Physicians Available (Ratio):
1/6,600

Education
Adult Literacy Rate: 57.3%
Compulsory (Ages): 7–16

COMMUNICATION
Telephones: 5,500 main lines
Internet Service Providers: 1
(1999)

TRANSPORTATION
Highways in Miles (Kilometers):
522 (870)
Railroads In Miles (Kilometers): none
Usable Airfields: 4

GOVERNMENT
Type: republic
Independence Date: July 6, 1975 (from
France)
Head of State/Government: President
Azali Assoumani; Prime Minister
Bianrifi Tarmidi
Political Parties: Rassemblement
National pour le Development; Front
National pour la Justice
Suffrage: universal at 18

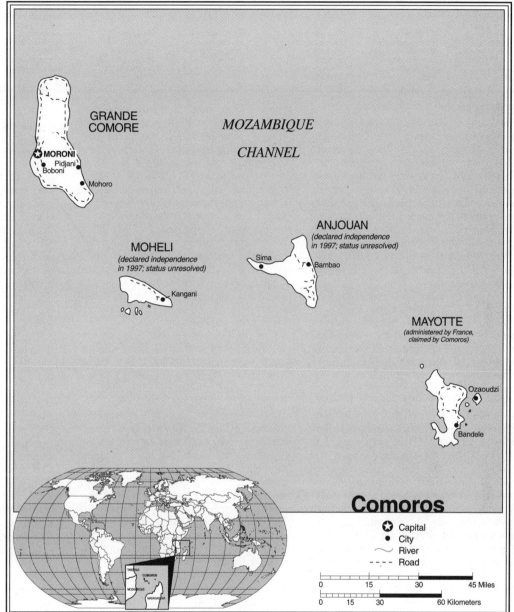

Comoros

★ Capital
● City
〜 River
- - - - Road

MILITARY
Current Disputes: Comoros claims the
French-administered island of Mayotte;
Moheli and Anjouan seek independence

ECONOMY
Currency ($ U.S. Equivalent): 297 Comoran
francs = $1
Per Capita Income/GDP: $725/$410 million
GDP Growth Rate: 0%
Inflation Rate: 4%
Unemployment Rate: 20%; extreme
underemployment
Labor Force: 144,000
Natural Resources: negligible

Agriculture: perfume essences; copra;
coconuts; cloves; vanilla; cinnamon;
yams; rice
Industry: tourism; perfume distillation;
textiles; furniture; jewelry; construction
materials; beverages
Exports: $9.3 million (primary partners
France, United States, Germany)
Imports: $49.5 million (primary partners
France, South Africa, Kenya)

 http://www.sas.upenn.edu/
African_Studies/Country_Specific/
Comoros. html
http://www.africaindex.africainfo.no/
africaindex/africaindex1/countries/
comoros.html

Various groups settle in the islands, which become part of a Swahili trading network
1500s

A French protectorate over the remaining Comoros islands is proclaimed
1886

The islands are ruled as part of the French colony of Madagascar
1914–1946

Independence is followed by a mercenary coup, which installs Ali Soilih
1975

Ali Soilih is overthrown by mercenaries; Ahmed Abdullah is restored
1978

Abdullah proclaims a one-party state; real power remains in the hands of mercenary leader Bob Denard
1980s

The assassination of Abdullah leads to the removal of Denard and to multiparty elections
1990s

2000s

The status of Anjouan and Moheli remains unsettled

Azali Assoumani is installed as president after a bloodless coup

COMOROS

The Comoros is a small archipelago consisting of three main islands: Grande Comore, Moheli, and Anjouan (a fourth island, Mayotte, has opted to remain under French rule). The country has been effectively divided since 1997, when separatists seized control of Anjouan, subsequently declaring independence. Separatists have also been active on the island of Moheli. Efforts by the Organization of African Unity and other outside mediators have since failed to restore unity and stability to the islands.

The years since independence from France, in 1975, have not been kind to the Comoros, which has been consistently listed by the United Nations as one of the world's least-developed countries. Lack of economic development has been compounded at times by natural disasters, eccentric and authoritarian leadership, political violence, and external interventions. The 1990 restoration of multi-party democracy, along with subsequent elections in 1992–1993, have so far failed to provide a basis for national consensus.

Meanwhile, the entire archipelago remains impoverished. While many Comorans remain underemployed as subsistence farmers, more than half of the country's food is imported. As a result, many Comorans have questioned the wisdom of independence, but appeals by Anjouan and Moheli islanders for a return of French control have been rejected by Paris.

The Comoros archipelago was populated by a number of Indian Ocean peoples, who—by the time of the arrival of Europeans during the early 1500s—had combined to form the predominantly Muslim, Swahili-speaking society found on the islands today. In 1886, the French proclaimed a protectorate over the three main islands that currently constitute the Federal Islamic Republic of the Comoros (France had ruled Mayotte since 1843). Throughout the colonial period,

the Comoros were especially valued by the French, for strategic reasons. A local elite of large landholders prospered from the production of cash crops. Life for most Comorans, however, remained one of extreme poverty.

A month after independence, the first Comoran government, led by Ahmed Abdullah Abderemane, was overthrown by mercenaries, who installed Ali Soilih in power. He promised a socialist transformation of the nation and began to implement land reform, but he rapidly lost support both at home and abroad—under his leadership, gangs of undisciplined youths terrorized society, while the basic institutions and services of government all but disappeared. In 1977, the situation was made even worse by a major volcanic eruption, which left 20,000 people homeless, and by the arrival of 16,000 Comoran refugees following massacres in neighboring Madagascar.

In 1978, another band of mercenaries—this time led by the notorious Bob Denard, whose previous exploits in Zaire, Togo, and elsewhere had made his name infamous throughout Africa—overthrew Soilih and restored Abdullah to power. Denard, however, remained the true power behind the throne.

The Denard–Abdullah government enjoyed close ties with influential right-wing elements in France and South Africa. Connections with Pretoria were manifested through the use of the Comoros as a major conduit for South African supplies to the Renamo rebels in Mozambique. Economic ties with South Africa, especially in tourism and sanctions-busting, also grew. The government also established good relations with Saudi Arabia, Kuwait, and other conservative Arab governments while attracting significant additional aid from the international donor agencies.

In 1982, the country legally became a one-party state. Attempted coups in 1985 and 1987 aggravated political tensions.

Many Comorans particularly resented the overbearing influence of Denard and his men. By November 1989, this group included President Abdullah himself. With the personal backing of President François Mitterand of France and President F. W. de Klerk of South Africa, Abdullah moved to replace Denard's mercenaries with a French-approved security unit. But before this move could be implemented, Abdullah was murdered following a meeting with Denard.

The head of the Supreme Court, Said Mohamed Djohar, was appointed interim president in the wake of the assassination. After a period of some confusion, during which popular protests against Denard swelled, Djohar quietly sought French intervention to oust the mercenaries. With both Paris and Pretoria united against him, Denard agreed to relinquish power, in exchange for safe passage to South Africa. The removal of Denard and temporary stationing of a French peacekeeping force was accompanied by the lifting of political restrictions in preparation for presidential elections. In 1990, a runoff resulted in a 55 percent electoral mandate for Djohar.

In September 1995, Denard's men returned to overthrow Djohar. But the mercenaries were soon forced to surrender to French forces, who installed Caambi el Yachourtu, rather than Djohar, as acting president. At the end of 1996, Mohamed Taki Abdulkarim replaced Yachourtu as president. In November 1998, Taki died suddenly and was replaced by Tadjiddine Ben Said Massounde as the head of a ruling military committee. Massounde's government was overthrown in a bloodless coup on April 30, 1999. Azali Assoumani was subsequently installed as president.

DEVELOPMENT

One of the major projects undertaken since independence has been the ongoing expansion of the port at Mutsamundu, to allow large ships to visit the islands. Vessels of up to 25,000 tons can now dock at the harbor. In recent years, there has been a significant expansion of tourism to the Comoros.

FREEDOM

Freedom was abridged after independence under both Ahmed Abdullah and Ali Soilih. The government elected in 1990 ended human-rights abuses.

HEALTH/WELFARE

Health statistics improved during the 1980s, but a recent World Health Organization survey estimated that 10% of Comoran children ages 3 to 6 years are seriously malnourished and another 37% are moderately malnourished.

ACHIEVEMENTS

Comoros has long been the world's leading exporter of ylang-ylang, an essence used to make perfume. It is also the second-leading producer of vanilla and a major grower of cloves. Together, these cash crops account for more than 95% of export earnings. Unfortunately, the international prices of these crops have been low for the past 2 decades.

Djibouti (Republic of Djibouti)

GEOGRAPHY
Area in Square Miles (Kilometers):
8,492 (22,000) (about the size
of Massachusetts)
Capital (Population): Djibouti
(383,000)
Environmental Concerns:
insufficient potable water;
desertification
Geographical Features: coastal
plain and plateau, separated
by central mountains
Climate: desert

PEOPLE

Population
Total: 452,000
Annual Growth Rate: 1.45%
Rural/Urban Population Ratio:
18/82
Major Languages: French;
Arabic; Somali; Saho-Afar
Ethnic Makeup: 60% Somali;
35% Afar; 5% French, Arab,
Ethiopian, Italian
Religions: 94% Muslim; 6%
Christian

Health
Life Expectancy at Birth: 49
years (male); 53 years (female)
Infant Mortality Rate (Ratio):
103.3/1,000
Physicians Available (Ratio):
1/3,790

Education
Adult Literacy Rate: 46.2%

COMMUNICATION
Telephones: 8,000 main lines
Televisions: 43 per 1,000 people
Internet Service Providers: na

TRANSPORTATION
Highways in Miles (Kilometers):
1,801 (2,906)
Railroads in Miles (Kilometers):
60 (97)
Usable Airfields: 11
Motor Vehicles in Use: 16,000

GOVERNMENT
Type: republic
Independence Date: June 27, 1977 (from
France)
Head of State/Government: President
Ishmail Omar Guellah; Prime Minister
Barkat Gourad Hamadou
Political Parties: People's Progress
Assembly; Democratic Renewal Party;
Democratic National Party
Suffrage: universal for adults

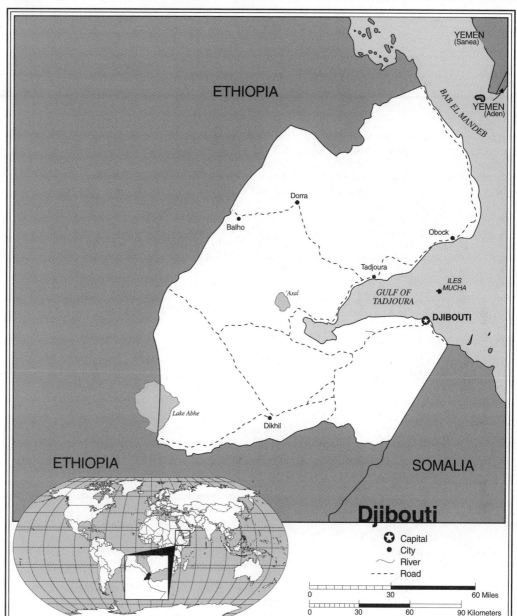

Djibouti

Capital
City
River
Road

MILITARY
Military Expenditures (% of GDP): 4.5%
Current Disputes: ethnic conflict; border
clashes with Eritrea

ECONOMY
Currency ($ U.S. Equivalent): 177.7
Djibouti francs = $1
Per Capita Income/GDP: $1,200/$550
million
GDP Growth Rate: 2%
Inflation Rate: 0%
Unemployment Rate: 40%–50%
Labor Force: 282,000
Natural Resources: geothermal areas

Agriculture: goats; sheep; camels; fruits;
vegetables
Industry: port and maritime support;
construction
Exports: $260 million (primary partners
Somalia, Yemen, Ethiopia)
Imports: $440 million (primary partners
France, Ethiopia, Italy)

http://www.sas.upenn.edu/African_
Studies/Country_Specific/
Djibouti.html
http://www.192.203.180.62/mlas/
djibouti.html

The underground
Union of
Movements for
Democracy is
formed as an
interethnic,
antigovernment
coalition
1980s

Civil war rends
the country;
Ishmail Omar
Guellah is elected
to replace
President Hassan
Gouled Aptidon
1990s

France buys the
port of Obock
1862

France acquires
the port of
Djibouti
1888

The Addis
Ababa-Djibouti
Railroad is
completed
1917

Djibouti votes to
remain part of
Overseas France
1958

Independence;
the Ogaden War
1977

2000s

Ethnic conflict continues

DJIBOUTI

In April 1999, Ishmail Omar Guellah was elected as Djibouti's second president, replacing the aging Hassan Gouled Aptidon, who retired due to ill health. Guellah's principal opponent, Musa Ahmed Idriss, was subsequently arrested after claiming massive fraud in the poll. The new president has since consolidated his authority, building on the national-reconciliation process begun under his predecessor. In 1997, a power-sharing agreement was reached between the long-ruling Issa-Somali–dominated Popular Rally for Progress Party (RPP) and a faction of the largely Afar-speaking armed movement Front for the Restoration of Unity (FRUD). FRUD won all 65 seats in December 1997 legislative elections. But, as with earlier elections in 1992–1993, the vote was boycotted by militant sections of FRUD, which launched new attacks. Political conflict, largely mirroring the country's ethnic division between Afars and Somalis, continues to threaten Djibouti's fragile unity.

Since achieving its independence from France, Djibouti has had to strike a cautious balance between the competing interests of its larger neighbors, Ethiopia and Somalia. Most of the nation's citizens are divided between Afar- and Somali-speakers. In the past, Somalia has claimed ownership of the territory, based on the numerical preponderance of Djibouti's Somali population, variously estimated at 50 to 70 percent. However, local Somalis as well as Afars also have strong ties to communities in Ethiopia. Furthermore, Djibouti's location at the crossroads of Africa and Eurasia has made it a focus of continuing strategic concern to nonregional powers, particularly France, which maintains a large military presence in the country.

Modern Djibouti's colonial genesis is a product of mid-nineteenth-century Euro-pean rivalry over control of the Red Sea. In 1862, France occupied the town of Obock, across the harbor from the city of Djibouti. This move was taken in anticipation of the 1869 opening of the Suez Canal, which transformed the Red Sea into the major shipping route between Asia, East Africa, and Europe. In 1888, Paris, having acquired Djibouti city and its hinterland, proclaimed its authority over French Somaliland, the modern territory of Djibouti.

The independence of France's other mainland African colonies by 1960, along with the formation in that year of the Somali Democratic Republic, led to local agitation for an end to French rule. To counter the effects of Somali nationalism, the French began to favor the Afar minority in local politics and employment. French president Charles de Gaulle's 1966 visit was accompanied by large, mainly Somali, pro-independence demonstrations. As a result, a referendum was held on the question of independence. Colonial control of voter registration assured a predominantly Afar electorate, who, fearful of Somali domination, opted for continued French rule. French Somaliland was then transformed into the self-governing "Territory of Afars and Issas." The name reflected a continuing colonial policy of divide-and-rule; members of the Issas clan constituted just over half of the area's Somali-speakers.

By the 1970s, neither Ethiopia nor France was opposed to Djibouti's independence but, for their own strategic reasons, both countries backed the Afar community in its desire for assurances that the territory would not be incorporated into Somalia. An ethnic power-sharing arrangement was established that in effect acknowledged local Somali preponderance. The empowerment of local Somalis, in particular the Issa, was accompanied by diminished pan-Somali sentiment. On June 27, 1977, the Republic of Djibouti became independent. French troops remained in the country, however, supposedly as a guarantee of its sovereignty. Internally, political power was divided by means of ethnically balanced cabinets.

War broke out between Ethiopia and Somalia a few months after Djibouti's independence. Djibouti remained neutral, but ethnic tensions mounted with the arrival of Somali refugees. In 1981, the Afar-dominated Djiboutian Popular Movement was outlawed. The Issa-dominated Popular Rally for Progress (RPP) then became the country's sole legal party.

Refugees have poured into Djibouti for years now, fleeing conflict and famine in Ethiopia, Somalia, and Sudan. The influx has swelled the country's population by about one third and has deepened Djibouti's dependence on external food aid. Massive unemployment among Djibouti's largely urbanized population remains a critical problem.

DEVELOPMENT

Recent discoveries of natural-gas reserves in Djibouti could result in a surplus for export. A number of small-scale irrigation schemes have been established. There is also a growing, though still quite small, fishing industry.

FREEDOM

The government continues to harass and detain its critics. While limiting freedom of speech and association. Prison conditions are harsh, with the sexual assault of female prisoners being commonplace.

HEALTH/WELFARE

Progress has been made in reducing infant mortality, but health services are strained in this very poor country. However, on the positive side, school enrollment has expanded by nearly one third since 1987.

ACHIEVEMENTS

Besides feeding its own refugees, the government of Djibouti has played a major role in assisting international efforts to relieve the effects of recurrent famines in Ethiopia, Somalia, and Sudan.

Eritrea (State of Eritrea)

GEOGRAPHY

Area in Square Miles (Kilometers):
46,829 (121,320) (about the size of Pennsylvania)

Capital (Population): Asmara (431,000)

Environmental Concerns: deforestation; desertification; soil erosion; overgrazing

Geographical Features: north-south–trending highlands, descending on the east to a coastal desert plain, on the northwest to hilly terrain, and on the southwest to flat-to-rolling plains

Climate: hot, dry desert on the seacoast; cooler and wetter in the central highlands; semiarid in western hills and lowlands

PEOPLE

Population

Total: 4,136,000

Annual Growth Rate: 3.86%

Rural/Urban Population Ratio: 83/17

Major Languages: various, including Tigrinya, Tigre, Kunama, Arabic, Amharic, and Afar

Ethnic Makeup: 50% ethnic Tigrinya; 40% Tigre and Kunama; 4% Afar; 3% Saho; 3% others

Religions: Muslim; Coptic Christian; Roman Catholic; Protestant

Health

Life Expectancy at Birth: 53 years (male); 58 years (female)

Infant Mortality Rate (Ratio): 76.6/1,000

Physicians Available (Ratio): 1/36,000

Education

Adult Literacy Rate: 25%

Compulsory (Ages): 7–13; free

COMMUNICATION

Telephones: 24,300 main lines

Televisions: 6 per 1,000 people

Internet Service Provider: 1 (1999)

TRANSPORTATION

Highways in Miles (Kilometers): 2,436 (3,930)

Railroads in Miles (Kilometers): 191 (307)

Usable Airfields: 21

GOVERNMENT

Type: transitional government

Independence Date: May 24, 1993 (from Ethiopia)

Head of State/Government: President Isaias Aferweki is both head of state and head of government

Political Parties: People's Front for Democracy and Justice (only recognized party)

MILITARY

Military Expenditures (% of GDP): 28.6%

Current Disputes: border disputes with Yemen; uneasy cease-fire with Ethiopia

ECONOMY

Currency ($ U.S. Equivalent): TK nakfa = $1

Per Capita Income/GDP: $750/$2.9 billion

GDP Growth Rate: 3%

Inflation Rate: 9%

Natural Resources: gold; potash; zinc; copper; salt; probably petroleum; fish

Agriculture: sorghum; lentils; vegetables; maize; cotton; tobacco; coffee; sisal; livestock; fish

Industry: food processing; beverages; clothing and textiles

Exports: $52.9 million (primary partners Ethiopia, Sudan, Italy)

Imports: $489.4 million (primary partners Saudi Arabia, Italy, United Arab Emirates)

 http://www.sas.upenn.edu/
African_Studies/Country_Specific/
Eritrea.html
http://www.eritrea.org

Italians occupy the Eritrean port of Assab
1869

Italians occupy all of Eritrea
1889

Italians use Eritrea as a springboard for conquest of Ethiopia
1935–1936

Great Britain occupies Eritrea
1941–1952

Eritrea is federated with Ethiopia
1952

The ELF begins the liberation struggle
1961

Federation ends; Eritrea is a province of Ethiopia
1962

99.8% vote yes for Eritrea's independence; Isaias Aferweki becomes the newly independent nation's first president
1990s

2000s

Eritrea signs a cease-fire agreement with Ethiopia

ERITREA

In June 2000, Ethiopia and Eritrea signed a cease-fire agreement, following the success of an Ethiopian military offensive the previous month. It is too early to know if ongoing mediation efforts will bring a permanent end to the fighting between the two nations over their disputed border. The two-year conflict resulted in the deaths of thousands of people, along with the massive displacement of civilians from the war zone. Large areas that are indisputably part of Eritrea remain occupied by Ethiopia.

The recent military reverses have been a harsh blow for Eritrea, which became Africa's newest nation in May 1993, ending 41 years of union with Ethiopia. The origins of Eritrea's separation date back to September 1961, when a small group of armed men calling themselves the Eritrean Liberation Front (ELF) began a bitter independence struggle that would last for three decades.

Between 60,000 and 70,000 people perished as a result of that war, while another 700,000—then about one fifth of the total population—went into exile. What had been one of the continent's most sophisticated light-industrial infrastructures was largely reduced to ruins. Yet the war has also left a positive legacy, in the spirit of unity, self-reliance, and sacrifice that it engendered among Eritreans.

There is no clear-cut reason why a nationalist sentiment should have emerged in Eritrea. Like most African countries, the boundaries of Eritrea are an artificial product of the late-nineteenth-century European scramble for colonies. Between 1869 and 1889, the territory fell under the rule of Italy. Italian influence survives today, especially in the overcrowded but elegant capital city of Asmara, which was developed as a showcase of neo-Roman imperialism. Italian rule came to an abrupt end in 1941, when British troops occupied the territory in World War II. The British withdrew only in 1952. In accordance with the wishes of the United Nations Security Council, the territory was then federated as an autonomous state within the "Empire of Ethiopia."

The federation did not come about through the wishes of the Eritreans. It was, rather, based on the dubious Ethiopian claim that Eritrea was an integral part of the Empire that had been alienated by the Italians. Among the Christians, there were historic cultural ties with their Ethiopian coreligionists, though the Tigrinya-speaking Copts of Eritrea were ethnically distinct from the Empire's then–politically dominant Amharic-speakers. The Muslim lowland areas had never been under any form of Ethiopian control. But, perhaps more important, developments under Italian rule had laid the basis for a sense that Eritrea had its own identity.

In the face of growing dissatisfaction inside the territory, Ethiopia's emperor, Haile Selassie, ended Eritrea's autonomous status in 1962. Fighting intensified in the early 1970s, after a faction ultimately known as the Eritrean Popular Liberation Front (EPLF) split from the ELF. The 1974 overthrow of Selassie briefly brought hopes of a peaceful settlement. But Ethiopia's new military rulers, known as the Dergue, committed themselves to securing the area by force. The ELF faded as the EPLF became increasingly effective in pinning down larger numbers of Ethiopian troops. In a major break with tradition, a large proportion of the EPLF's "Liberation Army," including many in command positions, was made up of women. In areas liberated by the EPLF, women were given the right to own land and choose their husbands, while the practice of female circumcision was discouraged.

Had it not been for the massive military support that the Dergue received from the Soviet Union and its allies, the conflict would have ended sooner. In the late 1980s, the EPLF began to work more closely with other groups inside Ethiopia proper that had taken up arms against their government. This resulted in an alliance between the EPLF and the Ethiopian People's Revolutionary Democratic Front (EPRDF), which was facilitated by the fact that leading members of both groups spoke Tigrinya. In May 1991, the Dergue collapsed, with the EPLF taking Asmara in the same month that EPRDF troops entered the Ethiopian capital of Addis Ababa. In July, the new EPRDF government agreed in principle to Eritrea's right to self-determination.

In 1997, the EPLF, transformed as the People's Front for Democracy and Justice, claimed an overwhelming mandate in elections in which there was little effective opposition. A number of smaller parties, including remnants of the ELF, had joined the Front. Former EPLF leader Isaias Aferweki was confirmed as president of Eritrea.

The renewal of war win Ethiopia has had a devastating effect on Eritrea's economy, which had been making significant progress in the years following independence. The rehabilitation of the port of Massawa and other infrastructure had boosted trade. Light industries, mostly based in Asmara, had recovered. International investors have shown increased interest in the country's mineral wealth, especially offshore oil. In July 1997, the country introduced its own currency, the nakfa, which replaced the Ethiopian birr. Resulting exchange disputes between the two nations led to a souring of relations prior to the outbreak of the border war.

DEVELOPMENT

Since liberation, the government has concentrated its efforts on restoring agricultural and communications infrastructure. The railway and ports of Assab and Massawa are being rehabilitated. In 1991, 80% of the country was dependent on food aid, but subsequent good rains helped boost crop production.

FREEDOM

The Eritrean government has pledged to uphold a bill of rights. While the government is dominated by the former EPLF, other parties and organizations participate in the 105-seat Provisional Council. Multiparty elections in 1997 confirmed former EPLF leader Isaias Aferweki as president.

HEALTH/WELFARE

A major challenge for the government has been the repatriation of hundreds of thousands of war refugees, mostly from neighboring Sudan. Rebuilding efforts were spearheaded by ex-combatants of the Liberation Army, who continued to work for virtually no pay. The EPLF established its own medical and educational services during the war.

ACHIEVEMENTS

Eritrea's independence struggle and ongoing national development efforts have been carried out against overwhelming odds, and with very little external support. During the war, self-reliance was manifested in the fact that most weapons and ammunition used by the EPLF were captured from Ethiopian forces.

Ethiopia (Federal Democratic Republic of Ethiopia)

GEOGRAPHY

Area in Square Miles (Kilometers):
435,071 (1,127,127) (about twice the size of Texas)

Capital (Population): Addis Ababa (2,431,000)

Environmental Concerns: deforestation; overgrazing; soil erosion; desertification

Geographical Features: a high plateau with a central mountain range divided by the Great Rift Valley

Climate: tropical monsoon with wide topographic-induced variation

PEOPLE

Population

Total: 64,118,000*

Annual Growth Rate: 2.76%

Rural/Urban Population Ratio: 84/16

Major Languages: Amharic; Tigrinya; Oromo; Somali; Arabic; Italian; English

Ethnic Makeup: 40% Oromo; 32% Amhara and Tigre; 9% Sidamo; 19% others

Religions: 45%–40% Muslims; 35%–40% Ethiopian Orthodox Christian; 12% animist; remainder others

Health

Life Expectancy at Birth: 44 years (male); 46 years (female)*

Infant Mortality Rate (Ratio): 101.2/1,000*

Physicians Available (Ratio): 1/36,600

Education

Adult Literacy Rate: 35.5%

Compulsory (Ages): 7–13; free

COMMUNICATION

Telephones: 157,000 main lines

Televisions: 4 per 1,000 people

Internet Service Providers: 1 (1999)

TRANSPORTATION

Highways in Miles (Kilometers): 17,016 (28,360)

Railroads in Miles (Kilometers): 425 (681)

Usable Airfields: 85

Motor Vehicles in Use: 66,000

GOVERNMENT

Type: federal republic

Independence Date: oldest independent country in Africa (at least 2,000 years)

Head of State/Government: President Ngesso Gidada; Prime Minister Meles Zenawi

Political Parties: Ethiopian People's Revolutionary Democratic Front; many others

Suffrage: universal at 18

MILITARY

Military Expenditures (% of GDP): 2.5%

Current Disputes: border war with Somalia; uneasy cease-fire with Eritrea

ECONOMY

Currency ($ U.S. Equivalent): 5.95 birrs = $1

Per Capita Income/GDP: $560/$33.3 billion

GDP Growth Rate: 0%

Inflation Rate: 4%

Natural Resources: gold; platinum, copper; potash; natural gas; hydropower

Agriculture: cereals; pulses; coffee; oilseed; sugarcane; vegetables; livestock

Industry: food processing; beverages; textiles; cement; building materials; hydropower

Exports: $420 million (primary partners Germany, Japan, Italy)

Imports: $1.25 billion (primary partners Italy, United States, Japan)

 http://www.state.gov/www/ background_notes/ ethiopia_0398_bgn.html
http://www.sas.upenn.edu/ African_Studies/Country_Specific/ Ethiopia.html

*Note: These estimates explicitly take into account the effects of excess mortality due to AIDS.

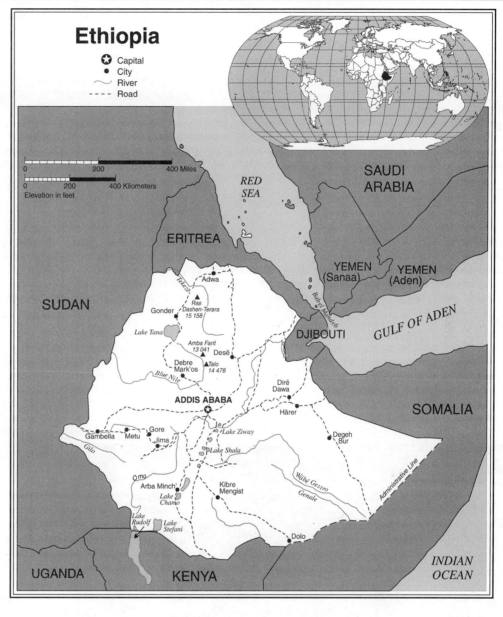

Ethiopia

⊛ Capital
● City
〜 River
- - - Road

ETHIOPIA

In May 2000, the government of Prime Minister Meles Zenawi celebrated two controversial victories. On the battlefield, Ethiopian forces gained the advantage in a debilitating two-year border war with Eritrea, raising hope for the restoration of peace. And at the polls, Zenawi's Ethiopian People's Revolutionary Democratic Front (EPRDF) won an easy victory in legislative elections against some 25 opposition parties. In almost half of the constituencies, EPRDF candidates ran unopposed.

Following equally overwhelming and controversial election victories in 1994–1995, the EPRDF remains the country's dominant political group. The movement initially came to power in 1991 as an armed movement, following the successful overthrow of Ethiopia's Marxist-oriented military dictatorship, after years of struggle.

Since coming to power, the EPRDF has faced a wide spectrum of opponents. Some critics see its transformation of Ethiopia into a multiethnic federation of 14 self-governing regions as a threat to national unity. Others contend that its devolutionary structures are a sham designed to obscure its own determination to rule from the center as a virtual one-party state. International as well as domestic supporters, however, see Ethiopia's new Constitution as a bold experiment in institutionalizing a new model of multiethnic statehood.

The EPRDF had emerged in the 1980s as an umbrella movement fighting to liberate Ethiopia from the repressive misrule by the Provisional Military Administrative Council, popularly known as the *Dergue* (Amharic for "Committee"). The Dergue had come to power through a popular uprising against the country's former imperial order. Time will tell whether Ethiopia's second revolution in two decades will succeed where its first one failed.

Political instability has reduced Ethiopia from a developing breadbasket to a famine-ridden basket case. Interethnic conflict among an increasingly desperate population, many of whom have long had better access to arms and ammunition than to food and medicine, could lead to the state's disintegration. In the late 1990s, the problems facing the EPRDF government were intensified by the outbreak of a border war with Eritrea, which compromised the landlocked country's access to the sea. The two countries signed a cease-fire agreement in 2000.

IMPERIAL PAST

Ethiopia rivals Egypt as Africa's oldest country. For centuries, its kings claimed direct descent from the biblical King Solomon and the Queen of Sheba. Whether Ethiopia was the site of Sheba is uncertain, as is the local claim that, prior to the birth of Christ, the country became the final resting place of the Ark of the Covenant holding the original Ten Commandments given to Moses (the Ark is said to survive in a local monastery).

Local history is better established from the time of the Axum empire, which prospered from the first century. During the fourth century, the Axumite court adopted the Coptic Christian faith, which has remained central to the culture of Ethiopia's highland region. The Church still uses the Geez, the ancient Axumite tongue from which the modern Ethiopian languages of Amharic and Tigrinya are derived, in its services.

From the eighth century, much of the area surrounding the highlands fell under Muslim control, all but cutting off the Copts from their European coreligionists. (Today, most Muslim Ethiopians live in the lowlands.) For many centuries, Ethiopia's history was characterized by struggles among the groups inhabiting these two regions and religions. Occasionally a powerful ruler would succeed in making himself truly "King of Kings" by uniting the Christian highlands and expanding into the lowlands. At other times, the mountains would be divided into weak polities that were vulnerable to the raids of both Muslim and non-Muslim lowlanders.

Modern Ethiopian history began in the nineteenth century, when the highlands became politically reunited by a series of kings, culminating in Menilik II, who built up power by importing European armaments. Once the Coptic core of his kingdom was intact, Menilik began to spread his authority across the lowlands, thus uniting most of contemporary Ethiopia. In 1889 and 1896, Menilik also defeated invading Italian armies, thus preserving his empire's independence during the European partition of Africa.

From 1916 to 1974, Ethiopia was ruled by Ras Tafari (from which is derived the term *Rasta,* or *Rastafarian*), who, in 1930, was crowned Emperor Haile Selassie. The late Selassie remains a controversial figure. For many decades, he was seen both at home and abroad as a reformer who was modernizing his state. In 1936, after his kingdom had been occupied by Benito Mussolini, he made a memorable speech before the League of Nations, warning the world of the price it would inevitably pay

(United Nations photo by Muldoon)

From 1916 to 1974, Ethiopia was ruled by Haile Selassie, also known as Ras Tafari (from which today's term *Rastafarian* is derived). He is pictured above, on the left, shaking hands with the infamous Idi Amin of Uganda.

for appeasing Fascist aggression. At the time, many African-Americans and Africans outside of Ethiopia saw Selassie as a great hero in the struggle of black peoples everywhere for dignity and empowerment. Selassie returned to his throne in 1941 and thereafter served as an elder statesman to the African nationalists of the 1950s and 1960s. However, by the latter decade, his own domestic authority was being increasingly questioned.

In his later years, Selassie could not, or would not, move against the forces that were undermining his empire. Despite its trappings of progress, the Ethiopian state remained quasi-feudal in character. Many of the best lands were controlled by the nobility and the Church, whose leading members lived privileged lives at the expense of the peasantry. Many educated people grew disenchanted with what they perceived as a reactionary monarchy and social order. Urban workers resented being paid low wages by often foreign owners. Within the junior ranks of the army and civil service, there was also great dissatisfaction with the way in which their superiors were able to siphon off state revenues for personal enrichment. But the empire's greatest weakness was its inability to accommodate the aspirations of the various ethnic, regional, and sectarian groupings living within its borders.

Ethiopia is a multiethnic state. Since the time of Menilik, the dominant group has been the Coptic Amhara-speakers, whose preeminence has been resented by their Tigrinya coreligionists as well as by predominantly non-Coptic groups such as the Afars, Gurages, Oromo, and Somalis. In recent years, movements fighting for ethnoregional autonomy have emerged among the Tigrinya of Tigray, the Oromo, and, to a lesser extent, the Afars, while many Somalis in Ethiopia's Ogaden region have long struggled for union with neighboring Somalia. Somali irredentism led to open warfare between the two principal Horn of Africa states in 1963–1964 and again in 1977–1978.

The former northern coastal province of Eritrea was a special case. From the late nineteenth century until World War II, it was an Italian colony. After the war, it was integrated into Selassie's empire. Thereafter, a local independence movement, largely united as the Eritrean People's Liberation Front (EPLF), waged a successful armed struggle, which led to Eritrea's full independence in 1993.

REVOLUTION AND REPRESSION

In 1974, Haile Selassie was overthrown by the military, after months of mounting unrest throughout the country. A major factor

(United Nations photo by John Isaac)

Ethiopians experienced a brutal civil war from 1974 to 1991. The continuous fighting displaced millions of people. The problems of this forced migration were compounded by drought and starvation. The drought victims pictured above are gathered at one of the many relief camps.

triggering the coup was the government's inaction in 1972–1974, when famine swept across the northern provinces, claiming 200,000 lives. Some accused the Amhara government of using the famine as a way of weakening the predominantly Tigrinya areas of the empire. Others saw the tragedy simply as proof of the venal incompetence of Selassie's administration.

The overthrow of the old order was welcomed by most Ethiopians. Unfortunately, what began as a promising revolutionary transformation quickly degenerated into a repressive dictatorship, which pushed the nation into chronic instability and distress. By the end of 1974, after the first in a series of bloody purges within its ranks, the Dergue had embraced Marxism as its guiding philosophy. Revolutionary measures followed. Companies and lands were nationalized. Students were sent into the countryside to assist in land reforms and to teach literacy. Peasants and workers were organized into cooperative associations, called *kebeles*. Initial steps were also taken to end Amhara hegemony within the state.

Progressive aspects of the Ethiopian revolution were offset by the murderous nature of the regime. Power struggles within the Dergue, as well as its determination to eliminate all alternatives to its authority, contributed to periods of "red terror," during which thousands of supporters of the revolution as well as those associated with the old regime were killed. By 1977, the Dergue itself had been transformed from a collective decision-making body to a small clique loyal to Colonel Mengistu Haile Mariam, who became a presidential dictator.

Mengistu sought for years to legitimize his rule through a commitment to Marxist-Leninism. He formally presided over a Commission for Organizing the Party of the Working People of Ethiopia, which, in 1984, announced the formation of a single-party state, led by the new Workers' Party. But real power remained in the hands of Mengistu's Dergue.

CIVIL WAR

From 1974 to 1991, Ethiopians suffered through civil war. In the face of oppressive central authority, ethnic-based resistance movements became increasingly effective in their struggles throughout much of the country. In the late 1970s, the Mengistu regime began to receive massive military aid from the Soviet bloc in its campaigns against the Eritreans and Somalis. Some 17,000 Cuban troops and thousands of other military personnel from the Warsaw Pact countries allowed the government temporarily to gain the upper hand in the fighting. The Ethiopian Army grew to

								The Mengistu regime is overthrown by EPRDF rebels; Eritrea achieves independence of Ethiopia **1990s**
Emperor Tewodros begins the conquest and development of modern Ethiopia **1855**	Ethiopia defeats Italian invaders at the Battle of Adowa **1896**	Fascist Italy invades Ethiopia and rules until 1941 **1936**	The Eritrean liberation struggle begins **1961**	Famines in Tigray and Welo Provinces result in up to 200,000 deaths **1972–1973**	Emperor Haile Selassie is overthrown; the PMAC is established **1974**	Diplomatic realignment and a new arms agreement with the Soviet Union **1977**	Massive famine, resulting from both drought and warfare **1980s**	

2000s

Interethnic political tensions continue

Ethiopia and Eritrea sign a cease-fire for a border war that begain in the late 1990s

more than 300,000 men under arms at any given time, the largest military force on the continent. Throughout the 1980s, military expenditures claimed more than half of the national budget.

Despite the massive domestic and international commitment on the side of the Mengistu regime, the rebels gradually gained the upper hand. Before 1991, almost all of northern Eritrea, except its besieged capital city of Asmara, had fallen to the EPLF, which had built up its own powerful arsenal, largely from captured government equipment. Local rebels had also liberated the province of Tigray and, as part of the EPRDF coalition, pushed south toward Ethiopia's capital city of Addis Ababa. In the south, independent Oromo and Somali rebels challenged government authority. There was also resistance to Mengistu from within the ranks of the national army. A major rebellion against his authority in 1989 was crushed, devastating military morale in the process. The regime was further undermined by the withdrawal of remaining Cuban and Soviet bloc support.

Ethiopians have paid a terrible price for their nation's conflicts. Tens of thousands have been killed in combat, while many more have died from the side effects of war. In 1984–1985, the conscience of the world was moved by the images of mass starvation in the northern war zone. (At the time, however, the global media and concerned groups like Band Aid paid relatively little attention to the nonenvironmental factors that contributed to the crisis.) Up to 1 million lives were lost before adequate relief supplies reached the famine areas. Although drought and other environmental factors, such as soil erosion, contributed to the catastrophe, the fact that people continued to starve despite the availability of international relief can be attributed only to the use of food as a weapon of war.

There were other political constraints on local crop production. Having seized the lands of the old ruling class, the Mengistu regime, in accordance with its Marxist-Leninist precepts, invested most of its agricultural inputs in large state farms, whose productivity was abysmal. Peasant production also fell in nondrought areas, due to insecure tenure, poor producer prices, lack of credit, and an absence of consumer goods. Ethiopia's rural areas were further disrupted by the government's heavy-handed villagization and relocation schemes. In 1984–1985, thousands died when the government moved some 600,000 northerners to what were supposedly more fertile regions in the southwest. Many considered the scheme to be part of the central government's war effort against local communities resistant to its authority. By the same token, villagization has long been associated with counterinsurgency efforts; concentrated settlements allow occupying armies to exert greater control over potentially hostile populations.

UNCERTAIN PROSPECTS
The Dergue's demise has not as yet been accompanied by national reconciliation. Opposition to the EPRDF's attempt to transform Ethiopia into a multiethnic federation has been especially strong among Amharas, many of whom support the All-Amhara People's Organization. Others accuse the EPRDF—or, more especially, former Stalinists within the Tigrean People's Liberation Front (TPLF), which has been its predominant element—of trying to create its own monopoly of power.

In 1992, fighting broke out between the EPRDF and the forces of its former rebel partner, the Oromo Liberation Front (OLF), which claims to represent Ethiopia's largest ethnic group (Oromos constitute 40 percent of the population). The OLF was prominent among those who boycotted June 1992 local-government elections, which were further marred by allegations of vote-rigging and intimidation on behalf of the EPRDF. In December 1993, the OLF joined a number of other movements in a Council of Alternative Forces for Peace and Democracy (CAFPD). At its inaugural meeting, seven CAFPD delegates were detained for allegedly advocating the armed overthrow of the government. In April, another antigovernment coalition, the Ethiopian National Democratic party, was formed. Both movements called for an election boycott.

Another source of resistance to the EPRDF was the Ogadeni National Liberation Front (ONLF), which won strong support from Ogadeni Somalis in the June 1992 elections. In April, the Transitional Government removed ONLF's Hassan Jireh from power as the Ogaden region's elected administrator; in May, he was arrested. As a result, clashes occurred between the ONLF and EPRDF in the area, with the former boycotting the subsequent polls. Smaller uprisings and acts of terror, such as a January 1996 bombing of an Addis Ababa hotel, have posed further challenges for the government, which has also had to cope with drought. But while the extent of its electoral mandate is disputed, the EPRDF has demonstrated that it retains strong popular support, while its opposition is divided.

DEVELOPMENT

There has been some progress in the country's industrial sector in recent years, after a sharp decline during the 1970s. Soviet-bloc investment resulted in the establishment of new enterprises in such areas as cement, textiles, and farm machinery.

FREEDOM

Despite its public commitment to freedom of speech and association, the EPRDF government has resorted to authoritarian measures against its critics. In 1995, Ethiopia had the highest number of jailed journalists in Africa. Basic freedoms are also compromised.

HEALTH/WELFARE

Ethiopia's progress in increasing literacy during the 1970s was undermined by the severe dislocations of the 1980s. By 1991, Ethiopia had some 500 government soldiers for every teacher.

ACHIEVEMENTS

With a history spanning 2 millennia, the cultural achievements of Ethiopia are vast. Today, Addis Ababa is the site of the headquarters of the Organization of African Unity. Ethiopia's Kefe Province is the home of the coffee plant, from whence it takes its name.

Kenya (Republic of Kenya)

GEOGRAPHY

Area in Square Miles (Kilometers):
224,900 (582,488) (twice the
size of Nevada)

Capital (Population): Nairobi
(2,000,000)

Environmental Concerns: water
pollution; deforestation; soil
erosion; poaching

Geographical Features: low
plains rise to central highlands
bisected by the Great Rift
Valley; fertile plateau in the
west

Climate: tropical to arid

PEOPLE

Population

Total: 30,340,000
Annual Growth Rate: 1.53%
Rural/Urban Population Ratio:
70/30

Major Languages: English;
Kiswahili; Maasai; others

Ethnic Makeup: 22% Kikuyu; 14%
Luhya; 13% Luo; 12% Kalenjin;
11% Kamba; 28% others

Religions: 38% Protestant; 28%
Catholic; 26% indigenous
beliefs; 8% others

Health

Life Expectancy at Birth: 47
years (male); 49 years (female)

Infant Mortality Rate (Ratio):
68.7/1,000

Physicians Available (Ratio):
1/5,999

Education

Adult Literacy Rate: 78%
Compulsory (Ages): 6–14; free

COMMUNICATION

Telephones: 272,000 main lines
Televisions: 18 per 1,000 people
Internet Service Providers: 8
(1999)

TRANSPORTATION

Highways in Miles (Kilometers): 38,198
(63,663)

Railroads in Miles (Kilometers): 1,654
(2,650)

Usable Airfields: 230
Motor Vehicles in Use: 357,000

GOVERNMENT

Type: republic

Independence Date: December 12, 1963
(from the United Kingdom)

Head of State/Government: President
Daniel arap Moi is both head of state
and head of government

Political Parties: Kenya African National
Union; Forum for the Restoration of

Democracy; Democratic Party of
Kenya; others

Suffrage: universal at 18

MILITARY

Military Expenditures (% of GDP): 3.9%

Current Disputes: border conflict with
Sudan; civil unrest and interethnic
violence

ECONOMY

Currency ($ U.S. Equivalent): 44.48
Kenya shillings = $1

Per Capita Income/GDP: $1,600/$45.1 billion
GDP Growth Rate: 1.5%
Inflation Rate: 6%
Unemployment Rate: 50%

Labor Force: 9,200,000

Natural Resources: gold; limestone; soda
ash; salt barites; rubies; fluorspar;
garnets; wildlife; hydropower

Agriculture: coffee; tea; corn; wheat;
sugarcane; fruit; vegetables; livestock
and dairy products

Industry: small-scale consumer goods;
agricultural processing; oil refining;
cement; tourism

Exports: $2.2 billion (primary partners
Uganda, United Kingdom, Tanzania)

Imports: $3.3 billion (primary partners United
Kingdom, United Arab Emirates, Japan)

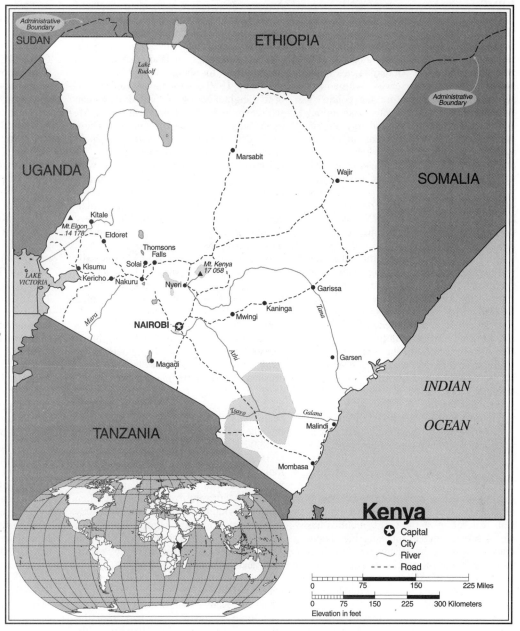

KENYA

In 1999, long-serving President Daniel arap Moi surprised many observers by appointing one of his best-known critics, the internationally renowned archaeologist and conservationist Richard Leakey, as head of Kenya's civil service, with an apparent mandate to restore the country's flagging economic fortunes by rooting out endemic corruption and lethargy in the public sector. After a year in office, Leakey and his "Recovery Team" could claim some progress in shaking up the system. But the reform effort is being met with serious resistance by a growing body of entrenched interests. In the meantime, hopes for accelerated recovery have been dealt a further blow by the onset of severe drought.

In August 1998, the world's attention was focused on the bombing of the U.S. Embassy building in Nairobi, Kenya's capital city. Scores of people in the vicinity of the blast were killed or injured. For Kenyans, it was an unprecedented act of international terrorism on their soil. It was also a further blow to the country's troubled tourist industry, which has been hard hit by a continuing upward spiral of both criminal and political violence. The strength of the tourist industry—a critical foreign-exchange earner—coupled with years of growth in manufacturing and services have made Kenya, and especially Nairobi, the commercial center of East Africa. But today, after nearly four decades of independence, most Kenyans remain the impoverished citizens of a state struggling to develop as a nation. And the recent restoration of multiparty politics has so far served only to intensify interethnic conflict, without diminishing the positions of those in the ruling Kenya African National Union (KANU) party who have plundered Kenya's wealth through their abuse of state power.

In the precolonial past, Kenyan communities belonged to relatively small-scale, but economically interlinked, societies. Predominantly pastoral groups, such as the Maasai and Turkana, exchanged cattle for the crops of the Kalinjin, Kamba, Kikuyu, Luo, and others. Swahili city-states developed on the coast. In the 1800s, caravans of Arab as well as Swahili traders stimulated economic and political changes. However, the outsiders who had the greatest modern impact on the Kenyan interior were European settlers, who began to arrive in the first decade of the twentieth century. By the 1930s, much of the temperate hill country around Nairobi had become the "White Highlands." More than 6 million acres of land—Maasai pasture and Kikuyu and Kamba farms—were stolen by the settlers.

African communities were often displaced to increasingly overcrowded reserves. Laborers, mostly Kikuyu migrants from the reserves, worked for the new European owners, sometimes on lands that they had once farmed for themselves.

By the 1950s, African grievances had been heightened by increased European settlement and the growing removal of African "squatters" from their estates. There were also growing class and ideological differences among Africans, leading to tensions between educated Christians with middle-class aspirations and displaced members of the rural underclass. Many members of the latter group, in particular, began to mobilize themselves in largely Kikuyu oathing societies, which coalesced into the Mau Mau movement.

Armed resistance by Mau Mau guerrillas began in 1951, with isolated attacks on white settlers. In response, the British proclaimed a state of emergency, which lasted for 10 years. Without any outside support, the Mau Mau held out for years by making effective use of the highland forests as sanctuaries. Nonetheless, by 1955, the uprising had largely been crushed. Although the name Mau Mau became for many outsiders synonymous with antiwhite terrorism, only 32 European civilians actually lost their lives during the rebellion. In contrast, at least 13,000 Kikuyu were killed. Another 80,000 Africans were detained by the colonial authorities, and more than 1 million were resettled in controlled villages. While the Mau Mau were overwhelmed by often ruthless counterinsurgency measures, they achieved an important victory: The British realized that the preservation of Kenya as a white-settler–dominated colony was militarily and politically untenable.

In the aftermath of the emergency, the person who emerged as the charismatic leader of Kenya's nationalist movement was Jomo Kenyatta, who had been detained and accused by the British—without any evidence—of leading the resistance movement. At independence, in 1963, he became the president. He held the office until his death in 1978.

To many, the situation in Kenya under Kenyatta looked promising. His government encouraged racial harmony, and the slogan *Harambee* (Swahili for "Pull together") became a call for people of all ethnic groups and races to work together for development. Land reforms provided plots to 1.5 million farmers. A policy of Africanization created business opportunities for local entrepreneurs, and industry grew. Although the Kenya African National Union was supposedly guided by a policy of "African Socialism," the nation

was seen by many as a showcase of capitalist development.

POLITICAL DEVELOPMENT

Kenyatta's Kenya quickly became a de facto one-party state. In 1966, the country's first vice-president, Oginga Odinga, resigned to form an opposition party, the Kenyan People's Union (KPU). Three years later, however, the party was banned and its leaders, including Odinga, were imprisoned. Thereafter KANU became the focus of political competition, and voters were allowed to remove sitting members of Parliament, including cabinet ministers. But politics was marred by intimidation and violence, including the assassinations of prominent critics within government, most notably Economic Development Minister Tom Mboya, in 1969, and Foreign Affairs Minister J. M. Kariuki, in 1975. Constraints on freedom of association were justified in the interest of preventing ethnic conflict—much of the KPU support came from the Luo group. However, ethnicity has always been important in shaping struggles within KANU itself.

Under Daniel arap Moi, Kenyatta's successor, the political climate grew steadily more repressive. In 1982, his government was badly shaken by a failed coup attempt, in which about 250 people died and approximately 1,500 others were detained. The old air force was disbanded and the university, whose students came out in support of the coup-makers, was temporarily closed.

In the aftermath of the coup, all parties other than KANU were formally outlawed. Moi followed this step by declaring, in 1986, that KANU was above the government, the Parliament, and the judiciary. Press restrictions, detentions, and blatant acts of intimidation became common. Those Members of Parliament brave enough to be critical of Moi's imperial presidency were removed from KANU and thus Parliament. Political tensions were blamed on the local agents of an ever-growing list of outside forces, including Christian missionaries and Muslim fundamentalists, foreign academics and the news media, and Libyan and U.S. meddlers.

A number of underground opposition groups emerged during the mid-1980s, most notably the socialist-oriented Mwakenya movement, whose ranks included such prominent exiles as the writer Ngugi wa Thiong'o. In 1987, many of these groups came together to form the United Movement for Democracy, or UMOJA (Swahili for "unity"). But in the immediate aftermath of the 1989 KANU elections, which in many areas were blatantly rigged, Moi's grip on power appeared strong.

The British East
African
Protectorate is
proclaimed
1895

British colonists
begin to settle in
the Highlands
area
1900–1910

Mau Mau, a
predominately
Kikuyu
movement,
resists
colonial rule
1951

Kenya gains
independence
under the
leadership of
Jomo Kenyatta
1963

Daniel arap Moi
becomes
president upon
the death of
Kenyatta
1978

A coup attempt
by members of
the Kenyan Air
Force is crushed;
political
repression grows
1980s

Prodemocracy agitation
leads to a return of
multiparty politics; interethnic
violence threatens
democratic transition;
President Daniel arap Moi is
reelected; the U.S. Embassy
building in Nairobi is bombed
1990s

2000s

Kenya seeks to root
out public corruption

Kenya works to
strengthen its economy
and international
reputation

The early months of 1990, however, witnessed an upsurge in antigovernment unrest. In February, the murder of Foreign Minister Robert Ouko touched off rioting in Nairobi and his home city of Kisumu. Another riot occurred when squatters were forcibly evicted from the Nairobi shantytown of Muoroto. Growing calls for the restoration of multiparty democracy fueled a cycle of unrest and repression. The detention in July of two former cabinet ministers, Kenneth Matiba and Charles Rubia, for their part in the democracy agitation sparked nationwide rioting, which left at least 28 people dead and 1,000 arrested. Opposition movements, most notably the Forum for the Restoration of Democracy (FORD), began to emerge in defiance of the government's ban on their activities.

Under mounting external pressure from Western donor countries as well as from his internal opponents, Moi finally agreed to the legalization of opposition parties, in December 1991. Unfortunately, this move failed to diffuse Kenya's increasingly violent political, social, and ethnic tensions.

Continued police harassment of the opposition triggered renewed rioting throughout the country. There was also a rise in interethnic clashes in both the rural and urban areas, which many, even within KANU, attributed to government incitement. In the Rift Valley, armed members of Moi's own Kalinjin grouping attacked other groups for supposedly settling on their land. Hundreds were killed and thousands injured and displaced in the worst violence since the Mau Mau era. In the face of the government's cynical resort to divide-and-rule tactics, the fledgling opposition movement betrayed the hopes of many of its supporters by becoming hopelessly splintered. New groups, such as the Islamic Party of Kenya, openly appealed for support along ethnoreligious lines. More significantly, a leadership struggle in

the main FORD grouping between Matiba and the veteran Odinga split the party into two, while a proposed alliance with Mwai Kibaki's Democratic Party failed to materialize. Although motivated as much by personal ambitions and lingering mistrust between KANU defectors and long-term KANU opponents, the FORD split soon took on an ethnic dimension, with many Kikuyu backing Matiba, while Luo remained solidly loyal to Odinga.

Taking skillful advantage of his opponents' disarray, Moi called elections in December 1992, which resulted in his plurality victory, with 36 percent of the vote. KANU was able to capture 95 of the 188 parliamentary seats that were up for grabs. The two FORD factions won 31 seats each, while the Democratic Party captured 23 seats. Notwithstanding voting irregularities, most independent observers blamed the divided opposition for sowing the seeds of its own defeat. The death of the widely respected Odinga in January 1994 coincided with renewed attempts to form a united opposition to KANU. In 1996, a group of opposition Members of Parliament was established.

Kenya's politics reflects class as well as ethnic divisions. The richest 10 percent of the population own an estimated 40 percent of the wealth, while the poorest 30 percent own only 10 percent. Past economic growth has failed to alleviate poverty. Kenya's relatively large middle class has grown resentful of increased repression and the evident corruption at the very top, but it is also fearful about perceived anarchy from below.

Although its rate of growth has declined during much of the past two decades, the Kenyan economy has expanded since independence. Nairobi is now the leading center of industrial and commercial activity in East Africa. While foreign capital has played an important role in industrial development, the largest share of invest-

ment has come from government and the local private sector.

A significant percentage of foreign-exchange earnings has come from agriculture. A wide variety of cash crops is exported, a diversity that has buffered the nation's economy to some degree from the uncertainties associated with single-commodity dependence. While large plantations—now often owned by wealthy Kenyans—have survived from the colonial era, much of the commercial production is carried out by small landholders.

Tourism has accounted for much of Kenya's foreign-exchange earnings, but its immediate prospects are not good. The sector has suffered from a combination of increased competition from other African destinations, widely publicized attacks on visitors, the current political unrest, fears about AIDS, and threats to the wildlife population.

Another major challenge to Kenya's well-being has been its rapidly expanding population. Although there are some hopeful signs that women are beginning to plan for fewer children than in the past, the nation has been plagued with one of the highest population growth rates in the world, until very recently hovering around 3 percent per year. More than half of all Kenyans are under age 15. Pressure on arable land is enormous. It will be difficult to create nonagricultural employment for the burgeoning rural-turned-urban workforce, even in the context of democratic stability and renewed economic growth.

DEVELOPMENT

Under its director Richard Leakey, the Kenyan Wildlife Service during the early 1990s cracked down on poachers while placing itself in the forefront of the global campaign to ban all ivory trading. As a result, local wildlife populations began to recover.

FREEDOM

In 1997–1998, Kenya's already poor human-rights record deteriorated, with extra-judicial killings, beatings, and torture by the police. The National Youth Service, intended to provide young Kenyans with vocational training, has been co-opted to block opposition political meetings. The worst atrocities, however, are linked to interethnic violence.

HEALTH/WELFARE

Kenya's social infrastructure has been burdened by the influx of some 300,000 refugees from the neighboring states of Ethiopia, Somalia, and Sudan. In addition to mounting relief efforts to feed and settle the new arrivals, the government has had to combat growing lawlessness in its border regions.

ACHIEVEMENTS

Each year, Kenya devotes about half of its government expenditures to education. Most Kenyan students can now expect 12 years of schooling. Tertiary education is also expanding.

Madagascar (Republic of Madagascar)

GEOGRAPHY

Area in Square Miles (Kilometers): 226,658 (587,041) (about twice the size of Arizona)

Capital (Population): Antananarivo (876,000)

Environmental Concerns: soil erosion resulting from deforestation and overgrazing; desertification; water contamination; endangered species

Geographical Features: narrow coastal plain; high plateau and mountains in the center; the world's fourth-largest island

Climate: tropical along the coast; temperate inland; arid in the south

PEOPLE

Population

Total: 15,507,000

Annual Growth Rate: 3.02%

Rural/Urban Population Ratio: 73/27

Major Languages: Malagasy; French

Ethnic Makeup: Malayo-Indonesian; Cotiers; French; Indian; Creole; Comoran

Religions: 52% indigenous beliefs; 41% Christian; 7% Muslim

Health

Life Expectancy at Birth: 53 years (male); 57 years (female)

Infant Mortality Rate (Ratio): 85.2/1,000

Physicians Available (Ratio): 1/8,628

Education

Adult Literacy Rate: 80%

Compulsory (Ages): for 5 years between 6–13

COMMUNICATION

Telephones: 43,000 main lines

Daily Newspaper Circulation: 4 per 1,000 people

Televisions: 20 per 1,000 people

Internet Service Providers: 3 (1999)

TRANSPORTATION

Highways in Miles (Kilometers): 29,900 (49,837)

Railroads in Miles (Kilometers): 530 (883)

Usable Airfields: 133

Motor Vehicles in Use: 76,000

GOVERNMENT

Type: republic

Independence Date: June 26, 1960 (from France)

Head of State/Government: President Didier Ratsiraka; Prime Minister Tantely Rene Gabriot Andrianarivo

Political Parties: Movement for the Progress of Madagascar; Renewal of the Social Democratic Party; others

Suffrage: universal at 18

MILITARY

Military Expenditures (% of GDP): 1%

Current Disputes: territorial disputes with France

ECONOMY

Currency ($ U.S. Equivalent): 3,718 Malagasy francs = $1

Per Capita Income/GDP: $780/$11.5 billion

GDP Growth Rate: 4.5%

Inflation Rate: 9.5%

Labor Force: 7,000,000

Natural Resources: graphite; chromite; coal; bauxite; salt; quartz; tar sands; semiprecious stones; mica; fish; hydropower

Agriculture: coffee; vanilla; sugarcane; cloves; cocoa; rice; cassava (tapioca); beans; bananas; livestock products

Industry: meat processing; soap; breweries; tanneries; sugar; textiles; glassware; cement; automobile assembly; paper; petroleum; tourism

Exports: $600 million (primary partners France, United States, Germany)

Imports: $881 million (primary partners France, Japan, Hong Kong)

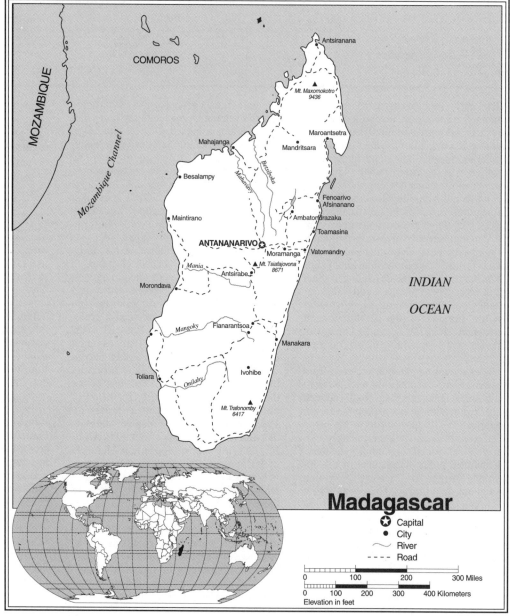

Madagascar

- ⊛ Capital
- • City
- ∼ River
- --- Road

MADAGASCAR

Madagascar has been called the "smallest continent"; indeed, many geologists believe that it once formed the core of a larger landmass, whose other principal remnants are the Indian subcontinent and Australia. The world's fourth-largest island remains a world unto itself in other ways. Botanists and zoologists know it as the home of flora and fauna not found elsewhere. The island's culture is also distinctive. The Malagasy language, which with dialectical variations is spoken throughout the island, is related to the Malay tongues of distant Indonesia. But despite their geographic separation from the African mainland and their Asiatic roots, the Malagasy are very aware of their African identity.

While the early history of Madagascar is the subject of much scholarly debate, it is clear that by the year A.D. 500, the island was being settled by Malay-speaking peoples, who may have migrated via the East African coast rather than directly from Indonesia. The cultural imprint of Southeast Asia is also evident in such aspects as local architecture, music, cosmology, and agricultural practices. African influences are equally apparent. During the precolonial period, the peoples of Madagascar were in communication with communities on the African mainland, and the waves of migration across the Mozambique channel contributed to the island's modern ethnic diversity.

During the early nineteenth century, most of Madagascar was united by the rulers of Merina. In seeking to build up their realm and preserve the island's independence, the Merina kings and queens welcomed European (mostly English) missionaries, who helped introduce new ideas and technologies. As a result, many Malagasy, including the royalty, adopted Christianity. The kingdom had established diplomatic relations with the United States and various European powers and was thus a recognized member of the international community. Foreign businesspeople were attracted to invest in the island's growing economy, while the rapid spread of schools and medical services, increasingly staffed by Malagasy, brought profound changes to the society.

The Merina court hoped that its "Christian civilization" and modernizing army would deter European aggression. But the French were determined to rule the island. The 1884–1885 Franco–Malagasy War ended in a stalemate, but a French invasion in 1895 led to the Merina kingdom's destruction. It was not an easy conquest. The Malagasy army, with its artillery and modern fortifications, held out for many months; eventually, however, it was outgunned by the invaders. French sovereignty was proclaimed in 1896, but "pacification" campaigns continued for another decade.

French rule reduced what had been a prospering state into a colonial backwater. The pace of development slowed as the local economy was restructured to serve the interests of French settlers, whose numbers had swelled to 60,000 by the time of World War II. Probably the most important French contribution to Madagascar was the encouragement their misrule gave to the growth of local nationalism. By the 1940s, a strong sense of Malagasy identity had been forged through common hatred of the colonialists.

The local overthrow of Vichy power by the British in 1943 created an opening for Malagasy nationalists to organize themselves into mass parties, the most promi-

(United Nations photo by L. Rajaonina)

Madagascar has a unique ethnic diversity, influenced by migrations from the African mainland and Southeast Asia. The varied ethnic makeup of the population can be seen in the faces of these schoolchildren.

| Merina rulers gain sovereignty over other peoples of the island **1828** | Franco–Malagasy War **1884–1885** | The French complete the conquest of the island **1904** | A revolt is suppressed by the French, with great loss of life **1947–1948** | Independence from France; Philibert Tsiranana becomes the first president **1960** | A coup leads to the fall of the First Malagasy Republic **1972** | Didier Ratsiraka becomes president by military appointment **1975** | Economic problems intensify **1980s** | Elections in 1989–1990 strengthen multiparty democracy **1990** |

2000s

Ratsiraka holds on to power after suffering some political reverses in the 1990s

nent of which was the Malagasy Movement for Democratic Renewal (MRDM). In 1946, the MRDM elected two overseas deputies to the French National Assembly, on the basis of its call for immediate independence. France responded by instructing its administrators to "fight the MRDM by every means." Arrests led to resistance. In March 1947, a general insurrection began. Peasant rebels, using whatever weapons they could find, liberated large areas from French control. French troops countered by destroying crops and blockading rebel areas, in an effort to starve the insurrectionists into surrendering. Thousands of Malagasy were massacred. By the end of the year, the rebellion had been largely crushed, although a state of siege was maintained until 1956. No one knows precisely how many Malagasy lost their lives in the uprising, but contemporary estimates indicate about 90,000.

INDEPENDENCE AND REVOLUTION

Madagascar gained its independence in 1960. However, many viewed the new government, led by Philibert Tsiranana of the Social Democratic Party (PSD), as a vehicle for continuing French influence; memories of 1947 were still strong. Lack of economic and social reform led to a peasant uprising in 1971. This Maoist-inspired rebellion was suppressed, but the government was left weakened. In 1972, new unrest, this time spearheaded by students and workers in the towns, led to Tsiranana's overthrow by the military. After a period of confusion, radical forces consolidated power around Lieutenant Commander Didier Ratsiraka, who assumed the presidency in 1975.

Under Ratsiraka, a new Constitution was adopted that allowed for a controlled

process of multiparty competition, in which all parties were grouped within the National Front. Within this framework, the largest party was Ratsiraka's Vanguard of the Malagasy Revolution (AREMA). Initially, all parties were expected to support the president's Charter of the Malagasy Revolution, which called for a Marxist-oriented socialist transformation. In accordance with the Charter, foreign-owned banks and financial institutions were nationalized. A series of state enterprises were also established to promote industrial development, but few proved viable.

Although 80 percent of the Malagasy were employed in agriculture, investment in rural areas and concerns was modest. The government attempted to work through *fokonolas* (indigenous village-management bodies). State farms and collectives were also established on land expropriated from French settlers. While these efforts led to some improvements, such as increased mechanization, state marketing monopolies and planning constraints contributed to shortfalls. Efforts to keep consumer prices low were blamed for a drop in rice production, the Malagasy staple, while cash-crop production, primarily coffee, vanilla, and cloves, suffered from falling world prices.

Since 1980, Madagascar has experienced grave economic difficulties, which have given rise to political instability. Food shortages in towns have led to rioting, while frustrated peasants have abandoned their fields. Ratsiraka's government turned increasingly from socialism to a greater reliance on market economics. But the economy has remained impoverished.

In 1985, having abandoned attempts to make the National Front into a vehicle for a single-party state, Ratsiraka presided over a loosening of his once-authoritarian control. In February 1990, most remaining

restrictions on multiparty politics were lifted. But the regime's opponents, including a revived PSD, became militant in their demands for a new constitution. After six months of crippling strikes and protests, Ratsiraka formally ceded many of his powers to a transitional government, headed by Albert Zafy, in November 1991. In February 1993, Zafy won the presidency by a large margin. But subsequent divisions with Parliament over his rejection of an International Monetary Fund austerity plan, accompanied by allegations of financial irregularities, led to his impeachment in August 1996. In elections held at the end of the year, Ratsiraka made a comeback, narrowly defeating Zafy. More than half of the population, however, stayed away from the polls.

DEVELOPMENT

In 1989, "Export Processing Zones" were established to attract foreign investment through tax and currency incentives. The government especially hopes to attract business from neighboring Mauritius, whose success with such zones has led to labor shortages and a shift toward more value-added production.

FREEDOM

Respect for human rights has improved since 1993, and there has been little political violence since the 1996 election. There are isolated reports of police brutality against criminal suspects and detainees, as well as instances of arbitrary arrest and detention. Prison conditions are often life threatening, with women experiencing abuse, including rape. New judges are being appointed in an effort to relieve the overburdened judiciary.

HEALTH/WELFARE

Primary-school enrollment is now universal. Thirty-six percent of the appropriate age group attend secondary school, while 5% of those ages 20 to 24 are in tertiary institutions. Malaria remains a major health challenge. Madagascar's health and education facilities are underfunded.

ACHIEVEMENTS

A recently established wildlife preserve will allow the unique animals of Madagascar to survive and develop. Sixty-six species of land animals are found nowhere else on earth, including the aye-aye, a nocturnal lemur that has bat ears, beaver teeth, and an elongated clawed finger, all of which serve the aye-aye in finding food.

Mauritius (Republic of Mauritius)

GEOGRAPHY

Area in Square Miles (Kilometers):
720 (1,865) (about 11 times
the size of Washington, D.C.)
Capital (Population): Port Louis
(146,000)
Environmental Concerns: water
pollution; population pressures
on land and water resources
Geographical Features: small
coastal plain rising to discon-
tinuous mountains encircling
a central plateau
Climate: tropical

PEOPLE

Population
Total: 1,179,500
Annual Growth Rate: 0.89%
Rural/Urban Population Ratio:
59/41
Major Languages: English;
Creole; French; Hindi; Urdu;
Hakka; Bojpoori
Ethnic Makeup: 68% Indo-
Mauritian; 27% Creole; 3%
Sino-Mauritian; 2%
Franco-Mauritian
Religions: 52% Hindu; 28%
Christian; 17% Muslim; 3%
others

Health
Life Expectancy at Birth: 67
years (male); 75 years (female)
Infant Mortality Rate (Ratio):
17.7/1,000
Physicians Available (Ratio):
1/1,182

Education
Adult Literacy Rate: 83%
Compulsory (Ages): 5–12

COMMUNICATION
Telephones: 244,000 main lines
Daily Newspaper Circulation:
49 per 1,000 people
Televisions: 150 per 1,000 people
Internet Service Provider: 1 (1999)

TRANSPORTATION
Highways in Miles (Kilometers): 1,126
(1,877)
Railroads in Miles (Kilometers): none
Usable Airfields: 5
Motor Vehicles in Use: 82,500

GOVERNMENT
Type: parliamentary democracy
Independence Date: March 12, 1968
(from the United Kingdom)
Head of State/Government: President
Cassam Uteem; Prime Minister
Aneerood Jugnauth

Political Parties: Mauritian Labor Party;
Mauritian Militant Movement; Militant
Socialist Movement; Mauritian Militant
Renaissance; Mauritian Social Demo-
cratic Party; Organization of the People
of Rodrigues; Hizbullah
Suffrage: universal at 18

MILITARY
Military Expenditures (% of GDP): 0.3%
Current Disputes: territorial disputes with
France and the United Kingdom

ECONOMY
Currency ($ U.S. Equivalent): 17.75 rupees = $1
Per Capita Income/GDP: $10,400/$12.3
billion
GDP Growth Rate: 4%

Inflation Rate: 6.8%
Unemployment Rate: 2%
Labor Force: 514,000
Natural Resources: arable land; fish
Agriculture: sugarcane; tea; corn; potatoes;
bananas; pulses; cattle; goats; fish
Industry: food processing; textiles;
apparel; chemicals; metal products;
transport equipment; nonelectrical
machinery; tourism
Exports: $1.7 billion (primary partners
United Kingdom, France, United States)
Imports: $2.1 billion (primary partners
France, South Africa, India)

  http://www.sas.upenn.edu/
African_Studies/Country_Specific/
Mauritius.html

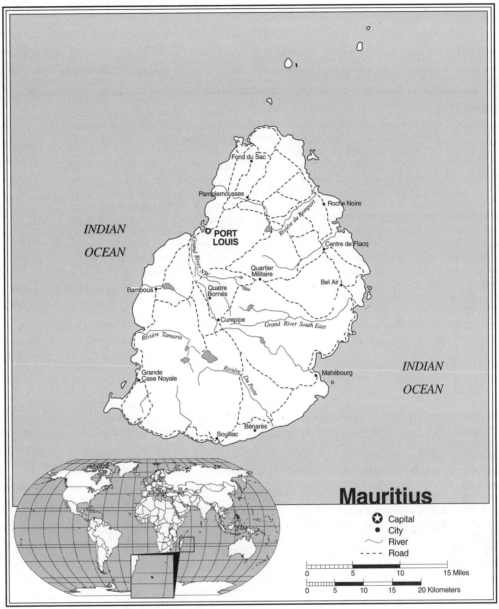

The Dutch claim, but abandon, Mauritius
1600s

French settlers arrive, and slaves imported from the African mainland
1722

The Treaty of Paris formally cedes Mauritius to the British
1814

Slavery is abolished; South Asians arrive
1835

Rioting on sugar estates shakes the political control of the Franco-Mauritian elite
1937

An expanded franchise allows greater democracy
1948

Independence
1968

A cyclone destroys homes as well as much of the sugar crop
1979

Aneerood Jugnauth replaces Seewoosagar Ramgoolam as prime minister
1982

Mauritius becomes a republic; Mauritius becomes the 12th member of the SADC
1990s

2000s

Jugnauth regains the prime ministership in a landslide electoral victory

Mauritius continues its focus on market economics

MAURITIUS

Although it was not permanently settled until 1722, today Mauritius is home to more than 1.1 million people of South Asian, Euro-African, Chinese, and other origins. Out of this extraordinary human diversity has emerged a society that in recent decades has become a model of democratic stability and economic growth as well as ethnic, racial, and sectarian tolerance.

Mauritius was first settled by the French, some of whom achieved great wealth by setting up sugar plantations. From the beginning, the plantations prospered through their exploitation of slave labor imported from the African mainland. Over time, the European and African communities merged into a common Creole culture; that membership currently accounts for one quarter of the Mauritian population. A small number claim pure French descent. For decades, members of this latter group have formed an economic and social elite. More than half the sugar acreage remains the property of 21 large Franco–Mauritian plantations; the rest is divided among nearly 28,000 small landholdings. French cultural influence remains strong. Most of the newspapers on the island are published in French, which shares official-language status with English. Most Mauritians also speak a local, French-influenced, Creole language. Most Mauritian Creoles are Roman Catholics.

In 1810, Mauritius was occupied by the British; they ruled the island until 1968. (After years of debate, in 1992, the country cut its ties with Great Britain to become a republic.) When the British abolished slavery, in 1835, the plantation owners turned to large-scale use of indentured labor from what was then British India. Today nearly two thirds of the population are of South Asian descent and

have maintained their home languages. Most are Hindu, but a substantial minority are Muslim. Other faiths, such as Buddhism, are also represented.

Although the majority of Mauritians gained the right to vote after World War II, the island has maintained an uninterrupted record of parliamentary rule since 1886. Ethnic divisions have long been important in shaping political allegiances. But ethnic constituency-building has not led, in recent years, to communal polarization. Other factors—such as class, ideology, and opportunism—have also been influential. All postindependence governments have been multiethnic coalitions.

While government in Mauritius has been characterized by shifting coalitions, with no single party winning a majority of seats, there has been relative stability in leadership at the top. Over the past half-century, Mauritius has had only three prime ministers. In September 2000, a coalition led by former prime minister Sir Aneerood Jugnauth won a landslide victory, ousting the rival coalition of Navin Ramgoolam, who had ousted Jugnauth five years earlier. Jugnauth had first come to power in 1982 by defeating Seewoosagar Ramgoolam, Navin's father.

Although most major political parties have in the past espoused various shades of socialism, Mauritius's economic success in recent decades has created a strong consensus in favor of export-oriented market economics. Until the 1970s, the Mauritian economy was almost entirely dependent on sugar. While 45 percent of the island's total landmass continues to be planted with the crop, sugar now ranks below textiles and tourism in its contribution to export earnings and gross domestic product. The transformation of Mauritius from monocrop dependency into a fledging industrial state with a strong service

sector has made it one of the major economic success stories of the developing world. Mauritian growth has been built on a foundation of export-oriented manufacturing. At the core of the Mauritian take-off is its island-wide Export Processing Zone (EPZ), which has attracted industrial investment through a combination of low wages, tax breaks, and other financial incentives. Although most of the EPZ output has been in the field of cheap textiles, the economy has begun to diversify into more capital- and skill-intensive production. In 1989, Mauritius also entered the international financial services market by launching Africa's first offshore banking center.

The success of the Mauritian economy is measured in relative terms. Mauritius is still considered a middle-income country. In reality, however, there are, as with most developing societies, great disparities in the distribution of wealth. Nonetheless, quality-of-life indicators confirm a rising standard of living for the population as a whole. While great progress has been made toward eliminating poverty and disease, concern has also grown about the environmental capacity of the small, crowded country to sustain its current rate of development. There is also a general recognition that Mauritian prosperity is—and will for the foreseeable future remain—extremely vulnerable to global-market forces.

DEVELOPMENT

The success of the Mauritian EPZ along with the export-led growth of various Asian economies has encouraged a growing number of other African countries, such as Botswana, Cape Verde, and Madagascar, to launch their own export zones.

FREEDOM

Political pluralism and human rights are respected on Mauritius, but problem areas remain. There are reports of police abuse of suspects and delayed acess to defense counsel. Child labor exists. Legislation outlawing domestic violence has been passed recently. The nation has more than 30 political parties, of which about a half dozen are important at any given time. The Mauritian labor movement is one of the strongest in all of Africa.

HEALTH/WELFARE

Medical and most educational expenses are free. Food prices are heavily subsidized. Rising government deficits, however, threaten future social spending. Mauritius has a high life expectancy rate and a low infant mortality rate. Human-rights education has been introduced in secondary schools.

ACHIEVEMENTS

Perhaps Mauritius's most important modern achievement has been its successful efforts to reduce its birth rate. This has been brought about by government-backed family planning as well as by increased economic opportunities for women.

Rwanda (Rwandese Republic)*

GEOGRAPHY
Area in Square Miles (Kilometers):
10,169 (26,338) (about the size of Maryland)
Capital (Population): Kigali (235,000)
Environmental Concerns: deforestation; overgrazing; soil exhaustion and erosion; poaching
Geographical Features: mostly grassy uplands and hills; landlocked
Climate: temperate

PEOPLE

Population
Total: 7,229,000
Annual Growth Rate: 1.14%
Rural/Urban Population Ratio: 94/6
Major Languages: Kinyarwanda; French; Kiswahili; English
Ethnic Makeup: 84% Hutu; 15% Tutsi; 1% Twa
Religions: 65% Roman Catholic; 25% indigenous beliefs; 9% Protestant; 1% Muslim

Health
Life Expectancy at Birth: 39 years (male); 40 years (female)
Infant Mortality Rate (Ratio): 120/1,000
Physicians Available (Ratio): 1/50,000

Education
Adult Literacy Rate: 60.5%
Compulsory (Ages): 7–14

COMMUNICATION
Telephones: 15,000 main lines
Internet Service Provider: 1 (1999)

TRANSPORTATION
Highways in Miles (Kilometers): 7,200 (12,000)
Railroads in Miles (Kilometers): none
Usable Airfields: 8
Motor Vehicles in Use: 28,000

GOVERNMENT
Type: republic
Independence Date: July 1, 1962 (from Belgian-administered UN trusteeship)
Head of State/Government: President Paul Kagame; Prime Minister Bernard Mazuka
Political Parties: Rwandan Patriotic Front; National Republican Movement for Democracy and Development; Democratic Republican Movement; Liberal Party; Democratic and Socialist Party; others
Suffrage: universal at 18

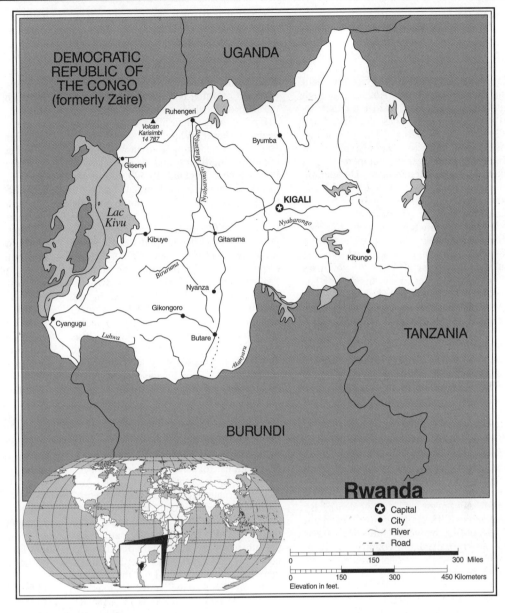

MILITARY
Military Expenditures (% of GDP): 3.8%
Current Disputes: continued internal ethnic violence; conflicts in the Democratic Republic of the Congo

ECONOMY
Currency ($ U.S. Equivalent): 145 Rwanda francs = $1
Per Capita Income/GDP: $720/$5.9 billion
GNP Growth Rate: 5.3%
Inflation Rate: 10%
Labor Force: 3,600,000
Natural Resources: tungsten ore; tin; cassiterite; methane; hydropower; arable land
Agriculture: coffee; tea; pyrethrum; bananas; sorghum; beans; potatoes; livestock

Industry: agricultural-products processing; mining; light consumer goods
Exports: $70.8 million (primary partners Brazil, Germany, Belgium)
Imports: $242 million (primary partners Kenya, Tanzania, United States)

*Note: Many of these statistics reflect conditions in Rwanda before the war that has destroyed much of the country and decimated its population. Population statistics explicitly take into account the effects of excess mortality due to AIDS.

http://www.sas.upenn.edu/
   African_Studies/Country_Specific/
   Rwanda. html

RWANDA

In April 2000, Paul Kagame was inaugurated as Rwanda's president, following the resignation of the incumbent, Pasteur Bizimungu. The change at the top had little immediate effect. As vice-president and minster of defense, Kagame, through his largely Tutsi-controlled Rwandan Patriotic Front (RPF), has dominated the "Government of National Unity" since its installation in 1994. The resignation of Bizimungu and other members of the mainly Hutu Republican Democratic Movement (RDM) has raised eyebrows, however, though the RDM itself has remained within the government.

Rwanda's Government of National Unity seized power to put an end to an anti-Tutsi campaign of genocide carried out by militant members of the country's Hutu majority. Since then, the regime has continued to battle armed, largely Hutu, opponents in the neighboring Democratic Republic of the Congo (Congo-Kinshasa; formerly Zaire) as well as in Rwanda itself. In the process, much of eastern Congo-Kinshasa has come under Rwandan occupation.

The 1994 genocide in Rwanda is one of the world's greatest tragedies. A small country, only about the size of Maryland, Rwanda had 8 million inhabitants early in 1994, making it continental Africa's most densely populated state. This population was divided into three groups: the Hutu majority (89 percent); the Tutsis (10 percent); and the Twas, commonly stereotyped as "pygmies" (1 percent). By September 1994, civil war involving genocidal conflict between Hutus and Tutsis had nearly halved the country's resident population while radically altering its group demography.

THE 1994 GENOCIDE

The genocide began within a half-hour of the April 6, 1994, death of the country's democratizing dictator, President Juvenal Habyarimana. Along with president Cyprien Ntaryamira of neighboring Burundi, Habyarimana was killed when his plane was shot down. While the identity of the culprits remains a matter of speculation, Belgian troops reported that rockets were fired from Kanombe military base, which was then controlled by the country's Presidential Guard, known locally as the Akuza. In broadcasts over the independent Radio Libre Mille Collins, Hutu extremists then openly called for the destruction of the Tutsis—"The graves are only half full, who will help us fill them up?" Because the tirades were in idiomatic Kinyarwanda, the national language, they initially escaped the attention of most international journalists on the spot. Meanwhile, Akuza and regular army units set up roadblocks and began systematically to massacre Tutsi citizens in the capital, Kigali. Even greater numbers perished in the countryside, because their names appeared on death lists that had been prepared with the help of local Hutu chiefs.

By July, more than 500,000 people had been murdered. While most were Tutsi, Hutus who had supported moves toward ethnic reconciliation and democratization had also been targeted. In addition to elements within the Hutu-dominated military, the killings were carried out by youth-wing militias of the ruling party, the National Revolutionary Movement for Development (MRND) and the Coalition for Defense of Freedom (CDR). Known respectively as the Interahamwe and Impuzamugambi, the ranks of these two all-Hutu militias had mushroomed in the aftermath of an August 1993 agreement designed to return the country to multiparty rule. The extent of the killings was apparent in neighboring Tanzania, where thousands of corpses were televised being carried downstream by the Kagara River. At a rate of 80 an hour, they entered Lake Victoria, more than 100 miles from the Rwandan border.

SYSTEMATIC PLANS FOR MASS MURDER

Preparations for the genocide had been going on for months. According to Amnesty International, Hutu "Zero Network" death squads had already murdered some 2,300 people in the months leading up to the crisis. Although this information was the subject of press reports, no action was taken by the 2,500 peacekeeping troops who had been stationed in the country since June 1993 as the United Nations Assistance Mission to Rwanda (UNAMIR). Once the crisis began, most of UNAMIR's personnel were hastily withdrawn. French and Belgian paratroopers arrived for a brief time to evacuate their nationals.

Rwanda's genocide did not end with the destruction of a third or more of the Tutsi minority. Enraged by the massacres of their brethren, the 14,000-man Tutsi-dominated Rwanda Patriotic Front (RPF), which had been waging an armed struggle against the Habyarimana regime since October, launched a massive offensive. The 35,000-man regular army, along with the militias, crumbled. In July 1994, the RPF took full control of Kigali and drove the remnants of the government and its army eastward into Zaire. Two million panic-stricken Hutu civilians also fled across the border. By then, about 1 million Rwandans were already in exile. Another 2.5 million people were crowded into a "safe zone" created by the French military. As the French prepared to pull out, the fate of these refugees was uncertain.

In depopulated Kigali, the RPF set up a "Provisional Government" with a Hutu president, Pasteur Bizimungu, and prime minister Faustin Twagiramungu. Its most powerful figure, however, was the RPF commander, Major General Paul Kagame, who became vice president and minister of defense.

HUTUS AND TUTSIS

The roots of Hutu–Tutsi animosity in Rwanda (as well as Burundi) run deep. Yet it is not easy for an outsider to differentiate between the two groups. Their members both speak Kinyarwanda and look the same physically, notwithstanding the stereotype of the Tutsis being exceptionally tall; intermarriage between the two groups has taken place for centuries. By some accounts, the Tutsi arrived as northern Nilotic conquerors, perhaps in the fifteenth century. But others believe that the two groups have always been defined by class or caste rather than by ethnicity.

In the beginning, according to one epic Kinyarwanda poem, the godlike ruler Kigwa fashioned a test to choose his successor. He gave each of his sons a bowl of milk to guard during the night. His son Gatwa drank the milk. Yahutu slept and spilled the milk. Only Gatutsi guarded it well. The myth justifies the old Rwandan social order, in which the Twas were the outcasts, the Hutus servants, and the Tutsis aristocrats. Historically, Hutu serfs herded cattle and performed various other services for their Tutsi "protectors." At the top of the hierarchy was the Mwami, or king.

THE COLONIAL ERA: HUTU AND TUTSI ANIMOSITIES CONTINUE

Rwanda's feudal system survived into the colonial era. German and, later, Belgian administrators opted to rule through the existing order. But the social order was subtly destabilized by the new ideas emanating from the Catholic mission schools and by the colonialists' encouragement of the predominantly Hutu peasantry to grow cash crops, especially coffee. Discontent grew also due to the ever-increasing pressure of people and herds on already crowded lands.

In the late 1950s, under UN pressure, Belgium began to devolve political power to Rwandans. The death of the Mwami in 1959 sparked a bloody Hutu uprising against the Tutsi aristocracy. Tens of thousands, if not hundreds of thousands, were killed. Against this violent backdrop, pre-independence elections were held in 1961.

Mwami Kigeri Rwabugiri expands and consolidates the kingdom A.D. 1860–1895	Belgium rules Rwanda as a mandate of the League of Nations 1916	The Hutu rebellion 1959	Rwanda becomes independent; Gregoire Kayibana is president 1962	Juvenal Habyarimana seizes power 1973	The National Revolutionary Movement for Development is formed 1975	A new Constitution is approved in a nationwide referendum; Habyarimana is reelected president 1978	Genocidal conflict results in a dramatic drop in the country's resident population; millions are killed or displaced; French relief workers withdraw from Rwanda; Tutsi massacre of Hutu at Kibeho refugee camp 1990s	2000s

Paul Kagame becomes president upon the resignation of Pasteur Bizimungu

Rwandans occupy much of eastern Democratic Republic of the Congo

These resulted in a victory for the first president, Gregoire Kayibanda's, Hutu Emancipation Movement, better known as Parmehutu. Thus, at independence, in 1962, Rwanda's traditionally Tutsi-dominated society was suddenly under a Hutu-dominated government.

In 1963 and 1964, the continued interethnic competition for power exploded into more violence, which resulted in the flight of hundreds of thousands of ethnic Tutsi to neighboring Burundi, Tanzania, and Uganda. Along with their descendants, this refugee population today numbers about 1 million. Successive Hutu-dominated governments have barred their return, questioning their citizenship and citing extreme land pressure as barriers to their reabsorption. But the implied hope that the refugees would integrate into their host societies has failed to materialize. The RPF was originally formed in Uganda by Tutsi exiles, many of whom were hardened veterans of that country's past conflicts. The repatriation of all Rwandan Tutsis has been a key RPF demand.

HABYARIMANA TAKES POWER
Major General Juvenal Habyarimana, a Hutu from the north, seized power in a military coup in 1973. Two years later, he institutionalized his still army-dominated regime as a one-party state under the MRND, in the name of overcoming ethnic divisions. Yet hostility between the Hutus and Tutsis remained. Inside the country, a system of ethnic quotas was introduced, which formally limited the remaining Tutsi minority to a maximum of 14 percent of the positions in schools and at the workplace. In reality, the Tutsis were often allocated less, while the MRND's critics maintained that the best opportunities

were reserved for Hutus from Habyarimana's northern home area of Kisenyi.

POPULAR DISCONTENT
In the 1980s, many Hutus, as well as Tutsis, grew impatient with their government's corrupt authoritarianism. The post-1987 international collapse of coffee prices, Rwanda's major export-earner, led to an economic decline, further fueling popular discontent. Even before the armed challenge of the RPF, the MRND had agreed to give up its monopoly of power, though this pledge was compromised by continued repression. Prominent among the new parties that then emerged were the Democratic Republic Movement (MDR), the Social Democrats (PSD), and the Liberals (PL). The PL and PSD were able to attract both Hutu and Tutsi support. As a result, many of their Hutu as well as Tutsi members were killed in 1994. The MDR was associated with southern-regional Hutu resentment at the MRND's supposed northern bias.

A political breakthrough occurred in March 1992 with the formation of a "Transitional Coalition Government," headed by the MDR's Dismas Nsengiyaremye, which also included MRND, PSD, and PL ministers. Habyarimana remained as president. With French military assistance, including the participation of several hundred French "advisers," Habyarimana's interim government of national unity was able to halt the RPF's advance in 1992. A series of cease-fires was negotiated with the RPF, leading up to the promise of (now aborted) UN-supervised elections in 1994. But from the beginning, progress toward national reconciliation was compromised by hard-line Hutus within the ruling military/MRND establishment and the ex-

tremist CDR. Ironically, these elements, who conspired to carry out the anti-Tutsi genocide in order to maintain control, were pushed out of the country by the RPF. These Hutu officials, soldiers, and militarymen, thought to be responsible for massacring hundreds of thousands of Tutsis and moderate Hutus during the 1994 Civil War, were exiled to camps in Zaire and Tanzania. Soon these militants returned and began a two-month wave of killings in western Rwanda in an apparent attempt to stop the Tutsis from testifying at genocide trials being conducted by the Rwandan government and the United Nations.

As Rwanda civil unrest intensified, refugees continued to flow into strife-torn Zaire. Estimates are that between 100,000 and 350,000 Hutu citizens are still in camps there. In March 1997, some 70,000 Rwandan Hutu refugees were gathered in Ubunda, a town 80 miles south of Kisangani on the Zaire River. But civil war in the Democratic Republic of the Congo has caused these people to be pushed back into Rwanda, where they are faced with the persistent and serious unrest in their home country.

DEVELOPMENT

Hydroelectric stations meet much of the country's energy needs. Before the 1994 genocide, plans were being made to exploit methane-gas reserves under Lake Kivu.

FREEDOM

The Rwandan government and its opponents continue to be responsible for serious human-rights abuses, including massacres. More than 120,000 prisoners are in overcrowded jails, most accused of participating in the 1994 genocide. Genocide trials, which began at the end of 1996, have made little progress and are expected to take years to complete. Hutu death squads, composed of members of the defeated former Rwandan Armed Forces and Interahamwe genocide gangs, continue to target Tutsis and foreigners.

HEALTH/WELFARE

The health system has collapsed. International relief agencies in Rwanda and neighboring countries are attempting to feed and care for the population. Diseases, like cholera have spread rapidly, to deadly effect.

ACHIEVEMENTS

Abbé Alexis Kagame, a Rwandan Roman Catholic churchman and scholar, has written studies of traditional Rwandan poetry and has written poetry about many of the traditions and rituals. Some of his works have been composed in Kinyarwanda, an official language of Rwanda, and translated into French. He has gained an international reputation among scholars.

Seychelles (Republic of Seychelles)

GEOGRAPHY
Area in Square Miles (Kilometers):
185 (455) (2.5 times the size
of Washington, D.C.)
Capital (Population): Victoria
(25,000)
Environmental Concerns:
uncertain freshwater supply
Geographical Features: Mahé
Group is granitic, narrow
coastal strip; rocky, hilly;
other islands are coral, flat,
elevated reefs
Climate: tropical marine

PEOPLE

Population
Total: 79,400
Annual Growth Rate: 0.5%
Rural/Urban Population Ratio:
45/55
Major Languages: English;
French; Creole
Ethnic Makeup: Seychellois
(mixture of Asians, Africans,
and Europeans)
Religions: 98% Christian; 2%
others

Health
Life Expectancy at Birth: 65
years (male); 76 years (female)
Infant Mortality Rate (Ratio):
17.7/1,000
Physicians Available (Ratio):
1/906

Education
Adult Literacy Rate: 58%
Compulsory (Ages): 6–15; free

COMMUNICATION
Telephones: 19,000 main lines
Daily Newspaper Circulation:
41 per 1,000 people
Televisions: 173 per 1,000 people
Internet Service Provider: 1
(1999)

TRANSPORTATION
Highways in Miles (Kilometers): 162 (270)
Railroads in Miles (Kilometers): none
Usable Airfields: 14
Motor Vehicles in Use: 8,600

GOVERNMENT
Type: republic
Independence Date: June 29, 1976 (from
the United Kingdom)
Head of State/Government: President
France Albert René is both head of
state and head of government
Political Parties: Seychelles People's Pro-
gressive Front; New Democratic Party;

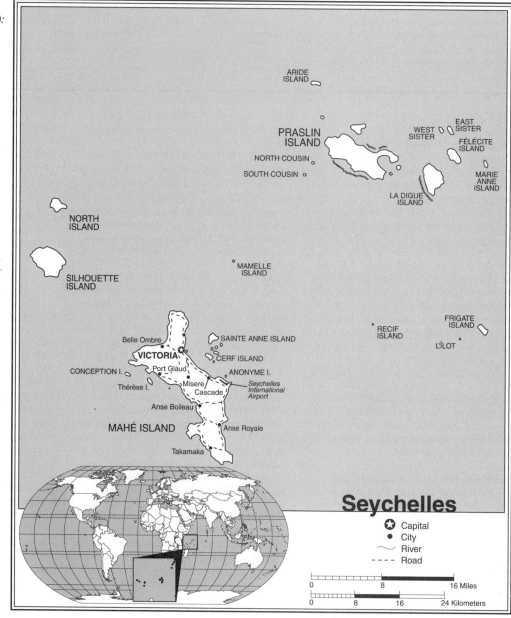

Democratic Party; United Opposition
(coalition)
Suffrage: universal at 17

MILITARY
Military Expenditures (% of GDP): 2.8%
Current Disputes: claims Chagos Archipelago

ECONOMY
Currency ($ U.S. Equivalent): 4.94
rupees = $1
Per Capita Income/GDP: $7,500/$590 million
GDP Growth Rate: 1.8%
Inflation Rate: 3%
Labor Force: 26,000
Natural Resources: fish; copra;
cinnamon trees

Agriculture: vanilla; coconuts; sweet
potatoes; cinnamon; cassava; bananas;
chickens; fish
Industry: tourism; fishing; copra and
vanilla processing; coconut oil; boat
building; printing; furniture; beverages
Exports: $91 million (primary partners
France, United Kingdom, Netherlands)
Imports: $403 million (primary partners
South Africa, United Kingdom,
Singapore)

http://www.sas.upenn.edu/
African_Studies/Country_Specific/
Seychelles.html
http://www.tbc.gov.bc.ca/cwgames/
country/Seychelles/seychelles.html

| French settlement begins 1771 | British rule is established 1814 | The British end slavery 1830 | Seychelles is detached from Mauritius by the British and made a Crown colony 1903 | Legislative Council with qualified suffrage is introduced 1948 | Universal suffrage 1967 | Independence 1976 | An Albert René coup against James Mancham 1977 | An Amnesty International report alleges government fabrication of drug-possession cases for political reasons 1980s | René agrees to a multiparty system; René and his party are approved in presidential and parliamentary elections 1990s | 2000s |

The tourism sector accounts for 30% of Seychellois employment and 70% of hard-currency earnings

The government seeks to diversify the economy

SEYCHELLES

Africa's smallest country in terms of both size and population, the Republic of the Seychelles consists of a number of widely scattered archipelagos off the coast of East Africa. Over the last quarter-century, Seychellois have enjoyed enormous economic and social progress. But for an equally long time, the country's politics was bitterly polarized between supporters of President James Mancham and his successor, Albert René. The holding of multiparty elections in 1992 and 1993, after 15 years of single-party rule under René, was accompanied by a significant degree of reconciliation between the partisans of these two long-time rivals.

The roots of Seychelles' modern political economy go back to 1963, when Mancham's Democratic Party and René's People's United Party were established. The former originally favored private enterprise and the retention of the British imperial connection, while the latter advocated an independent socialist state. Electoral victories in 1970 and 1974 allowed Mancham to pursue his dream of turning Seychelles into a tourist paradise and a financial and trading center by aggressively seeking outside investment. Tourism began to flourish following the opening of an international airport on the main island of Mahe in 1971, fueling an economic boom. Between 1970 and 1980, per capita income rose from nearly $150 to $1,700 (today it is about $7,500).

In 1974, Mancham, in an about-face, joined René in advocating the islands' independence. The Democratic Party, despite its modest electoral and overwhelming parliamentary majority, set up a coalition government with the People's United Party. On June 29, 1976, Seychelles became independent, with Mancham as president and René as prime minister.

On June 5, 1977, with Mancham out of the country, René's supporters, with Tanzanian assistance, staged a successful coup in which several people were killed. Thereafter René assumed the presidency and suspended the Constitution. A period of rule by decree gave way in 1979, without the benefit of referendum, to a new constitutional framework in which the People's Progressive Front, successor to the People's United Party, was recognized as the nation's sole political voice. The first years of one-party government were characterized by continued economic growth, which allowed for an impressive expansion of social-welfare programs.

Political power since the coup has largely remained concentrated in the hands of René. The early years of his regime, however, were marked by unrest. In 1978, the first in a series of unsuccessful countercoups was followed, several months later, by violent protests against the government's attempts to impose a compulsory National Youth Service, which would have removed the nation's 16- and 17-year-olds from their families in order to foster their sociopolitical indoctrination in accordance with the René government's socialist ideals. Another major incident occurred in 1981, when a group of international mercenaries, who had the backing of authorities in Kenya and South Africa as well as exiled Seychellois, were forced to flee in a hijacked jet after an airport shootout with local security forces. Following this attempt, Tanzanian troops were sent to the islands. A year later, the Tanzanians were instrumental in crushing a mutiny of Seychellois soldiers.

Despite its success in creating a model welfare state, which undoubtedly strengthened its popular acceptance, for years René continued to govern in a repressive manner. Internal opposition was not tolerated by his government, and exiled activists were largely neutralized. About one fifth of the islands' population now live overseas (not all of these people left the country, however, for political reasons).

In 1991, René gave in to rising internal and external pressures for a return to multiparty democracy. In July 1992, his party won 58 percent of the vote for a commission to rewrite the Constitution. Mancham's Democrats received just over a third of the vote. But in November 1992, voters heeded Mancham's call, rejecting the revised constitution proposed by the pro-René commission. Faced with a possible deadlock, the two parties reached consensus on new proposals, which were ratified in a June 1993 referendum. Presidential and parliamentary elections held the following month confirmed majority support for René's party. In subsequent elections, in March 1998, René and the SPPF gained a renewed mandate. The latter contest was perhaps more significant for the emergence of the United Oppostion coalition, led by Wavel Ramkalawan, with the aging Mancham's Democrats slipping to a distant third place.

DEVELOPMENT

Seychelles has declared an Exclusive Economic Zone of 200 miles around all of its islands in order to promote the local fishing industry. Most of the zone's catch is harvested by foreign boats, which are supposed to pay licensing fees to the Seychelles.

FREEDOM

Since the restoration of multiparty democracy, there has been greater political freedom in Seychelles. The opposition nonetheless continues to complain of police harassment and to protest about the government's control over the broadcast media.

HEALTH/WELFARE

A national health program has been established; private practice has been abolished. Free-lunch programs have raised nutritional levels among the young. Education is also free up to age 15.

ACHIEVEMENTS

Seychelles has become a world leader in wildlife preservation. An important aspect of the nation's conservation efforts has been the designation of one island as an international wildlife refuge.

69

Somalia

GEOGRAPHY

Area in Square Miles (Kilometers):
246,331 (638,000) (about the
size of Texas)

Capital (Population): Mogadishu
(997,000)

Environmental Concerns:
famine; contaminated water;
deforestation; overgrazing; soil
erosion; desertification

Geographical Features: mostly
flat to undulating plain, rising
to hills in the north

Climate: arid to semiarid

PEOPLE

Population

Total: 7,253,200*

Annual Growth Rate: 3.03%

Rural/Urban Population Ratio:
74/26

Major Languages: Somali;
Arabic; Italian; English

Ethnic Makeup: 85% Somali;
Bantu; Arab

Religion: Sunni Muslim

Health

Life Expectancy at Birth: 45
years (male); 48 years (female)

Infant Mortality Rate (Ratio):
125.8/1,000

Physicians Available (Ratio):
1/19,071

Education

Adult Literacy Rate: 24%

Compulsory (Ages): 6–14; free

COMMUNICATION

Telephones: 15,000 main lines

Televisions: 18 per 1,000 people

Internet Service Providers: na

TRANSPORTATION

Highways in Miles (Kilometers):
13,702 (22,100)

Railroads in Miles (Kilometers):
none

Usable Airfields: 61

Motor Vehicles in Use: 20,000

GOVERNMENT

Type: no functioning government

Independence Date: July 1, 1960 (from a
merger of British Somaliland and
Italian Somaliland)

Head of State/Government: Interim
President Abdiqassim Salad Hassan

Political Parties: none

Suffrage: universal at 18

MILITARY

Current Disputes: ongoing civil war;
border and territorial disputes with
Ethiopia

ECONOMY

Currency ($ U.S. Equivalent): 5,000
Somali shillings = $1

Per Capita Income/GDP: $600/$4.3 billion

Labor Force: 3,700,000

Natural Resources: uranium; iron ore; tin;
gypsum; bauxite; copper; salt

Agriculture: livestock; bananas; sugarcane;
cotton; cereals; corn; sorghum;
mangoes; fish

Industry: sugar refining; textiles; limited
petroleum refining

Exports: $187 million (primary partners
Saudia Arabia, United Arab Emirates, Italy)

Imports: $327 million (primary partners
Djibouti, Kenya, Belarus)

http://www.state.gov/www/
background_notes/
somalia_0798_bgn.html

http://www.cs.indiana.edu/hyplan/
dmulholl/somalia/somalia.html

http://www.sas.upenn.edu/
African_Studies/Country_Specific
Somalia.html

*Note: Population counting in Somalia is compli-
cated by the large number of nomads and by refugee movements in response to famine and clan
warfare.

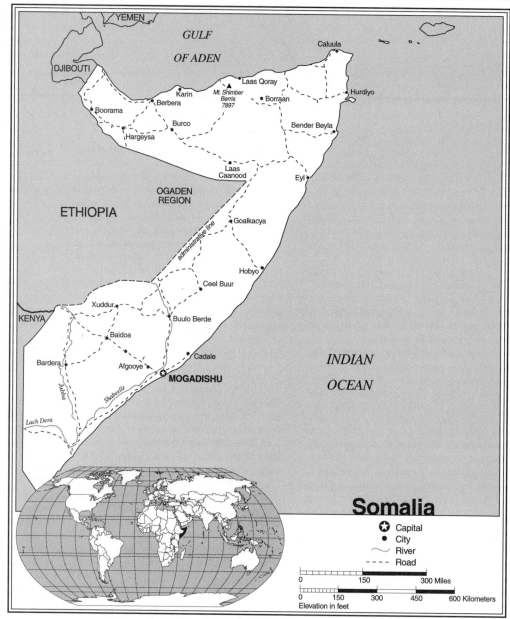

SOMALIA

In July–August 2000, progress was reported at a peace conference among various competing Somali factions, convened by Djibouti's President Guellah. But many key groupings boycotted the talks. The prospect for the restoration of a national government seemed elusive.

In August 2000, however, Abdiqassim Salad Hassan entered the war-battered capital city of Mogadishu as the newly designated "interim president" of Somalia. Ignoring threats from militia leaders who refused to recognize his leadership, Hassan was greeted by ecstatic crowds. The overwhelming public welcome gave further encouragement to the hope that after a decade without any effective government, Somalia may at last be on the road to normalcy.

But many challenges remain. Hassan was elected by a "Transitional National Assembly," which had been formed at an internationally backed peace conference in neighboring Djibouti. After months of negotiations, the new government was accepted by a broad cross-section of Somali society. But a number of key groupings, in addition to still-powerful military leaders, remain outside of the accord. The northern "Puntland" and "Somaliland" governments were among those that boycotted the talks. The latter administration has declared itself an independent state, in the face of international opposition. Time will tell whether Hassan's transitional government will succeed where others have failed in restoring peace and unity to Somalia.

For much of the outside world, Somalia has become a symbol of failure of both international peacekeeping operations and the postcolonial African state. For the Somalis themselves, Somalia is an ideal that has ceased to exist—but may yet be re-created. Since the January 1991 overthrow of the dictatorial regime of Mohammed Siad Barre, the country has been without any effective central government or formal economy. The territory is now divided by dozens of armed factions, organized on the basis of local clan loyalties, that are obedient only to the law of the gun and their warlords' own self-interests.

Literally hundreds of thousands of Somalis starved to death in 1991–1992 before a massive U.S.-led United Nations intervention—officially known as UNITAF but labeled "Operation Restore Hope" by the Americans—assured the delivery of relief supplies. The 1994 withdrawal of most UN forces (the last token units left in March 1995), following UNITAF's failure to disarm local militias while supporting the creation of a Transitional National Council, led to the termination of relief efforts in many areas, but widespread famine was averted in 1994–1995. Meanwhile, repeated attempts to reach a settlement between the various armed factions have ended in failure, despite the death in August 1996 of Somalia's most powerful warlord, General Mohammed Farah Aideed.

SOMALI SOCIETY

The roots of Somalia's suffering run deep. Somalis have lived with the threat of famine for centuries, as the country is arid even in good years. Traditionally, most Somalis were nomadic pastoralists, but in recent years, this way of life has declined dramatically. Prior to the 1990s crisis, about half the population were still almost entirely reliant on livestock. Somali herds have sometimes been quite big: In the early 1980s, more than 1 million animals, mostly goats and sheep, were exported annually. Large numbers of cattle and camels have also been kept. But hundreds of thousands of animals were lost due to lack of rain during the mid-1980s; and since 1983, reports of rinderpest led to a sharp drop in exports, due to the closing of the once-lucrative Saudi Arabian market to East African animals.

A quarter of the Somali population have long combined livestock-keeping with agriculture. Cultivation is possible in the area between the Juba and Shebelle Rivers and in portions of the north. Although up to 15 percent of the country is potentially arable, only about 1 percent of the land has been put to plow at any given time. Bananas, cotton, and frankincense have been major cash crops, while maize and sorghum are subsistence crops. Like Somali pastoralists, farmers walk a thin line between abundance and scarcity, for locusts as well as drought are common visitors.

The delicate nature of Somali agriculture helps to explain recent urbanization. One out of every four Somalis lives in the large towns and cities. The principal urban center is Mogadishu, which, despite being divided by war, still houses nearly a million people. Unfortunately, as Somalis have migrated in from the countryside, they have found little employment. Even before the recent collapse, the country's manufacturing and service sectors were small. By 1990, more than 100,000 Somalis had become migrant workers in the Arab Gulf states. (In 1990–1991, many were repatriated as a result of the regional conflict over Kuwait.)

Until recently, many outsiders assumed that Somalia possessed a greater degree of national coherence than most other African states. Somalis do share a common language and a sense of cultural identity. Islam is also a binding feature. However, competing clan and subclan allegiances have long played a divisive political role in the society. Membership in all the current armed factions is congruent with blood loyalties. Traditionally, the clans were governed by experienced, wise men. But the authority of these elders has now largely given way to the power of younger men with a surplus of guns and a surfeit of education and a lack of moral decency.

Past appeals to greater Somali nationalism have also been a source of conflict by encouraging irredentist sentiments against Somalia's neighbors. During the colonial era, contemporary Somalia was divided. For about 75 years, the northern region was governed by the British, while the southern portion was subject to Italian rule. These colonial legacies have complicated efforts at nation-building. Many northerners feel that their region has been neglected and would benefit from greater political autonomy or independence.

Somalia became independent on July 1, 1960, when the new national flag, a white, five-pointed star on a blue field, was raised in the former British and Italian territories. The star symbolized the five supposed branches of the Somali nation—that is, the now-united peoples of British and Italian Somalilands and the Somalis still living in French Somaliland (modern Djibouti), Ethiopia, and Kenya.

THE RISE AND FALL OF SIAD BARRE

Siad Barre came to power in 1969, through a coup promising radical change. As chairman of the military's Supreme Revolutionary Council, Barre combined Somali nationalism and Islam with a commitment to "scientific socialism." Some genuine efforts were made to restructure society through the development of new local councils and worker management committees. New civil and labor codes were written. The Somali Revolutionary Socialist Party was developed as the sole legal political party.

Initially, the new order seemed to be making progress. The Somali language was alphabetized in a modified form of Roman script, which allowed the government to launch mass-literacy campaigns. Various rural-development projects were also implemented. In particular, roads were built, which helped to break down isolation among regions.

The promise of Barre's early years in office gradually faded. Little was done to follow through the developments of the early 1970s, as Barre increasingly bypassed the participatory institutions that he had helped to create. His government became one of personal rule; he took on emergency powers, relieved members of the governing council of their duties, surrounded himself with members of his own Marehan branch of the Darod clan, and isolated himself

The British take control of northern regions of present-day Somalia
1886–1887

Italy establishes a protectorate in the eastern areas of present-day Somalia
1889

Somalia is formed through a merger of former British and Italian colonies under UN Trusteeship
1960

Siad Barre comes to power through an army coup; the Supreme Revolutionary Council is established
1969

The Ogaden war in Ethiopia results in Somalia's defeat
1977–1978

SNM rebels escalate their campaign in the north; government forces respond with genocidal attacks on the local Issaq population
1980s

The fall of Barre leaves Somalia without an effective central government; U.S.–led UN intervention feeds millions while attempting to restore order

In the face of mounting losses, foreign troops pull out of Somalia

1990s

2000s

Chaos still reigns in Somalia, causing untold suffering

Abdiqassim Salad Hassan is named interim president

from the public. Barre also isolated Somalia from the rest of Africa by pursuing irredentist policies that would unite the other points of the Somali star under his rule. To accomplish this task, he began to encourage local guerrilla movements among the ethnic Somalis living in Kenya and Ethiopia.

In 1977, Barre sent his forces into the Ogaden region to assist the local rebels of the Western Somali Liberation Front. The invaders achieved initial military success against the Ethiopians, whose forces had been weakened by revolutionary strife and battles with Eritrean rebels. However, the intervention of some 17,000 Cuban troops and other Soviet bloc personnel on the side of the Ethiopians quickly turned the tide of battle. At the same time, the Somali incursion was condemned by all members of the Organization of African Unity.

The intervention of the Soviet bloc on the side of the Ethiopians was a bitter disappointment to Barre, who had enjoyed Soviet support for his military buildup. In exchange, he had allowed the Soviets to establish a secret base at the strategic northern port of Berbera. However, in 1977, the Soviets decided to shift their allegiances decisively to the then–newly established revolutionary government in Ethiopia. Barre in turn tried to attract U.S. support with offers of basing rights at Berbera, but the Carter administration was unwilling to jeopardize its interests in either Ethiopia or Kenya by backing Barre's irredentist adventure. American–Somali relations became closer during the Reagan administration, which signed a 10-year pact giving U.S. forces access to air and naval facilities at Berbera, for which the United States increased its aid to Somalia, including limited arms supplies.

In 1988, Barre met with Ethiopian leader Mengistu Mariam. Together, they pledged to respect their mutual border. This understanding came about in the context of growing internal resistance to both regimes. By 1990, numerous clan-based armed resistance movements—the Somali Salvation Democratic Front (SSDF), the Somalia Democratic Movement (SDM), the Somali National Movement (SNM), the Somalia Patriotic Movement (SPM), the United Somali Front (USF), the United Somali Party (USP), and the 16-faction United Somali Congress (USC)—were enjoying success against Barre.

Growing resistance was accompanied by massive atrocities on the part of government forces. Human-rights concerns were cited by the U.S. and other governments in ending their assistance to Somalia. In March 1990, Barre called for national dialogue and spoke of a possible end to one-party rule. But continuing atrocities, including the killing of more than 100 protesters at the national stadium, fueled further armed resistance.

In January 1991, Barre fled Mogadishu, which was seized by USC forces. The USC set up an interim administration, but its authority was not recognized by other groups. By the end of the year, the USC itself had split into two warring factions. A 12-faction "Manifesto Group" recognized Ali Mahdi as the country's president. But Mahdi's authority was repudiated by the four-faction Somali National Alliance (SNA), led by Farah Aideed. Much of Mogadishu was destroyed in inconclusive fighting between the two groupings. Other militias, including forces still loyal to Barre (that is, the Somali National Front, or SNF), have also continued to fight one another. In the north, the Somali National Movement declared its zone's sovereign independence as "Somaliland."

Continued fighting coincided with drought. As failed crops and dying livestock resulted in countrywide famine, international relief efforts were unable to supply sufficient quantities of outside food to those most in need, due to the prevailing state of lawlessness. In mid-1992, the International Red Cross estimated that, of southern Somalia's 4.5 million people, 1.5 million were in danger of starvation. Another 500,000 or so had fled the country. More than 300,000 children under age five were reported to have perished.

As Somalia's suffering grew and became publicized in the Western media, many observers suggested the need for the United Nations to intervene. A small UN presence, known as UNISOM, was established in August 1992, but its attempts to police the delivery of relief supplies proved to be ineffectual. Conceived as a massive U.S.–led military operation, initially consisting of 30,000 troops (22,000 Americans), UNITAF (Operation Restore Hope) averted catastrophe by assuring the delivery of food and medical supplies to Somalia's starving millions. Still, the foreign troops' mission was unclear.

In March 1993, a UN–sponsored agreement was reached among most of the southern Somali factions to form a Transitional National Council. But subsequent UNITAF attempts to enforce the agreement by disarming the militias ended in total failure. A bloody clash between Aideed's SNA militia and Pakistani troops in Mogadishu led to full-scale armed conflict. Efforts by UNITAF forces to capture Aideed and neutralize his men were unsuccessful. After a U.S. helicopter was shot down in October 1993, President Bill Clinton decided to end American involvement in UNITAF by March 1994. By then, much higher losses had been suffered by several other nations participating in the UNITAF–UNISOM coalition, causing them also to reassess their commitments. Outgunned and demoralized, the remaining UN forces (officially labeled UNISOM II) remained largely confined to their compounds until their withdrawal.

DEVELOPMENT

Most development projects have ended. Somalia's material infrastructure has largely been destroyed by war and neglect, though some local rebuilding efforts are under way, especially in the more peaceful central and northern parts of the country. In 1996, the European Union agreed to finance the reconstruction of the port of Berbera.

FREEDOM

Plagued by persistent hunger and internal violence, and with the continuing threat of governance by the anarchic greed of the warlords, the living have no true freedom in Somalia.

HEALTH/WELFARE

Somalia's small health service has almost completely disappeared, leaving the country reliant on a handful of international health teams. By 1986, education's share of the national budget had fallen to 2%. Somalia had 525 troops per teacher, the highest such ratio in Africa.

ACHIEVEMENTS

Somalia has been described as a "nation of poets." Many scholars attribute the strength of the Somali poetic tradition not only to the nomadic way of life, which encourages oral arts, but to the role of poetry as a local social and political medium.

Sudan (Republic of the Sudan)

GEOGRAPHY
Area in Square Miles (Kilometers):
967,247 (2,505,810) (about ¼
the size of the United States)
Capital (Population): Khartoum
(948,000)
Environmental Concerns:
insufficient potable water;
excessive hunting of wildlife;
soil erosion; desertification
Geographical Features: generally
flat, featureless plain; mountains
in the east and west
Climate: arid desert to tropical

PEOPLE

Population
Total: 35,080,000
Annual Growth Rate: 2.84%
Rural/Urban Population Ratio:
68/32
Major Languages: Arabic;
Sudanic languages; Nubian;
English; others
Ethnic Makeup: 52% black; 39%
Arab; 6% Beja; 3% others
Religions: 70% Sunni Muslim,
especially in north; 25%
indigenous beliefs;
5% Christian

Health
Life Expectancy at Birth: 55
years (male); 58 years (female)
Infant Mortality Rate (Ratio):
70.3/1,000
Physicians Available (Ratio):
1/11,300

Education
Adult Literacy Rate: 46%

COMMUNICATION
Telephones: 162,000 main lines
Daily Newspaper Circulation:
21 per 1,000 people
Televisions: 8.2 per 1,000 people
Internet Service Provider: 1 (1999)

TRANSPORTATION
Highways in Miles (Kilometers): 7,198
(11,610)
Railroads in Miles (Kilometers): 3,425 (5,516)
Usable Airfields: 61
Motor Vehicles in Use: 75,000

GOVERNMENT
Type: transitional
Independence Date: January 1, 1956
(from Egypt and the United Kingdom)
Head of State/Government: President
Omar Hasan Ahmad al-Bashir is both
head of state and head of government

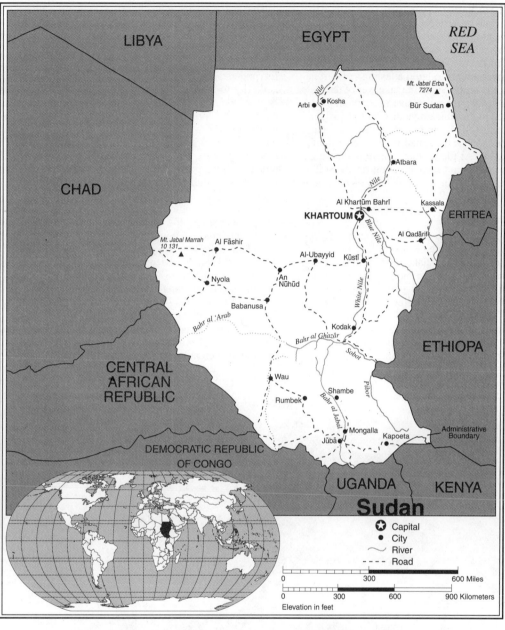

Political Parties: parties are banned,
but political "associations" have been
allowed since 1999
Suffrage: universal for adults

MILITARY
Current Disputes: civil war; border
disputes and clashes with Egypt and
Kenya

ECONOMY
Currency ($ U.S. Equivalent): 434.8
Sudanese pounds = $1
Per Capita Income/GDP: $940/$32.6
billion
GDP Growth Rate: 3%
Inflation Rate: 20%
Unemployment Rate: 30%

Labor Force: 11,000,000
Natural Resources: petroleum; iron ore;
chromium ore; copper; zinc; tungsten;
mica; silver; gold; hydropower
Agriculture: cotton; sesame; gum arabic;
sorghum; millet; wheat; sheep; groundnuts
Industry: textiles; cement; cotton ginning;
edible oils; soap; sugar; shoes; petroleum
refining
Exports: $580 million (primary partners
Italy, Saudi Arabia, Germany)
Imports: $1.4 billion (primary partners
China, France, United Kingdom)

 http://www.sas.upenn.edu/
African_Studies/Country_Specific/
Sudan.html
http://www.sudan.net/contents.shtml

SUDAN

Sudan is Africa's largest country. Its tremendous size as well as its great ethnic and religious diversity have frustrated the efforts of successive postindependence governments to build a lasting sense of national unity. Since the takeover of the state in 1989 by a repressive military clique allied to the fundamentalist National Islamic Front (NIF), the polarization of Sudanese society has deepened to an unprecedented extent. At the moment, there is little hope for unity and reconciliation for the suffering people in this vast land of enormous potential.

HISTORY

Sudan, like its northern neighbor Egypt, is a gift of the Nile. The river and its various branches snake across the country, providing water to most of the 80 percent of Sudanese who survive by farming. From ancient times, the Upper Nile region of northern Sudan has been the site of a series of civilizations, whose histories are closely intertwined with those of Egypt. There has been constant human interaction between the two zones. Some groups, such as the Nubians, expanded northward into the Egyptian lower Nile.

The last ruler to unite the Nile Valley politically was the nineteenth-century Turko–Egyptian ruler Muhammad Ali. After absorbing northern Sudan, by then predominantly Arabized Muslim, into his Egyptian state, Ali gradually expanded his authority to the south and west over non-Arabic and, in many cases, non-Muslim groups. This process, which was largely motivated by a desire for slave labor, united for the first time the diverse regions that today make up Sudan. In the 1880s, much of Sudan fell under the theocratic rule of the Mahdists, a local anti-Egyptian Islamic movement. The Mahdists were defeated by an Anglo–Egyptian force in 1898. Thereafter, the British dominated Sudan until its independence, in 1956.

Sudanese society has remained divided ever since. There has been strong pan-Arab sentiment in the north, but 60 percent of Sudanese (concentrated in the south and west) are non-Arab. About a third of Sudanese, especially in the south, are also non-Muslim. Despite this fact, many, but by no means all, Sudanese Muslims have favored the creation of an Islamic state. Ideological divisions among various socialist- and non-socialist-oriented factions have also been important. Sudan has long had a strong Communist Party (whether legal or not), drawing on the support of organized labor, and an influential middle class.

The division between northern and southern Sudan has been especially deep. A mutiny by southern soldiers prior to independence escalated into a 17-year rebellion by southerners against what they perceived to be the hegemony of Muslim Arabs. Some 500,000 southerners perished before the Anya Nya rebels and the government reached a compromise settlement, recognizing southern autonomy in 1972.

In northern Sudan, the first 14 years of independence saw the rule of seven different civilian coalitions and six years of military rule. Despite this chronic instability, a tradition of liberal tolerance among political factions was generally maintained. Government became increasingly authoritarian during the administration of Jaafar Nimeiri, who came to power in a 1969 military coup.

Nimeiri quickly moved to consolidate his power by eliminating challenges to his government from the Islamic right and the Communist left. His greatest success was ending the Anya Nya revolt, but his sub-

(United Nations photo by Milton Grant)

Millions of Sudanese have been displaced by warfare and drought. The effect on the population has been devastating, and even the best efforts of the international community have met with only limited success.

Egypt invades
northern Sudan
1820

The Mahdist
Revolt begins
1881

Independence
1956

Jaafar Nimeiri
comes to power
1969

Hostilities end
in southern
Sudan
1972

Islamic law
replaces the
former penal
code; renewed
civil war in the
south
1980s

Nimeiri is
overthrown in
a popular coup;
an elected
government is
installed

The hard-line
Islamic
fundamentalist
regime installed
in 1989 becomes
increasingly
repressive
1990s

2000s

Famine threatens
large segments of
the population

Omar al-Bashir claims
victory in a boycotted
1996 election

sequent tampering with the provisions of the peace agreement led to renewed resistance. In 1983, Nimeiri decided to impose Islamic law throughout Sudanese society. This led to the growth of the Sudanese People's Liberation Army (SPLA), under the leadership of John Garang, which quickly seized control of much of the southern Sudanese countryside. Opposition to Nimeiri had also been growing in the north, as more people became alienated by the regime's increasingly heavy-handed ways and inability to manage the declining economy. Finally, in 1985, he was toppled in a coup.

The holding of multiparty elections in 1986 seemed to presage a restoration of Sudan's tradition of pluralism. With the SPLA preventing voting in much of the south, the two largest parties were the northern-based Umma and Democratic Union (DUP). The National Islamic Front was the third-largest vote-getter, with eight other parties plus a number of independents gaining parliamentary seats. The major challenge facing the new coalition government, led by Umma, was reconciliation with the SPLA. Because the SPLA, unlike the earlier Anya Nya, was committed to national unity, the task did not appear insurmountable. However, arguments within the government over meeting key SPLA demands, such as the repeal of Islamic law, caused the war to drag on. A hard-line faction within Umma and the NIF sought to resist a return to secularism. In March 1989, a new government, made up of Umma and the DUP, committed itself to accommodating the SPLA. However, a month later, on the day the cabinet was to ratify an agreement with the rebels, there was a coup by pro-NIF officers.

Besides leading to a breakdown in all efforts to end the SPLA rebellion, the NIF/military regime has been responsible for establishing the most intolerant, re-pressive government in Sudan's modern history. Extra-judicial executions have become commonplace. Instances of pillaging and enslavement of non-Muslim communities by government-linked militias have increased. NIF-affiliated security groups have become a law unto themselves, striking out at their perceived enemies and intimidating Muslims and non-Muslims alike to conform to their fundamentalist norms. Islamic norms are also being invoked to justify a radical campaign to undermine the status of women.

In 1990, most of the now-banned political parties (including Umma, the DUP, and the Communists) aligned themselves with the SPLA as the National Democratic Alliance. But opposition by the northern-based parties proved ineffectual, leading to the formation of a new, Eritrean-based armed movement—the Sudan Alliance of Forces, headed by Abdul Azizi Khalid.

Beginning in 1991, the SPLA was weakened by a series of splits. Two factions—Kerubino Kuanyin Bol's SPLA–Bahr al-Ghazal group and Riek Macher's Southern Sudan Independence Army (SSIA)—accepted a government peace plan in April 1996. But the plan was rejected by John Garang's SPLA (Torit faction), which remains the most powerful southern group. After a number of years of being on the defensive, Garang's forces began making significant advances in 1996, partially as a result of increased support from neighboring countries that have come to look upon the Khartoum regime as a regional threat. (In June 1995, the regime was implicated in an attempt to assassinate Egyptian president Hosni Mubarak in Ethiopia, which resulted in the imposition of UN antiterrorism sanctions. Border clashes have since occurred with Eritrea, Kenya, and Uganda as well as Egypt.)

There is no immediate prospect of an end to the internal fighting, which has been accompanied by atrocities on all sides, including by a number of regional militias with shifting loyalties. By 1998, the conflict had claimed more than 1.5 million lives.

ECONOMIC PROSPECTS

Although it has great potential, political conflict has left Sudan one of the poorest nations in the world. The country's under-utilized water resources have led to talk of creating the "breadbasket of the Arab world," while untapped oil reserves in the south could transform the country from an energy importer to an exporter. However, persistent warfare and lack of financing are blocking needed infrastructural improvements. Sudan's unwillingness to pay its foreign debt has led to calls for its expulsion from the International Monetary Fund.

Nearly 7 million Sudanese (out of a total population then of 23 million) had been displaced by 1988—more than 4 million by warfare, with drought and desertification contributing to the remainder. Sudan has been a major recipient of international emergency food aid for years, but warfare, corruption, and genocidal indifference have often blocked help from reaching the needy. In 1994, the United Nations estimated that 700,000 southern Sudanese faced the prospect of starvation.

DEVELOPMENT

Many ambitious development plans have been launched since independence, but progress has been limited by political instability. The periodic introduction and redefinition of "Islamic" financial procedures have complicated long-term planning.

FREEDOM

The current regime rules through massive repression. In 1992, Africa Watch accused it of practicing genocide against the Nuba people. Elsewhere, tales of massacres, forced relocations, enslavement, torture, and starvation are commonplace. The insurgent groups have also been responsible for numerous atrocities.

HEALTH/WELFARE

Civil strife and declining government expenditures have resulted in rising rates of infant mortality. Warfare has also prevented famine relief from reaching needy populations, resulting in instances of mass starvation.

ACHIEVEMENTS

Although his music is banned in his own country, Mohammed Wardi is probably Sudan's most popular musician. Now living in exile, he has been imprisoned and tortured for his songs against injustice, which also appeal to a large international audience, especially in North Africa and the Middle East.

Tanzania (United Republic of Tanzania)

GEOGRAPHY

Area in Square Miles (Kilometers):
363,950 (939,652) (about
twice the size of California)
Capital (Population): Dar es
Salaam (1,747,000); Dodoma
(to be new capital) (1,238,000)
Environmental Concerns: soil
degradation; deforestation;
desertification; destruction of
coral reefs and marine
environment
Geographical Features: plains
along the coast; central
plateau; highlands in the north
and south
Climate: tropical to temperate

PEOPLE

Population
Total: 35,306,000*
Annual Growth Rate: 2.57%*
Rural/Urban Population Ratio:
75/25
Major Languages: Kiswahili;
Chagga; Gogo; Ha; Haya;
Luo; Maasai; English; others
Ethnic Makeup: 99% African;
1% others
Religions: indigenous beliefs;
Muslim; Christian; Hindu

Health
Life Expectancy at Birth: 51 years
(male); 53 years (female)*
Infant Mortality Rate (Ratio):
81/1,000*
Physicians Available (Ratio):
1/20,511

Education
Adult Literacy Rate: 79.4%
Compulsory (Ages): 7–14; free

COMMUNICATION
Telephones: 122,000 main lines
Televisions: 2.8 per 1,000 people
Internet Service Providers: 7 (1999)

TRANSPORTATION
Highways in Miles (Kilometers): 52,800
(85,161)
Railroads in Miles (Kilometers): 2,141 (3,453)
Usable Airfields: 129
Motor Vehicles in Use: 134,000

GOVERNMENT
Type: republic
Independence Date: December 9, 1961
(from United Nations trusteeship)
Head of State/Government: President
Benjamin William Mkapa is both head
of state and head of government
Political Parties: Revolutionary Party;
National Convention for Construction

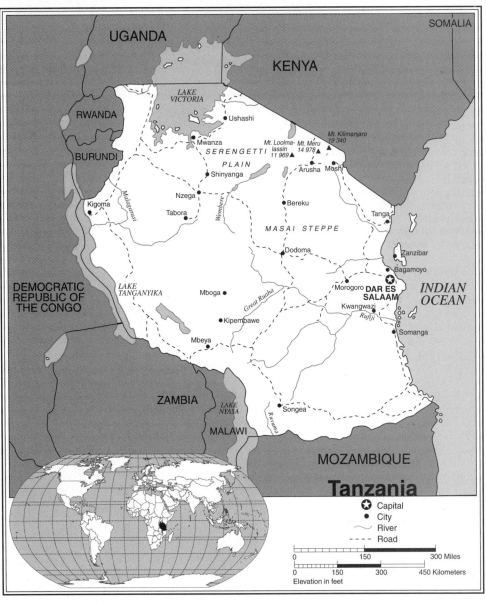

and Reform; Civic United Front; Union
for Multiparty Democracy; Democratic
Party; United Democratic Party; others
Suffrage: universal at 18

MILITARY
Military Expenditures (% of GDP): 0.2%
Current Disputes: boundary dispute with Malawi

ECONOMY
Currency ($ U.S. Equivalent): 523.4
Tanzanian shillings = $1
Per Capita Income/GDP: $550/$23.3 billion
GDP Growth Rate: 4%
Inflation Rate: 8.8%
Labor Force: 13,495,000
Natural Resources: hydropower; tin;
phosphates; iron ore; coal; diamonds;
gemstones; gold; natural gas; nickel

Agriculture: coffee; sisal; tea; cotton;
pyrethrum; cashews; tobacco; cloves;
wheat; fruits; vegetables; livestock
Industry: agricultural processing; mining;
oil refining; shoes; cement; textiles;
wood products; fertilizer; salt
Exports: $828 million (primary partners
India, Germany, Japan)
Imports: $1.44 billion (primary partners
South Africa, Kenya, United Kingdom)

http://www.sas.upenn.edu/
African_Studies/Country_Specific/
Tanzania.html
http://www.tanzania_online.gov.uk

*Note: Estimates explicitly take into account the
effects of excess mortality due to AIDS.

TANZANIA

In October 1999, more than 3 million Tanzanians joined leaders from around the world in filing through a temporary mausoleum housing the body of the country's late first president, Julius Nyerere. It was an overwhelming tribute to the man who was known at home and abroad as *Mwalimu*—Swahili for "teacher." Nyerere voluntarily relinquished power in 1985, but the legacy of his nation-building efforts can be found throughout the country. Since independence, Tanzania has enjoyed internal unity and an expansion of social services. The Kiswahili language has helped bind the nation together. But economic growth has remained modest.

After a period of harsh German rule followed by paternalistic British trusteeship, the Tanzanian mainland gained its independence, as Tanganyika, in 1961. In 1964, it merged with the small island state of Zanzibar, which had been a British protectorate, to form the "United Republic of Tanzania." Political activity in Tanzania was restricted to the ruling Revolutionary or Chama Cha Mapinduzi (CCM) Party, which joined the former Tanganyika African National Union with its Zanzibar partner, the Afro-Shirazi Party.

In February 1992, the CCM agreed to compete with other "national parties"—provided they did not "divide the people along tribal, religious or racial lines." Multiparty elections were held in October–December 1995, with the CCM claiming victory over a divided opposition in a poll characterized by massive irregularities. The disputed official results were CCM, 60 percent of the vote and 187 members of Parliament (MPs), including 128 seats where the results were still being legally contested months later; the National Committee for Constitutional Reform (NCCR), 25 percent of the vote and 15 MPs; and the Civic United Front, 24 MPs but only a small percentage of the vote, concentrated in Zanzibar and Pemba Islands. The new CCM leader, Ben Mkapa, replaced as president Ali Hassan Mwinyi, who was forced to step down after having served two terms. The dominant personality in the CCM, however, remained former president Nyerere.

By 1967, the CCM's predecessors had already eliminated legal opposition, when they proclaimed their commitment to the Arusha Declaration, a blueprint for "African Socialism." At the time, Tanzania was one of the least-developed countries in the world. It has remained so. Beyond this fact, there is much controversy over the degree to which the goals of the Declaration have been achieved. To some critics, the Arusha experiment has been responsible for reducing a potentially well-off country to ruin. Supporters often counter that it has led to a stable society in which major strides have been made toward greater democracy, equality, and human development. Both sides exaggerate.

Like many African states, Tanzania has a primarily agrarian economy that is constrained by a less than optimal environment. Although some 90 percent of the population are employed in agriculture, only 8 percent of the land is under cultivation. Rainfall for most of the country is low and erratic, and soil erosion and deforestation are critical problems in many areas. But geography and environmental problems are only one facet of Tanzania's low agricultural productivity. There has also been instability in world-market de-

(UN photo by Ray Witlin)

The Tanzanian economy is primarily agriculture-based. However, rainfall for most of the country is sporadic. This, coupled with wide swings in world-market demand for its cash crops, has led to economic pressures affecting food crops. These men in the village of Lumeji are receiving seed grains needed to develop Tanzania's food production.

The sultan of Oman transfers the capital to Zanzibar as Arab commercial activity increases
1820

Germany declares a protectorate over the area
1885

The Maji Maji rebellion unites many ethnic groups against German rule
1905–1906

Tanganyika becomes a League of Nations mandate under the United Kingdom
1919

Tanganyika becomes independent; Julius Nyerere is the leader
1961

Tanzania is formed of Tanganyika and Zanzibar
1964

The Arusha Declaration establishes a Tanzanian socialist program for development
1967

Nyerere retires; Ali Hassan Mwinyi succeeds as president
1985

The CCM wins disputed multiparty elections
1990s

2000s

Tanzania continues to look for ways to strengthen and diversify its economy

mand for the nation's principal cash crops: coffee, cotton, cloves, sisal, and tobacco. The cost of imported fuel, fertilizers, and other inputs has risen simultaneously.

Government policies have also been responsible for underdevelopment. Perhaps the greatest policy disaster was the program of villagization. Tanzania hoped to relocate its rural and unemployed urban populations into *ujaama* (Swahili for "familyhood") villages, which were to become the basis for agrarian progress. In the early 1970s, coercive measures were adopted to force the pace of resettlement. Agricultural production is estimated to have fallen as much as 50 percent during the initial period of ujaama dislocation, transforming the nation from a grain exporter to a grain importer.

Another policy constraint was the exceedingly low official produce prices paid by the government to farmers. Many peasants withdrew from the official market, while others turned to black-market sales. Since 1985, the official market has been liberalized, and prices have risen. This has been accompanied by a modest rise in production, yet the lack of consumer goods in rural areas is widely seen as a disincentive to greater development.

All sectors of the Tanzanian economy have suffered from deteriorating infrastructure. Here again there are both external and internal causes. Balanced against rising imported-energy and equipment costs have been inefficiencies caused by poor planning, barriers to capital investment, and a relative neglect of communications and transport. Even when crops or goods are available, they often cannot reach their destination. Tanzania's few bituminized roads have long been in a chronic state of disrepair, and there have been frequent shutdowns of its

railways. In particular, much of the southern third of the country is isolated from access to even inferior transport services.

Manufacturing declined from 10 to 4 percent of gross domestic product in the 1980s, with most sectors operating at less than half of their capacity. Inefficiencies also grew in the nation's mining sector. Diamonds, gold, iron, coal, and other minerals are exploited, but production has been generally falling and now accounts for less than 1 percent of GDP. Lack of capital investment has led to a deterioration of existing operations and an inability to open up new deposits.

As with agriculture, the Tanzanian government has in recent years increasingly abandoned socialism in favor of market economics, in its efforts to rehabilitate and expand the industrial and service sectors of the economy. A number of state enterprises are being privatized, and better opportunities are being offered to outside investors. Tourism is now being actively promoted, after decades of neglect.

Tanzania has made real progress in extending health, education, and other social services to its population since independence, though the statistical evidence is inadequate and official claims exaggerated. Some 1,700 health centers and dispensaries have been built since 1961, but they have long been plagued by shortages of medicines, equipment, and even basic supplies such as bandages and syringes. Although the country has a national health service, patients often end up paying for material costs.

Much of the progress that has been made in human services is a function of outside donations. Despite the Arusha Declaration's emphasis on self-reliance, Tanzania has for decades been either at or near the top of the list of African countries

in its per capita receipt of international aid. By 1987, aid, primarily from Western countries, accounted for more than one third of the gross national product.

Even before the recent opening to multipartyism, Tanzania's politics was in a state of transition. Political life has been dominated since the 1950s by Julius Nyerere, who was the driving personality behind the Arusha experiment. However, in 1985, he gave up the presidency in favor of Ali Hassan Mwinyi, and, in 1990, Nyerere resigned as chairman of the CCM, without having to give up his leading influence in the party.

The move to multiparty politics is complicated by the omnipresent CCM. The party has sought to control all organized social activity outside of religion. A network of community and workplace cells has assured that all Tanzanians have at least one party official responsible for monitoring their affairs.

In 1993, a dozen new opposition parties were registered, though others, notably the Democratic Party of Reverend Christopher Mtikila, remain banned. Opposition disunity contributed to subsequent CCM election victories. In addition, the CCM still enjoys a near media monopoly, occasionally invoking the National Security Act to harass independent journalists. Overt political repression has been most notable on Zanzibar and Pemba Islands, where the CCM claimed a narrow 50.2 percent victory over CUP in October 1996, amid allegations of electoral fraud. Resulting civil unrest on the islands led to a government crackdown, with some 600 arrests.

DEVELOPMENT

In 1990, the World Bank approved a $200 million loan to assist Tanzania in the radical restructuring of its agricultural marketing system. Unprofitable state farms were to be sold off, the cereal marketing board was to be abolished, and the role of cash-crop marketing boards was to be reduced.

FREEDOM

Civil rights in Tanzania, especially on the island of Zanzibar, remain circumscribed, with police often harassing supporters of the political opposition. Arbitrary arrest and torture remain commonplace on the island, but on the mainland there has been a steady opening up of society since 1995, though there still exist restrictions on freedoms of speech and association.

HEALTH/WELFARE

The Tanzanian Development Plan calls for the government to give priority to health and education in its expenditures. This reflects a recognition that early progress in these areas has been undermined to some extent in recent years. Malnutrition remains a critical problem.

ACHIEVEMENTS

The government has had enormous success in its program of promoting the use of Kiswahili (Swahili) as the national language throughout society. Mass literacy in Kiswahili has facilitated the rise of a national culture, helping to make Tanzania one of the more cohesive African nations.

Uganda (Republic of Uganda)

GEOGRAPHY

Area in Square Miles (Kilometers):
91,076 (235,885) (about the size of Oregon)
Capital (Population): Kampala (954,000)
Environmental Concerns: draining of wetlands; deforestation; overgrazing; soil erosion; widespread poaching
Geographical Features: mostly plateau, with a rim of mountains
Climate: generally tropical, but semiarid in the northeast

PEOPLE

Population

Total: 23,318,000
Annual Growth Rate: 2.72%
Rural/Urban Population Ratio: 87/13
Major Languages: English; Swahili; Bantu languages; Nilotic languages
Ethnic Makeup: Bantu; Nilotic; Nilo-Hamitic; Sudanic
Religions: 66% Christian; 18% indigenous beliefs; 16% Muslim

Health

Life Expectancy at Birth: 39 years (male); 40 years (female)
Infant Mortality Rate (Ratio): 93.2/1,000
Physicians Available (Ratio): 1/20,700

Education

Adult Literacy Rate: 62%

COMMUNICATION

Telephones: 54,000 main lines
Televisions: 27 per 1,000 people
Internet Service Providers: 3 (1999)

TRANSPORTATION

Highways in Miles (Kilometers): 16,200 (27,000)
Railroads in Miles (Kilometers): 745 (1,241)
Usable Airfields: 26
Motor Vehicles in Use: 51,000

GOVERNMENT

Type: republic
Independence Date: October 9, 1962 (from the United Kingdom)
Head of State/Government: President Yoweri Kaguta Museveni is both head of state and head of government; Prime Minister Kintu Musoke assists the president
Political Parties: National Resistance Movement (only organization allowed public political activities); unrecognized: Democratic Party; Conservative Party; Ugandan People's Congress; others

Suffrage: universal at 18

MILITARY

Military Expenditures (% of GDP): 1.9%
Current Disputes: Ugandan military forces are supporting rebel forces in the former Zaire

ECONOMY

Currency ($ U.S. Equivalent): 1,165 Uganda shillings = $1
Per Capita Income/GDP: $1,060/$24.2 billion
GDP Growth Rate: 5.5%
Inflation Rate: 7%
Labor Force: 8,361,000
Natural Resources: copper; cobalt; salt; limestone; hydropower; arable land

Agriculture: coffee; tea; cotton; tobacco; cassava; potatoes; corn; millet; pulses; livestock
Industry: sugar; brewing; tobacco; textiles; cement
Exports: $471 million (primary partner Europe)
Imports: $1.1 billion (primary partners Kenya, United Kingdom, Japan)

http://www.mbendi.co.za/cyugcy.htm
http://www.sas.upenn.edu/African_ Studies/Country_Specific/Uganda. html
http://www.state.gov/www/background_ notes/uganda_0298_bgn.html
http://www.uganda.co.ug/

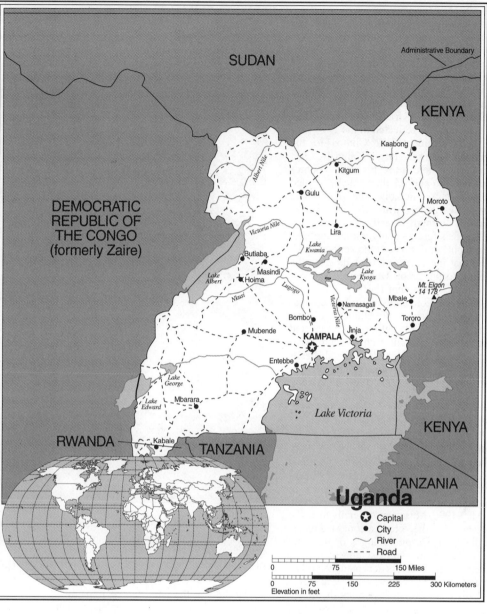

UGANDA

With his apparent sponsorship of two rebellions in the neighboring Democratic Republic of the Congo, insurgency in southern Sudan, and earlier mentorship of the Rwandan Patriotic Front (RPF) victory in Rwanda, Uganda's president, Yoweri Museveni, has emerged as a major power broker on the African continent. His prominence was reflected in the 1998 visit by U.S. president Bill Clinton to the Ugandan capital city, Kampala. Yet Museveni's hold over his own country continues to be challenged by armed groups, most notably the murderous Lord's Resistance Army, which terrorizes much of northern Uganda.

Uganda's foreign and domestic conflicts pose a potential threat to the very real progress that the country has made since the coming to power of Museveni's National Resistance Movement (NRM).

After years of repressive rule accompanied by massive interethnic violence, Uganda is still struggling for peace and reconciliation. A land rich in natural and human resources, Uganda suffered dreadfully during the despotic regimes of Milton Obote (1962–1971, 1980–1985) and Idi Amin (1971–1979). Under these two dictators, hundreds of thousands of Ugandans were murdered by the state.

The country had reached a state of general social and political collapse by 1986, when the NRM seized power. The new government soon made considerable progress in restoring a sense of normalcy in most of the country, except for the north. In May 1996, Museveni officially received 74 percent of the vote in a contested presidential poll. Despite charges of fraud by his closest rival, Paul Ssemogerere, most independent observers accepted the poll as an endorsement of Museveni's leadership, including his view that politics should remain organized on a nonparty basis. Museveni was reelected in March 2001.

HISTORIC GEOGRAPHY

The breakdown of Uganda is an extreme example of the disruptive role of ethnic and sectarian competition, which was fostered by policies of both its colonial and postcolonial governments. Uganda consists of two major zones: the plains of the northeast and the southern highlands. It has been said that you can drop anything into the rich volcanic soils of the well-watered south and it will grow. Until the 1960s, the area was divided into four kingdoms—Buganda, Bunyoro, Ankole, and Toro—populated by peoples using related Bantu languages.

The histories of these four states stretch back hundreds of years. European visitors

(UN photo by T. Chen)

Uganda is a land rich in natural and human resources, with tremendous potential for economic growth and improved quality of life. A major problem has been overcoming the abuses of Uganda's despotic regimes. Idi Amin, above, was dictator from 1971 to 1979. Under his infamously repressive rule, hundreds of thousands of Ugandans were murdered by the state.

of the nineteenth century were impressed by their sophisticated social orders, which the Europeans equated with the feudal monarchies of medieval Europe. When the British took over, they integrated the ruling class of the southern highlands into a system of "indirect rule." By then, missionaries had already succeeded in converting many southerners to Christianity; indeed, civil war among Protestants, Catholics, and Muslims within Buganda had been the British pretext for establishing their overrule.

The Acholi, Langi, Karamojang, Teso, Madi, and Kakwa peoples, who are predominant in the northeast, lack the political heritage of hierarchical state-building found in the south. These groups are also linguistically separate, speaking either Nilotic or Nilo-Hamitic languages. The two regions were united by the British as the

Uganda Protectorate during the 1890s (the name *Uganda*, which is a corruption of "Buganda," has since become the accepted term for the larger entity). But the zones developed separately under colonial rule.

Cash-crop farming, especially of cotton, by local peasants spurred an economic boom in the south. The Bugandan ruling class benefited in particular. Increasing levels of education and wealth led to the European stereotype of the "progressive" Bugandans as the "Japanese of Africa." A growing class of Asian entrepreneurs also played an important role in the local economy, although its prosperity, as well as that of the Bugandan elite, suffered from subordination to resident British interests.

The south's growing economy stood in sharp contrast to the relative neglect of the northeast. Forced to earn money to pay taxes, many northeasterners became mi-

Establishment
of the oldest
Ugandan kingdom,
Bunyoro, followed
by the formation of
Buganda and
other kingdoms
1500s

A British
protectorate
over Uganda
is proclaimed
1893

Uganda
becomes
independent
1962

Milton Obote
introduces
a new unitary
Constitution and
forces Bugandan
compliance
1966

Idi Amin
seizes power
1971

Amin invades
Tanzania;
Tanzania invades
Uganda and
overturns Amin's
government
1978—1979

The rise and fall
of the second
Obote regime;
the NRM takes
power under
Yoweri Museveni
1980s

Recovery
produces slow
gains; unrest
continues in
the northeast
1990s

2000s

Uganda addresses
the HIV/AIDS
pandemic

Museveni retains
power

grant workers in the south. They were also recruited, almost exclusively, to serve in the colonial security forces.

As independence approached, many Bugandans feared that their interests would be compromised by other groups. Under the leadership of their king, Mutesa II, they sought to uphold their separate status. Other groups feared that Buganda wealth and educational levels could lead to their dominance. A compromise federal structure was agreed to for the new state. At independence, the southern kingdoms retained their autonomous status within the "United Kingdom of Uganda." The first government was made up of Mutesa's royalist party and the United People's Congress (UPC), a largely non-Bugandan coalition, led by Milton Obote, a Langi. Mutesa was elected president and Obote prime minister.

THE REIGN OF TERROR

In 1966, the delicate balance of ethnic interests was upset when Obote used the army—still dominated by fellow north-easterners—to overthrow Mutesa and the Constitution. In the name of abolishing "tribalism," Obote established a one-party state and ruled in an increasingly dictatorial fashion. However, in 1971, he was overthrown by his army chief, Idi Amin. Amin began his regime with widespread public support but alienated himself by favoring fellow Muslims and Kakwa. He expelled the 40,000-member Asian community and distributed their property to his cronies. The Langi, suspected of being pro-Obote, were also early targets of his persecution, but his attacks soon spread to other members of Uganda's Christian community, at the time about 80 percent of the total population. Educated people

in particular were purged. The number of Ugandans murdered by Amin's death squads is unknown; the most commonly cited figure is 300,000, but estimates range from 50,000 to 1 million. Many others went into exile. Throughout the world, Amin's name became synonymous with despotic rule.

A Ugandan military incursion into Tanzania led to war between the two countries in 1979. Many Ugandans joined with the Tanzanians in defeating Amin's army and its Libyan allies. Unfortunately, the overthrow of Amin, who fled into exile, did not lead to better times.

In 1980, Obote was returned to power, through a fraudulent vote count. His second administration was characterized by a continuation of the violence of the Amin years. An estimated 300,000 people, mostly southerners, were massacred by Obote's security forces; an equal number fled the country. Much of the killing occurred in the Bugandan area known as the Luwero triangle, which was completely depopulated; its fields are still full of skeletons today. As the killings escalated, so did the resistance of Museveni's NRM guerrillas, who had taken to the bush in the aftermath of the failed election. In 1985, a split between Ancholi and Langi officers led to Obote's overthrow and yet another pattern of interethnic recrimination. Finally, in 1986, the NRM gained the upper hand.

THE STRUGGLE CONTINUES

Museveni's National Resistance Movement administration has faced enormous challenges in trying to bring about national reconstruction. The task has been complicated by continued warfare in the northeast by armed factions representing elements of the former regimes, inde-

pendent Karamojong communities, and followers of prophetic religious movements. In 1987, an uprising of the Holy Spirit rebels of Alice Lakwena was crushed, at the cost of some 15,000 lives.

Currently, there is cause for both hope and despair in Uganda. A sense of civil society has been returning to much of the country. Since 1990, the level of insurgency has been low. With peace has come economic growth, which has made up for some of the past decline.

While rebuilding their shattered country, Ugandans have had to cope with an especially severe outbreak of AIDS. Thousands have died of the disease in the last decade; it is believed that literally hundreds of thousands of Ugandans are HIV-positive. The government's bold acknowledgment of the seriousness of the crisis has given rise to (mostly internal) criticism as well as praise.

A new political order is emerging. Museveni has consistently advocated a "no party government," resisting agitation for a restoration of multiparty democracy. His position was strengthened in March 1994, when elections to a Constituent Assembly, which will endorse a new constitution, resulted in his supporters' capturing at least 150 of the 214 seats. In another controversial initiative, Museveni allowed the restoration of traditional offices, including Bugandan kingship.

DEVELOPMENT

Uganda's economy has been growing at an average annual rate of about 5%, boosted by increased investment. Foreign economic assistance nonetheless accounts for approximately 29% of government spending.

FREEDOM

The human-rights situation in Uganda remains poor, with government security forces linked to torture, extra-judicial executions, and other atrocities. Freedom of speech and association are curtailed. Insurgent groups are also associated with atrocities; the Lord's Resistance Army continues to kill, torture, maim, and abduct large numbers of civilians, enslaving numerous children.

HEALTH/WELFARE

Millions of Ugandans live below the poverty line. Uganda's traditionally strong school system was damaged but not completely destroyed under Amin and Obote. In 1986, some 70% of primary-school children attended classes. The killing and exiling of teachers have resulted in a serious drop of standards at all levels of the education system, but progress is under way. The adult literacy rate has risen to 62%.

ACHIEVEMENTS

The Ugandan government was one of the first countries in Africa (and the world) to acknowledge the seriousness of the AIDS epidemic within its borders. It has instituted public-information campaigns and welcomed outside support. In urban areas, the seropositive rate is 25%.

North Africa

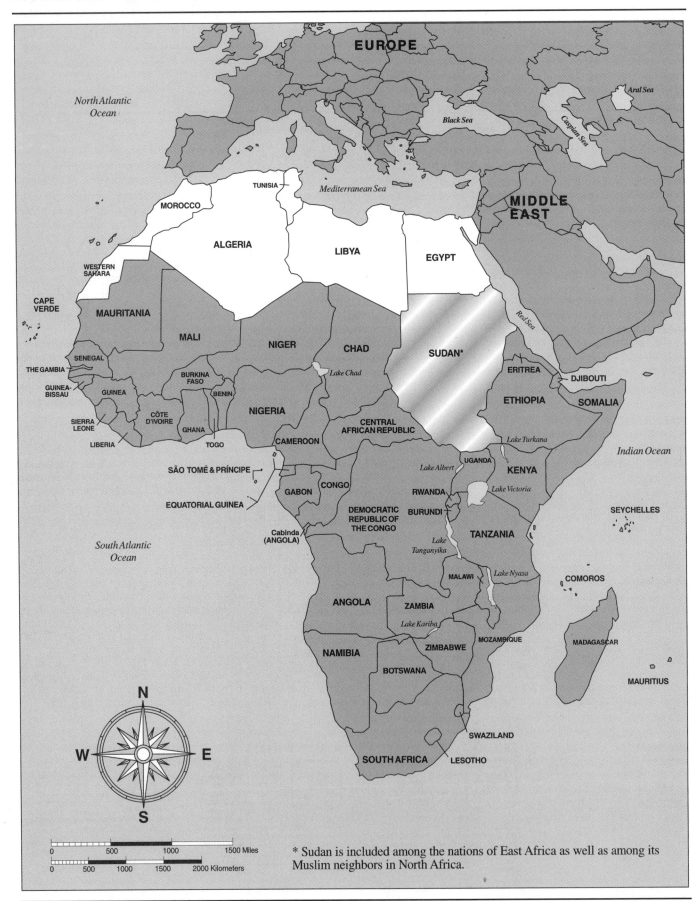

EUROPE

North Atlantic Ocean

Black Sea

Aral Sea

Caspian Sea

TUNISIA

Mediterranean Sea

MOROCCO

MIDDLE EAST

ALGERIA

LIBYA

EGYPT

WESTERN SAHARA

Red Sea

CAPE VERDE

MAURITANIA

MALI

NIGER

CHAD

SUDAN*

ERITREA

DJIBOUTI

SENEGAL

Lake Chad

ETHIOPIA

SOMALIA

THE GAMBIA

BURKINA FASO

GUINEA-BISSAU

GUINEA

BENIN

NIGERIA

CENTRAL AFRICAN REPUBLIC

Lake Turkana

SIERRA LEONE

CÔTE D'IVOIRE

GHANA

TOGO

CAMEROON

Indian Ocean

LIBERIA

UGANDA

KENYA

SÃO TOMÉ & PRÍNCIPE

Lake Albert

Lake Victoria

GABON

CONGO

RWANDA

SEYCHELLES

EQUATORIAL GUINEA

DEMOCRATIC REPUBLIC OF THE CONGO

BURUNDI

South Atlantic Ocean

Cabinda (ANGOLA)

TANZANIA

Lake Tanganyika

COMOROS

MALAWI

Lake Nyasa

ANGOLA

ZAMBIA

Lake Kariba

MOZAMBIQUE

MADAGASCAR

ZIMBABWE

NAMIBIA

BOTSWANA

MAURITIUS

SWAZILAND

SOUTH AFRICA

LESOTHO

N

W   E

S

| 0 | 500 | 1000 | 1500 Miles |
| 0 | 500 | 1000 | 1500 | 2000 Kilometers |

* Sudan is included among the nations of East Africa as well as among its Muslim neighbors in North Africa.

North Africa: The Crossroads of the Continent

Located at the geographical and cultural crossroads between Europe, Asia, and the rest of Africa, North Africa has served since ancient times as a link between the civilizations of sub-Saharan Africa and the rest of the world. Traders historically carried the continent's products northward, either across the Sahara Desert or up the Nile River and Red Sea, to the great port cities of the Mediterranean coast. Goods also flowed southward. In addition, the trade networks carried ideas: Islam, for example, spread from coastal North Africa across much of the rest of the continent to become the religion of at least one third of all Africans.

North Africa's role as the continent's principal window to the world gradually declined after the year A.D. 1500, as the trans-Atlantic trade increased. (The history of East Africa's participation in Indian Ocean trade goes back much further.) However, the countries of North Africa have continued to play an important role in the greater continent's development.

The countries of North Africa—Morocco, Algeria, Tunisia, Libya, and Egypt—and their millions of people differ from one another, but they share a predominant, overarching Arab-Islamic culture that both distinguishes them from the rest of Africa and unites them with the Arabic-speaking nations of the Middle East. To begin to understand the societies of North Africa and their role in the rest of the continent, it is helpful to examine the area's geography. The region's diverse environment has long encouraged its inhabitants to engage in a broad variety of economic activities: pastoralism, agriculture, trading, crafts, and, later, industry.

GEOGRAPHY AND POPULATION

Except for Tunisia, which is relatively small, the countries of North Africa are sprawling nations. Algeria, Libya, and Egypt are among the biggest countries on the African continent, and Morocco is not far behind. Their size can be misleading, for much of their territories are encompassed by the largely barren Sahara Desert. The approximate populations of the five states today range from Egypt's 67 million people to Libya's 5 million; Morocco has 30 million, Algeria 31 million, and Tunisia 9.5 million citizens. All these populations are increasing at a rapid rate; indeed, well over half of the region's citizens are under age 21.

Due to its scarcity, water is the region's most precious resource, so most people live either in valleys near the Mediterranean coast or along the Nile. The latter courses through the desert for thousands of miles, creating a narrow green ribbon that is the home of the 95 percent of Egypt's population who live within 12 miles of its banks. More than 90 percent of the people of Algeria, Libya, Morocco, and Tunisia live within 200 miles of either the Mediterranean or, in the case of Morocco, the Atlantic coast.

Besides determining where people live, the temperate, if often too dry, climate of North Africa has always influenced

(United Nations photo)

Geography has been less of a barrier to regional cohesiveness in North Africa than have politics and ideology.

local economies and lifestyles. There is intensive agriculture along the coasts and rivers. Algeria, Morocco, and Tunisia are well known for their tree and vine crops, notably citrus fruits, olives, and wine grapes. The intensively irrigated Nile Valley has been a leading source of high-quality cotton as well as locally consumed foodstuffs since the time of the American Civil War, which temporarily removed U.S.–produced fiber from the world market. In the oases that dot the Sahara Desert, date palms are grown for their sweet fruits, which are almost a regional staple. Throughout the steppelands between the fertile coasts and the desert, pastoralists follow flocks of sheep and goats or herds of cattle and camels in constant search of pasture. Although now few in number, it was these nomads who in the past developed the trans-Saharan trade. As paved roads and airports have replaced their caravan routes, long-distance nomadism has declined. But the traditions it bred, including a love of independence, remain an important part of North Africa's cultural heritage.

Urban culture has flourished in North Africa since the ancient times of the Egyptian pharaohs and the mercantilist rulers of Carthage. Supported by trade and local industries, the region's medieval cities, such as Cairo, Fez, and Kairouan, were the administrative centers of great Islamic empires, whose civilizations shined during Europe's dark ages. In the modern era, the urban areas are bustling industrial centers, ports, and political capitals.

Geography—or, more precisely, geology—has helped to fuel economic growth in recent decades. Although agriculture continues to provide employment in Algeria and Libya for as much as a third of the labor force, discoveries of oil and natural gas in the 1950s dramatically altered these two nations' economic structures. Between 1960 and 1980, Libya's annual per capita income jumped from $50 to almost $10,000, transforming it from among the poorest to among the richest countries in the world. Algeria has also greatly benefited from the exploitation of hydrocarbons, although less dramatically than Libya. Egypt and Tunisia have developed much smaller oil industries, which nonetheless provide for their domestic energy needs and generate much needed foreign exchange. The decline in oil prices during the 1980s, however, reduced revenues, increased unemployment, and contributed to social and political unrest, especially in Algeria. While it has no oil, Morocco profits from its possession of much of the world's phosphate production.

CULTURAL AND POLITICAL HERITAGES

The vast majority of the inhabitants of North Africa are Arabic-speaking Muslims. Islam and Arabic both became established in the region between the seventh and eleventh centuries A.D. Thus, by the time of the Crusades in the eastern Mediterranean, the societies of North Africa were thoroughly incorporated into the Muslim world, even though the area had earlier been the home of many Christian scholars. Except for Egypt, where about 5 percent of the population remain loyal to the Coptic Church, there is virtually no Christianity among modern North Africans. Until recently, important Jewish communities existed in all the region's countries, but their numbers have dwindled as a result of mass immigration to Israel.

With Islam came Arabic, the language of the Koran—the holy book of Islam. Today, Egypt and Libya are almost exclusively Arabic-speaking. In Algeria, Morocco, and Tunisia, Arabic coexists with various local minority languages, which are collectively known as Berber (from which the term "Barbary," as in Barbary Coast, was derived). As many as a third of the Moroccans speak a form of Berber as their first language. Centuries of interaction between the Arabs and Berbers as well as their common adherence to Islam have promoted a sense of cultural unity between the two communities, although ethnic disputes have developed in Algeria and Morocco over demands that Berber be included in local school curriculums. As was the case almost everywhere else on the continent, the linguistic situation in North Africa was further complicated by the introduction of European languages during the colonial era. Today, French is particularly important as a language of technology and administration in Algeria, Morocco, and Tunisia.

Early in the nineteenth century, all the countries of North Africa, except Morocco, were autonomous provinces of the Ottoman Empire, which was based in present-day Turkey and also incorporated most of the Middle East. Morocco was an independent state; indeed, it was one of the earliest to recognize the independence of the United States from England. From 1830, the European powers gradually encroached upon the Ottoman Empire's North African realm. Thus, like most of their sub-Saharan counterparts, all the states of North Africa fell under European imperial control. Algeria's conquest by the French began in 1830 but took decades to accomplish, due to fierce local resistance. France also seized Tunisia in 1881 and, along with Spain, partitioned Morocco in 1912. Britain occupied Egypt in 1882, and Italy invaded Libya in 1911, although anti-Italian resistance continued until World War II, when the area was liberated by Allied troops.

The differing natures of their European occupations have influenced the political and social characters of each North African state. Algeria, which was directly incorporated into France as a province for 120 years, did not win its independence until 1962, after a protracted and violent revolution. Morocco, by contrast, was accorded independence in 1956, after only 44 years of Franco–Spanish administration, during which the local monarchy continued to reign. Tunisia's 75 years of French rule also ended in 1956, as a strong nationalist party took the reins of power. Egypt, although formally independent of Great Britain, did not win genuine self-determination until 1952, when a group of nationalist army officers came to power by overthrowing the British-supported monarchy. Libya became a temporary ward of the United Nations after Italy was deprived of its colonial empire during World

War II. The nation was granted independence by the United Nations in 1951, under a monarch whose religious followers had led much of the anti-Italian resistance.

NATIONAL POLITICS

Egypt

Egypt reemerged as an important actor on the world stage soon after Gamal Abdel Nasser came to power, in the aftermath of the overthrow of the monarchy. One of the major figures in the post-World War II Non-aligned Movement, Nasser gave voice to the aspirations of millions in the Arab world and Africa, through his championing of pan-Arab and pan-African anti-imperialist sentiments. Faced with the problems of his nation's burgeoning population and limited natural resources, Nasser nonetheless refused to let his government become dependent on a single foreign power. Domestically, he adopted a policy of developmental socialism.

Because of mounting debts, spurred by enormous military spending, and increasing economic problems, many Egyptians had already begun to reassess some aspects of Nasser's policies by the time of his death in 1970. His successor, Anwar al-Sadat, reopened Egypt to foreign investment in hopes of attracting much-needed capital and technology. In 1979, Sadat drew Egypt closer to the United States by signing the Camp David Accords, which ended more than three decades of war with Israel. Egypt has since been one of the largest recipients of U.S. economic and military aid.

Sadat's increasingly authoritarian rule, as well as his abandonment of socialism and foreign policy initiatives, made him a target of domestic discontent, and in 1981, he was assassinated. His successor, Hosni Mubarak, has modestly liberalized Egyptian politics and pursued what are essentially moderate internal and external policies. While maintaining peace with Israel, Mubarak has succeeded in reconciling Egypt with other Arab countries, which had strongly objected to the Camp David agreement. In 1990–1991, he took a leading role among the majority of Arab leaders opposed to Iraq's seizure of Kuwait. However, rapid urbanization, declining per capita revenues, debt, and unemployment, all linked to explosive population growth, have continued to strain the Egyptian economy and fuel popular discontent. Some of this discontent has in recent years been channeled into violence by extremist Islamic groups, which now threaten to destroy the traditional tolerance that has existed between Egypt's Muslim majority and Christian minority. Domestic terrorism has also had a negative impact on Egypt's tourism industry, the country's largest foreign-exchange earner. Particularly detrimental was a 1997 massacre by Islamic extremists of 58 foreign tourists at the ancient ruins of Luxor.

Libya

Libya was ruled for years by a pious, autocratic king whose domestic legitimacy was always in question. After 1963, the nation came under the heavy influence of foreign oil companies, which discovered and produced the country's only substantial resource. In 1969, members of the military, led by Colonel Muammar al-Qadhafi, overthrew the monarchy. Believed to be about age 27 at the time of the coup, Qadhafi was an ardent admirer of Nasser's vision of pan-Arab nationalism and anti-imperialism. Qadhafi invested billions of dollars, earned from oil, in ambitious domestic development projects, successfully ensuring universal health care, housing, and education for his people by the end of the 1970s. He also spent billions more on military equipment and aid to what he deemed "nationalist movements" throughout the world. Considered a maverick, he came into conflict with many African and Arab rulers as well as with outside powers like the United States. Despite Qadhafi's persistent efforts to forge regional alliances, political differences, economic pressures, and the expulsion of expatriate workers (due to declining oil reve-

(United Nations photo by Y. Nagata)

The Egyptian president, Hosni Mubarak, continues the legacy of his predecessor, Anwar al-Sadat.

nues) have increased tensions between Libya and its neighbors as well as between the country's own military and middle class.

Strained relations between Libya and the United States over Qadhafi's activist foreign policy and support for international terrorists culminated in a U.S. air raid on Tripoli in 1986. In that year, the United States required American businesses and citizens to leave Libya and since then has sought other ways to undermine Qadhafi's ambitions. With the support of the United States and other powers, the Hisséne Habré government of Chad was able in 1987 to expel the Libyan military from its northern provinces. In 1991, Libya came under greater international pressure when the UN Security Council backed American and British demands for the extradition of two alleged Libyan agents suspected of complicity in the 1987 blowing up of a Pan Am passenger jet over Lockerbie, Scotland. The Qadhafi government's failure to submit to this decision led to the imposition of international sanctions barring other countries from maintaining air links with or selling arms to Libya.

Since 1998, Qadhafi has broken out of his regime's international isolation. UN sanctions on Libya were lifted after Qadhafi turned over the Lockerbie suspects for trial under Scottish law at The Hague, Netherlands, seat of the International Court of Justice. Qadhafi has also put himself forward as a promoter of African integration. In 1999, he hosted a special Organization of African Unity conference, where his call for a new "African Union" was adopted in principle. But on the domestic front, there are increasing signs of disillusionment with the status quo, particularly among the nation's youth, many of whom face unemployment.

Tunisia

Although having the fewest natural resources of the North African countries, Tunisia enjoyed a high degree of political stability and economic development during the first three decades that followed the restoration of its independence, in 1956. Habib Bourguiba, leader of the local nationalist party known as the Neo-Destour, led the country to independence while retaining cordial economic and political ties with France as well as other Western countries. Bourguiba's government was a model of pragmatic approaches to both economic growth and foreign policy. A mixed economy was developed, and education's contribution to development was emphasized. The nation's Mediterranean coast was transformed into a vacation spot for European tourists.

However, in the 1980s, amid economic recession and after 30 years of single-party rule, Tunisians became increasingly impatient with their aging leader's refusal to recognize opposition political parties. Strikes, demonstrations, and opposition from Muslim fundamentalists as well as underground secular movements were the context for Bourguiba's forced retirement in 1987 (he died in 2000, at age 96). He was succeeded by his prime minister, Zine al-Abidine ben Ali,

whose efforts in 1988 to release jailed Muslim activists and to open political dialogue led to a period of optimism and widespread support. By the middle of that year, he had replaced most of the cabinet ministers who had served under Bourguiba. Multiparty elections were held in 1989, but they were marred by opposition charges of fraud. This pattern was repeated in 1994, when Ben Ali was reelected unopposed, while his party captured all but 19 of the 163 parliamentary seats. In October 1999, it was announed that Ben Ali had been reelected by 99.4 percent of the vote! To the BBC, outspoken Tunisian journalist Taoufik Ben Brik noted: "How can I answer the question were the elections free? when we lack freedom of expression, freedom of organisation, even freedom of movement."

Economically, Tunisia continued to make substantial progress through an export-oriented market strategy based on manufactures, tourism, agriculture, and petroleum. In 1999, real per capita income grew by 5 percent, with the majority of Tunisians enjoying a middle-class lifestyle. The country benefits from high literacy, relatively low population growth, and wide distribution of health care.

Algeria

Algeria, wracked by the long and destructive revolution that preceded independence in 1962, was long ruled by a coalition of military and civilian leaders who rose to power as revolutionary partisans of the National Liberation Front (FNL) during the war. Although FNL leaders have differed over what policies and programs to emphasize, in the past they were able to forge a governing consensus in favor of secularism (but with respect for Islam's special status), a socialist domestic economy, and a foreign policy based on nonalignment. The country's substantial oil and gas revenues were invested in large-scale industrial projects, which were carried out by the state sector. But by the end of the 1970s, serious declines in agricultural productivity and growing urban unemployment, partially due to the country's high overall rate of population growth, sent hundreds of thousands of Algerian workers to France in search of jobs. As a result, cautious encouragement began to be given to private-sector development.

In 1988, rising bread prices led to severe rioting, which left more than 100 people dead. In the aftermath, the FNL's long period of one-party rule came to an end, with the legalization of opposition parties. In the 1990 local elections, the Islamic Salvation Front (FIS), a coalition group of Muslim fundamentalists, managed to take control of about 80 percent of the country's municipal and departmental councils. This triumph was followed by FIS success in the first round of voting for a new National Assembly in December 1991; the Front captured 187 out of 230 seats. But, just before a second round of voting could be held, in January 1992, the military seized power in a coup. A state of emergency was declared, and thousands of FIS supporters and other opponents of the new

(United Nations photo by Bill Graham)

Nomadic traditions, including loyalty to family and love of independence, are still integral to the cultures of North Africa.

regime were detained. In response, some turned to armed resistance. In June 1992, the political temperature was raised further by the mysterious assassination of Mohamed Boudiaf, a veteran nationalist who had been installed by the military's High State Committee as the president. In 1993, elements of the Islamic resistance began an increasingly effective campaign of isolating Algeria internationally by assassinating foreign expatriates residing in the country. In 1995, Liamine Zeroual was elected president in a poll boycotted by the FIS and other major opposition parties. He cited the relatively high voter turnout as a mandate for a peaceful settlement based on dialogue. But the nation has remained polarized by civil war, whose death toll is now estimated to be in excess of 80,000.

In the aftermath of the 1995 election, armed self-styled Islamists turned to massacring large numbers of civilians of all ages, in apparent retaliation against villages and extended families who ceased providing support to them. There are also credible accusations that some mass killings have been carried out by government forces. In an effort to push forward a political settlement, in February 1999, President Zeroual stepped down. He was replaced by Abdelaziz Bouteflika, who in April received 73 percent of the vote in a poll in which leading opponents dropped out of the race. In September 1999, Bouteflika received a greater mandate when a majority of Algerians voted in favor of new peace policies aimed at bringing an end to the years of bloodshed.

Internationally, Algeria has been known for its troubleshooting role in difficult diplomatic negotiations. In 1980, it mediated the release of the U.S. hostages held in Iran. After years of tension, largely over the war in Western Sahara, Algeria resumed diplomatic relations with its western neighbor, Morocco, in 1988.

Morocco

In August 1999, Morocco's King Hassan II, who had ruled since 1961, died. He was succeeded by his son Muhammad VI, who has since encouraged a degree of political and economic liberalization in the kingdom. Under Hassan II, the political parties that developed during the struggle against French rule (led by the current king's grandfather, Muhammad V) had continued to contest elections. But Hassan rarely permitted them to have any genuine influence in policy making, preferring to reserve the role for himself and his advisers. As in Tunisia, Moroccan agricultural development has been based on technological innovations rather than on land reform. (The latter, while it could raise productivity, would also likely anger the propertied supporters of the king. Elites also oppose business-tax reforms, yet the government needs revenues to repay its multibillion-dollar debt.) Much of the country's economic development has been left to the private sector. High birth rates and unemployment have led many Moroccans to join the Algerians and Tunisians in seeking employment in Europe.

By the mid-1990s, Morocco's three-decade-long war to retain control of the phosphate-rich Western Sahara—a former Spanish colony whose independence is being fought for by a local nationalist movement known as Polisario—had become an unsettled stalemate, with Morocco controlling most of the Western Sahara. By the late 1980s, Moroccan forces had become increasingly effective in frustrating the infiltration of Polisario guerrillas in the main centers of the territory by enclosing them behind a network of security walls. These walls have also effectively shut out some 120,000 refugees (the number is bitterly disputed by the contestants) living in Polisario-controlled camps in Algeria. A UN peace plan calling for a referendum over the territory's future was agreed to by both sides in 1990. But, though the two parties have generally maintained a cease-fire since 1991, other provisions of the plan have not been implemented, largely as a result of continued Moroccan intransigence. In 1995, Polisario formally renounced the agreement. But, with waning international support and the Moroccan forces now well dug in, Polisario's short-term prospects of making either a political or a military breakthrough appear unpromising.

Morocco maintains a mixed economy based largely on agriculture, fishing, light industry, phosphate mining, tourism, and remittances from citizens working abroad. The illegal cultivation of cannabis is also an important source of income for many Moroccans. Economic growth is highly

(United Nations photo by Saw Lwin)

Morocco's King Hassan II was a leader whose influence was often pivotal in North African regional planning.

dependent on agricultural output and has experienced wide fluctuations in recent years, due to drought.

REGIONAL AND CONTINENTAL LINKS

There have been many calls for greater regional integration in North Africa since the 1950s. Under Nasser, Egypt was the leader of the pan-Arab movement; it even joined Syria in a brief political union, from 1958 to 1961. Others have attempted to create a union of the countries of the *Maghrib* (Arabic for "west") region—that is, Algeria, Morocco, and Tunisia. Recently, these three countries, along with the adjacent states of Libya and Mauritania, agreed to work toward an economic community, but they continue to be politically divided. At one time or another, Qadhafi has been accused of subverting all the region's governments; Algeria and Morocco have disagreed over the disposition of the Western Sahara; and each country has closed its borders to its neighbors' citizens. Still, the logic of closer political and economic links and the example of increasing European unity on the other side of the Mediterranean will likely keep the issue of regional unity alive.

Both as members of the Organization of African Unity (OAU) and as individual states, the North African countries

(United Nations photo by J. Slaughter)

Creating economic and political integration has been a goal of North African countries for a number of years. Economic unification would have the benefits of wider markets, diversified products, and expanded employment; political unification, however, is more problematic, due to the historical and cultural diversity of the area. The Moroccan port of Casablanca, pictured above, is clearly an economic asset to the region.

have had strong diplomatic and political ties to the rest of the continent. They are, however, also deeply involved in regional affairs outside Africa, particularly those of the Arab and Mediterranean worlds. There have also been some modest tensions across the Sahara. Requests by the North African nations that other OAU countries break diplomatic relations with Israel were promptly met in the aftermath of the 1974 Arab–Israeli War. Many sub-Saharan countries hoped that, in return for their solidarity, the Arab nations would extend development aid to help them, in particular to cope with rising oil prices. Although some aid was forthcoming (mostly from the Persian Gulf countries rather than the North African oil producers), it was less generous than many had expected. During the 1980s, a number of sub-Saharan countries resumed diplomatic relations with Israel.

Border disputes, ideological differences, and internal conflicts have caused additional tensions. The Polisario cause in Western Sahara, for example, badly divided the Organization of African Unity. When the OAU recognized the Polisario's exiled government in 1984, Morocco, along with Zaire, withdrew from membership in the body. However, the OAU has also had significant regional successes. In 1974, for example, its mediation led to a settlement of a long-standing border dispute between Algeria and Morocco.

In recent years, the states of North Africa have begun to seek greater economic ties with Europe as well as with one another. In 1998, Algeria, Egypt, Morocco, and Tunisia signed accords with the European Union, agreements that are intended to promote free trade across the Mediterranean over the coming decade.

Southern Africa

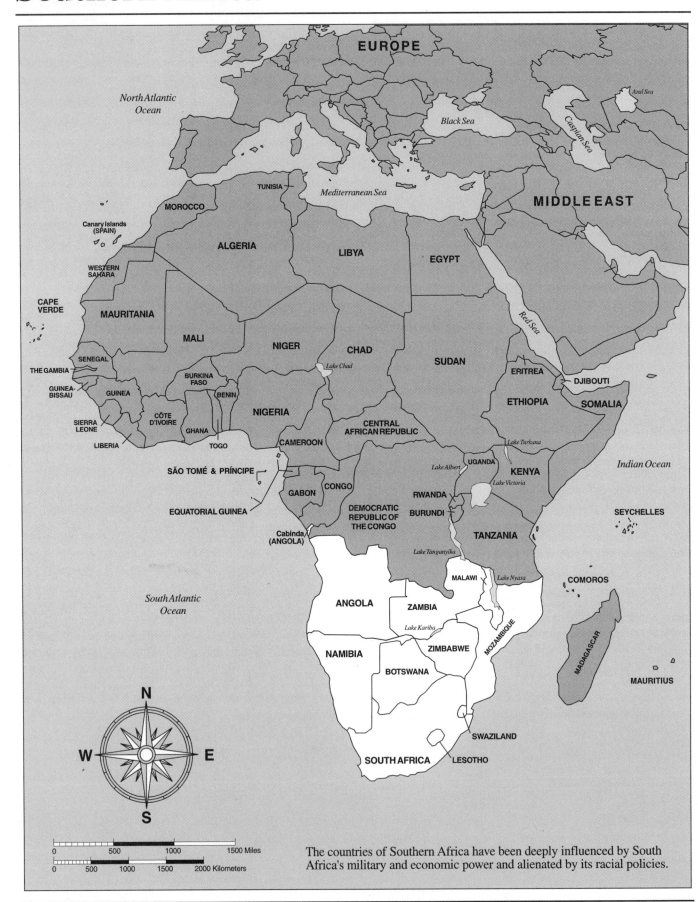

EUROPE

North Atlantic Ocean

Aral Sea

Black Sea

Caspian Sea

TUNISIA

Mediterranean Sea

MIDDLE EAST

MOROCCO

Canary Islands (SPAIN)

ALGERIA

LIBYA

EGYPT

WESTERN SAHARA

CAPE VERDE

MAURITANIA

Red Sea

MALI

NIGER

CHAD

SUDAN

Lake Chad

ERITREA

DJIBOUTI

SENEGAL

THE GAMBIA

BURKINA FASO

GUINEA-BISSAU

GUINEA

BENIN

ETHIOPIA

SOMALIA

SIERRA LEONE

CÔTE D'IVOIRE

NIGERIA

CENTRAL AFRICAN REPUBLIC

Lake Turkana

LIBERIA

GHANA

TOGO

CAMEROON

Lake Albert

UGANDA

KENYA

SÃO TOMÉ & PRÍNCIPE

CONGO

Lake Victoria

Indian Ocean

GABON

RWANDA

EQUATORIAL GUINEA

DEMOCRATIC REPUBLIC OF THE CONGO

BURUNDI

SEYCHELLES

Cabinda (ANGOLA)

TANZANIA

Lake Tanganyika

South Atlantic Ocean

MALAWI

Lake Nyasa

COMOROS

ANGOLA

ZAMBIA

Lake Kariba

MOZAMBIQUE

MADAGASCAR

NAMIBIA

ZIMBABWE

MAURITIUS

BOTSWANA

SWAZILAND

SOUTH AFRICA

LESOTHO

N
W   E
S

0   500   1000   1500 Miles
0   500   1000   1500   2000 Kilometers

The countries of Southern Africa have been deeply influenced by South Africa's military and economic power and alienated by its racial policies.

Southern Africa: The Continuing Struggle for Self-Determination

Southern Africa—which includes the nations of Angola, Botswana, Lesotho, Malawi, Mozambique, Namibia, South Africa, Swaziland, Zambia, and Zimbabwe—is a diverse region made up of savannas and forest, snow-topped mountains and desert, temperate Mediterranean and torrid tropical climates. Southern African identity is, however, as much defined by the region's peoples and their past and present interactions as by its geographic features. An appreciation of local history is crucial to understanding the forces that both divide and unite the region today.

EUROPEAN MIGRATION AND DOMINANCE
A dominant theme in the modern history of Southern Africa has been the evolving struggle of the region's indigenous black African majority to free itself of the racial hegemony of white settlers from Europe and their descendants. By the eighth century A.D., but probably earlier, the southernmost regions of the continent were populated by a variety of black African ethnic groups who spoke languages belonging to the Bantu as well as the Khoisan linguistic classifications. Members of these two groupings practiced both agriculture and pastoralism; archaeological evidence indicates that livestock keeping in Southern Africa pre-dates the time of Christ. Some, such as the BaKongo of northern Angola and the Shona peoples of the Zimbabwean plateaux, had, by the fifteenth century, organized strong states; others, like most Nguni-speakers prior to the early 1800s, lived in smaller

communities. Trade networks existed throughout the region, linking various local peoples not only to one another but also to the markets of the Indian Ocean and beyond. For example, porcelains from China have been unearthed in the grounds of the Great Zimbabwe, a stone-walled settlement that flourished in the fifteenth century.

In the 1500s, small numbers of Portuguese began settling along the coasts of Angola and Mozambique. A century later, in 1652, the Dutch established a settlement at Africa's southernmost tip, the Cape of Good Hope. While the Portuguese flag generally remained confined to coastal enclaves until the late 1800s, the Dutch colony expanded steadily into the interior throughout the 1700s, seizing the land of local Khoisan communities. Unlike the colonial footholds of the Portuguese and other Europeans on the continent, which prior to the 1800s were mostly centers for the export of slaves, the Dutch Cape Colony imported slaves from Asia as well as from elsewhere in Africa. Although not legally enslaved, conquered Khoisan were also reduced to servitude. In the process, a new society evolved at the Cape. Much like the American South before the U.S. Civil War, the Cape Colony was racially divided between free white settlers and subordinated peoples of mixed African and Afro-Asian descent.

During the Napoleonic Wars, Britain took over the Cape Colony. Shortly thereafter, in 1820, significant numbers of English-speaking colonists began arriving in the region. The arrival of the British coincided with a period of political

(United Nations photo by Ray Witlin)

Countries throughout Southern Africa are developing projects to employ laborers who might otherwise migrate to urban centers in South Africa—a pattern established in colonial times. These workers are building a highway in Lesotho.

(United Nations photo by J. P. Laffont)

Angolan youths celebrated when the nation became independent in 1974.

realignment throughout much of Southern Africa that is commonly referred to as the "Mfecane." Until recently, the historical literature has generally attributed this upheaval to dislocations caused by the rise of the Zulu state, under the great warrior prince Shaka. However, more recent scholarship on the Mfecane has focused on the disruptive effects of increased traffic in contraband slaves from the interior to the Cape and the Portuguese stations of Mozambique, following the international ban on slave trading.

In the 1830s, the British abolished slavery throughout their empire and extended limited civil rights to nonwhites at the Cape. In response, a large number of white Dutch-descended Boers, or Afrikaners, moved into the interior, where they founded two republics that were free of British control. This migration, known as the Great Trek, did not lead the white settlers into an empty land. The territory was home to many African groups, who lost their farms and pastures to the superior firepower of the early Afrikaners, who often coerced local communities into supplying corvee labor for their farms and public works. But a few African polities, like Lesotho and the western Botswana kingdoms, were able to preserve their independence by acquiring their own firearms.

In the second half of the nineteenth century, white migration and dominance spread throughout the rest of Southern Africa. The discovery of diamonds and gold in northeastern South Africa encouraged white exploration and subsequent occupation farther north. In the 1890s, Cecil Rhodes's British South Africa Company occupied modern Zambia and Zimbabwe, which then became known as the Rhodesias. British traders, missionaries, and settlers also invaded the area now known as Malawi. Meanwhile, the Germans seized Namibia, while the Portuguese began to expand inland from their coastal enclaves. Thus, by 1900, the entire region had fallen under white colonial control.

With the exception of Lesotho and Botswana, which were occupied as British "protectorates," all of the European colonies in Southern Africa had significant populations of white settlers, who in each case played a predominant political and economic role in their respective territories. Throughout the region, this white supremacy was fostered and maintained through racially discriminatory policies of land alienation, labor regulation, and the denial of full civil rights to nonwhites. In South Africa, where the largest and longest-settled white population resided, the Afrikaners and English-speaking settlers were granted full self-government in 1910—with a Constitution that left the country's black majority virtually powerless.

BLACK NATIONALISM AND
SOUTH AFRICAN DESTABILIZATION

After World War II, new movements advocating black self-determination gained ascendancy throughout the region. However, the progress of these struggles for majority rule and independence was gradual. By 1968, the countries of Botswana, Lesotho, Malawi, Swaziland, and Zambia had gained their independence. The area was then polarized between liberated and nonliberated nations. In 1974, a military uprising in Portugal brought statehood to Angola and Mozambique, after long armed struggles by liberation forces in the two territories. Wars of liberation also led to the overthrow of white-settler rule in Zimbabwe, in 1980, and the independence of Namibia, in 1990. Finally, in 1994, South Africa completed a negotiated transition to a nonracial government.

South Africa's liberation has far-reaching implications for the entire Southern African subcontinent as well as the country's own historically oppressed masses. Since the late nineteenth century, South Africa has been the region's economic hub. Today, it accounts for about 80 percent of the total Southern African gross domestic product. Most of the subcontinent's roads and rails also run through South Africa. For generations, the country has recruited expatriate as well as local black African workers for its industries and mines. Today, it is the most economically developed country on the continent, with manufactured goods and agricultural surpluses that are in high demand elsewhere. By the late 1980s, when the imposition of economic sanctions against the then–apartheid regime was at its height, some 46 African countries were importing South African products. With sanctions now lifted, South Africa's economic role on the continent is likely to increase substantially.

A significant milestone was South Africa's admittance in 1994 as the 11th member of the Southern African Development Community (SADC). This organization's ultimate goal is to emulate the European Union (formerly called the European Community or Common Market) by promoting economic integration and political coordination among Southern Africa's states (including Tanzania). While South Africa is expected to be at the center of the Community, SADC's roots lie in past efforts by its other members to reduce their ties to that country. The organization grew out of the Southern African Development Coordination Conference (SADCC), which was created by the region's then–black-ruled states in 1980 to lessen their dependency on white-ruled South Africa. Each SADCC government assumed responsibility for research and planning in a specific developmental area: Angola for energy, Mozambique for transport and communication, Tanzania for industry, and so on.

In its first decade, SADCC succeeded in attracting considerable outside aid for building and rehabilitating its member states' infrastructure. The organization's greatest success was the Beira corridor project, which enabled the Mozambican port to serve once more as a major regional transit point. Other successes included telecommunications independence of South Africa, new regional power grids, and the upgrading of Tanzanian roads to carry Malawian goods to the port of Dar es Salaam. In 1992, with South Africa's liberation on the horizon, the potential for a more ambitious and inclusive SADC grouping became possible.

In 1996, South African president Nelson Mandela replaced Botswana's president, Sir Ketumile Masire, as SADC chairman, while Pretoria became the headquarters of a new SADC "Organ for Politics Defense and Security." The new South Africa's role as security coordinator within SADC was especially ironic: Before 1990, it had been the violent destabilizing policies of South Africa's military that had sabotaged efforts toward building greater regional cooperation. SADCC members, especially those that were further linked as the so-called Frontline States (Angola, Botswana, Mozambique, Tanzania, Zambia, and Zimbabwe), were then hostile to South Africa's racial policies. To varying degrees, they provided havens for those oppressed by these policies. South Africa responded by striking out against its exiled opponents through overt and covert military operations, while encouraging insurgent movements among some of its neighbors, most notably in Angola and Mozambique.

In Angola, South Africa (along with the United States) backed the rebel movement UNITA, while in Mozambique, it assisted RENAMO. Both of these movements resorted to the destruction of the railways and roads in their operational areas, a tactic that greatly increased the dependence on South African communications of the landlocked states of Botswana, Malawi, Zambia, and Zimbabwe. It is estimated that in the 1980s, the overall monetary cost to the Frontline States of South Africa's destabilization campaign was about $60 billion. (The same countries' combined annual gross national product was only about $25 billion in 1989.) The human costs were even greater: Hundreds of thousands of people were killed; at least equal numbers were maimed; and in Mozambique alone, more than 1 million people became refugees.

In the Southern African context, South Africa remains a military superpower. Despite the imposition of a United Nations arms embargo between 1977 and 1994, the country's military establishment was able to secure both the arms and sophisticated technology needed to develop its own military/industrial complex. Now a global arms exporter, South Africa is nearly self-sufficient in basic munitions, with a vast and advanced arsenal of weapons. Whereas in 1978 it imported 75 percent of its weapons, today that figure is less than 5 percent. By the 1980s, the country had also developed a nuclear arsenal, which it now claims to have dismantled. However, the former embargo was not entirely ineffective—

while South African industry produced many sophisticated weapons systems, it found it increasingly difficult to maintain its regional superiority in such high-technology fields as fighter aircraft. By 1989, the increasing edge of Angolan pilots and air-defense systems was a significant factor in the former South African regime's decision to disengage from the Angolan Civil War. The economic costs of South African militarization were also steep. In addition to draining some 20 percent of its total budget outlays, the destabilization campaign contributed to increased international economic sanctions, which between 1985 and 1990 cost its own economy at least $20 billion. Today, both South Africa and its neighbors hope to benefit from a "peace dividend." But after a generation of militarization, progress in shifting resources from lethal to peaceful pursuits will be gradual.

Throughout the 1980s, South Africa justified its acts of aggression by claiming that it was engaged in counterinsurgency operations against guerrillas of the African National Congress (ANC) and Pan Africanist Congress (PAC), which were then struggling for the regime's overthrow. In fact, the various Frontline States took a cautious attitude toward the activities of South African political refugees, generally forbidding them from launching armed attacks from across their borders. In 1984, both Angola and Mozambique formally signed agreements of mutual noninterference with South Africa. But within a year, these accords had repeatedly and blatantly been violated by South Africa.

Drought, along with continued warfare, has resulted in recurrent food shortages in much of Southern Africa in recent decades—again especially in Angola and Mozambique. The early 1980s' drought in Southern Africa neither lasted as long as nor was as widely publicized as those of West Africa and the Horn, yet it was as destructive. Although some countries, such as Botswana, Mozambique, and Zimbabwe, as well as areas of South Africa, suffered more from nature than others, the main features of the crisis were the same: water reserves were depleted; cattle and game died; and crop production declined, often by 50 percent or more.

Maize and cereal production suffered everywhere. South Africa and Zimbabwe, which are usually grain exporters, had to import food. The countries of Angola, Botswana, and Lesotho each had more than half a million people who were affected by the shortfalls, while some 2 million were malnourished in Mozambique. But in 1988, the rains returned to the region, raising cereal production by 40 percent. Zimbabwe was able not only to export but also to provide food aid to other African countries. However, South African destabilization contributed to continuing food scarcities in many parts of Angola and Mozambique.

In 1991–1992, the entire region was once more pushed toward catastrophe, with the onset of the worst single drought year in at least a century. Although most of the region experienced improved rainfall in 1993–1994, many areas are still afflicted by food shortages, while the entire region

(United Nations photo by Jerry Frank)

South Africa's economic and military and economic dominance overshadows the region's planning. Pictured above is Cape Town, South Africa's chief port and the country's legislative capital.

remains vulnerable to famine. Up to 4.5 million people remain at risk of starvation in Mozambique, and another 3 million in Angola, while Malawi has had to struggle to feed hundreds of thousands of Mozambican refugees along with its own population.

A NEW ERA

Recent events have given rise to hopes for a new era of peace and progress in the region. In 1988, Angola, Cuba, and South Africa reached an agreement, with U.S. and Soviet support, that led to South Africa's withdrawal from Namibia and the removal of Cuban troops from Angola, where they had been supporting government forces. In 1990, Namibia gained its independence under the elected leadership of SWAPO—the liberation movement that had fought against local South African occupation for more than a quarter of a century. In Mozambique, two decades of fighting between the FRE-LIMO government and South African–backed RENAMO rebels ended in a peace process that has resulted in the successful holding of two multiparty elections. In Zambia and Malawi, multiparty democracy was restored, resulting in the electoral defeat of long-serving authoritarian rulers. The most significant development in the region, however, has been South Africa's transformation. There, the 1990 release of prominent political prisoners, particularly Nelson Mandela, the unbanning of the ANC and PAC, and the lifting of internal state-of-emergency restrictions resulted in extended negotiations that led to an end to white-minority rule.

Southern Africa has also experienced some reversals. After an on-again/off-again start, direct negotiations between the Angolan government and UNITA rebels led in 1991 to a UN–supervised peace process based on multiparty elections. But this agreement collapsed in 1992, when UNITA rejected the election results. Although external support for UNITA is now minimal, casualties in the renewed fighting are as high as ever. Lesotho is also being rocked by (less violent) political turmoil as a result of continuing military opposition to the 1993 emergence of the nation's first freely elected government in two decades.

Having finally come to the end of its epoch of struggle against white-minority rule, Southern Africa as a whole may be on the threshold of sustained growth. Besides their now-shared commitment to nonracialism, cooperation among the states is being facilitated by their new-found, yet still tenuous, commitment to democracy. Economic thinking within the region has also converged toward a consensus favorable to the growth of market economies. While Angola, Mozambique,

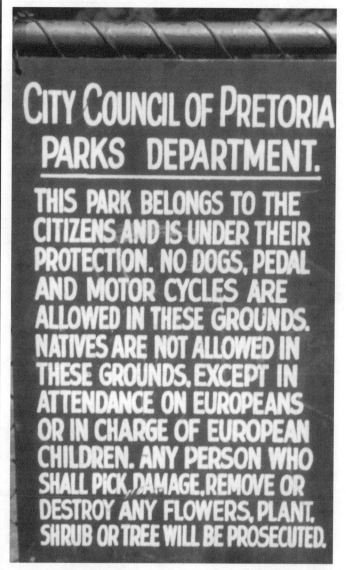

(United Nations photo)

This sign, once displayed in a park in Pretoria, South Africa, reflected the restrictions of apartheid, formerly the South African government's official policy of racial discrimination.

Tanzania, Zambia, and Zimbabwe have all moved away from past commitments to various shades of state-centered socialism, the South African economy is being freed from the statist distortions of apartheid. While reconstruction will take time, its resource base and human as well as physical infrastructure could make Southern Africa a major global nexus in the twenty-first century.

Angola (Republic of Angola)

GEOGRAPHY

Area in Square Miles (Kilometers):
481,351 (1,246,699) (about
twice the size of Texas)
Capital (Population): Luanda
(2,081,000)
Environmental Concerns: soil
erosion; desertification;
deforestation; loss of habitat
and biodiversity; water
pollution
Geographical Features: a narrow
coastal plain rises abruptly to
a vast interior plateau
Climate: semiarid in south and
along coast to Luanda; the
north has a cool, dry season
and then a hot, rainy season

PEOPLE

Population

Total: 10,146,000
Annual Growth Rate: 2.15%
Rural/Urban Population Ratio: 68/32
Major Languages: Portuguese;
Bantu and other African languages
Ethnic Makeup: 37% Ovimbundu;
25% Kimbundu; 13%
Bakongo; 25% others
Religions: 47% indigenous
beliefs; 38% Roman Catholic;
15% Protestant

Health

Life Expectancy at Birth: 37
years (male); 40 years (female)
Infant Mortality Rate (Ratio):
196/1,000
Physicians Available (Ratio):
1/15,136

Education

Adult Literacy Rate: 42%
Compulsory (Ages): 7–15; free

COMMUNICATION

Telephones: 72,000 main lines
Daily Newspaper Circulation:
11 per 1,000 people
Televisions: 48 per 1,000 people
Internet Service Providers: 2 (1999)

TRANSPORTATION

Highways in Miles (Kilometers): 47,508 (76,626)
Railroads in Miles (Kilometers): 1,982 (3,189)
Usable Airfields: 249
Motor Vehicles in Use: 223,000

GOVERNMENT

Type: transitional government
Independence Date: November 11, 1975
(from Portugal)
Head of State/Government: President José
Edouardo dos Santos is both head of
state and head of government

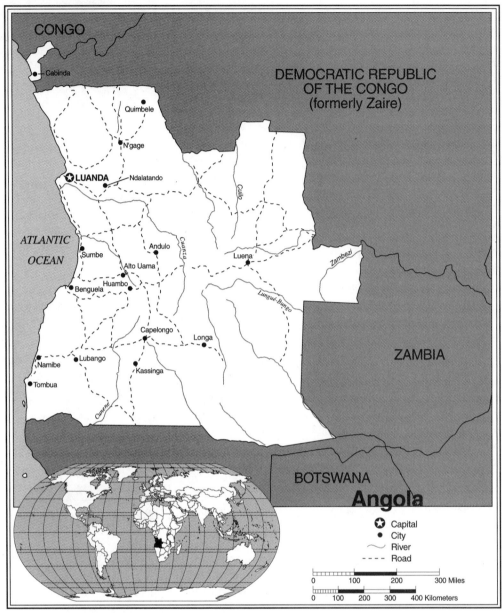

Political Parties: Popular Movement for the
Liberation of Angola; National Front for
the Liberation of Angola; others
Suffrage: universal at 18

MILITARY

Military Expenditures (% of GDP): 25%
Current Disputes: civil war

ECONOMY

Currency ($ U.S. Equivalent): 900,000
kwanzas = $1
Per Capita Income/GDP: $1,030/$11.6 billion
GDP Growth Rate: 4%
Inflation Rate: 270%
Unemployment Rate: unemployment and
underemployment affect more than half
the population

Labor Force: 5,000,000
Natural Resources: petroleum; diamonds;
phosphates; iron ore; copper; feldspar;
gold; bauxite; uranium
Agriculture: coffee; sisal; cotton; sugarcane;
tobacco; vegetables; bananas;
plantains; livestock; forest products; fish
Industry: petroleum; minerals; fish processing;
brewing; tobacco products; textiles;
food processing; construction; others
Exports: $5 billion (primary partners United
States, Europe, China)
Imports: $3 billion (primary partners
Portugal, United States, South Africa)

http://www.sas.upenn.edu/
African_Studies/Country_Specific/
Angola.html

ANGOLA

Throughout much of 1999 and 2000, the government of Angola was able to take the military offensive against the rebel Union for Total Independence of Angola (UNITA). This followed the September 1998 break-off of talks between the two sides as a result of UNITA's continuing refusal to disarm. Notwithstanding the capture of a number of UNITA strongholds and the increasing success of international sanctions against the movement, the three-decade-long civil war, which has decimated the country's population, shows little sign of being resolved in the near future.

In 1996, hopes for a cease-fire had been raised when UNITA agreed in principle to join the governing Popular Movement for the Liberation of Angola (MPLA) in forming a "government of National Unity," but a settlement has never been implemented. Instead, both sides have maintained their military capacities while supporting proxy forces in neighboring states. With friendly governments now installed in Congo and the Deomcratic Republic of the Congo, the Angolan authorities seem to believe that they can gain the military advantage over their UNITA foes. History, however, suggests that there may be no military solution to Angola's long-standing political problems.

Since 1975, more than half a million Angolans have perished as a result of fighting between the two movements, including many passive victims of land mines. Up to 1 million others have fled the country, while another 1 million or so have been internally displaced. According to a report by the human-rights organization Africa Watch, tens of thousands of Angolans have lost their limbs "because of the indiscriminate use of landmines by both sides of the conflict." Angola's small and impoverished population could not have perpetuated such carnage were it not for decades of external interference in the nation's internal affairs. The United States, the former Soviet Union, South Africa, Cuba, Zaire, and many others have helped to create and sustain this tragedy.

Since 1991, with the end of the Cold War and the demise of South Africa's apartheid regime, there has been an almost complete cutoff of outside support for the conflict. An agreement in April 1991 between the MPLA and UNITA to participate in United Nations–sponsored elections led to a dramatic decline in violence during 16 months of "phony peace." The successful holding of elections in September 1992 further raised hopes of a new beginning for Angola. While the MPLA appeared to have topped the poll, UNITA and the smaller National Front for the Liberation of Angola (FNLA) secured a considerable vote. But hopes for a new beginning under an all-party government of national unity were quickly dashed by UNITA's rejection of the election result. As a result, the country was plunged into renewed civil war.

THE COLONIAL LEGACY

The roots of Angola's long suffering lie in the area's colonial underdevelopment. The Portuguese first made contact with the peoples of the region in 1483. They initially established peaceful trading contact with the powerful Kongo kingdom and other coastal peoples, some of whom were converted to Catholicism by Jesuit missionaries. But from then to the mid-1800s, the outsiders primarily saw the area as a source of slaves. Angola has been called the "mother of Brazil" because up to 4 million Angolans were carried away from its shores to that country, chained in the holds of slave ships. With the possible exception of Nigeria, no African territory lost more of its people to the trans-Atlantic slave trade.

Following the nineteenth-century suppression of the slave trade, the Portuguese introduced internal systems of exploitation that very often amounted to slavery in all but name. Large numbers of Angolans were pressed into working on coffee plantations owned by a growing community of white settlers. Others were forced to labor in other sectors, such as diamond mines or public-works projects.

Although the Portuguese claimed that they encouraged Angolans to learn Portuguese and practice Catholicism, thus becoming "assimilated" into the world of the colonizers, they actually made little effort to provide education. No more than 2 percent of the population ever achieved the legal status of *assimilado*. The assimilados, many of whom were of mixed race, were concentrated in the coastal towns. Of the few interior Angolans who became literate, a large proportion were the products of Protestant, non-Portuguese, mission schools. Because each mission tended to operate in a particular region and teach from its own syllabus, usually in the local language, an unfortunate by-product of these schools was the reinforcement (the creation, some would argue) of ethnic rivalries among the territory's educated elite.

In the late colonial period, the FNLA, MPLA, and UNITA emerged as the three major liberation movements challenging Portuguese rule. Although all three sought a national following, each built up an ethnoregional core of support by 1975. The FNLA grew out of a movement whose original focus was limited to the northern Kongo-speaking population, while UNITA's principal stronghold has been the largely Ovimbundu-speaking south-central plateaux. The MPLA has its strongest following among assimilados and Kimbundu speakers, who are predominant in Luanda, the capital, and the interior to the west of the city. From the beginning, all three movements have cultivated separate sources of external support.

The armed struggle against the Portuguese began in 1961, with a massive FNLA–inspired uprising in the north and MPLA–led unrest in Luanda. To counter the northern rebellion, the Portuguese resorted to the saturation bombing of villages. In the first year of fighting, this left an estimated 50,000 dead (about half the

(United Nations photo by J. P. Laffont)

Angola's war for independence from Portugal led to the creation of a one-party state.

The Kongo state develops **1400s**	The Portuguese make contact with the Kongo state **1483**	Queen Nzinga defends the Mbundu kingdom against the Portuguese **1640**	The MPLA is founded in Luanda **1956**	The national war of liberation begins **1961**	Angola gains independence from Portugal **1975**	South African–initiated air and ground incursions into Angola **1976**	President Agostinho Neto dies; José dos Santos becomes president **1979**	Jonas Savimbi visits the United States; U.S. "material and moral" support for UNITA resumes **1986**	Talks for national reconciliation break down; multiparty elections are held **1990s**

2000s

Civil war continues

total number killed throughout the anti-colonial struggle). The liberation forces were as much hampered by their own disunity as by the brutality of Portugal's counterinsurgency tactics. Undisciplined rebels associated with the FNLA, for example, were known to massacre not only Portuguese plantation owners but many of their southern workers as well. Such incidents contributed to UNITA's split from the FNLA in 1966. There is also evidence of UNITA forces cooperating with the Portuguese in attacks on the MPLA. Besides competition with its two rivals, the MPLA also encountered some difficulty in keeping its urban and rural factions united.

CIVIL WAR

The overthrow of Portugal's fascist government in 1974 led to Angola's rapid decolonization. Attempts to create a transitional government of national unity among the three major nationalist movements failed. The MPLA succeeded in seizing Luanda, which led to a loose alliance between the FNLA and UNITA. As fighting between the groups escalated, so did the involvement of their foreign backers. Meanwhile, most of Angola's 300,000 or more white settlers fled the country, triggering the collapse of much of the local economy. With the notable exception of Angola's offshore oil industry, most economic sectors have since failed to recover their preindependence output as a result of the war.

While the chronology of outside intervention in the Angolan conflict is a matter of dispute, it is nonetheless clear that, by October 1975, up to 2,000 South African troops were assisting the FNLA–UNITA forces in the south. In response, Cuba dispatched a force of 18,000 to 20,000 to assist the MPLA, which earlier had gained control of Luanda. These events proved decisive during the war's first phase. On

the one hand, collaboration with South Africa led to the withdrawal of Chinese and much of the African support for the FNLA–UNITA cause. It also contributed to the U.S. Congress' passage of the Clarke Amendment, which abruptly terminated the United States' direct involvement. On the other hand, the arrival of the Cubans allowed the MPLA quickly to gain the upper hand on the battlefield. Not wishing to fight a conventional war against the Cubans by themselves, the South Africans withdrew their conventional forces in March 1976.

By 1977, the MPLA's "People's Republic" had established itself in all of Angola's provinces. It was recognized by the United Nations and most of its membership as the nation's sole legitimate government, the United States numbering among the few that continued to withhold recognition. However, the MPLA's apparent victory did not bring an end to the hostilities. Although the remaining pockets of FNLA resistance were overcome following an Angola–Zaire rapprochement in 1978, UNITA maintained its largely guerrilla struggle. Until 1989, UNITA's major supporter was South Africa, whose destabilization of the Luanda government was motivated by its desire to keep the Benguela railway closed (thus diverting traffic to its own system) and harass Angola-based SWAPO forces. Besides supplying UNITA with logistical support, the South Africans repeatedly invaded southern Angola and on occasion infiltrated sabotage units into other areas of the country. South African aggression in turn justified Cuba's maintenance (by 1988) of some 50,000 troops in support of the government. In 1986, the U.S. Congress approved the resumption of "covert" U.S. material assistance to UNITA via Zaire.

An escalation of the fighting in 1987 and 1988 was accompanied by a revival of negotiations for a peace settlement among representatives of the Angolan government, Cuba, South Africa, and the United States. In 1988, South African forces were checked in a battle at the Angolan town of Cuito Cuanavale. South Africa agreed to withdraw from Namibia and end its involvement in the Angolan conflict. It was further agreed that Cuba would complete a phased withdrawal of its forces from the region by mid-1991.

The scaling back of external support, in the context of a relaxation of Cold War tensions around the world, provided a basis for further contacts between the warring parties themselves. An agreement in April 1991 between the MPLA president, Eduardo dos Santos, and the UNITA leader, Jonas Savimbi, led to the establishment of a UN–supervised cease-fire and a national reconciliation process. This process culminated in the September 1992 elections. After initially fierce fighting, the renewed civil war degenerated into a bloody stalemate.

UNITA currently occupies up to 75 percent of the countryside, but most of the population is crowded into government-controlled areas. A series of meetings between MPLA and UNITA resulted in a fragile peace in late 1994. The United Nations hoped to inaugurate a new peacekeeping operation in Angola, but the prospects for a lasting peace remain uncertain.

DEVELOPMENT

Most of Angola's export revenues currently come from oil. There are important diamond and iron mines, but their output has suffered due to the war, which has also prevented the exploitation of the country's considerable reserves of other minerals. Angola has enormous agricultural potential, but only about 2% of its arable land is under cultivation.

FREEDOM

Despite new constitutional guarantees, pessimists note that neither UNITA nor MPLA has demonstrated a strong commitment to democracy and human rights in the past. Within UNITA, Jonas Savimbi's word has been law; he has been known to have critics within his movement burned as "witches." For a time UNITA had its own Internet address, perhaps the first armed faction to do so.

HEALTH/WELFARE

Civil war has caused a serious deterioration of Angola's health services, resulting in lower life expectancy and one of the highest infant mortality rates in the world.

ACHIEVEMENTS

Between 1975 and 1980, the Angolan government claimed that it had tripled the nation's primary-school enrollment, to 76%. That figure subsequently dropped as a result of war.

Botswana (Republic of Botswana)

GEOGRAPHY

Area in Square Miles (Kilometers): 231,804 (600,372) (about the size of Texas)

Capital (Population): Gaborone (184,000)

Environmental Concerns: overgrazing; desertification; limited freshwater resources

Geographical Features: mainly flat to gently rolling tableland; Kalahari Desert in the southwest

Climate: semiarid; warm winters and hot summers

PEOPLE

Population

Total: 1,576,500*

Annual Growth Rate: 0.76%*

Rural/Urban Population Ratio: 37/63

Major Languages: English; Setswana

Ethnic Makeup: 95% Batswana; 4% Basarwa, Kalanga, and Kgalagadi; 1% white

Religions: 50% indigenous beliefs; 50% Christian

Health

Life Expectancy at Birth: 37 years (male); 40 years (female)

Infant Mortality Rate (Ratio): 61.9/1,000*

Physicians Available (Ratio): 1/4,395

Education

Adult Literacy Rate: 70%

COMMUNICATION

Telephones: 86,000 main lines

Daily Newspaper Circulation: 29 per 1,000 people

Televisions: 24 per 1,000 people

Internet Service Providers: 2 (1999)

TRANSPORTATION

Highways in Miles (Kilometers): 11,459 (18,482)

Railroads in Miles (Kilometers): 583 (940)

Usable Airfields: 92

Motor Vehicles in Use: 100,000

GOVERNMENT

Type: parliamentary republic

Independence Date: September 30, 1966 (from the United Kingdom)

Head of State/Government: President Festus Mogae is both head of state and head of government

Political Parties: Botswana Democratic Party; Botswana Alliance Movement (Coalition); Botswana National Front; Botswana Congress Party; Botswana People's Party

Suffrage: universal at 18

MILITARY

Military Expenditures (% of GDP): 1.2%

Current Disputes: territorial dispute with Namibia

ECONOMY

Currency ($ U.S. Equivalent): 1.71 pulas = $1

Per Capita Income/GDP: $3,900/$5.7 billion

GDP Growth Rate: 6.5%

Inflation Rate: 7.7%

Unemployment Rate: 20%–40%

Natural Resources: diamonds; copper; nickel; salt; soda ash; potash; coal; iron ore; silver

Agriculture: sorghum; maize; millet; pulses; peanuts; cowpeas; beans; sunflower seeds; livestock

Industry: diamonds; copper; nickel; salt; soda ash; potash; tourism; livestock processing

Exports: $2.36 billion (primary partners Europe, Southern Africa)

Imports: $2.05 billion (primary partners Southern Africa, Europe)

 http://www.sas.upenn.edu/ African_Studies/Country_Specific/ Botswana.html

*Note: These estimates explicitly take into account the effects of excess mortality due to AIDS.

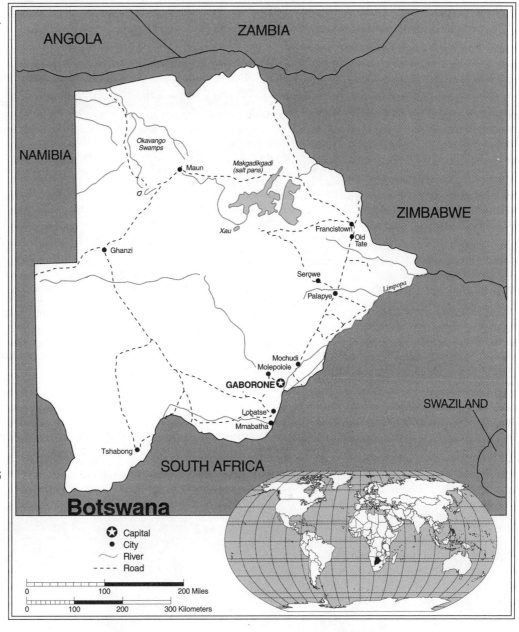

BOTSWANA

Since its independence in 1966, Botswana has enjoyed one of the highest average economic growth rates in the world. This has resulted in a better life for many of its citizens. But serious challenges remain if the country is to realize the ambitious goals contained within its "Vision 2016" program of national development. Economic growth has not been accompanied by equity. More than 40 percent of households remain below the official poverty line. The country also shares with its neighbors South Africa and Zimbabwe the sad distinction of having the highest HIV infection rates in the world. A third concern is the feeling of many Batswana that their country's private sector continues to be dominated by noncitizens.

The man currently leading Botswana in the face of the above challenges is the country's third president, Festus Mogae, who was inaugurated in April 1998 following the retirement of the long-serving Sir Ketumile Masire (1980–1998). In October 1999, Mogae and his Botswana Democratic Party won an easy victory in national elections, against a divided opposition. But his government was subsequently rocked by conflict between several veteran members of the cabinet and the youthful, charismatic vice-president, Ian Khama, a former army commander and the son of the country's first president, Sir Seretse Khama (1966–1980). In August 2000, it was announced that Ian Khama would be given a new co-

ordinating role to assure adequate performance by various ministries, leading many local commentators to proclaim him as Botswana's first "prime minister."

Over the past four decades, Botswana has been hailed as a model of postcolonial development in Africa. When the country emerged from 81 years of British colonial occupation, it was ranked as one of the 10 poorest countries in the world, with an annual per capita income of just $69. In the years since, the nation's economy has grown at an average annual rate of 9 percent. Social services have been steadily expanded, and infrastructure has been created. Whereas at independence the country had no significant paved roads, most major towns and villages are now interlinked by ribbons of asphalt and tarmac. The nation's capital, Gaborone, has emerged as a vibrant city. Schools, hospitals, and businesses dot the landscape, while the country's all-digital telecommunications network is among the most advanced in the world. But the failure of such gowth to promote greater equity has also led to a rise in social tension.

Botswana's economic success has come in the context of its unbroken postindependence commitment to political pluralism, respect for human rights, and racial and ethnic tolerance. Freedoms of speech and association have been upheld. In October 1994, the nation held its seventh successive multiparty elections. The Botswana Democratic Party, which has ruled since independence, won with a greatly reduced majority. As a result, a genuine

two-party competition has now emerged, with the left-leaning opposition Botswana National Front taking on the role of an alternative government-in-waiting. The Botswana Democratic Party won its eighth consecutive victory in national elections in 1999.

Most of Botswana's people share Setswana as their first language—a tongue that is commonly spoken in much of South Africa. There also exist a number of sizable minority communities—Kalanga, Herero, Khalagari, Khoisan groups, and others—but contemporary ethnic conflict is relatively modest. In the nineteenth century, most of Botswana was incorporated into five Tswana states, each centering around a large settlement of 10,000 people or more. These states, which incorporated non-Tswana communities, survived through agropastoralism, hunting, and their control of trade routes linking Southern and Central Africa.

Lucrative dealing in ivory and ostrich feathers allowed local rulers to build up their arsenals and thus deter the aggressive designs of South African whites. An attempt by white settlers to seize control of southeastern Botswana was defeated in an 1852–1853 war. However, European missionaries and traders were welcomed, leading to a growth of Christian education and the consumption of industrial goods.

A radical transformation took place after the imposition of British overrule in 1885. Colonial taxes and economic decline stimulated the growth of migrant la-

(United Nations photo by E. Darroch)

Botswana, like many other African nations, is susceptible to periodic drought. The country, however, has a good supply of underground water and the governmental competence to utilize this resource. In this photograph, antelopes drink from a hole dug to allow water seepage.

| Emergence of the Tswana trading center at Toutswemogala **700s** | Kololo and Ndebele invaders devastate the countryside **1820s** | Tswana begin to acquire guns through trade in ivory and other game products **1830s** | Batswana defeat Boer invaders **1852–1853** | The British establish colonial rule over Botswana **1885** | Botswana regains its independence **1966** | Elections in 1984 and 1989 result in landslide victories for the Democratic Party; the National Front is the major opposition party **1980s** | The ruling Democratic Party wins the 1994 and 1999 elections, but the opposition National Front makes significant gains **1990s** |

2000s

Despite astounding national economic growth, many Batswana remain poor

HIV/AIDS crisis

bor to the mines and industries of South Africa. (In some regions, migrant earnings remain the major source of income to this day.) Although colonial rule brought much hardship and little benefit, the twentieth-century relationship between the people of Botswana and the British was complicated by local fears of being incorporated into South Africa. For many decades, leading nationalists championed continued rule from London as a shield against their powerful, racially oppressive neighbor.

ECONOMIC DEVELOPMENT

Economic growth since independence has been largely fueled by the rapid expansion of mining activity. Botswana has become one of the world's leading producers of diamonds, which typically account for 80 percent of its export earnings. Local production is managed by Debswana Corporation, an even partnership between the Botswana government and DeBeers, a South Africa-based global corporation; DeBeers' Central Selling Organization has a near monopoly on diamond sales worldwide. The Botswana government has a good record of maximizing the local benefits of Debswana's production.

The nickel/copper/cobalt mining complex at Selibi-Pikwe is the largest nongovernment employer in Botswana. Falling metal prices and high development costs have reduced the mine's profitability, but high operating efficiency has assured its survival. However, given that mining can make only a modest contribution to local employment, and because of the potential vulnerability of the diamond market, Botswana is seeking to expand its small manufacturing and service sectors. Meat processing is currently the largest industrial activity outside minerals, but efforts are under way to attract overseas invest-

ment in both private and parastatal production. Botswana already has a liberal foreign exchange policy and has established an Export Processing Zone at Selibi-Pikwe. Small-scale production is encouraged through government subsidies.

Tourism is of growing importance. Northern Botswana is particularly noted for its bountiful wildlife and stunning scenery. The region includes the Okavango Delta, a vast and uniquely beautiful swamp area, and the Chobe National Park, home of the world's largest elephant herds.

Agriculture is still the leading economic activity for most Botswana citizens. The standard Tswana greeting, *Pula* ("Rain"), reflects the significance attached to water in a society prone to its periodic scarcity. Botswana suffered severe droughts between 1980 and 1987 and again in 1991 and 1992, which—despite the availability of underground water supplies—had a devastating effect on both crops and livestock. Up to 1 million cattle are believed to have perished. Small-scale agropastoralists, who make up the largest segment of the population, were particularly hard hit. However, government relief measures prevented famine. The government provides generous subsidies to farmers, but environmental constraints hamper efforts to achieve food self-sufficiency even in non-drought years.

Commercial agriculture is dominated by livestock. The Lobatse abbatoir, opened in 1954, stimulated the growth of the cattle industry. Despite periodic challenges from disease and drought, beef exports have become relatively stable. Much of the output of the Botswana Meat Commission has preferential access to the European Union. There is some concern about the potential for future reductions in the European quota. Because most of Botswana's herds are grazed in communal lands, questions

about the allocation of pasture are a source of local debate. There is also a growing, but largely misinformed, international concern that wildlife are being threatened by overgrazing livestock.

SOUTH AFRICA

Until recently, Botswana's progress has taken place against a backdrop of political hostility on the part of its powerful neighbor, South Africa. Since the nineteenth-century, Botswana has sheltered refugees from racist oppression elsewhere in the region. This led to periodic acts of aggression against the country, especially during the 1980s, when Botswana became the repeated victim of overt military raids and covert terrorist operations. The establishment of a nonracial democracy in South Africa has led to a normalization of relations. In 1992, the two countries established formal diplomatic ties for the first time. Botswana has, nonetheless, continued to increase its military spending in recent years, stirring public controversy.

Gaborone is the headquarters of the Southern African Development Community, which was originally conceived to reduce the economic dependence of its 10 member nations on the South African apartheid state. SADC now plans to transform itself into a common market that could eventually include a democratic South Africa. Despite the countries' political differences, Botswana has maintained a customs union with South Africa that dates back to the colonial era.

DEVELOPMENT

The United Nations' 1990 Human Development Report singles out Botswana among the nations of Africa for significantly improving the living conditions of its people. In 1989, President Masire was awarded The Hunger Project's leadership prize, based on Botswana's record of improving rural nutritional levels during the 1980s despite 7 years of severe drought.

FREEDOM

Democratic pluralism has been strengthened by the growth of a strong civil society and an independent press. Concern has been voiced about social and economic discrimination against Khoisan-speaking communities living in remote areas of the Kalahari, who are known to many outsiders as "Bushmen."

HEALTH/WELFARE

After years of being praised as a model of primary health-care delivery, Botswana's public-health service has come under increased criticism for a perceived decline in quality. Botswana's high HIV-positive rate has placed the system under serious stress.

ACHIEVEMENTS

In 1999, Botswana's Mpule Kwelagobe was crowned as Miss Universe. In July 2000, Botswana launched its first national television service. A UN report ranked Botswana first in Africa in its percentage of women holding middle- and senior-level managerial positions.

Lesotho (Kingdom of Lesotho)

GEOGRAPHY

Area in Square Miles (Kilometers):
11,716 (30,344) (about the
size of Maryland)

Capital (Population): Maseru
(400,200)

Environmental Concerns:
overgrazing; soil erosion; soil
exhaustion; desertification;
water pressures

Geographical Features: mostly
highland, with plateaus, hills,
and mountains; landlocked

Climate: temperate

PEOPLE

Population

Total: 2,143,200
Annual Growth Rate: 1.65%
Rural/Urban Population Ratio:
75/25
Major Languages: English; Sesotho
Ethnic Makeup: 99.7% Sotho
Religions: 80% Christian; 20%
indigenous beliefs

Health

Life Expectancy at Birth: 49
years (male); 54 years (female)
Infant Mortality Rate (Ratio):
83/1,000
Physicians Available (Ratio):
1/14,306

Education

Adult Literacy Rate: 71.3%
Compulsory (Ages): 6–13; free

COMMUNICATION

Telephones: 20,000 main lines
Daily Newspaper Circulation: 7
per 1,000 people
Televisions: 7 per 1,000 people
Internet Service Providers: 1
(1999)

TRANSPORTATION

Highways in Miles (Kilometers):
2,973 (4,955)
Railroads in Miles (Kilometers):
1.6 (2.6)
Usable Airfields: 29
Motor Vehicles in Use: 23,000

GOVERNMENT

Type: parliamentary constitutional monarchy
Independence Date: October 4, 1966
(from the United Kingdom)
Head of State/Government: King Letsie
III; Prime Minister Pakalitha Mosisili
Political Parties: Basotho National Party;
Basutoland Congress Party; Marematlou
Freedom Party; United Democratic
Party; others
Suffrage: universal at 18

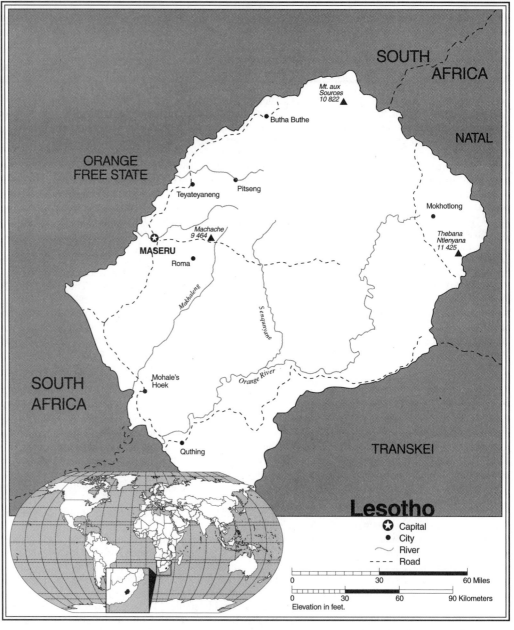

MILITARY

Current Disputes: none

ECONOMY

Currency ($ U.S, Equivalent): 3.54
malotis = $1
Per Capita Income/GDP: $2,240/$4.7 billion
GDP Growth Rate: –10%
Inflation Rate: 8%
Unemployment Rate: substantial unemploy-
ment and underemployment, affecting
more than half of the labor force
Labor Force: 689,000
Natural Resources: water; agricultural and
grazing land; some diamonds and other
minerals

Agriculture: corn; wheat; sorghum; pulses;
barley; livestock
Industry: food and beverages; textiles;
handicrafts; construction; tourism
Exports: $235 million (primary partners
Southern Africa, North America)
Imports: $700 million (primary partners
Southern Africa, Asia)

 http://www.mbendi.co.za/cylecy.htm
http://www.sas.upenn.edu/
African_Studies/Country_Specific/
Lesotho. html

| Lesotho emerges as a leading state in Southern Africa 1820s | Afrikaners annex half of Lesotho 1866 | The Sotho successfully fight to preserve local autonomy under the British 1870–1881 | Independence is restored 1966 | The elections and Constitution are declared void by Leabua Jonathan 1970 | An uprising against the government fails 1974 | The Lesotho Liberation Army begins a sabotage campaign 1979 | South African destabilization leads to the overthrow of Jonathan by the military 1986 | Troops from South Africa and Botswana intervene in Lesotho to avert a coup 1990s |

2000s

The country prepares for elections

LESOTHO

In February 2000, the people of Lesotho united in celebrating the wedding of King Letsie to Karabo Motsoeneng. The event allowed them to briefly take their minds off their country's difficulties. Since October 1998, the country has been ruled by a transitional executive that is preparing for elections in 2001, under a revised Constitution. The arrangement was put in place following the September 1998 intervention of Botswana and South African troops in support of the previous government, which had claimed that it was about to be ousted by a military coup. Large segments of Lesotho's defense force resisted the intervention, causing scores of deaths on both sides. In the process, many businesses in the capital city, Maseru, and other centers were heavily looted by rioters, who directed much of their anger against Asians.

Listed by the United Nations as one of the world's "least-developed" nations, each year the lack of opportunity at home causes up to half of Lesotho's adult males to seek employment in neighboring South Africa, where jobs are becoming increasingly scarce. The retrenchment of Basotho mineworkers has led to a local unemployment rate of nearly 50 percent. This dire economic situation is aggravated by Lesotho's chronic political instability.

Lesotho is one of the most ethnically homogeneous nations in Africa; almost all of its citizens are Sotho. The country's emergence and survival were largely the product of the diplomatic and military prowess of its nineteenth-century rulers, especially its great founder, King Moshoeshoe I. In the 1860s, warfare with South African whites led to the loss of land and people as well as an acceptance of British overrule. For nearly a century, the British preserved the country but also taxed the inhabitants and generally neglected their interests. Consequently, Lesotho remained dependent on South Africa. However, despite South African attempts to incorporate the country politically as well as economically, Lesotho's independence was restored by the British in 1966.

Lesotho's politicians were bitterly divided at independence. The conservative Basotho National Party (BNP) had won an upset victory in preindependence elections, with strong backing from the South African government and the local Roman Catholic Church—Lesotho's largest Christian denomination. The opposition, which walked out of the independence talks, was polarized between a pro-royalist faction, the Marematlou Freedom Party (whose regional sympathies largely lay with the African National Congress of South Africa), and the Basotho Congress Party (or BCP, which was allied with the rival Pan-Africanist Congress).

Soon after independence, the BNP prime minister, Leabua Jonathan, placed the king, Moshoeshoe II, under house arrest. (Later, the king was temporarily exiled.) The BCP won the 1970 elections, but Jonathan, possibly at the behest of South Africa, declared a state of emergency and nullified the results.

In the early 1980s, armed resistance to Jonathan's dictatorship was carried out by the Lesotho Liberation Army (LLA), an armed faction of the BCP. The Lesotho government maintained that the LLA was aided and abetted by South Africa as part of that country's regional destabilization efforts. By 1983, both the South African government and the Catholic Church hierarchy were becoming nervous about Jonathan's establishment of diplomatic ties with various Communist-ruled countries and the growing sympathy within the BNP, in particular its increasingly radical youth wing, for the ANC. South African military raids and terrorist attacks targeting anti-apartheid refugees in Lesotho became increasingly common. Finally, a South African blockade of Lesotho in 1986 led directly to Jonathan's ouster by his military.

Lesotho's new ruling Military Council, initially led by Major General Justinus Lekhanya, was closely linked to South Africa. In 1990, Lekhanya had Moshoeshoe II exiled (for the second time), after he refused to agree to the dismissals of several senior officers. Moshoeshoe's son Letsie was installed in his place. In 1991, Lekhanya was himself toppled by the army. The new leader, General Elias Rameama, promised to hold multiparty elections. In 1992, Moshoeshoe returned, to a hero's welcome, but he was prevented from resuming his role as monarch. His status was uncertain after elections in March 1993 brought the BCP back to power.

Under its aging leader, Ntsu Mokhele, the BCP faced military opposition to its rule. An outbreak of internal fighting within the RLDF culminated, in April 1994, in the assassination of the deputy prime minister and the kidnapping of cabinet members by mutinous soldiers. In August, King Letsie tried to dismiss the government and suspend the constitution. In the face of growing unrest, Botswana, South Africa, and Zimbabwe acted on behalf of the Southern African Development Community as mediators—and subsequently as guarantors—of constitutional rule. The BCP and Moshoeshoe were both restored to power; the latter was killed in January 1996 in an auto accident. In June 1997, a schism in the BCP's ranks led Mokhele to establish the new Lesotho Congress for Democracy (LCD) Party, taking most of the BCP with him. The LCD won a landslide victory in May 1998 elections, but the remnants of the BCP and other opposition parties refused to accept the result, inciting King Letsie and the military to intervene. The resulting mutiny within the RLDF led to the South African/Botswana intervention to restore order.

DEVELOPMENT

Despite an infusion of international aid, Lesotho's economic dependence on South Africa has not decreased since independence; indeed, it has been calculated that the majority of outside funds have actually ended up paying for South African services.

FREEDOM

In Lesotho, basic freedoms and rights are compromised by continuing political instability. Basotho journalists have come out against proposed measures that they say will gag Lesotho's vigorous independent press.

HEALTH/WELFARE

With many of Lesotho's young men working in the mines of South Africa, much of the resident population relies on subsistence agriculture. Despite efforts to boost production, malnutrition, aggravated by drought, is a serious problem.

ACHIEVEMENTS

Lesotho has long been known for the high quality of its schools, which for more than a century and a half have trained many of the leading citizens of Southern Africa.

Malawi (Republic of Malawi)

GEOGRAPHY

Area in Square Miles (Kilometers):
45,747 (118,484) (about the
size of Pennsylvania)
Capital (Population): Lilongwe
(395,500)
Environmental Concerns:
deforestation; land degradation;
water pollution; siltation of
fish spawning grounds
Geographical Features: narrow,
elongated plateau with rolling
plains, rounded hills, some
mountains; landlocked
Climate: subtropical

PEOPLE

Population
Total: 10,386,000
Annual Growth Rate: 1.61%
Rural/Urban Population Ratio:
86/14
Major Languages: Chichewa;
English; regional languages
Ethnic Makeup: 90% Chewa;
10% Nyanja, Lomwe, other
Bantu groups
Religions: 75% Christian; 20%
Muslim; 5% indigenous
beliefs

Health
Life Expectancy at Birth: 37
years (male); 38 years (female)
Infant Mortality Rate (Ratio):
122.2/1,000
Physicians Available (Ratio):
1/47,634

Education
Adult Literacy Rate: 58%
Compulsory (Ages): 6–14

COMMUNICATION
Telephones: 37,400 main lines
Internet Service Providers: 1
(1999)

TRANSPORTATION
Highways in Miles (Kilometers): 17,608
(28,400)
Railroads in Miles (Kilometers): 489 (789)
Usable Airfields: 44
Motor Vehicles in Use: 55,000

GOVERNMENT
Type: multiparty democracy
Independence Date: July 6, 1964 (from
the United Kingdom)
Head of State/Government: President
Bakili Muluzi is both head of state and
head of government
Political Parties: United Democratic
Front; Malawi Congress Party; Alliance
for Democracy; Malawi Democratic
Party; Social Democratic Party
Suffrage: universal at 18

MILITARY
Military Expenditures (% of GDP): 0.8%
Current Disputes: boundary dispute with
Tanzania

ECONOMY
Currency ($ U.S. Equivalent): 7.84
kwachas = $1
Per Capita Income/GDP: $940/$9.4 billion
GDP Growth Rate: 4.2%
Inflation Rate: 45%
Labor Force: 3,500,000

Natural Resources: limestone; uranium;
coal; bauxite; arable land; hydropower
Agriculture: tobacco; tea; sugarcane;
cotton; potatoes; cassava; sorghum;
pulses; livestock
Industry: tobacco; sugar; tea; sawmill
products; cement; consumer goods
Exports: $510 million (primary partners
South Africa, United States, Germany)
Imports: $512 million (primary partners
South Africa, Zimbabwe, Zambia)

http://www.sas.upenn.edu/
African_Studies/Country_Specific/
Malawi.html

[Map of Malawi]

TANZANIA

Karonga

Livingstonia

ZAMBIA

Mzuzu · *Lake*
Chinteche *Nyasa*
Mzimba

Nkhota
Kota

Mchinji
LILONGWE

MOZAMBIQUE

MOZAMBIQUE

Mangoche
*Lake
Malombe*
*Lake
Chilwa*
Zomba

Blantyre

Chiromo

Malawi

*Mozambique
Channel*

⊕ Capital
● City
〰 River
--- Road

| 0 | 100 | 200 Miles |
| 0 | 100 | 200 | 300 Kilometers |

Malawi trading kingdoms develop **1500s**

Explorer David Livingstone arrives along Lake Malawi; missionaries follow **1859**

The British protectorate of Nyasaland (present-day Malawi) is declared **1891**

Reverend John Chilembwe and followers rise against settlers and are suppressed **1915**

The Nyasaland African Congress, the first nationalist movement, is formed **1944**

Independence, under the leadership of Hastings Banda **1964**

Diplomatic ties are established with South Africa **1967**

"Ngwazi" Hastings Kamuzu Banda becomes president-for-life **1971**

Bakili Muluzi is elected president, ending Banda's 30-year dictatorship **1990s**

2000s

The Malawi economy continues to struggle   Political liberalization

MALAWI

In June 1999, President Bakili Muluzi narrowly won reelection, while his United Democratic Front (UDF) won a plurality of seats in Malawi's second multiparty elections since moving away from 30 years of dictatorial rule under its first president, Dr. Hastings Banda. Muluzi defeated the then–96-year-old Banda in the 1994 elections, which brought an end to what had been one of Africa's most repressive regimes. But since Banda's death in 1997, a degree of nostalgia has emerged regarding his era, perhaps relecting the failure of political liberalization to bring improvement to the country's weak economy, which is largely dependent on tobacco production. The spread of the HIV/AIDS pandemic and a rising crime rate have also shaken public confidence. While the old political order has been swept aside, the new order has yet to deliver better conditions for most Malawians.

Since the early months of independence in 1964, when he purged his cabinet and ruling Malawi Congress Party (MCP) of most of the young politicians who had promoted him to leadership in the nationalist struggle, Banda had ruthlessly used his secret police and MPC's militia, the Malawi Young Pioneers (MYP), to eliminate potential alternatives to his highly personalized dictatorship. Generations of Malawians, including those living abroad, have grown up with the knowledge that voicing critical thoughts about the self-proclaimed "Life President," or *Ngwazi* ("Great Lion"), could prove fatal. Only senior army officers, Banda's long-time "official state hostess" Tamanda Kadzamira, and her uncle John Tembo, the powerful minister of state, survived Ngwazi's jealous exercise of power.

In 1992, Banda's grip began to weaken. Unprecedented antigovernment unrest gave rise to an internal opposition, spearheaded by clergy, underground trade unionists, and a new generation of dissident politicians. By 1993, this opposition had coalesced into two major movements: the southern-based UDF, and the northern-based Alliance for Democracy (AFORD). The detention of AFORD's leader, Chakufwa Chihana, and others failed to stem the tide of opposition. A referendum in June showed two-to-one support for a return to multiparty politics. In November, while Banda was hospitalized in South Africa, young army officers seized the initiative by launching a crackdown against the MYP while purging a number of senior officers from their own ranks. Thereafter, the army played a neutral role in assuring the success of the election.

While the ruthless efficiency of its security apparatus contributed to past perceptions of Malawi's stability, Banda did not survive by mere repression. A few greatly benefited from the regime. Until 1979, the country enjoyed an economic growth rate averaging 6 percent per year. Almost all this growth came from increased agricultural production. The postindependence government favored large estates specializing in exported cash crops. While in the past the estates were almost exclusively the preserve of a few hundred white settlers, today many are controlled by either the state or local individuals.

In the 1970s, the prosperity of the estates helped to fuel a boom in industries involved in agricultural processing. Malawi's limited economic success prior to the 1980s came at the expense of the vast majority of its citizens, who survive as small landholders growing food crops. By 1985, some 86 percent of rural households farmed on less than five acres. Overcrowding has contributed to serious soil depletion while marginalizing most farmers to the point where they can have little hope of generating a significant surplus. In addition to land shortage, peasant production has suffered from low official produce prices and lack of other inputs. The northern half of the country, which has almost no estate production, has been relatively neglected in terms of government expenditure on transport and other forms of infrastructure. Many Malawian peasants have for generations turned to migrant labor as a means of coping with their poverty, but there have been far fewer opportunities for them in South Africa and Zimbabwe in recent years.

Under pressure from the World Bank, the Malawian government has since 1981 modestly increased its incentives to the small landholders. Yet these reforms have been insufficient to overcome the continuing impoverishment of rural households, which has been aggravated in recent decades by a decline in migrant-labor remittances. The maldistribution of land in many areas remains a major challenge. On a more positive note, peace in Mozambique has reopened Malawi's access to the Indian Ocean ports of Beira and Nacala while reducing the burden of dealing with what once numbered 600,000 refugees. Communications infrastructure to the ports, damaged by war, is now being repaired.

DEVELOPMENT

As in other parts of Africa, there is increasing recognition in Malawi that rural development must be addressed from a perspective that recognizes the key role of women, especially in arable agriculture. Securing property rights for women has become an important development as well as human-rights issue.

FREEDOM

Although greatly improved since the end of the Banda era, serious human-rights problems remain, including the abuse and death of detainees by police. Prison conditions are poor. Lengthy pretrial detention, an inefficient judicial system, and limited resources have called into question the ability of defendants to receive timely and fair trials. High levels of crime have prompted a rise in vigilante justice.

HEALTH/WELFARE

Malawi's health service is considered exceptionally poor even for an impoverished country. The country has one of the highest child mortality rates in the world, and more than half of its children under age 5 are stunted by malnutrition.

ACHIEVEMENTS

Although it is the poorest, most overcrowded country in the region, Malawi's response to the influx of Mozambican refugees was described by the U.S. Committee for Refugees as "no less than heroic."

Mozambique (Republic of Mozambique)

GEOGRAPHY

Area in Square Miles (Kilometers):
309,494 (801,590) (about
twice the size of California)
Capital (Population): Maputo
(2,212,000)
Environmental Concerns: civil
war and drought have had
adverse consequences on the
environment; water pollution;
desertification
Geographical Features: mostly
coastal lowlands; uplands in
center; high plateaus in
northwest; mountains in west
Climate: tropical to subtropical

PEOPLE

Population
Total: 19,105,000
Annual Growth Rate: 1.47%
Rural/Urban Population Ratio:
65/35
Major Languages: Portuguese;
indigenous dialects
Ethnic Makeup: nearly 100%
indigenous groups
Religions: 50% indigenous
beliefs; 30% Christian; 20%
Muslim

Health
Life Expectancy at Birth: 38
years (male); 37 years (female)
Infant Mortality Rate (Ratio):
139.8/1,000
Physicians Available (Ratio):
1/131,991

Education
Adult Literacy Rate: 40.1%
Compulsory (Ages): 7–14

COMMUNICATION
Telephones: 75,000 main lines
Daily Newspaper Circulation:
8 per 1,000 people
Televisions: 3.5 per 1,000 people
Internet Service Providers: 2 (1999)

TRANSPORTATION
Highways in Miles (Kilometers): 17,886
(29,810)
Railroads in Miles (Kilometers): 1,879
(3,131)
Usable Airfields: 170
Motor Vehicles in Use: 89,000

GOVERNMENT
Type: republic
Independence Date: June 25, 1975 (from
Portugal)
Head of State/Government: President
Joaquim Chissano; Prime Minister
Alberto Pascoal Mocumbi

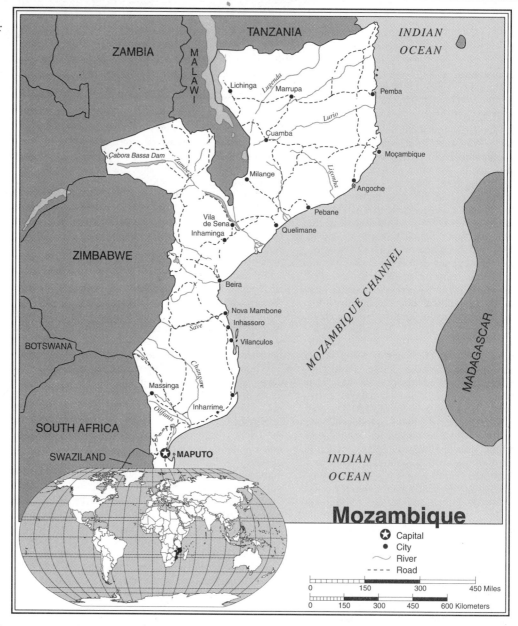

Mozambique

 Capital
● City
〜 River
--- Road

Political Parties: Front for the Liberation of
Mozambique; (Frelimo); Mozambique
National Resistance—Electoral Union
Suffrage: universal at 18

MILITARY
Military Expenditures (% of GDP): 4.7%
Current Disputes: none

ECONOMY
Currency ($ U.S. Equivalent):
5,220 meticais = $1
Per Capita Income/GDP: $1,000/$18.7 billion
GDP Growth Rate: 10%
Inflation Rate: 4%
Natural Resources: coal; titanium; natural
gas; hydropower

Agriculture: cotton; cassava; cashews;
sugarcane; tea; corn; rice; fruits; livestock
Industry: processed foods; textiles;
beverages; chemicals; tobacco; cement;
glass; asbestos; petroleum products
Exports: $300 million (primary partners
Spain, South Africa, Portugal)
Imports: $1.6 billion (primary partners
South Africa, Zimbabwe, Saudi Arabia)

http://www.africaindex.africainfo.no/
africaindex1/countries/
mozambique.html
http://www.sas.upenn.edu/
African_Studies/Country_Specific/
Mozambique.html

MOZAMBIQUE

In February 2000, the eyes of the world focused on devastating floods in Mozambique. In some places, the country's two main rivers, the Limpopo and Save, expanded miles beyond their normal banks, engulfing hundreds of villages and destroying property and infrastructure. Many Mozambicans were left homeless. This enormous disaster was a serious setback for the nation, which in recent years had been making steady economic progress after three decades of civil war. A 1992 cease-fire agreement, followed by the holding of multiparty elections in 1994 and 1999, has seemingly brought peace to the country, though the opposition Mozambique National Resistance Movement or Renamo, which narrowly lost both polls, has rejected the most recent (1999) electoral outcome.

Even before the floods, Mozambique (which remains one of the world's poorest countries) faced immense economic, political, and social challenges. Since the 1994 elections, the ruling Mozambique Liberation Front, or Frelimo, which has governed the country since independence in 1975, has faced a large opposition bloc in Parliament from its old civil-war adversary, the Mozambique National Resistance—MNR, or Renamo. Renamo currently controls 117 out of 250 seats.

A now-peaceful Renamo is, arguably, less of a challenge to the government than the dictates of international donors, upon whose funding it now depends. While the government must be concerned about improving the dismal living conditions endured by the majority of its people, the donors have insisted on fiscal austerity and a privatization program that has led to retrenchments as well as a loss of government influence.

Frelimo originally came to power as a result of a liberation war. Between 1964 and 1974, it struggled against Portuguese colonial rule. At a cost of some 30,000 lives, Mozambique gained its independence in 1975 under Frelimo's leadership. Although the new nation was one of the least-developed countries in the world, many were optimistic that the lessons learned in the struggle could be applied to the task of building a dynamic new society based on Marxist-Leninist principles.

Unfortunately, hopes for any sort of postindependence progress were quickly dashed by Renamo, which was originally established as a counterrevolutionary fifth column by the Rhodesian (Zimbabwe) Central Intelligence Organization. More than 1 million people died due to the rebellion, a large proportion murdered in cold blood by Renamo forces. It is further estimated that, out of a total population of 17 million, some 5 million people were internally displaced, and about 2 million others fled to neighboring states. No African nation paid a higher price in its resistance against white supremacy.

Although some parts of Mozambique were occupied by the Portuguese for more than 400 years, most of the country came under colonial control only in the early twentieth century. The territory was developed as a dependency of neighboring colonial economies rather than that of Portugal itself. Mozambican ports were linked by rail to South Africa and the interior colonies of British Central Africa—that is, modern Malawi, Zambia, and Zimbabwe. In the southern provinces, most men, and many women, spent time as migrant laborers in South Africa. The majority of the males worked in the gold mines.

Most of northern Mozambique was granted to three predominantly British concessions companies, whose abusive policies led many to flee the colony. For decades, the colonial state and many local enterprises also relied on forced labor. After World War II, new demands were put on Mozambicans by a growing influx of Portuguese settlers, whose numbers swelled during the 1960s, from 90,000 to more than 200,000. Meanwhile, even by the dismal standards of European colonialism in Africa, there continued to be a notable lack of concern for human development. At independence, 93 percent of the African population in Mozambique were illiterate. Furthermore, most of those who had acquired literacy or other skills had done so despite the Portuguese presence.

Although a welcome event in itself, the sudden nature of the Portuguese empire's collapse contributed to the destabilization of postindependence Mozambique. Because Frelimo had succeeded in establishing itself as a unified nationalist front, Mozam-

(United Nations photo by Kate Truscott)

The drain resulting from civil war on natural resources, the displacement of approximately one fifth of the population, persistent drought, and, most recently, devastating floods, have led to the need for Mozambique to import food to stave off famine.

Portuguese
explorers land in
Mozambique
1497

The Northern
Nguni of
Shosagaane
invade southern
Mozambique,
establishing the
Gaza kingdom
1820s

The Frelimo
liberation
movement is
officially launched
1962

Frelimo's leader,
Eduardo
Mondlane, is
killed by a parcel
bomb
1969

The liberation
struggle is
successful when
the Portuguese
revolution brings
independence
1975

Increased Renamo attacks
on civilian and military
targets; President Samora
Machel is killed in a
mysterious airplane crash;
Joaquim Chissano
becomes president
1980s

Renamo agrees
to end fighting,
participate in
multiparty
elections
1990s

2000s

Floods lead to
enormous prices in life,
property, and
infrastructure

Former first lady Graca
Machel marries South
African leader Nelson
Mandela

bique was spared an immediate descent into civil conflict, such as that which engulfed Angola, Portugal's other major African possession. However, the economy was already bankrupt due to the Portuguese policy of running Mozambique on a nonconvertible local currency. The rapid transition to independence compounded this problem by encouraging the sudden exodus of almost all the Portuguese settlers.

Perhaps even more costly to Mozambique in the long term was the polarization between Frelimo and African supporters of the former regime, who included about 100,000 who had been active in its security forces. The rapid Portuguese withdrawal was not conducive to the difficult task of reconciliation. While the "compromised ones" were not subjected by Frelimo to bloody reprisals, their rights were circumscribed, and many were sent, along with prostitutes and other "antisocial" elements, to "reeducation camps." While the historically pro-Portuguese stance of the local Catholic hierarchy would have complicated its relations with the new state under any circumstance, Frelimo's Marxist rejection of religion initially alienated it from broader numbers of believers.

A TROUBLED INDEPENDENCE
Frelimo assumed power without the benefit or burden of a strong sense of administrative continuity. While it had begun to create alternative social structures in its "liberated zones" during the anticolonial struggle, these areas had encompassed only a small percentage of Mozambique's population and infrastructure. But Frelimo was initially able to fill the vacuum and launch aggressive development efforts. Health care and education were expanded, worker committees successfully ran many of the enterprises abandoned by the set-

tlers, and communal villages coordinated rural development. However, efforts to promote agricultural collectivization as the foundation of a command economy generally led to peasant resistance and economic failure. Frelimo's ability to adapt and implement many of its programs under trying conditions was due largely to its disciplined mass base (the party's 1990 membership stood at about 200,000).

No sooner had Mozambique begun to stabilize itself from the immediate dislocations of its decolonization process than it became embroiled in the Rhodesian conflict. Mozambique was the only neighboring state to impose fully the "mandatory" United Nations economic sanctions against Rhodesia. Between 1976 and 1980, this decision led to the direct loss of half a billion dollars in rail and port revenues. Furthermore, Frelimo's decision to provide bases for the fighters of the Patriotic Front led to a state of undeclared war with Rhodesia as well as its Renamo proxies.

Unfortunately, the fall of Rhodesia did not bring an end to externally sponsored destabilization. Renamo had the support of South Africa. By continuing Renamo's campaign of destabilization, the Pretoria regime gained leverage over its hostile neighbors, for the continued closure of Mozambique's ports meant that most of their traffic had to pass through South Africa. In 1984, Mozambique signed a nonaggression pact with South Africa, which should have put an end to the latter's support of Renamo. However, captured documents and other evidence indicate that official South African support for Renamo continued at least until 1989, while South African supplies were still reaching the rebels under mysterious circumstances. In response, Zimbabwe, and

to a lesser extent Malawi and Tanzania, contributed troops to assist in the defense of Mozambique.

In its 1989 Congress, Frelimo formally abandoned its commitment to the primacy of Marxist-Leninist ideology and opened the door to further political and economic reforms. Multipartyism was formally embraced in 1991. With the help of the Catholic Church and international mediators, the government opened talks with Renamo. In October 1992, Renamo's leader, Alfonso Dlakama, signed a peace accord that called for UN–supervised elections. The cease-fire finally came into actual effect in the early months of 1993, by which time the UN personnel on the ground reported that some 3 million Mozambicans were suffering from famine.

Besides their mutual distrust, reconciliation between Renamo and Frelimo was troubled by their leaderships' inability to control their armed supporters. With neither movement able to pay its troops, apolitical banditry by former fighters for both sides increased. International financial and military support, mobilized through the United Nations, was inadequate to meet this challenge. In June and July 1994, a number of UN personnel, along with foreign-aid workers, were seized as hostages. The near-complete collapse of the country, however, has so far encouraged Mozambique's political leaders to sustain the peace drive.

DEVELOPMENT

To maintain minimum services and to recover from wartime and flood destruction, Mozambique relies on the commitment of its citizens and international assistance. Western churches have sent relief supplies, food aid, and vehicles.

FREEDOM

While the status of political and civil liberties has improved, the government's overall human-rights record continues to be marred by security-force abuses (including extra-judicial killings, excessive use of force, torture, and arbitrary detention) and an ineffective and only nominally independent judicial system.

HEALTH/WELFARE

Civil strife, widespread Renamo attacks on health units, and food shortages drastically curtailed health care goals and led to Mozambique's astronomical infant mortality rate.

ACHIEVEMENTS

Between 1975 and 1980, the illiteracy rate in Mozambique declined from 93% to 72% while classroom attendance more than doubled. Progress slowed during the 1980s due to Renamo attacks. Today, the overall literacy rate stands at about 40%.

Namibia (Republic of Namibia)

GEOGRAPHY

Area in Square Miles (Kilometers):
318,261 (824,292) (about half the size of Alaska)

Capital (Population): Windhoek (190,000)

Environmental Concerns: very limited natural freshwater resources; desertification

Geographical Features: mostly high plateau; desert along coast and in east

Climate: desert

PEOPLE

Population

Total: 1,772,000

Annual Growth Rate: 1.57%

Rural/Urban Population Ratio: 63/37

Major Languages: English; Ovambo; Kavango; Nama/Damara; Herero; Khoisan; German; Afrikaans

Ethnic Makeup: 50% Ovambo; 9% Kavango; 7% Herero; 7% Damara; 27% others

Religions: 80%–90% Christian; 10%–20% indigenous beliefs

Health

Life Expectancy at Birth: 44 years (male); 41 years (female)

Infant Mortality Rate (Ratio): 70.8/1,000

Physicians Available (Ratio): 1/4,594

Education

Adult Literacy Rate: 76%

Compulsory (Ages): 6–16

COMMUNICATION

Telephones: 101,000 main lines

Daily Newspaper Circulation: 27 per 1,000 people

Televisions: 28 per 1,000 people

Internet Service Providers: 4 (1999)

TRANSPORTATION

Highways in Miles (Kilometers): 39,220 (63,258)

Railroads in Miles (Kilometers): 1,429 (2,382)

Usable Airfields: 135

Motor Vehicles in Use: 129,000

GOVERNMENT

Type: republic

Independence Date: March 21, 1990 (from South African mandate)

Head of State/Government: President Samuel Nujoma is both head of state and head of government

Political Parties: South West Africa People's Organization; Democratic Turnhalle Alliance of Namibia; United Democratic Front; Monitor Action Group

Suffrage: universal at 18

MILITARY

Military Expenditures (% of GDP): 2.6%

Current Disputes: civil unrest; border dispute over at least one island in the Linyanti River

ECONOMY

Currency ($ U.S. Equivalent):
3.54 Namibian dollars = $1

Per Capita Income/GDP: $4,300/$7.1 billion

GDP Growth Rate: 3%

Inflation Rate: 8.5%

Unemployment Rate: 30%–40%

Labor Force: 500,000

Natural Resources: diamonds; gold; tin; copper; lead; zinc; uranium; salt; cadmium; lithium; natural gas; possible oil, coal reserves; fish; vanadium; hydropower

Agriculture: millet; sorghum; peanuts; livestock; fish

Industry: meat packing; dairy products; fish processing; mining

Exports: $1.4 billion (primary partners United Kingdom, South Africa, Spain)

Imports: $1.5 billion (primary partners South Africa, Germany, United States)

 http://www.sas.upenn.edu/ African_Studies/Country_Specific/ Namibia.html

http://www.republicofnamibia.com

NAMIBIA

In August 1999, Namibians were shocked when a small group of self-proclaimed separatists launched an armed attack on the town of Katima Mulilo. Subsequent attacks along the border with war-torn Angola and the involvement of Namibian forces in the war in the Democratic Republic of the Congo (Congo-Kinshasa) have further shaken the country's peaceful international image. The incidents, however, have not as yet fundamentally disturbed Namibia's steady progress in the decade since its liberation from South African rule.

Namibia became independent in 1990, after a long liberation struggle. Its transition from the continent's last colony to a developing nation-state marked the end of a century of often brutal colonization, first by Germany and later South Africa. The German colonial period (1884–1917) was marked by the annihilation of more than 60 percent of the African population in the southern two thirds of the country, during the uprising of 1904–1907. The South African period (1917–1990) saw the imposition of apartheid as well as a bitter 26-year war for independence between the South African Army (SADF) and the South West Africa People's Organization (SWAPO). During that war, countless civilians, especially in the northern areas of the country, were harassed, detained, and abused by South African–created death squads, such as the *Koevoet* (the Afrikaans word for "crowbar").

Namibia's final liberation was the result of South African military misadventures and U.S.–Soviet cooperation in reducing tensions in the region. In 1987, as it had done many times before, South Africa invaded Angola to assist Jonas Savimbi's UNITA movement. Its objective was Cuito Cuanavale, a small town in southeastern Angola where the Luanda government had set up an air-defense installation to keep South African aircraft from supplying UNITA troops. The SADF met with fierce resistance from the Angolan Army and eventually committed thousands of its own troops to the battle. In addition, black Namibian soldiers were recruited and given UNITA uniforms to fight on the side of the SADF. Many of these proxy UNITA troops later mutinied because of their poor treatment at the hands of white South African soldiers.

South Africa failed to capture Cuito Cuanavale, and its forces were eventually surrounded. Faced with military disaster, the Pretoria government bowed to decades of international pressure and agreed to withdraw from its illegal occupation of Namibia. In return, Angola and its ally Cuba agreed to send home troops sent by Havana in 1974 after South Africa invaded Angola for the first time. Key brokers of the cease-fire, negotiations, and implementation of this agreement were the United States and the Soviet Union. This was the first instance of their post–Cold War cooperation.

A plebiscite was held in Namibia in 1989. Under United Nations supervision, more than 97 percent of eligible voters cast their ballots—a remarkable achievement given the vast distances that many had to travel to reach polling stations. SWAPO emerged as the clear winner, with 57 percent of the votes cast. The party's share of the vote increased to 73 percent in the subsequent 1995 elections; support for its main political rival, the Democratic Turnhalle Alliance, dropped to 15 percent.

CHALLENGES AND PROSPECTS

Namibia is a sparsely populated land. More than half of its more than 1.7 million residents live in the northern region

(United Nations photo by J. Isaac)

The importance of developing agricultural production in arable parts of Namibia is key to the country's economic future. The international economic sanctions that applied before independence have been lifted, and Namibia is now free to enter the potentially profitable markets of Europe and North America. This man working in a cornfield near Grootfontein is part of Namibia's crucial agricultural economy.

| Germany is given rights to colonize Namibia at the Conference of Berlin **1884–1885** | Herero, Nama, and Damara rebellions against German rule **1904–1907** | The UN General Assembly revokes a 1920 South African mandate; SWAPO begins war for independence **1966** | Bantustans, or "homelands," are created by South Africa **1968** | A massive strike paralyzes the economy **1971** | An internal government is formed by South Africa **1978** | Defeat at Cuito Cuanavale leads to a South African agreement to withdraw from Namibia; SWAPO wins UN-supervised elections; a new Constitution is approved **1980s** | More than 1,000 refugees flee to Botswana from Namibia's Caprivi regions **1990s** |

2000s

The International Court of Justice awards the disputed Kasikili/Sedudu Island to Botswana

Namibian involvement in the Congo-Kinshasa war

Unrest follows attacks by separatists

known as Ovamboland. Rich in minerals, Namibia is a major producer of diamonds, uranium, copper, silver, tin, and lithium. A large gold mine recently began production, and the end of hostilities has opened up northern parts of the country to further mineral explorations.

Much of Namibia is arid. Until recently, pastoral farming was the primary agricultural activity, with beef, mutton, and goat meat the main products. Independence brought an end to international sanctions applied when South Africa ruled the country, giving Namibian agricultural goods access to the world market. Although some new investment has been attracted to the relatively well-watered but historically neglected northern border regions, most of Namibia's rural majority are barely able to eke out a living, even in nondrought years.

Despite the economic promise, the fledgling government of Namibia faces severe problems. It inherits an economy structurally perverted by apartheid to favor the tiny white minority. With a glaring division between fabulously wealthy whites and the oppressively poor black majority, the government is faced with the daunting problem of promoting economic development while encouraging the redistribution of wealth. Apartheid ensured that managerial positions were filled by whites, leaving a dearth of qualified and experienced nonwhite executives in the country. This past pattern of discrimination has contributed to high levels of black unemployment today.

The demobilization of 53,000 former SWAPO and South African combatants and the return of 44,000 exiles aggravated this problem. A few former soldiers—notably the Botsotsos, made up of former Koevoet members—turned to organized crime. Having already inherited a civil service bloated by too many white sine-

cures, the SWAPO administration resisted the temptation of trying to hire its way out of the problem. In 1991–1992, several thousand ex-combatants received vocational training in Development Brigades, modeled after similar initiatives in Botswana and Zimbabwe, but inadequate funding and preparation limited the program's success.

Another major problem lies in Namibia's economic dependence on South Africa. Before independence, Namibia had been developed as a captive market for South African goods, while its resources had been depleted by overexploitation on the part of South African firms. In 1990, all rail and most road links between Namibia and the rest of the world ran through South Africa. But South Africa's March 1, 1994, return of Walvis Bay, Namibia's only port, has greatly reduced this dependence. The port has now been declared a free trade area. Namibia has also been linked to South Africa through a Common Monetary Area. In 1994, a new Namibian dollar was introduced, replacing the South African rand. But, at least for the time being, the currency's value remains tied to the rand.

The government of President Samuel Nujoma has taken a hard look at these and other economic problems and embarked on a program to solve them. SWAPO surprised everyone during the election campaign by modifying its previously strident socialist rhetoric and calling for a market-oriented economy. Since taking power, it has joined the International Monetary Fund and proposed a code for foreign investors that includes protection against undue nationalizations. Since independence, the Ministry of Finance has pursued conservative policies, which have calmed the country's largely white business community but have been criticized as insufficient

to transform the economy for the greater benefit of the impoverished masses.

The government recognizes the need to attract significant foreign investment to overcome the colonial legacy of underdevelopment. In 1993, a generous package of manufacturing incentives was introduced by the Ministry of Trade and Industry. In the same year, the Namibia National Development Corporation was established to channel public investment into the economy. It is too early to assess the success of these initiatives.

NAMIBIA'S FISHING INDUSTRY
Namibia's fishing sector has made an impressive recovery after years of decline. The country's coastal waters had long supported exceptionally high concentrations of sea life due to the upwelling of nutrients by the cold offshore current. But in the years before independence, overfishing, mostly by foreign vessels, had nearly wiped out many species. Since then, the government has established a 200-nautical-mile Exclusive Economic Zone along Namibia's coast and passed a Sea Fisheries Act designed to promote the conservation and controlled exploitation of the country's marine resources. These measures have been backed up by effective monitoring on the part of the new Ministry of Fisheries and Marine Resources and the creation of a National Fisheries Research and Information Centre. A rapid recovery in fish stocks has led to an annual growth of 35 percent in the sector's value.

DEVELOPMENT

The Nujoma government has instituted English as the medium of instruction in all schools. (Before independence, English was discouraged for African schoolchildren, a means of controlling their access to skills necessary to compete in the modern world.) This effort requires new curricula and textbooks for the entire country.

FREEDOM

In line with Namibia's liberal Constitution, human rights are generally respected. There are some problem areas: Demonstrations that do not have prior police approval are banned. The president and other high officials have repeatedly attacked the independent press. There has not been a full accounting of missing detainees who were in SWAPO camps before independence. Security forces have admitted to cases of extrajudicial killing along the Angolan border.

HEALTH/WELFARE

The social-service delivery system of Namibia must be rebuilt to eliminate the structural inequities of apartheid. Health care for the black majority, especially those in remote rural areas, will require significant improvements. Public-health programs for blacks, nonexistent prior to independence, must be created.

ACHIEVEMENTS

The government of President Sam Nujoma has received high praise for its efforts at racial and political reconciliation after a bitter 26-year war for independence. Nujoma has led these efforts and has impressed many observers with his exceptional political and consensus-building skills.

South Africa (Republic of South Africa)*

GEOGRAPHY
Area in Square Miles (Kilometers): 437,872 (1,222,480) (about twice the size of Texas)

Capital (Population): Pretoria (administrative) (1,080,000); Cape Town (legislative) (2,350,000); Bloemfontein (judicial) (na)

Environmental Concerns: water and air pollution; acid rain; soil erosion; desertification; lack of fresh water

Geographical Features: vast interior plateau rimmed by rugged hills and a narrow coastal plain

Climate: mostly semiarid; subtropical along the east coast

PEOPLE

Population
Total: 43,421,000
Annual Growth Rate: 0.5%
Rural/Urban Population Ratio: 50/50
Major Languages: Afrikaans; English; Ndebele; Pedi; Sotho; Swati; Tsonga; Tswana; Venda; Xhosa; Zulu
Ethnic Makeup: 75% black; 14% white; 9% Colored; 2% Indian
Religions: 68% Christian; 28.5% indigenous beliefs and animist; 2% Muslim; 1.5% Hindu

Health
Life Expectancy at Birth: 50 years (male); 52 years (female)
Infant Mortality Rate (Ratio): 59/1,000
Physicians Available (Ratio): 1/1,529

Education
Adult Literacy Rate: 82%
Compulsory (Ages): 7–16

COMMUNICATION
Telephones: 4,645,000 main lines
Daily Newspaper Circulation: 29 per 1,000 people
Televisions: 84 per 1,000 people
Internet Service Providers: 58 (1999)

TRANSPORTATION
Highways in Miles (Kilometers): 331,161 (534,131)
Railroads in Miles (Kilometers): 12,859 (21,431)
Usable Airfields: 744
Motor Vehicles in Use: 6,000,000

GOVERNMENT
Type: republic

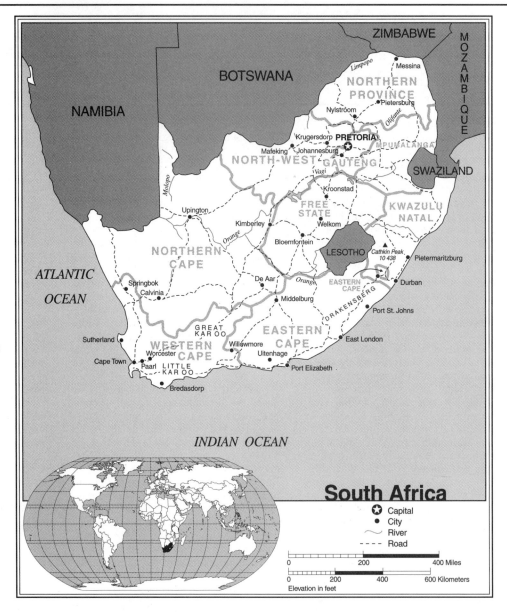

South Africa

- ⊗ Capital
- ● City
- ⌇ River
- --- Road

Independence Date: May 31, 1910 (from the United Kingdom)
Head of State/Government: President Thabo Mbeki is both head of state and head of government
Political Parties: African National Congress; New National Party; Inkatha Freedom Party; African Christian Democratic Party; Freedom Front; Pan Africanist Congress; others
Suffrage: universal at 18

MILITARY
Military Expenditures (% of GDP): 1.5%
Current Disputes: civil unrest; territorial issues with Swaziland

ECONOMY
Currency ($ U.S. Equivalent): 4.42 rands = $1
Per Capita Income/GDP: $6,900/$296.1 billion

GDP Growth Rate: 0.6%
Inflation Rate: 5.5%
Unemployment Rate: 30%
Labor Force: 15,000,000
Natural Resources: gold; chromium; coal; antimony; iron ore; manganese; nickel; phosphates; tin; diamonds; others
Agriculture: corn; wheat; sugarcane; fruits; vegetables; livestock products
Industry: mining; automobile assembly; metalworking; machinery; textiles; iron and steel; chemicals; fertilizer; foodstuffs
Exports: $28 billion (primary partners United Kingdom, Italy, Japan)
Imports: $26 billion (primary partners Germany, United States, United Kingdom)

*Note: When separated, figures for blacks and whites vary greatly.

112

SOUTH AFRICA

In 1999, South Africa entered a new era when its first post-apartheid president, Nelson Mandela, retired. He handed over power to his deputy, Thabo Mbeki. The new administration subsequently won a decisive mandate, in the country's second post-apartheid elections. Mandela, however, remains as a unifying father figure to most South Africans, both black and white. His retirement ended an extraordinary period in which South Africa struggled to come to terms with its new status as a nonracial democracy, after a long history of white-minority rule.

In April 1994, millions of South Africans turned out to vote in their country's first nonracial elections. Most waited patiently for hours to cast their ballots for the first time. The result was a landslide victory for the African National Congress (ANC), which, under the new interim Constitution, would nonetheless cooperate with two of its long-standing rivals, the National Party (NP) and the Inkatha Freedom Party (IFP), in a "Government of National Unity" (GNU). On May 10, the ANC's leader was sworn in as South Africa's first black president. Despite the history of often violent animosity between its components, the GNU survived for two years, facilitating national reconciliation. In July 1996, the NP pulled out of the GNU, giving the ANC a freer hand to pursue its ambitious but largely unrealized program of "Reconstruction and Development."

With the emergence of an elected nonracial government, South Africa has decisively turned away from its long, tragic history of racism. For nearly 3½ centuries, the territory's white minority expanded and entrenched its racial hegemony over the nonwhite majority. After 1948, successive NP governments consolidated white supremacy into a governing system known as *apartheid* ("separatehood"). But in a dramatic political about-face, the NP government, under the new leadership of F. W. de Klerk, committed itself in 1990 to a negotiated end to apartheid. Political restrictions inside the country were significantly relaxed through the unbanning of anti-apartheid resistance organizations, most notably the ANC, the Pan Africanist Congress (PAC), and the South African Communist Party (SACP). Thereafter, three years of on-again, off-again negotiations, incorporating virtually all sections of public opinion, resulted in a 1993 consensus in favor of a five-year, nonracial, interim Constitution.

Notwithstanding its remarkable political progress in recent years, South Africa remains a deeply divided country. In general, whites continue to enjoy relatively affluent, comfortable lives, while the vast majority of nonwhites survive in a state of impoverished deprivation. The boundary between these two worlds remains deep. Under the pre-1990 apartheid system, nonwhites were legally divided as members of three officially subordinate race classifications: "Bantu" (black Africans), "Coloureds" (people of mixed race), or "Asians." (*Note:* Many members of these three groups prefer the common label of "black," which the government now commonly uses in place of Bantu as an exclusive term for black Africans, hereafter referred to in this text as *blacks*.)

THE ROOTS OF APARTHEID

White supremacy in South Africa began with the Dutch settlement at Cape Town in 1652. For 1½ centuries, the domestic economy of the Dutch Cape Colony, which gradually expanded to include the southern third of modern South Africa, rested on a foundation of slavery and servitude. Much like the American South before the Civil War, Cape Colonial society was racially divided between free white settlers and nonwhite slaves and servants. Most of the slaves were Africans imported from outside the local region, although a minority were taken from Asia. The local blacks, who spoke various Khiosan languages, were not enslaved. However, they were robbed by the Europeans of their land and herds. Many were also killed either by European bullets or diseases. As a result, most of the Cape's Khiosan were reduced to a status of servitude. Gradually, the servant and slave populations, with a

(United Nations photo)

The system of apartheid made it impossible for most black South Africans to share in their country's economic prosperity.

considerable admixture of European blood, merged to form the core of the so-called Coloured group.

At the beginning of the nineteenth century, the Cape Colony reverted to British control. In the 1830s, the British abolished slavery and extended legal rights to servants. But, as with the American South, emancipation did not end racial barriers to the political and economic advancement of nonwhites. Nonetheless, even the limited reforms that were introduced upset many of the white "Cape Dutch" (or "Boers"), whose society was evolving its own "Afrikaner" identity. (Today, some 60 percent of the whites and 90 percent of the Coloureds in South Africa speak the Dutch-derived Afrikaans language.) In the mid-nineteenth century, thousands of Afrikaners, accompanied by their Coloured clients, escaped British rule by migrating into the interior. They established two independent republics, the Transvaal and the Orange Free State, whose Constitutions recognized only whites as having any civil rights.

The Afrikaners, and the British who followed them, did not settle an empty land. Then, as now, most of the people living in the area beyond the borders of the old Dutch Cape Colony were blacks who spoke languages linguistically classified as Bantu. While there are nine officially recognized Bantu languages in South Africa, all but two (Tsonga and Venda) belong to either the Sotho-Tswana (Pedi, Sotho, Tswana) or Nguni (Ndebele, Swati, Xhosa, and Zulu) subgroupings of closely related dialects.

Throughout the 1700s and 1800s, the indigenous populations of the interior and the eastern coast offered strong resistance to the white invaders. Unlike the Khiosan of the Cape, these communities were able to preserve their ethnolinguistic identities. However, the settlers eventually robbed them of most of their land as well as their independence. Black subjugation served the economic interests of white farmers, and later industrialists, who were able to coerce the conquered communities into providing cheap and forced labor. After 1860, many Asians, mostly from what was then British-ruled India, were also brought into South Africa to work for next to nothing on sugar plantations. As with the blacks and Coloureds, the Asians were denied civil rights.

The lines of racial stratification were already well entrenched at the turn of the twentieth century, when the British waged a war of conquest against the Afrikaner republics. During this South African, or Boer, War, tens of thousands of Afrikaners, blacks, and Coloureds died while interned in British concentration camps. The camps helped to defeat the Afrikaner resistance but left bitter divisions between the resistance and pro-British English-speaking whites. However, it was the nonwhites who were the war's greatest losers. A compromise peace between the Afrikaners and the British Empire paved the way for the emergence, in 1910, of a self-governing Union of South Africa, made up of the former British colonies and Afrikaner republics. In this new state, political power remained in the hands of the white minority.

"GRAND APARTHEID"

In 1948, the Afrikaner-dominated Nationalist Party was voted into office by the white electorate on a platform promising apartheid. Under this system, existing patterns of segregation were reinforced by a vast array of new laws. "Pass laws," which had long limited the movement of blacks in many areas, were extended to apply throughout the country. Black men and women were required to carry "passbooks" at all times to prove their right to be residing in a particular area. Under the Group Areas Act, more than 80 percent of South Africa was reserved for whites (who now make up no more than 14 percent of the population). In this area, blacks were confined to townships or white-owned farms, where, until recently, they were considered to be temporary residents. If they lacked a properly registered job, they were subject to deportation to one of the 10 "homelands."

Under apartheid, the homelands—poor, noncontiguous rural territories that together account for less than 13 percent of South Africa's land—were the designated "nations" of South Africa's blacks, who make up more than 70 percent of the population. Each black was assigned membership in a particular homeland, in accordance with ethnolinguistic criteria invented by the white government. Thus, in apartheid theory, there was no majority in South Africa but, rather, a single white nation—which in reality remained divided among speakers of Afrikaans, English, and other languages, and 10 separate black nations. The Coloureds and the Asians were consigned a never clearly defined intermediate position as powerless communities associated with, but segregated from, white South Africa. The apartheid "ideal" was that each black homeland would eventually become "independent," leaving white South Africa without the "burden" of a black majority. Of course, black "immigrants" could still work for the "white economy," which would remain reliant on black labor. To assure that racial stratifi-cation was maintained at the workplace, a system of job classification was created that reserved the best positions for whites, certain middle-level employments for Asians and Coloureds, and unskilled labor for blacks.

Before 1990, the NP ruthlessly pursued its ultimate goal of legislating away South Africa's black majority. Four homelands—Bophutatswana, Ciskei, Transkei, and Venda—were declared independent. The 9 million blacks who were assigned as citizens of these pseudo-states (which were not recognized by any outside country) did not appear in the 1989 South African Census, even though most lived outside of the homelands. Indeed, despite generations of forced removals and influx control, today there is not a single magistrate's district (the equivalent of a U.S. county) that has a white majority.

While for whites apartheid was an ideology of mass delusion, for blacks it meant continuous suffering. In the 1970s alone, some 3.5 million blacks were forcibly relocated because they were living in "black spots" within white areas. Many more at some point in their lives fell victim to the pass laws. Within the townships and squatter camps that ringed the white cities, families survived from day to day not knowing when the police might burst into their homes to discover that their passbooks were not in order.

Under apartheid, blacks were as much divided by their residential status as by their assigned ethnicity. In a relative sense, the most privileged were those who had established their right to reside legally within a township like Soweto. Township dwellers had the advantage of being able to live with their families and seek work in a nearby white urban center. Many of their coworkers lived much farther away, in the peri-urban areas of the homelands. Some in this less fortunate category spent as much as one third of their lives on Putco buses, traveling to and from their places of employment. Still, the peri-urban homeland workers were in many ways better off than their colleagues who were confined to crowded worker hostels for months at a time while their families remained in distant rural homelands. There were also millions of female domestic workers who generally earned next to nothing while living away from their children in the servant quarters of white households. Many of these conditions still persist in South Africa.

Further down the black social ladder were those living in the illegal squatter camps that existed outside the urban areas. Without secure homes or steady jobs, the squatters were frequent victims of night-time police raids. When caught, they were generally transported back to their homelands, from whence they would usually try once more to escape. The relaxation of influx-control regulations eased the tribulations of many squatters, but their lives remained insecure.

Yet even the violent destruction of squatter settlements by the state did not stem their explosive growth. For many blacks, living without permanent employment in a cardboard house was preferable to the hardships of the rural homelands. Nearly half of all blacks live in these areas today. Unemployment there tops 80 percent, and agricultural production is limited by marginal, overcrowded environments.

Economic changes in the 1970s and 1980s tended further to accentuate the importance of these residential patterns. Although their wages on average were only a fraction of those enjoyed by whites, many township dwellers saw their wages rise over several decades, partially due to their own success in organizing strong labor federations. At the same time, however, life in the homelands became more desperate as their populations mushroomed.

Apartheid was a totalitarian system. Before 1994, an array of security legislation gave the state vast powers over individual citizens, even in the absence of a state of emergency, such as existed throughout much of the country between 1985 and 1990. Control was more subtly exercised through the schools and other public institutions. An important element of apartheid was "Bantu Education." Beyond being segregated and unequal, black educational curricula were specifically designed to assure underachievement, by preparing most students for only semi-skilled and unskilled occupations. The schools were also divided by language and ethnicity. A student who was classified as Zulu was taught in the Zulu language to be loyal to the Zulu nation, while his or her playmates might be receiving similar instruction in Tsonga or Sotho. Ethnic divisions were also often encouraged at the workplace. (At the mines, even today, ethnicity generally determines the job and hostel to which one is assigned.)

LIMITED REFORMS

In 1982 and 1983, there was much official publicity about reforming apartheid. Yet the Nationalist Party's moves to liberalize the system were limited and were accompanied by increased repression. Some changes were simply semantic. In official publications, the term "apartheid" was replaced by "separate development," which was subsequently dropped in favor of "plural democracy."

A bill passed in the white Parliament in 1983 brought Asian and Coloured representatives into the South African government—but only in their own separate chambers, which remained completely subordinate to the white chamber. The bill also concentrated power in the office of the presidency, which eroded the oversight prerogatives of white parliamentarians. Significantly, the new dispensation completely excluded blacks. Seeing the new Constitution as another transparent attempt at divide-and-rule while offering them nothing in the way of genuine empowerment, most Asians and Coloureds refused to participate in the new political order. Instead, many joined together with blacks and a handful of progressive whites in creating a new organization, the United Democratic Front (UDF), which opposed the Constitution.

In other moves, the NP gradually did away with many examples of "petty" apartheid. In many areas, signs announcing separate facilities were removed from public places; but, very often, new, more subtle signs were put up to assure continued segregation. Many gas stations in the Transvaal, for example, had their facilities marked with blue and white figures to as-

(United Nations photo)

Millions of black South Africans were forcibly resettled in villages. The formation of these so-called black homelands represented the largest forced movement of people in peacetime history.

Migration of Bantu speakers into Southern Africa **1000–1500**	The first settlement of Dutch people in the Cape of Good Hope area **1652**	The first Khiosan attempt to resist white encroachment **1659**	The British gain possession of the Cape Colony **1815**	Shaka develops the Zulu nation and sets in motion the wars and migrations known as the Mfecane **1820s**	The Boer War: the British fight the Afrikaners (Boers) **1899–1902**	The Union of South Africa gives rights of self-government to whites **1910**	The African National Congress is founded **1912**

sure that everyone continued to know his or her place. Another example of purely cosmetic reform was the legalization of interracial marriage—although it was no longer a crime for a man and a woman belonging to different racial classifications to be wed, before 1992 it remained an offense for such a couple to live in the same house. In 1986, the hated passbooks were replaced with new "identity cards." Unions were legalized in the 1980s, but in the Orwellian world of apartheid, their leaders were regularly arrested. The UDF was not banned but, rather, was forbidden from holding meetings. Although such reforms were meaningless to most nonwhites living within South Africa, some outsiders, including the Reagan administration, were impressed by the "progress."

BLACK RESISTANCE
Resistance to white domination dates back to 1659, when the Khiosan first attempted to counter Dutch encroachments on their pastures. In the first half of the twentieth century, the African National Congress (founded in 1912 to unify what until then had been regionally based black associations) and other political and labor organizations attempted to wage a peaceful civil-rights struggle. An early leader within the Asian community was Mohandas (the Mahatma) Gandhi, who pioneered his strategy of passive resistance in South Africa while resisting the pass laws. In the 1950s, the ANC and associated organizations adopted Gandhian tactics on a massive scale, in a vain attempt to block the enactment of apartheid legislation. Although ANC president Albert Luthuli was awarded a Nobel Peace Prize, the NP regime remained unmoved.

The year 1960 was a turning point. Police massacred more than 60 persons when they fired on a passbook-burning demonstration at Sharpeville. Thereafter, the government assumed emergency powers, banning the ANC and the more recently formed Pan Africanist Congress. As underground movements, both turned to armed struggle. The ANC's guerrilla organization, the Umkonto we Sizwe ("Spear of the Nation"), attempted to avoid taking human lives in its attacks. Poqo ("Ourselves Alone"), the PAC's armed wing, was less constrained in its choice of targets but proved less able to sustain its struggle. By the mid-1960s, with the capture of such figures as Umkonto leader Nelson Mandela, active resistance had been all but fully suppressed.

A new generation of resistance emerged in the 1970s. Many nonwhite youths were attracted to the teachings of the Black Consciousness Movement (BMC), led by Steve Biko. The BMC and like-minded organizations rejected the racial and ethnic classifications of apartheid by insisting on the fundamental unity of all oppressed black peoples (that is, all nonwhites) against the white power structure. Black consciousness also rejected all forms of collaboration with the apartheid state, which brought the movement into direct opposition with homeland leaders like Gatsha Buthelezi, whom they looked upon as sellouts. In the aftermath of student demonstrations in Soweto, which sparked months of unrest across the country, the government suppressed the BMC. Biko was subsequently murdered while in detention. During the crackdown, thousands of young people fled South Africa. Many joined the exiled ANC, helping to reinvigorate its ranks.

Despite the government's heavyhanded repression, internal resistance to apartheid continued to grow. Hundreds of new and revitalized organizations—community groups, labor unions, and religious bodies—emerged to contribute to the struggle. Many became affiliated through coordinating bodies such as the United Democratic Front, the Congress of South African Trade Unions (COSATU), and the South African Council of Churches (SACC). SACC leader Archbishop Desmond Tutu became the second black South African to be awarded a Nobel Peace Prize for his nonviolent efforts to bring about change. But in the face of continued oppression, black youths, in particular, became increasingly willing to use whatever means necessary to overthrow the oppressors.

The year 1985 was another turning point. Arrests and bannings of black leaders led to calls to make the townships "ungovernable." A state of emergency was

(United Nations photo)

Resistance groups gained international recognition in their struggle against the South African apartheid regime.

The Nationalist Party comes to power on an apartheid platform
1948

The Sharpeville Massacre: police fire on demonstration; more than 60 deaths result
1960

Soweto riots are sparked off by student protests
1976

Unrest in the black townships leads to the declaration of a state of emergency; thousands are detained while violence escalates; F. W. de Klerk replaces P. W. Botha as president; anti-apartheid movements are unbanned; political prisoners are released
1980s

Negotiations begin for a nonracial interim Constitution; nonracial elections in May 1994 result in an ANC-led Government of National Unity; Nelson Mandela becomes president
1990s

2000s

Thabo Mbeki is inaugurated as president

Mbeki calls on South Africans to help build an "African Renaissance"

proclaimed by the government in July, which allowed for the increased use of detention without trial. By March 1990, some 53,000 people, including an estimated 10,000 children, had been arrested. Many detainees were tortured while in custody. Stone-throwing youths nonetheless continued to challenge the heavily armed security forces sent into the townships to restore order. By 1993, more than 10,000 people had died during the unrest.

TOWARD A NEW SOUTH AFRICA

Despite the Nationalist Party's ability to marshall the resources of a sophisticated military–industrial complex to maintain its totalitarian control, it was forced to abandon apartheid along with its four-decade-long monopoly of power. Throughout the 1980s, South Africa's advanced economy was in a state of crisis due to the effects of unrest and, to a lesser extent, of sanctions and other forms of international pressure. Under President P. W. Botha, the NP regime stubbornly refused to offer any openings to genuine reform. However, Botha's replacement in 1989 by F. W. de Klerk opened up new possibilities. The unbanning of the ANC, PAC, and SACP was accompanied by the release of many political prisoners. As many had anticipated, after gaining his freedom in March 1990, ANC leader Nelson Mandela emerged as the leading advocate for change. More surprising was the de Klerk government's willingness to engage in serious negotiations with Mandela and others. By August 1990, the ANC felt that the progress being made justified the formal suspension of its armed struggle.

Many obstacles blocked the transition to a postapartheid state. The NP initially advocated a form of power sharing that fell short of the concept of one person, one vote in a unified state. The ANC, UDF (disbanded in 1991), COSATU, and SACP, which were associated as the Mass Democratic Movement (MDM), however, remained steadfast in their loyalty to the nonracial principles of the 1955 Freedom Charter. Many members of the PAC and other radical critics of the ANC initially feared that the apartheid regime was not prepared to agree to its dismantlement and that the ongoing talks could only serve to weaken black resistance. On the opposite side of the spectrum were still-powerful elements of the white community who remained openly committed to continued white supremacy. In addition to the Conservative Party, the principal opposition in the old white Parliament, there were a number of militant racist organizations, which resorted to terrorism in an attempt to block reforms. Some within the South African security establishment also sought to sabotage the prospects of peace. In March 1992, these far-right elements suffered a setback when nearly 70 percent of white voters approved continued negotiation for democratic reform.

Another troublesome factor was Mangosuthu Buthelezi's Inkatha Freedom Party and other, smaller black groups that had aligned themselves in the past with the South African state. Prior to the elections, thousands were killed in clashes between Inkatha and ANC/MDM supporters, especially in the Natal/Kwazulu region. As the positions of the ANC and NP began to converge in 1993, the IFP delegation walked out of the negotiations and formed a "Freedom Alliance" with white conservatives and the leaders of the Bophutatswana and Ciskei homelands. It collapsed in March 1994, following the violent overthrow of the Bophutatswana regime and the defeat of groups of armed white right-wingers that rallied to its defense. Following this debacle, the IFP and more moderate white conservatives—the "Freedom Front"—agreed to participate in national elections. Attempts by more extreme right-wingers to disrupt the elections through a terrorist bombing campaign were crushed in a belated security crackdown.

The elections and the subsequent installation of the GNU were remarkably peaceful, despite organizational difficulties and instances of voting irregularities. In the end, all major parties accepted the result in which the ANC (incorporating MDM) attracted 63 percent of the vote, the NP 20 percent, IFP 10 percent, the Freedom Front 2.2 percent, and the PAC a disappointing 1.2 percent.

Although the Government of National Unity got off to a good start, it faced many challenges. Under even the best of circumstances, it will not be easy for South Africans to dismantle the legacies of apartheid.

DEVELOPMENT

The Government of National Unity's major priority was the implementation of the comprehensive Reconstruction and Development Plan. A major aspect of the plan was a government commitment to build 1 million low-cost houses each year for 5 years.

FREEDOM

The government is committed to upholding human rights, which are generally respected. Members of the security forces have committed abuses, including torture and excessive use of force. Action has been taken to punish some of those involved. The Truth and Reconciliation Commission, created to investigate apartheid-era human-rights abuses, completed its investigations in 1998. It made recommendations for reparations for victims and granted amnesty for full disclosure of politically motivated crimes.

HEALTH/WELFARE

Public-health and educational facilities are being desegregated. In its first 100 days, the new government introduced free child healthcare and AIDS-prevention programs. A 10-year program of schooling is to be free to all pupils. Students have returned to school in large numbers. Crime remains a major problem, with a recent study concluding that South Africa is the most murderous country in the world.

ACHIEVEMENTS

With the end of international cultural and sporting boycotts, South African artists and athletes have become increasingly prominent. In 1993, Nelson Mandela and F. W. de Klerk were awarded the Nobel Peace Prize, following in the footsteps of their countrymen Albert Luthuli and Desmond Tutu.

Swaziland (Kingdom of Swaziland)

GEOGRAPHY

Area in Square Miles (Kilometers):
6,704 (17,366) (about the size
of New Jersey)
Capital (Population): Mbabane
(administrative) (47,000);
Lobanta (legislative) (na)
Environmental Concerns:
depletion of wildlife populations;
overgrazing; soil degradation;
soil erosion; limited potable
water
Geographical Features: mostly
mountains and hills; some
sloping plains; landlocked
Climate: from tropical to temperate

PEOPLE

Population
Total: 1,083,300*
Annual Growth Rate: 1.96%*
Rural/Urban Population Ratio:
68/32
Major Languages: English;
SiSwati
Ethnic Makeup: 97% African;
3% European
Religions: 60% Christian; 40%
indigenous beliefs

Health
Life Expectancy at Birth: 40
years (male); 41 years (female)*
Infant Mortality Rate (Ratio):
109/1,000*
Physicians Available (Ratio):
1/9,265

Education
Adult Literacy Rate: 76.7%

COMMUNICATION

Telephones: 29,000 main lines
Televisions: 96 per 1,000 people
Internet Service Providers: 2 (1999)

TRANSPORTATION

Highways in Miles (Kilometers):
1,769 (2,853)
Railroads in Miles (Kilometers): 184 (297)
Usable Airfields: 18
Motor Vehicles in Use: 37,000

GOVERNMENT

Type: monarchy; independent member of
the British Commonwealth
Independence Date: September 6, 1968
Head of State/Government: King Mswati
III; Prime Minister Sibusiso Barnabas
Dlamini
Political Parties: Convention for Full
Democracy in Swaziland; Swaziland
Democratic Alliance (coalition); others
Suffrage: not known

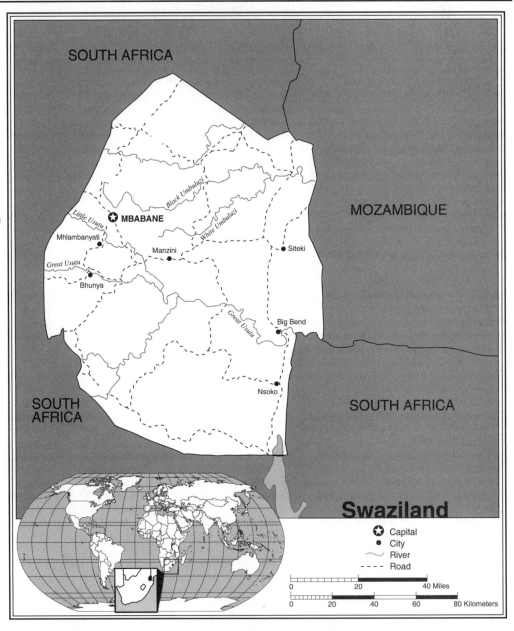

MILITARY

Military Expenditures (% of GDP): 1.9%
Current Disputes: territorial issues with
South Africa

ECONOMY

Currency ($ U.S. Equivalent): 3.54
emalangenis = $1
Per Capita Income/GDP: $4,200/$4.2 billion
GDP Growth Rate: 3.1%
Inflation Rate: 6%
Unemployment Rate: 22%
Natural Resources: iron ore; asbestos;
coal; clay; hydropower; forests; gold;
diamonds; quarry stone; talc

Agriculture: corn; livestock; sugarcane;
fruits; cotton; rice; sorghum; tobacco;
peanuts
Industry: sugar processing; mining; wood
pulp; beverages
Exports: $825 million (primary partners
South Africa, Europe, Mozambique)
Imports: $1.05 billion (primary partners
South Africa, Europe, Japan)

http://www.sas.upenn.edu/
African_Studies/Country_Specific/
Swaziland.html
http://www.realnet.co.sz

*Note: Population figures for Swaziland
explicitly take into account the effects of excess
mortality due to AIDS.

| Zulu and South African whites encroach on Swazi territory **1800s** | A protectorate is established by the British **1900** | Britain assumes control over Swaziland **1903** | Independence is restored **1968** | Parliament is dissolved and political parties are banned **1973** | King Sobuza dies **1982** | King Mswati III is crowned, ending the regency period marked by political instability **1986** | Swaziland's relationship with South Africa shifts; pressures mount for increased democracy **1990s** |

2000s

AIDS is recognized as a formidable threat to the Swazi people

Pressure continues for multipartyism

SWAZILAND

Swaziland is a small, landlocked kingdom sandwiched between the much larger states of Mozambique and South Africa. Casual observers have tended to look upon the country as a peaceful island of traditional Africa that has been immune to the continent's contemporary conflicts. This image is a product of the country's status as the only precolonial monarchy in sub-Saharan Africa to have survived into the modern era. Swazi sociopolitical organization is ostensibly governed in accordance with age-old structures and norms. But below this veneer of timelessness lies a dynamic society that has been subject to internal and external pressures.

The holding of restricted, nonparty elections in 1993 and 1998 has not quelled the debate over the country's political future between defenders of the status quo and those who advocate a restoration of multiparty democracy. During the 1993 elections, a "stay-away" campaign in favor of reform, accompanied by quiet diplomacy by neighboring states, helped push the Swazi government toward dialogue on the issue. In 1996, King Mswati announced the appointment of a committee to draw up a new constitution. But progress has since been stalled. The offically banned People's United Democratic Movement (PU-DEMO) and other civil-society groups have long called for a repeal of the 1973 royal decree that abolished constitutional rule, including the guarantee of basic freedoms.

From 1903 until the restoration of independence in 1968, the country remained a British colonial protectorate, despite sustained pressure for its incorporation into South Africa. Throughout the colonial period, the ruling Dlamini dynasty, which was led by the energetic Sobuza II after 1921, served successfully as a rallying point for national self-assertion on the key issues of regaining control of alienated land and opposing union with South Africa. Sobuza's personal leadership in both struggles contributed to the overwhelming popularity of his royalist Imbokodvo Party in the elections of 1964, 1967, and 1972. In 1973, faced with a modest but articulate opposition party, the Ngwane National Liberatory Congress, Sobuza dissolved Parliament and repealed the Westminster-style Constitution, characterizing it as "un-Swazi." In 1979, a new, nonpartisan Parliament was chosen; but authority remained with the king, assisted by his advisory council, the Liqoqo.

Sobuza's death in 1982 left many wondering if Swaziland's unique monarchist institutions would survive. A prolonged power struggle increased tensions within the ruling order. Members of the Liqoqo seized effective power and appointed a new "Queen Regent," Ntombi. However, palace intrigue continued until Prince Makhosetive, Ntombi's teenage son, was installed as King Mswati III in 1986, at age 18. The new king approved the demotion of the Liqoqo back to its advisory status and has ruled through his appointed prime minister and cabinet.

One of the major challenges facing any Swazi government is its relationship with South Africa. Under Sobuza, Swaziland managed to maintain its political autonomy while accepting its economic dependence on its powerful neighbor. The king also maintained a delicate balance between the apartheid state and the forces opposing it. In the 1980s, this balance became tilted, with a greater degree of cooperation between the two countries' security forces in curbing suspected African National Congress (ANC) activists. In an abrupt reversal of fortunes, Swaziland's prodemocracy activists now look to the new ANC–led government in South Africa for support.

Swaziland's economy, like its politics, is the product of both internal and external initiatives. Since independence, the nation has enjoyed a high rate of economic growth, led by the expansion and diversification of its agriculture. Success in agriculture has promoted the development of secondary industries, such as a sugar refinery and a paper mill. There has also been increased exploitation of coal and asbestos. Another important source of revenue is tourism, which depends on weekend traffic from South Africa.

Swazi development has relied on capital-intensive, rather than labor-intensive, projects. As a result, disparities in local wealth and dependence on South African investment have increased. Only 16 percent of the Swazi population, including migrant workers in South Africa, were in formal-sector employment by 1989. Until recently the economy was boosted by international investors looking for a politically preferable window to the South African market. An example is Coca Cola's decision to move its regional headquarters and concentrate plant from South Africa to Swaziland; the plant employs only about 100 workers but accounts for 20 percent of all foreign-exchange earnings. The current reform process in South Africa, however, is reducing Swaziland's attraction as a center for corporate relocation and sanctions-busting. It has also increased pressure for greater democracy.

DEVELOPMENT

Much of Swaziland's economy is managed by the Tibiyo TakaNgwana, a royally controlled institution established in 1968 by Sobuza. It is responsible for the financial assets of the communal lands (upon which most Swazis farm) and mining operations.

FREEDOM

The current political order restricts many forms of opposition, although its defenders claim that local councils, *Tikhudlas,* allow for popular participation in decision making. The leading opposition group is the People's United Democratic Movement.

HEALTH/WELFARE

Swaziland's low life expectancy and high infant mortality rates have resulted in greater public-health budget allocations. A greater emphasis has also been placed on preventive medicine. However, a high rate of HIV/AIDS poses severe and long-term threats to the nation.

ACHIEVEMENTS

The University of Swaziland was established in the 1970s and now offers a full range of degree and diploma programs.

Zambia (Republic of Zambia)

GEOGRAPHY

Area in Square Miles (Kilometers):
290,724 (752,972) (about the
size of Texas)

Capital (Population): Lusaka
(1,317,000)

Environmental Concerns: air
pollution; acid rain; poaching;
deforestation; soil erosion;
desertification; lack of
adequate water treatment

Geographical Features: mostly
high plateau with some hills
and mountains; landlocked

Climate: tropical; modified by
altitude

PEOPLE

Population

Total: 9,582,500*

Annual Growth Rate: 1.95%*

Rural/Urban Population Ratio:
57/43

Major Languages: English;
Bemba; Nyanja; Ila-Tonga;
Lozi; others

Ethnic Makeup: 99% African

Religions: 50% Christian;
48% indigenous beliefs; 2%
Hindu, Muslim, and others

Health

Life Expectancy at Birth: 37
years (male); 37 years (female)*

Infant Mortality Rate (Ratio):
92.3/1,000*

Physicians Available (Ratio):
1/10,917

Education

Adult Literacy Rate: 78.2%

Compulsory (Ages): 7–14

COMMUNICATION

Telephones: 76,700 main lines

Daily Newspaper Circulation:
13 per 1,000 people

Televisions: 32 per 1,000 people

Internet Service Providers: 3 (1999)

TRANSPORTATION

Highways in Miles (Kilometers): 41,404
(66,781)

Railroads in Miles (Kilometers): 1,294
(2,087)

Usable Airfields: 112

Motor Vehicles in Use: 215,000

GOVERNMENT

Type: republic

Independence Date: October 24, 1964
(from the United Kingdom)

Head of State/Government: President
Frederick Chiluba is both head of state
and head of government

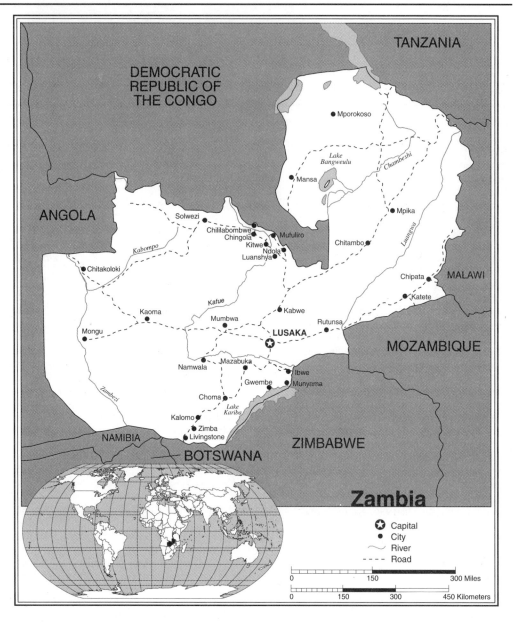

Political Parties: Movement for Multiparty
Democracy; United National
Independence Party; others

Suffrage: universal at 18

MILITARY

Military Expenditures (% of GDP): 1.8%

Current Disputes: boundary disputes with
several countries

ECONOMY

Currency ($ U.S. Equivalent): 672.8
kwachas = $1

Per Capita Income/GDP: $880/$8.5 billion

GDP Growth Rate: 1.5%

Inflation Rate: 27.4%

Unemployment Rate: 25%

Labor Force: 3,400,000

Natural Resources: copper; zinc; lead; cobalt;
coal; emeralds; gold; silver; uranium;
hydropower

Agriculture: corn; sorghum; rice; tobacco;
cotton; seeds; cassava; peanuts; sugarcane

Industry: livestock; mining; foodstuffs;
beverages; chemicals; textiles; fertilizer

Exports: $900 million (primary partners
Japan, Saudi Arabia, India)

Imports: $1.15 billion (primary partners
South Africa, Saudi Arabia, United
Kingdom)

 http://www.state.gov/www/
background_notes/
zambia_0997_bgn.html

*Note: Population figures for Zambia explicitly
take into account the effects of excess mortality
due to AIDS.

| Rhodes' South African Company is chartered by the British government A.D. 1889 | Development of the Copperbelt 1924–1934 | Federation of Northern Rhodesia, Southern Rhodesia, and Nyasaland is formed; still part of British Empire 1953–1963 | Zambia gains independence 1964 | Zambia becomes a one-party state under the United National Independence Party 1972 | South African military raids on Zambia 1980s | President Kenneth Kaunda is defeated in multiparty elections; Frederick Chiluba becomes the nation's second president; a coup attempt is thwarted; the government imposes a state of emergency 1990s |

2000s

The country grapples with the AIDS pandemic

ZAMBIA

On the morning of October 28, 1997, a Zambian Army captain took control of the national radio station and announced a coup. The plot had little support and was quickly crushed. In its aftermath, the president (and prime minister), Frederick Chiluba, proposed—and Parliament approved—a 90-day state of emergency, during which time 86 prominent critics of the government, including former president Kenneth Kaunda, were detained on allegations of involvement in the coup. Domestic and international human-rights groups reported serious abuses throughout the period.

The "Emergency" served to further polarize Zambian politics and society, which had already been divided by controversial elections in November 1996. President Chiluba and his Movement for Multiparty Democracy (MMD) were reelected in a poll that had been boycotted by the former ruling party, the United National Independence Party (UNIP), amid reports of voter-registration irregularities and the enactment of a law barring UNIP's leader, Kaunda, and others from running on account of their being "foreigners" (Kaunda's father had been born before colonial boundaries in what is today Malawi). The fairness of the elections was also compromised by MMD's use of state resources, especially the public media, in its campaign, and by the charging of Kaunda and nine other UNIP members with treason following a brief bombing campaign by an otherwise still shadowy group calling itself the Black Mambas (after an especially poisonous snake).

Recent events are a disappointment to those who saw the MMD's defeat of UNIP in 1991 as the beginning of a new era of democracy and development. Chiluba's victory had given hope that, after decades of decline, Zambia's hour had come. Chiluba's government has had to contend with high inflation; shrinking gross domestic product; the social and economic effects of a high rate of HIV/AIDS; expo-

sures of high-level corruption, including drug trafficking; and desertions from the MMD to the new National Party. Thousands of educated Zambians have left their country in search of opportunities elsewhere.

The roots of Zambia's woes lie in Kaunda's 27-year rule. During much of that period, the nation's economy steadily declined. Kaunda consistently blamed his country's setbacks on external forces rather than on his government's failings. There was some justification for his position. The high rate of return on exported copper made the nation one of the most prosperous in Africa until 1975. Since then, fluctuating, but generally depressed, prices for the metal—and the disruption of landlocked Zambia's traditional sea outlets as a result of strife in neighboring states—have had disastrous economic consequences. Nonetheless, internal factors have also contributed to Zambia's decay.

From the early years of Zambia's independence, Kaunda and UNIP showed little tolerance for political opposition. In 1972, the country was legally transformed into a one-party state in which power was concentrated in the hands of Kaunda and his fellow members of UNIP's Central Committee. After 1976, the government ruled with emergency powers. Although Zambia was never as repressive as such neighboring states as Malawi and Zaire, torture and political detention without trial were common.

In its rule, UNIP was supposedly guided by the philosophy of "humanism," a term that became synonymous with the "thoughts of Kaunda." The party also claimed adherence to socialism. Although it was once a mass party that spearheaded Zambia's struggle for majority rule and independence, UNIP came to stand for little other than the perpetuation of its own power.

An underlying economic problem has been the decline of rural production, despite Zambia's considerable agricultural

potential. The underdevelopment of agriculture is rooted in the colonial policies that favored mining to the exclusion of other sectors. Since independence, the rural areas have continued to be neglected in terms of infrastructural investment. Until recently Zambian farmers were paid little for their produce, with government subsidization of imported food. The result has been a continuous influx of individuals into urban areas, despite a lack of jobs, and falling food production.

Zambia's rural decline has severely constrained the government's ability to meet the challenge imposed by the depressed international price of copper. Falling prices have resulted in severe shortages of foreign exchange and mounting indebtedness. After years of relative inertia, the government, during the 1980s, devoted greater attention to rural development. Agricultural production rose modestly in response to increased incentives. But the size and desperate condition of the urban population discouraged the government from decontrolling prices altogether; rising maize prices in 1986 set off riots that left at least 30 people dead. The new MMD government ended the subsidies.

By 1990, the government's continuing economic crisis had dovetailed with rising agitation for a return to multiparty democracy. Despite the president's attempts to label multiparty advocates as "misfits, malcontents, drug-peddlers and dissidents," the movement grew, with the support of Zambia's major labor federation, its powerful Catholic Church, and a number of prominent UNIP backbenchers. In June–July 1990, severe riots culminated in a coup attempt, which, although unsuccessful, exposed the weakness of Kaunda's regime, forcing it finally to agree to free and fair elections.

DEVELOPMENT

Higher producer prices for agriculture, technical assistance, and rural-resettlement schemes are part of government efforts to raise Zambia's agricultural production. The agricultural sector has shown growth.

FREEDOM

Under the MMD, police have continued to commit extra-judicial killings and other abuses. The government has continued to try to limit press freedom, while failing to honor its 1991 promise to privatize the public media.

HEALTH/WELFARE

Life expectancy rates have increased in Zambia since independence, as a result of improved health-care facilities. However, AIDS increasingly looms as a critical problem in Zambia.

ACHIEVEMENTS

Zambia has long played a major role in the fight against white supremacy in Southern Africa. From 1964 until 1980, it was a major base for Zimbabwe nationalists.

Zimbabwe (Republic of Zimbabwe)

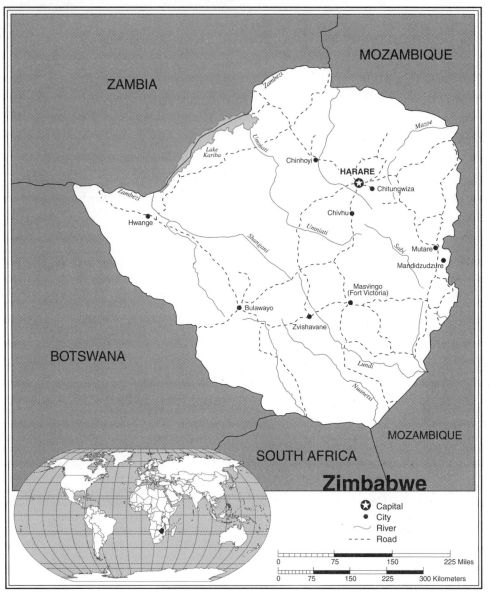

GEOGRAPHY

Area in Square Miles (Kilometers):
150,873 (390,759) (about the size of Montana)

Capital (Population): Harare (1,410,000)

Environmental Concerns: deforestation; soil erosion; land degradation; air and water pollution; poaching

Geographical Features: high plateau with higher central plateau (high veld); mountains in the east; landlocked

Climate: tropical; moderated by altitude

PEOPLE

Population

Total: 11,342,500*

Annual Growth Rate: 0.26%*

Rural/Urban Population Ratio: 67/33

Major Languages: English; Shona; Ndebele; Sidebele

Ethnic Makeup: 71% Shona; 16% Ndebele; 11% other African; 2% others

Religions: 50% syncretic (part Christian, part indigenous beliefs); 25% Christian; 24% indigenous beliefs; 1% Muslim

Health

Life Expectancy at Birth: 39 years (male); 36 years (female)

Infant Mortality Rate (Ratio): 62.2/1,000

Physicians Available (Ratio): 1/6,909

Education

Adult Literacy Rate: 85%

Compulsory (Ages): 6–13

COMMUNICATION

Telephones: 212,000 main lines

Daily Newspaper Circulation: 17 per 1,000 people

Televisions: 12 per 1,000 people

Internet Service Providers: 10 (1999)

TRANSPORTATION

Highways in Miles (Kilometers): 11,369 (18,338)

Railroads in Miles (Kilometers): 1,655 (2,759)

Usable Airfields: 459

Motor Vehicles in Use: 358,000

GOVERNMENT

Type: parliamentary democracy

Independence Date: April 18, 1980 (from the United Kingdom)

Head of State/Government: Executive President Robert Mugabe is both head of state and head of government

Political Parties: Zimbabwe African National Union–Patriotic Front; Zimbabwe African National Union–NDONGA; Movement for Democratic Change; Zimbabwe Unity Movement; Democratic Party; Forum Party; others

Suffrage: universal at 18

MILITARY

Military Expenditures (% of GDP): 3.1%

ECONOMY

Currency ($ U.S. Equivalent): 8.38 Zimbabwe dollars = $1

Per Capita Income/GDP: $2,400/$26.5 billion

GDP Growth Rate: 0%

Inflation Rate: 59%

Unemployment Rate: 50%

Labor Force: 5,000,000

Natural Resources: coal; minerals and metals

Agriculture: coffee; tobacco; corn; sugarcane; peanuts; wheat; cotton; livestock

Industry: mining; steel; textiles

Exports: $2 billion (primary partners South Africa, United Kingdom, Germany)

Imports: $2 billion (primary partners South Africa, United Kingdom, United States)

 http://www.sas.upenn.edu/African-Studies/Country-Specific/Zimbabwe.html
http://www.zimweb.com/Dzimbabwe.html

*Note: These estimates explicitly take into account the effects of excess mortality due to AIDS.

ZIMBABWE

In the year 2000, Zimbabwe was thrust into the international spotlight after its aging president, Robert Mugabe, gave his blessing to the occupation of white-owned commercial farms by supposed veterans of Zimbabwe's liberation war, which had ended two decades earlier. The occupation campaign began in April 2000, after Mugabe suffered an unexpected defeat in a constitutional referendum. In July, his ruling Zimbabwe African National Union–Patriotic Front (ZANU–PF) party won 62 out of 120 contested National Assembly seats in an election marked by state-sanctioned violence and intimidation against Mugabe's opponents. The newly formed Movement for Democratic Change (MDC) captured 57 seats. The MDC's relative success was a breakthrough in galvanizing electoral opposition to two decades of rule by Mugabe's ZANU–PF. But it did little to halt Zimbabwe's decline as "the world's fastest-shrinking economy." In adopting mob tactics toward the emotive issue of land—where there is a longstanding and widely accepted need for redistributive reform—Mugabe has bought his regime some additional time. But Zimbabwe's reputation as a law-abiding society, along with its economy, lies in tatters. Many have chosen to leave the country, usually illegally, in search for survival in South Africa or Botswana.

Zimbabwe achieved its formal independence in April 1980, after a 14-year armed struggle by its disenfranchised black African majority. Before 1980, the country had been called Southern Rhodesia—a name that honored Cecil Rhodes, the British imperialist who had masterminded the colonial occupation of the territory in the late nineteenth century. For its black African majority, Rhodesia's name was thus an expression of their subordination to a small minority of privileged white settlers whose racial hegemony was the product of Rhodes's conquest. The new name of Zimbabwe was symbolic of the greatness of the nation's precolonial roots.

THE PRECOLONIAL PAST

By the fifteenth century, Zimbabwe had become the center of a series of states that prospered through their trade in gold and other goods with Indian Ocean merchants. These civilizations left as their architectural legacy the remains of stone settlements known as *zimbabwes*. The largest of these, the so-called Great Zimbabwe, lies near the modern town of Masvingo. Within its massive walls are dozens of stella, topped with distinctive carved birds whose likeness has become a symbol of the modern state. Unfortunately, early European fortuneseekers and archaeologists destroyed much of the archaeological evidence of this site, but what survives confirms that the state had trading contacts as far afield as China.

From the sixteenth century, the Zimbabwean civilizations seem to have declined, possibly as a result of the disruption of the East African trading networks by the Portuguese. Nevertheless, the states themselves survived until the nineteenth century, while their cultural legacy is very much alive today, especially among the 71 percent of Zimbabwe's population who speak Shona.

Zimbabwe's other major ethnolinguistic community are the Ndebele-speakers, who today account for about 16 percent of the population. This group traces its local origin to the mid-nineteenth-century conquest of much of modern Zimbabwe by invaders from the south under the leadership of Umzilagazi, who established a militarily strong Ndebele kingdom, which subsequently was ruled by his son.

WHITE RULE

Zimbabwe's colonial history is unique in that it was never under the direct rule of a European power. In 1890, the lands of the Ndebele and Shona were invaded by agents of Rhodes's British South Africa Company (BSACO). In the 1890s, both groups put up stiff resistance to the encroachments of the BSACO settlers, but eventually they succumbed to the invaders. In 1924, the BSACO administration was dissolved and Southern Rhodesia became a self-governing British Crown colony. "Self-government" was, in fact, confined to the white-settler community, which grew rapidly but never numbered more than 5 percent of the population.

In 1953, Southern Rhodesia was federated with the British colonial territories of Northern Rhodesia (Zambia) and Nyasaland (Malawi). This Central African Federation was supposed to evolve into a "multiracial" dominion; but from the beginning, it was perceived by the black majority in all three territories as a vehicle for continued white domination. As the Federation's first prime minister put it, the partnership of blacks and whites in building the new state would be analogous to a horse and its rider—no one had any illusions as to which race group would continue to be the beast of burden.

In 1963, the Federation collapsed as a result of local resistance. Black nationalists established the independent "nonracial" states of Malawi and Zambia. For a while, it appeared that majority rule would also come to Southern Rhodesia. The local black community was increasingly well organized and militant in demanding full citizenship rights. However, in 1962, the white electorate responded to this challenge by voting into office the Rhodesia Front (RF), a party determined to uphold white supremacy at any cost. Using already-existing emergency powers, the new government moved to suppress the two major black nationalist movements: the Zimbabwe African People's Union (ZAPU) and the Zimbabwe African National Union (ZANU).

RHODESIA DECLARES INDEPENDENCE

In a bid to consolidate white power along the lines of the neighboring apartheid regime of South Africa, the RF, now led by Ian Smith, made its 1965 Unilateral Declaration of Independence (UDI) of any ties to the British Crown. Great Britain, along with the United Nations, refused to recognize this move. In 1967, the United Nations imposed mandatory economic sanctions against the "illegal" RF regime. But the sanctions were not fully effective, largely due to the fact that they were flouted by South Africa and the Portuguese authorities who controlled most of Mozambique until 1974. The United States continued openly to purchase Rhodesian chrome for a number of years, while many states and individuals engaged in more covert forms of sanctions-busting. The Rhodesian economy initially benefited from the porous blockade, which encouraged the development of a wide range of import-substitution industries.

With the sanctions having only a limited effect and Britain and the rest of the international community unwilling to engage in more active measures, it soon became clear that the burden of overthrowing the RF regime would be borne by the local population. ZANU and ZAPU, as underground movements, began to engage in armed struggle beginning in 1966. The success of their attacks initially was limited; but from 1972, the Rhodesian Security Forces were increasingly besieged by the nationalists' guerrilla campaign. The 1974 liberation of Mozambique from the Portuguese greatly increased the effectiveness of the ZANU forces, who were allowed to infiltrate into Rhodesia from Mozambican territory. Meanwhile, their ZAPU comrades launched attacks from bases in Zambia. In 1976, the two groups became loosely affiliated as the Patriotic Front.

Unable to stop the military advance of the Patriotic Front, which was resulting in a massive white exodus, the RF attempted to forge a power-sharing arrangement that preserved major elements of settler privilege. Although rejected by ZANU or ZAPU, this "internal settlement" was implemented in 1978–1979. A predominantly black government took office, but real power remained in white hands, and the fighting only intensified. Finally, in 1979, all the belligerent parties, meeting at Lancaster House in London, agreed to a compromise peace, which opened the door to majority rule while containing a number of constitutional provisions designed to reassure the white minority. In the subsequent elections, held in 1980, ZANU captured 57 and ZAPU 20 out of the 80 seats elected by the "common roll." Another 20 seats, which were reserved for whites for seven years as a result of the Lancaster House agreement, were captured by the Conservative Alliance (the new name for the RF). ZANU leader Robert Mugabe became independent Zimbabwe's first prime minister.

THE RHODESIAN LEGACY
The political, economic, and social problems inherited by the Mugabe government were formidable. Rhodesia had essentially been divided into two "nations": one black, the other white. Segregation prevailed in virtually all areas of life, with those facilities open to blacks being vastly inferior to those open to whites. The better half of the national territory had also been reserved for white ownership. Large commercial farms prospered in this white area, growing maize and tobacco for export as well as a diversified mix of crops for domestic consumption. In contrast, the black areas, formally known as Tribal Trust Lands, suffered from inferior soil and rainfall, overcrowding, and poor infrastructure. Most black adults had little choice but to obtain seasonal work in the white areas. Black workers on white plantations, together with the large number of

domestic servants, were particularly impoverished. But until the 1970s, there were also few opportunities for skilled blacks as a result of a de facto "color bar," which reserved the best jobs for whites.

Despite its stated commitment to revolutionary socialist objectives, since 1980, the Mugabe government has taken an evolutionary approach in dismantling the socioeconomic structures of old Rhodesia. This cautious policy is, in part, based on an appreciation that these same structures support what, by regional standards, is a relatively prosperous and self-sufficient economy. Until 1990, the government's hands were also partially tied by the Lancaster House accords, wherein private property, including the large settler estates, could not be confiscated without compensation. In its first years, the government nevertheless made impressive progress in improving the livelihoods of the Zimbabwean majority by redistributing some of the surplus of the still white-dominated private sector. With the lifting of sanctions, mineral, maize, and tobacco exports expanded and import restrictions eased. Workers' incomes rose, and a minimum wage, which notably covered farm employees, was introduced. Rising consumer purchasing power initially benefited local manufacturers. Health and educational facilities were expanded, while a growing number of blacks began to occupy management positions in the civil service and, to a lesser extent, in businesses.

Zimbabwe had hoped that foreign investment and aid would pay for an ambitious scheme to buy out many white farmers and to settle African peasants on their land. However, funding shortfalls have resulted in only modest resettlement. Approximately 4,000 white farmers own more than one third of the land. In 1992,

the government passed a bill that allows for the involuntary purchase of up to 50 percent of this land at an officially set price. While enjoying overwhelming domestic support, this land-redistribution measure has come under considerable external criticism for violating the private-property and judicial "rights" of the large-scale farmers. Others have pointed out that, besides producing large surpluses of food in nondrought years, many jobs are tied to the commercial estates. Revelations in 1993–1994 that some confiscated properties had been turned over to leading ZANU politicians gave rise to further controversy.

While gradually abandoning its professed desire to build a socialist society, the Zimbabwean government has continued to face a classic dilemma of all industrializing societies: whether to continue to use tight import controls to protect its existing manufacturing base or to open up its economy in the hopes of enjoying a takeoff based on export-oriented growth. While many Zimbabwean manufacturers would be vulnerable to greater foreign competition, there is now a widespread consensus that limits of the local market have contributed to stagnating output and physical depreciation of local industry in recent years.

POLITICAL DEVELOPMENT
The Mugabe government has promoted reconciliation across the racial divide. Although the reserved seats for whites were abolished in 1987, the white minority (whites now make up less than 2 percent of the population) is well represented within government as well as business. Unfortunately, Mugabe's ZANU administration has shown less tolerance of its political opponents, especially ZAPU. ZANU was originally a breakaway faction

(Oxfam America photo)

As in many African institutions, decisions in Zimbabwean organizations are often made by consensus, arrived at after long discussions.

Heyday of the gold trade and Great Zimbabwe 1400s–1500s	The Ndebele state emerges in Zimbabwe 1840s	The Pioneer Column: arrival of the white settlers 1890	Chimurenga: rising against the white intruders, ending in repression by whites 1895–1897	Local government in Southern Rhodesia is placed in the hands of white settlers 1924	Unilateral Declaration of Independence 1965	Armed struggle begins 1966	ZANU leader Robert Mugabe becomes Zimbabwe's first prime minister 1980	ZANU and ZAPU merge and win the 1990 elections; elections in 1995 result in a landslide victory for the ruling ZANU-PF 1990s

2000s

Mugabe sanctions occupation of white-owned commercial farms

of ZAPU. At the time of this split, in 1963, the differences between the two movements had largely been over tactics. But elections in 1980 and 1985 confirmed that the followings of both movements have become ethnically based, with most Shona supporting ZANU and Ndebele supporting ZAPU.

Initially, ZANU agreed to share power with ZAPU. However, in 1982, the alleged discoveries of secret arms caches, which ZANU claimed ZAPU was stockpiling for a coup, led to the dismissal of the ZAPU ministers. Some leading ZAPU figures were also detained. The confrontation led to violence that very nearly degenerated into a full-scale civil war. From 1982 to 1984, the Zimbabwean Army, dominated by former ZANU and Rhodesian units, carried out a brutal counterinsurgency campaign against supposed ZAPU dissidents in the largely Ndebele areas of western Zimbabwe. Thousands of civilians were killed—especially by the notorious Fifth Brigade, which operated outside the normal military command structure. Many more fled to Botswana, including, for a period, the ZAPU leader, Joshua Nkomo.

Until 1991, Mugabe's stated intention was to create a one-party state in Zimbabwe. With his other black and white opponents compromised by their past association with the RF and its internal settlement, this largely meant coercing ZAPU into dissolving itself into ZANU. However, the increased support for ZAPU in its core Ndebele constituencies during the 1985 elections led to a renewed emphasis on the carrot over the stick in bringing about the union. In 1987, ZAPU formally merged into ZANU, but their shotgun wedding has made for an uneasy marriage.

With the demise of ZAPU, new forces have emerged in opposition to Mugabe and the drive for a one-party state. Principal among these is the Zimbabwe Unity Movement (ZUM), led by former ZANU member Edger Tekere. In the 1990 elections, ZUM received about 20 percent of the vote, in a poll that saw a sharp drop in voter participation. The election was also marred by serious restrictions on opposition activity and blatant voter intimidation. The deaths of ZUM supporters in the period before the election reinforced the message of the government-controlled media that a vote for the opposition was an act of suicide. A senior member of the Central Intelligence Organization and a ZANU activist were subsequently convicted of the murder of ZUM organizing secretary Patrick Kombayi. However, they were pardoned by Mugabe.

Mugabe initially claimed that his 1990 victory was a mandate to establish a one-party state. But in 1991, the changing international climate, the continuing strength of the opposition, and growing opposition within ZANU itself caused him to shelve the project. Under 1992 election law, however, ZANU alone was made eligible for state funding.

The survival of political pluralism in Zimbabwe reflects the emergence of a civil society that is increasingly resistant to the concentration of power. Independent nongovernmental organizations have successfully taken up many social human-rights issues. Less successful have been attempts to promote an independent press, which has remained almost entirely in government/ZANU hands.

In 1992, the Forum Party, a new opposition movement, was launched, under the leadership of former chief justice Enoch Dumbutshena. But it failed to break the mold of Zimbabwean politics due to its own internal splits and failure to unite with other groups. As a result, Mugabe was easily reelected in March 1996 in a low voter turnout (it was ultimately boycotted by the entire opposition).

Notwithstanding its continuing electoral success, public confidence in the ZANU government has been greatly eroded by its relative failure in handling the 1992 drought crisis. Despite warning signs of the impending catastrophe, little attempt was made to stockpile food. This failure resulted in widespread hunger and dependence on expensive food imports. Long-neglected waterworks, especially those serving Bulawayo, the country's second-largest city, proved to be inadequate. The government also lost support due to its seeming insensitivity to the plight of ordinary Zimbabweans suffering from high rates of unemployment and inflation. With inflation at 22 percent, a civil servants strike was sparked in August 1996 by an across-the-board 6 percent raise for ordinary workers as compared to a 130 percent raise for members of Parliament.

While the welfare of ordinary Zimbabweans may have improved since 1980, popular frustration with the status quo is increasing. In 1998, resentment against the government, resulting from continued economic decline, was aggravated in some quarters by Mugabe's decision to dispatch nearly 3,000 troops to the Democratic Republic of the Congo (Zaire) to defend the embattled regime of Laurent Kabila. With formal-sector unemployment in excess of 50 percent and inflation approaching 200 percent, it was a foreign adventure that the country could ill afford.

DEVELOPMENT

Peasant production has increased dramatically since independence, creating grain reserves and providing exports for the region. The contribution of communal farmers has been recognized both within Zimbabwe and internationally.

FREEDOM

Since the 1990 lifting of the state of emergency that had been in effect since the days of the Federation, Zimbabwe's human-rights record has generally improved. Some government institutions, however, especially the Central Intelligence Organization, are still accused of extra-judicial abuses.

HEALTH/WELFARE

Public expenditure on health and education has risen dramatically since independence. Most Zimbabweans now enjoy access to medical facilities, while primary-school enrollment has multiplied fourfold. Higher education has also been greatly expanded. But the advances are threatened by downturns in the economy, and school fees have been reintroduced.

ACHIEVEMENTS

Zimbabwe's capital city of Harare has become an arts and communications center for Southern Africa. Many regional as well as local filmmakers, musicians, and writers based in the city enjoy international reputations. And the distinctive malachite carvings of Zimbabwean sculptors are highly valued in the international art market.

West Africa

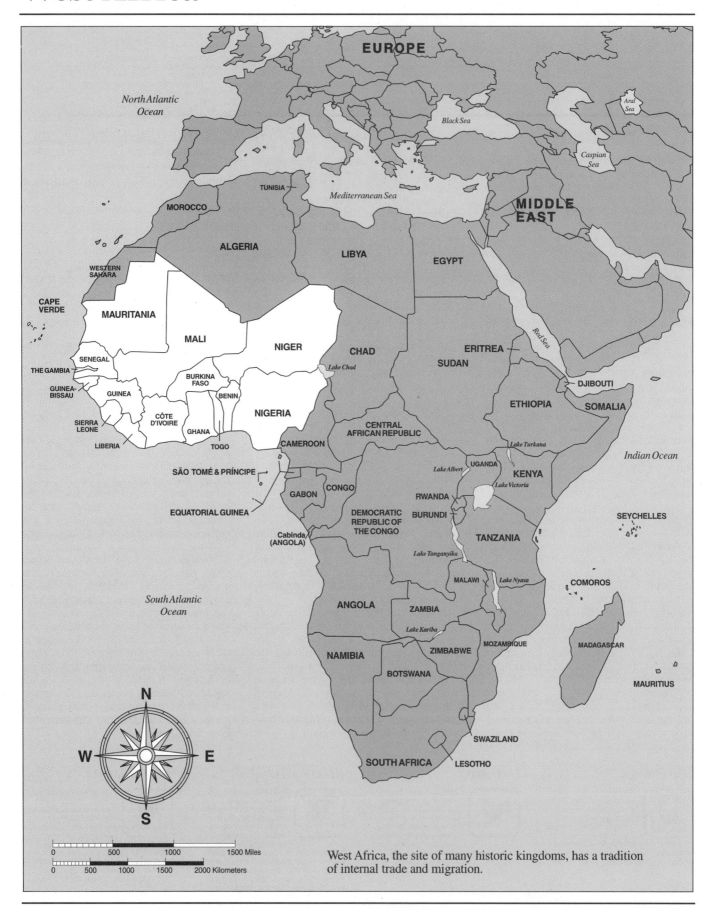

North Atlantic
Ocean

EUROPE

Black Sea

Aral
Sea

Caspian
Sea

TUNISIA

MOROCCO

Mediterranean Sea

MIDDLE
EAST

ALGERIA

LIBYA

EGYPT

WESTERN
SAHARA

CAPE
VERDE

MAURITANIA

MALI

NIGER

CHAD

Red Sea

ERITREA

SUDAN

SENEGAL

Lake Chad

DJIBOUTI

THE GAMBIA

GUINEA-
BISSAU

GUINEA

BURKINA
FASO

BENIN

ETHIOPIA

SOMALIA

SIERRA
LEONE

CÔTE
D'IVOIRE

GHANA

NIGERIA

CENTRAL
AFRICAN REPUBLIC

Lake Turkana

LIBERIA

TOGO

CAMEROON

Indian Ocean

SÃO TOMÉ & PRÍNCIPE

Lake Albert

UGANDA

KENYA

Lake Victoria

EQUATORIAL GUINEA

GABON

CONGO

RWANDA

DEMOCRATIC
REPUBLIC OF
THE CONGO

BURUNDI

SEYCHELLES

Cabinda
(ANGOLA)

TANZANIA

Lake Tanganyika

South Atlantic
Ocean

MALAWI

Lake Nyasa

COMOROS

ANGOLA

ZAMBIA

Lake Kariba

MOZAMBIQUE

MADAGASCAR

NAMIBIA

ZIMBABWE

BOTSWANA

MAURITIUS

N

SWAZILAND

W   E

SOUTH AFRICA

LESOTHO

S

| 0 | 500 | 1000 | 1500 Miles |

| 0 | 500 | 1000 | 1500 | 2000 Kilometers |

West Africa, the site of many historic kingdoms, has a tradition
of internal trade and migration.

West Africa: Seeking Unity in Diversity

Anyone looking at a map of Africa can identify West Africa as the great bulge on the western coast of the continent. It is a region bound by the Sahara Desert to the north, the Atlantic Ocean to the south and west, and, in part, by the Cameroonian Mountains to the east. Each of these boundaries has historically been a bridge rather than a barrier, in that the region has long been linked through trade to the rest of the world.

At first glance, West Africa's great variety is more striking than any of its unifying features. It contains the environmental extremes of desert and rain forest. While most of its people rely on agriculture, every type of occupation can be found, from herders to factory workers. Hundreds of languages are spoken; some are as different from one another as English is from Arabic or Japanese. Local cultural traditions and the societies that practice them are also myriad.

Yet the more closely one examines West Africa, the more one is impressed with the features that give the nations of the region a degree of coherence and unity. Some of the common characteristics and features of West Africa as a whole include the vegetation belts that stretch across the region from west to east, creating a similar environmental mix among the region's polities; the constant movement of peoples across local and national boundaries; and efforts being made by West African governments toward greater integration in the region, primarily through economic organizations. West Africans also share elements of a common history.

With the exception of Liberia, all the contemporary states of West Africa were the creations of competing European colonial powers—France, Germany, Great Britain, and Portugal—that divided most of the area during the late 1800s. Before this partition, however, much of the region was linked by the spread of Islam and patterns of trade, including the legacy of intensive involvement between the sixteenth and nineteenth centuries in the trans-Atlantic slave trade. From ancient times, great kingdoms expanded and contracted across the West African savanna and forest, giving rise to sophisticated civilizations.

WEST AFRICAN VEGETATION AND CLIMATE ZONES

Traveling north from the coastlines of such states as Nigeria, Ghana, and Côte d'Ivoire, one encounters tropical rain forests, which give way first to woodland savanna and then to more arid, more open plains. In Mali, Niger, and other landlocked countries to the north, the savanna gives way to the still drier Sahel environment, and finally to the Sahara Desert itself.

Whatever their ethnicity or nationality, the peoples living within each of these vegetation zones generally share the benefits and problems of similar livelihoods. For instance, cocoa, coffee, yams, and cassava are among the cash and food crops planted in the cleared forest and woodland zones, which stretch from Guinea to Nigeria. Groundnuts, sorghum, and millet are commonly harvested in the savanna belt that runs from Senegal to northern Nigeria. Herders in the Sahel, who historically could not go too far south with their cattle because of the presence of the deadly tsetse fly in the forest, continue to cross state boundaries in search of pasture.

People throughout West Africa have periodically suffered from drought. The effects of drought have often been aggravated in recent years by population pressures on the land. These factors have contributed to environmental changes and degradation. The condition of the Sahel in particular has deteriorated through a process of desertification, leading to large-scale relocations among many of its inhabitants. The eight Sahelian countries—Cape Verde, The Gambia, Burkina Faso, Mali, Senegal, Niger, Chad (in Central Africa), and Mauritania—have consequently formed a coordinating Committee for Struggle Against Drought in the Sahel (CILSS).

Farther to the south, large areas of woodland savanna have turned into grasslands as their forests have been cut down by land-hungry farmers. Drought has also periodically resulted in widespread brushfires in Ghana, Côte d'Ivoire, Togo, and Benin, which have transformed forests into savannas and savannas into deserts. Due to the depletion of forest, the Harmattan (a dry wind that blows in from the Sahara during January and February) now reaches many parts of the coast that in the recent past did not feel its breath. Its dust and haze have become a sign of the new year—and of new agricultural problems—throughout much of West Africa.

The great rivers of West Africa, such as The Gambia, Niger, Senegal, and Volta, along with their tributaries, have become increasingly important both as avenues of travel and trade and for the water they provide. Countries have joined together in large-scale projects designed to harness their waters for irrigation and hydroelectric power through regional organizations, like the Mano River grouping of Guinea, Liberia, and Sierra Leone and the Organization for the Development of the Senegal River, composed of Mali, Mauritania, and Senegal.

THE LINKS OF HISTORY AND TRADE

The peoples of West Africa have never been united as members of a single political unit. Yet some of the precolonial kingdoms that expanded across the region have great symbolic importance for those seeking to enhance interstate cooperation. The Mali empire of the thirteenth to fifteenth centuries, the Songhai empire of the sixteenth century, and the nineteenth-century Fulani caliphate of Sokoto, all based in the savanna, are widely remembered as examples of past supranational glory. The kingdoms of the southern forests, such as the Asante Confederation, the Dahomey kingdom, and the Yoruba city-states, were smaller than the great savanna empires to their north. Although generally later in origin and different in character from the northern states, the forest kingdoms are, nonetheless, sources of greater regional identity.

The precolonial states of West Africa gave rise to great urban centers, interlinked through extensive trade networks.

This development was probably the result of the area's agricultural productivity, which supported a relatively high population density from early times. Many modern settlements have long histories. Present-day Timbuctu and Gao, in Mali, were important centers of learning and commerce in medieval times. Some other examples include Ouagadougou, Ibadan, Benin, and Kumasi, all in the forest zone. These southern centers prospered in the past by sending gold, kola, leather goods, cloth—and slaves—to the northern savanna and southern coast.

The cities of the savannas linked West Africa to North Africa. Beginning in the eleventh century, the ruling groups of the savanna increasingly turned to the universal vision of Islam. While Islam also spread to the forests, the southernmost areas were ultimately more strongly influenced by Christianity, which was introduced by Europeans, who became active along the West African coast in the fifteenth century. For centuries, the major commercial link among Europe, the Americas, and West Africa was the trans-Atlantic slave trade; during the 1800s, however, legitimate commerce in palm oil and other tropical products replaced it. New centers such as Dakar, Accra, and Freetown emerged—resulting either from the slave trade or from its suppression.

THE MOVEMENT OF PEOPLES

Despite the (incorrect) view of many who see Africa as being a continent made up of isolated groups, one constant characteristic of West Africa has been the transregional migration of its people. Herders have moved east and west across the savanna and south into the forests. Since colonial times, many professionals as well as laborers have sought employment outside their home areas.

Some of the peoples of West Africa, such as the Malinke, Fulani, Hausa, and Mossi, have developed especially well-established heritages of mobility. In the past, the Malinke journeyed from Mali to the coastal areas in Guinea, Senegal, and The Gambia. Other Malinke traders made their way to Burkina Faso, Liberia, and Sierra Leone, where they came to be known as Mandingoes.

The Fulani have developed their own patterns of seasonal movement. They herd their cattle south across the savanna during the dry season and return to the north during the rainy season. Urbanized Fulani groups have historically journeyed from west to east, often serving as agents of Islamization as well as promoters of trade. More recently, many Fulani have been forced to move southward as a result of the deterioration

(IFC/World Bank photo by Ray Witkin)

A worker cuts cloth at a textile mill in Côte d'Ivoire. The patterns shown here are similar to indigenous regional patterns. Most of the cloth made in Côte d'Ivoire is exported.

of their grazing lands. The Hausa, who live mostly in northern Nigeria and Niger, are found throughout much of West Africa. Indeed, their trading presence is so widespread that some have suggested that the Hausa language be promoted as a lingua franca, or common language, for West Africa.

Millions of migrant laborers are regularly attracted to Côte d'Ivoire and Ghana from the poorer inland states of Burkina Faso, Mali, and Niger, thus promoting continuing economic interdependence between these states. Similar large-scale migrations also occur elsewhere. The drastic expulsion of aliens by the Nigerian government in 1983 was startling to the outside world, in part because few had realized that so many Ghanaians, Nigeriens, Togolese, Beninois, and Camerooni-ans had taken up residence in Nigeria. Such immigration is not new, though its scale into Nigeria was greatly increased by that country's oil boom. Peoples such as the Yoruba, Ewe, and Vai, who were divided by colonialism, have often ignored modern state boundaries in order to maintain their ethnic ties. Other migrations also have roots in the colonial past. Sierra Leonians worked as clerks and craftspeople throughout the coastal areas of British West Africa, while Igbo were recruited to serve in northern Nigeria. Similarly, Beninois became the assistants of French administrators in other parts of French West Africa, while Cape Verdians occupied intermediate positions in Portugal's mainland colonies.

WEST AFRICAN INTEGRATION

Many West Africans recognize the weaknesses inherent in the region's national divisions. The peoples of the region would benefit from greater multilateral political cooperation and economic integration. Yet there are many obstacles blocking the growth of pan-regional development. National identity is probably even stronger today than it was in the days when Kwame Nkrumah, the charismatic Ghanaian leader, pushed for African unity but was frustrated by parochial interests. The larger and more prosperous states, such as Nigeria and Côte d'Ivoire, are reluctant to share their relative wealth with smaller countries, which, in turn, fear being swallowed.

One-party rule and more overt forms of dictatorship have recently been abandoned throughout West Africa. However, for the moment, the region is still politically divided between those states that have made the transition to multiparty constitutional systems of government and those that are still under effective military control. Overlapping ethnicity is also sometimes more a source of suspicion rather than a source of unity between states. Because the countries were under the rule of different colonial powers, French, English, and Portuguese serve today as official languages of the different na-

tions, which also inherited different administrative traditions. Moreover, during colonial times, independent infrastructures were developed in each country; these continue to orient economic activities toward the coast and Europe rather than encouraging links among West African countries.

Political changes also affect regional cooperation and domestic development. Senegambia, the now-defunct confederation of Senegal and The Gambia, was dominated by Senegal and resented by many Gambians. The Liberian Civil War has also led to division between the supporters and opponents of the intervention of a multinational peacekeeping force.

Despite the many roadblocks to unity, a number of multinational organizations have developed in West Africa, stimulated in large part by the severity of the common problems that the countries face. The West African countries have a good record of cooperating to avoid armed conflict and to settle their occasional border disputes. In addition to the multilateral agencies that are coordinating the struggle against drought and the development of various river basins, there are also various regional commodity cartels, such as the five-member Groundnut Council. The West African Examinations Council standardizes secondary-school examinations in most of the countries where English is an official language, and most of the Francophonic states have the same currency.

The most ambitious and broad organization in the region is the Economic Organization of West African States (ECOWAS), which includes all the states incorporated in the West African section of this text. Established in 1975 by the Treaty of Lagos, ECOWAS aims to promote trade, cooperation, and self-reliance. The progress of the organization in these areas has thus far been limited. But ECOWAS can point to some significant achievements. Several joint ventures have been developed; steps toward tariff reduction are being taken; competition between ECOWAS and the Economic Community of West Africa (CEAO), an economic organization of former French colonies, has been lessened by limiting CEAO; and ECOWAS members have agreed in principle to eventually establish a common currency. Through its multinational peacekeeping force, ECOMOG, some members of ECOWAS have jointly intervened to try to settle internal conflicts in Liberia and Sierra Leone. The belated success of this force in Liberia points to the pivotal role that must be played by Nigeria, which has sustained the force, in any move toward greater regional cooperation. With about half of West Africa's population and economic output, a revitalized Nigeria has the potential for leadership—but only if it makes progress toward overcoming its own internal political and economic weaknesses.

Benin (Republic of Benin)

GEOGRAPHY

Area in Square Miles (Kilometers):
43,483 (112,620) (about the
size of Pennsylvania)
Capital (Population): official:
Porto-Novo (200,000); de
facto: Cotonou (750,000)
Environmental Concerns:
drought; insufficient potable
water; poaching; deforestation;
desertification
Geographical Features: mostly
flat to undulating plain; some
hills and low mountains
Climate: tropical to semiarid

PEOPLE

Population

Total: 6,396,000
Annual Growth Rate: 3.03%
Rural/Urban Population Ratio:
61/39
Major Languages: French; Fon;
Yoruba; others
Ethnic Makeup: 99% African
(most important groupings
Fon, Adja, Yoruba, and
Bariba); 1% European
Religions: 70% indigenous
beliefs; 15% Muslim; 15%
Christian

Health

Life Expectancy at Birth: 49
years (male); 51 years (female)
Infant Mortality Rate (Ratio):
90.8/1,000
Physicians Available (Ratio):
1/14,216

Education

Adult Literacy Rate: 37%
Compulsory (Ages): 6–12; free

COMMUNICATION

Telephones: 38,400 main lines
Daily Newspaper Circulation: 2
per 1,000 people
Televisions: 4 per 1,000 people
Internet Service Providers: na

TRANSPORTATION

Highways in Miles (Kilometers): 4,208
(6,787)
Railroads in Miles (Kilometers): 360 (578)
Usable Airports: 5
Motor Vehicles in Use: 55,000

GOVERNMENT

Type: republic
Independence Date: August 1, 1960 (from
France)
Head of State/Government: President
Mathieu Kérékou is both head of state
and head of government

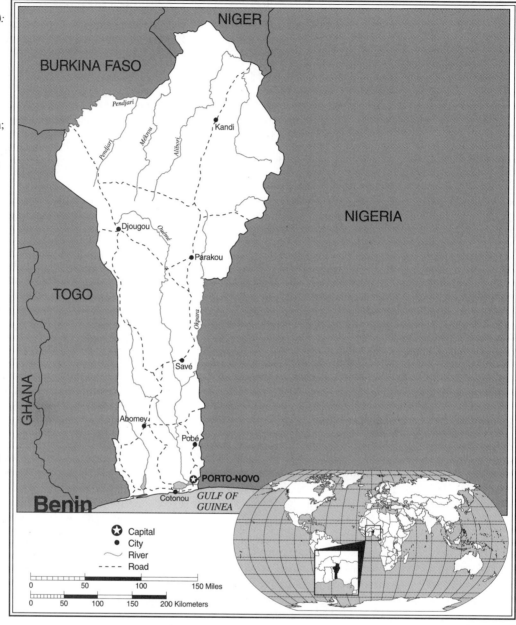

Benin

- ⊗ Capital
- ● City
- ∼ River
- --- Road

Political Parties: Popular Revolutionary
Party of Benin; Alliance for Democracy
and Progress; Front for Renewal and
Development; African Movement for
Democracy and Progress; many others
Suffrage: universal at 18

MILITARY

Military Expenditures (% of GDP): 1.2%
Current Disputes: none

ECONOMY

Currency ($ U.S. Equivalent): 529.43
CFA francs = $1
Per Capita Income/GDP: $1,300/$8.1 billion
GDP Growth Rate: 5%

Inflation Rate: 3%
Natural Resources: small offshore oil
deposits; limestone; marble; timber
Agriculture: palm products; cotton; corn;
rice; yams; cassava; beans; sorghum;
livestock
Industry: textiles; construction materials;
food; cigarettes; petroleum
Exports: $396 million (primary partners
Brazil, Libya, Indonesia)
Imports: $566 million (primary partners
France, China, United Kingdom)

http://www.sas.upenn.edu/
African_Studies/Country_Specific/
Benin.htm

BENIN

On August 1, 2000, Benin marked 40 years of independence. During this period, the country has experienced a series of shifts in political and economic policy that have so far failed to lift most Beninoise out of chronic poverty. In this respect, Benin's ongoing struggle for development can be seen as a microcosm of the challenges facing much of the African continent.

Politically, Benin has been in the forefront of those nations on the continent making the transition away from an authoritarian centralized state toward greater democracy and market reforms. This process has not as yet been accompanied by a decisive shift toward a new generation of leadership. In March 1996, former president Mathieu Kérékou returned to power with 52 percent of the vote, defeating incumbent Nicephore Soglo in Benin's second ballot since the 1990 restoration of multiparty democracy. Five years earlier, Soglo had defeated Kérékou, who had ruled the country as a virtual dictator for 17 years before agreeing to a democratic transition. In the past, Kérékou styled himself as a Marxist-Leninist and presided over a one-party state. Today, he presents himself as a Christian Democrat, affirming that there can be no turning back to the old order. In Parliament, his Popular Revolutionary Party of Benin (PRPB) shares power with other groupings whose existence is primarily a reflection of ethnoregional rather than ideological divisions.

Kérékou's restoration did not result in any significant moves away from his predecessor's economic reforms, which had resulted in a modest rise in gross domestic product, increased investment, reduced inflation, and an easing of the country's debt burden. He is under pressure, however, to raise the living standards of Benin's impoverished masses, who so far have not benefited from the reforms.

THE OLD ORDER FALLS

Kérékou's first reign began to unravel in late 1989. Unable to pay its bills, his government found itself increasingly vulnerable to mounting internal opposition and, to a lesser extent, to external pressure to institute sweeping political and economic reforms.

A wave of strikes and mass demonstrations swept through Cotonou, the country's largest city, in December 1989. This upsurge in prodemocracy agitation was partially inspired by the overthrow of Central/Eastern Europe's Marxist-Leninist regimes; ironically, the Stalinist underground Communist Party of Dahomey (PCD) also played a role in organizing much of the unrest. Attempts to quell the demonstrations with force only increased public anger toward the authorities.

In an attempt to defuse the crisis, the PRPB's state structures were forced to give up their monopoly of power by allowing a representative gathering to convene with the task of drawing up a new constitution. For 10 days in February 1990, the Beninois gathered around their television sets and radios to listen to live broadcasts of the "National Conference of Active Forces of the Nation." The conference quickly turned into a public trial of Kérékou and his PRPB. With the eyes and ears of the nation tuned in, critics of the regime, who had until recently been exiled, were able to pressure Kérékou into handing over effective power to a transitional government. The major task of this new, civilian administration was to prepare Benin for multiparty elections while trying to stabilize the deteriorating economy.

The political success of Benin's "civilian coup d'etat" placed the nation in the forefront of the democratization process then sweeping Africa. But liberating a nation from poverty is a much more difficult process.

A COUNTRY OF MIGRANTS

Benin is one of the least-developed countries in the world. Having for decades experienced only limited economic growth,

(United Nations photo)

Benin is one of the least-developed countries in the world. Beninois must often fend for themselves in innovative ways. The peddler pictured above moves among the lake dwellings of a Beninois fishing village, selling cigarettes, spices, rice, and other commodities.

The kingdom of
Dahomey is
established
1625

The French
conquer
Dahomey
and declare it
a French
protectorate
1892

Dahomey
becomes
independent
1960

Mathieu Kérékou
comes to power
in the sixth
attempted
military coup
since
independence
1972

The name of
Dahomey is
changed to Benin
1975

Kérékou announces the
abandonment of
Marxism-Leninism as
Benin's guiding ideology;
multiparty elections are held;
Kérékou loses power to
Nicephore Soglo; Kérékou
is reelected 5 years later
1990s

2000s

Benin marks its 40th year
of independence

in recent years the nation's real gross domestic product has actually declined.

Emigration has become a way of life for many. The migration of Beninois in search of opportunities in neighboring states is not a new phenomenon. Before 1960, educated people from the then-French colony of Dahomey (as Benin was called until 1975) were prominent in junior administrative positions throughout other parts of French West Africa. But as the region's newly independent states began to localize their civil-service staffs, most of the Beninois expatriates lost their jobs. Their return increased bureaucratic competition within Benin, which, in turn, led to heightened political rivalry among ethnic and regional groups. Such local antagonisms contributed to a series of military coups between 1963 and 1972. These culminated in Kérékou's seizure of power.

While Beninois professionals can be found in many parts of West Africa, the destination of most recent emigrants has been Nigeria. The movement from Benin to Nigeria is facilitated by the close links that exist among the large Yoruba-speaking communities on both sides of the border. After Nigeria, the most popular destination has been Côte d'Ivoire. This may change, however, as economic recession in both of those states has led to heightened hostility against the migrants.

THE ECONOMY
Nigeria's urban areas have also been major markets for food. This has encouraged Beninois farmers to switch from cash crops (such as cotton, palm oil, cocoa beans, and coffee) to food crops (such as yams and cassava), which are smuggled across the border to Nigeria. The emergence of this parallel export economy has

been encouraged by the former regime's practice of paying its farmers among the lowest official produce prices in the region. Given that agriculture, in terms of both employment and income generation, forms the largest sector of the Beninois economy, the rise in smuggling activities has inevitably contributed to a growth of graft and corruption.

Benin's small industrial sector is primarily geared toward processing primary products, such as palm oil and cotton, for export. It has thus been adversely affected by the shift away from producing these cash crops for the local market. Small-scale manufacturing has centered around the production of basic consumer goods and construction materials. The biggest enterprises are state-owned cement plants. One source of hope is that with privatization and new exploration, the country's small oil industry will undergo expansion.

Transport and trade are other important activities. Many Beninois find legal as well as illegal employment carrying goods. Due to the relative absence of rain forest (an impediment to travel), Benin's territory has historically served as a trade corridor between the coastal and inland savanna regions of West Africa. Today the nation's roads are comparatively well developed, and the railroad carries goods from the port at Cotonou to northern areas of the country. An extension of the railroad will eventually reach Niamey, the capital of Niger. The government has also tried, with little success, to attract tourists in recent years, through such gambits as selling itself as the "home of Voodoo."

POLITICS AND RELIGION
Kérékou's narrow victory margin in 1996 amid charges and countercharges of elec-

toral fraud underscored the continuing north–south division of Beninois politics and society. Although he is now a self-proclaimed Christian, Kérékou's political base remains the mainly Muslim north, while Soglo enjoyed majority support in the more Christianized south. Religious allegiance in Benin is complicated, however, by the prominence of the indigenous belief system known as Voodoo. Having originated in Benin, belief in Voodoo spirits has taken root in the Americas, especially Haiti, as well as elsewhere in West Africa. During his first presidency, Kérékou sought to suppress Voodoo, which he branded as "witchcraft." Soglo, on the other hand, publicly embraced Voodoo, which was credited with helping him recover from a serious illness in 1992. On the eve of the 1996 election, Soglo recognized Voodoo as an official religion, proclaiming January 10 as "Voodoo National Day." (This move may have politically backfired, however, as it was condemned by the influential Catholic archbishop of Cotonou.)

A more decisive factor in Soglo's fall was the failure of his free-market reforms to revive the Beninois economy. Modest initial growth was seriously undermined in 1994 by the massive devaluation of the CFA franc, while privatization led to the retrenchment of 10,000 public workers. It was unlikely, however, that Kérékou would be tempted to return to his own failed policies of "Marxist-Beninism."

DEVELOPMENT

Palm-oil plantations were established in Benin by Africans in the mid-nineteenth century. They have continued to be African-owned and capitalist-oriented. Today, there are some 30 million trees in Benin, and palm-oil products are a major export used for cooking, lighting, soap, margarine, and lubricants.

FREEDOM

Since 1990, political restrictions have been lifted and prisoners of conscience freed. More recently, however, a number of citizens have been arrested for supposedly inciting people against the government and encouraging them not to pay taxes.

HEALTH/WELFARE

One-third of the national budget of Benin goes to education, and the number of students receiving primary education has risen to 50% of the school-age population. College graduates serve as temporary teachers through the National Service System, but more teachers and higher salaries are needed.

ACHIEVEMENTS

Fon appliquéd cloths have been described as "one of the gayest and liveliest of the contemporary African art forms." Formerly these cloths were used by Dahomeyan kings. Now they are sold to tourists, but they still portray the motifs and symbols of past rulers and the society they ruled.

Burkina Faso

GEOGRAPHY

Area in Square Miles (Kilometers):
106,000 (274,500) (about the size of Colorado)
Capital (Population):
Ouagadougou (824,000)
Environmental Concerns:
drought; desertification; overgrazing; soil erosion; deforestation
Geographical Features: mostly flat to dissected, undulating plains; hills in west and southeast
Climate: tropical

PEOPLE

Population
Total: 11,947,000
Annual Growth Rate: 2.71%
Rural/Urban Population Ratio:
84/16
Major Languages: French; Mossi; Senufo; Fula; Bobo; Mande; Gurunsi; Lobi
Ethnic Makeup: about 40% Mossi; Gurunsi; Senufo; Lobi; Bobo; Mande; Fulani
Religions: 50% Muslim; 40% indigenous beliefs; 10% Christian

Health
Life Expectancy at Birth: 46 years (male); 47 years (female)
Infant Mortality Rate (Ratio):
108.5/1,000
Physicians Available (Ratio):
1/27,158

Education
Adult Literacy Rate: 19.2%
Compulsory (Ages): 7–14; free

COMMUNICATION
Telephones: 41,600 main lines
Televisions: 4.4 per 1,000 people
Internet Service Provider: 1 (1999)

TRANSPORTATION
Highways in Miles (Kilometers): 7,504 (12,506)
Railroads in Miles (Kilometers): 385 (622)
Usable Airfields: 33
Motor Vehicles in Use: 26,000

GOVERNMENT
Type: parliamentary
Independence Date: August 5, 1960 (from France)
Head of State/Government: President (Captain) Blaise Compaoré; Prime Minister Kadré Désiré Ouédraogo

Political Parties: Popular Democratic Organization—Worker's Movement; Congress for Democracy and Progress; Alliance for Democracy and Federation; others
Suffrage: universal

MILITARY
Military Expenditures (% of GDP): 2%
Current Disputes: none

ECONOMY
Currency ($ U.S. Equivalent): 529.43 CFA francs = $1
Per Capita Income/GDP: $1,100/$12.4 billion
GDP Growth Rate: 5.5%
Inflation Rate: 2.5%

Natural Resources: manganese; limestone; marble; gold; antimony; copper; bauxite; nickel; lead; phosphates; zinc; silver
Agriculture: peanuts; shea nuts; cotton; sesame; millet; sorghum; corn; rice; livestock
Industry: cotton lint; beverages; agricultural processing; soap; cigarettes; textiles; gold
Exports: $311 million (primary partners Côte d'Ivoire, Taiwan, France)
Imports: $572 million (primary partners Côte d'Ivoire, France, Senegal)

http://www.sas.upenn.edu/ African_Studies/Country_Specific/ Burkina.html

BURKINA FASO

Much of Burkina Faso's (formerly Upper Volta) four decades of independence has been characterized by chronic political instability, with civilian rule being interrupted by the military on seven different occasions. The restoration of multiparty democracy in 1991 under the firm guidance of former military ruler Blaise Compaoré seemed to usher in an era of greater political stability. Compaoré's reelection in November 1998 was accepted as legitimate by international observers. But the assassination a month later of independent journalist Robert Zongo touched off a wave of violent strikes and protests. Since then, there have been sustained calls for more fundamental political and social reform from an emerging generation of activists within civil society, including the traditionally powerful trade unions. An umbrella body known as the Collective of Democratic Organizations for the Masses and Political Parties has been formed to challenge the status quo. Notwithstanding some notable achievements, especially in the utilization of the Volta River and the area of promoting indigenous culture, Burkina Faso remains an impoverished country searching for a governing consensus.

Since 1987, real power has remained in the hands of Compaoré, who has proven to be a master of political survival. Along with his party, the Popular Democratic Organization—Worker's Movement (ODP-MT), he won elections against fragmented opposition in 1991 and again in 1995. But in the 1998 elections, the majority of Burkinabé failed to vote. Local indifference to the poll may in part stem from the failure of successive governments to rescue the nation from its chronic poverty.

Before adopting the mantle of democracy, Compaoré rose to power through a series of coups, the last of which resulted in the overthrow and assassination of the charismatic and controversial Thomas Sankara. A man of immense populist appeal for many Burkinabé, Sankara remains as a martyr to their unfulfilled hopes. By the time of its overthrow, his radical regime had become the focus of a great deal of external as well as internal opposition.

Of the three men directly responsible for Sankara's toppling, two—Boukari Lingani and Henri Zongo—were executed following a power struggle with the third—Compaoré. It is in this context of sanguinary political competition that the assassination of a prominent media critic has once more called into question the government's commitment to political pluralism.

DEBILITATING DROUGHTS

At the time of its independence from France, in 1960, the landlocked country then named the Republic of Upper Volta inherited little in the way of colonial infrastructure. Since independence, progress has been hampered by prolonged periods of severe drought. As a result, much of the country has been forced at times to depend on international food aid. To counteract some of the negative effects of this circumstance, efforts have been made to integrate relief donations into local development schemes. Of particular note have been projects instituted by the traditional rural cooperatives known as *naam,* which have been responsible for such small-scale but often invaluable local improvements as new wells and pumps, better grinding mills, and distribution of tools and medical supplies.

Despite such community action, the effects of drought have been devastating. Particularly hard-hit has been pastoral production, long a mainstay of the local economy, especially in the north. It is estimated that the most recent drought destroyed about 90 percent of the livestock in Burkina Faso.

(United Nations photo by John Isaac)

Since Burkina Faso gained its independence from France, its progress has been hampered by prolonged periods of drought. Local cooperatives have been responsible for small-scale improvements such as the construction of the water barrage or barricade pictured above.

						Captain Thomas Sankara seizes power and changes the country's name to Burkina (Mossi for "land of honest men") Faso (Dioula for "democratic republic"); Sankara is assassinated in a coup; Blaise Compaoré succeeds as head of state	Compaoré introduces multipartyism, but his critics are skeptical
The first Mossi kingdom is founded 1313	The French overcome Mossi resistance and claim Upper Volta 1896	Upper Volta is divided among adjoining French colonies 1932	Upper Volta is reconstituted as a colony 1947	Independence under President Maurice Yameogo 1960		1980s	1990s

2000s

The country marks 4 decades of independence

To counteract the effects of drought while promoting greater development, the Burkinabé government has developed two major hydroelectric and agricultural projects over the past decade. The Bagre and Kompienga Dams, located east of Ouagadougou, have significantly reduced the country's dependence on imported energy, while also supplying water for large-scale irrigation projects. This has already greatly reduced the need for imported food.

Most Burkinabé continue to survive as agriculturalists and herders, but many people are dependent on wage labor. In the urban centers, there exists a significant working-class population that supports the nation's politically powerful trade-union movement. The division between this urban community and rural population is not absolute, for it is common for individuals to combine wage labor with farming activities. Another population category—whose numbers exceed those of the local wage-labor force—are individuals who seek employment outside of the country. At least 1 million people work as migrant laborers in other parts of West Africa. This is part of a pattern that dates back to the early twentieth century. Approximately 700,000 of these Burkinabé regularly migrate to Côte d'Ivoire. Returning workers have infused the rural areas with consumer goods and a working-class consciousness.

UNIONS FORCE CHANGE

As is the case in much of Africa, it is the salaried urban population (at least, next to the army) who have exercised the greatest influence over successive Burkinabé regimes. Trade-union leaders representing these workers have been instrumental in forcing changes in government. They have spoken out vigorously against government efforts to ban strikes and restrain unions.

They have also demanded that they be shielded from downturns in the local economy. Although many unionists have championed various shades of Marxist-Leninist ideology, they, along with their natural allies in the civil service, arguably constitute a conservative element within the local society. During the mid-1980s, they became increasingly concerned about the dynamic Sankara's efforts to promote a nationwide network of grassroots Committees for the Defense of the Revolution (CDRs) as vehicles for empowering the nation's largely rural masses.

To many unionists, the mobilization and arming of the CDRs was perceived as a direct challenge to their own status. This threat seemed all the more apparent when Sankara began to cut urban salaries, in the name of a more equitable flow of revenue to the rural areas. When several union leaders challenged this move, they were arrested on charges of sedition. Sankara's subsequent overthrow thus had strong backing from within organized labor and the civil service. These groups, along with the military, remain the principal supporters of Compaoré's ODP–MT and its policy of "national rectification." Yet despite this support base, the government has moved to restructure the until recently all-encompassing public sector of the economy by reducing its wage bill. This effort has impressed international creditors.

Beyond its core of support, the ODP–MT government has generally been met with sentiments ranging from hostility to indifference. While Compaoré claimed—with some justification—that Sankara's rule had become too arbitrary and that he had resisted forming a party with a set of rules, many people mourned the fallen leader's death. In the aftermath of the coup, the widespread use of a new cloth pattern, known locally as "homage to Sankara," became an informal barometer of popular dissatisfaction. Compaoré has also been challenged by the high regard that has been accorded Sankara outside Burkina Faso, as a symbol of a new generation of African radicalism.

Compaoré, like Sankara, has sometimes resorted to sharp anti-imperialist rhetoric. However, his government has generally sought to cultivate good relations with France (the former colonial power) and other members of the Organization for Economic Cooperation and Development, as well as the major international financial institutions. But he has alienated himself from some of his West African neighbors, as well as the Euro–North American diplomatic consensus, through his close ties to Libya and past military support for Charles Taylor's National Patriotic Front in Liberia. Along with Taylor, Compaoré has more recently been accused of, but denies, providing support for the Revolutionary United Front rebels in Sierra Leone. To many outsiders, as well as the Burkinabé people themselves, the course of Compaoré's government remains ambiguous.

DEVELOPMENT

Despite political turbulence, Burkina Faso's economy has recorded positive, albeit modest, annual growth rates for more than a decade. Most of the growth has been in agriculture. New hydroelectric projects have significantly reduced the country's dependence on imported energy.

FREEDOM

There has been a surprisingly strong tradition of pluralism in Burkina Faso despite the circumscribed nature of human rights under successive military regimes. Freedom of speech and association are still curtailed, and political detentions are common. The Burkinabé Movement for Human Rights has challenged the government.

HEALTH/WELFARE

The inadequacy of the country's public health measures is reflected in the low Burkinabé life expectancy. Mass immunization campaigns have been successfully carried out, but in an era of structural economic adjustment, the prospects for a dramatic improvement in health appear bleak.

ACHIEVEMENTS

In 1997, a record total of 19 feature films competed for the Etalon du Yennenga award, the highest distinction of the biannual Pan-African Film Festival, hosted in Ouagadougou. Over the past 3 decades, this festival has contributed significantly to the development of the film industry in Africa. Burkina Faso has nationalized its movie houses, and the government has encouraged the showing of films by African filmmakers.

Cape Verde (Republic of Cape Verde)

http://www.sas.upenn.edu/
African_Studies/Country_Specific/
C_Verde.html

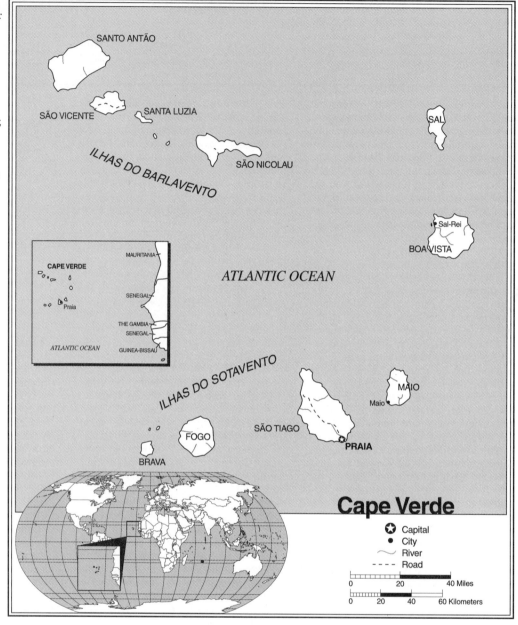

| Cape Verdean settlement begins 1462 | Slavery is abolished 1869 | Thousands of Cape Verdeans die of starvation during World War II 1940s | The PAIGC is founded 1956 | Warfare begins in Guinea-Bissau; Amilcar Cabral is assassinated 1973 | A coup in Lisbon initiates the Portuguese decolonization process 1974 | Independence 1975 | The PAICV is defeated by the MPD in the country's first multiparty elections; Cape Verde adopts a new Constitution 1990s | 2000s |

Cape Verdeans celebrate
25 years of independence

THE REPUBLIC OF CAPE VERDE

On July 5, 2000, Cape Verdeans proudly celebrated a quarter-century of economic, political, and social progress since independence from Portugal. Despite a late start and unfavorable environmental conditions, the country has emerged as one of postcolonial Africa's tangible success stories. This has been accompanied by a change in political direction. In 1992, Cape Verde adopted a new flag and Constitution, reflecting the country's transition to political pluralism. After 15 years of single-party rule by the African Party for the Independence of Cape Verde (PAICV), rising agitation led to the legalization of opposition groups in 1990. In January 1991, a quickly assembled antigovernment coalition, the Movement for Democracy (MPD), stunned the political establishment by gaining 68 percent of the votes and 56 out of 79 National Assembly seats. A month later, the MPD candidate, Antonio Mascarenhas Monteiro, defeated the long-serving incumbent, Aristides Pereira, in the presidential election. It is a credit to both the outgoing administration and its opponents that this dramatic political transformation occurred without significant violence or rancor. Parliamentary elections in December 1995 resulted in the MPD retaining power, albeit with a reduced majority.

The Republic of Cape Verde is an archipelago located about 400 miles west of the Senegalese Cape Verde, or "Green Cape," after which it is named. Unfortunately, green is a color that is often absent in the lives of the islands' citizens. Throughout its history, Cape Verde has suffered from periods of prolonged drought, which before the twentieth century were often accompanied by extremely high mortality rates (up to 50 percent). The last severe drought lasted from 1968

to 1984. Even in normal years, though, rainfall is often inadequate.

When the country gained independence, in 1975, there was little in the way of nonagricultural production. As a result, the new nation had to rely for its survival on foreign aid and the remittances of Cape Verdeans working abroad, but the post-independence period has been marked by a genuine improvement in the lives of most Cape Verdeans.

Cape Verde was ruled by Portugal for nearly 500 years. Most of the islanders are the descendants of Portuguese colonists, many of whom arrived as convicts, and African slaves who began to settle on the islands shortly after their discovery by Portuguese mariners in 1456. The merging of these two groups gave rise to the distinct Cape Verdean Kriolu language (which is also spoken in Guinea-Bissau). Under Portuguese rule, Cape Verdeans were generally treated as second-class citizens, although a few rose to positions of prominence in other parts of the Portuguese colonial empire. Economic stagnation, exacerbated by cycles of severe drought, caused many islanders to emigrate elsewhere in Africa, Western Europe, and the Americas.

In 1956, the African Party for the Independence of Guinea-Bissau and Cape Verde (PAIGC) was formed under the dynamic leadership of Amilcar Cabral, a Cape Verdean revolutionary who, with his followers, hoped to see the two Portuguese colonies form a united nation. Between 1963 and 1974, PAIGC waged a successful war of liberation in Guinea-Bissau and led to the independence of both territories. Although Cabral was assassinated by the Portuguese in 1973, his vision was preserved during the late 1970s by his successors, who, while ruling the two countries separately, maintained the

unity of the PAIGC. This arrangement, however, began to break down in the aftermath of a 1980 coup in Guinea-Bissau and resulted in the party's division along national lines. In 1981, the Cape Verdean PAIGC formally renounced its Guinean links, becoming the PAICV.

After independence, the PAIGC/CV government was challenged by the colonial legacy of economic underdevelopment, exacerbated by drought. Massive famine was warded off through a reliance on imported foodstuffs, mostly received as aid. The government attempted to strengthen local food production and assist the 70 percent of the local population engaged in subsistence agriculture. Its efforts took the forms of drilling for underground water, terracing, irrigating, and building a water-desalinization plant with U.S. assistance. Major efforts were also devoted to tree-planting schemes as a way to cut back on soil erosion and eventually make the country self-sufficient in wood fuel.

With no more than 15 percent of the islands' territory potentially suitable for cultivation, the prospect of Cape Verde developing self-sufficiency in food appears remote. The few factories that exist on Cape Verde are small-scale operations catering to local needs. Only textiles have enjoyed modest success as an export. Another promising area is fishing.

DEVELOPMENT

In a move designed to attract greater investment from overseas, especially from Cape Verdean Americans, the country has joined the International Finance Corporation. Efforts are under way to promote the islands as an offshore banking center for the West African (ECOWAS) region.

FREEDOM

The new Constitution should entrench the country's recent political liberalization. Opposition publications have emerged to complement the state- and Catholic Church–sponsored media.

HEALTH/WELFARE

Greater access to health facilities has resulted in a sharp drop in infant mortality and a rise in life expectancy. Clinics have begun to encourage family planning. Since independence, great progress has taken place in social services. Nutrition levels have been raised, and basic health care is now provided to the entire population.

ACHIEVEMENTS

Cape Verdean Kriolu culture has a rich literary and musical tradition. With emigrant support, Cape Verde bands have acquired modest followings in Western Europe, Lusophone Africa, Brazil, and the United States. Local drama, poetry, and music are showcased on the national television service.

Côte d'Ivoire (Republic of Côte d'Ivoire)

GEOGRAPHY

Area in Square Miles (Kilometers):
124,503 (323,750) (about the size of New Mexico)

Capital (Population): Abidjan (administrative) (2,793,000); Yamoussoukro (political) (120,000)

Environmental Concerns: water pollution; deforestation

Geographical Features: mostly flat to undulating plains; mountains in the northwest

Climate: tropical to semiarid

PEOPLE

Population

Total: 15,981,000

Annual Growth Rate: 2.58%

Rural/Urban Population Ratio: 56/44

Major Languages: French; Dioula; many indigenous dialects

Ethnic Makeup: 23% Baoule; 18% Bete; 15% Senoufou; 11% Malinke; 33% others

Religions: 60% Muslim; 22% Christian; 18% indigenous

Health

Life Expectancy at Birth: 44 years (male); 47 years (female)

Infant Mortality Rate (Ratio): 95/1,000

Physicians Available (Ratio): 1/11,745

Education

Adult Literacy Rate: 48.5%

Compulsory (Ages): 7–13; free

COMMUNICATION

Telephones: 170,000 main lines

Televisions: 57 per 1,000 people

Internet Service Providers: na

TRANSPORTATION

Highways in Miles (Kilometers): 30,240 (50,400)

Railroads in Miles (Kilometers): 408 (660)

Usable Airfields: 36

Motor Vehicles in Use: 255,000

GORNMENT

Type: republic

Independence Date: August 7, 1960 (from France)

Head of State/Government: President (General) Laurent Gbagbo is both head of state and head of government

Political Parties: Democratic Party of Côte d'Ivoire; Ivoirian Popular Front; Rally of the Republicans; Ivoirian Workers' Party; others

Suffrage: universal at 21

MILITARY

Military Expenditures (% of GDP): 1%

Current Disputes: civil strife

ECONOMY

Currency ($ U.S. Equivalent): 529.43 CFA francs = $1

Per Capita Income/GDP: $1,600/$25.7 billion

GDP Growth Rate: 5%

Inflation Rate: 2.5%

Natural Resources: petroleum; diamonds; manganese; iron ore; cobalt; bauxite; copper; hydropower

Agriculture: coffee; cocoa beans; bananas; palm kernels; corn; rice; manioc; sweet potatoes; sugar; cotton; rubber; timber

Industry: foodstuffs; beverages; oil refining; wood products; textiles; automobile assembly; fertilizer; construction materials; electricity

Exports: $3.9 billion (primary partners France, the Netherlands, United States)

Imports: $2.6 billion (primary partners France, United States, Italy)

http://www.sas.upenn.edu/
African_Studies/Country_Specific/
Cote.html
http://geography.miningco.com/
library/maps/blcote.htm
http://www.africanews.org/west/
ivorycoast/

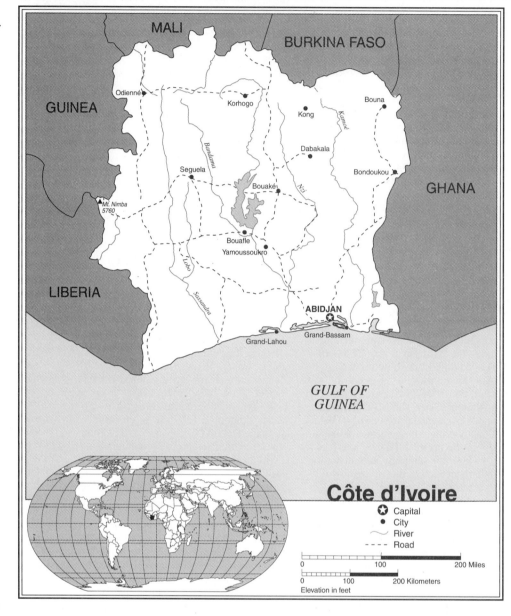

Côte d'Ivoire

★ Capital
● City
River
Road

0   100   200 Miles
0   100   200 Kilometers
Elevation in feet

CÔTE d'IVOIRE

On December 23, 1999, automatic gunfire broke out in the center of Abidjan, the capital city of Côte d'Ivoire, signaling the onset of a military coup d'etat. Twenty-four hours later, General Robert Guei appeared at a news conference to announce that the government of Henri Konan Bedie had been overthrown and that Guei was now the acting president. Bedie found refuge at a French military base and was subsequently escorted out of the country. While military interventions have been commonplace in a number of neighboring states, for Côte d'Ivoire (French for "Ivory Coast"), the coup was an unprecedented interruption of nearly four decades of civilian rule under the Democratic Party of Côte d'Ivoire (PDCI). For most of that period, until his death in 1993, the country was led by its able if autocratic first president, Félix Houphouët-Boigny.

Initial international condemnation of the coup was muted by the obvious jubilation with which it was greeted by many Ivoirians. Since the death of Houphouët-Boigny, Ivoirian politics and society had become increasingly polarized along ethnic and religious lines. In October 1995, Houphouët-Boigny's successor, Bedie, retained power in an election boycotted by supporters of his main rival, Allassane Ouattera, who was banned from running for office due to a new law mandating that both parents of presidential candidates must be born in Côte d'Ivoire. The boycott enjoyed widespread support in the predominantly Muslim north, which is Ouaterra's home area. For the first time since independence, immigrants—who account for up to 40 percent of the population—were banned from voting. Violent protests before the poll were accompanied by increased governmental repression.

In the wake of the coup, there was initial hope that the societal divisions of the Bedie era were being laid to rest. Guei reached out to Ouattera and his supporters, as well as to members of the PDCI. A new Constitution was drafted and accepted in a referendum. But a last-minute reintroduction of the provision that both parents of presidential candidates must be Ivoirian by birth raised concerns that Guei intended to assure his own election by once more excluding Ouattera. A failed second coup and the postponement of elections to October 2000 increased the uncertainty.

For more than half a century, Ivoirians had lived under the certainty of Houphouët-Boigny's leadership. He had been a dominant figure not only in Côte d'Ivoire but throughout Francophonic Africa. A pioneering pan-Africanist, he had served for three years as a French cabinet minister before leading his country to independence, in 1960. Under him, Ivoirians had enjoyed stability and economic growth that were the envy of their neighbors. But his paternalistic autocracy, exercised through the PDCI, had started to break down before his death. Ivoirian politics has fluctuated between reform and repression since 1990.

REFORM AND REPRESSION

The political life of Côte d'Ivoire entered a new phase in 1990. Months of mounting prodemocracy protests and labor unrest led to the legalization of previously banned opposition parties as well as to the emergence within the PDCI itself of a strong progressive wing seemingly committed to liberalization. Although the first multiparty presidential and, especially, legislative elections in October 1990 were widely regarded as having been less than free and fair, many nevertheless believed that the path was open for further reform. Houphouët-Boigny garnered 82 percent of the vote against a challenger named Laurent Gbagbo, while the PDCI captured 163 out of 175 National Assembly seats. In November, the outgoing National Assembly passed a constitutional amendment to allow its speaker to take over the presidency in the event of a vacancy. This move brought about premature speculation that Houphouët-Boigny was preparing to step aside in favor of Bedie. Another amendment provided for the naming of a prime minister, a post that was subsequently filled by Ouattara, an able technocrat. But the octogenarian president refused to give up power. As his health declined, his actions became more erratic. The reform process was probably further paralyzed by a power struggle between Bedie and Ouattara. Bedie clearly came out ahead: In 1994, Ouattara lost his position.

In February 1992, a mass demonstration called by the main opposition party, Gbagbo's Ivoirian Popular Front (FPI), and the Ivoirian Human Rights League turned into a riot. The violence provided the government with a pretext to jail Gbagbo, along with Human Rights League head Degny Segui and dozens of other prominent political and community leaders, including members of another opposition movement, the Ivoirian Workers' Party (PIT), as well as journalists and students. Gbagbo, Segui, and 10 others were subsequently convicted of being "responsible" for "acts of violence," although state prosecutors acknowledged that they had not been personally involved in any criminal activity. Others were imprisoned on charges ranging from "harboring criminals" to putting forward "outrageous arguments." Denouncing what was characterized as an "undeclared state of siege," the FPI temporarily withdrew from the National Assembly, making it once more the sole preserve of the PDCI.

In the year 2000, Laurent Gbagbo gained the presidency in elections marred by popular demonstrations and charges of fraud.

ECONOMIC DOWNTURN

Reform and repression have been taking place against the backdrop of a prolonged deterioration in Côte d'Ivoire's once-vibrant economy. The primary explanation for this downturn is the decline in revenue from cocoa and coffee, which have long been the country's principal export earners. This has led to mounting state debt, which in turn has pressured the government to adopt unpopular austerity measures.

The economy's current problems and prospects are best understood in the context of its past performance. During its first two decades of independence, Côte d'Ivoire enjoyed one of the highest economic growth rates in the world. This growth was all the more notable in that, in contrast to many other developing-world "success stories" during the same period, it had been fueled by the expansion of commercial agriculture.

Although prosperity gave way to recession during the 1980s, the average per capita income of the country is still one of Africa's highest. Statistics also indicate that, on average, Ivoirians live longer and better than people in many neighboring states. But the creation of a productive, market-oriented economy has not eliminated the harsh reality of widespread poverty, leading some to question whether the majority of Ivoirians have derived reasonable benefit from their nation's wealth. To the dismay of many young Ivoirians struggling to enter the country's tight job market, much of the political and economic life of Côte d'Ivoire is controlled by its large and growing expatriate population, largely comprised of French and Lebanese.

Commercial farmers, who include millions of medium- and small-scale producers, have also prospered. About two thirds of the workforce are employed in agriculture, with coffee alone being the principal source of income for some 2.5 million people. In addition to coffee, Ivoirian planters grow cocoa, bananas, pineapples, sugar, cotton, palm oil, and other cash crops for export. While some farmers are quite wealthy, most have only modest incomes.

In recent years, the circumstance of Ivoirian coffee and cocoa planters has become much more precarious, due to fluctuations in commodities prices. In this respect, the growers, along with their colleagues elsewhere, are to some extent victims of their own success. Their productivity, in response to international demand, has been a factor in depressing prices through increased supply. In 1988, Houphouët-Boigny held cocoa in storage in an attempt to force a price rise, but the effort failed, aggravating the nation's economic downturn. As a result, the government took a new approach, scrapping plans for future expansion in cocoa production in favor of promoting food crops such as yams, corn, and plantains, for which there is a regional as well as a domestic market.

Ivoirian planters often hire low-paid laborers from other West African countries. There are about 2 million migrant laborers in Côte d'Ivoire, employed throughout the economy. Their presence is not a new phenomenon but goes back to colonial times. Many laborers come from Burkina Faso, which was once a part of Côte d'Ivoire. Today, Burkinabé as well as citizens of other former colonies of French West Africa have the advantage of being paid in a regional currency, the CFA franc, as well as sharing the colonial vernacular. A good road system and the Ivoirian railroad (which extends to the Burkinabé capital of Ouagadougou) facilitate the travel of migrant workers to rural as well as urban areas.

DEBT AND DISCONTENT
Other factors determine how much an Ivoirian benefits from the country's development. Residents of Abidjan, the capital, and its environs near the coast receive more services than do citizens of interior areas. Professionals in the cities make better salaries than do laborers on farms or in small industries. Yet persistent inflation and recession have made daily life difficult for the middle class as well as poorer peasants and workers. In 1983, teachers went on strike to protest the discontinuance of their housing subsidies. The gov-

ernment refused to yield and banned the teachers' union; the teachers went back to work. The ban has since been lifted, but the causes of discontent. Teachers deeply resent the fact that other civil servants, ministers, and French *cooperants* (helpers on the Peace Corps model) did not have their subsidies cut back, and they demand a more even "distribution of sacrifices." In 1987, teachers' leaders were detained by the government.

The nonagricultural sectors of the economy have also been experiencing difficulties. Many state industries are unable to make a profit due to their heavy indebtedness. Brush fires, mismanagement, and the clearing of forests for cash-crop plantations have put the nation's once-sizable timber industry in jeopardy. Out of a former total of 12 million hectares of forest, 10½ million have been lost. Plans for expansion of offshore oil and natural-gas production were delayed due to an inability to raise investment capital. In 1994, however, significant discoveries were announced, which should allow for fuel self-sufficiency in coming years.

Difficulty in raising capital for oil and gas development is a reflection of the debt crisis that has plagued the country since the collapse of its cocoa and coffee earnings. Finding itself in the desperate situation of being forced to borrow to pay interest on its previous loans, the government suspended most debt repayments in 1987. Subsequent rescheduling of negotiations with international creditors resulted in a Structural Adjustment Plan (SAP). This plan has resulted in a reduction in the prices paid to farmers and a drastic curtailment in public spending, leading to severe salary cuts for public and parastatal workers. Recent pressure on the part of the lending agencies for the Ivoirian government to cut back further on its commitment to cash crops is particularly ironic, given the praise that they

bestowed on the same policies in the not-too-distant past.

THE SEARCH FOR STABILITY
The government's ability to gain popular acceptance for its austerity measures has been compromised by corruption and extravagance at the top. A notorious example of the latter is the basilica that was recently constructed at Yamoussoukro, the home village of Houphouët-Boigny, which is to become the nation's new capital city. This air-conditioned structure, patterned after the papal seat of St. Peter's in Rome, is the largest Christian church building in the world. Supposedly a personal gift from Houphouët-Boigny to the Vatican (a most reluctant recipient), its construction is believed to have cost hundreds of millions of dollars.

Côte d'Ivoire's current period of political upheaval comes after decades of stability. Houphouët-Boigny was adept at striking a balance among the country's diverse regions and ethnic groups. Despite his authoritarianism, he also generally preferred to deal with internal opponents by offering the proverbial carrot rather than the stick. In contrast, Bedie sought to suppress dissent, arresting scores of journalists before his overthrow in December 1999. Massive opposition protests in September 1998 underscored the weakness of his regime, but it was another 14 months before the army moved in to "end corruption" and "restore the betrayed legacy of Houphouët-Boigny." During his first months in office, Guei spoke in favor of pan-Africanism and against Bedie's xenophobic policies. What tack Gbagbo takes remains to be seen.

DEVELOPMENT

It has been said that Côte d'Ivoire is "power hungry." The Soubre Dam, being developed on the Sassandra River, is the sixth and largest hydroelectric project in Côte d'Ivoire. It will serve the eastern area of the country. Another dam is planned for the Cavalla River, between Côte d'Ivoire and Liberia.

FREEDOM

Former President Konan Bedie showed little tolerance for dissent, within either the PDCI or society as a whole. Journalists by the score were jailed for such "offenses" as writing "insulting" articles. Six Ivoirian gendarmes were charged in connection with a mass grave discovered near Abidjan in 2000.

HEALTH/WELFARE

Côte d'Ivoire has one of the lowest soldier-to-teacher ratios in Africa. Education absorbs about 40% of the national budget. The National Commission to Combat AIDS has reported significant success in its campaign to promote condom use, by targeting especially vulnerable groups.

ACHIEVEMENTS

Ivoirian textiles are varied and prized. Block printing and dyeing produce brilliant designs; woven cloths made strip by strip and sewn together include the white Korhogo tapestries, covered with Ivoirian figures, birds, and symbols drawn in black. The Ivoirian singer Alpha Blondy has become an international superstar as the leading exponent of West African reggae.

The Gambia (Republic of The Gambia)

GEOGRAPHY

Area in Square Miles (Kilometers):
(4,361) (11,295) (about twice the size of Delaware)
Capital (Population): Banjul (42,400)
Environmental Concerns: deforestation; desertification; water-borne diseases
Geographical Features: floodplain of The Gambia River flanked by some low hills
Climate: tropical; hot rainy season, cooler dry season

PEOPLE

Population

Total: 1,368,000
Annual Growth Rate: 3.2%
Rural/Urban Population Ratio: 70/30
Major Languages: English; Mandinka; Wolof; Fula; Sarakola; Diula; others
Ethnic Makeup: 42% Mandinka; 18% Fula; 16% Wolof; 24% others (99% African; 1% non-Gambian)
Religions: 90% Muslim; 9% Christian; 1% indigenous beliefs

Health

Life Expectancy at Birth: 51 years (male); 55 years (female)
Infant Mortality Rate (Ratio): 79.3/1,000
Physicians Available (Ratio): 1/14,536

Education

Adult Literacy Rate: 38.6%
Compulsory (Ages): 7–13; free

COMMUNICATION

Telephones: 25,600 main lines
Internet Service Providers: 2 (1999)

TRANSPORTATION

Highways in Miles (Kilometers): 1,584 (2,640)
Railroads in Miles (Kilometers): none
Usable Airfield: 1
Motor Vehicles in Use: 9,000

GOVERNMENT

Type: republic
Independence Date: February 18, 1965 (from the United Kingdom)
Head of State/Government: President (Lieutenant) Yahya Jemmeh is both head of state and head of government
Political Parties: Alliance for Patriotic Reorientation and Construction; United Democratic Party; National Reconciliation Party; People's Democratic Organization for Independence and Socialism; others
Suffrage: universal at 18

MILITARY

Military Expenditures (% of GDP): 2%
Current Disputes: internal conflicts; boundary dispute with Senegal

ECONOMY

Currency ($ U.S. Equivalent): 9.56 dalasis = $1
Per Capita Income/GDP: $1,030/$1.4 billion
GDP Growth Rate: 4.2%
Inflation Rate: 2.5%
Natural Resources: fish
Agriculture: peanuts; millet; sorghum; rice; corn, cassava; livestock; fish and forest resources
Industry: processing peanuts, fish, and hides; tourism; beverages; agricultural machinery assembly; wood- and metal-working; clothing
Exports: $132 million (primary partners Benelux countries, Japan, United Kingdom)
Imports: $201 million (primary partners Hong Kong, United Kingdom, the Netherlands)

http://www.gambia.com/gambia.html
http://www.sas.upenn.edu/ African_Studies/Country_Specific/ Gambia.html

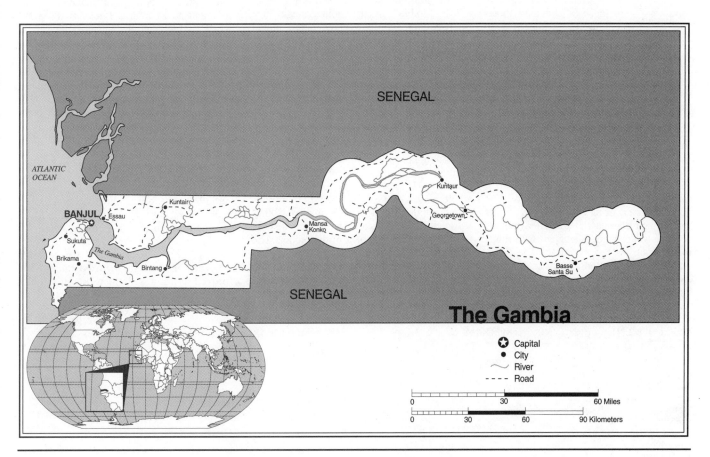

The British build
Fort James at the
current site of
Banjul, on the
Gambia River
1618

The Gambia is
ruled by the
United Kingdom
through Sierra
Leone
1807

Independence
1965

Dawda Jawara
comes to power
1970

An attempted coup
against President
Dawda Jawara; the
rise and fall of the
Senegambia
Confederation
1980s

Jawara is
overthrown by
a military coup;
Yahya Jammeh
becomes head
of state
1990s

2000s

Government security
forces kill 14 people
during student protests

THE GAMBIA

In April 2000, Gambians were shocked when student protests in the capital city, Banjul, resulted in the killing of 14 people and the wounding of many more by government security forces. Many interpreted the violence as an ominous official response to the re-emergence in recent years of independent voices within the media and civil society, which have been pushing for greater openness and accountability in government.

In July 1994, The Gambia's armed forces overthrew the government of Sir Dawda Jawara, bringing to an abrupt end what had been postcolonial West Africa's only example of uninterrupted multiparty democracy. Under international pressure, the new military ruler, Yahya Jammeh, held elections in September 1996 and January 1997 after many delays. These elections resulted in victories for himself and his new party, the Alliance for Patriotic Reorientation and Construction. But the process was marred by the regime's continuing intolerance of genuine opposition. Since the failure of an alleged coup attempt in January 1995, critical voices have been largely silenced by an increasingly powerful National Intelligence Agency. Meanwhile, The Gambia's already weak economy has suffered from reduced revenues from tourism and foreign donors.

The Gambia is Africa's smallest noninsular nation. Except for a small seacoast, it is entirely surrounded by its much larger neighbor, Senegal. The two nations' separate existence is rooted in the activities of British slave traders who, in 1618, established a fort at the mouth of The Gambia River, from which they gradually spread their commercial and, later, political dominance upstream. Gambians have much in common with Senegalese. The Gambia's three major ethnolinguistic groups—the Mandinka, Wolof, and Fula (or Peul)—are found on both sides of the bor-

der. The Wolof language serves as a lingua franca in both the Gambian capital of Banjul and the urban areas of Senegal. Islam is the major religion of both countries, while each also has a substantial Christian minority. The economies of the two countries are also similar, with each being heavily reliant on the cultivation of groundnuts as a cash crop.

In 1981, the Senegalese and Gambian governments were drawn closer together by an attempted coup in Banjul. While Jawara was in London, dissident elements within his Paramilitary Field Force joined in a coup attempt with members of two small, self-styled revolutionary parties. Based on a 1965 mutual-defense agreement, Jawara received assistance from Senegal in putting down the rebels. Constitutional rule was restored, but the killing of 400 to 500 people during the uprising and the subsequent mass arrest of suspected accomplices left Gambians bitter and divided.

In the immediate aftermath of the coup, The Gambia agreed to join Senegal in a loose confederation, which some hoped would lead to a full political union. But from the beginning, the Senegambia Confederation was marred by the circumstances of its formation. The continued presence of Senegalese soldiers in their country led Gambians to speak of a "shotgun wedding." Beyond fears of losing their local identity, many believed that proposals for closer economic integration, through a proposed monetary and customs union, would be to The Gambia's disadvantage. Underlying this concern was the role played by Gambian traders in providing imports to Senegal's market. Other squabbles, such as a long-standing dispute over the financing of a bridge across The Gambia River, finally led to the Confederation's formal demise in 1989. But the two countries still recognize a need to develop alternative forms of cooperation.

The Gambia was modestly successful in rebuilding its politics in the aftermath of the 1981 coup attempt. Whereas the 1982 elections were arguably compromised by the detention of the main opposition leader, Sherif Mustapha Dibba, on (later dismissed) charges of complicity in the revolt, the 1987 and 1992 polls restored most people's confidence in Gambian democracy. In both elections, opposition parties significantly increased their share of the vote, while Jawara's People's Progressive Party retained majority support.

Instances of official corruption had compromised the Jawara government's ability to use its electoral mandate to implement an Economic Recovery Program (ERP), which included austerity measures. The Gambia has always been a poor country. During the 1980s, conditions worsened as a result of bad harvests and falling prices for groundnuts, which usually account for half of the nation's export earnings. The tourist industry was also disrupted by the 1981 coup attempt. Faced with mounting debt, the government submitted to International Monetary Fund pressure by cutting back its civil service and drastically devaluing the local currency. The latter step initially led to high inflation, but prices have become more stable in recent years, and the economy as a whole has begun to enjoy a gross domestic product growth rate of up to 5 percent per year. As elsewhere, the negative impact of Structural Adjustment has proved especially burdensome to urban dwellers.

DEVELOPMENT

Since independence, The Gambia has developed a tourist industry. Whereas in 1966 only 300 individuals were recorded as having visited the country, the figure for 1988–1989 was over 112,000. Tourism is now the second-biggest sector of the economy.

FREEDOM

Despite the imposition of martial law in the aftermath of the 1981 coup attempt, The Gambia has had a strong record of respect for individual liberty and human rights. Under its current regime, the Gambia has forfeited its model record of respect for freedoms of speech and association.

HEALTH/WELFARE

Forty percent of Gambian children remain outside the primary-school setup. Economic Recovery Program austerity has made it harder for the government to achieve its goal of education for all.

ACHIEVEMENTS

Gambian *griots*—hereditary bards and musicians such as Banna and Dembo Kanute—have maintained a traditional art. Formerly, griots were attached to ruling families; now, they perform over Radio Gambia and are popular throughout West Africa.

Ghana (Republic of Ghana)

GEOGRAPHY
Area in Square Miles (Kilometers):
92,100 (238,536) (about the size of Oregon)
Capital (Population): Accra (1,673,000)
Environmental Concerns: drought; deforestation; overgrazing; soil erosion; threatened wildlife populations; water pollution; insufficient potable water
Geographical Features: low plains with dissected plateau
Climate: tropical

PEOPLE

Population
Total: 19,534,000
Annual Growth Rate: 1.87%
Rural/Urban Population Ratio: 64/36
Major Languages: English; Akan; Ewe; Ga
Ethnic Makeup: nearly 100% African
Religions: 38% indigenous beliefs; 30% Muslim; 24% Christian; 8% others

Health
Life Expectancy at Birth: 56 years (male); 59 years (female)
Infant Mortality Rate (Ratio): 57.4/1,000
Physicians Available (Ratio): 1/22,452

Education
Adult Literacy Rate: 64.5%
Compulsory (Ages): 6–16

COMMUNICATION
Telephones: 105,500 main lines
Daily Newspaper Circulation: 64 per 1,000 people
Televisions: 15 per 1,000 people
Internet Service Providers: 2 (1999)

TRANSPORTATION
Highways in Miles (Kilometers): 24,428 (39,400)
Railroads in Miles (Kilometers): 592 (953)
Usable Airfields: 12
Motor Vehicles in Use: 135,000

GOVERNMENT
Type: constitutional democracy
Independence Date: March 6, 1957 (from the United Kingdom)
Head of State/Government: President J. A. Kufuor is both head of state and head of government
Political Parties: National Democratic Congress; New Patriotic Party; People's Convention Party; Every Ghanaian Living Elsewhere; others
Suffrage: universal at 18

MILITARY
Military Expenditures (% of GDP): 0.7%
Current Disputes: internal conflicts

ECONOMY
Currency ($ U.S. Equivalent): 1,046.74 cedis = $1
Per Capita Income/GDP: $1,900/$35.5 billion
GDP Growth Rate: 4.3%
Inflation Rate: 12.8%
Unemployment Rate: 20%
Labor Force: 4,000,000
Natural Resources: gold; timber; industrial diamonds; bauxite; manganese; fish; rubber; hydropower
Agriculture: cocoa beans; rice; coffee; cassava; peanuts; corn; shea nuts; bananas; timber
Industry: mining; lumbering; light manufacturing; fishing; aluminum smelting; food processing
Exports: $1.7 billion (primary partners Togo, United Kingdom, Italy)
Imports: $2.5 billion (primary partners United Kingdom, Nigeria, United States)

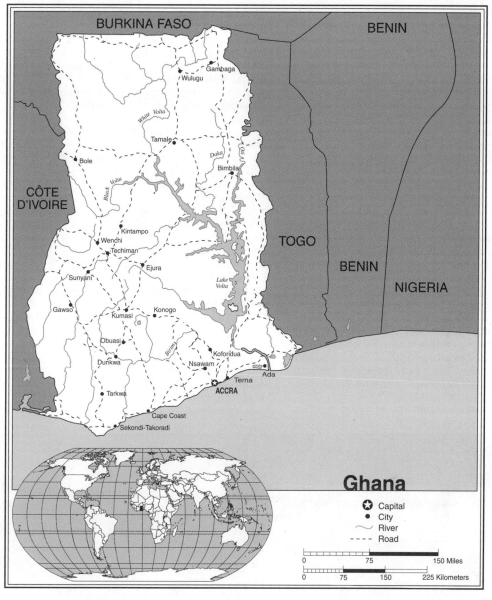

Ghana

⭐ Capital
● City
〜 River
--- Road

| 0 | 75 | 150 Miles |
| 0 | 75 | 150 | 225 Kilometers |

http://www.state.gov/www/
    background_notes/
    ghana_0298_bgn.html
http://www.ghana-embassy.org/
http://www.ghanaweb.com/
    GhanaHomePage/ghana.html

GHANA

In December 2000, Ghanaians went to the polls to elect a new president, bringing to an end two decades of rule by the incumbent Jerry Rawlings. Under Rawlings's guidance, in recent years Ghana made gradual but steady progress in rebuilding its economy and political culture, after decades of decline. For many Ghanaians, these recent gains have been of modest benefit. The country has achieved economic growth, while implementing a socially painful World Bank/International Monetary Fund–sponsored Economic Recovery Program (ERP). Yet when adjusted for inflation, per capita income remains below the level that existed in 1957, when Ghana became the first colony in sub-Saharan Africa to obtain independence.

The country is also overcoming the legacy of political instability brought about by revolving-door military coups. In March 1992, Rawlings marked the country's 35th anniversary of independence by announcing an accelerated return to multiparty rule. Eight months later, he was elected by a large majority as the president of what has been hailed as Ghana's "Fourth Republic." Although the election received the qualified endorsement of international monitors, its result was re-

jected by the main opposition, the New Patriotic Party (NPP). The NPP subsequently boycotted parliamentary elections, allowing an easy victory for Rawlings's National Democratic Congress (NDC), which captured 189 out of 200 seats, with a voter turnout of just under 30 percent. After months of bitter standoff, the political climate has eased since December 1993, when the NPP agreed to enter into a dialogue with the government about its basic demand that the interests of the ruling party be more clearly separated from those of the state.

Ghana's political transformation was a triumph for Rawlings, who ruled since 1981, when he and other junior military officers seized power as the Provisional National Defense Council (PNDC). In the name of ending corruption, they overthrew Ghana's previous freely elected government after it had been in office for less than two years. Rawlings was dismissive of elections at that time: "What does it mean to stuff bits of paper into boxes?" But political success seems to have altered his opinion.

At its independence, Ghana assumed a leadership role in the struggle against colonial rule elsewhere on the continent. Both its citizens and many outside ob-

servers were optimistic about the country's future. As compared to many other former colonies, the country seemed to have a sound infrastructure for future progress. Unfortunately, economic development and political democracy have proven to be elusive goals.

The "First Republic," led by the charismatic Kwame Nkrumah, degenerated into a bankrupt and an increasingly authoritarian one-party state. Nkrumah had pinned his hopes on an ambitious policy of industrial development. When substantial overseas investment failed to materialize, he turned to socialism. His efforts led to a modest rise in local manufacturing, but the sector's productivity was compromised by inefficient planning, limited resources, expensive inputs, and mounting government corruption. The new state enterprises ended up being financed largely from the export earnings of cocoa, which had emerged as Ghana's principal cash crop during the colonial period. Following colonial precedent, Nkrumah resorted to paying local cocoa farmers well below the world market price for their output in an attempt to expand state revenues.

Nkrumah was overthrown by the military in 1966. Despite his regime's short-

(United Nations photo)

The resources of the sea are important to the Ghanaian economy. The form of fishing shown in this photograph demands both power and skill; the men in the surf have to throw the weighted net far out in the water.

| A Portuguese fort is built at Elmina 1482 | The establishment of the Asante Confederation under Osei Tutu 1690s | The "Bonds" of 1844 signed by British officials and Fante chiefs as equals 1844 | The British conquer the Asante, a final step in British control of the region 1901 | Ghana is the first of the colonial territories in sub-Saharan Africa to become independent 1957 | Kwame Nkrumah is overthrown by a military coup 1966 | The first coup of Flight Lieutenant Jerry Rawlings 1979 | The second coup by Rawlings; the PNDC is formed 1980s | World Bank and IMF austerity measures; prodemocracy agitation leads to a transition to multiparty rule 1990s |

2000s

Ghanaians elect J. A. Kufuor of the opposition NPP as president, ending Rawlings's 2-decade rule

comings, he is still revered by many as the leading pan-African nationalist of his generation. His warnings about the dangers of neo-imperialism have proved prophetic.

Since Nkrumah's fall, the army has been Ghana's dominant political institution, although there were brief returns to civilian control in 1969–1972 and again in 1979–1981. Both the military and the civilian governments abandoned much of Nkrumah's socialist commitment, but for years they continued his policy of squeezing the cocoa farmers, with the long-term result of encouraging planters both to cut back on their production and to attempt to circumvent the official prices through smuggling. This situation, coupled with falling cocoa prices on the world market and rising import costs, helped to push Ghana into a state of severe economic depression during the 1970s. During that period, real wages fell by some 80 percent. Ghana's crisis was then aggravated by an unwillingness on the part of successive governments to devalue the country's currency, the cedi, which encouraged black-market trading.

RAWLINGS'S RENEWAL

By 1981, many Ghanaians welcomed the PNDC, seeing in Rawlings's populist rhetoric the promise of change after years of corruption and stagnation. The PNDC initially tried to rule through People's Defense Committees, which were formed throughout the country to act as both official watchdogs and instruments of mass mobilization. Motivated by a combination of idealism and frustration with the status quo, the vigilantism of these institutions threatened the country with anarchy until, in 1983, they were reined in. Also in 1983, the country faced a new crisis, when the Nigerian government suddenly expelled

nearly 1 million Ghanaian expatriates, who had to be resettled quickly.

Faced with an increasingly desperate situation, the PNDC, in a move that surprised many, given its leftist leanings, began to implement the Economic Recovery Program. Some 100,000 public and parastatal employees were retrenched, the cedi was progressively devalued, and wages and prices began to reflect more nearly their market value. These steps have led to some economic growth, while annually attracting $500 million in foreign aid and soft loans and perhaps double that amount in cash remittances from the more than 1 million Ghanaians living abroad.

The human costs of ERP have been a source of criticism. Many ordinary Ghanaians, especially urban salary-earners, have suffered from falling wages coupled with rising inflation. Unemployment has also increased in many areas (today it is estimated at about 20 percent). Yet a recent survey found surprisingly strong support among "urban lower income groups" for ERP and the government in general. In the countryside, farmers have benefited from higher crop prices and investments in rural infrastructure, while there has been a countrywide boom in legitimate retailing.

ERP continues to have its critics, but it gained substantial support from politicians aligned with Ghana's three principal political tendencies: the Nkrumahists, loyal to the first president's pan-African socialist vision; the Danquah-Busia grouping, named after two past statesmen who struggled against Nkrumah for more liberal economic and political policies; and those loyal to the PNDC. In the November 1992 presidential election, the NPP emerged as the main voice of the Danquah-Busia camp, while Rawlings's NDC attracted substantial support from Nkrumahists as

well as those sympathetic to his own legacy. There was also a body of opinion that was critical of all three historic tendencies, characterizing the NPP and NDC as fronts for power-hungry men fighting yesterday's battles. During the April 1992 referendum to approve the new Constitution, more than half the registered voters (many Ghanaians complained that they were denied registration) failed to participate, despite the government and opposition's joint call for a large "yes" vote. Many also boycotted the November presidential poll. In December 1996, in a poll widely judged to have been fair, Rawlings was reelected. He narrowly defeated his former vice-president, John Kufuor, who enjoyed the backing of both the New Patriotic Party and the Convention People's Party.

DEVELOPMENT

In the 1960s, Ghana invested heavily in schooling, resulting in perhaps the best-educated population in Africa. Today, hundreds of thousands of professionals who began their schooling under Nkrumah work overseas, annually remitting an estimated $1 billion to the Ghanaian economy.

FREEDOM

The move to multipartyism has promoted freedom of speech and assembly. Dozens of independent periodicals have emerged. But government opponents claim harassment and arbitrary arrests, especially by progovernment paramilitary groups in rural areas.

HEALTH/WELFARE

In 1991, the African Commission of Health and Human Rights Promoters established a branch in Accra to help rehabilitate victims of human-rights violations from throughout Anglophone Africa. The staff deals with both the psychological and physiological after-effects of abused ex-detainees.

ACHIEVEMENTS

In 1993, Ghana celebrated the 30th anniversary of the School of the Performing Arts at the University of Legon. Integrating the world of dance, drama, and music, the school has trained a generation of artists committed to perpetuating Ghanaian, African, and international traditions in the arts.

Guinea (Republic of Guinea)

GEOGRAPHY

Area in Square Miles (Kilometers):
95,000 (246,048) (about the size of Oregon)
Capital (Population): Conakry (1,558,000)
Environmental Concerns: deforestation; insufficient potable water; desertification; soil erosion and contamination; overfishing; overpopulation
Geographical Features: mostly flat coastal plain; hilly to mountainous interior
Climate: tropical

PEOPLE

Population

Total: 7,467,400
Annual Growth Rate: 1.95%
Rural/Urban Population Ratio: 70/30
Major Languages: French; many tribal languages
Ethnic Makeup: 40% Peuhl; 30% Malinke; 20% Soussou; 10% other African groups
Religions: 85% Muslim; 8% Christian; 7% indigenous beliefs

Health

Life Expectancy at Birth: 43 years (male); 48 years (female)
Infant Mortality Rate (Ratio): 131/1,000
Physicians Available (Ratio): 1/9,732

Education

Adult Literacy Rate: 40%
Compulsory (Ages): 7–13; free

COMMUNICATION

Telephones: 36,800 main lines
Televisions: 10 per 1,000 people
Internet Service Providers: na

TRANSPORTATION

Highways in Miles (Kilometers): 18,060 (30,100)
Railroads in Miles (Kilometers): 651 (1,086)
Usable Airfields: 15
Motor Vehicles in Use: 33,000

GOVERNMENT

Type: republic
Independence Date: October 2, 1958 (from France)
Head of State/Government: President (General) Lansana Conté; Prime Minister Lamine Sidime

Political Parties: Party for Unity and Progress; Union for the New Republic; Rally for the Guinean People; others
Suffrage: universal at 18

MILITARY

Military Expenditures (% of GDP): 1.4%
Current Disputes: none

ECONOMY

Currency ($ U.S. Equivalent): 810.94 Guinean francs = $1
Per Capita Income/GDP: $1,200/$9.2 billion
GDP Growth Rate: 3.7%
Inflation Rate: 4.5%
Labor Force: 2,400,000

Natural Resources: bauxite; iron ore; diamonds; gold; uranium; hydropower; fish
Agriculture: rice; cassava; millet; sweet potatoes; coffee; bananas; palm products; pineapples; livestock
Industry: bauxite; gold; diamonds; alumina refining; light manufacturing and agricultural processing
Exports: $695 million (primary partners Russia, United States, Benelux Countries)
Imports: $560 million (primary partners France, Côte D'Ivoire, United States)

 http://www.sas.upenn.edu/
African_Studies/Country_Specific/
Guinea.html

Map

SENEGAL
MALI
GUINEA BISSAU
Massif du Tomgue 7310
Danea
Tombadonkeo
Labe
Dinguiraye
Siguiri
Télimélé
Dabola
Kouroussa
Fria
Konkouré
Mamou
Kankan
Boffa
Kindia
Faranah
Sankarani
NORTH
ATLANTIC
OCEAN
SIERRA LEONE
Kissidougou
Kérouané
Pic de Tio 4934
Macenta
Beyla
LIBERIA
Nzérékoré
CÔTE D'IVOIRE
Yomou
CONAKRY
Niger
Milo
Dion

Guinea
★ Capital
● City
— River
--- Road

0   100   200 Miles
0   100   200   300 Kilometers
Elevation in feet

A major Islamic kingdom is established in the Futa Djalon
1700s

Samori Touré is defeated by the French
1898

Led by Sekou Touré, Guineans reject continued membership in the French Community; an independent republic is formed
1958

French president Giscard d'Estaing visits Guinea: the beginning of a reconciliation between France and Guinea
1978

Sekou Touré's death is followed by a military coup; the introduction of SAP leads to urban unrest
1980s

President Lansana Conté begins to establish a multiparty democracy; multiparty elections are held for the presidency; Conté claims victory
1990s

2000s

Guinea stays the course of Structural Adjustment despite severe hardships

Fears intensify regarding a regional conflict

GUINEA

In recent years, Guinea has managed to maintain internal peace in the face of armed conflict along its borders. But the collapse in April 2000 of the peace process in neighboring Sierra Leone and a subsequent revival of cross-border tensions with Liberia have revived fears that the country could yet be dragged into a wider regional conflict. At home, the harassment of journalists and opposition leaders has underscored the government's continued insecurity despite the 1992 transition to multiparty politics. In 1996, order was barely restored when some 2,000 soldiers rioted for two days in the streets of the capital city, Conakry, after failing to receive their pay. With a weak economy and the influx of more than half a million refugees from across its borders, the challenges facing any government of Guinea are formidable.

Since 1984, the country has been governed by Lansana Conté, who has proven to be more adept at surviving challenges to his authority than at charting a progressive course for his country. In April 1992, Conté announced that a new Constitution guaranteeing freedom of association would take immediate effect. Within a month, more than 30 political parties had been formed. Conté's initiative was a political second chance for a nation whose potential had been mismanaged for decades, under the dictatorial rule of its first president, Sekou Touré.

From his early years as a radical trade-union activist in the late 1940s until his death in office in 1984, Sekou Touré was Guinea's dominant personality. A descendent of the nineteenth-century Malinke hero Samori Touré, who fiercely resisted the imposition of French rule, Sekou Touré was a charismatic but repressive leader. In 1958, he inspired Guineans to vote for immediate independence from France. At the time, Guinea was the only territory to opt out of Charles de Gaulle's newly established French Community. The French reacted spitefully, withdrawing all aid, personnel, and equipment from the new nation, an event that heavily influenced Guinea's postindependence path. The ability of Touré's Democratic Party of Guinea (PDG) to step into the administrative vacuum was the basis for the quick transformation into the African continent's first one-party socialist state, a process that was encouraged by the Soviet bloc.

Touré's rule was characterized by economic mismanagement and the widespread abuse of human rights. It is estimated that 2 million people—at the time about one out of every four Guineans —fled the country during his rule. At least 2,900 individuals disappeared under detention.

By the late 1970s, Touré, pressured by rising discontent and his own apparent realization of his country's poor economic performance, began to modify both his domestic and foreign policies. This shift led to better relations with Western countries but little improvement in the lives of his people. In 1982, Amnesty International publicized the Touré regime's dismal record of political killings, detentions, and torture, but the world remained largely indifferent.

On April 3, 1984, a week after Touré's death, the army stepped in, claiming that it wished to end all vestiges of the late president's dictatorial regime. The bloodless coup was well received by Guineans. Hundreds of political prisoners were released; and the once-powerful Democratic Party of Guinea, which during the Touré years had been reduced from a mass party into a hollow shell, was disbanded. A new government was formed, under the leadership of then-colonel Conté; and a 10-point program for national recovery was set forth, including the restoration of human rights and the renovation of the economy.

Faced with an empty treasury, the new government committed itself to a severe Structural Adjustment Program (SAP).

This has led to a dismantling of many of the socialist structures that had been established by the previous government. While international financiers have generally praised it, the government has had to weather periodic unrest and coup attempts. In spite of these challenges, however, it has remained committed to SAP.

Guinea is blessed with mineral resources, which could lead to a more prosperous future. The country is rich in bauxite and has substantial reserves of iron and diamonds. New mining agreements, leading to a flow of foreign investment, have already led to a modest boom in bauxite and diamond exports. Small-scale gold mining is also being developed.

Guinea's greatest economic failing has been the poor performance of its agricultural sector. Unlike many of its neighbors, the country enjoys a favorable climate and soils. But, although some 80 percent of Guineans are engaged in subsistence farming, only 3 percent of the land is cultivated, and foodstuffs remain a major import. Blame for this situation largely falls on the Touré regime's legacy of an inefficient, state-controlled system of marketing and distribution. In 1987, the government initiated an ambitious plan of road rehabilitation, which, along with better produce prices, has begun to encourage farmers to produce more for the domestic market.

DEVELOPMENT

A measure of economic growth in Guinea is reflected in the rising traffic in Conakry harbor, whose volume rose 415% over a 4-year period. Plans are being made to improve the port's infrastructure.

FREEDOM

Human rights continue to be restricted in Guinea, with the government's security forces being linked to disappearances, abuse of prisoners and detainees, torture by military personnel, and inhumane prison conditions.

HEALTH/WELFARE

The life expectancy of Guineans is among the lowest in the world, reflecting the stagnation of the nation's health service during the Sekou Touré years.

ACHIEVEMENTS

More than 80% of the programming broadcast by Guinea's television service is locally produced. This output has included more than 3,000 movies. A network of rural radio stations is currently being installed.

Guinea-Bissau (Republic of Guinea-Bissau)

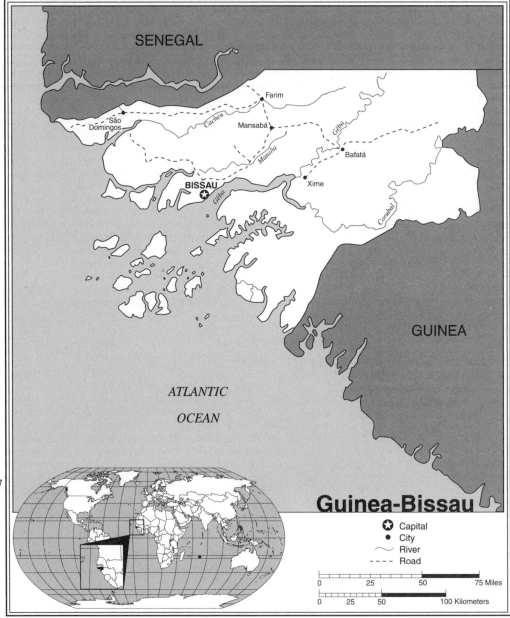

Guinea-Bissau

- ⊛ Capital
- • City
- ~ River
- --- Road

GEOGRAPHY
Area in Square Miles (Kilometers): 13,948 (36,125) (about 3 times the size of Connecticut)
Capital (Population): Bissau (197,600)
Environmental Concerns: soil erosion; deforestation; overgrazing; overfishing
Geographical Features: mostly low coastal plain, rising to savanna in the east
Climate: tropical

PEOPLE

Population
Total: 1,286,000
Annual Growth Rate: 2.4%
Rural/Urban Population Ratio: 78/22
Major Languages: Portuguese; Kriolo; various African languages
Ethnic Makeup: 30% Balanta; 20% Fula; 14% Manjaca; 13% Mandinka; 23% others (99% African; 1% others)
Religions: 65% indigenous beliefs; 30% Muslim; 5% Christian

Health
Life Expectancy at Birth: 47 years (male); 51 years (female)
Infant Mortality Rate (Ratio): 112.2/1,000
Physicians Available (Ratio): 1/9,477

Education
Adult Literacy Rate: 54%
Compulsory (Ages): 7–13

COMMUNICATION
Telephones: 8,100 main lines
Internet Service Providers: na

TRANSPORTATION
Highways in Miles (Kilometers): 2,610 (4,350)
Railroads in Miles (Kilometers): none
Usable Airfields: 30
Motor Vehicles in Use: 6,000

GOVERNMENT
Type: republic
Independence Date: September 10, 1974 (from Portugal)
Head of State/Government: President Koumba Yalla; Prime Minister Caetana N'tchama
Political Parties: African Party for the Independence of Guinea-Bissau and Cape Verde; Front for the Liberation of Guinea; United Social Democratic Party; Social Renovation Party; Democratic Convergence; others
Suffrage: universal at 15

MILITARY
Military Expenditures (% of GDP): 2.8%
Current Disputes: none

ECONOMY
Currency ($ U.S. Equivalent): 14,482 pesos = $1
Per Capita Income/GDP: $900/$1.1 billion
GDP Growth Rate: 9.5%
Inflation Rate: 5.5
Labor Force: 480,000
Natural Resources: fish; timber; phosphates; bauxite; petroleum
Agriculture: corn; beans; cassava; cashew nuts; cotton; fish and forest products; peanuts; rice; palm kernels
Industry: agricultural-products processing; beverages
Exports: $26.8 million (primary partners India, Singapore, Italy)
Imports: $22.9 million (primary partners Portugal, France, Senegal)

 http://www.sas.upenn.edu/ African_Studies/Country_Specific/ G_Bissau.html

Portuguese ships arrive; claimed as Portuguese Guinea; slave trading develops 1446	Portugal gains effective control over most of the region 1915	The African Party for the Independence of Guinea-Bissau and Cape Verde is formed 1956	Liberation struggle in Guinea-Bissau under the PAIGC and Amilcar Cabral 1963–1973	Amilcar Cabral is assassinated; the PAIGC declares Guinea-Bissau independent 1973	Revolution in Portugal leads to recognition of Guinea-Bissau's independence 1974	João Vieira comes to power through a military coup, ousting Luis Cabral 1980	The country moves toward multipartyism; Government of National Unity 1990s

The PAIGC candidate is defeated by Koumba Yala

GUINEA-BISSAU

In February 2000, Koumba Yala of the Social Renewal Party took 72 percent of the vote in the second round of presidential voting, defeating the candidate of the former ruling African Party for the Independence of Guinea-Bissau and Cape Verde (PAIGC). The new government of Guinea-Bissau now faces the unenviable challenge of promoting economic development: Since independence, the country has consistently been listed as one of the world's five least-developed societies.

Yala's election was the culmination of an 18-month process that has brought political peace to the country, which in 1998 appeared to be heading toward civil war. Two months of fighting, which had resulted in the displacement of up to a third of the country's population, was brought to an end in August 1998 with the signing of a cease-fire accord between government and rebel soldiers. This was followed up in November of that year by the establishment of a "Government of National Unity," which presided over a transition to genuine multiparty politics.

To many outsiders, the nation has been better known for its prolonged liberation war, from 1962 to 1974, against Portuguese colonial rule. Mobilized by the PAIGC, the freedom struggle in Guinea-Bissau played a major role in the overthrow of the fascist dictatorship in Portugal itself and the liberation of its other African colonies.

The origins of Portuguese rule in Guinea-Bissau go back to the late 1400s. The area was raided for centuries as a source of slaves, who were shipped to Portugal and its colonies of Cape Verde and Brazil. With the nineteenth-century abolition of slave trading, the Portuguese began to impose forced labor within Guinea-Bissau itself.

In 1956, six *assimilados*—educated Africans who were officially judged to have assimilated Portuguese culture—led by Amilcar Cabral, founded the PAIGC as a vehicle for the liberation of Cape Verde as well as Guinea-Bissau. From the beginning, many Cape Verdeans, such as Cabral,

played a prominent role within the PAIGC. But the group's largest following and main center of activity were in Guinea-Bissau. In 1963, the PAIGC turned to armed resistance and began organizing itself as an alternative government. By the end of the decade, the movement was in control of two thirds of the country.

In its liberated areas, the PAIGC was notably successful in establishing its own marketing, judicial, and educational as well as political institutions. Widespread participation throughout Guinea-Bissau in the 1973 election of a National Assembly encouraged a number of countries to formally recognize the PAIGC declaration of state sovereignty.

INDEPENDENCE

Since 1974, the leaders of Guinea-Bissau have tried to confront the problems of independence while maintaining the idealism of their liberation struggle. The nation's weak economy has limited their success. Guinea-Bissau has little in the way of mining or manufacturing, although explorations have revealed potentially exploitable reserves of oil, bauxite, and phosphates. More than 80 percent of the people are engaged in agriculture, but urban populations depend on imported foodstuffs. This situation has been generally attributed to the poor infrastructure and a lack of incentives for farmers to grow surpluses. Efforts to improve the rural economy during the early years of independence were hindered by severe drought. Only 8 percent of the small country's land is cultivated.

Under financial pressure, the government adopted a Structural Adjustment Program (SAP) in 1987. The peso was devalued, civil servants were dismissed, and various subsidies were reduced. The effects of these SAP reforms on urban workers were cushioned somewhat by external aid.

In 1988, in a desperate move, the government signed an agreement with Intercontract Company, allowing the firm to use its territory for five years as a major dump site for toxic waste from Britain, Switzerland, and the United States. In return, the government was

to earn up to $800 million. But the deal was revoked after it was exposed by members of the country's exiled opposition; a major environmental catastrophe would have resulted had it gone through.

POLITICAL DEVELOPMENT

Following the assassination of Amilcar Cabral, in 1973, his brother, Luis Cabral, succeeded him as the leader of the PAICG, thereafter becoming Guinea-Bissau's first president. Before 1980, both Guinea-Bissau and Cape Verde were separately governed by a united PAIGC, which had as its ultimate goal the forging of a political union between the two territories. But in 1980, Luis Cabral was overthrown by the military, which accused him of governing through a "Cape Verdean clique." João Vieira, a popular commander during the liberation war who had also served as prime minister, was appointed as the new head of state. As a result, relations between Cape Verde and Guinea-Bissau deteriorated, leading to a breakup in the political links between the two nations.

The PAIGC under Vieira continued to rule Guinea-Bissau as a one-party state for 10 years. The system's grassroots democracy, which had been fostered in its liberated zones during the war, gave way to a centralization of power around Vieira and other members of his military-dominated Council of State. Several coup attempts resulted in increased authoritarianism.

But the government reversed course, and in 1991, the country formally adopted multipartyism. Progress has been slow. An alleged coup attempt in 1993 led to the detention and subsequent trial of a leading opposition figure, João da Costa, on charges of plotting the government's overthrow. Elections finally occurred in July 1994. The vote resulted in a narrow second-round victory for Vieira against a very divided opposition.

DEVELOPMENT

With help from the UN Development Program, Guinea-Bissau has improved the tourism infrastructure of the 40-island Bijagos Archipelago in the hopes of bringing in much-needed revenues.

FREEDOM

The police have engaged in arbitrary arrests and torture. The fighting between government and rebel troops resulted in some 13,000 civilian casualties during the 1990s.

HEALTH/WELFARE

Guinea-Bissau's health statistics remain appalling: an overall 48-year life expectancy, 12% infant mortality, and more than 90% of the population infected with malaria.

ACHIEVEMENTS

With Portuguese assistance, a new fiber-optic digital telephone system is being established in Guinea-Bissau.

Liberia (Republic of Liberia)

GEOGRAPHY

Area in Square Miles (Kilometers): 43,000 (111,370) (about the size of Tennessee)

Capital (Population): Monrovia (962,000)

Environmental Concerns: soil erosion; deforestation; loss of biodiversity; water pollution

Geographical Features: mostly flat to rolling coastal plains, rising to rolling plateau and low mountains in the northeast

Climate: tropical

PEOPLE

Population

Total: 3,165,000

Annual Growth Rate: 1.94%

Rural/Urban Population Ratio: 54/46

Major Languages: English; Kpelle; Grio; Kru; Krahn; others

Ethnic Makeup: 95% indigenous groups; 5% Americo-Liberian

Religions: 40% indigenous beliefs; 40% Christian; 20% Muslim

Health

Life Expectancy at Birth: 50 years (male); 52 years (female)

Infant Mortality Rate (Ratio): 134.6/1,000

Physicians Available (Ratio): 1/8,333

Education

Adult Literacy Rate: 38.3%

Compulsory (Ages): 7–16; free

COMMUNICATION

Telephones: 6,400 main lines

Daily Newspaper Circulation: 15 per 1,000 people

Televisions: 20 per 1,000 people

Internet Service Providers: na

TRANSPORTATION

Highways in Miles (Kilometers): 6,180 (10,300)

Railroads in Miles (Kilometers): 306 (490)

Usable Airfields: 45

Motor Vehicles in Use: 28,000

GOVERNMENT

Type: republic

Independence Date: July 26, 1847

Head of State/Government: President Charles Ghankay Taylor is both head of state and head of government

Political Parties: National Patriotic Party; National Democratic Party of Liberia; Liberian Action Party; Liberian People's Party; United People's Party; others

Suffrage: universal at 18

MILITARY

Military Expenditures (% of GDP): 2%

Current Disputes: civil strife

ECONOMY

Currency ($ U.S. Equivalent): 1 Liberian dollar = $1

Per Capita Income/GDP: $1,000/$2.85 billion

GDP Growth Rate: 0.5%

Inflation Rate: 3%

Unemployment Rate: 70%

Natural Resources: iron ore; timber; diamonds; gold; hydropower

Agriculture: rubber; rice; palm oil; cassava; coffee; cocoa beans; sugarcane; bananas; sheep; goats; timber

Industry: rubber processing; food processing; diamonds

Exports: $39 million (primary partners Benelux countries, Norway, Ukraine)

Imports: $142 million (primary partners South Korea, Japan, Italy)

 http://www.blackworld.com/country/liberia.htm

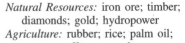

Map labels

SIERRA LEONE

GUINEA

CÔTE D'IVOIRE

Vonjama

Yekepa

Sanniquellie

Gahnpa

Ting Dowuli

Gbarnga

Robertsport

Brewerville

Tapeta

MONROVIA

Buchanan

Zwerdu

Greenville

Harper

ATLANTIC OCEAN

Lofa

Saint Paul

Farmington

Saint John

Cestos

Cavally

Liberia

★ Capital
● City
∿ River
- - - Road

0   50   100 Miles

0   50   100   150 Kilometers

LIBERIA

In August 2000, Liberian president Charles Taylor declared a state of emergency as fighting intensified in the north of the country. The success of the rebels, along with renewed fighting in neighboring Sierra Leone, whose rebels are alleged to enjoy Taylor's backing, has raised the specter of a return to civil war in Liberia. Between 1989 and 1996, some 200,000 people were killed in a civil war. Among the survivors, approximately 750,000 fled the country as refugees, while another 1.2 million were internally displaced, out of a total population of only 2.6 million people. The war ended in July 1997 with Taylor and his National Patriotic Front of Liberia (NPFL) receiving about three quarters of the vote in internationally supervised elections. These elections were the culmination of a year-long process to restore peace to the country. Taylor's subsequent inauguration brought stability to the country—but it is now under renewed threat.

The restoration of peace in Liberia after July 1997 was overseen by a West African regional military force (ECOMOG) of just over 10,000. The force was deployed throughout the country to provide the security, facilitate the disarmament and demobilization of local combatants, and protect returning refugees. Its relative success in carrying out these functions came about after years of frustration. When the force finally withdrew in 1998, it left behind 10,000 to 25,000 locally fathered children. ECOMOG's security role has been taken over by the reconstituted Armed Forces of Liberia, an uneasy mix of former civil-war rivals.

A major challenge facing Taylor's new government was Liberia's war-ravaged economy, with little formal-sector employment, some $2.2 billion in debts, and a collapsed infrastructure. In December 1997, the president announced that a new currency would be introduced in 1998 to replace the two separate currencies that were in use in different parts of the country in addition to the U.S. dollar, which is also legal tender.

AFRICAN-AMERICAN-AFRICANS

Among the African states, Liberia shares with Ethiopia the distinction of having avoided European rule. Between 1847 and 1980, Liberia was governed by an elite made up primarily of descendants of African Americans who had begun settling along its coastline two decades earlier. These "Americo-Liberians" make up only 5 percent of the population. But they dominated politics for decades through their control of the governing True Whig Party (TWP). Although the republic's

Constitution was ostensibly democratic, the TWP rigged the electoral process.

Most Liberians belong to indigenous ethnolinguistic groups, such as the Kpelle, Bassa, Grio, Kru, Krahn, and Vai, who were conquered by the Americo-Liberians during the 1800s and early 1900s. Some individuals from these subjugated communities accepted Americo-Liberian norms. Yet book learning, Christianity, and an ability to speak English helped an indigenous person to advance within the state only if he or she accepted its social hierarchy by becoming a "client" of an Americo-Liberian "patron." In a special category were the important interior "chiefs," who were able to maintain their local authority as long as they remained loyal to the republic.

During the twentieth century, Liberia's economy was transformed by vast Firestone rubber plantations, iron-ore mining, and urbanization. President William Tubman (1944–1971) proclaimed a Unification Policy, to promote national integration, and an Open-Door Policy, to encourage outside investment in Liberia. However, most of the profits that resulted from the modest external investment that did occur left the country, while the wealth that remained was concentrated in the hands of the TWP elite.

During the administration of Tubman's successor, William Tolbert (1971–1980), Liberians became more conscious of the inability of the TWP to address the inequities of the status quo. Educated youths

from all ethnic backgrounds began to join dissident associations rather than the regime's patronage system.

As economic conditions worsened, the top 4 percent of the population came to control 60 percent of the wealth. Rural stagnation drove many to the capital city of Monrovia (named after U.S. president James Monroe), where they suffered from high unemployment and inflation. The inevitable explosion occurred in 1979, when the government announced a 50 percent price increase for rice, the national food staple. Police fired on demonstrators, killing and wounding hundreds. Rioting, which resulted in great property damage, led the government to appeal to neighboring Guinea for troops. It was clear that the TWP was losing its grip. Thus Sergeant Samuel Doe enjoyed widespread support when, in 1980, he led a successful coup.

DOE DOESN'T DO

Doe came to power as Liberia's first indigenous president, a symbolically important event that many believed would herald substantive changes. Some institutions of the old order, such as the TWP and the Masonic Temple (looked upon as Liberia's secret government) were disbanded. The House of Representatives and Senate were suspended. Offices changed hands, but the old administrative system persisted. Many of those who came to power were members of Doe's own ethnic group, the Krahn, who had long been prominent in the lower ranks of the army.

(United Nations photo by N. van Praag)

The Liberian Civil War left the country destitute. Political anarchy destroyed much of the infrastructure, economy, and culture. Nearly a tenth of the population were killed, many more displaced from their homes.

| The Vai move onto the Liberian coast from the interior **1500s** | The first African-American settlers arrive from the United States **1822** | The first coup exchanges one Americo-Liberian government for another **1871** | The League of Nations investigates forced-labor charges **1931** | President William Tubman comes to office **1944** | William Tolbert becomes president **1971** | Tolbert is assassinated; a military coup brings Samuel Doe to power **1980s** | Civil war leads to the execution of Doe, anarchy, and foreign intervention; Charles Taylor and the NPFL win power in internationally supervised elections; the Civil War ends **1990s** | **2000s** |

Civil strife intensifies; President Taylor declares a state of emergency

Doe declared a narrow victory for himself in the October 1985 elections, but there was widespread evidence of ballot tampering. A month later, exiled General Thomas Quiwonkpa led an abortive coup attempt. During and after the uprising, thousands of people were killed, mostly civilians belonging to Quiwonkpa's Grio group who were slaughtered by loyalist (largely Krahn) troops. Doe was inaugurated, but opposition-party members refused to take their seats in the National Assembly. Some, fearing for their lives, went into exile.

During the late 1980s, Doe became increasingly dictatorial. Many called on the U.S. government, in particular, to withhold aid until detainees were freed and new elections held. The U.S. Congress criticized the regime but authorized more than $500 million in financial and military support. Meanwhile, Liberia suffered from a shrinking economy and a growing foreign debt, which by 1987 had reached $1.6 billion.

Doe's government was not entirely to blame for Liberia's dire financial condition. When Doe came to power, the Liberian treasury was already empty, in large part due to the vast expenditures incurred by the 1979 Organization of African Unity Conference. The rising cost of oil and decline in world prices for natural rubber, iron ore, and sugar had further crippled the economy. But government corruption and instability under Doe made the bad situation worse.

DOE'S DOWNFALL
Liberia's descent into violent anarchy began on December 24, 1989, when a small group of insurgents, led by Charles Taylor, who had earlier fled the country amid corruption charges, began a campaign to overthrow Doe. As Taylor's NPFL rebels gained ground, the war developed into an increasingly vicious interethnic struggle among groups who had been either victimized by or associated with the regime. Thousands of civilians were thus massacred by ill-disciplined gunmen on both sides; hundreds of thousands began to flee for their lives. By June 1990, with the rump of Doe's forces besieged in Monrovia, a small but efficient breakaway armed faction of the NPFL, under the ruthless leadership of a former soldier named Prince Johnson, had emerged as a deadly third force.

By August, with the United States unwilling to do more than evacuate foreign nationals from Monrovia (the troops of Doe, Johnson, and Taylor had begun kidnapping expatriates and violating diplomatic immunity), members of the Economic Community of West African States decided to establish a framework for peace by installing an interim government, with the support of a regional peacekeeping force known as ECOMOG: the ECOWAS Monitoring Group. The predominantly Nigerian force, which also included contingents from Ghana, Guinea, Sierra Leone, The Gambia, and, later, Senegal, landed in Monrovia in late August. This coincided with the nomination, by a broad-based but NPFL–boycotted National Conference, of Amos Sawyer, a respected academic, as the head of the proposed interim administration.

Initial hopes that ECOMOG's presence would end the fighting proved to be naïve. On September 9, 1990, Johnson captured Doe by shooting his way into ECOMOG headquarters. The following day, Doe's gruesome torture and execution were videotaped by his captors. This "outrage for an outrage" did not end the suffering. Protected by a reinforced ECOMOG, Sawyer was able to establish his interim authority over most of Monrovia, but the rest of the country remained in the hands of the NPFL or of local thugs.

Repeated attempts to get Johnson and Taylor to cooperate with Sawyer in establishing an environment conducive to holding elections have so far proved fruitless. While most neighboring states have supported ECOMOG's mediation efforts, some have provided support (and, in the case of Burkina Faso, troops) to the NPFL, which has encouraged Taylor in his on-again, off-again approach toward national reconciliation.

In September 1991, a new, fiercely anti-NPLF force, the United Liberation Movement of Liberia (ULIMO), emerged from bases in Sierra Leone. The group is identified with former Doe supporters. Subsequent clashes between ULIMO and NPFL on both sides of the Liberian–Sierra Leonean border contributed to the April 1992 overthrow of the Sierra Leonean government as well as the failure of an October 1991 peace accord brokered by the Côte d'Ivoire's late president Felix Houphouët-Boigny.

In October 1992, ECOWAS agreed to impose sanctions on the NPFL for blocking Monrovia. ECOMOG then joined ULIMO and remnants of the Armed Forces of Liberia (AFL) in a counteroffensive. In 1993, yet another armed faction, the Liberia Peace Council (LPC), emerged to challenge Taylor for control of southeastern Liberia. In March 1994, an all-party interim State Council, agreed to in principle eight months earlier, was finally sworn in. But it quickly collapsed, while a violent split in ULIMO contributed to further anarchy.

DEVELOPMENT

Liberia's economic and social infrastructure was devastated by the war. Today people are surviving primarily through informal-sector bartering and trading.

FREEDOM

The Taylor government has tried to reestablish the rule of law. The various government security forces continue to be linked to abuses. In 1998, Taylor accused rivals of plotting a coup and jeopardizing continued efforts to build postwar reconciliation in the country. In 2000, he declared a state of emergency when civil fighting intensified in the north of the country.

HEALTH/WELFARE

Outside aid and local self-help efforts were mobilized against famine in Liberia in 1990–1991. But the long and brutal Civil War took a dreadful toll on Liberians' health and well-being.

ACHIEVEMENTS

Through a shrewd policy of diplomacy, Liberia managed to maintain its independence when Great Britain and France conquered neighboring areas during the late nineteenth century. It espoused African causes during the colonial period; for instance, Liberia brought the case of Namibia to the World Court in the 1950s.

Mali (Republic of Mali)

GEOGRAPHY
Area in Square Miles (Kilometers):
478,819 (1,240,142) (about twice the size of Texas)
Capital (Population): Bamako (810,000)
Environmental Concerns: soil erosion; deforestation; desertification; insufficient potable water; poaching
Geographical Features: mostly flat to rolling northern plains covered by sand; savanna in the south; rugged hills in the northeast
Climate: subtropical to arid

PEOPLE

Population
Total: 10,686,000
Annual Growth Rate: 2.98%
Rural/Urban Population Ratio: 72/28
Major Languages: French; Bambara; numerous African languages
Ethnic Makeup: 50% Mande; 17% Peul; 12% Voltaic; 6% Songhai; 10% Tuareg and Maur (Moor); 5% others
Religions: 90% Muslim; 9% indigenous beliefs; 1% Christian

Health
Life Expectancy at Birth: 46 years (male); 48 years (female)
Infant Mortality Rate (Ratio): 124/1,000
Physicians Available (Ratio): 1/18,376

Education
Adult Literacy Rate: 31%
Compulsory (Ages): 7–16; free

COMMUNICATION
Telephones: 26,800 main lines
Televisions: 12 per 1,000 people
Internet Service Providers: 1 (1999)

TRANSPORTATION
Highways in Miles (Kilometers): 9,362 (15,100)
Railroads in Miles (Kilometers): 452 (729)
Usable Airfields: 28
Motor Vehicles in Use: 41,000

GOVERNMENT
Type: republic
Independence Date: September 22, 1960 (from France)
Head of State/Government: President Alpha Oumar Konare; Prime Minister Ibrabima Boubacar Keita

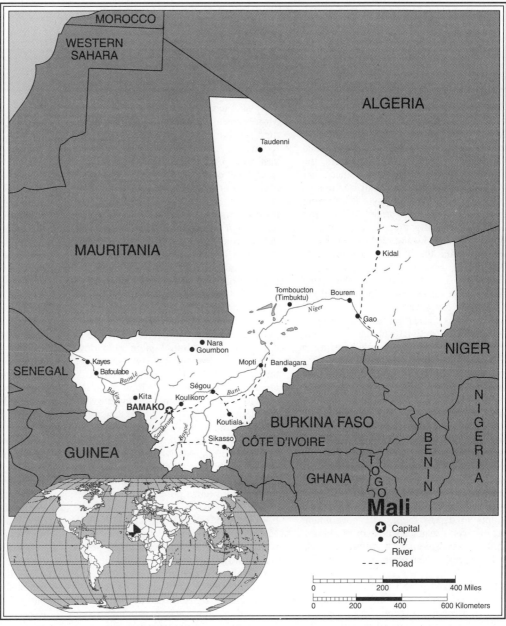

Political Parties: Alliance for Democracy; National Congress for Democratic Initiative; Sudanese Union/African Democratic Rally; others
Suffrage: universal at 21

MILITARY
Military Expenditures (% of GDP): 2%
Current Disputes: none

ECONOMY
Currency ($ U.S. Equivalent): 529.43 CFA francs = $1
Per Capita Income/GDP: $820/$8.5 billion
GDP Growth Rate: 5%
Inflation Rate: 3%

Natural Resources: hydropower; bauxite; iron ore; manganese; tin; phosphates; kaolin; salt; limestone; gold; uranium; copper
Agriculture: millet; sorghum; corn; rice; sugar; cotton; peanuts; livestock
Industry: food processing; construction; phosphate and gold mining; consumer-goods production
Exports: $640 million (primary partners Thailand, Italy, China)
Imports: $650 million (primary partners CFA Franc Zone and Europe)

 http://www.cia.gov/cia/publications/factbook/geos/ml/html

The Mali empire extends over much of the upper regions of West Africa
1250–1400s

The Songhai empire controls the region
late 1400s– late 1500s

The French establish control over Mali
1890

The Mali Confederation
1960

Moussa Traoré and the Military Committee for National Liberation grab power
1968

Traoré's Democratic Union of the Malian People is the single ruling party
1979

School strikes and demonstrations; teachers and students are detained
1979–1980

The country's first multiparty elections are held; economic problems stir civic unrest
1990s

2000s

The Konare government explores ways to strengthen the economy

MALI

In May 1997, Malians reelected Dr. Alpha Konare as their president. While the election was marred by a heavy-handed clampdown on opposition protesters, the human-rights situation has since improved, easing fears that Mali was returning to its authoritarian past. The current government was inaugurated a year after a coup ended the dictatorial regime of Moussa Traoré. Like his predecessor, Modibo Keita, the first president of Mali, Traoré had governed Mali as a single-party state. True to their word, the young officers who seized power in 1991 following bloody antigovernment riots presided over a quick transition to civilian rule. Konare is an activist scholar who, like many Malians, finds political inspiration in his country's rich heritage.

Konare's efforts to rebuild Mali were hampered by a weak economy, aggravated by the 1994 collapse in value of the CFA franc. In 1994 and 1995, violence occurred between security forces and university students protesting against economic hardship. The plight of Malian economic refugees in France gained international attention in 1996, when a number sought sanctuary in a Parisian church and went on a hunger strike in protest against attempts to deport them. The government has enjoyed greater success in reaching a (still fragile) settlement with Tuareg rebels in the country's far north.

AN IMPERIAL PAST

The published epic of Sundiata Keita, the thirteenth-century A.D. founder of the great Mali empire, is recognized throughout the world as a masterpiece of classical African literature. In Mali itself, Sundiata remains a source of national pride and unity.

Sundiata's state was one of three great West African empires whose centers lay in modern Mali. Between the fourth and thirteenth centuries, the area was the site of the prosperous, ancient Ghana. The Malian empire was superseded by that of Songhai, which was conquered by the Moroccans at the end of the sixteenth century. All these empires were in fact confederations. Although they encompassed vast areas united under a single supreme ruler, local communities generally enjoyed a great deal of autonomy.

From the 1890s until 1960, another form of imperial unity was imposed over Mali (then called the French Sudan) and the adjacent territories of French West Africa. The legacy of broader colonial and precolonial unity as well as its landlocked position have inspired Mali's postcolonial leaders to seek closer ties with neighboring countries.

Mali formed a brief confederation with Senegal during the transition period to independence. This initial union broke down after only a few months, but since then, the two countries have cooperated in the Organization for the Development of the Senegal River and other regional groupings. The Senegalese port of Dakar, which is linked by rail to Mali's capital city, Bamako, remains the major outlet for Malian exports. Mali has also sought to strengthen its ties with nearby Guinea. In 1983, the two countries signed an agreement to harmonize policies and structures.

ENVIRONMENTAL CHALLENGES

Mali is one of the poorest countries in the world. More than 85 percent of the people are employed in (mostly subsistence) agriculture, but the government usually has to rely on international aid to make up for local food deficits. Most of the country lies within either the expanding Sahara Desert or the semiarid region known as the Sahel, which has become drier as a result of recurrent drought. Much of the best land lies along the Senegal and Niger Rivers, which support most of the nation's agropastoral production. In earlier centuries, the Niger was able to sustain great trading cities such as Timbuctu and Djenne, but today, most of its banks do not even support crops. Efforts to increase cultivation have so far been met with limited overall success.

Mali's frequent inability to feed itself has been largely blamed on locust infestation, drought, and desertification. The inefficient state-run marketing and distribution system, however, has also had a negative impact. Low official produce prices have encouraged farmers either to engage in subsistence agriculture or to sell their crops on the black market. Thus, while some regions of the country remain dependent on international food donations, crops continue to be smuggled across Mali's borders. Recent policy commitments to liberalize agricultural trading, as part of an International Monetary Funding–approved Structural Adjustment Program (SAP), have yet to take hold.

In contrast to agriculture, Mali's mining sector has experienced promising growth. The nation exports modest amounts of gold, phosphates, marble, and uranium. Potentially exploitable deposits of bauxite, manganese, iron, tin, and diamonds exist.

For decades, Mali was officially committed to state socialism. Its first president, Keita, a descendant of Sundiata, established a command economy and one-party state during the 1960s. His attempt to go it alone outside the CFA Franc Zone proved to be a major failure. Under Traoré, socialist structures were modified but not abandoned. Agreements with the IMF ended some government monopolies, and the country adopted the CFA franc as its currency. But the lack of a significant class of private entrepreneurs and the role of otherwise unprofitable public enterprises in providing employment discouraged radical privatization.

DEVELOPMENT

In 1989, the government received international funding to overhaul its energy infrastructure. The opening of new gold mines has provided the economy with a boost.

FREEDOM

The human-rights situation in Mali has improved in recent years, though international attention was drawn to the suppression of opposition demonstrations in the run-up to the 1997 election.

HEALTH/WELFARE

About a third of Mali's budget is devoted to education. A special literacy program in Mali teaches rural people how to read and write, by using booklets that concern fertilizers, measles, and measuring fields.

ACHIEVEMENTS

For centuries, the ancient Malian city of Timbuctu was a leading center of Islamic learning and culture. Chronicles published by its scholars of the Middle Ages still enrich local culture.

Mauritania (Islamic Republic of Mauritania)

GEOGRAPHY
Area in Square Miles (Kilometers):
398,000 (1,030,700) (about 3
times the size of New Mexico)
Capital (Population):
Nouakchott (735,000)
Environmental Concerns:
overgrazing; deforestation;
soil erosion; desertification;
very limited natural freshwater
resources; overfishing
Geographical Features: mostly
barren, flat plains of the
Sahara; some central hills
Climate: desert

PEOPLE

Population
Total: 2,668,000
Annual Growth Rate: 2.94%
Rural/Urban Population Ratio: 47/53
Major Languages: Hasanixa;
Soninke; Arabic; Pular; Wolof
Ethnic Makeup: 40% mixed Maur/
black; perhaps 30% Maur;
30% black
Religions: 100% Muslim

Health
Life Expectancy at Birth: 49
years (male); 53 years (female)
Infant Mortality Rate (Ratio):
78.1/1,000
Physicians Available (Ratio):
1/11,085

Education
Adult Literacy Rate: 37.7%
Compulsory (Ages): 6–12

COMMUNICATION
Telephones: 13,500 main lines
Internet Service Providers: na

TRANSPORTATION
Highways in Miles (Kilometers):
4,560 (7,600)
Railroads in Miles (Kilometers):
422 (704)
Usable Airfields: 26
Motor Vehicles in Use: 26,500

GOVERNMENT
Type: republic
Independence Date: November 28, 1960
(from France)
Head of State/Government: President
(Colonel) Maaouya Ould Sid Ahmed
Taya; Prime Minister Cheik El Afia
Ould Mohamed Khouna
Political Parties: Democratic and Social
Republican Party; Union of Democratic
Forces–New Era; Assembly for
Democracy and Unity; Popular Social

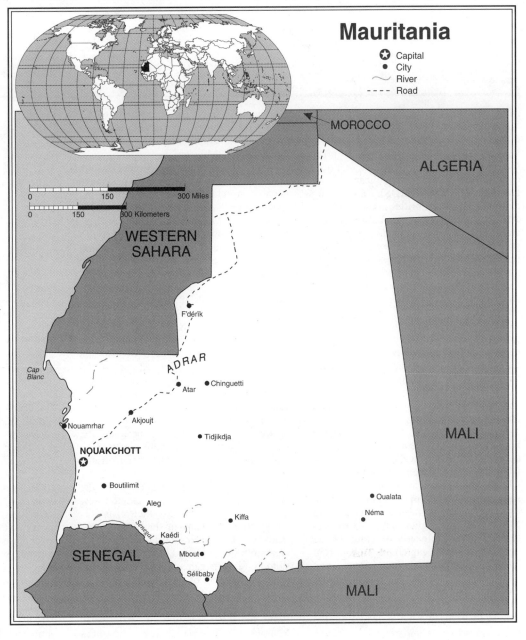

Mauritania

and Democratic Union; National
Avant-Garde Party; Action for Change
Suffrage: universal at 18

MILITARY
Military Expenditures (% of GDP): 2.7%
Current Disputes: ethnic tensions

ECONOMY
Currency ($ U.S. Equivalent): 125.91
ouguiyas = $1
Per Capita Income/GDP: $1,910/$4.9 billion
GDP Growth Rate: 3.7%
Inflation Rate: 9.8%
Unemployment Rate: 23%

Labor Force: 465,000
Natural Resources: iron ore; gypsum;
fish; copper; phosphates
Agriculture: millet; sorghum; dates; root
crops; cattle and sheep; fish products
Industry: iron-ore and gypsum mining;
fish processing
Exports: $425 million (primary partners
Japan, Italy, France)
Imports: $444 million (primary partners
France, Spain Germany)

http://www.cia.gov/cia/publications/
factbook/geos/mr.html

The Almoravids spread Islam in the Western Sahara areas through conquest
1035–1055
●

The Mauritanian area becomes a French colony
1920
●

Mauritania becomes independent under President Moktar Ould Daddah
1960
●

A military coup brings Khouma Ould Haidalla and the Military Committee for National Recovery to power
1978
●

The Algiers Agreement: Mauritania makes peace with Polisario and abandons claims to Western Sahara
1979
●

Slavery is formally abolished
1980
●

Multiparty elections are boycotted by the opposition; tensions continue between Mauritania and Senegal
1990s
●

2000s

Desertification takes its toll on the environment and the economy

It is estimated that 90,000 Mauritanians still live in servitude, despite the abolishment of slavery

Senegal and Mauritania seek better relations

MAURITANIA

Since the adoption of its current Constitution in 1991, Mauritania has legally been a multiparty democracy. But in practice, power remains in the hand of President Ould Taya's Republican Social Democratic Party (PRDS). The ruling party won large majorities in the 1992 and 1997 elections, which in both instances were boycotted by the leading opposition grouping, the Union of Democratic Forces (UDF). Multipartyism has so far failed to assure either social harmony or a respect for human rights. Neither has it resolved the country's severe social and economic problems.

For decades, Mauritania has grown progressively drier. Today, about 75 percent of the country is covered by sand. Less than 1 percent of the land is suitable for cultivation, 10 percent for grazing. To make matters worse, the surviving arable and pastoral areas have been plagued by grasshoppers and locusts.

In the face of natural disaster, people have moved. Since the mid-1960s, the percentage of urban dwellers has swelled, from less than 10 percent to 53 percent, while the nomadic population during the same period has dropped, from more than 80 percent to perhaps 20 percent. In Nouakchott, the capital city, vast shantytowns now house nearly a quarter of the population. As the capital has grown, from a few thousand to more than three quarters of a million in a single generation, its poverty—and that of the nation as a whole—has become more obvious. People seek new ways to make a living away from the land, but there are few jobs.

Mauritania's faltering economy has coincided with an increase in racial and ethnic tensions. Since independence, the government has been dominated by the Maurs (or Moors), who speak Hasaniya Arabic. This community has historically been divided between the aristocrats and commoners, of Arab and Berber origin, and their black African slaves who have been assimilated into Maurish culture but remain socially segregated as "Haratine." Together the Maurs account for anywhere from 30 to 60 percent of the citizenry (the government has refused to release comprehensive data from the last two censuses).

The other half of Mauritania's population is composed of the "blacks," who mostly speak Pulaar, Soninke, or Wolof. Like the Maurs, all these groups are Muslim. Thus Mauritania's rulers have stressed Islam as a source of national unity. The country proclaimed itself an Islamic republic at independence, and since 1980 the Shari'a, the Islamic penal code, has been the law of the land.

Muslim brotherhood has not been able to overcome the divisions between the northern Maurs and southern blacks. One major source of friction has been official Arabization efforts, which are opposed by most southerners. In recent years, the country's desertification has created new sources of tension. As their pastures turned to sand, many of the Maurish nomads who did not find refuge in the urban areas moved southward. There, with state support, they began in the 1980s to deprive southerners of their land.

Growing oppression of blacks has been met with resistance from the underground Front for the Liberation of Africans in Mauritania (FLAM). Black grievances were also linked to an unsuccessful coup attempt in 1987. In 1989, interethnic hostility exploded when a border dispute with Senegal led to race riots that left several hundred "Senegalese" dead in Nouakchott. In response, the "Moorish" trading community in Senegal became the target of reprisals. Mauritania claimed that 10,000 Maurs were killed, but other sources put the number at about 70. Following this bloodshed, more than 100,000 refugees were repatriated across both sides of the border. Mass deportations of "Mauritanians of Senegalese origin" have fueled charges that the Nouakchott regime is trying to eliminate its non-Maurish population.

Tensions between Mauritania and Senegal have persisted, but a visit in June 2000 by newly elected Senegalese president Abdoulaye Wade has revived hopes for better relations. This could help to bring an end to the occasional cross-border raids by deported Mauritanians. Genuine peace, however, will require greater reform within Mauritania itself. In recent years, the regime in Nouakchott has sent out conflicting signals. Although the government has legalized opposition parties, it has also continued to pursue its Arabization program and has clamped down on genuine dissent. Maur militias have been armed, and the army has been expanded with assistance from Arab countries.

DEVELOPMENT

Mauritania's coastal waters are among the richest in the world. During the 1980s, the local fishing industry grew at an average annual rate of more than 10%. Many now believe that the annual catch has reached the upper levels of its sustainable potential.

FREEDOM

The Mauritanian government is especially sensitive to continuing allegations of the existence of chattel slavery in the country. While slavery is outlawed, there is credible evidence of its continued existence. In 1998, five members of a local advocacy group SOS–Esclaves (Slaves) were sentenced to 13 months imprisonment for "activities within a non-authorized organization."

HEALTH/WELFARE

There have been some modest improvements in the areas of health and education since the country's independence, but conditions remain poor. Mauritania has received low marks regarding its commitment to human development.

ACHIEVEMENTS

There is a current project to restore ancient Mauritanian cities, such as Chinguette, which are located on traditional routes from North Africa to Sudan. These centers of trade and Islamic learning were points of origin for the pilgrimage to Mecca and were well known in the Middle East.

Niger (Republic of Niger)

GEOGRAPHY

Area in Square Miles (Kilometers): 489,191 (1,267,000) (about twice the size of Texas)

Capital (Population): Niamey (420,000)

Environmental Concerns: overgrazing; deforestation; soil erosion; desertification; poaching and habitat destruction

Geographical Features: mainly desert plains and sand dunes; flat to rolling plains in the south; hills in the north

Climate: desert; tropical in the extreme south

PEOPLE

Population

Total: 10,076,000

Annual Growth Rate: 2.75%

Rural/Urban Population Ratio: 81/19

Major Languages: French; Hausa; Djerma

Ethnic Makeup: 56% Hausa; 22% Djerma; 8% Fula; 8% Tuareg; 6% others

Religions: 80% Muslim; 20% indigenous beliefs and Christian

Health

Life Expectancy at Birth: 41 years (male); 41 years (female)

Infant Mortality Rate (Ratio): 125/1,000

Physicians Available (Ratio): 1/35,141

Education

Adult Literacy Rate: 13.6%

Compulsory (Ages): 7–15, free

COMMUNICATION

Telephones: 18,000 main lines

Televisions: 2.8 per 1,000 people

Internet Service Provider: 1 (1999)

TRANSPORTATION

Highways in Miles (Kilometers): 6,262 (10,100)

Railroads in Miles (Kilometers): none

Usable Airfields: 27

Motor Vehicles in Use: 51,500

GOVERNMENT

Type: republic

Independence Date: August 3, 1960 (from France)

Head of State/Government: President Mamadou Tandja is both head of state and head of government

Political Parties: National Movement for a Developing Society–Nassara; Democratic and Social Convention–Rahama; Nigerien Party for Democracy and Socialism; Nigerien Alliance for Democracy and Social Progress–Zaman-lahia; others

Suffrage: universal at 18

MILITARY

Military Expenditures (% of GDP): 1.1%

Current Disputes: territorial dispute with Libya; boundary disputes over Lake Chad

ECONOMY

Currency ($ U.S. Equivalent): 529.43 CFA francs = $1

Per Capita Income/GDP: $1,000/$9.6 billion

GDP Growth Rate: 2%

Inflation Rate: 4.8%

Natural Resources: uranium; coal; iron ore; tin; phosphates; gold; petroleum

Agriculture: millet; sorghum; peanuts; cotton; cowpeas; cassava; livestock

Industry: cement; brick; textiles; chemicals; agricultural products; food processing; uranium mining

Exports: $269 million (primary partners United States, Greece, Japan)

Imports: $295 million (primary partners France, Côte d'Ivoire, United States)

 http://www.cia.gov/cia/publications/factbook/geos/ng.html

NIGER

In August 2000, Niger marked four decades of independence with a financially bankrupt and politically insecure government. In November 1999, President Mamadou Tandja was elected under a new Constitution. But ultimate power remains in the hands of the military, which, in January 1996, overthrew Niger's last elected government. In July 1996, the leader of the coup, Colonel Ibrahim Bare Mainassara, had claimed victory in an election that was widely condemned as fraudulent. Mainassara's subsequent assassination, in April 1999, opened the door to a return to civilian rule, but at this writing, a military committee under strongman Major Daouda Mallam-Wanke continues to wield influence over the government.

DROUGHT AND DESERTIFICATION

Most Nigeriens subsist through small-scale crop production and herding. Yet farming is especially difficult in Niger. Less than 10 percent of the nation's vast territory is suitable for cultivation even during the best of times. Most of the cultivable land lies along the banks of the Niger River. Unfortunately, much of the past four decades has been the worst of times. During this period, Nigeriens have been constantly challenged by recurrent drought and an ongoing process of desertification.

Drought had an especially catastrophic effect during the 1970s. Most Nigeriens were reduced to dependency on foreign food aid, while about 60 percent of their livestock perished. Some people believe that the ecological disaster that afflicted Africa's Sahel region (which includes southern Niger) during that period was of such severity as to disrupt the delicate long-term balance between desert and savanna. Others, however, have concluded that the intensified desertification of recent years is primarily rooted in human, rather than natural, causes, which can be reversed. In particular, many attribute environmental degradation to the introduction of inappropriate forms of cultivation, overgrazing, deforestation, and new patterns of human settlement.

Ironically, much of the debate on people's negative impact on the Sahel environment has been focused on some of the agricultural-development schemes that once were perceived as the region's salvation. In their attempts to boost local food production, international aid agencies often promoted so-called Green Revolution programs. These were designed to increase per acre yields, typically through the intensive planting of new, higher-yielding seeds and reliance on imported fertilizers and pesticides. Such projects often led to higher initial local outputs that proved unsustainable, largely due to expensive overhead. In addition, many experts promoting the new agricultural techniques failed to appreciate the value of traditional technologies and forms of social organization in limiting desertification while allowing people to cope with drought. It is now appreciated that patterns

(United Nations photo)

Drought and desertification in Niger have been amplified by inappropriate forms of cultivation, overgrazing, deforestation, and human settlement. Attempted "improvements" to increase local food production have discouraged the traditional nomadic pattern of life in Niger and, in consequence, have upset the delicate long-term balance between desert and savanna.

The Mali Empire includes territories and peoples of current Niger areas
1200s–1400s

Hausa states develop in the south of present-day Niger
1400s

The area is influenced by the Fulani Empire, centered at Sokoto, now in Nigeria
1800s

France consolidates rule over Niger
1906

Niger becomes independent
1960

A military coup brings Colonel Seyni Kountché and a Supreme Military Council to power
1974

President Kountché dies and is replaced by Ali Saibou
1987

The Nigerien National Conference adopts multipartyism; President Ibrahim Bare Mainassara is assassinated
1990s

2000s

President Mamadou Tandja holds power under the new Constitution, but the military retains significant influence

of cultivation long championed by Nigerien farmers allowed for soil conservation and reduced the risks associated with pests and poor climate.

The government's recent emphasis has been on helping Niger's farmers to help themselves through the extension of credit, better guaranteed minimum prices, and improved communications. Vigorous efforts have been made in certain regions to halt the spread of desert sands by supporting village tree-planting campaigns. Given the local inevitability of drought, the government has also increased its commitment to the stockpiling of food in granaries. But, for social and political as much as economic reasons, government policy has continued to discourage the flexible, nomadic pattern of life that has long characterized many Nigerien communities.

The Nigerien government's emphasis on agriculture has, in part, been motivated by the realization that the nation could not rely on its immense uranium deposits for future development. The opening of uranium mines in the 1970s resulted in the country becoming the world's fifth-largest producer. By the end of that decade, uranium exports accounted for some 90 percent of Niger's foreign-exchange earnings. Depressed international demand throughout the 1980s, however, resulted in substantially reduced prices and output. Although uranium still accounts for 75 percent of foreign-exchange earnings, its revenue contribution in recent years is only about a third of what it was prior to the slump.

MILITARY RULE

For nearly half of its existence after its independence, Niger was governed by a civilian administration, under President Hamani Diori. In 1974, during the height of drought, Lieutenant Colonel (later, Major General) Seyni Kountché took power in a bloodless coup. Kountché ruled as the leader of a Supreme Military Council, which met behind closed doors. Ministerial portfolios, appointed by the president, were filled by civilians as well as military personnel. In 1987, Kountché died of natural causes and was succeeded by Colonel Ali Saibou.

A National Movement for the Development of Society (MNSD) was established in 1989 as the country's sole political party, after a constitutional referendum in which less than 4 percent of the electorate participated. But, as was the case in many other countries in Africa, the year 1990 saw a groundswell of local support for a return to multipartyism. In Niger, this prodemocracy agitation was spearheaded by the nation's labor confederation, which organized a widely observed 48-hour general strike. Having earlier rejected the strikers "as a handful of demagogues," in 1991, President Saibou agreed to the formation of a National Conference to prepare a new constitution.

The conference ended its deliberations with the appointment of an interim government, headed by Amadou Cheffou, which led the country to multiparty elections in February–March 1993. After two rounds of voting, the presidential contest was won by Mahamane Ousmane. Ousmane's Alliance of Forces for Change (AFC) opposition captured 50 seats in the new 83-seat National Assembly, while the MNSD became the major opposition party, with 29 seats.

Ousmane's government made a promising start by reaching peace agreements with two rebel movements, the Tuareg Front for the Liberation of Air and Azaouad and the Organization of Army Resistance. But the nation's economic crisis deepened with the 1994 devaluation of the CFA franc. Naturally, Ousmane's political status was weakened. In February 1995, the opposition coalition, led by Hama Amadou, gained control of the National Assembly, resulting in an uneasy government of "cohabitation." Serious student unrest was followed by the military coup in January 1996 that resulted in the installation of Colonel Ibrahim Bare Mainassara as president. Under international pressure, Mainassara agreed to early elections, which were seen to have been fraudulent.

The political turn is likely to further poison interethnic relations in Niger. Since independence, members of the Zarma group have been especially prominent in the government, MNSD, and military. The deposed Ousmane has been Niger's first Hausa leader (the Hausa constitute the country's largest ethnolinguistic group).

DEVELOPMENT

Nigerien village cooperatives, especially marketing cooperatives, pre-date independence and have grown in size and importance in recent years. They have successfully competed with well-to-do private traders for control of the grain market.

FREEDOM

Nigeriens have been effectively disenfranchised by the 1996 coup and subsequent fraudulent presidential election. Security forces are known to beat and intimidate opposition political figures. The private media are a target of repression, with a number of journalists having been detained. Opposition meetings and demonstrations are often banned.

HEALTH/WELFARE

A national conference on educational reform stimulated a program to use Nigerien languages in primary education and integrated the adult literacy program into the rural development efforts. The National Training Center for Literacy Agents is crucial to literacy efforts.

ACHIEVEMENTS

Niger has consistently demonstrated a strong commitment to the preservation and development of its national cultures through its media and educational institutions, the National Museum, and events such as the annual youth festival at Agades.

Nigeria (Federal Republic of Nigeria)

GEOGRAPHY

Area in Square Miles (Kilometers):
356,669 (923,768) (twice the size of California)
Capital (Population): Abuja (na)
Environmental Concerns: soil degradation; deforestation; desertification; drought
Geographical Features: southern lowlands merge into central hills and plateaus; mountains in southeast; plains in north
Climate: varies from equatorial to arid

PEOPLE

Population
Total: 123,338,000
Annual Growth Rate: 2.67%
Rural/Urban Population Ratio: 60/40
Major Languages: English; Hausa; Yoruba; Ibo; Fulani
Ethnic Makeup: about 21% Hausa; 21% Yoruba; 18% Ibo; 9% Fulani; 31% others
Religions: 50% Muslim; 40% Christian; 10% indigenous beliefs

Health
Life Expectancy at Birth: 52 years (male); 52 years (female)
Infant Mortality Rate (Ratio): 74.8/1,000
Physicians Available (Ratio): 1/4,496

Education
Adult Literacy Rate: 57%
Compulsory (Ages): 6–15; free

COMMUNICATION

Telephones: 413,000 main lines
Daily Newspaper Circulation: 18 per 1,000 people
Televisions: 38 per 1,000 people
Internet Service Providers: 5 (1999)

TRANSPORTATION

Highways in Miles (Kilometers): 120,524 (194,394); but much of the road system is barely usable
Railroads in Miles (Kilometers): 2,226 (3,567)
Usable Airfields: 71
Motor Vehicles in Use: 954,000

GOVERNMENT

Type: republic in transition from military rule
Independence Date: October 1, 1960 (from the United Kingdom)
Head of State/Government: President Olusegun Obasanjo is both head of state and head of government

Political Parties: People's Democratic Party; Alliance for Democracy; All People's Party
Suffrage: universal at 18

MILITARY

Military Expenditures (% of GDP): 0.7%
Current Disputes: civil strife; various border disputes

ECONOMY

Currency ($ U.S. Equivalent): 21.99 naira = $1
Per Capita Income/GDP: $970/$110.5 billion
GDP Growth Rate: 2.7%
Inflation Rate: 12.5%
Unemployment Rate: 28% (1992 est.)
Labor Force: 42,844,000

Natural Resources: petroleum; tin; columbite; iron ore; coal; limestone; lead; zinc; natural gas; hydropower
Agriculture: cocoa; peanuts; rubber; yams; cassava; sorghum; palm oil; millet; corn; rice; livestock; timber; fish
Industry: mining; petroleum; food processing; textiles; cement; building materials; chemicals; agriculture products; printing; steel
Exports: $13.1 billion (primary partners United States, Spain, India)
Imports: $10 billion (primary partners United Kingdom, United States, Germany)

 http://www.africanews.org/west/nigeria/
http://www.sas.upenn.edu/African_Studies/Country_Specific/Nigeria.html

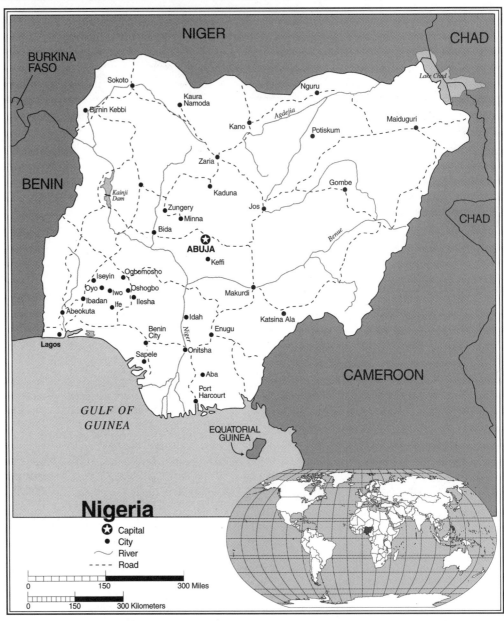

Nigeria

⊛ Capital
● City
〰 River
--- Road

0 150 300 Miles
0 150 300 Kilometers

NIGERIA

In February 1999, former general Olusegun Obasanjo was elected Nigeria's first civilian president in 15 years. His government has struggled to push forward with the immense task of governing the diverse communities that make up Africa's most populous country. In the early months of 2000, attempts to introduce Shari'a (Islamic) law in northern areas of the country touched off severe violence between Muslim and Christian communities. But tensions have since subsided, giving hope that Nigeria is entering a new era of democratic pluralism after decades of military dictatorship.

Nigeria's transition to civilian rule followed the unexpected deaths of its last dictator, General Sani Abacha, and his most famous political prisoner, Chief Mashood Abiola. (The latter was considered by many to have won an annulled 1993 presidential election.) In the wake of the deaths, a caretaker administration under General Abdulsalem Abubakar promised to restore democracy in cooperation with previously repressed sections of civil society.

The Nigerian government's credibility at home and abroad was enhanced by the freeing of political prisoners and Abubakar's personal paying of respects to the late Abiola. Among those freed was Obasanjo, who had briefly served as Nigeria's military ruler in the 1970s, before handing over power to civilians. Besides the jailing of such figures as Abiola and Obasanjo, the Abacha regime had reduced Nigeria to the status of a pariah state through its execution of dozens of political opponents, including the internationally prominent writer, ecologist, and human-rights activist Ken Saro Wiwa.

Since Nigeria's independence, in 1960, its citizens have been through an emotional, political, and material rollercoaster ride. It has been a period marred by interethnic violence, economic downturns, and mostly military rule. But there have also been impressive levels of economic growth, cultural achievement, and human development. To some people, this land of great extremes typifies both the hopes and frustrations of its continent.

With the elephant as a symbol, many Nigerians like to think of their country as the giant of Africa. In 1992, its status as Africa's most populous country was confirmed by the first seemingly successful census since 1963. With a 2000 population of more than 123 million, Nigeria still far outranks second-place Egypt's 68 million. But the country is far less crowded than has been suggested by commonly quoted pre-census estimates.

Nigeria's hardworking population is also responsible for Africa's second-largest economy, as measured by gross domestic product, which stands at $110.5 billion, below only South Africa. But per capita income is still at only $970 per year, which is about average for the globe's most impoverished continent but down from Nigeria's estimated 1980 per capita income of $1,500.

A decade ago, it was common to equate Nigeria's wealth with its status as Africa's leading oil producer, but oil earnings have since plummeted. Although hydrocarbons still account for about 90 percent of the country's export earnings and 75 percent of its government revenue, the sector's current contribution to total GDP is a more modest 20 percent.

NIGERIA'S ROOTS

For centuries, the river Niger, which cuts across much of Nigeria, has facilitated long-distance communication among various communities of West Africa's forest and savanna regions. This fact helps to account for the rich variety of cultures that have emerged within the territory of Nigeria over the past millennium. Archaeologists and historians have illuminated the rise and fall of many states whose cultural legacies continue to define the nation.

Precolonial Nigeria produced a wide range of craft goods, including leather, glass, and metalware. The cultivation of cotton and indigo supported the growth of a local textiles industry. During the mid-nineteenth century, southern Nigeria prospered through palm-oil exports, which lubricated the wheels of Europe's Industrial Revolution. Earlier, much of the country was disrupted through its participation in the slave trade. Most African Americans have Nigerian roots.

Today, more than 250 languages are spoken in Nigeria. Pidgin, which combines an English-based vocabulary with local grammar, is widely used as a lingua franca in the cities and towns. Roughly two-thirds of Nigerians speak either Hausa, Yoruba, or Igbo as a home language. During and after the colonial era, the leaders of these three major ethnolinguistic groups clashed politically from their separate regional bases.

The British, who conquered Nigeria in the late nineteenth and early twentieth centuries, administered the country through a policy of divide-and-rule. In the predominantly Muslim, Hausa-speaking north, they co-opted the old ruling class while virtually excluding Christian missionaries. But in the south, the missionaries, along with their schools, were encouraged, and Christianity and formal education spread rapidly. Many Yoruba farmers of the southwest profited through their cultivation of cocoa. Although most remained as farmers, many of the Igbo of the southeast became prominent in nonagricultural pursuits, such as state employees, artisans, wage workers, and traders. As a result, the Igbo tended to migrate in relatively large numbers to other parts of the colony.

REGIONAL CONFLICTS

At independence, the Federal Republic of Nigeria was composed of three states: the Northern Region, dominated by Hausa speakers; the Western Region, of the Yoruba; and the predominantly Igbo Eastern Region. National politics quickly deteriorated into conflict among these three regions. At one time or another, politicians in each of the areas threatened to secede from the federation. In 1966, this strained situation turned into a crisis following the overthrow by the military of the first civilian government.

In the coup's aftermath, the army itself was divided along ethnic lines; its ranks soon became embroiled in an increasingly violent power struggle. The unleashed tensions culminated in the massacre of up to 30,000 Igbos living in the north. In response, the Eastern Region declared its independence, as the Republic of Biafra. The ensuing civil war between Biafran partisans and federal forces lasted for three years, claiming an estimated 2 million lives. During this time, much of the outside world's attention became focused on the conflict through visual images of the mass starvation that was occurring in rebel-controlled areas under federal blockade. Despite the extent of the war's tragedy, the collapse of Biafran resistance was followed by a largely successful process of national reconciliation. The military government of Yakubu Gowon (1966–1975) succeeded in diffusing ethnic politics, through a restructured federal system based on the creation of new states. The oil boom, which began soon after the conflict, helped the nation-building process by concentrating vast resources in the hands of the federal government in Lagos.

CIVILIAN POLITICS

Thirteen years of military rule ended in 1979. A new Constitution was implemented, which abandoned the British parliamentary model and instead adopted a modified version of the U.S balance-of-powers system. In order to encourage a national outlook, Nigerian presidential candidates needed to win a plurality that included at least one-fourth of the vote in two-thirds of the states.

Five political parties competed in the 1979 elections. They all had similar plat-

(United Nations photo)

Nigeria experienced a tremendous influx of money when its oil industry took advantage of the 1970s' worldwide oil panics. The huge increase in cash resources led to the growth of a middle class and a flurry of expensive new projects. One such project was the Kainji Dam, shown above, which supplies a significant amount of energy to agriculture, industry, and the populace.

forms, promising social welfare for the masses, support for Nigerian business, and a foreign policy based on nonalignment and anti-imperialism. Ideological differences tended to exist within the parties as much as among them, although the People's Redemption Party (PRP) of Aminu Kano became the political home for many Socialists. The most successful party was the somewhat right-of-center National Party of Nigeria (NPN), whose candidate, Shehu Shagari, won the presidency.

New national elections took place in August and September 1983, in which Shagari received more than 12 million of 25.5 million votes. However, the reelected government did not survive long. On December 31, 1983, there was a military coup, led by Major General Muhammad Buhari. The 1979 Constitution was suspended, Shagari and others were arrested, and a federal military government was reestablished. Although no referendum was ever taken on the matter, it is clear that many Nigerians welcomed the coup: this initial response was a reflection of widespread disillusionment with the Second (civilian) Republic.

The political picture seemed very bright in the early 1980s. A commitment to national unity was well established. Although marred by incidents of political violence, two elections had successfully taken place. Due process of law, judicial independence, and press freedom—never entirely eliminated under previous military rulers—had been extended and were seemingly entrenched. But the state was increasingly seen as an instrument of the privileged that offered little to the impoverished masses, with an electoral system that, while balancing the interests of the elite in different sections of the country, failed to empower ordinary citizens. A major reason for this failing was pervasive corruption. People lost confidence as certain officials and their cro-

nies became millionaires overnight. Transparent abuses of power had also occurred under the previous military regime. Conspicuous kleptocracy (rule by thieves) had been tolerated during the oil-boom years of the 1970s, but it became the focus of popular anger as Nigeria's economy contracted during the 1980s.

OIL BOOM—AND BUST

Nigeria, as a leading member of the Organization of Petroleum Exporting Countries, experienced a period of rapid social and economic change during the 1970s. The recovery of oil production after the Civil War and the subsequent hike in its prices led to a massive increase in government revenue. This allowed for the expansion of certain types of social services. Universal primary education was introduced, and the number of universities increased from five (in 1970) to 21 (in 1983). A few Nigerians became very wealthy, while a growing middle class was able to afford what previously had been luxuries.

Oil revenues had already begun to fall off when the NPN government embarked upon a dream list of new prestige projects, most notably the construction of a new federal capital at Abuja, in the center of the country. While such expenditures provided lucrative opportunities for many businesspeople and politicians, they did little to promote local production.

Agriculture, burdened by inflationary costs and low prices, entered a period of crisis, leaving the rapidly growing cities dependent on foreign food. Nonpetroleum exports, once the mainstay of the economy, either virtually disappeared or declined drastically.

While gross indicators appeared to report impressive industrial growth in Nigeria, most of the new industry depended heavily on foreign inputs and was geared toward direct consumption rather than the production

of machines or spare parts. Selective import bans led merely to the growth of smuggling.

The golden years of the 1970s were also banner years for inappropriate expenditures, corruption, and waste. For a while, given the scale of incoming revenues, it looked as if these were manageable problems. But GDP fell drastically in the 1980s with the collapse of oil prices. As the economy worsened, populist resentment grew.

In 1980, an Islamic movement condemning corruption, wealth, and private property defied authorities in the northern metropolis of Kano. The army was called in, killing nearly 4,000. Similar riots subsequently occurred in the cities of Maiduguri, Yola, and Gombe. Attempts by the government to control organized labor by reorganizing the union movement into one centralized federation sparked unofficial strikes (including a general strike in 1981). In an attempt to placate the growing number of unemployed Nigerians, more than 1 million expatriate West Africans, mostly Ghanaians, were suddenly expelled, a domestically popular but essentially futile gesture.

REFORM OR RETRIBUTION?

Buhari justified the military's return to power on the basis of the need to take drastic steps to rescue the economy, whose poor performance he blamed almost exclusively on official corruption. A "War against Indiscipline" was declared, which initially resulted in the trial of a number of political leaders, some of whose economic crimes were indeed staggering. The discovery of large private caches of naira (the Nigerian currency) and foreign exchange fueled public outrage. Tribunals sentenced former politicians to long jail terms. In its zeal, the government looked for more and more culprits, while jailing journalists and others who questioned aspects of its program. In 1985, Major General Ibrahim Babanguida led a successful military coup, charging Buhari with human-rights abuses, autocracy, and economic mismanagement.

Babanguida released political detainees. In a clever strategy, he also encouraged all Nigerians to participate in national forums on the benefits of an International Monetary Fund (IMF) loan and Structural Adjustment Program (SAP). The government turned down the loan but used the consultations to legitimize the implementation of "home-grown" austerity measures consistent with IMF and World Bank prescriptions.

The 1986 budget signaled the beginning of SAP. The naira was devalued, budgets were restricted, and the privatization of many state-run industries was planned. Because salaries remained the same while

| | | | | | Muhammed Buhari's military coup ends the Second Republic; later, Buhari is toppled by Ibrahim Babanguida; lean times; austerity measures provoke protests and strikes | Babanguida resigns; Sani Abacha takes the reins; civil unrest and violence intensify; military strongman Abdulsalam Abubakar takes power; elections bring civilian Olusegun Obasanjo to power |
| Ancient life flourishes 1100–1400 | The first British protectorate is established at Lagos 1851 | Nigeria becomes independent as a unified federal state 1960 | Military seizure of power; proclamation of Biafra; civil war 1966–1970 | Elections restore civilian government 1979 | 1980s | 1990s |

2000s

Ethnic and religious conflict

Hopes for democratic pluralism in Nigeria revive

prices rose, the cost of basic goods rose dramatically, with painful consequences for middle- and working-class Nigerians as well as for the poor.

Although the international price of oil improved somewhat in the late 1980s, there was no immediate return to prosperity. Continued budgetary excesses on the part of the government (which heaped perks on its officer corps and created more state governments to soak up public coffers), coupled with instability, undermined SAP sacrifices. In 1988, the government attempted a moderate reduction in local fuel subsidies. But when, as a result, some transport owners raised fares by 50 to 100 percent, students and workers protested, and bank staff and other workers went on strike. Police killed demonstrators in Jos. Domestic fuel prices have since remained among the lowest in the world, encouraging a massive smuggling of petroleum to neighboring states. This has recently led to the ironic situation of a severe local petroleum shortage.

The Babanguida government faced additional internal challenges while seeking to project an image of stability to foreign investors. Coup attempts were foiled in 1985 and 1991, while chronic student unrest led to the repeated closure of university campuses. Religious riots between Christians and Muslims became endemic in many areas, leading to hundreds, if not thousands, of deaths.

In 1986, Babanguida promised a phased return to full civilian control. But his program of guided democratization degenerated into a farce. Local nonparty elections were held in 1987, and a (mostly elected) Constituent Assembly subsequently met and approved modifications to Nigeria's 1979 Constitution. Despite the trappings of electoral involvement, the Transitional Program was tightly controlled. Many politicians were banned as Babanguida tried to impose a two-party system on what traditionally had been a multiparty political culture. When none of 13 potential parties gained his approval, the general decided to create two new parties of his own: the "a little to the left" Social Democratic Party (SDP) and the "a little to the right" National Republican Convention (NRC).

Doubts about the military in general and Babanguida's grasp on power in particular were raised in 1990, when a group of dissident officers launched yet another coup. In radio broadcasts, the insurrectionists announced the expulsion of five northern states from the federal republic, thus raising the specter of a return to interethnic civil war. The uprising was crushed.

A series of national elections were held in 1992 between the two officially sponsored parties. But public indifference and/or fear of intimidation, institutionalized by the replacement of the (ideally, secret) ballot with a procedure of publicly lining up for one's candidate, compromised the results. Allegations of gross irregularities led to the voiding of first-round presidential primary elections and the banning of all the candidates. After additional delays, accompanied by a serious antigovernment rioting in Lagos and other urban areas, escalating intercommunal violence, and further clampdowns on dissent, a presidential poll was finally held in June 1993 between two government-approved candidates: Mashood Abiola and Bashir Tofa. The result was a convincing 58 percent victory for the SDP's Abiola, though an estimated 70 percent of the electorate refused to participate in the charade.

Babanguida annulled the results before they had been officially counted (the final results were released by local officials in defiance of Babanguida's regime). Instead, in August 1992, he resigned and installed an interim government led by an ineffectual businessman, Ernest Shonekan. Growing unrest—aggravated by an overnight 600 percent increase in domestic fuel prices and a dramatic airline hijacking by a group calling itself the Movement for the Advancement of Democracy (MAD)—led to the interim regime's rapid collapse. In November, the defense minister, General Sani Abacha, reimposed full military rule.

Resistance to military rule steadily increased throughout 1994. Abiola was arrested in June after proclaiming himself president. His detention touched off nationwide strikes, which shut down the oil industry and other key sectors of the economy. In August, Abacha suspended the unions, but workers refused to call off their campaign. While gaining momentum, agitation to install Abiola became increasingly colored by ethnicity.

CULTURAL PROMINENCE

Nigeria is renowned for its arts. Contemporary giants include Wole Solyinka, who received the Nobel Prize for Literature for his work—plays such as "The Trials of Brother Jero" and "The Road," novels such as *The Interpreters,* and poems and nonfiction works. Two other literary giants are Chinua Achebe, author of *Things Fall Apart, A Man of the People,* and *Anthills of the Savannah;* and the feminist writer Buchi Emecheta, whose works include *The Joy of Motherhood.* The legendary Fela Anikulado Kuti's "Afro-Beat" sound and critical lyrics have made him a local hero and international music megastar. Also prominent is "King" Sunny Ade, who has brought Nigeria's distinctive Juju music to international audiences.

DEVELOPMENT

Nigeria hopes to mobilize its human and natural resources to encourage labor-intensive production and self-sufficient agriculture. Recent bans on food imports will increase local production, and restrictions on imported raw materials should encourage research and local input for industry.

FREEDOM

Under Abacha, Nigeria had one of the world's worst human-rights records. In 1998, the Nigerian Advocacy Group for Human Rights joined other inernational groups in issuing a statement insisting that nothing essentially changed after Abubakar succeeded Abacha. With the transition to civilian rule under former political detainee Obasanjo, the situation should improve.

HEALTH/WELFARE

Nigeria's infant mortality rate is now believed to have dropped to about 75 per 1,000. (Some estimate it to be as high as 150 per 1,000.) While social services grew rapidly during the 1970s, Nigeria's strained economy since then has led to cutbacks in health and education.

ACHIEVEMENTS

When many of their leading writers, artists, and intellectuals were exiled and the once-lively press was suppressed, Nigerians found some solace in the success of their world-class soccer team and other athletes.

Senegal (Republic of Senegal)

GEOGRAPHY

Area in Square Miles (Kilometers):
76,000 (196,840) (about the size of South Dakota)
Capital (Population): Dakar (1,642,000)
Environmental Concerns: poaching; deforestation; overgrazing; soil erosion; desertification; overfishing
Geographical Features: low, rolling plains, foothills in the southeast; Gambia is almost an enclave of Senegal
Climate: tropical

PEOPLE

Population
Total: 9,988,000
Annual Growth Rate: 2.94%
Rural/Urban Population Ratio: 56/44
Major Languages: French; Wolof; Pulaar; Diola; Mandinka
Ethnic Makeup: 43% Wolof; 24% Pular; 15% Serer; 18% others
Religions: 92% Muslim; 6% indigenous beliefs; 2% Christian

Health
Life Expectancy at Birth: 61 years (male); 64 years (female)
Infant Mortality Rate (Ratio): 58/1,000
Physicians Available (Ratio): 1/14,825

Education
Adult Literacy Rate: 43%
Compulsory (Ages): 7–13

COMMUNICATION
Telephones: 130,500 main lines
Televisions: 6.9 per 1,000 people
Internet Service Providers: 4 (1999)

TRANSPORTATION
Highways in Miles (Kilometers): 8,746 (14,576)
Railroads in Miles (Kilometers): 565 (905)
Usable Airfields: 20
Motor Vehicles in Use: 160,000

GOVERNMENT
Type: republic
Independence Date: April 4, 1960 (from France)
Head of State/Government: President Abdoulaye Wade; Prime Minister Niasse Moustapha
Political Parties: Socialist Party; Senegalese Democratic Party; Democratic League–Labor Party

Movement; Independence and Labor Party; Senegalese Democratic Union–Renewal; others
Suffrage: universal at 18

MILITARY
Military Expenditures (% of GDP): 1.4%
Current Disputes: civil unrest; boundary issue with The Gambia; tensions with Mauritania and Guinea-Bissau

ECONOMY
Currency ($ U.S. Equivalent): 529.43 CFA francs = $1
Per Capita Income/GDP: $1,650/$16.6 billion
GDP Growth Rate: 5%

Inflation Rate: 2%
Unemployment Rate: high and chronic
Natural Resources: fish; phosphates; iron ore
Agriculture: peanuts; millet; sorghum; corn; rice; cotton; vegetables; livestock; fish
Industry: agricultural and fish processing; phosphate mining; fertilizer production; petroleum refining; construction materials
Exports: $925 million (primary partners France, Italy, India)
Imports: $1.2 billion (primary partners France, other European countries, Nigeria)

http://www.sas.upenn.edu/
African_Studies/Country_Specific/
Senegal.html

Map Legend
- ✪ Capital
- • City
- 〜 River
- - - - Road

SENEGAL

In March 2000, Senegalese politics entered a new era with the electoral victory of veteran opposition politician Abdoulaye Wade over incumbent Abdou Diouf. Wade became the country's third president. Like his predecessors, Wade faces daunting challenges. Much of Senegal's youthful, relatively well-educated population remains unemployed. Widespread corruption and a long-running separatist rebellion in the southern region of Casamance will also test the new regime. But, also like his predecessors, Wade should be able to draw upon the underlying strength of Senegal's culturally rich multiethnic society, which has maintained its cohesion through decades of adversity.

THE IMPACT OF ISLAM

The vast majority of Senegalese are Muslim. Islam was introduced into the region by the eleventh century A.D. and was spread through trade, evangelism, and the establishment of a series of theocratic Islamic states from the 1600s to the 1800s.

Today, most Muslims are associated with one or another of the Islamic Brotherhoods. The leaders of these Brotherhoods, known as marabouts, often act as rural spokespeople as well as the spiritual directors of their followers. The Brotherhoods also play an important economic role. For example, the members of Mouride Brotherhood, who number about 700,000, cooperate in the growing of the nation's cash crops.

FRENCH INFLUENCE

In the 1600s, French merchants established coastal bases to facilitate their trade in slaves and gum. As a result, the coastal communities have been influenced by French culture for generations. More territory in the interior gradually fell under French political control.

Although Wolof is used by many as a lingua franca, French continues to be the common language of the country, and the educational system maintains a French character. Many Senegalese migrate to France, usually to work as low-paid laborers. The French maintain a military force near the capital, Dakar, and are major investors in the Senegalese economy. Senegal's judiciary and bureaucracy are modeled after those of France.

POLITICS

Under Diouf, Senegal strengthened its commitment to multipartyism. After succeeding Leopold Senghor, the nation's scholarly first president, Diouf liberalized the political process by allowing an increased number of opposition parties

(United Nations photo by Purcell/AB)

The potential for drought is an ongoing concern in the Sahel zone of Senegal. It is an ever-present factor in any agricultural program. The young herder shown above with his starving cattle is an all-too-familiar image.

The French occupy present-day St. Louis and, later, Gorée Island
1659

The Jolof kingdom controls much of the region
1700s

All Africans in four towns of the coast vote for a representative to the French Parliament
1848

Interior areas are added to the French colonial territory
1889

Senegal becomes independent as part of the Mali Confederation; shortly afterward, it breaks from the Confederation
1960

President Leopold Senghor retires and is replaced by Abdou Diouf; Senegalese political leaders unite in the face of threats from Mauritania
1980s

Serious rioting breaks out in Dakar protesting the devaluation of the CFA franc
1990s

2000s

Tensions remain between Senegal and Guinea-Bissau

Senegal and Mauritania try to improve relations, but hostility remains

Abdoulaye Wade wins the presidency

effectively to compete against his own ruling Socialist Party (PS). He also restructured his administration in ways that were credited with making it less corrupt and more efficient. Some say that these moves did not go far enough, but Diouf, who inclined toward reform, had to struggle against reactionary elements within his own party.

In national elections in 1988, Diouf won 77 percent of the vote, while the Socialists took 103 out of 120 seats. Outside observers believed that the election had been plagued by fewer irregularities than in the past. However, opposition protests against alleged fraud touched off serious rioting in Dakar. As a result, the city was placed under a three-month state of emergency. Diouf's principal opponent, Abdoulaye Wade of the Democratic Party (PD), was among those arrested and tried for incitement. But subsequent meetings between Diouf and Wade resulted in an easing of tensions. Indeed, in 1991, Wade shocked many by accepting the post of minister of state in Diouf's cabinet. Elections in 1993 were less controversial, with Diouf being reelected with 58 percent of the vote. PS representation dropped to 84 seats.

In March 1995, a new, multiparty "Government of National Unity" was formed, which survived despite the defection of one of its members, the Independent Labor Party, in September 1996. But interparty tension grew in the face of Diouf's failure to appoint an independent elections commission in preparation for elections in November 1996.

THE ECONOMY
Many believe that the *Sopi* (Wolof for "change") riots of 1988 were primarily motivated by popular frustration with Senegal's weak economy, especially among its youth (about half of the Senegalese are under age 21), who face an uncertain future. Senegal's relatively large (44 percent) urban population has suffered from rising rates of unemployment and inflation, which have been aggravated by the country's attempt to implement an International Monetary Fund–approved Structural Adjustment Program (SAP). In recent years, the economy has grown modestly but has so far failed to attract the investment needed to meet ambitious privatization goals. Among rural dwellers, drought and locusts have also made life difficult. Fluctuating world market prices and disease as well as drought have undermined groundnut exports.

Senegal has also been beset by difficulties in its relations with neighboring states. The Senegambia Confederation, which many hoped would lead to greater cooperation with The Gambia, was dissolved in September 1989. Relations with Guinea-Bissau are strained as a result of that nation's failure to recognize the result of international arbitration over disputed, potentially oil-rich waters. Senegalese further suspect that individuals in Guinea-Bissau may be linked to separatist unrest in Senegal's Casamance region. There some 1,000 people died in an insurgency campaign between the Senegalese Army and the guerrillas of the Movement of Democratic Forces of Casamance. In July 1993, the rebels agreed to a cease-fire, but the cease-fire collapsed in 1995. In August 2000, the rebels agreed to reopen talks with Wade's new administration.

But the major source of cross-border tension has been Mauritania. In 1989, long-standing border disputes between the two countries led to a massacre of Senegalese in Mauritania, setting off widespread revenge attacks against Mauritanians in Senegal. More than 200,000 Senegalese and Mauritanians were repatriated. Relations between the two countries have remained tense, in large part due to the persecution of Mauritania's "black" communities by its Maur-dominated military government. Many Mauritanians belonging to the persecuted groups have been pushed into Senegal, leading to calls for war, but in April 1992, the two countries agreed to restore diplomatic, air, and postal links.

DEVELOPMENT

The recently built Diama and Manantali Dams will allow for the irrigation of many thousands of acres for domestic rice production. At the moment, large amounts of rice are imported to Senegal, mostly to feed the urban population.

FREEDOM

Senegal's generally favorable human-rights record is marred by persistent violence in its southern region of Casamance, where rebels are continuing to fight for independence. A 2-year cease-fire broke down in 1995 after an army offensive was launched against the rebel Movement of Democratic Forces of Casamance.

HEALTH/WELFARE

Like other Sahel countries, Senegal has a high infant mortality rate and a low life expectancy rate. Health facilities are considered to be below average, even for a country of Senegal's modest income, but recent child-immunization campaigns have been fairly successful.

ACHIEVEMENTS

Dakar, sometimes described as the "Paris of West Africa," has long been a major cultural center for the region. Senegalese writers such as former president Leopold Senghor were founders of the Francophonic African tradition of Negritude.

Sierra Leone (Republic of Sierra Leone)

GEOGRAPHY

Area in Square Miles (Kilometers):
27,925 (72,325) (about the size of South Carolina)
Capital (Population): Freetown (669,000)
Environmental Concerns: soil exhaustion; deforestation; overfishing; population pressures
Geographical Features: a coastal belt of mangroves; wooded, hilly country; upland plateau; mountains in the east
Climate: tropical; hot, humid

PEOPLE

Population
Total: 5,233,000
Annual Growth Rate: 3.67%
Rural/Urban Population Ratio: 66/34
Major Languages: English, Krio, Temne, Mende
Ethnic Makeup: 30% Temne; 30% Mende; 30% other African; 10% others
Religions: 60% Muslim; 30% indigenous beliefs; 10% Christian

Health
Life Expectancy at Birth: 42 years (male); 48 years (female)
Infant Mortality Rate (Ratio): 148.6/1,000
Physicians Available (Ratio): 1/10,832

Education
Adult Literacy Rate: 31.4%

COMMUNICATION
Telephones: 17,400 main lines
Internet Service Providers: na

TRANSPORTATION
Highways in Miles (Kilometers): 7,020 (11,700)
Railroads in Miles (Kilometers): 52 (84)
Usable Airfields: 10
Motor Vehicles in Use: 44,000

GOVERNMENT
Type: constitutional democracy
Independence Date: April 27, 1961 (from the United Kingdom)
Head of State/Government: President Ahmad Tejan Kabbah is both head of state and head of government
Political Parties: Sierra Leone People's Party; National Unity Party; others
Suffrage: universal at 18

MILITARY
Military Expenditures (% of GDP): 2%
Current Disputes: civil war

ECONOMY
Currency ($ U.S. Equivalent): 618 leones = $1
Per Capita Income/GDP: $500/$2.5 billion
GDP Growth Rate: −10%
Inflation Rate: 30%
Labor Force: primarily subsistence agriculture
Natural Resources: diamonds; titanium ore; bauxite; gold; iron ore; chromite
Agriculture: coffee; cocoa; palm kernels; rice; palm oil; peanuts; livestock; fish
Industry: mining; petroleum refining; small-scale manufacturing
Exports: $41 million (primary partners Belgium, United States, Spain)
Imports: $166 million (primary partners Europe, Côte d'Ivoire)

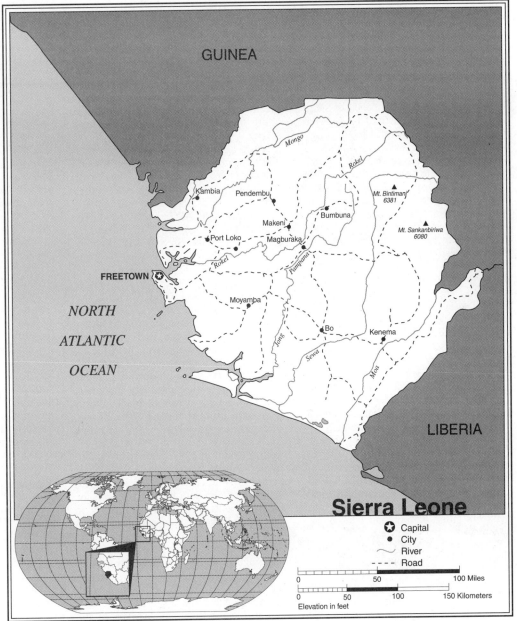

http://www.africanews.org/west/ sierraleone/
http://www.sas.upenn.edu/ African_Studies/Country_Specific/ S_Leone.html

Early inhabitants arrive from Africa's interior
1400–1750

Settlement by people from the New World and recaptured slave ships
1787

Sierra Leone is a Crown colony
1801

Mende peoples unsuccessfully resist the British in the Hut Tax War
1898

Independence
1961

The new Constitution makes Sierra Leone a one-party state
1978

President Siaka Stevens steps down; Joseph Momoh, the sole candidate, is elected
1985

Debt-servicing cost mounts; SAP; Liberian rebels destabilize Sierra Leone; Momoh is overthrown
1990s

2000s

Ahmed Kabbah holds onto power, but peace remains elusive

SIERRA LEONE

For more than a decade, the people of Sierra Leone have been traumatized by endemic political violence. Hopes that the (in many quarters unexpected) successful holding of democratic elections in February–March 1996 would lead to peace and reconciliation were dashed in May 1997, when dissident junior officers overthrew the elected government of President Ahmed Tejan Kabbah. An Armed Forces Revolutionary Council (AFRC), led by Major Johnny Paul Koroma, who had been awaiting trial on charges stemming from an earlier coup attempt, banned political parties and all public demonstrations and meetings and announced that all legislation would be made by military decree. The AFRC soon revealed itself to be a vehicle of the rebel Revolutionary United Front (RUF) as well as of elements within the military unwilling to accept a return to civilian control.

The AFRC/RUF regime attracted overwhelming regional condemnation, with the international community sanctioning efforts by the Economic Community of West African States (ECOWAS) to restore Kabbah to power. This was finally achieved in February 1998, when military units of ECOMOG, the Nigerian-led ECOWAS peace-monitoring force, attacked and routed the junta's forces in the capital city, Freetown, after Koroma abandoned his agreement to step down peacefully.

Subsequent ECOMOG offensives pushed back the RUF, which agreed to abide by a 1999 Lomé Peace Agreement, after assurances of amnesty. In accordance with the agreement, the RUF leader, Foday Sankoh, was brought into a transitional government pledged to restoring democracy, law, and order, with UN peacekeeper assistance. But the outbreak of renewed violence in April 2000 has since cast doubt over the peace process. While UN peacekeepers (temporarily reinforced by British military units) were able to secure Freetown and place Sankoh in detention, efforts to secure an enduring peace remain elusive.

Sierra Leone's period of political instability began in April 1992, when Captain Valentine Strasser announced the overthrow of the long-governing All People's Congress (APC). The coup was initially welcomed, as the APC governments of the deposed president Joseph Momoh and his predecessor Siaka Stevens had been renowned for their institutionalized corruption and economic incompetence. But disillusionment grew as the Strasser-led National Provisional Ruling Council postponed holding multiparty elections, while sinking into its own pattern of corruption. The emergence of the RUF insurgency brought further misery, with both the rebels and army being accused of atrocities.

Sierra Leone is the product of a unique colonial history. Its capital city, Freetown, was founded by waves of black settlers who were brought there by the British. The first to arrive were the so-called Black Poor, a group of 400 people sent from England in 1787. Shortly thereafter, former slaves from Jamaica and Nova Scotia arrived. These former slaves had gained their freedom by fighting with the British, against their American masters, in the U.S. War of Independence. About 40,000 Africans who were liberated by the British and others from slave ships captured along the West African coast were also settled in Freetown and the surrounding areas in the first half of the nineteenth century. The descendants of Sierra Leone's various black settlers blended African and British ways into a distinctive *Krio*, or Creole, culture. Besides speaking English, they developed their own Krio language, which has become the nation's lingua franca. Today, the Krio make up only about 5 percent of Sierra Leone's multiethnic population.

As more people were given the vote in the 1950s, the indigenous communities ended Krio domination in local politics. The first party to win broad national support was the Sierra Leone People's Party (SLPP), under Sir Milton Margai, which led the country to independence in 1961. During the 1967 national elections, the SLPP was narrowly defeated by Stevens' APC. From 1968 to 1985, Stevens presided over a steady erosion of Sierra Leone's economy and civil society.

The APC's increasingly authoritarian control coincided with the country's economic decline. Although rich in its human as well as natural resources at independence, today Sierra Leone is one of the world's poorest countries. Revenues from diamonds, which formed the basis for prosperity during the 1950s, and gold have steadily fallen due to the depletion of old diggings and massive smuggling.

The two thirds of Sierra Leone's labor force employed in agriculture have suffered the most from the nation's faltering economy. Poor producer prices, coupled with an international slump in demand for cocoa and robusta coffee, have cut into rural incomes. Momoh's promise to improve producer prices as part of a "Green Revolution" program was largely unfulfilled. Like its minerals, much of Sierra Leone's agricultural production has been smuggled out of the country. In 1989, the cost of servicing Sierra Leone's foreign debt was estimated to be 130 percent of the total value of its exports. This grim figure led to the introduction of an International Monetary Fund–supported Structural Adjustment Program (SAP), whose austerity measures have made life even more difficult for urban dwellers.

DEVELOPMENT

The recently relaunched Bumbuna hydroelectric project should reduce Sierra Leone's dependence on foreign oil, which has accounted for nearly a third of its imports. In response to threats of boycotting, the country's Lungi International Airport was upgraded. Persistent inflation and unemployment have taken a severe toll on the country's people.

FREEDOM

The deposed AFCR/RUF regime unleashed a terror campaign, including extra-judicial killings, torture, mutilation, rape, beatings, arbitrary arrest, and the detention of unarmed civilians. Junta forces killed and/or amputated the arms of detainees. Prior to the coup, RUF was infamous for its murderous attacks on civilians during raids in which children were commonly abducted and forced to commit atrocities against their relatives as a form of psychological conditioning.

HEALTH/WELFARE

Life expectancy for both males and females in Sierra Leone is only in the 40s, while the infant mortality rate, 148.6 per 1,000, remains appalling. In 1990, hundreds, possibly thousands, of Sierra Leone children were reported to have been exported to Lebanon on what amounted to slave contracts. The UNEP Human Development Index rates Sierra Leone last, out of 174 countries.

ACHIEVEMENTS

The Sande Society, a women's organization that trains young Mende women for adult responsibilities, has contributed positively to life in Sierra Leone. Beautifully carved wooden helmet masks are worn by women leaders in the society's rituals. Ninety-five percent of Mende women join the Society.

Togo (Togolese Republic)

GEOGRAPHY

Area in Square Miles (Kilometers):
21,853 (56,600) (about the
size of West Virginia)
Capital (Population): Lomé
(513,000)
Environmental Concerns:
drought; deforestation
Geographical Features: gently
rolling savanna in north; central
hills; southern plateau; low
coastal plain with extensive
lagoons and marshes
Climate: tropical to semiarid

PEOPLE

Population

Total: 5,019,000
Annual Growth Rate: 2.7%
Rural/Urban Population Ratio:
69/31
Major Languages: French;
Ewe; Mina; Dagomba;
Kabye; Dasomsa
Ethnic Makeup: 99% African—
Ewe; Mina; Kabye; many others
Religions: 70% indigenous
beliefs; 20% Christian; 10%
Muslim

Health

Life Expectancy at Birth: 53
years (male); 57 years (female)
Infant Mortality Rate (Ratio):
71.5/1,000
Physicians Available (Ratio):
1/11,270

Education

Adult Literacy Rate: 51.7%
Compulsory (Ages): 6–12

COMMUNICATION

Telephones: 31,400 main lines
Televisions: 36 per 1,000 people
Internet Service Provider: 1
(1999)

TRANSPORTATION

Highways in Miles (Kilometers): 4,512 (7,520)
Railroads in Miles (Kilometers): 352 (532)
Usable Airfields: 9
Motor Vehicles in Use: 109,000

GOVERNMENT

Type: republic under transition to
multiparty democratic rule
Independence Date: April 27, 1960 (from
French-administered UN trusteeship)
Head of State/Government: President
Gnassingbé Eyadéma; Prime Minister
Eugene Koffi Adoboli
Political Parties: Rally of the Togolese
People; Coordination des Forces
Nouvelles; Action Committee for

Renewal; Patriotic Pan-African
Convergence; Union of Forces for
Change; others
Suffrage: universal for adults

MILITARY

Military Expenditures (% of GDP): 2%
Current Disputes: civil unrest

ECONOMY

Currency ($ U.S. Equivalent): 529.43
CFA francs = $1
Per Capita Income/GDP: $1,300/$8.6 billion
GDP Growth Rate: 4%
Inflation Rate: 3%
Labor Force: primarily agriculture

Natural Resources: phosphates; limestone;
marble; arable land
Agriculture: coffee; cocoa; yams; cassava;
millet; sorghum; rice; livestock; fish
Industry: phosphates mining; textiles;
handicrafts; agricultural processing;
cement; beverages
Exports: $400 million (primary partners
Canada, Philippines, Ghana)
Imports: $450 million (primary partners
Ghana, France, Côte d'Ivoire)

http://www.republicoftogo.com/
http://www.sas.upenn.edu/African_
Studies/Country_Specific/Togo.html

Map labels

BURKINA FASO
Dapango
Kanté
Niamtougou
Lama-Kara
Bossari
Mo River
Sokodé
GHANA
BENIN
NIGERIA
Blitta
Mono
Anie
Atakpamé
Mono
Amou
Tabligbo
Aného
BIGHT OF BENIN
LOMÉ

Togo

⊛ Capital
● City
〜 River
- - - - Road

0   60   120 Miles
0   60   120   180 Kilometers

MALI
NIGER
BURKINA FASO
BENIN
CÔTE D'IVOIRE
NIGERIA
GHANA
TOGO

TOGO

In the year 2000, Togo marked its 40th anniversary of independence. For most of that time, the Togolese have lived under the rule of General Gnassingbé Eyadéma (who in July 2000 achieved the distinction of becoming chairman of the Organization of African Unity). In July 1998, Eyadéma claimed victory with 52 percent of the vote in presidential elections. The result was all but assured by the continued dominance of his Assembly of the Togolese People (RPT) party and its military backers over the political process. In recent years, Togo has become a prime example of the fragility of prodemocracy forces in the face of determined resistance by a ruling clique with a strong ethnic support base. Togo's army set a sad regional precedent in 1963 by assassinating the nation's first president, Sylvanus Olympio. After a subsequent period of instability, power was seized by Gnassingbé Eyadéma. In 1969, Eyadéma institutionalized his increasingly dictatorial regime as a one-party state. All Togolese have been required to belong to his Coalition of the Togolese People (RPT). But in 1991, faced with mass prodemocracy demonstrations in Lomé, the capital city, Eyadéma acquiesced to opposition calls for a "National Conference" that would end the RPT's monopoly of power. Since then, Eyadéma has survived Togo's turbulent return to multiparty politics with characteristic ruthlessness, skillfully taking advantage of the weakness of his divided opponents.

DEMOCRACY VS. DICTATORSHIP

Meeting in July–August 1991, the National Conference turned into a public trial of the abuses of the ruling regime. Resisting the president's attempts to dissolve it, the Conference appointed Kokou Koffigoh as the head of an interim government, charged with preparing the country for multiparty elections. The RPT was to be disbanded, and Eyadéma himself was barred from standing for reelection.

In November–December 1991, however, soldiers loyal to Eyadéma launched a bloody attack on Koffigoh's residence. The French, whose troops had intervened in the past to keep Eyadéma in power, refused Koffigoh's plea for help. Instead, the coup attempt ended with the now-almost-irrelevant Koffigoh and Eyadéma agreeing to maintain their uneasy cohabitation. Elections were henceforth to include the RPT. Despite the "compromise," there was an upsurge in political violence in 1992, which included the May shooting of Gilchrist Olympio (the son of Sylvanus) and other Eyadéma opponents. In September, "rebel" soldiers once more held the government hostage.

A January 1993 massacre of the prodemocracy demonstrators pushed the country even further to the brink. Some 300,000 southern Togolese, mostly Ewe-speakers, fled the country, fearing "ethnic cleansing" by the largely northern, Kabye-speaking army. In 1993–1994, exiled anti-Eyadéma militants—many of whom coalesced as the Front of the National Committee for the Liberation of the Togolese People (FNCL)—began to fight back. The army chief of staff was among those killed during a daring raid on the main military headquarters in Lomé, in which grenades were also thrown into Eyadéma's bedroom.

In July 1993, Eyadéma and his more moderate opponents signed a peace accord in Burkina Faso, pledging renewed movement toward election. A month later, however, the opposition boycotted a snap presidential poll. Thereafter, Eyadéma

gave ground, agreeing to internationally supervised legislative elections in February 1994. After two rounds of voting, amid escalating violence, Eyadéma's RPT and the main opposition—Action Committee for Renewal (CAR), led by Yaovi Agboyibor—each controlled about 35 seats in the 75-seat Assembly. (The situation was clouded by judicial reviews of the results in five constituencies.) The balance of power rested with former Organization of African Unity secretary general Edem Kodjo's Togo Union for Democracy (UTD), which had entered the election allied with CAR. But in May, Kodjo became prime minister, with Eyadéma's backing. The failure of the moderate opposition to capitalize on its apparent victory in undoubtedly flawed elections strengthened the determination of the militants to carry on by other means.

(United Nations photo by Anthony Fisher)

Potable water is not universally available in Togo. While food production in Togo is officially said to be adequate, outside observers contend that the drought-prone north is uncomfortably reliant on the more agriculturally productive southern areas.

Germany
occupies Togo
1884

Togo is mandated
to the United
Kingdom and
France by the
League of Nations
following
Germany's defeat
in World War I
1919

UN plebiscites
result in the
independence of
French Togo and
incorporation of
British Togo into
Ghana
1956–1957

Independence is
achieved
1960

Murder of
President
Sylvanus
Olympio; a new
civilian
government is
organized after
the coup
1963

The coup of
Colonel Etienne
Eyadéma, now
President
Gnassingbé
Eyadéma
1967

The Coalition of
the Togolese
People becomes
the only legal
party in Togo
1969

Prodemocracy
demonstrations lead to
interim government and
the promise of multiparty
elections; Eyadéma
survives escalating
violence and
controversial elections
1990s

2000s

Eyadéma retains power   Eyadéma is named
                               chairman of the OAU

STRUCTURAL ADJUSTMENT

Togo's political crisis has taken place against a backdrop of economic restructuring. In 1979, Togo adopted an economic-recovery strategy that many consider to have been a forerunner of other Structural Adjustment Programs (SAPs) introduced throughout most of the rest of Africa. Faced with mounting debts as a result of falling export revenue, the government began to loosen the state's grip over the local economy. Since 1982 a more rigorous International Monetary Fund/World Bank–supported program of privatization and other market-oriented reforms has been pursued. Given this chronology, Togo's economic prospects have become a focus of attention for those looking for lessons about the possible effects of SAP. Both proponents and opponents of SAP have grounds for debate.

Supporters of Togo's SAP point out that since 1985, the country has enjoyed an average growth in gross domestic product of 3.3 percent per year. While this statistic is an improvement over the 1.7 percent rate recorded between 1973 and 1980, however, it is well below the 7.2 percent growth that prevailed from 1965 to 1972. (The GDP growth rate in 2000 was estimated at 4 percent.) During the 1980s, there was a rise in private consumption, 7.6 percent per year, and a drop in inflation, from about 13 percent in 1980 to an estimated 2 percent in 1989. A rate of 3 percent was estimated for 2000.

The livelihoods of certain segments of the Togolese population have materially improved during the past decade. Beneficiaries include some of the two thirds of the workforce employed in agriculture. Encouraged by increased official purchase prices, cash-crop farmers have expanded their outputs of cotton and coffee. This is especially true in the case of cotton pro-

duction, which tripled between 1983 and 1989. Nearly half the nation's small farmers now grow the crop.

Balanced against the growth of cotton has been a decline in cocoa, which emerged as the country's principal cash crop under colonialism. Despite better producer prices during the mid-1980s, output fell as a result of past decisions not to plant new trees. Given the continuing uncertainty of cocoa prices, this earlier shift may prove to have been opportune. The long-term prospects of coffee are also in doubt, due to a growing global preference for the arabica beans of Latin America over the robusta beans that thrive throughout much of West Africa. As a result, the government had to reverse course in 1988, drastically reducing its prices for both coffee and cocoa, a move that it hopes will prove to be only temporary.

Eyadéma's regime has claimed great success in food production, but its critics have long countered official reports of food self-sufficiency by citing the importation of large quantities of rice, a decline in food production in the cotton-growing regions, and widespread childhood malnutrition. The country's food situation is complicated by an imbalance between the drought-prone northern areas and the more productive south. In 1992, famine threatened 250,000 Togolese, mostly northerners.

There have been improvements in transport and telecommunications. The national highway system, largely built by the European Development Fund, has allowed the port of Lomé to develop as a transshipment center for exports from neighboring states as well as Togo's interior. At the same time, there has been modest progress in cutting the budget deficit. But it is in precisely this area that the cost of Togo's SAP is most apparent. Public expenditures in health and education de-

clined by about 50 percent between 1982 and 1985. Whereas school enrollment rose from 40 percent to more than 70 percent during the 1970s, it has slipped back below 60 percent in recent years.

The ultimate justification for Togo's SAP has been to attract overseas capital investment. In addition to sweeping privatization, a Free Trade Zone has been established. But overseas investment in Togo has always been modest. There have also been complaints that many foreign investors have simply bought former state industries on the cheap rather than starting up new enterprises. Furthermore, privatization and austerity measures are blamed for unemployment and wage cuts among urban workers. One third of the state-divested enterprises have been liquidated.

Whatever the long-term merits of Togo's SAP, it is clear that it has so far resulted in neither a clear pattern of sustainable growth nor an improved standard of living for most Togolese. For the foreseeable future, the health of Togo's economy will continue to be tied to export earnings derived from three commodities—phosphates, coffee, and cocoa—whose price fluctuations have been responsible for the nation's previous cycles of boom and bust.

DEVELOPMENT

Much hope for the future of Togo is riding on the recently created Free Trade Zone at Lomé. Firms within the zone are promised a 10-year tax holiday if they export at least three quarters of their output. The project is backed by the U.S. Overseas Private Investment Corporation.

FREEDOM

Togo continues to have a poor human-rights record. Its progovernment security forces have been responsible for extra-judicial killings, beatings, arbitrary detentions, and interference with citizens' rights to movement and privacy. Freedom of speech and of the press are restricted. Interethnic killings have led to major population displacements.

HEALTH/WELFARE

The nation's health service has declined as a result of austerity measures. Juvenile mortality is 15%. Self-induced abortion now causes approximately 17% of the deaths among Togolese women of child-bearing age. School attendance has dropped in recent years.

ACHIEVEMENTS

The name of Togo's capital, Lomé, is well known in international circles for its association with the Lomé Convention, a periodically renegotiated accord through which products from various African, Caribbean, and Pacific countries are given favorable access to European markets.

Annotated Table of Contents for Articles

Topic Guide to Articles

TOPIC AREA	TREATED IN	TOPIC AREA	TREATED IN
Abortion	1. Sub-Saharan Africa: At the Turning Point	**Economic Reform**	1. Sub-Saharan Africa: At the Turning Point 11. Maritius: Rethinking the Miracle
Agriculture	1. Sub-Saharan Africa: At the Turning Point	**Economy**	2. Emerging Africa: Coming to Terms With an Overlooked Continent 10. Freedom to Farm—and Starve—in Kenya
AIDS	1. Sub-Saharan Africa: At the Turning Point 8. Death Stalks a Continent		
		Elections	3. Africa: Prospects for the Future
Arts	1. Sub-Saharan Africa: At the Turning Point	**Ethnicity**	4. Africa United: Not Hopeless, Not Helpless
Civil War	7. Ending Africa's Wars 14. Signs of Hope in Africa: World Donors Have Ignored Somaliland as It Slowly Rebuilds	**Exports**	11. Mauritius: Rethinking the Miracle
		Foreign Investment	2. Emerging Africa: Coming to Terms With an Overlooked Continent 11. Mauritius: Rethinking the Miracle
Conservation	1. Sub-Saharan Africa: At the Turning Point		
		Foreign Relations	2. Emerging Africa: Coming to Terms With an Overlooked Continent 6. End to Africa's Wars: Rethinking International Intervention 7. Ending Africa's Wars
Current Leaders	1. Sub-Saharan Africa: At the Turning Point 3. Africa: Prospects for the Future 6. End to Africa's Wars: Rethinking International Intervention 7. Ending Africa's Wars 9. In the Heart of Darkness 10. Freedom to Farm—and Starve—in Kenya 14. Signs of Hope in Africa: World Donors Have Ingored Somaliland as It Slowly Rebuilds		
		Health Care	8. Death Stalks a Continent
		History	1. Sub-Saharan Africa: At the Turning Point 4. Africa United: Not Hopeless, Not Helpless 9. In the Heart of Darkness
Democracy	1. Sub-Saharan Africa: At the Turning Point 3. Africa: Prospects for the Future 11. Maritius: Rethinking the Miracle 12. Nigeria: The Politics of Marginalization	**HIV/AIDS**	8. Death Stalks a Continent
		Human Rights	3. Africa: Prospects for the Future 13. Faith's Unbreakable Force
		Leadership	3. Africa: Prospects for the Future 6. End to Africa's Wars: Rethinking International Intervention 9. In the Heart of Darkness 10. Freedom to Farm—and Starve—in Kenya 11. Maritius: Rethinking the Miracle 12. Nigeria: The Politics of Marginalization
Economic Development	1. Sub-Saharan Africa: At the Turning Point 2. Emerging Africa: Coming to Terms With an Overlooked Continent 3. Africa: Prospects for the Future 5. Making the Connection: Africa and the Internet 11. Maritius: Rethinking the Miracle 13. Faith's Unbreakable Force 14. Signs of Hope in Africa: World Donors Have Ignored Somaliland as It Slowly Rebuilds		

TOPIC AREA	TREATED IN	TOPIC AREA	TREATED IN
Natives	8. Death Stalks a Continent	**Population**	1. Sub-Saharan Africa: At the Turning Point
Political Reform	1. Sub-Saharan Africa: At the Turning Point 3. Africa: Prospects for the Future 4. Africa United: Not Hopeless, Not Helpless 12. Nigeria: The Politics of Marginalization	**Regional Integration**	1. Sub-Saharan Africa: At the Turning Point 4. Africa United: Not Hopeless, Not Helpless
		Religion	13. Faith's Unbreakable Force
Political Unrest	6. End to Africa's Wars: Rethinking International Intervention 7. Ending Africa's Wars 9. In the Heart of Darkness 12. Nigeria: The Politics of Marginalization	**Technology**	5. Making the Connection: Africa and the Internet
		Tourism	1. Sub-Saharan Africa: At the Turning Point
Politics	2. Emerging Africa: Coming to Terms With an Overlooked Continent 3. Africa: Prospects for the Future 4. Africa United: Not Hopeless, Not Helpless 6. End to Africa's Wars: Rethinking International Intervention 7. Ending Africa's Wars 10. Freedom to Farm—and Starve—in Kenya	**Turmoil**	9. In the Heart of Darkness 10. Freedom to Farm—and Starve—in Kenya
		Violence	4. Africa United: Not Hopeless, Not Helpless 9. In the Heart of Darkness
		War	6. End to Africa's Wars: Rethinking International Intervention 7. Ending Africa's Wars 9. In the Heart of Darkness

Article 1   *The Humanist,* July/August 1998

Sub-Saharan Africa
At the Turning Point
by Shanti R. Conly

The woman at the Kaneshie Polyclinic in suburban Accra, Ghana, was in her mid-forties. She was a tall, spare woman with an anxious expression and a little boy—immaculately dressed in starched shirt and shorts—leaning against her knee. She had all kinds of misconceptions and fears about modern contraceptives. Indeed, she belonged to a generation of African women who went through their childbearing years knowing little about modern contraception. She and her husband were using withdrawal—not a very reliable family planning method; the little boy at her knee was a child she had not planned to have. Now her period was late again. She had borne six children and had come to the clinic because another pregnancy had become more frightening to her than modern contraception.

Like most African women, she had to wait for her husband, who was away on business, to come home to give her permission and money to go to the family planning clinic. When she got there, the clinic staff explained she had to have a pregnancy test before they could give her a contraceptive. She could not bear the thought of another pregnancy: "I'm so afraid. My health cannot take it. If I'm pregnant, will they help me take it out?"

Across the continent, in a one-room hut in Uchiru village near Nairobi, Kenya, thirty-year-old "Sara" was scheduling an appointment for a tubal ligation. She and her husband have three children—ages twelve, six, and two—all planned with the help of birth control pills and an IUD. She wanted to give her children a decent life and an education, which is increasingly costly in Kenya. She did not want any more children and wanted a more permanent method of birth control—this in a region where, just five years earlier, experts had said voluntary sterilization would never be accepted. Her story is increasingly typical of younger African women, especially in Kenya, which has one of the oldest and most effective family planning programs in the region.

These two women are a study in contrasts. Born fifteen years and a generation apart, their different life patterns have been shaped in large part by their access to contraception: the older woman in Ghana has been worn down by frequent pregnancies and the burden of raising a large family; the younger Kenyan woman is taking charge of her life and shaping her family's future. They represent the dual challenge of rapid population growth and poor reproductive health confronting sub-Saharan Africa. Nowhere in the world is the situation further from the ideal.

The Challenges

With Kenya, South Africa, Botswana, and Zimbabwe leading the way, the countries of sub-Saharan Africa are at a critical turning point in their efforts to effect dramatic changes in government policies regarding family planning programs and fundamental shifts in people's attitudes toward childbearing.

For more than twenty years, population growth of almost 3 percent a year has outpaced economic gains as well as increases in food production, leaving sub-Saharan Africans 22 percent poorer than in 1975.

Sub-Saharan Africa's population has doubled in just twenty-five years to 620 million—and is projected to double again in less than three decades, even after taking into account declining birthrates and rising deaths from AIDS. For more than twenty years, population growth of almost 3 percent a year has outpaced economic gains as well as increases in food production, leaving sub-Saharan Africans, on average, 22 percent poorer than in 1975. These farmers would have to increase production *fivefold* just to meet the region's basic food needs in the year 2050. Even sooner, by 2025, six out of ten Africans are projected to live in countries classified as water scarce, hampering food production and industrialization.

Women bear the greatest burden of frequent high-risk pregnancies, raising large families, and, increasingly, the AIDS epidemic. They also must perform household chores and most agricultural work. Together, these conditions have had devastating consequences for the health and well-being not only of African women but also their families:

- Just one in ten of the world's women live in sub-Saharan Africa, but the region accounts for 40 percent of all pregnancy-related deaths worldwide—215,000 deaths every year, or one every two and a half minutes. Childbearing is riskier in Africa than anywhere else—one woman dies for every 100 births—and most women have numerous pregnancies. Less than half of women receive any kind of skilled maternity care and half are anemic. During her lifetime, an African woman has a one in fifteen chance of dying from reasons related to pregnancy—odds over 200 times greater than those faced by women in the United States. The risks are somewhat lower in southern Africa, where incomes are higher than elsewhere in the region, access to health care is better, and women bear fewer children.
- Young women face heavy social pressure to marry and bear children early; more than half give birth by age twenty—a proportion that has remained substantially unchanged over the years. Early childbearing increases the risks of complications during pregnancy and reduces the chances of survival for children. It also shortens the span between generations, contributing to greater population momentum and higher rates of population growth.
- Although the chances of survival for African children improved markedly over the past four decades, one in six children still does not live to see her or his fifth birthday. Moreover, the regionwide economic slump has slowed progress in battling child deaths in Africa since 1980. Child immunization rates of 50 percent—already the lowest in the developing world—are only slowly rising. Fewer than half of pregnant women are adequately immunized against tetanus, resulting in the deaths of thousands of newborn infants annually.

In addition, about 22,000 African women die each year from unsafe abortion, reflecting both legal restrictions on abortion and limited access to contraception. Meanwhile, the AIDS epidemic has already killed more than four million Africans, and an estimated 21 million adults and children are infected with HIV and AIDS. Progress is lagging in the incorporation of AIDS education into family planning and maternal health services. A study in ten countries revealed that health staff discuss sexually transmitted diseases with only one in ten family planning clients and AIDS with just one in fourteen. Such

services are often the only contact women have with the health system and thus an important opportunity for educating women about protecting themselves from HIV and AIDS. Further jeopardizing women's health is the traditional practice of female genital mutilation, affecting 110 million women in the region.

Perhaps most foretelling of sub-Saharan Africa's populous future, however, is the record number of adolescents entering their childbearing years. The number of women in the region aged fifteen to nineteen is projected to almost double to 62 million by the year 2020. Although pregnancy rates in this age group have fallen, they remain extremely high and the declines have been less steep than in other developing regions. More than one in seven African adolescents give birth each year—more than twice the average for other developing countries and two and a half times the rate in the United States. Adolescents are also at high risk of unsafe abortion and HIV infection, as the provision of sexual and reproductive health information and services to young people remains highly controversial in most countries. Laws and policies often restrict their access to such services. In Kenya, the Roman Catholic church has vigorously opposed sexuality education in schools.

The Changes

Despite the setbacks, there is strong evidence of a fundamental shift in attitudes toward childbearing in Africa:

- Over the past two decades, ideal family size has decreased considerably across the region. The decline has been particularly steep in Kenya, where desired family size has dropped from seven to four, and in Nigeria and Senegal, where it's dropped from eight to six. Roughly a quarter of married women surveyed—triple the proportion in the 1970s—want no more children. In Kenya, the percent is over half, and in Madagascar and Uganda, over a third want to limit family size.
- Demand for family planning has increased dramatically in some African countries, although contraceptive use is still quite low for the region as a whole. Use of family planning in such countries as Botswana, Kenya, and Zimbabwe grew rapidly in the 1980s and 1990s, and now approaches or exceeds 40 percent—levels similar to those observed in Bangladesh and India. As a result, overall contraceptive use for the region has grown at about 1 percent per year—a modest increment compared to other regions but nevertheless a notable improvement after decades of little or no progress. Still, just 18 percent of married women of childbearing age use family planning—one-third the average for other developing regions; use of modern methods, at 12 percent, is even lower.
- Changes in desired family size and increased contraceptive use have stimulated a substantial fall in birthrates in a number of African countries—a trend that is spreading rapidly. While, for the region as a whole, average family size is about six, a few countries have experienced substantially larger declines. In Kenya, family size has fallen from eight in the 1970s to 5.4; Zimbabwe has seen fertility decrease

by a third since the 1980s to 4.3 children; between the 1980s and 1990s, smaller but still important declines on the order of 10 to 30 percent have taken place in at least six other countries. Both the size and speed of these declines are strikingly similar to those in other developing countries early in their transition to low fertility. Furthermore, in Africa as elsewhere, couples in cities are leading the downward trend in childbearing; family size is one to two children lower in urban areas compared to rural areas.

The potential beneficial impact of this shift in attitudes on the health of women and children is enormous. As women bear fewer children, their exposure to the risks of pregnancy decreases; the children they have are more likely to survive and live a better life.

And because of this desire for smaller families, some African governments are now making substantial headway in improving reproductive health services in the region—answering critics skeptical of development aid for Africa:

- More countries now have **outreach efforts** at the local community level to help improve acceptance for and access to family planning. In Kenya, a leader in developing such programs, there are now twenty-five programs employing about 17,000 workers—women and men who take contraceptive services directly to their clients. In communities served, nearly 60 percent of men and women know a field worker.
- **Voluntary sterilization** for women—considered even five years ago to be culturally unacceptable—is becoming more widely available and is rapidly gaining popularity, although vasectomy has yet to gain acceptance.
  - **Mass media campaigns** are increasing knowledge of family planning, as well as AIDS and other reproductive health issues. Radio programs geared to young people in Kenya, Nigeria, and Uganda transmit messages on sexual responsibility and information on prevention of both pregnancy and AIDS.
  - Today, more than twenty countries are making **subsidized, low-cost condoms** available through commercial sales outlets. Condom sales in sub-Saharan Africa quadrupled between 1991 and 1995 to 166 million annually—one-quarter of the worldwide total for so-called social marketing of condoms.
  - In Uganda, a vigorous **AIDS prevention campaign** has led to a decline in HIV prevalence (rates of infection), showing that there is real potential for bringing the AIDS epidemic under control.
  - Ghana, Kenya, and Nigeria have introduced programs on a national scale to improve **emergency treatment** for women suffering from complications of unsafe abortion.

The Choices

An effective partnership among governments in the region, donor nations, and the private sector is key to addressing sub-Saharan Africa's population and reproductive health challenges. Governments must further expand basic health services in order to increase access to family planning and other reproductive health services and to build up their capacity to deliver high quality reproductive health services. Governments also need to reach out beyond health clinics to local communities, further strengthen basic management systems—especially in the area of contraceptive supply—and tap into the substantial expertise of both nonprofit and for-profit private organizations. Other areas for government action include:

Unmet Need for Contraception
Sub-Saharan African Countries and Selected Regions

Percent of Married Women of Childbearing Age

Women with Unmet Need
Women Using Contraception

SOURCE: *Africa's Population Challenge: Accelerating Progress in Reproductive Health.* Population Action International, 1998.

- **improving the quality of services** by removing unnecessary obstacles to contraceptive use and providing the broadest possible range of contraceptive methods

- **breaking the taboo on providing services to unmarried adolescents,** to ensure they have the means to protect themselves from unwanted pregnancy, AIDS, and other sexually transmitted diseases

- **expanding campaigns aimed at increasing male involvement** in both family planning and prevention of STDs, especially AIDS

- **strengthening links between family planning and related health services**—in particular, AIDS and STD prevention and post-abortion care

- **improving emergency care for women** who experience complications during delivery, through community education, training of health staff, and upgrading of health facilities

- **intensifying efforts to raise women's status** by increasing school enrollment among girls, removing legal and other barriers to women's economic participation, and halting the practice of female genital mutilation.

Carrying out the ambitious agenda outlined above will require enormous effort by African governments, particularly with regard to financial resources. Most countries in the region are extremely poor, and current funding falls far short of the estimated $2 billion needed in order to meet family planning and other reproductive health needs. In 1990, these governments spent only about $200 million of their own money for all preventive health services, including family planning. The lack of resources in the region highlights the need for continued assistance from wealthy donor nations. Indeed, donors need to increase support for family planning and related health care from the current $500 million to at least $1 billion by the year 2000.

Historically, the United States—the world's wealthiest country—has led the way in assisting family planning and reproductive health programs in Africa, providing some $127 million in 1996 for training, supplies, and other hands-on assistance. Other large-scale donors are the United Nations Population Fund, Germany, and Great Britain. But future prospects for population assistance are uncertain because U.S. leadership on population and reproductive health is slipping. Worldwide, U.S. funding for population programs is now 30 percent lower than in 1995. In Africa, the U.S. Agency for International Development, which administers population assistance, has closed nine country offices since 1994 and reduced the number of population and health experts in the field by more than one-third.

Prospects for Success

The present time is a moment of opportunity on the African continent. Africa is making new headway: democracy and economic reform are revitalizing the continent, and a number of countries are experiencing dynamic economic growth. With greater political openness, African governments are increasingly seeking to address the health and education needs of their people.

These governments need to emphasize three key strategies to improve individual well-being and slow population growth. The first priority should be to expand reproductive health and family planning services to meet existing unmet needs. The second, to expand educational and economic opportunities, especially for women, both to improve the lives of individuals and help encourage a desire for smaller families. The third, to slow the momentum of future population growth through education and reproductive health programs that help young people choose to delay childbearing.

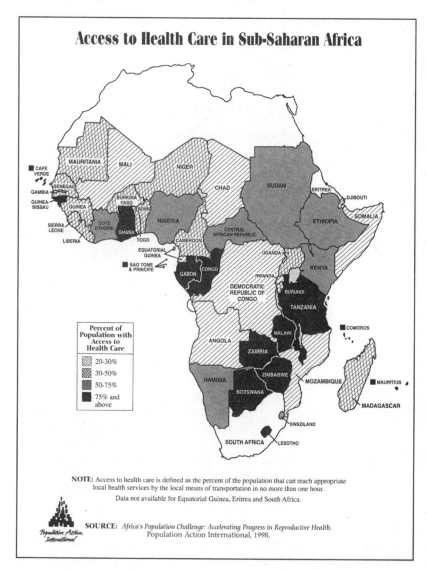

Access to Health Care in Sub-Saharan Africa

Percent of Population with Access to Health Care
- 20-30%
- 30-50%
- 50-75%
- 75% and above

NOTE: Access to health care is defined as the percent of the population that can reach appropriate local health services by the local means of transportation in no more than one hour.

Data not available for Equatorial Guinea, Eritrea and South Africa.

SOURCE: *Africa's Population Challenge: Accelerating Progress in Reproductive Health.*
Population Action International, 1998.

Africa's relatively recent establishment of population policies and programs has given it the chance to learn from both the mistakes and achievements of other regions which have grappled with the problem of rapid population growth. African countries—with help from the world community—have the potential to build on these experiences and create their own success story.

In 1994, at the International Conference on Population and Development in Cairo, virtually every nation in the world endorsed a statement calling for universal access to the information and means to plan families. At the time, the United States and a number of other wealthy nations said they would increase their spending to help reach this goal. The future for women like Sara in Kenya—and the potential for achieving environmentally sustainable development for the world as a whole—depends in large part on the extent to which donor countries fulfill this commitment.

Shanti R. Conly is director of policy research at Population Action International based in Washington, D.C. She has over fifteen years of international development experience and has lived in Bangladesh, Egypt, Pakistan, Niger, and Nigeria. This article is adapted from her study, "Africa's Population Challenge: Accelerating Progress in Reproductive Health," coauthored with James Rosen and available on PAI's website at www.populationaction.org.

Article 2   *Harvard Magazine*, March/April 1999

Emerging
AFRICA

Coming to terms with an overlooked continent

by Matt O'Keefe

❝IF YOU SUBJECT AN EGG AND A STONE TO THE SAME EXTERNAL ENVIRONMENT," SAYS KWESI Botchwey, "after a while, under the heat of the sun, a chicken will break out of the egg, but not out of the stone." The folkloric metaphor at first sounds odd, coming from an accomplished economic bureaucrat like Botchwey, who was finance minister of Ghana for 13 years before coming to Cambridge in 1995, where he now directs a new research program on development in Africa. But as he talks, it begins to seem exactly right: the perfect symbol for the changes he sees emerging as some nations of sub-Saharan Africa evolve in ways that may make them succeed in joining the world's economic and political communities.

It has always been a mistake, if perhaps a pardonable one, to imagine Africa as a homogeneous place. "When we're here, we speak about Africa and it has meaning," says Robert H. Bates, Eaton professor of the science of government and a faculty fellow in the Harvard Institute for International Development (HIID). "But when you're in Africa," where he has done extensive research and to which he travels twice a year to teach—"it makes no sense to speak about Africa. The internal variation is enormous. You can't write the story of Africa by going to Sudan during the drought or Zaire during the war." That is particularly so today, when alongside the long-running horrors of an Angola or Rwanda or Sudan one also finds political change coming to nations like The Gambia and Madagascar, and signs of economic growth in countries as diverse as Botswana and Mauritius.

The problems are still legion. New governments may have only a few years, or months, to prove that they can work. Economies based on exporting commodities—coffee, copper, gold, oil—can collapse when prices fall or when credit, already dearer than desert rain, vanishes as financial crises sweep through the more developed developing markets of Asia, Eastern Europe, and Latin America. As some African nations struggle to put behind them their unwanted role as proxies in the Cold War, and to move beyond the legacy of colonialism, they need traditional kinds of help—money and medicine—as well as education and good advice.

At the same time, they become fertile new ground for academicians eager to study everything from the equatorial home of the AIDS pathogen to art forms and ways of thought until now too little understood by developed nations' students of the humanities. With the emergence of new possibilities in Africa—the sorting out of Botchwey's eggs from the stones—has come an unheralded emergence of African studies and expertise at Harvard. Portraits of some of the practitioners and their work are presented here.

"THE CHALLENGES POSED BY THE DEVELOPING NATIONS ANIMATE both self-interest and conscience," wrote Bates in 1996. His conclusion—"It is Africa that constitutes the development challenge of our time"—now resonates even more loudly.

That belief certainly animates much of the new work on Africa under way at Harvard. In fact, the occasion for Nelson Mandela's historic visit to the University last September was the launching of Botchwey's "Emerging Africa" program, an ambitious effort to rethink—and improve—the course of economic development in the continent below the Sahara.

"East Asia and Africa were not that significantly different through the 1960s," Botchwey says, but they began to diverge in the early 1970s, and the gap widened into a chasm in the following decade. Now, the East Asian nation much of Africa most resembles is Bangladesh—not China nor Hong Kong, Singapore, South Korea, nor Taiwan, not even Indonesia and Malaysia, where (until recently) economic progress had become increasingly widespread. The data are stark: a 1997 report by HIID notes that "for the last two decades real per capita incomes have declined" in most sub-Saharan nations; from 1961 to 1995, food production per person rose 71 percent in Asia and 31 percent in Latin America—but fell in Africa; countries such as Congo, Mozambique, and Tanzania each had gross domestic product per capita of $135 or less in 1996.

"Obviously," Botchwey says, "geography, climate, and disease have an impact on development that is not always acknowledged. This," he is at pains to point out, "is not to suggest any kind of determinism—that since these countries are in the tropics, they are doomed." Rather, in explaining Africa's past and prospects, he insists that "it is important to see the complexity of the problems and the interrelatedness of all these factors" with culture and institutions. But in the end, he says, "Policies make a difference. Human action through mobilization makes a difference."

Much of that action, including many of those policies, has been misguided, Botchwey says. For all the development funds spent in Africa, "a lot of the aid went not to support good policies, but to support the geopolitical interests of the donors." In Zaire, to take a notorious example, "Everyone knew Mobutu wasn't using the resources wisely, but they saw him as a Cold War ally." There and elsewhere, Botchwey says, foreign aid "shored up despots, postponing the day of reckoning."

Now that day of reckoning has arrived. With their national economies looted or ruined by civil wars, many of the despots have been deposed. Bates has found extensive, if not always firmly rooted, political reform since the mid 1970s—what he calls "a deepening of institutionalized political competition."

As a result, and facing the end of the aid that flowed during the Cold War, Botchwey figures, two-thirds of the 48 sub-Saharan countries have begun to adopt policies more conducive to economic growth. The "macroeconomic stabilization" measures he applied in Ghana—letting the market determine the currency's foreign-exchange rate, attacking inflation, collecting tax revenues, and balancing the budget—have become more commonplace.

But necessary as those steps were, they weren't and aren't sufficient to encourage sustained growth. "We had taxied to the end of the runway," Botchwey says of Ghana's experience, "but we weren't taking off." And so, "emotionally and intellectually drained"—and, ironically, finding that the country's liberalized governance made economic policymaking more subject to politicking—Botchwey decided to head for the academy, to reflect on his experiences and examine their larger implications.

"IN THE OLD STORY, THE PEASANT GOES TO THE PRIEST FOR ADVICE ON saving his dying chickens," wrote Jeffrey Sachs '76, Ph.D. '80, Jf '81, Stone professor of international trade, in a 1996 article for the *Economist*. "The priest recommends prayer, but the chickens continue to die. The priest then recommends music for the chicken coop, but the deaths continue unabated." And so on, until, finally, "all the chickens die. 'What a shame,' the priest tells the peasant. 'I had so many more good ideas.' "

After decades of feckless aid, the African development challenge demands new thinking about "the interlinkages of economic growth with health, education, geography, environment, demography, macroeconomic policy, and institutions," as the Emerging Africa prospectus puts it. Many underpinnings for that new thinking have come out of HIID, where Sachs has been paying much attention to Africa since becoming director in 1995. HIID conducts practical research and provides economic and policy advice to nonindustrial nations and those making the transition to market economies. Emerging Africa, engaged in broader research questions, is housed in a new Center for International Development, itself an HIID-Kennedy School of Government venture focused on pioneering new approaches to beginning, and sustaining, economic growth. Botchwey's enterprise, therefore, is poised somewhere between the hands-on approach of HIID's field staff and the Kennedy School's scholar-policymakers, and, like them, promotes international collaboration and extensive exchange with academicians and government officials from other nations.

Sachs embodies this modus operandi. Now the man who would save Africa, he has previously been the man who would save Bolivia, Poland, and Russia. He went to these nations at their governments' behest, a wunderkind economist whose turn-on-a-dime policies earned him the nickname "Dr. Shock" (see "The Revolutionary Jeffrey Sachs," November–December 1992, page 48). In Bolivia, he slashed hyperinflation. In Poland, he converted a socialist economy into a market economy. In Russia, he tried to do both, and people still argue about whether the failure was his.

"It is not as if Africa rose to the top of the radar screen for American foreign policy, it just rose from the bottom." Jeffrey Sachs

His prescriptions for Africa contain elements of all these prior experiences, beginning with an economist's interpretation of recent political history and new opportunity. "The rise of President Mandela and the end of apartheid were watersheds in African history," Sachs says. "An economic powerhouse [South Africa] began to play a broader role in overall African economic growth. A number of countries turned the corner on economic development. Africa's shortcomings and potentialities became evident simultaneously." In the Cold War's aftermath, he continues, it became possible to see Africa not as a strategic chessboard, but as "a place in need of attention in its own right. It's not as if Africa rose to the top of the radar screen for American foreign policy, it just rose from the bottom."

Part of that rise is attributable to an HIID paper, "A New Partnership for Growth in Africa," which subsequently transmogrified into the African trade bill passed by the House of Representatives just before President Clinton's historic visit to the continent last March. Although it ultimately failed to become law, the bill began to set forth a market-oriented new vision for development assistance: it would have eliminated duties and quotas on exports to the United States for the next 10 years and encouraged the establishment of free-trade zones. Those benefits were tied to one of Sachs's core beliefs—that it is worth extending "timely support for new democracies." To qualify for the benefits of the bill, countries would have had to prove a commitment to democracy, human rights, and a market economy, limiting eligibility to a handful of nations, including Botswana, Ethiopia, the Ivory Coast, South Africa, and Uganda.

Sachs has expressed other core beliefs that repudiate the prevailing wisdom about how to help Africa develop. His proclamation in the *Economist* went after the pillars of the development community: "The IMF [International Monetary Fund] is so obsessed with price stability it doesn't think very hard about anything else. The World Bank, on the other hand, has hundreds of good ideas but no priorities": calling for feeble and indebted governments to "introduce value-added taxes, new customs administration, civil-service reform, decentralized public administration and many other wonderful things—often within months." It is a critique Kwesi Botchwey can visualize with painful vividness.

To judge how far the continent must travel, one need only consult *The Africa Competitiveness Report 1998,* published by HIID and the World Economic Forum last spring, the first assessment of its kind. From 1991 to 1995, Botchwey notes in one essay, Africa attracted less than 2 percent of foreign direct investment funds worldwide—and three quarters of that was concentrated in the African oil-exporting nations. With 10 percent of the world's population, sub-Saharan Africa accounts for only 2 percent of world economic output, and a third of that meager share is South Africa's.

AS THE ONLY REMEDY, SACHS ADVOCATES SUSTAINED, RAPID growth—say 5 percent per year—like the revolution that transformed so many Asian economies. In theory, the key to such growth lies in reintegration into the world economy, based on political willingness to overcome prejudices against open trade and foreign investment instilled by not-so-distant memories of colonialism. So Botchwey's mission becomes a search for the best ways to put the HIID's new general theories into practice in Africa. Given his mantra that the development issues must be seen in their "multisidedness," that promises to be a daunting challenge, comprising infrastructure, institutions, and industrialization.

He notes, for example, that "everyone bemoans the small flow of international capital into Africa." But, given that the continent's "infrastructure is *so* underdeveloped," investors' inability, or reluctance, to put funds to work there is understandable. Whatever the causes—Botchwey cites government policies hostile to some kinds of investment, cumbersome statist procedures, and corruption—he is most concerned about the effect: "The fact that telephone density is so low, and that so many countries are landlocked and the road network and rails and ports and airlines are so relatively undeveloped, means that productivity is affected." Richard H. Goldman, an HIID agricultural policy adviser who has worked in Kenya and Malawi, gives a dramatic illustration: "In Kenya, even over the cheaper routes, it cost more to move maize from Mombasa to Nairobi, only 250 miles, than it did to move it from Louisiana to Mombasa."

Clearly, problems like these cannot be resolved solely through economic administration, by controlling inflation or correcting skewed exchange rates. Focusing on those priorities, Botchwey concedes, has done "some good," but most such efforts have fallen short because "for a *long* time, there has been no recognition that, along with sound policies, you need governments that could deliver them."

In much of sub-Saharan Africa, public functions taken for granted in the industrial world—educating workers, securing property rights, ensuring the privacy of domestic banking "so people could put their money there without a politician who doesn't like you coming and seizing it"—are not even a prospect. The vulnerability of private assets is especially costly for capital-starved African countries. It is in this context that Sachs's criticism of the World Bank's lack of priorities takes on its bitter meaning. In Botchwey's gentler formulation, this is just another symptom of development schemes too fragmented and superficial to sustain growth.

Instead, Botchwey prescribes comprehensive "strategic, long-term change," predicated on a fundamental shift "away from primary commodity exports to exports of manufactured goods and services"—nothing less than industrialization. Intellectually, this means deferring the classic short-term stabilization measures (raising taxes and tariffs) used to balance national budgets: "That's the worst thing you can do for a country," he says. Practically, it means creating the conditions that attract foreign capital investments to support long-term growth, mimicking East Asia's transformation. "So far, after 15 years of reform," Botchwey says, "hardly *any* country in Africa has made that shift to higher growth from real exports of manufactured goods."

For the first time it makes sense to ask seriously, "What would it take to make Africa an emerging region in the same way as Asia?"
Kwesi Botchwey

What, then, must be done? First, he says, "the change has to start within the countries themselves," through better governance—the transformation from stones to eggs. "Without that," Botchwey says, "no amount of external aid can help." Then, international institutions like the World Bank must direct their support to those countries that have changed—not to all needy African nations indiscriminately—and within these countries, must support "critical things"—not glamorous projects like massive dams, but the subtler factors essential for economic progress: education and training, eradication of disease, and regional infrastructure schemes (telephony, coastal access roads) that are too taxing for local private investors.

Once the foundations are in place, Emerging Africa hopes to show how certain industries can thrive in specific locales. As Asian nations move up from labor-intensive exports, such as textiles, to higher-technology manufacturing, Botchwey sees the opportunity for African nations to succeed them, establishing free-trade zones to exploit their own comparative advantages, based, for example, on the availability of local cotton crops and inexpensive labor. Over the next two years, he plans rigorous studies on how exactly the obstacles to growth could be overcome in a few nations, enabling a few industries to take hold and succeed.

Despite the discouraging history to date, Botchwey is not on a fool's errand. The competitiveness report cites Mauritius, for example, which has overcome its one-time dependence on sugar sales to sustain 6 percent annual economic growth over three decades, elevating per capita gross national product to about $4,000. Isolated from the mainland (and from major markets), the country has evolved what the report calls "one of the most firmly rooted liberal democracies in Africa"—the necessary institutional context—and has successfully pursued a strategy of encouraging tourism and of processing textiles for export through a modern commercial harbor. If anything, the most pressing constraint on growth is the shortage of labor: unemployment now hovers around 2 percent.

"We are used to thinking of Africa as a region of gloom and doom, where nothing works," Botchwey says. But he believes that Africa can work in economic terms, once its people and governments determine to succeed, and once those who wish to help have acknowledged the complexity of the challenge. He calls what he sees "a turnaround," where for the first time it makes sense to ask seriously, "What would it take to make Africa an emerging region in the same way as Asia?"

A NIGERIAN ATTENDS AN OPEC CONFERENCE IN INDONESIA. Admiring his host's palatial estate, the visitor asks, "How can you afford this spread on your government salary?"

The Indonesian gestures toward a highway in the distance. "Do you see that road?" he says.

The Nigerian nods.

The Indonesian says, "Exactly."

A few years later, the Indonesian attends a conference in Nigeria, arranged by his former guest. Indicating his host's new mansion and lavish gardens with a sweep of his arm, the Indonesian says, "So, I see you took my advice. My only question is, where's the road?"

The Nigerian says, "Exactly." Smita Singh, who is studying the politics of economic policymaking in Jakarta and Lagos as part of her doctoral research, tells the joke to illustrate a truism: in corrupt Asian countries, personal enrichment accompanied public investment, while in Africa, the looted funds all ended up in private pockets or offshore bank accounts.

The consequences for the affected citizens have been devastating. Nigeria, an oil-rich nation like Indonesia, was widely expected 30 years ago to power Africa's economies. Instead, according to the *Africa Competitiveness Report,* Nigeria's 1996 economic output per capita was $240—11 percent *below* the sub-Saharan average. Its economic landscape is a virtual metaphor for unfinished business. Singh describes Lagos as "post-apocalyptic," littered with abandoned construction projects, skeletal skyscrapers, highways that simply end. Power goes out in large sections of the city every night. Phones are often down. A company hoping to erect a new factory might also have to build and maintain its own power source and roads. "All people can do is sell things on the road," she says. "It's a country that is deindustrializing."

HABITATS FOR THE HUMANITIES

An Africa on its feet economically might more easily share its cultural riches with the rest of the world. Few scholars at Harvard know more about those riches, or how hard it can be to sample them, than Kay Kaufman Shelemay, who chairs the department of music, which she joined in 1992. She still speaks with intensity about the chance encounter with Ethiopian music in 1970 that transformed her studies from a consuming interest in Western art music to a passion for world music, folk music, and anthropology. Three years later, she pursued that interest to its origins for her doctoral research. "In finding Ethiopia," Shelemay says, "I found my field, ethnomusicology," and in finding that intellectual focus, she also found "not only a husband but a revolution"—an intellectual, personal, and political odyssey recounted in her 1991 book, *A Song of Longing: An Ethiopian Journey.*

Shelemay's scholarship has as its center communities within communities, a situation to which Ethiopia is uniquely hospitable. "Ethiopia," she says, "is the country no one wants to acknowledge as part of Africa." Isolated by a rugged highland plateau in the Horn of Africa, it was colonized, if the term applies at all, only during the Italian occupation form 1935 to 1941. Otherwise, it was ruled by a succession of emperors from biblical times until 1974, when Haile Selassie was deposed. Shelemay went to study the country's anomalous cultures—particularly the Ethiopian Jewish community, Beta Israel—not its politics.

She traveled by bus and horse to Amobober, a small Beta Israel village, where she witnessed the rituals performed on the eve of the New Year, as the glow of an oil lamp lit a silkscreen of Jerusalem while five priests, in white gowns and turbans, chanted a prayer services in Ge'ez. The musical accompaniment included a repetitive rhythm on a flat, circular metal gong and a large kettledrum, "covered with the same bright, flowered cloth I had seen in Ethiopian Christian churches." As a foreign researcher, Shelemay was granted access to many rituals normally little attended by women, and she was able to tape-record all the ceremonies to which she was invited.

In 1974 she married Jack Shelemay in Tel Aviv, and the couple returned to his home city, Addis Ababa, where Kay resumed her research as "a revolution of hope" began. But as shifting curfews enforced by excitable soldiers made civilians loath to leave their homes, she began frantically shipping research materials out of the country.

In 1975, as she became interested in studying the music of the Ethiopian Christian church, the new government nationalized all the land and buildings in urban centers. Local militias, called *kebele,* were charged with preserving order throughout the capital. The revolution veered toward becoming a bloodbath as the militias and their opponents fought in the streets. In December, Kay Shelemay left for the United States. To get her remaining tapes past the government censor, she played him a recording of *tezzeta,* a type of sentimental Ethiopian love song. It would be three years before her husband would be permitted to join her.

Even though she was now cut off from the sources of her research, Shelemay harvested the materials she had gathered to produce a series of articles and books on Ethiopian musical and religious culture. *Music, Ritual, and Falasha History,* based on her dissertation, untangled the intermingling of Beta Israel and Ethiopian Christian liturgy, revealing the Beta Israel to be not some isolated outpost of Judaism in the heart of a Christian nation, but rather practitioners of a hybrid religion, descended from a centuries-old Ethiopian Judeo-Christianity—a controversial finding during their emigration to Israel under the Law of Return.

"One reason I was able to work during the revolution is that I was a musicologist and everyone thought I was harmless," Shelemay says. "But music opens a window on history." Another such window opened as a result of her frantic 1975 researches. With Peter Jeffery of Princeton, Shelemay edited and published between 1993 and 1997 the three-volume anthology *Ethiopian Christian Liturgical Chant.* Among its revelations: although indigenous sub-Saharan African music was thought to exist only orally, this particular Ethiopian music, at least, has a long-established form of notation, dating from the sixteenth century, when Islamic invasion threatened the Church, forcing its adherents to invent a way to record its vital traditions.

Having "lost my field for many years," Shelemay remains interested in Boston's vibrant Ethiopian community, with its churches, restaurants, and frequent dance parties. "There are a lot of immigrants here who were displaced by the revolution," she says. "So I've been able to follow my work from Africa into the African diaspora," the subject of a recent graduate-level ethnomusicology seminar.

Nothing brought Africa nearer to Harvard than Nelson Mandela's visit to Tercentenary Theatre, for which Shelemay arranged the rousing introductory drumming chorus. ("You made me feel at home," Mandela told the performers.) Less dramatically, the scholarship of her faculty colleagues on the Committee on African Studies (see box, "African Studies") sustains her ties to a country she has not visited since 1978. "Just in the humanities," she says, "the quality of the people who are here with African specializations and interests is extraordinary."

Now, as Shelemay completes a textbook on world music in North America and introduces a new Core course, "Soundscapes: World Music at Home and Aborad," she is beginning a new research project, on the influence of Ethiopian culture on Italy (Ethiopians first visited Rome in the fifteenth century, she notes, and Ethiopian chant was performed at the Ravenna festival last year) and vice versa. As always, she says, she is engaged by "borderlands, where people and cultures run into each other." With her term as chair of the music department coming to an end, and a sabbatical year in prospect, Shelemay plans to cross a significant border of her own by returning to Ethiopia in 2000, to resume her fieldwork there for the first time in more than 20 years.

Even as Shelemay has documented written musical notation where none was known to exist, one of her fellow humanists at Harvard has been probing Africa's oral cultures. K. Anthony Appiah, professor of Afro-American studies and of philosophy, is currently working to connect Africa's philosophical traditions to those of the rest of the world, extracting evidence of early African thought from secondary sources within the culture, most notably from the spoken word.

Appiah—coeditor with Henry Louis Gates Jr. of *The Dictionary of Global Culture* and of *Encarta Africana,* a CD-ROM encyclopedia of Africa—says that for a philosopher accustomed to the rewritten tradition, his new inquiry is a fascinating challenge. "The construction is analogous to what Plato was doing," he says. "Plato made famous a man called Socrates who existed entirely in the oral mode. Socrates spoke and Plato wrote it down. But Plato had to decide what to write down. In shaping his account of what Socrates said, he was shaping fundamental philosophical question. And that's what we're doing, asking which of these questions are worth continuing with, which of these answers are worth holding on to."

In other words, just what one would expect after years of brutal military government and the dashed hopes following the annulment of the 1993 election and the 1994 imprisonment of the winner, Chief Moshood Abiola (whose daughter, Hafsat '96, was then an undergraduate). Naturally, this political atmosphere affects government and business decisionmakers alike, says Singh: "When your time horizon is very short, you're not going to make long-term investments. You can see why people would rather put their money in Swiss bank accounts."

Overcoming that predilection, ingrained by decades of chaos, would obviously go far toward securing for much of Africa a more promising future. So what are the prospects for more humane governance in a continent where a traditional leader like Haile Selassie has more often been succeeded by a murderous Mengistu Haile Mariam and a junta than by an elected president and a parliament?

Much as the studies published by Jeffrey Sachs and others at HIID underlie the Emerging Africa initiative, new analyses by Singh, Robert Bates, and other students of government support Sachs's championing of Africa's "new democracies." What they are finding extends well beyond Nelson Mandela's transformed South Africa.

In an initial paper on "democratic transition in Africa," published in 1995, Bates found from a review of 46 countries that their political systems "more frequently exhibited attributes of democracy" in 1991 than in 1975—that evidence of political transition was "widespread." He also noted, however, that many of the changes were superficial "window dressing," applied like rouge by dictators eager to present a prettier public face to the world.

Subsequent papers by Bates and graduate students Singh, Karen Ferree, and others who have worked in Africa provide much deeper understanding of the real political changes under way there. Comparing the data over time reveals, for example, that for 46 sub-Saharan countries, the number of chief executives at least nominally elected rose from 18 in 1975 to 28 in 1991. Over that period, Botswana, Madagascar, and Mauritius enjoyed fully competitive legislative elections, and Benin and Zimbabwe moved dramatically in that direction. On the other hand, Mauritania, which had contested multiparty elections in 1975, had abolished them by 1991.

In the aggregate, Bates and his colleagues find "a deepening of institutionalized political competition in Africa during the period in question," but not uniform change, because a substantial fraction of the least competitive political systems remained that way—most often, mired in armed insurrections. The result: "an increasing level of heterogeneity in the political systems of Africa," and comparable divergence in nations' economic growth. In the precise language of statistical analysis, the Bates group is now quantifying the relationship between political change and economic performance. As Kwesi Botchwey might put it, the differences attributable to human choices are beginning to appear, and with them distinctions between stones and eggs.

Although these papers emerge from the comfortable confines of Cambridge, the data and observations underpinning them derive from fieldwork often conducted under challenging, even severe, conditions. Bates caught the Africa bug while he was still a student at the Pomfret School, in Connecticut. A progressive headmaster put together a program, funded by a wealthy parent, that sent Bates, several classmates, and students from other secondary schools to Kenya and South Africa, where he recalls seeing for the first time a weapon being loaded with the intention, if necessary, of killing people. He remembers being moved by "the incredible humanity of the people in the face of conditions that would challenge any of us to remain decent. When I came back, like so many others who have experienced Africa, I knew what I wanted to do with my life. It was that simple."

Bates went to graduate school, he says, because he discovered that professors could be paid to go to Africa. He has conducted research with his wife, Margaret (now dean of student life at MIT), in the mining townships of Zambia, and returned to study the life in a village on the Zambia-Zaire (now Congo) border. He remembers his hut there—"It was made out of clay bricks, with a wooden door frame and a thatch roof"—as fondly as village life: "Biologically, that's the way we're supposed to live. It's a very rich life."

From those earlier experiences comes a profusion of new scholarship today. With colleagues at Oxford, the University of Ibadan, Nigeria, and the University of Dar es Salaam, Tanzania, Bates is launching in March a project entitled "The Economic Development of Modern Africa, 1945–2000." Under their direction, 30 researchers throughout Africa will prepare volumes for publication by Cambridge University Press—volumes that may have special credibility because of their indigenous origins. Meanwhile, Bates and a team of undergraduate and graduate students continue to collect data for the research that forms the subject of his course on "The Politics and Economics of Policy Reform." With a separate group of graduate students, he is beginning to study political conflict in Africa—particularly the worrisome recent rise of cross-border conflicts, as opposed to the civil wars that ripped through the continent but were contained within national borders by the superpowers during the Cold War.

Each of those inquiries depends on, and expands, a network of colleague-scholars here and in Africa. And so, enthusiastically, Bates sends his students out to do fieldwork, just as he and Kay Shelemay did (see box, "Habitats for the Humanities"). At around the time that Singh was avoiding being "shaken down" by police and armed robbers in Lagos (an experience she maintains was less physically challenging than earlier anthropological research in India, where she slept on a floor with 10 other people, enduring pecks from a chicken that also used the premises), Melissa Thomas, Ph.D. '98, was studying the rule of law in Mali. Thomas, who was in the graduate political economy and government program at Harvard and now works at the World Bank, found it prudent to stockpile food and water in case revolution broke out anew. And Karen Ferree, a graduate student in government and economics, learned that one of the risks of observing South Africa's party system was the likelihood of a violent bank robbery in her Johannesburg neighborhood every week or two.

For all that, Bates insists on the value of wearing out shoe leather. "It's just too easy to sit back here and grind numbers and make announcements," he says. "You think you're on to something, but if it doesn't resonate with your experience, it has a high probability of being wrong or silly. And the worst thing is, you'll never know that. The one thing I'm proudest of is my students in the field."

The other thing he and many Africanists are excited about—yes, even proud about—is the belief that they are in a position to help new ways of life emerge. "For a very long time after independence," Jeffrey Sachs says, "most countries had one-party rule. In the 1990s, there has been a shift to democracy, which is always difficult in low-income countries. The situation is highly desirable on the one hand, but reversible and subject to violence. Democratization and economic reform go hand in hand. There is not a case for sequencing them. You can't take for granted that democracy will function or survive. You need to help at fragile moments."

Matt O'Keefe, a freelance writer and occasional contributor to this magazine, recently moved from Cambridge to North Carolina.

AFRICAN STUDIES

Africa and the Disciplines, published in 1993, was a landmark in African studies. The volume sought to justify the place of African studies in the American university, not on the basis of Afrocentricity or multiculturalism, but because, it claimed, work done in Africa was already vital to the core disciplines. The book's subtitle, "The contributions of research in Africa to the social sciences and humanities," suggested the breadth of the potential contributions to knowledge, and the book's contributors—an all-star team of premier Africanists—personified the academic potential already focused on the continent. Of the book's three editors and seven essayist, only anthropologist Sally Falk Moore (then Thomas professor of anthropology, and now curator of African ethnology in the Peabody Museum) was a Harvard faculty member. But philosopher K. Anthony Appiah, political scientist Robert H. Bates, and art historian Suzanne P. Blier have since joined the Harvard roster. Says Bates proudly, "We do Africa at least as well as anybody in the country."

Nonetheless, student Africanists must be resourceful in order to pursue an academic program at Harvard. Unlike many other area-studies programs, African studies does not reside in its own center. Nor is it an undergraduate concentration, although undergraduates in other concentrations who satisfactorily complete eight approved half-courses (including an honors thesis) receive an honors certificate in African studies.

Why the lack of institutional support? Some say it's because Harvard, wary of overexpanding, can't be expected to do everything. Others suggest that Africa isn't a sufficiently promising source for donations. Taking the latter view, professor of history Leroy Vail says succinctly: "If you're talking about Harvard, within another sentence or two, you have to use the word 'money.' "

So Africanists at Harvard make do with what they have, operating through the Committee on African Studies, a 15-member group of scholars appointed by the dean of the Faculty of Arts and Sciences. The committee oversees the African studies certificate program and disburses summer travel grants that enable students to conduct fieldwork for their theses. Such funds have recently grown with two gifts from Jennifer Ward Oppenheimer '89, J.D. '93, totaling $600,000 including matching funds; the money will be used for graduate-student fellowships, preferably to assist sub-Saharan students enrolled in FAS, and for general research support for undergraduate and graduate-student projects focusing on that region. In addition, from a small cluster of offices in Coolidge Hall, on Cambridge Street, Rita Breen, the committee's executive officer, maintains a website with links to all things African and academic Harvard and at institutions around the world ("http://www.fas.harvard.edu/~cafrica/").

Appiah, the committee's chair, appears untroubled by the lack of an institutional anchor. "The problem of not having a center is theoretical," he says. "The other departments themselves have been hiring Africanists quite happily." He adds that "a student who just takes the courses available can do a lot," noting that several courses drawing on African materials are now a part of the Core curriculum. Appiah does identify one major weakness in Harvard's offerings: a lack of languages. Those available in Swahili, in which courses are supervised by Ali Asani, professor of the practice of Indo-Muslim languages and cultures, and Ge'ez (classical Ethiopic), taught by professor of semitic philology John Huehnergard. Students who wish to learn other African languages must look elsewhere, most notably to Boston University and its prominent African Studies Center. Apart from that, Appiah says, "We can do everything Harvard's other regional centers can do."

Other members of the committee are far from satisfied. Allan G. Hill, Andelot professor of demography at the School of Public Health, points to the relationship between the study of Africa and the development of Africa. Reflecting on his own studies of population growth in polygamous villages in The Gambia, Hill says, "It's important to see things from the inside. You have to understand why polygamy is important to that culture, the role it plays in cementing relationships." Forming sound policies sensitive to problems like these depends on conducting good research, he says—and this is where he sees Harvard fitting in. "Do we, as one of the richest institutions in the Western world, have an obligation to use our wherewithal to develop poorer regions? Yes, yes we do."

But for the moment, Appiah chooses to focus on the strengths of African studies at Harvard, even citing the scattered nature of the discipline as a positive. "We're here to pursue our own intellectual agendas and train students who have the tools to think about the questions," he says. "Most people [working here] put together a bundle of tools. I think it's an intellectual advantage, even when it's an institutional disadvantage."

Africa:
prospects for the future

The renaissance in Africa presents its leaders with many challenges.
What are U.S. interests in Africa? What role should the U.S. play?

by Peter J. Schraeder

PETER J. SCHRAEDER *is associate professor in the Department of Political Science at Loyola University Chicago, and author, most recently, of* African Politics and Society: A Mosaic in Transformation (*Boston/New York: College Division of Bedford/St. Martin's, 2000*).

A N "AFRICAN RENAISSANCE" of historic proportions is under way. The 1994 inauguration of Nelson Mandela as South Africa's first democratically elected president symbolized the efforts of thousands of prodemocracy groups to instill democratic practices throughout the African continent. Mandela's willingness to embrace his former captors embodied the vision of a new generation of leaders committed to multiracial and multiethnic societies based on tolerance, universal human rights and the rule of law. Policymakers, technocrats and private entrepreneurs are also at the forefront of restructuring once moribund economies to unleash the African entrepreneurial spirit. This renaissance is perhaps best captured by the flourishing of the media and literature as they enjoy the progressive decline of state censorship. A new generation of journalists, writers and scholars remains firmly committed to strengthening the democratic achievements of the last decade of the 20th century.

As Americans begin debating U.S. foreign policy as part of the 2000 presidential election, the time is ripe for a reassessment of U.S.-Africa relations. Though the African mosaic is diverse, with 53 independent countries and a number of complex issues, one question

stands out: Should the next U.S. President draw upon America's traditional role as aid-giver and play an activist role in the African renaissance, or will budgetary constraints and competing interests in other regions reinforce what is viewed by some as a policy of neglect, at best?

Democratization

Dozens of countries in Africa, Asia, Latin America, and Eastern and Southern Europe made transitions from authoritarian to more democratic forms of governance during the last quarter of the 20th century. This trend has prompted visions of a "third wave of democratization" (the first began in the 1820s and the second in the 1940s). In the case of Africa, this third wave coincided with the fall of the Berlin Wall in 1989. The collapse of single-party regimes throughout Eastern Europe and the former Soviet Union set powerful precedents for African pro-democracy activists who already had begun organizing against human-rights abuses and political repression against the backdrop of severe economic stagnation in their respective countries. The most notable outcome, often referred to as "Africa's second independence" or "Africa's second liberation," was the discrediting of more than 30 years of experimentation with single-party political systems in favor of more democratic forms of governance based on multiparty politics and the protection of human rights.

In the early 1980s, truly competitive elections were held in only five African

countries: Botswana, Gambia, Mauritius, Senegal and Zimbabwe. But between 1990 and 1994, more than 38 countries held competitive elections. Most important, 29 of the multiparty contests of this period constituted "founding elections" in which the office of the head of government is openly contested following a period during which multiparty political competition was impossible.

Optimism or pessimism?

The prospect of a new wave of democratization has fostered both optimism and pessimism: optimism generated by a host of democratic successes that culminated in what numerous observers have referred to as the South African "miracle," and pessimism based on the simple reality that several transitions resulted in "democratic decay," often ending in military coups d'état and a return to authoritarianism. Colonel Ibrahim Maïnassara Baré of Niger achieved the dubious honor of leading the first successful coup d'état against a democratically elected government in francophone West Africa since the beginning of the third wave of democratization. In a throwback to an earlier reign, Colonel Baré announced that there would be multiparty elections in 1996, presented himself as the "civilian" candidate of the ruling party and won what international observers agreed was a grossly flawed electoral contest.

Even when a successful transition to more democratic governance is made, newly elected leaders are confronted

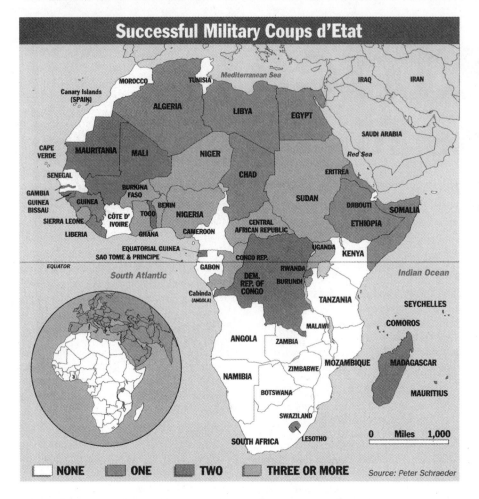

Successful Military Coups d'Etat

NONE ONE TWO THREE OR MORE

Source: Peter Schraeder

shared following multiparty elections. When the weak Zambian state was saddled with even the minimal checks and balances of a democratic system, economic progress was stymied, and weariness and disenchantment grew.

Although largely trained within an authoritarian tradition, Chiluba is now expected to abide by the "rules of the game" of Zambia's multiparty political system. When strict adherence to those rules threatened to seal his political fate in the 1996 presidential elections, however, he put them aside, especially after Kaunda accepted opposition backing and entered the race. To fend off his opponents, Chiluba oversaw the ratification of two constitutional amendments that harked back to the authoritarian excesses of his predecessor and undermined the very democratic political system he had sought to create. The first requires that the parents of any presidential candidate be Zambians by birth. The second limits presidential candidates to two terms of office. Since Kaunda's parents were born in neighboring Malawi, and he had ruled Zambia for 27 years (1964–91), he was forced to withdraw from the race. Chiluba's political maneuvering removed the only serious challenge to his rule and ensured his reelection.

Some proponents of democratization argue that the true test of Africa's newly established systems is their ability to foster an "alternation of power" between rival political parties. Benin stands out as the best example of a newly established, multiparty democracy that has successfully weathered an alternation of power via the ballot box. Following a 1990 national conference, founding elections were held in 1991 in which a technocrat, Nicéphore Soglo, was elected president. Mathieu Kérékou, the former Marxist dictator, graciously accepted defeat and retired from politics only to return as the leading opposition candidate in the 1996 presidential elections. With Soglo's reelection campaign severely hampered by the poor performance of the economy and public perceptions of his disregard for the average citizen, Kérékou overcame the odds, emerged victorious and now serves as a powerful example of the consolidation of democratic practices on the African continent.

with the long-term challenge of ensuring the consolidation of democratic practices in still-fragile political systems. "The frequency of democratic breakdowns in this century—and the difficulties of consolidating new democracies—must give serious pause to those who would argue . . . for the inevitability of global democracy," explains Larry Diamond, a senior research fellow at the Hoover Institution. "As a result, those concerned about how countries can move 'beyond authoritarianism and totalitarianism' must also ponder the conditions that permit such movement to endure. . . . To rid a country of an authoritarian regime or dictator is not necessarily to move it fundamentally beyond authoritarianism.

The authoritarian-democratic paradox

In 1991 Zambia made a successful transition from a single-party system headed by President Kenneth Kaunda to a mul-

tiparty system under the leadership of President Frederick Chiluba of the Movement for Multiparty Democracy. Eighteen months after achieving victory, Chiluba reinstated a "state of emergency" that had existed throughout Kaunda's rule, and arrested and detained without charges 14 members of the official opposition, the United National Independence party. Critics drew parallels between Kaunda's use of states of emergency during the 1970s and the 1980s to silence political opponents and Chiluba's use of them to curb rising criticism of his regime's inability to resolve economic problems.

Chiluba's predicament illustrates Africa's new authoritarian-democratic paradox. As with the first generation of African leaders, who took office beginning in the 1950s, Chiluba and the other newly elected leaders of the 1990s are confronted with popular expectations that higher wages and better living conditions will be widely and quickly

Whether democratic consolidation will overcome democratic decay largely depends on how the newly elected elites respond to the authoritarian-democratic paradox. Will they graciously accept defeat and join the ranks of the "loyal opposition," as was the case in Soglo's defeat in 1996, or will they increasingly turn to a variety of authoritarian tactics to keep themselves in power at any cost, as did Chiluba?

Civilian militaries

African militaries emerged from the shadows during the 1950s to become some of the most important institutions in politics and society. The main way they achieved power was the coup d'état: the sudden and illegal overthrow of an existing government by a portion of the state's armed forced. By the end of the 1960s, more than two dozen successful coups had ushered in a period that soon left more than 50% of all African countries governed by military regimes. Even in cases where they led

their troops back to the barracks after turning over power to elected civilian regimes, military leaders maintained—and often enhanced—their newfound levels of political influence. Once they enjoyed the fruits of power, these so-called leaders in khaki were prone to return to presidential mansions in subsequent coups, leading foreign observers to characterize African militaries as the primary forces for change throughout the continent.

Most African countries have experienced at least one attempted or successful military coup, and several have experienced two or more. The record for the greatest number (six) is jointly held by Benin, Burkina Faso and Nigeria. Only six African countries—Botswana, Djibouti, Cape Verde, Eritrea, Namibia and South Africa—have never faced armed challenges from their military, police or other security personnel. Nonetheless, the common assumption in Africa is that civilian-dominated systems constitute the norm. Even military leaders intent on staying in power are

forced to offer, at minimum, rhetorical support for an eventual "return" to civilian rule, usually accompanied by some sort of time-table. The notion of "demilitarization," sometimes referred to as promoting the "civilianization" of military regimes, became increasingly important in the post-1989 era as policymakers and citizen movements sought firmer transitions to democracy.

In contrast to the 1960s, when military coups reached their peak, the second half of the 1980s and the 1990s have witnessed a sharp decline in military intervention. This trend may suggest a growing strength among democratic transitions in the post-cold-war era. At the same time, it is important to note that the transition to civilian governments during the 1950s ultimately stalled, only to be followed by an explosion of coups that made the 1960s the "decade of the military." Today's civilian leaders thus view the potential reemergence of African militaries—the so-called khaki contagion—as a threat to the democratization process throughout Africa.

Article 4

New Internationalist, August 2000

Africa united: Not hopeless, not helpless.

Chris Brazier champions the Pan-African alternative

Boys with guns. A rebel army which cuts off people's limbs. A civil war only kept under control by heroic white soldiers (Sierra Leone). Aggressive ex-combatants seizing farms. White farmers murdered. A wild-eyed leader who will do anything to hold on to power (Zimbabwe). Devastating floods. People stranded and starving. Western helicopters rushing to the rescue (Mozambique).

These images come from the last few months of media coverage of Africa. They are important stories which deserve our attention and concern. And of course the media thrive on bad news. But negative news stories about our own countries will be balanced by culture, sport, political intrigue and humour. They also appear in the context of ordinary life as we experience it—a life in which we take our children to school,

do our shopping, and walk in the park; a life generally free from danger and violence.

Right across Africa, the vast majority of people also do these things every day but you would never know it from the reporting: news items full of violence and disaster are the only stories told. Small wonder that the average Westerner might feel inclined to give up on the continent.

The Sierra Leone story no more represents the entire African continent today than the Mandela story did in 1994

Indeed sometimes we are even told to do so. On the cover of *The Economist* in May there appeared a photo of a man with a rocket-launcher over his shoulder. He fills the whole outline of Africa; the issue title is 'The hopeless continent'. With one stark phrase, Africans, from diligent farmers in the Sahel to wise elders in the Rift Valley, from *fellahin* in Egypt to bankers in Botswana, are summarily dismissed from the ranks of our common humanity. Africa is reduced to one single, terrible reality: violence.

To understand the outrage such dismissiveness provokes in Africa itself you should perhaps imagine what it would be like to have a copy of *African Agenda* drop through your letterbox with a picture of a violent British soccer fan superimposed on an outline of Europe, and the title 'The hooligan continent'. Except that, of course, *African Agenda,* good magazine though it may be, could never be thought to have the global establishment behind it and does not carry *The Economist*'s dead weight of power.

When the *Economist* issue emerged I was subscribing to an e-mail conference called 'African Realities' organized by the UN Economic Commission on Africa. This involved contributions from people all over the world interested in debating the state of Africa from economics to education, democracy to peace. But these more sober considerations were forgotten for a fortnight as people expressed their outrage at the grotesque misrepresentation. Eventually

a collective protest letter was composed and mailed to the magazine.

'Your articles,' it said, 'reflect the tendency for one sensational story to "epitomize" the continent, as you note Sierra Leone does today. This is precisely what prevents the policy-makers and the public from understanding the diversity of a continent more than three times the size of Europe. The "Sierra Leone" story no more represents the entire African continent today than the "Mandela" story did in 1994.

'It is important to provide readers with a balanced view of both African success stories and crises. Reinforcing stereotypes of "backwardness" and "hopelessness" is not conducive to finding solutions to any of Africa's problems. It is also not an honest portrayal of the complex realities.'

It is not an honest portrayal. But it certainly reflects the Western world's dominant attitude to Africa.

It is true that the situation is bleak, even to those of us who love Africa. Development there has conspicuously failed. Over the two decades that I have worked for the *New Internationalist* if there has been one consistently encouraging global trend it has been the decline in child mortality and rise in life expectancy right across the developing world. We have become accustomed to immunization and generally higher standards of public health and nutrition delivering on the most fundamental level: giving people more years of life.

And that is broadly still the case across the developing world—except in Africa south of the Sahara. Here, average life expectancy increased from 40 years in 1960 to 52 in 1990. But it has now gone into reverse, currently standing at around 48, just as it did in 1980. The average sub-Saharan African now can expect to live 14 years less than someone in the next-poorest region, South Asia—and fully 30 years less than someone in the rich world. In Zimbabwe and Uganda, devastated by aids, life expectancy has sunk to below what it was when the 'development decades' began, in 1960.[1]

In economic terms the indicators have also been going into reverse. Gross national product is a thoroughly inadequate measure of human well-being. But it is the chosen yardstick of the World

Bank and the International Monetary Fund (IMF) and, by its lights, their own policies and programmes in Africa have demonstrably failed.

While every other region of the world has made steady progress on this front over the last two decades, the income per head for Africa as a whole is, at $665, lower than it was in 1980. Meanwhile average income in the rich world has shown stratospheric growth. The average Westerner in 1980 earned 15 times more than the average African; now they earn 50 times more.[2]

Africans looking at these figures could be forgiven for concluding that there has been a conspiracy at work to boost the wealth of the West at the expense of its former colonial subjects. These, after all, were the two decades in which African nations were forced by debt and desperation to submit to the unyielding economic orthodoxy of the World Bank and the IMF. They have followed the rules, more or less to the letter. By cutting public expenditure and government subsidies, opening up their country to transnational corporations, they have put their citizens through enormous pain, supposedly in the name of future gain. Such suffering has even passed into the language. In francophone West Africa, since the devaluation of the local currency, the popular term used to describe any person in difficulty is 'adjusted'.[3]

There may be no conspiracy as such but the effect is pretty much the same. Each IMF-inspired budget cut, each market liberalization, serves to turn the local economy into a more effective supplier of raw materials, of export crops and minerals—and indeed of debt interest payments—to the industrialized world.

The finesse would be almost admirable for its style were it not so morally repugnant. Direct colonial exploitation being now unfashionable, the West has evolved a way of forcing African countries to service its interests— *apparently of their own free will.* 'Look,' the visiting financiers say: 'the national flag flies, the President is there in his pomp; we are here by invitation. What's more, we are only here because we are trying to help.'

But finally the mirror has cracked. After four decades of national independence, African governments are being forced by the depth and scale of the continent's crisis to accept that this cannot go on. The dream that independent nation-states could aspire, via heavy doses of education and industrialization, to affluence and influence is in tatters. Nation-states in Africa are barely worthy of the term 'independent'; they now have no room for manoeuvre at all. Sad to say, in all too many cases, the only room for manoeuvre many of its leaders have wished for has involved use of a torture cell and a Swiss bank account.

As a result, in a phenomenon unlooked for even as recently as 1990, another African dream has been revived: that of Pan-African unity. The ideas of Pan-Africanism have been so discounted, so marginalized since the 1960s that few people in the West are aware of them and of the rich heritage that lies behind them.

Born of the yearning of exiled slaves for their ancestral land, Pan-Africanism had by the dawn of the twentieth century become a nascent movement resisting the colonial dismemberment of the continent (for the early history of Pan-Africanism see article here). By the 1950s, in the hands of Kwame Nkrumah, it had become an alternative path to freedom.

When Nkrumah led Ghana (the former Gold Coast) to independence from Britain in 1957, he inspired Africans resisting colonialism and seeking freedom all over the continent. His firm conviction, however, was that national independence was not enough and he spent much of his energy pursuing the possibility of a united Africa.

As another great leader, Julius Nyerere, recalled, full of regret in the last decade of his life for the missed opportunity of a united Africa: 'Kwame Nkrumah was the great crusader for African unity. He wanted the Accra summit of 1965 to establish a Union Government for the whole of independent Africa. But we failed. The minor reason is that Kwame, like all great believers, underestimated the degree of suspicion and animosity which his crusading passion had created among a substantial number of his fellow heads of state. The major reason was linked to the first: already

too many of us had a vested interest in keeping Africa divided ...'[4]

The idea of a united Africa seemed to have been consigned to the past. But in the 1990s it was born again

---

Nkrumah was toppled by a coup in 1966 and lived thereafter in exile in Guinea until his death cancer in 1972; his Pan-African ambitions seemed lost with him. During the 1970s and 1980s the influence and coherence of the Pan-African movement waned. The Organization of African Unity (OAU) became a painfully ineffective regional body, too often presided over by dictators who made a mockery of paper concern for human rights and social justice. National leaders ferociously defended the colonial borders they had inherited—there was a fear that if once these were broken open all hell might let loose. The idea of a united Africa seemed to have been consigned to the past.

Yet in the 1990s the notion of Pan-African union was born again. The liberation of South Africa helped it back to life. The failure to overcome the apartheid state had been one of the OAU's worst failures. But when freedom finally came, it unlocked new possibilities—for the first time the unity of the continent from Cape Town to Cairo could at least be conceived.

The 'sanctity' of the colonial borders has now been breached too, by Eritrea's long-sought independence from Ethiopia in 1993—though the OAU continues to resist the plausible case for another such breach in Somaliland, which has formed its own coherent but utterly unrecognized government in a breakaway from the still-chaotic Somalia.

The sheer absurdity of the existing borders has become ever more evident. In many parts of the continent these borders are plainly and quite rightly ig-

nored, as people trade the way they have for centuries, within and between ethnic groupings, irrespective of the lines on the colonizers' map that have divided them. From one point of view these traders are 'smugglers'; from another they are 'Pan-African entrepreneurs'.[5] African leaders, too, have become more conscious than ever before that their own nation-states are unsustainable—at least within the current world economic and political arrangements. Yes, they still have their ten-gun salutes and their military parades, their presidential palaces and their motorcades. But the more intelligent among them have realized that their power to change their people's circumstances is severely circumscribed, and that if they want to make a difference they will have no alternative but to swim in a bigger pool.

The main influence propelling Africans towards greater economic and political unity, however, is globalization. Faced with a trading system which insists on transnational capital having *carte blanche,* Africans are increasingly recognizing that they will have to stand together if they are to defend (or advance) their own interests. As individual nation-states within artificial borders they can too easily be picked off or played against each other by the corporations and the global accountants in a post-colonial version of divide-and-rule.

Both the threat and the example of the European Union have given the idea of an African Union new impetus—and an African bloc incorporating the economic weight of both South Africa and the oil states of the Maghreb would have infinitely more clout than even the most populous nation, Nigeria, let alone minnows like Togo or Cape Verde. There is little likelihood, for example, of a permanent seat on the UN Security Council being granted to any single African country—but an African Union representing a tenth of the world's people could hardly be denied it.

At the OAU summit in Abuja, Nigeria, in 1991, a treaty was signed establishing an African Economic Community and holding out the prospect of 'Africawide monetary union' and a continental Parliament by the year 2025. But the long timetable led to understandable suspicion that this was mere rhetoric. As the

Pan-African scholar Julius O Ihonvbere wrote in 1994: 'Given that none of the current leaders will be in office by 2025, the current decision to finalize arrangements for a regional community in 34 years appears to be an attempt to buy time and give the impression that something was being done as a response to the crisis.'[6]

The headlong onrush of globalization in the 1990s has, however, made it clear that this leisurely pace towards a united Africa is inadequate. Prompted by the Libyan leader, Muammar Qadhafi, the OAU held an extraordinary summit in Sirte, Libya, in September 1999, and committed itself to a fast-track process. The Sirte Declaration decided to establish an African Union, to 'ensure the speedy establishment of . . . the African Central Bank, the African Monetary Union, the African Court of Justice and, in particular, the Pan-African Parliament. We aim to establish that Parliament by the year 2000.'

This deadline looks to be too ambitious but it signals the new sense of urgency. As we go to press the draft treaty for an African union—which would completely replace the OAU—has been approved by an extra-ordinary ministerial council and will be put to a summit meeting in Lomé in July. Such radical moves toward international unity only ever tend to come to fruition after a cataclysm, just as painful memories of the Second World War provided the motivating force for both the United Nations and the European Union. But make no mistake: Africa has undergone a disaster equivalent in scale to a world war over the last two decades, and unity may well be the eventual result here too.

Of course there will be all kinds of obstacles in the road over the next few years. The Francophone countries, for instance, have historically been the least keen on the notion of Pan-African union. But even that negative consensus, based on a special relationship with Paris and a direct link to the French franc, has been undermined in the last few years by another example of continental unity—when France entered the European single currency it was unable to take its former African colonies' currencies along for the ride.

> # There is a chance that Pan-African institutions could help unlock some of the continent's more intractable problems

Ironically one of the main stumbling blocks may be a development which in itself underlines the slow death of the African nation-state: the move towards regional unity. The most notable example of this is, like Pan-Africanism, a resurrection of an old idea: Tanzania, Kenya and Uganda have agreed to form an East African Union like that first planned by Nyerere, Kenyatta and Obote in the early 1960s; an East African passport is envisaged, together with eventual expansion to include Rwanda and Burundi. This makes a great deal of sense but may detract from the momentum towards a wider union.

Even if it eventually comes about, a United States of Africa would not, needless to say, be a panacea for all the continent's ills. If it were to work, power would have not only to be handed upwards to a federal administration but also transferred downwards to local areas and communities, enhancing genuine participation and democracy. Realizing that greater unity carries with it the nightmare possibility of a bigger stage for the kind of despots with which too many African nations have been blighted, the OAU last year established a new rule which will from now on exclude from its table and its consultations any leader who has come to power by military coup. A simple rule—but one which betokens a dramatic sea change since the 1980s when most of the continent's leaders owed their position to the gun.

There is a chance that Pan-African institutions and sensibilities could help unlock some of the continent's more in-

tractable problems. It is at least arguable that there would be less scope for ethnic conflict or national rivalry within an African Union than at present—countries are often chronically destabilized in part by a colonial border which divides an ethnic group in two or three. The current peace process in Burundi—a painstaking programme overseen first by Nyerere and now by Mandela—is in itself an encouraging example of a Pan-African initiative aimed at forestalling another genocide (see article). On the AIDS front, meanwhile, it is much easier to imagine a coherent programme of action emerging from a federal government than from national leaders, too many of whom have adopted an ostrich mentality (see article).

This may be over-optimistic. But we would rather err on the side of hope than of despair. And while *The Economist* and a hundred other leader-writers in the West would have us believe that Foday Sankoh's atrocities in Sierra Leone sum up the continent, we would rather focus on the resilience and resourcefulness of the millions of Africans who have never held a gun. This silent majority could shake the world if it spoke with a single voice.

In one tiny, though fascinating, way it already has. The BBC World Service recently conducted its own poll asking people from the continent who was the greatest African of the twentieth century. The result, they thought, would be a foregone conclusion: yet more eulogies to Nelson Mandela were planned. Instead they were shocked to find that Kwame Nkrumah won by a mile, an index of the rising stock of the Pan-Africanism he embodied. Nkrumah did not live to see it, but 'Africa United' may well be an idea whose time has finally come.

Notes

1. UNICEF State of the World's Children 1982, 1992, 1997 and 2000.
2. World Bank World Development Report 1982; UNICEF State of the World's Children 2000.
3. Rabia Abdelkrim-Chikh, 'African Realities' electronic digest, 2000.
4. Speech in Accra on the 40th anniversary of Ghana's independence, 6 March 1997.
5. I am indebted for this thought to Tajudeen Abdul-Raheem.
6. Keynote address to The All-African Students' Conference, University of Guelph, Canada, 27 May 1994.

Making the Connection: Africa and the Internet

"The development of the Internet is at a critical point in Africa. Web-based services could help accelerate the continent's economic growth and aid poverty alleviation, but these tools place large demands on an underlying infrastructure that is currently incapable of servicing them."

MIKE JENSEN

MIKE JENSEN *is an independent consultant based in Port St. Johns, South Africa who has advised development agencies on information and communication technologies in more than 35 African countries. He cofounded Canada's national Internet service provider for nongovernmental organizations in 1986 and was a member of the African Conference of Ministers working group that developed the African Information Society Initiative in 1996.*

Amid talk of the growing digital divide between rich and poor countries, Africa has shown encouraging signs that it is rapidly adopting the Internet and making innovative use of the technology. Nevertheless, the continent is still well behind other developing regions of the world in taking advantage of the information and communication revolution. The main reasons for this are the limited and expensive telecommunication infrastructure, small markets, and lack of skills and awareness.

ACCESS TO THE NET

At the end of 1996, just 11 of Africa's 54 countries had local Internet access, but by February 2000 all of the continent's countries had access in the capital cities. Excluding South Africa, the number of computers permanently connected to the Internet in Africa exceeded 10,000 early in 1999. By January 2000, the total had increased to about 25,000, which means Africa, with an estimated population of 780 million people,

has about as many Internet-connected computers (hosts) as Latvia, which only has a population of 2.5 million.

Measuring the actual number of Internet users is difficult, but figures for the number of dial-up accounts supplied by Internet service providers (ISPs) show that Africa has more than 500,000 subscribers. Each computer with an Internet or e-mail connection supports an average of three users, a recent study by the UN Economic Commission for Africa (ECA) has found. This puts current estimates of the number of African Internet users at somewhere around 1.5 million. Most are in South Africa (approximately 1 million), leaving only about 500,000 among the remaining 734 million people on the continent. This works out to about 1 Internet user for every 1,500 people, compared to a global average of about 1 user for every 38 people, and a North American and European average of about 1 in 4. No studies of the number of rural versus urban users have been conducted in Africa, but undoubtedly users in cities and towns vastly outnumber those in rural regions.[1]

Africa now has about 26 countries with 1,000 or more dial-up subscribers, but only about 9 countries with 5,000 or more: Egypt, Morocco, Kenya, Ghana, Mozambique, South Africa, Tunisia, Uganda, and Zimbabwe. Clearly countries such as those in North Africa and southern Africa have more highly developed economies and better infrastructures, which would naturally result in larger populations of Internet users. Most of these countries were also among the first on the continent to obtain Internet access, and so have had the most time to develop the market.

The average cost of using a local dial-up Internet account for 5 hours a month in Africa is $60.

The average cost of using a local dial-up Internet account for five hours a month in an African country is about $60 (usage fees and telephone time included, but not telephone line rental). According to the Organization for Economic Cooperation and Development, 20 hours of Internet access in the United States costs $29 a month, including telephone charges. Although monthly European costs are higher ($74 in Germany, $52 in France, $65 in Britain, and $53 in Italy, for example), these costs are for four times the amount of access, and all these Western countries have per capita incomes at least ten times greater than the African average. Moreover, ISP charges in Africa vary greatly—between $10 and $100 a month, largely reflecting the different levels of the markets' maturity, the varying tariff policies of the public telecommunication operators (PTOs), and the different national policies on access to international telecommunications bandwidth.

Most African capitals—which is where Internet access on the continent has been largely confined—now have more than one ISP; by early 1999 over 300 public ISPs had sprung up across the continent. Seven countries had 10 or more ISPs—Egypt, Kenya, Morocco, Nigeria, South Africa, Tanzania, and Zimbabwe—while 20 countries had only one ISP. Although Ethiopia and Mauritius are the only countries in which private companies are barred by the monopoly telecom operator from reselling Internet services, single-ISP service remains the rule in other countries, predominantly in the Sahel subregion, where markets are small.

In some countries the PTOs provide local-call Internet access facilities for ISPs across the entire country by establishing a special area code for Internet access that is charged as a local call. This allows Internet providers to immediately roll out a network with national coverage. Although it massively reduces costs for those in remote areas, only 15 African countries have adopted this strategy (Benin, Burkina Faso, Cape Verde Islands, Chad, Ethiopia, Gabon, Malawi, Mali, Mauritania, Mauritius, Morocco, Senegal, Togo, Tunisia, and Zimbabwe).

In response to the high cost of full Internet-based services and slow access speeds, lower cost e-mail–only services have been launched by many ISPs. Similarly, because of the relatively high cost of local electronic mailbox services from Af-

rican ISPs, a large proportion of African e-mail users use free web-based services such as Hotmail, Yahoo!, or Excite, most of which are based in the United States. E-mail–only and free web-based services can be more costly and cumbersome than standard e-mail software, however, since extra on-line time is needed to maintain the connection to the remote site. These services do provide the added advantages of anonymity and greater perceived stability than a local ISP, which may not be operating the following year.

Interest is also growing in using kiosks (small, stand-alone Internet access units found in public places), cybercafés, and other forms of public Internet access, such as adding computers to community phone shops (which provide voice phone services for the public), schools, police stations, and clinics that can share the cost of equipment and access among a larger number of users. Many existing phone shops are now adding Internet access to their services, even in remote towns where a call to the nearest dial-up access point is long distance. In addition, a growing number of hotels and business centers provide a PC with Internet access.

WHO USES THE INTERNET—AND WHAT FOR?

In a recent survey carried out by the UN Economic Commission for Africa (ECA), the greatest number of users belongs to nongovernmental organizations, private companies, and universities. Most user were male: 86 percent in Ethiopia, 83 percent in Senegal, and 64 percent in Zambia. The majority of users were well educated: 87 percent in Zambia and 98 percent in Ethiopia had university degrees. A recent South African survey of the Internet found similar results: the average user was male, 26 to 30 years old, spoke English, was high-school or university educated, and earned between $24,000 and $45,000 per year working in the computer industry (all of which indicates that most South African users are white).

Evidence gathered by the ECA suggests that the average level of Internet use in Africa is generally one incoming and one outgoing e-mail daily, averaging 3 to 4 pages, in communications that are most often with people outside the continent. Surveys indicate that about 25 percent of the e-mail has replaced faxes, while 10 percent has replaced phone calls; the other 65 percent are communications that would not have been made in the absence of an e-mail system. Thus, except for e-mail, the web is still a relatively underutilized resource, although 40 percent of Zambian users questioned had conducted literature searches on the web.

Universities were initially at the vanguard of Internet developments in Africa, and most provide e-mail services, yet in early 1999 only about 20 countries had universities with full Internet connectivity. Because of the limited resources and high costs of providing computer facilities and bandwidth, full Internet access at the universities where it exists is usually restricted to staff. Postgraduate students can often obtain access, but the general student population usually cannot.

The African web space is expanding rapidly, and almost all countries have some form of local or internationally hosted web server, unofficially or officially representing the country with varying degrees of comprehensiveness. But generally few institutions of any kind are using the web to deliver significant quantities of information. While progressively more organizations have web sites with basic descriptive and contact information, many are hosted by international development agency sites, and few use the web for their activities. This is partly explained by the small number of local people who have access to the Internet (and thus the relative unimportance of a web presence to the institution), the limited skills available for digitizing and coding pages, and the high costs of local web-hosting services.[2]

Although a few notable official government web sites exist, such as those of Angola, Egypt, Gabon, Mauritius, Morocco, Mozambique, Senegal, Togo, Tunisia, and Zambia, no discernible government use of the Internet for administrative purposes has been seen. The exception perhaps is in the area of public relations; the Zambian State House, for example, established a press release web site shortly after the local opposition paper, *The Post,* established its own web site. Use of the web by opposition groups is almost nonexistent outside of South Africa, largely due to the lack of penetration of the Internet among their potential constituencies.

Acquiring technology is still a dream for the majority of Africans who do not live in the capital cities and are not part of the elite.

Web presence is higher in sectors involved in tourism and foreign investment, which often have more mature sites aimed at developing an international market presence. While most ministries and national research centers may have access to electronic mail, few have web sites (reflecting the limited resources of the public sector, the ECA survey found that government employees made up 1 percent of users in Ethiopia and 6 percent in Zambia). Regional intergovernmental agencies have fared better; organizations such as the African Development Bank and the Southern Africa Development Conference (http://www.sadc.int) have built web sites providing substantial information on their activities and member states.

The news media are also relatively well represented on the web. The African studies department of Columbia University in New York has identified over 120 African newspapers and news magazines available on the Internet. Those countries best represented are again those with more advanced Internet sectors: Egypt, Ghana, Ivory Coast, Kenya, Senegal, South Africa, Tanzania, Zambia, and Zimbabwe. Also of note are the efforts to host daily newspapers by the ISP AfricaOnline, which has offices in six countries. Two major continentwide African news agencies extensively use electronic media: Inter Press Service and the Panafrican News Agency[3]

Business use of the web in Africa has increased rapidly over the last 18 months, although again mainly in tourism promotion rather than any inward business from the rest of the world. This is likely to change as teleservices draw more attention (in Togo, the world's first Internet-based call center is being set up to provide globally competitive telephone support services for companies with customers in North America). Craft makers around Africa are beginning to sell their wares through the web, usually hosted internationally at sites such as through Buy Afrika (http://www.buyafrica.com). In West Africa a women's fishing cooperative has set up a web site that enables its 7,350 members to promote their produce, monitor export markets, and negotiate prices with buyers overseas.

The Internet is also beginning to play a role in health care in Africa. Mozambique and Namibia are part of a growing number of countries where telemedicine is being used to transmit x-ray images and other graphical data through e-mail to experts at major hospitals. In Dakar, medical students are being taught by a team of expert doctors in Brussels using video linkups. Electronic distance education is growing in other areas also. In 24 university campuses across Africa, students are being linked to classrooms and libraries worldwide through satellite and will soon be able to obtain degrees in computer science, computer engineering, and electrical engineering through the African Virtual University project of the World Bank (http://www.avu.org).

BUILDING THE INFRASTRUCTURE

The communications and information infrastructure has improved dramatically in Africa in the past five years. The Internet, satellite television, and cellular phones are widespread. But acquiring this technology is still a dream for the majority of Africans who do not live in the capital cities and are not part of the elite. Access to telephones on the continent is still restricted—only 14 million lines have been installed, fewer than the number of telephones in Manhattan or Tokyo. Most of those lines are concentrated in urban areas, but over 70 percent of Africa's population is rural. Likewise, cellular phone coverage is usually confined to the capitals and secondary cities. And, as was noted, since ISPs are located primarily in the

HARDWARE AND SOFTWARE

MOST RECENT estimates of the number of PCs in Africa put the average at about 3 per 1,000 people in 1996, although some studies put the average at less than 1 per 1,000. Some of the wealthier countries such as Botswana, Mauritius, and South Africa have significantly higher levels of penetration, with at least 5 per 1,000 and perhaps up to 20 per 1,000 (but as many as 20 people may share a single computer).

Almost all the PC equipment uses Intel or Intel-compatible processors (the exception is the publishing industry, which generally uses Apple Macintosh PCs). Many of these non-Apple PCs are older machines powered by 386 and 486 microprocessors. Microsoft Windows is the dominant operating system, but large numbers of DOS-based systems are still in use. Poor maintenance and insufficient skills to diagnose system problems and to swap parts have led to many out-of-commission machines that could easily be reactivated.

Underutilization of existing computer resources is also common, the result of the preponderance of many standalone PCs in the same office unconnected to local area networks (LANS). Often an office may have many machines, but only one with a modem connecting to the Internet. This usually means competition for the machine and a shared e-mail account.

M. J.

capital cities, an Internet dial-up call for most of the (predominantly rural) public is long distance.

Still, the rate of expansion and modernization of fixed telecommunication networks has increased, and the number of main lines is growing at about 10 percent annually across the Africa. Much of the growth is in the urban areas, where the overall teledensity is still about 1 per 200 inhabitants (continentwide the figure is 0.52 per 100 in 1996, the latest year for which data exists). Between 1990 and 1995, teledensity actually decreased in Liberia, Ghana, Republic of Congo, Sudan, Sierra Leone, and Guinea. Furthermore, 50 percent of the available lines are concentrated in the capital cities. In some countries, notably Eritrea, Guinea-Bissau, Central African Republic, Sierra Leone, Burundi, and Chad, the International Telecommunication Union (ITU) has found that between 80 and 95 percent of the lines are in the main cities.

A considerable degree of variability can be found in the existing telephone networks of various countries. Some governments have made telecommunications a priority and are installing digital switches with fiber optic intercity backbones and the newest cellular and mobile technology. Among the world's most sophisticated national networks are Botswana and Rwanda, where 100 percent of the main lines are digital, compared with 49.5 percent in the United States. At the other end of the scale, large parts of the network in countries such as Madagascar and Uganda are old analog systems with poor national links among urban centers. Surprisingly, the proportion of digital lines in sub-Saharan Africa in 1996 was 69 percent—close to the world average of 79 percent.

Even if telecom infrastructure is beginning to spread, a much smaller proportion of the population can actually afford a private telephone. The cost of renting a connection averaged almost 20 percent of the 1995 GDP per capita. The average world cost is 9 percent; in high-income countries the cost is only 1 percent. Despite this, the number of public telephones is still much lower in Africa than elsewhere—about 1 for every 17,000 people (compared with a world average of 1 for 600 and a high-income-country average of 1 for 200). Because progressively more operators are now passing the maintenance of public telephones to the private sector, a rapid growth of phone shops has occurred in some countries; Senegal, for example, now has more than 10,000 commercially run public phone points. While most of these are in urban areas, a growing number are being established in more remote locations, especially with the PTO Sonatel's aggressive rollout of backbone infrastructure, which now links 2,000 villages and towns by fiber optic cable.

A large variation exists among countries in the costs of installation, line rental, and call tariffs. In 1996 the average business connection in Africa cost $112 to install, $6 a month to rent, and $0.11 per three-minute local call. But installation charges exceeded $200 in some countries (Benin, Mauritania, Nigeria, and Togo), line rentals ranged from $.80 to $20 a month, and call charges varied by a factor of almost 10—from $.60 an hour to over $5 an hour. Local-call tariffs in some countries have increased even further, to more than $8 an hour (as in Uganda, Gabon, and Chad).

Mobile cellular telephony has experienced rapid growth in Africa, expanding from a presence in only 6 countries 9 years ago to about 78 networks in 42 countries serving over 400,000 customers (excluding the 5 million in South Africa). Operators provide access mainly in the capital cities but also in some secondary towns and along major truck routes. A majority of the systems in use are now based on a digital standard, although international roaming agreements are virtually nonexistent and data communication facilities are often not available except on the older analog systems.

NEW CONNECTIONS

Communications ministers from over 40 African countries have provided high-level endorsement for telecommunications development policies, encapsulated in the African Connection (www.doc.org.za/docs/misc/africon.html), their common vision document published in 1998. Aimed at supporting the development of the underlying infrastructure required by the African Information Society Initiative (*AISI*), the goal is to lay 50 million telephone lines in Africa over the next 5 years. The project has been officially adopted by the Pan African Telecommunications Union (PATU).

The first concrete project of the African Connection was to hold a promotional and connectivity-awareness-raising car rally in which South African Minister of Telecommunications

Jay Naidoo drove from the northernmost tip of the continent in Tunisia to its southernmost point in South Africa. Accompanied by 40 journalists and a support crew, the rally passed through 11 countries and was escorted in each by the local minister of telecommunications (a diary of the trip and other information is available at www.africanconnection.org/rally/index.html).

The recent announcements of many international infrastructure-building initiatives also will substantially change the region's telecommunications with the rest of the world. One of the best-known projects is Columbia Technology's Africa ONE, which aims to put a fiber optic "necklace" around the continent. After some years of dormancy, the $1.6-billion project, originally led by AT&T, has been given the go-ahead and is expected to be completed in 2002.

Other satellite networks, such as East, Tachyon, SkyBridge, and Celestri promise multimedia voice and data communications, and an "Internet in the sky" using helium-supported stratospheric telecommunications platforms tethered above urban areas has been proposed. While some of these ideas are still some way off and the costs are unlikely to be within reach of the average African citizen until 2010, they will considerably reduce operating costs for ISPs wherever regulations allow. Various worldwide low-earth-orbit satellite networks have also been launched, or shortly will be, such as ICO, Globalstar, and Teledesic, which hold special promise for the subcontinent's widely dispersed population. These satellite networks will derive most of their income when they pass over developed countries, but developing regions of the world, including Africa, hope to take advantage of the satellites' orbit and plan to reduce tariffs to encourage consumer demand in these regions.

With the worldwide recognition of the importance of information and communication technologies (ICTS) in accelerating development, other recent development-assistance initiatives have improved the prospects for wider access to information and communication networks on the continent, especially in rural areas. In addition, to address the growing need for coordination and collaboration, donors and executing agencies involved in ICTs in Africa have agreed to establish an ongoing forum for information exchange on projects called the Partnership for Information and Communication Technologies in Africa (PICTA). Of the general projects identified, among the potentially most important include:

• The United States Agency for International Development Leland Initiative, which is helping develop Internet connectivity in 20 African countries in return for agreements to liberalize the market to third-party ISPs and to adopt policies that allow the unrestricted flow of information. New initiatives for Leland recently announced by Vice President Al Gore include a program for "1 million PCs for Africa, 1,000 schools connected and 100 universities connected." In June 1999, a new initiative to increase Internet access and use in developing countries was announced. Guatemala, Jamaica, Bulgaria, Egypt, Morocco, Ghana, Guinea, Uganda, South Africa, and Mozambique are the targeted developing countries. The United States is actively encouraging other interested countries to join this initiative, which is part of a broad American effort to foster the information industry worldwide. Through the initiative, these countries will collaborate with the United States government, the private sector, multilateral organizations, and nonprofits to use electronic commerce and the Internet as tools for economic development. Specific aims of the initiative include encouraging the deployment of Internet applications such as micro e-commerce (transactions that are generally less than one dollar), telemedicine, distance education, and improved access to government services.

• The World Bank's assistance to telecommunication and ICT development in approximately 25 countries in sub-Saharan Africa. Initiatives include the African Virtual University, Economic Toolkit and Workshops for Internet Connectivity in Africa, and the Global Connectivity for Africa Conference. The World Bank expects to be heavily involved in sector reforms and privatization over the next few years with a view to mobilizing private participation for public objectives, to help remove market imperfections, and, where necessary, to attract private investment. It will focus on the rural sector and on information strategies, building infrastructure, and applications.

• The ITU's program for Africa, which involves various rural, community telecenter, health, and satellite projects emanating from the Buenos Aires Action Plan.

• A number of UN agencies and UN-sponsored programs, such as the UN Special Initiative for Africa's Harnessing Information Technology for Development, a $11.5-million, five-year program supported by the various UN partners. UNESCO has launched the Creating Learning Networks for African Teachers project to help teacher-training colleges develop ICT literacy and use it in education and in connecting to the Internet. The UN Development Programs' Africa Bureau has agreed to a $6-million fund to improve Internet connectivity in Africa in the Internet Initiative for Africa project. The Development Program's Sustainable Development Network Program (SDNP) also has 10 operational nodes in Africa: Angola, Benin, Cameroon, Chad, Gabon, Malawi, Morocco, Mozambique, Togo, and Tunisia. National SDNP projects are funded for 2 to 3 years and are expected to provide seed money toward sustainability, either through sale of services or adoption within government budget.

• The Agence de la Francophonie and related international organizations, which are providing support for ICTs in Francophone countries, most of which are in Africa. Recently launched was the AFRiNET project, which provides web servers and related support at a ministerial level to Benin, Burkina Faso, Cameroon, Ivory Coast, Madagascar, Mali, Mauritania, Mauritius, and Senegal. In addition, the Banque internationale d'information sur les états francophones project is establishing web servers in Benin, Tunisia, Mauritius, and Morocco, where databases and information from other countries is hosted.

THE NET'S PROMISE

The development of the Internet is at a critical point in Africa. Web-based services could help accelerate the continent's economic growth and aid poverty alleviation, but these tools place large demands on an underlying infrastructure that is currently incapable of servicing them. The infrastructure is steadily improving, but not fast enough to accommodate the growth in demand for the multitude of services now available. It will require greater commitment by African leadership to open up the telecommunication sector to more competition to ensure that the potential of the Internet is fully exploited.

Notes

1. The proportions for other developing regions are 1 in 125 for Latin America and the Caribbean, 1 in 200 for Southeast Asia and the Pacific, 1 in 250 for East Asia, 1 in 500 for the Arab states, and 1 in 2,500 for South Asia.

2. Africa's French-speaking countries have a far higher profile on the web and greater institutional connectivity than the non-French-speaking countries. This is largely attributable to the strong assistance provided by the various Francophone support agencies, and the Canadian and French governments, which are concerned about the dominance of English on the Internet.

3. Radio remains the dominant mass medium in Africa, with ownership of radios far more common than for any other electronic device. In 1995 radio ownership was estimated by UNESCO at close to 18 per 100 inhabitants, compared to 3.5 televisions and 0.31 personal computers per 100. It should be noted, however, that large-scale sharing of information resources is an important feature of the African media landscape. Many people listen to one radio or watch one television at the same time (it is not uncommon to find most of a small village crowded around the only television set, often powered by a car battery or small generator). Similarly, readership of newspapers is often more than 10 people per paper.

Article 6

Harvard International Review, Winter 2001

PERSPECTIVES

An End to Africa's Wars: Rethinking International Intervention

MARINA OTTAWAY

MARINA OTTAWAY is co-director of the Democracy and Rule of Law Project at the Carnegie Endowment for International Peace.

From Eritrea to Angola, a large swath of Africa has been engulfed by war for several years. The situation is unlikely to improve any time soon, because the conflicts arise from the disintegration of postcolonial states and thus from the order that was imposed on Africa by outside states. Wars will continue to flare up until a new order emerges. Such an order could either be imposed and maintained with force by the international community—that is, industrialized countries and the United Nations—or it could be based on new territorial and political arrangements reflecting the balance of power among African forces.

No Winners

The international community has decided that it must help restore stability in Africa by promoting negotiations, providing peacekeepers to monitor the implementation of agreements, and shoring up and reconstructing crumbling states. This policy has been a failure: commitment of resources has not matched the rhetoric, and international intervention has not been sufficient to bring any African conflicts to an end. International intervention, however, has been sufficient to prevent conflicts from ending the way most conflicts do: through the victory of one side. The current policy of the international community does not help populations and does not even help the international community. The reputation of the United Nations is becoming seriously tarnished by its African failures, and there is much resentment among Africans towards the United States.

The major source of conflict in Africa at present is the political and economic decay of a growing number of postcolonial states. Political decay has created a power vacuum in many governments that have only nominal control over their territories and little power over means of coercion. Economic decay has worsened the situation because, in the absence of a viable legal-administrative structure, violence is the only way of securing access to resources—the major conflicts in Africa involve diamond-rich countries. Economic decay also provides the warring factions with an endless supply of fighters, including child-soldiers who see few other career prospects in war-torn nations. The lone exception to this scenario of decay-induced conflict is the war between Ethiopia and Eritrea, which stems from the two countries' ambition to build strong states; in other words, theirs is a classic war between states vying for power and economic advantage.

The Great Lakes region provides the most dramatic, but by no means the only, example of how decay breeds civil war, which can then expand into interstate war. The multiple, interlocked conflicts in the area stem from the implosion of the Democratic Republic of the Congo, formerly Zaire, after decades of mismanagement. With the government no longer controlling the country, border regions have become havens for both opposition movements and the armies of neighboring countries such as Uganda and Rwanda. This, in turn, has invited political and armed intervention from all neighbors in a tangle that has been dubbed Africa's first world war. A victorious warlord, Laurent Kabila, has been installed in Kinshasa as president and enjoys diplomatic recognition as the country's leader by virtue of being there; however, two armed opposition movements, the RCD (Congolese Rally for Democracy), which is itself divided into two antagonistic factions, and the MLC (Movement for the Liberation of the Congo) combine to wage war on the government and periodically on each other with the support of Uganda and Rwanda. Troops from these two countries operate in Congolese territory against the government. Other armed groups, including the indigenous Mai-Mai, the Rwandan Hutu Interahamwe, and the remnants of the pre-1994 Rwandan army, add to the complexity by simultaneously pursuing their own goals and those of Kabila.

Conflicts in Sierra Leone, Angola, Sudan, Rwanda, Burundi, and Somalia have also sprung from the decay plaguing the continent. Other countries, such as Nigeria, are highly vulnerable. Nigeria's return to civilian government in 1998 was a positive step, but not a guarantee that the country will succeed in avoiding further decay and possibly violent conflict. Even the future of the countries of southern Africa, until recently the most stable and promising, is threatened by a political crisis in Zimbabwe and by their staggering rates of HIV infection—around a quarter of the adult population—which is bound to affect their economies and most probably their politics with unpredictable consequences.

Lukewarm Interventions

The international community's response to the spreading conflict in Africa has lacked coherence, to a large extent because the fighting does not significantly threaten the security or economic interests of any major power. The international community has responded to conflict not because of any clear self-interest but instead for humanitarian reasons and a rather vague, general interest in keeping Africa from sinking into complete chaos and becoming a breeding ground for new diseases. Humanitarian interests and hazy predictions of future threats have not elicited strong and clear policy responses to Africa's predicament. Rather, they have led to a dangerous combination of the idealistic and thus ambitious goals rooted in humanitarian considerations and the scant resources, and lukewarm commitment associated with the absence of immediate, concrete interests on the part of most industrialized countries. Such a combination is a recipe for failed interventions. A scenario that is becoming typical in Africa is the signing, under pressure from the international community, of a peace agreement to which the warring factions are not seriously committed; the implementation of the agreement is therefore dependent on a UN presence which has rarely been sufficient to do the job.

Some of the interventions have been completely ineffectual, as in Sierra Leone, where peacekeepers have been unable to protect themselves from being kidnapped by the rebels, let alone fulfill their mandate. In other cases, the international community's approach has been not only ineffectual but morally outrageous, as in Rwanda, where the UN presence was reduced at the height of the genocide in 1994. Most major powers, including the United States, were unwilling to increase their symbolic commitment to the level necessary to protect the population. Finally, some international interventions aimed at ending conflict have simply made the situation worse, as in Angola, where the internationally-sponsored and monitored agreements have been used repeatedly by the rebels to rearm, reorganize, and eventually restart the fight.

The intervention in the Democratic Republic of the Congo at present also appears headed for futility or disaster—one can only hope for the former. The international community has supported negotiations and the resulting Lusaka agreement. This unrealistic pact is based on the assumptions that armed movements at war with each other can suddenly lay aside their differences, without any new developments having taken place on the ground; abide by a cease-fire agreement; and engage, together with representatives of civil society, in a national dialogue that will produce an agreement on a new political system in 45 days. The only concrete support the international community has provided for the Lusaka agreement so far is the deployment of a small number of observers with the pledge that 500 observers protected by 5,000 peacekeepers will be positioned in the country if the cease-fire is ever implemented. This is fewer than the number initially deployed in tiny Sierra Leone to support the Lome agreement; by September 2000, the United Nations was calling for an increase in the number of peacekeepers to 20,000, over three times the initial figure.

It is time to reassess the effectiveness of the international community's efforts to settle African conflicts and to rethink when and how interventions should take place, what the goal of intervention should be, and how intervention can best be managed. Only if the goals are realistic and the means are adequate can the international community have an impact on the conflicts in Africa.

Unlikely Conditions for Success

The purported goals of international intervention have matured during the last decade. In the "good old days" of the Cold War, it was enough to maintain the stability of pro-Western regimes and to deny access to the Soviet Union, and if these goals could be best attained by supporting a friendly dictator like south africa gave Sese Seko in Zaire, so be it. Fortunately, the international community has moved away from that position, but, as often happens, it has swung too far in the opposite direction: the goals now are to stop conflict immediately through negotiations, to restore democratic and accountable government—from bullets to ballots in one smooth transition—and to do so while preserving the territorial integrity of all post-colonial states within the boundaries established by the colonial powers.

Commendable goals indeed. Unfortunately, so far there is little evidence that they can be attained except under special circumstances. Namibia and Mozambique did indeed go from conflict to stability under international supervision, but success was based on an unusual combination of factors. In Namibia, the South African government simply gave up its fight to keep control of the territory, and the major opposition movement had no difficulty accepting an electoral process where it was certain to win by a very wide margin. Furthermore, the United Nations deployed over 8,000 military and civilian personnel to administer the transition, a large number for a country of one million people.

Mozambique was also blessed with special circumstances. The conflict was two-sided, and neither side had the resources to continue fighting: the opposition movement, Renamo, lost its outside support when South Africa gave up the attempt to preserve apartheid, and the government was highly dependent on the donor community, which had no intention of financing a war. By contrast, all active conflicts at present are multi-sided. Even in small Burundi there are at present 17 parties and two armed movements that need to sign on for any agreement to be implemented. Furthermore, in Angola, Sierra Leone, and the Democratic Republic of the Congo, the conflict is self-financed, supported on all sides by the sale of diamonds.

Since the present model only appears to work under special circumstances, what can the international community do elsewhere? Although theoretically it could impose the settlement it wants on any country, if it were willing to provide a presence comparable to that in Bosnia or Kosovo for an indefinite period of time, in practice this can happen only in exceptional cases. This is not because racist attitudes prevent the commitment, as many Africans have come to believe, but because the scale of the conflict, the size of the territories involved, and the logistical problems preclude such intervention in many countries. A very simplistic calculation, based on population size, suggests that an international presence in the Democratic Republic of the Congo comparable to that in Kosovo would require the deployment of some 900,000 military and civilian personnel. The figure should not be taken literally but is a sobering reminder of what robust intervention means in large, messy countries.

Selective Intervention

The key to more effective policy is to realign goals and commitment. This means increasing commitment in those cases where it is warranted and where it could be effective, and settling for more modest goals in the other, more numerous cases. When the international community opts for the immediate cessation of conflict, the preservation of the existing states, and their reconstruction as democratic entities, it must provide real rather than symbolic resources, and it must be prepared to sustain the commitment for a long period.

In all other cases, it would be more helpful, or at least less harmful, if the international community allowed conflicts to reach a decisive turning point before becoming involved, even if this implied that some post-colonial states might not survive.

At present, there is only one conflict in Africa where the international community should increase its commitment to fit presently stated goals, and that is in Sierra Leone. The present level of commitment has proven vastly insufficient, thus the choice is to increase it or to pull out altogether. Pulling out of Dierra Leone at this point would destroy once and for all the credibility of the United Nations in Africa, while making it impossible to get support for any kind of international intervention in the future. The failure in Somalia is still casting a long shadow, and another failure would be the final blow.

On the other hand, the small size of Sierra Leone makes it conceivable to provide sufficient peacekeepers and civilian personnel to end the conflict and to reconstruct the country. While it is proving difficult for the United Nations to get member states to commit sufficient troops to Sierra Leone, success is not impossible as it would be, for example, in the Congo. Finally, Sierra Leone would provide a manageable test case for the effectiveness of the international community's prescriptions for Africa. Does the international community know how to put an end to years of chaos without using undue force and hurting civilians? Can it bring the culprits to justice? Can it demobilize the combatants? Can it build the small, efficient, professional army it believes suitable for African countries? Can it develop a modern police force, an honest civil service, and an apolitical judiciary in a reasonable span of time? If it cannot be done in Sierra Leone, there is no point pretending it can be done elsewhere.

At the opposite extreme are the conflicts from which the international community should step back altogether until something clearly changes on the ground. Sudan is the prime example here. It has become obvious over the years that none of the parties in that war are ready for compromise and that negotiations are simply a game, an attempt by each participant to bamboozle the international community into believing in their good will and to put the blame on the other side. There is nothing to be gained by continuing this process. Stopping it will not bring the conflict to an end any faster, but it will at least send a signal to groups in other countries that the international community is not willing to participate in a game of perpetual negotiations.

Finally, there are cases, such as the Congo, where it is too early for the international community to pull back completely, but where massive intervention it neither warranted nor possible. If groups are still engaged in talks and outsiders can play a useful role, there is no reason not to continue—talk is cheap. But the international community must also make clear to all sides the limits of its willingness to engage. combatants needs to be told clearly that if he does not want to abide by the Lusaka agreement, he cannot count on the rest of the world to save his country from disintegration if the fortunes of war turn against him. If rebel movements have no interest in compromise, they must risk

defeat. The international community must clarify that is neither wants to, nor can, hold together a country whose leaders only want war and that it is up to them to make the choice. Even if the international community remains involved in the diplomatic effort to end the fighting, it must stop pushing for ideal frameworks and quick solutions, because they cannot work. The participants in the civil war in the Congo will never agree on a democratic political system in 45 days.

African conflicts will eventually come to an end, as conflicts always do. The ex-

ample of Somalia suggests that, left to their own devices, and without the hope of getting more resources from the international community, or protection in the form of a cease-fire when the going gets too tough, the warring factions will find their own solutions. They will not be ideal solutions based on territorial integrity for all countries and democracy in our lifetime. However, it is time that the international community stepped back, lest in trying to promote ideal solutions without providing even remotely sufficient resources, it prolongs conflict in Africa.

Article 7   *Foreign Affairs,* July/August 2000

Ending Africa's Wars

John Stremlau

COLD WAR, HOT WARS

FOLLOWING LAST YEAR'S military interventions in defense of human rights in Kosovo and East Timor, Western leaders proclaimed a new determination to stand up to similar abuses whenever they occur. On one continent, however, warfare still rages unchecked, and far too little is being done about it. Renewed clashes in Sierra Leone and on the Ethiopian-Eritrean border are two recent examples of deadly African conflicts that have killed and displaced millions of people. Yet despite occasional bursts of aid and attention, the United States and Europe have remained largely disengaged. The reasons for their lack of involvement in conflict prevention and peacekeeping there are fairly obvious. War in Africa seems to pose no clear and present danger to U.S. interests. Furthermore, most African conflicts are fought within, not between, states. The international norms, institutions, and political will to intervene in such hard-to-solve conflicts remain inadequate. So do Washington's defense doctrine, bureaucracy, and budgets, all of which are still dedicated to preventing or settling traditional conflicts between states.

Yet those who argue that Washington and its allies should become more involved in solving Africa's problems make a powerful case. Africa is a vast continent of 700 million people with abundant natural resources and deep historical and cultural ties to the United States. It is simply too big and too important to be neglected. The question should be not whether, but rather how, to intervene there.

Of course, preventing conflict in Africa is primarily a task for Africans. But the 1990s showed that outside help is needed. The nice-sounding nostrum of "African solutions for African problems" became an excuse for neglect, until the images of human suffering in Africa became impossible for the West to ignore—leaving humanitarian relief as the only real option.

There are alternatives, however. Preventing wars, rather than fighting them, has always appealed to American strategists, so long as no vital national interests are compromised. Washington's greatest foreign policy success—winning the Cold War peacefully through military deterrence and the building of a strong coalition of democracies—vindicated the strategy of containing conflicts before they erupt. That strategy should now be adapted for and applied to Africa, where most wars result from bad governance. Weak, authoritarian African governments lack the institutional capacity to manage factional struggles. They exclude majority or minority groups from power and suffer from poverty and gross income inequality. All of these tensions throw off sparks that can start a war.

Any strategy for preventing conflict in Africa must therefore address these fundamental flaws. In deciding how to do that, and how to do it affordably, Washington should remember the Cold War lesson that working closely with democratic partners spreads the burden and gives policies greater legitimacy. Although Africa has few ready candidates for such a partnership, the region's most politically capable and economically advanced state—South Africa—does share key interests and values with the United States. Developing a strategic partnership with Pretoria must therefore become the foundation for conflict prevention and democratic development in Africa.

Such a strategy will require serious U.S. backing for South Africa's lead. Much more generous engagement by the American government, the business community, and nongovernmental organizations is needed to help develop the economic foundations of South Africa's new democracy. Only then will South Africa be able to effectively inspire and support democracy elsewhere on the continent. A real partnership based on support and mutual respect—the kind America once created with postwar Europe and Japan—could profit the region tremendously. And it would be in Washington's interests as well. For although the world may have changed since the Cold War, America's broad goals of preventing conflict and promoting a liberal international order remain the same.

Focusing on these goals in Africa will also help the United States overcome the lingering effects of two of the worst failures of President Clinton's foreign policy: the 1993 military debacle in Somalia and the failure to prevent the 1994 genocide in Rwanda. Both disasters had a profound impact on Washington. Although the American public and Congress would never tolerate a repeat of the Somalia intervention, unease persists about not having done more to prevent the massacres in Rwanda. Devising a new threshold for intervention, somewhere between the extremes of Somalia and Rwanda, is now necessary. But any new strategy will be easier to sell, both in Africa and in America, if it is seen as part of a broader strategy involving reliable regional partners.

TWO STEPS FORWARD, TWO STEPS BACK

War and poverty remain dominant realities in Africa. According to the State Department, last year Africa had more major conflicts than any other continent. Wars causing at least 1,000 battle deaths per year plague Angola, both Congos, Eritrea, Ethiopia, Rwanda, Somalia, and Sudan. Meanwhile, low-intensity conflicts simmer in Burundi, Chad, Djibouti, Senegal, Sierra Leone, and Uganda. And several other countries, notably Nigeria, the region's most populous, suffer from internal instability that could erupt into greater civil strife. "Preventing such wars," wrote U.N. Secretary-General Kofi Annan in an unusually frank May 1998 report, "is no longer a matter of defending states or protecting allies [but] a matter of defending humanity itself."

Approximately 8.1 million of the world's 22 million cross-border refugees live in Africa, with many more millions having been displaced within their own countries. An August 1999 global assessment of humanitarian emergencies by the National Intelligence Council paints a very grim picture of the continent, noting that the overall "demand" for humanitarian assistance through 2000 will likely exceed the willingness of major donor countries to respond. Africa is home to 23 of the world's poorest countries, and an estimated 290 million Africans survive on less than $1 a day. External debt burdens (totaling more than $200 billion), weak governments, and widespread corruption complicate efforts to alleviate poverty. On top of this, another recent National Intelligence Council report estimates that half of the world's infectious disease

deaths take place in Africa, with old and new viruses posing global threats that governments must devise collective means to combat. 11. 5 million Africans have died of aids, and in 1998, 70 percent of the world's new aids infections occurred there.

Other trends point in more positive directions. Until the late 1980s Africa's only functioning multiparty democracies were Botswana, Senegal, tiny Gambia, and the island of Mauritius—and the first three had never managed to produce a change in government. But according to a recent Freedom House survey, 32 of 53 African countries are now either democratic or at least partly free, with elections of varying credibility.

In June 1999, sub-Saharan Africa's two most important countries celebrated major democratic rituals. President Thabo Mbeki succeeded Nelson Mandela in South Africa, and Nigerians ended 16 years of increasingly repressive military rule by electing Olusegun Obasanjo as president. The two new presidents then teamed up diplomatically in June, successfully persuading the Organization of African Unity to agree to sanction any African government that comes to power by military means.

Meanwhile, Senegal has moved closer to accepting human rights and democracy. In February, Senegal's High Court took the unprecedented decision to prosecute exiled former President Hissene Habre of Chad for "complicity in acts of torture" following complaints filed against him by several human rights organizations. And a month later, Senegal's long-serving President Abdou Diouf gracefully accepted defeat as voters ended 40 years of uninterrupted Socialist Party rule.

Economically, the world's poorest region is also showing some improvement. Negative rates of per capita growth in the 1980s have turned positive, with a three percent rise forecast for this year. More than 30 countries are implementing broad macroeconomic reforms, many for the first time. These include liberalizing trade and investment rules, reducing tariffs, rationalizing exchange rates, ending subsidies, stabilizing currencies, and privatizing state enterprises.

Yet setbacks are still occurring, and these highlight the need for preventive action. President Robert Mugabe's disregard for the rule of law in Zimbabwe, where he has sought to rewrite the constitution and has condoned both the intimidation of the opposition and the violent appropriation of white-owned farms, is one such example. Another is the renewed violence by warlord Foday Sankoh's Revolutionary United Front in Sierra Leone, which included the seizure of several hundred predominantly African U.N. troops in a bid to wreck an otherwise promising peacekeeping operation.

What all this means for Washington is that whichever party takes control of the White House early next year will have to take a fresh look at America's stakes in a changing Africa. To properly plan America's next move, however, requires understanding its past steps and missteps, starting with those taken by the Clinton administration.

WITH FRIENDS LIKE THESE

Old Africa hands were initially surprised and delighted by the amount of attention Bill Clinton paid to Africa. His original national security adviser, Anthony Lake, was the first Africa expert ever to hold the post. Within weeks of the inauguration, an unprecedented White House Conference on Africa was held to signal a new chapter in U.S.- Africa cooperation. Since then, a steady stream of cabinet-level delegations has gone to Africa at the rate of about one every eight weeks. In March 1998, Clinton made his own unprecedented eleven-day, six-nation tour.

But neither the frequent high-level visits nor special events, such as the first-ever U.S.-Africa Ministerial Meeting, held in March 1999 for representatives from 50 countries, have resulted in major new programs. The main achievement of the ministerial, for example, was a unanimous call for the U.S. Congress to pass the stalled African Growth and Opportunity Act that grants improved U.S. market access to African textiles and other products. Yet it took more than a year for the White House and its allies in Congress to overcome pressure from U.S. textile interests (who were opposed to doubling Africa's 0.8 percent of imports) and pass this modest measure. Given the preferences already enjoyed by Asian textile producers, the reluctance to fulfill American promises to help create jobs in the world's poorest region was seen in Africa as another example of U.S. hypocrisy.

Today, less than one percent of U.S. trade and investment is with sub-Saharan Africa. Of that, nearly 85 percent goes to just four countries. Three are oil producers—Angola, Gabon, and Nigeria—and the other is South Africa. The United States currently gets more than 16 percent of its oil from Africa, and oil accounts for America's nearly $7 billion trade deficit with the continent. Furthermore, with huge new discoveries in Angola, oil imports from Africa could surpass those from the Persian Gulf by 2010. Washington has rarely seemed to care what is done with the revenues from these sales, which have fueled war in Angola, enriched a corrupt clique in Gabon, and until last year, sustained military repression and horrific corruption in Nigeria. The oil sales also obscure the surplus that the United States runs with the majority of other sub-Saharan African countries, primarily with South Africa; in 1998 (the last year for which such figures are available) that surplus amounted to $1 billion.

A similar disparity between promises and performance has arisen over peacekeeping. Secretary of State Madeleine Albright and Assistant Secretary of State for African Affairs Susan Rice often speak about the seriousness of Africa's wars, calling the conflict in the Congo "one of the most dangerous in the world," and even comparing it to World War I. But neither their administration nor Congress has been willing to consider more than token funding for U.N. or regional peacekeeping forces, and each has consistently ruled out U.S. troop contributions under any circumstance.

When Secretary of Defense William Cohen visited Africa earlier this year—at the height of diplomatic activity to raise a U.N. force to implement the Lusaka peace accord for the Congo—he told journalists that the United States is "stretched so very thin" militarily that Washington could not be expected to play a role in African peacekeeping missions. Such comments have fueled African cynicism about American claims that Washington is doing all it can to bring peace. The problem is clearly one of will, not means, for any African with access to a television or newspaper knows the scale of the U.S. role

in Yugoslavia. African governments are similarly aware that the United States, with 1.4 million armed troops on active duty and an annual defense budget that equals 80 percent of the combined GDPs of all 48 sub-Saharan countries, could do more if it wanted.

To be fair, African leaders have also shown a reluctance to commit to peace operations. Richard Holbrooke, the U.S. Permanent Representative to the U.N., used his time as chair of the Security Council to declare January 2000 "Africa Month" and threw his weight behind resolving the Congo war. But after convening in New York, the key players in the conflict failed to take advantage of the opportunity to work out a peace accord.

Further complicating matters, the Clinton administration's pledges to support democracy have likewise been dogged by a credibility gap. Part of the problem is historical. Before the end of the Cold War, U.S. policy was aimed primarily at gaining and holding reliable allies, and what went on within those allied states hardly mattered. In the 1980s, the four biggest African recipients of U.S. assistance were three dictators— Samuel Doe of Liberia, Muhammed Siad Barre of Somalia, and Mobutu Sese Seko of Zaire—and the Angolan insurgent Jonas Savimbi. The Clinton administration has tried to distance itself from this past —witness its embrace of a new bloc of leaders in East and Central Africa during the mid-1990s—but to little effect. Those heralded as America's new partners were Rwanda's Paul Kagame, Ethiopia's Meles Zenawi, Eritrea's Isaias Afwerki, and Uganda's Yoweri Museveni. Washington hoped these undemocratic but market-oriented strongmen would bring stability to their countries and then liberalize, all the while accepting advice from the International Monetary Fund (IMF) and the World Bank. Yet human rights groups claimed that Washington had merely substituted international economic allegiance for anticommunism as its criterion for support. Currently all four "partners" are at war, Ethiopia and Eritrea with each other and Rwanda and Uganda backing insurgents in the Congo. The lesson learned should be that Washington must from now on apply standards of good governance, not merely economic performance, in choosing its partners, lest it seem to reward repressive and even aggressive behavior.

MONEY WHERE THEIR MOUTHS ARE

A NEW APPROACH to conflict prevention and democratic development in Africa will require changes in both the substance and tone of American foreign policy. The first and easiest step will be rhetorical: the next U.S. president should designate conflict prevention as a primary goal of U.S. foreign policy. This should be followed by a concerted effort to win the support of Congress and the public. The president should call for a truly national commitment, one involving business, labor, and a broad range of civil society.

States at risk, such as Nigeria today or South Africa in the waning days of apartheid, benefit from the involvement of human rights groups and nongovernmental organizations. These groups pressure troubled regimes to reform and to resolve factional differences through political means. American businesses can have a similarly powerful impact, showing their support for peaceful change through their investment decisions, and should be encouraged and backed by Washington to do so.

Internally, the U.S. government should take a number of steps to strengthen its approach to conflict prevention. Better interdepartmental communication and cooperation is necessary, especially between the State and Defense Departments. Early warning is rarely the problem. Rather, as in the case of Rwandan genocide, it is the failure to respond in time and with sufficient force. Current U.S. political and military programs, such as the African Crisis Response Initiative or the International Military Education and Training Program (IMET), are useful but much too small: Africa's biggest IMET program, in South Africa, amounted to only $800,000 last year. Funding for these programs must be increased to build their capacity for conflict prevention and peace enforcement while helping to ensure that African militaries remain accountable to civilian authorities. Another urgent reason to work with African militaries is to help them cope with aids infection rates that run as high as 50 to 60 percent among some forces—a human tragedy that threatens the viability of Africa's militaries.

On an organizational level, senior American bureaucrats and embassy personnel should be allowed greater flexibility and resources to initiate preventive diplomacy, including offering to broker domestic disputes and to provide quick support from democracy-building programs. Also necessary is a long-over-due reform of what is left of U.S. foreign assistance, bringing it into line with a foreign policy dedicated to conflict prevention. In a similar vein, the State Department's public affairs programs and the operations of the United States' foreign broadcasting services must adopt prevention as a central theme, countering local hate radio that, as in Rwanda, is often a precursor of deadly conflict.

Finally, new funds will have to be found under current U.S. budget caps. This year the United States will spend less than one percent of the federal budget on non-defense-related international affairs—about half what the Reagan administration invested in international affairs in the mid-1980s. This country cannot be a good partner, much less a leader, in conflict prevention when it has so little money to spend on it.

Apart from its own efforts, the United States should encourage the World Bank and other international donors to likewise stress conflict prevention in potentially troubled countries. The bank has already made good governance a priority, has embarked on several postconflict reconstruction efforts aimed at avoiding further fighting, and has begun cooperating with U.N. conflict-prevention efforts. But more could be done. International loans should be tied to demands for the protection of human rights, the rule of law, and transparency, while ensuring that they do not exacerbate conflict by favoring one faction over another.

Support for such moves exists in Africa itself. Subregional organizations in western and southern Africa are beginning to address abuses of power in Zimbabwe, Sierra Leone, and elsewhere. Such efforts deserve strong U.S. backing. More broadly, this new attitude was evident in May, at the first meeting of the Ministerial Conference on Security, Stability, Development, and Cooperation. The conference arose from a 1991 initiative by Obasanjo, Nigeria's current president, when he led a group of prominent Africans to adopt a set of human rights and good governance provisions modeled on those of the Conference on Security and Cooperation in Europe. Whether the fledgling body will match the CSCE's achievements, however, remains to be seen.

THE SOUTHERN STRATEGY

SOUTH AFRICA is of singular strategic significance to U.S. Africa policy. It is the continent's most advanced democracy by far, with an economy that accounts for 40 percent of sub-Saharan Africa's total GDP. Excluding oil imports, 60 percent of U.S. trade with Africa is with South Africa. The late U.S. Commerce Secretary Ron Brown included it in his list of the world's ten "Big Emerging Markets" vital to America's economic future. Such faith in the country as the economic engine of Africa appears well placed. Roughly half of South Africa's economy depends on trade, and its fastest growing export markets are in Africa. Two-way trade with the rest of the continent shot up 20 percent between 1996 and 1998. The total volume of Pretoria's Africa trade in 1998 was just under $4 billion, compared to $5.75 billion with its biggest partner that year, the United States. And although South Africa ran trade deficits with industrial countries, it achieved a surplus with Africa of over $2.7 billion—enough to cover its deficits with three of its major trade partners, the United States, the United Kingdom, and Japan. These economic ties to the rest of Africa are vital to Pretoria's attempt to pull the country out of its apartheid legacy of inequality and unemployment. Although South Africa's economy grew only one percent in 1999, it is projected to increase by six percent over the next two years as the result of a highly disciplined macroeconomic strategy.

Business and government leaders in South Africa assert that they have only begun to penetrate African markets. Leaders of the country's newly empowered black business community, drawing on personal networks that date back to the anti-apartheid struggle, claim to be doing especially well in quickly expanding joint ventures across the region. South African companies, which enjoy greater proximity and familiarity with African conditions than their Western competitors, are expanding rapidly in areas of infrastructure development, telecommunications, and mining in Central, West, and North Africa. In 1997, South Africa surpassed the United Kingdom as the biggest exporter to Kenya. And last year, the South African Broadcasting Corporation launched Africa's first all-Africa 24-hour news service, available to satellite subscribers throughout the continent.

All of this is relevant to conflict prevention, since South Africa now promotes democracy elsewhere to serve its vital interests. Simply put, the rule of law is good for South African business. More important, human rights and democracy are essential for stemming the deadly conflicts that create millions of refugees (many of whom could become a burden to Pretoria), divert and destroy scarce resources, and discredit Africa internationally. When South Africa's leaders call on governments to hold each other more accountable for their domestic behavior, they make clear that this is not merely a moral issue, nor an effort to export their domestic values. It is what Nelson Mandela called "democratic realism," noting,

The neglect of human rights is the certain recipe for internal and international disaster. The powerful secessionist movements that are found throughout the world are nurtured by neglect. The erosion of national sovereignty by global forces, from trade to communications, has paradoxically been accompanied by an increase in the means to ensure separateness: the right to differ has, tragically, become the fight to differ.

On balance, Pretoria is living up to its commitments. Earlier this year, Nkosazana Dlamini-Zuma, South Africa's Minister of Foreign Affairs, announced that two newly discovered covert slush funds from the apartheid era would be used to strengthen "electoral and conciliation skills for emerging democracies in Africa" with an initial $30 million grant—an amount nearly equal to what the U.S. Congress provides annually to the National Endowment for Democracy. Another investment in conflict prevention is the $140 million "lifeline" of emergency loans and credits to help stabilize Zimbabwe's economy and halt its slide toward authoritarianism and mass violence. Although its leverage in the Democratic Republic of the Congo and Angola is more limited, South Africa continues a strenuous diplomatic campaign seeking political, not military, solutions.

Globally, South Africa serves as a key bridge between North and South, promoting human rights and democracy as the chair of several important bodies, including the 113-nation Nonaligned Movement, the Board of Governors of the IMF, the 53-member Commonwealth, and the U.N. Conference on Trade and Development. In recent months, South Africa has sought to forge a coalition with Brazil, Egypt, India, and Nigeria to press for the resumption of world trade talks. South Africa is also the sole African member of the new "Group of 20" initiative proposed by the United States as a way of bringing together major industrial and developing countries.

In less than a decade, South Africa has gone from a pariah state to Africa's indispensable country. If the United States is to develop a network of politically capable states in Africa to help manage transnational threats such as terrorism, crime, drugs, and the spread of deadly diseases, then South Africa must become its strategic partner and the hub of that network. Yet so far, the U.S.-South African relationship has failed to live up to expectations.

MASAKANE

In March 1998 Bill Clinton became the first U.S. president to address the South African Parliament. He used the Sotho term *masakane*—"working together"—to describe the kind of relationship Washington seeks with Pretoria. This seemed natural given the oft-noted convergence of interests and values between the two countries, and on the surface relations do now appear very close. A 1999 opinion survey by the Chicago Council on Foreign Relations ranked South Africa among the top ten countries that Americans most admire, a view shared by leaders of both parties.

Most U.S. politicians grew up during the civil rights struggles of the 1960s and have a visceral understanding of the enormity of South Africa's political achievement, as well as the negative effects that images of mass violence there might have had on race relations in America. South Africa's first

universal election in April 1994 thus came as a relief and provided an encouraging contrast to the simultaneous failure of democratization elsewhere. That same month, genocide erupted in Rwanda and within weeks more than half a million civilians there were dead. In the Balkans, NATO aircraft mounted their first attacks in reaction to outbreaks of violent ethnic nationalism.

To show support for democratic South Africa, the United States provided $210 million in foreign assistance in 1995 and launched an extraordinary Binational Commission (BNC), chaired by Vice President Al Gore and South Africa's then deputy president, Thabo Mbeki. The BNC met every six months and included as many as seven cabinet ministers from each side. Since 1995 a plethora of bilateral committees and subcommittees have met under BNC auspices to discuss problems and propose new initiatives in the areas of trade and investment, education, energy, agriculture, science and technology, defense, and justice. But as with other aspects of U.S. Africa policy, the BNC has so far amounted to more symbolism than substance. It has produced highly publicized protocols, often with useful training and exchange components, but without the financial backing to effectively help South Africa overcome the legacies of apartheid.

By 1998, in fact, South Africans had grown so wary of binational initiatives that are expensive to administer but bring no substantial benefits that they insisted that Clinton's state visit be billed only as a "goodwill mission." They had good reason to do so: the U.S. Agency for International Development's South Africa budget, which pays the U.S. costs of the BNC, had dropped 80 percent, to about $47 million—an amount roughly equal to 8 percent of the U.S. trade surplus with South Africa that year. U.S. diplomats blame the budgetary straitjacket imposed by Congress but insist that the bilateral relationship has become a "normal one," similar to those with America's major Western partners.

Yet huge differences persist between the two countries, and the U.S.- South Africa partnership has a somewhat shaky foundation. It rests primarily on shared values but does not reflect similar needs or domestic capabilities. The U.S. economy is more than 50 times bigger than South Africa's and has just a tiny fraction of South Africa's unemployment rate. White South Africa enjoys a standard of living comparable to Spain's (24th in the world) whereas black South Africa gets by at the level of the Republic of the Congo (123rd in the world). Crime levels are among the highest anywhere. And the government's capacity to deal with these and other problems is being severely constrained by the skyrocketing costs and social impact of aids, which spreads to 1,700 new individuals each day. Meanwhile, South Africa's 86 percent black majority still owns less than 20 percent of the country's land. (Such unequal land distribution has inflamed conflict in neighboring Zimbabwe.) Social upheaval in South Africa remains a danger, despite the country's magnificent political achievements and sound economic policies. Assisting South Africa to reduce this danger should be a top priority of U.S. Africa policy.

The next U.S. administration should issue fewer empty pledges and back a new strategy of more substantial and comprehensive engagement, one involving business, civil society, and state and local governments to support South Africa's economic and social transformation. This will require returning the country to the centrality in U.S. Africa policy it had during the Reagan administration. Second, the BNC should be broadened and better funded, with more substantial public-private partnerships in such high-priority areas as education, health, crime prevention, micro-enterprise, and rural development. Third, a return to the assistance levels of the mid-1990s is necessary to encourage much greater private-sector and civil-society participation by Americans and South Africans. Such measures hardly seem extravagant when weighed against the basic values and long-term interests America has at stake in South Africa's democratic success.

A WHOLE NEW WORLD

SOUTH AFRICA today is a microcosm of global inequities and is trying to build a decent society against huge odds. It has escaped civil war, but the danger of a slide toward chaos or authoritarianism—however slight—must never be discounted. In light of this, U.S. reluctance to more generously help South Africa's domestic transformation seems dangerously shortsighted.

Substantial new support would be welcomed by Pretoria. South Africa also needs U.S. backing for debt forgiveness elsewhere in Africa, for cheaper access to lifesaving drugs—especially to combat aids—and for giving developing countries a greater voice in the policy debates of the IMF, the World Bank, and the U.N. (by expanding the Security Council). This would show Pretoria's critics that tangible benefits can result from a democratic North-South partnership.

South Africa's call for reform of the U.N. system reflects Mbeki's vision of a grand global bargain. Under it, developing countries would accept stricter international accountability for human rights and democracy locally, while wealthy nations would agree to broaden governance globally. The U.N. and international financial institutions, whose job it is to define and enforce stricter standards of national accountability, also must become more representative of the world's people. Until recently, South Africa's cry to the world was for freedom. Now it warns of the coming challenge: to rein in rising inequities that threaten not only its democracy but also the liberal international order that America is committed to uphold.

Seventy-five years ago, W. E. B. Du Bois wrote that the denial of democracy in Africa and Asia hinders its realization in Europe and America. Today it is no longer the simple creation of democracy in Africa but rather its development and entrenchment that should matter most to Europe and America. Only with lasting democracies—especially in South Africa and Nigeria, sub-Saharan Africa's major powers—will Africa have a realistic chance at conflict prevention. Achieving such democratization in Africa need not take as long or cost as much in blood or treasure as it did in Europe. But it may well, unless the United States and other Western nations realize that their best interests lie in helping Africans find a faster pathway to democracy and peace.

JOHN STREMLAU is a professor and the head of the Department of International Relations at the University of the Witwatersrand in Johannesburg, South Africa. From 1989 to 1994 he served as Deputy Director of the U.S. State Department's

---

Article 8   *Time*, February 12, 2001

DEATH STALKS A CONTINENT

In the dry timber of African societies, AIDS was a spark.
The conflagration it set off continues to kill millions. Here's why

BY JOHANNA MCGEARY

Imagine your life this way.

You get up in the morning and breakfast with your three kids. One is already doomed to die in infancy. Your husband works 200 miles away, comes home twice a year and sleeps around in between. You risk your life in every act of sexual intercourse. You go to work past a house where a teenager lives alone tending young siblings without any source of income. At another house, the wife was branded a whore when she asked her husband to use a condom, beaten silly and thrown into the streets. Over there lies a man desperately sick without access to a doctor or clinic or medicine or food or blankets or even a kind word. At work you eat with colleagues, and every third one is already fatally ill. You whisper about a friend who admitted she had the plague and whose neighbors stoned her to death. Your leisure is occupied by the funerals you attend every Saturday. You go to bed fearing adults your age will not live into their 40s. You and your neighbors and your political and popular leaders act as if nothing is happening.

Across the southern quadrant of Africa, this nightmare is real. The word not spoken is AIDS, and here at ground zero of humanity's deadliest cataclysm, the ultimate tragedy is that so many people don't know—or don't want to know—what is happening. As the HIV virus sweeps mercilessly through these lands—the fiercest trial Africa has yet endured—a few try to address the terrible depredation. The rest of society looks away. Flesh and muscle melt from the bones of the sick in packed hospital wards and lonely bush kraals. Corpses stack up in morgues until those on top crush the identity from the faces underneath. Raw earth mounds scar the landscape, grave after grave without name or number. Bereft children grieve for parents lost in their prime, for siblings scattered to the winds.

The victims don't cry out. Doctors and obituaries do not give the killer its name. Families recoil in shame. Leaders shirk responsibility. The stubborn silence heralds victory for the disease: denial cannot keep the virus at bay.

The developed world is largely silent too. AIDS in Africa has never commanded the full-bore response the West has brought to other, sometimes lesser, travails. We pay sporadic attention, turning on the spotlight when an international conference occurs, then turning it off. Good-hearted donors donate; governments acknowledge that more needs to be done. But think how different the effort would be if what is happening here were happening in the West.

HALF A MILLION AFRICAN CHILDREN WERE INFECTED WITH HIV LAST YEAR

By now you've seen pictures of the sick, the dead, the orphans. You've heard appalling numbers: the number of new infections, the number of the dead, the number who are sick without care, the number walking around already fated to die.

But to comprehend the full horror AIDS has visited on Africa, listen to the woman we have dubbed Laetitia Hambahlane in Durban or the boy Tsepho Phale in Francistown or the woman who calls herself Thandiwe in Bulawayo or Louis Chikoka, a long-distance trucker. You begin to understand how AIDS has struck Africa—with a biblical virulence that will claim tens of millions of lives—when you hear about shame and stigma and ignorance and poverty and sexual violence and migrant labor and promiscuity and political paralysis and the terrible silence that surrounds all this dying. It is a measure of the silence that some asked us not to print their real names to protect their privacy.

Theirs is a story about what happens when a disease leaps the confines of medicine to invade the body politic, infecting not just individuals but an entire society. As AIDS migrated to

man in Africa, it mutated into a complex plague with confounding social, economic and political mechanics that locked together to accelerate the virus' progress. The region's social dynamics colluded to spread the disease and help block effective intervention.

We have come to three countries abutting one another at the bottom of Africa—Botswana, South Africa, Zimbabwe—the heart of the heart of the epidemic. For nearly a decade, these nations suffered a hidden invasion of infection that concealed the dimension of the coming calamity. Now the omnipresent dying reveals the shocking scale of the devastation.

AIDS in Africa bears little resemblance to the American epidemic, limited to specific high-risk groups and brought under control through intensive education, vigorous political action and expensive drug therapy. Here the disease has bred a Darwinian perversion. Society's fittest, not its frailest, are the ones who die—adults spirited away, leaving the old and the children behind. You cannot define risk groups: everyone who is sexually active is at risk. Babies too, unwittingly infected by mothers. Barely a single family remains untouched. Most do not know how or when they caught the virus, many never know they have it, many who do know don't tell anyone as they lie dying. Africa can provide no treatment for those with AIDS.

They will all die, of tuberculosis, pneumonia, meningitis, diarrhea, whatever overcomes their ruined immune systems first. And the statistics, grim as they are, may be too low. There is no broad-scale AIDS testing: infection rates are calculated mainly from the presence of HIV in pregnant women. Death certificates in these countries do not record AIDS as the cause. "Whatever stats we have are not reliable," warns Mary Crewe of the University of Pretoria's Center for the Study of AIDS. "Everybody's guessing."

THE TB PATIENT

CASE NO. 309 IN THE TUGELA FERRY HOME-CARE program shivers violently on the wooden planks someone has knocked into a bed, a frayed blanket pulled right up to his nose. He has the flushed skin, overbright eyes and careful breathing of the tubercular. He is alone, and it is chilly within the crumbling mud walls of his hut at Msinga Top, a windswept outcrop high above the Tugela River in South Africa's KwaZulu-Natal province. The spectacular view of hills and veld would gladden a well man, but the 22-year-old we will call Fundisi Khumalo, though he does not know it, has AIDS, and his eyes seem to focus inward on his simple fear.

Before he can speak, his throat clutches in gasping spasms. Sharp pains rack his chest; his breath comes in shallow gasps. The vomiting is better today. But constipation has doubled up his knees, and he is too weak to go outside to relieve himself. He can't remember when he last ate. He can't remember how long he's been sick—"a long time, maybe since six months ago." Khumalo knows he has TB, and he believes it is just TB. "I am only thinking of that," he answers when we ask why he is so ill.

But the fear never leaves his eyes. He worked in a hair salon in Johannesburg, lived in a men's hostel in one of the cheap townships, had "a few" girlfriends. He knew other young men in the hostel who were on-and-off sick. When they fell too ill to work anymore, like him, they straggled home to rural villages like Msinga Top. But where Khumalo would not go is the hospital. "Why?" he says. "You are sick there, you die there."

"He's right, you know," says Dr. Tony Moll, who has driven us up the dirt track from the 350-bed hospital he heads in Tugela Ferry. "We have no medicines for AIDS. So many hospitals tell them, 'You've got AIDS. We can't help you. Go home and die.'" No one wants to be tested either, he adds, unless treatment is available. "If the choice is to know and get nothing," he says, "they don't want to know."

Here and in scattered homesteads all over rural Africa, the dying people say the sickness afflicting their families and neighbors is just the familiar consequence of their eternal poverty. Or it is the work of witchcraft. You have done something bad and have been bewitched. Your neighbor's jealousy has invaded you. You have not appeased the spirits of your ancestors, and they have cursed you. Some in South Africa believe the disease was introduced by the white population as a way to control black Africans after the end of apartheid.

Ignorance about AIDS remains profound. But because of the funerals, southern Africans can't help seeing that something more systematic and sinister lurks out there. Every Saturday and often Sundays too, neighbors trudge to the cemeteries for costly burial rites for the young and the middle-aged who are suddenly dying so much faster than the old. Families say it was pneumonia, TB, malaria that killed their son, their wife, their baby. "But you starting to hear the truth," says Durban home-care volunteer Busi Magwazi. "In the church, in the graveyard, they saying, 'Yes, she died of AIDS.' Oh, people talking about it even if the families don't admit it." Ignorance is the crucial reason the epidemic has run out of control. Surveys say many Africans here are becoming aware there is a sexually transmitted disease called AIDS that is incurable. But they don't think the risk applies to them. And their vague knowledge does not translate into changes in their sexual behavior. It's easy to see why so many don't yet sense the danger when few talk openly about the disease. And Africans are beset by so plentiful a roster of perils—famine, war, the violence of desperation or ethnic hatred, the regular illnesses of poverty, the dangers inside mines or on the roads—that the delayed risk of AIDS ranks low.

THE OUTCAST

TO ACKNOWLEDGE AIDS IN YOURSELF IS TO BE branded as monstrous. Laetitia Hambahlane (not her real name) is 51 and sick with AIDS. So is her brother. She admits it; he doesn't. In her mother's broken-down house in the mean streets of Umlazi township, though, Laetitia's mother hovers over her son, nursing him, protecting him, resolutely denying he has anything but TB, though his sister claims the sure symptoms of AIDS mark him. Laetitia is the outcast, first from her family, then from her society.

For years Laetitia worked as a domestic servant in Durban and dutifully sent all her wages home to her mother. She fell in love a number of times and bore four children. "I loved

that last man," she recalls. "After he left, I had no one, no sex." That was 1992, but Laetitia already had HIV.

She fell sick in 1996, and her employers sent her to a private doctor who couldn't diagnose an illness. He tested her blood and found she was HIV positive. "I wish I'd died right then," she says, as tears spill down her sunken cheeks. "I asked the doctor, 'Have you got medicine?' He said no. I said, 'Can't you keep me alive?'" The doctor could do nothing and sent her away. "I couldn't face the word," she says. "I couldn't sleep at night. I sat on my bed, thinking, praying. I did not see anyone day or night. I ask God, Why?"

Laetitia's employers fired her without asking her exact diagnosis. For weeks she could not muster the courage to tell anyone. Then she told her children, and they were ashamed and frightened. Then, harder still, she told her mother. Her mother raged about the loss of money if Laetitia could not work again. She was so angry she ordered Laetitia out of the house. When her daughter wouldn't leave, the mother threatened to sell the house to get rid of her daughter. Then she walled off her daughter's room with plywood partitions, leaving the daughter a pariah, alone in a cramped, dark space without windows and only a flimsy door opening into the alley. Laetitia must earn the pennies to feed herself and her children by peddling beer, cigarettes and candy from a shopping cart in her room, when people are brave enough to stop by her door. "Sometimes they buy, sometimes not," she says. "That is how I'm surviving."

Her mother will not talk to her. "If you are not even accepted by your own family," says Magwazi, the volunteer home-care giver from Durban's Sinoziso project who visits Laetitia, "then others will not accept you." When Laetitia ventures outdoors, neighbors snub her, tough boys snatch her purse, children taunt her. Her own kids are tired of the sickness and don't like to help her anymore. "When I can't get up, they don't bring me food," she laments. One day local youths barged into her room, cursed her as a witch and a whore and beat her. When she told the police, the youths returned, threatening to burn down the house.

But it is her mother's rejection that wounds Laetitia most. "She is hiding it about my brother," she cries. "Why will she do nothing for me?" Her hands pick restlessly at the quilt covering her paper-thin frame. "I know my mother will not bury me properly. I know she will not take care of my kids when I am gone."

Jabulani Syabusi would use his real name, but he needs to protect his brother. He teaches school in a red, dusty district of KwaZulu-Natal. People here know the disease is all around them, but no one speaks of it. He eyes the scattered huts that make up his little settlement on an arid bluff. "We can count 20 who died just here as far as we can see. I personally don't remember any family that told it was AIDS," he says. "They hide it if they do know."

Syabusi's own family is no different. His younger brother is also a teacher who has just come home from Durban too sick to work anymore. He says he has tuberculosis, but after six months the tablets he is taking have done nothing to cure him. Syabusi's wife Nomsange, a nurse, is concerned that her 36-year-old brother-in-law may have something worse. Syabusi finally asked the doctor tending his brother what is wrong. The doctor said the information is confidential and will not tell him. Neither will his brother. "My brother is not brave enough to tell me," says Syabusi, as he stares sadly toward the house next door, where his only sibling lies ill. "And I am not brave enough to ask him."

Kennedy Fugewane, a cheerful, elderly volunteer counselor, sits in an empty U.S.-funded clinic that offers fast, pinprick blood tests in Francistown, Botswana, pondering how to break through the silence. This city suffers one of the world's highest infection rates, but people deny the disease because HIV is linked with sex. "We don't reveal anything," he says. "But people are so stigmatized even if they walk in the door." Africans feel they must keep private anything to do with sex. "If a man comes here, people will say he is running around," says Fugewane, though he acknowledges that men never do come. "If a woman comes, people will say she is loose. If anyone says they got HIV, they will be despised."

Pretoria University's Mary Crewe says, "It is presumed if you get AIDS, you have done something wrong." HIV labels you as living an immoral life. Embarrassment about sexuality looms more important than future health risks. "We have no language to talk candidly about sex," she says, "so we have no civil language to talk about AIDS." Volunteers like Fugewane try to reach out with flyers, workshops, youth meetings and free condoms, but they are frustrated by a culture that values its dignity over saving lives. "People here don't have the courage to come forward and say, 'Let me know my HIV status,'" he sighs, much less the courage to do something about it. "Maybe one day . . ."

Doctors bow to social pressure and legal strictures not to record AIDS on death certificates. "I write TB or meningitis or diarrhea but never AIDS," says South Africa's Dr. Moll. "It's a public document, and families would hate it if anyone knew." Several years ago, doctors were barred even from recording compromised immunity or HIV status on a medical file; now they can record the results of blood tests for AIDS on patient charts to protect other health workers. Doctors like Moll have long agitated to apply the same openness to death certificates.

THE TRUCK DRIVER

HERE, MEN HAVE TO MIGRATE TO WORK, INSIDE their countries or across borders. All that mobility sows HIV far and wide, as Louis Chikoka is the first to recognize. He regularly drives the highway that is Botswana's economic lifeline and its curse. The road runs for 350 miles through desolate bush that is the Texas-size country's sole strip of habitable land, home to a large majority of its 1.5 million people. It once brought prospectors to Botswana's rich diamond reefs. Now it's the link for transcontinental truckers like Chikoka who haul goods from South Africa to markets in the continent's center. And now the road brings AIDS.

Chikoka brakes his dusty, diesel-belching Kabwe Transport 18-wheeler to a stop at the dark roadside rest on the edge of Francistown, where the international trade routes converge and at least 43% of adults are HIV-positive. He is a cheerful man even after 12 hard hours behind the wheel freighting rice from Durban. He's been on the road for two weeks and will reach

his destination in Congo next Thursday. At 39, he is married, the father of three and a long-haul trucker for 12 years. He's used to it.

Lighting up a cigarette, the jaunty driver is unusually loquacious about sex as he eyes the dim figures circling the rest stop. Chikoka has parked here for a quickie. See that one over there, he points with his cigarette. "Those local ones we call bitches. They always waiting here for short service." Short service? "It's according to how long it takes you to ejaculate," he explains. "We go to the 'bush bedroom' over there [waving at a clump of trees 100 yds. away] or sometimes in the truck. Short service, that costs you 20 rands [$2.84]. They know we drivers always got money."

Chikoka nods his head toward another woman sitting beside a stack of cardboard cartons. "We like better to go to them," he says. They are the "businesswomen," smugglers with gray-market cases of fruit and toilet paper and toys that they need to transport somewhere up the road. "They come to us, and we negotiate privately about carrying their goods." It's a no-cash deal, he says. "They pay their bodies to us." Chikoka shrugs at a suggestion that the practice may be unhealthy. "I been away two weeks, madam. I'm human. I'm a man. I have to have sex."

IN SOME AFRICAN COUNTRIES, THE INFECTION RATE OF TEEN GIRLS IS FOUR TIMES THAT OF BOYS

What he likes best is dry sex. In parts of sub-Saharan Africa, to please men, women sit in basins of bleach or saltwater or stuff astringent herbs, tobacco or fertilizer inside their vagina. The tissue of the lining swells up and natural lubricants dry out. The resulting dry sex is painful and dangerous for women. The drying agents suppress natural bacteria, and friction easily lacerates the tender walls of the vagina. Dry sex increases the risk of HIV infection for women, already two times as likely as men to contract the virus from a single encounter. The women, adds Chikoka, can charge more for dry sex, 50 or 60 rands ($6.46 to $7.75), enough to pay a child's school fees or to eat for a week.

Chikoka knows his predilection for commercial sex spreads AIDS; he knows his promiscuity could carry the disease home to his wife; he knows people die if they get it. "Yes, HIV is terrible, madam," he says as he crooks a finger toward the businesswoman whose favors he will enjoy that night. "But, madam, sex is natural. Sex is not like beer or smoking. You can stop them. But unless you castrate the men, you can't stop sex—and then we all die anyway."

Millions of men share Chikoka's sexually active lifestyle, fostered by the region's dependence on migrant labor. Men desperate to earn a few dollars leave their women at hardscrabble rural homesteads to go where the work is: the mines, the cities, the road. They're housed together in isolated males-only hostels but have easy access to prostitutes or a "town wife" with whom they soon pick up a second family and an ordinary STD and HIV. Then they go home to wives and girlfriends a few times a year, carrying the virus they do not know they have. The pattern is so dominant that rates of infection in many rural areas across the southern cone match urban numbers.

If HIV zeros in disproportionately on poor migrants, it does not skip over the educated or the well paid. Soldiers, doctors, policemen, teachers, district administrators are also routinely separated from families by a civil-service system that sends them alone to remote rural posts, where they have money and women have no men. A regular paycheck procures more access to extramarital sex. Result: the vital professions are being devastated.

Schoolmaster Syabusi is afraid there will soon be no more teachers in his rural zone. He has just come home from a memorial for six colleagues who died over the past few months, though no one spoke the word AIDS at the service. "The rate here—they're so many," he says, shaking his head. "They keep on passing it at school." Teachers in southern Africa have one of the highest group infection rates, but they hide their status until the telltale symptoms find them out.

Before then, the men—teachers are mostly men here—can take their pick of sexual partners. Plenty of women in bush villages need extra cash, often to pay school fees, and female students know they can profit from a teacher's favor. So the schoolmasters buy a bit of sex with lonely wives and trade a bit of sex with willing pupils for A's. Some students consider it an honor to sleep with the teacher, a badge of superiority. The girls brag about it to their peers, preening in their ability to snag an older man. "The teachers are the worst," says Jabulani Siwela, an AIDS worker in Zimbabwe who saw frequent teacher-student sex in his Bulawayo high school. They see a girl they like; they ask her to stay after class; they have a nice time. "It's dead easy," he says. "These are men who know better, but they still do it all the time."

THE PROSTITUTE

THE WORKINGWOMAN WE MEET DIRECTS OUR car to a reedy field fringing the gritty eastern townships of Bulawayo, Zimbabwe. She doesn't want neighbors to see her being interviewed. She is afraid her family will find out she is a prostitute, so we will call her Thandiwe. She looked quite prim and proper in her green calf-length dress as she waited for johns outside 109 Tongogaro Street in the center of downtown. So, for that matter, do the dozens of other women cruising the city's dim street corners: not a mini or bustier or bared navel in sight. Zimbabwe is in many ways a prim and proper society that frowns on commercial sex work and the public display of too much skin.

That doesn't stop Thandiwe from earning a better living turning tricks than she ever could doing honest work. Desper-

ate for a job, she slipped illegally into South Africa in 1992. She cleaned floors in a Johannesburg restaurant, where she met a cook from back home who was also illegal. They had two daughters, and they got married; he was gunned down one night at work.

She brought his body home for burial and was sent to her in-laws to be "cleansed." This common practice gives a dead husband's brother the right, even the duty, to sleep with the widow. Thandiwe tested negative for HIV in 1998, but if she were positive, the ritual cleansing would have served only to pass on the disease. Then her in-laws wanted to keep her two daughters because their own children had died, and marry her off to an old uncle who lived far out in the bush. She fled.

Alone, Thandiwe grew desperate. "I couldn't let my babies starve." One day she met a friend from school. "She told me she was a sex worker. She said, 'Why you suffer? Let's go to a place where we can get quick bucks.'" Thandiwe hangs her head. "I went. I was afraid. But now I go every night."

She goes to Tongogaro Street, where the rich clients are, tucking a few condoms in her handbag every evening as the sun sets and returning home strictly by 10 so that she won't have to service a taxi-van driver to get a ride back. Thandiwe tells her family she works an evening shift, just not at what. "I get 200 zim [$5] for sex," she says, more for special services. She uses two condoms per client, sometimes three. "If they say no, I say no." But then sometimes resentful johns hit her. It's pay-and-go until she has pocketed 1,000 or 1,500 Zimbabwe dollars and can go home—with more cash than her impoverished neighbors ever see in their roughneck shantytown, flush enough to buy a TV and fleece jammies for her girls and meat for their supper.

79% OF THOSE WHO DIED OF AIDS LAST YEAR WERE AFRICAN

"I am ashamed," she murmurs. She has stopped going to church. "Every day I ask myself, 'When will I stop this business?' The answer is, 'If I could get a job' . . ." Her voice trails off hopelessly. "At the present moment, I have no option, no other option." As trucker Chikoka bluntly puts it, "They give sex to eat. They got no man; they got no work; but they got kids, and they got to eat." Two of Thandiwe's friends in the sex trade are dying of AIDS, but what can she do? "I just hope I won't get it."

In fact, casual sex of every kind is commonplace here. Prostitutes are just the ones who admit they do it for cash. Everywhere there's premarital sex, sex as recreation. Obligatory sex and its abusive counterpart, coercive sex. Transactional sex: sex as a gift, sugar-daddy sex. Extramarital sex, second families, multiple partners. The nature of AIDS is to feast on promiscuity.

Rare is the man who even knows his HIV status: males widely refuse testing even when they fall ill. And many men who suspect they are HIV positive embrace a flawed logic: if I'm already infected, I can sleep around because I can't get it again. But women are the ones who progress to full-blown AIDS first and die fastest, and the underlying cause is not just sex but power. Wives and girlfriends and even prostitutes in this part of the world can't easily say no to sex on a man's terms. It matters little what comes into play, whether it is culture or tradition or the pathology of violence or issues of male identity or the subservient status of women.

Beneath a translucent scalp, the plates of Gertrude Dhlamini's cranium etch a geography of pain. Her illness is obvious in the thin, stretched skin under which veins throb with the shingles that have blinded her left eye and scarred that side of her face. At 39, she looks 70. The agonizing thrush, a kind of fungus, that paralyzed her throat has ebbed enough to enable her to swallow a spoon or two of warm gruel, but most of the nourishment flows away in constant diarrhea. She struggles to keep her hand from scratching restlessly at the scaly rash flushing her other cheek. She is not ashamed to proclaim her illness to the world. "It must be told," she says.

Gertrude is thrice rejected. At 19 she bore a son to a boy-friend who soon left her, taking away the child. A second boy-friend got her pregnant in 1994 but disappeared in anger when their daughter was born sickly with HIV. A doctor told Gertrude it was her fault, so she blamed herself that little Noluthando was never well in the two years she survived. Gertrude never told the doctor the baby's father had slept with other women. "I was afraid to," she says, "though I sincerely believe he gave the sickness to me." Now, she says, "I have rent him from my heart. And I will never have another man in my life."

Gertrude begged her relatives to take her in, but when she revealed the name of her illness, they berated her. They made her the household drudge, telling her never to touch their food or their cooking pots. They gave her a bowl and a spoon strictly for her own use. After a few months, they threw her out.

Gertrude sits upright on a donated bed in a cardboard shack in a rough Durban township that is now the compass of her world. Perhaps 10 ft. square, the little windowless room contains a bed, one sheet and blanket, a change of clothes and a tiny cooking ring, but she has no money for paraffin to heat the food that a home-care worker brings. She must fetch water and use a toilet down the hill. "Everything I have," she says, "is a gift." Now the school that owns the land under her hut wants to turn it into a playground and she worries about where she will go. Gertrude rubs and rubs at her raw cheek. "I pray and pray to God," she says, "not to take my soul while I am alone in this room."

Women like Gertrude were brought up to be subservient to men. Especially in matters of sex, the man is always in charge. Women feel powerless to change sexual behavior. Even when a woman wants to protect herself, she usually can't: it is not uncommon for men to beat partners who refuse intercourse or request a condom. "Real men" don't use them, so women who want their partners to must fight deeply ingrained taboos. Talk to him about donning a rubber sheath and be prepared for accusations, abuse or abandonment.

A nurse in Durban, coming home from an AIDS training class, suggested that her mate should put on a condom, as a kind of homework exercise. He grabbed a pot and banged loudly on it with a knife, calling all the neighbors into his house. He pointed the knife at his wife and demanded: "Where was she between 4 p.m. and now? Why is she suddenly suggesting this? What has changed after 20 years that she wants a condom?"

Schoolteacher Syabusi is an educated man, fully cognizant of the AIDS threat. Yet even he bristles when asked if he uses a condom. "Humph," he says with a fine snort. "That question is nonnegotiable." So despite extensive distribution of free condoms, they often go unused. Astonishing myths have sprung up. If you don one, your erection can't grow. Free condoms must be too cheap to be safe: they have been stored too long, kept too hot, kept too cold. Condoms fill up with germs, so they spread AIDS. Condoms from overseas bring the disease with them. Foreign governments that donate condoms put holes in them so that Africans will die. Education programs find it hard to compete with the power of the grapevine.

THE CHILD IN NO. 17

IN CRIB NO. 17 OF THE SPARTAN BUT CROWDED children's ward at the Church of Scotland Hospital in KwaZulu-Natal, a tiny, staring child lies dying. She is three and has hardly known a day of good health. Now her skin wrinkles around her body like an oversize suit, and her twig-size bones can barely hold her vertical as nurses search for a vein to take blood. In the frail arms hooked up to transfusion tubes, her veins have collapsed. The nurses palpate a threadlike vessel on the child's forehead. She mews like a wounded animal as one tightens a rubber band around her head to raise the vein. Tears pour unnoticed from her mother's eyes as she watches the needle tap-tap at her daughter's temple. Each time the whimpering child lifts a wan hand to brush away the pain, her mother gently lowers it. Drop by drop, the nurses manage to collect 1 cc of blood in five minutes.

The child in crib No. 17 has had TB, oral thrush, chronic diarrhea, malnutrition, severe vomiting. The vial of blood reveals her real ailment, AIDS, but the disease is not listed on her chart, and her mother says she has no idea why her child is so ill. She breast-fed her for two years, but once the little girl was weaned, she could not keep solid food down. For a long time, her mother thought something was wrong with the food. Now the child is afflicted with so many symptoms that her mother had to bring her to the hospital, from which sick babies rarely return.

She hopes, she prays her child will get better, and like all the mothers who stay with their children at the hospital, she tends her lovingly, constantly changing filthy diapers, smoothing sheets, pressing a little nourishment between listless lips, trying to tease a smile from the vacant, staring face. Her husband works in Johannesburg, where he lives in a men's squatter camp. He comes home twice a year. She is 25. She has heard of AIDS but does not know it is transmitted by sex, does not know if she or her husband has it. She is afraid this child will die soon, and she is afraid to have more babies. But she is afraid too to raise the subject with her husband. "He would not agree to that," she says shyly. "He would never agree to have no more babies."

Dr. Annick DeBaets, 32, is a volunteer from Belgium. In the two years she has spent here in Tugela Ferry, she has learned all about how hard it is to break the cycle of HIV transmission from mother to infant. The door to this 48-cot ward is literally a revolving one: sick babies come in, receive doses of rudimentary antibiotics, vitamins, food; go home for a week or a month; then come back as ill as ever. Most, she says, die in the first or second year. If she could just follow up with really intensive care, believes Dr. DeBaets, many of the wizened infants crowding three to a crib could live longer, healthier lives. "But it's very discouraging. We simply don't have the time, money or facilities for anything but minimal care."

Much has been written about what South African Judge Edwin Cameron, himself HIV positive, calls his country's "grievous ineptitude" in the face of the burgeoning epidemic. Nowhere has that been more evident than in the government's failure to provide drugs that could prevent pregnant women from passing HIV to their babies. The government has said it can't afford the 300-rand-per-dose, 28-dose regimen of AZT that neighboring nations like Botswana dole out, using funds and drugs from foreign donors. The late South African presidential spokesman Parks Mankahlana even suggested publicly that it was not cost effective to save these children when their mothers were already doomed to die: "We don't want a generation of orphans."

Yet these children—70,000 are born HIV positive in South Africa alone every year—could be protected from the disease for about $4 each with another simple, cheap drug called nevirapine. Until last month, the South African government steadfastly refused to license or finance the use of nevirapine despite the manufacturer's promise to donate the drug for five years, claiming that its "toxic" side effects are not yet known. This spring, however, the drug will finally be distributed to leading public hospitals in the country, though only on a limited basis at first.

The mother at crib No. 17 is not concerned with potential side effects. She sits on the floor cradling her daughter, crooning over and over, "Get well, my child, get well." The baby stares back without blinking. "It's sad, so sad, so sad," the mother says. The child died three days later.

The children who are left when parents die only add another complex dimension to Africa's epidemic. At 17, Tsepho Phale has been head of an indigent household of three young boys in the dusty township of Monarch, outside Francistown, for two years. He never met his father, his mother died of AIDS, and the grieving children possess only a raw concrete shell of a house. The doorways have no doors; the window frames no glass. There is not a stick of furniture. The boys sleep on piled-up blankets, their few clothes dangling from nails. In the room that passes for a kitchen, two paraffin burners sit on the dirt floor alongside the month's food: four cabbages, a bag of oranges and one of potatoes, three sacks of flour, some yeast, two jars of oil and two cartons of milk. Next to a dirty stack of plastic pans lies the mealy meal and rice that will provide their main sustenance for the month. A couple of bars of soap and two rolls of toilet paper also have to last the month. Tsepho

has just brought these rations home from the social-service center where the "orphan grants" are doled out.

Tsepho has been robbed of a childhood that was grim even before his mother fell sick. She supported the family by "buying and selling things," he says, but she never earned more than a pittance. When his middle brother was knocked down by a car and left physically and mentally disabled, Tsepho's mother used the insurance money to build this house, so she would have one thing of value to leave her children. As the walls went up, she fell sick. Tsepho had to nurse her, bathe her, attend to her bodily functions, try to feed her. Her one fear as she lay dying was that her rural relatives would try to steal the house. She wrote a letter bequeathing it to her sons and bade Tsepho hide it.

As her body lay on the concrete floor awaiting burial, the relatives argued openly about how they would divide up the profits when they sold her dwelling. Tsepho gave the district commissioner's office the letter, preventing his mother's family from grabbing the house. Fine, said his relations; if you think you're a man, you look after your brothers. They have contributed nothing to the boys' welfare since. "It's as if we don't exist anymore either," says Tsepho. Now he struggles to keep house for the others, doing the cooking, cleaning, laundry and shopping.

The boys look at the future with despair. "It is very bleak," says Tsepho, kicking aimlessly at a bare wall. He had to quit school, has no job, will probably never get one. "I've given up my dreams. I have no hope."

Orphans have traditionally been cared for the African way: relatives absorb the children of the dead into their extended families. Some still try, but communities like Tsepho's are becoming saturated with orphans, and families can't afford to take on another kid, leaving thousands alone.

Now many must fend for themselves, struggling to survive. The trauma of losing parents is compounded by the burden of becoming a breadwinner. Most orphans sink into penury, drop out of school, suffer malnutrition, ostracism, psychic distress. Their makeshift households scramble to live on pitiful handouts—from overstretched relatives, a kind neighbor, a state grant—or they beg and steal in the streets. The orphans' present desperation forecloses a brighter future. "They hardly ever succeed in having a life," says Siphelile Kaseke, 22, a counselor at an AIDS orphans' camp near Bulawayo. Without education, girls fall into prostitution, and older boys migrate illegally to South Africa, leaving the younger ones to go on the streets.

EVERY DAY SPENT IN THIS PART OF AFRICA IS ACUTELY depressing: there is so little countervailing hope to all the stories of the dead and the doomed. "More than anywhere else in the world, AIDS in Africa was met with apathy," says Suzanne LeClerc-Madlala, a lecturer at the University of Natal. The consequences of the silence march on: infection soars, stigma hardens, denial hastens death, and the chasm between knowledge and behavior widens. The present disaster could be dwarfed by the woes that loom if Africa's epidemic rages on. The human losses could wreck the region's frail economies, break down civil societies and incite political instability.

In the face of that, every day good people are doing good things. Like Dr. Moll, who uses his after-job time and his own fund raising to run an extensive volunteer home-care program in KwaZulu-Natal. And Busi Magwazi, who, along with dozens of others, tends the sick for nothing in the Durban-based Sinoziso project. And Patricia Bakwinya, who started her Shining Stars orphan-care program in Francistown with her own zeal and no money, to help youngsters like Tsepho Phale. And countless individuals who give their time and devotion to ease southern Africa's plight.

1 IN 4 SOUTH AFRICAN WOMEN AGES 20 TO 29 IS INFECTED WITH HIV

But these efforts can help only thousands; they cannot turn the tide. The region is caught in a double bind. Without treatment, those with HIV will sicken and die; without prevention, the spread of infection cannot be checked. Southern Africa has no other means available to break the vicious cycle, except to change everyone's sexual behavior—and that isn't happening.

The essential missing ingredient is leadership. Neither the countries of the region nor those of the wealthy world have been able or willing to provide it.

South Africa, comparatively well off, comparatively well educated, has blundered tragically for years. AIDS invaded just when apartheid ended, and a government absorbed in massive transition relegated the disease to a back page. An attempt at a national education campaign wasted millions on a farcical musical. The premature release of a local wonder drug ended in scandal when the drug turned out to be made of industrial solvent. Those fiascoes left the government skittish about embracing expensive programs, inspiring a 1998 decision not to provide AZT to HIV-positive pregnant women. Zimbabwe too suffers savagely from feckless leadership. Even in Botswana, where the will to act is gathering strength, the resources to follow through have to come from foreign hands.

AIDS' grip here is so pervasive and so complex that all societies—theirs and ours—must rally round to break it. These countries are too poor to doctor themselves. The drugs that could begin to break the cycle will not be available here until global pharmaceutical companies find ways to provide them inexpensively. The health-care systems required to prescribe and monitor complicated triple-cocktail regimens won't exist unless rich countries help foot the bill. If there is ever to be a vaccine, the West will have to finance its discovery and provide it to the poor. The cure for this epidemic is not national but international. The deep silence that makes African leaders and societies want to deny the problem, the corruption and incompetence that render them helpless is something the West cannot fix. But the fact that they are poor is not. The wealthy world must help with its zeal and its cash if southern Africa is ever to be freed of the AIDS plague.

Article 9

The Economist December 9, 2000

In the heart of darkness

GOMA, KINSHASA AND LUANDA

The war in Congo is the world's biggest, affecting at least ten countries and millions of people. Can anything be done?

THE hefty cargo plane grinds on across Africa, the deafening monotony of its engines never changing. The hold is stuffed with drums of fuel and crates of ammunition, spare parts for weapons and medical supplies. Perched among them are a dozen soldiers, one of whom is carrying a suitcase full of dollars. Three young women, one of them with a child, crouch among the drums with wrapped-up bundles, a couple of live chickens and several bunches of bananas.

The old Russian-made plane is flown by Ukrainians. They and the plane have been rented in Kiev by a Greek entrepreneur who also deals in coffee, timber and arms. This time he has hired it out to the Ugandan army, but it could have been made available to any one of the seven national armies at war in Congo. His business prospects look good. Peace is impossible just now.

Below, the forest stretches to the horizon in all directions, a vast head of dark trees broken only by slate-coloured rivers. Look down two hours later, and nothing has changed. It is as if the plane hasn't moved. Congo is big. Lay a map of Europe across Congo, with London at its western end, and the eastern border falls 200 miles beyond Moscow.

War in Congo does not involve huge armies and terrible battles, but a few guns can send hundreds of thousands fleeing their homes. It threatens Congo' nine neighbours with destabilisation, and with thousands of refugees pouring into their border areas. In the first week of December alone, by UN estimates, more than 60,000 refugees fled into Zambia from fighting that has just delivered the town of Pweto to Congo' anti-government rebels. War in Congo means a generation growing up without inoculation or education and the rapid spread of AIDS, the camp-follower of war in Africa. A recent United Nations report described Congo' war as one of the world' worst humanitarian crises, affecting some 16m people.

THE LEGACY OF GREED

Congo was only briefly a nation state. For most of history it was a blank on the map, luring in the greedy and unwary. It was first pillaged by the slave kingdoms and foreign slavers; then by predators looking for ivory, rubber, timber, copper, gold and diamonds. Leopold, king of the Belgians, grabbed it in 1885 to make himself a private kingdom. That sparked the imperial takeover of Africa by Europeans at the end of the 19th century.

Leopold' agents cut off hands and heads to force the inhabitants to deliver its riches to him. Then came Belgian state rulers. They built some roads and brought in health and education programmes, but blocked any political development. When Congo was pitched into independence in 1960, there was chaos.

Congo nearly broke up; then out of the chaos came Mobutu Sese Seko, one of the more grotesque rulers of independent Africa. America and Europe supported him because he was anti-communist; but he was Leopold' true successor, regarding the country as his personal possession. He renamed it Zaire, used the treasury as his bank account and ruled by allowing supporters and rivals to feed off the state. If they became too greedy or powerful, he would have them thrown into prison for a while before being given another post

to plunder. On two occasions he encouraged his unpaid, disgruntled soldiers to satisfy themselves by looting the cities. He built himself palaces and allowed the roads the Belgians had built to disintegrate. This helped break up Congo into fiefs. When Mobutu' rule ended in 1997, the nation state was dead. The only national organisation was the Catholic church.

One of his fiefs was Hutu-ruled Rwanda. Mobutu called its president, Juvenal Habyarimana, his baby brother. In 1994 Habyarimana was killed in a plane crash, and the rump of his regime carried out genocide against Rwanda' Tutsi minority. But, with Ugandan help, the Tutsis triumphed. The old Rwandan army and the gangs of killers fled into Congo, where Mobutu gave them shelter and weapons. In 1996 the new Tutsi-dominated Rwandan army crossed the border and attacked the Hutu camps, intending to set up a buffer zone to protect its western border. The attack worked better than anticipated and the Rwandans, Ugandans and their Congolese allies kept walking westwards until they took the capital, Kinshasa. Mortally ill, Mobutu fled and the Rwandans installed Laurent Kabila as president.

A year later, Mr Kabila tried to wriggle out of the control of the Rwandans and Ugandans. He allied himself with their enemies, the Hutu militias in eastern Congo. In response they launched another rebellion to try to dislodge him. But this time Angola, Zimbabwe, Namibia, Sudan and Chad sent troops to defend him. They said they were acting on principle, to protect a neighbouring state from invasion. The war reached a stalemate with the country divided. In the western half, Mr Kabila was backed by Zimbabwe, Angola and Namibia (Sudan and Chad withdrew). The east was controlled by three rebel movements and their creators and controllers, Uganda and Rwanda. Burundi also has troops in Congo allied to the Rwandans, but these stay close to the Burundi border.

In June and July last year, a peace agreement was signed in Lusaka by the government of Congo, the three rebel groups and five intervening nations. It provided a timetable for a ceasefire, the deployment of African military observers supported by UN monitors, the disarming of "negative forces" (the mi-

litia gangs that roam eastern Congo), and the eventual withdrawal of all foreign forces. It also prescribed a national dialogue between Mr Kabila and the armed and unarmed opposition.

NEIGHBOURS ON THE TAKE

Unsurprisingly, it has not worked. The ceasefire has been persistently broken by all sides, most recently with the fighting around Pweto. Although the defence chiefs of six of the intervening countries, led by Zimbabwe, and several rebel groups signed a deal in Harare on December 6th to pull back their forces from front-line positions, it is still unlikely to happen. The exploitation of the country by the intervening armies reinforces the imperialist nature of the invasion, as do their disparaging comments about the Congolese. "A hopeless people," remarked one senior Rwandan. "All they want to do is drink and dance."

Each of the interveners in Congo has complex and different reasons for being there. At one level, they have been sucked into the vacuum; social and population pressure east of Congo has drawn the neighbours towards a country with few people for its size and no state structures. But each also had internal political reasons for going to Congo.

The Rwandans want to track down the perpetrators of genocide and either drive them back to Rwanda or kill them. The success of the 1996 invasion and American support has made them overconfident. President Yoweri Museveni of Uganda also has ambitions bigger than his own country. He wants the economy of eastern Congo to link up with East Africa, and wants to replicate his own political system in Congo. The rebel Movement for the Liberation of Congo (MLC) was created by Uganda, and mimics Mr Museveni' political analysis and ideology.

On the other side, Mr Kabila' allies also have domestic reasons for being in Congo. Sudan, engaged in a proxy war with Uganda, wanted another way to attack it. Angola wanted to get into Congo to stop its own rebel movement, UNITA, from using Congolese territory as a supply route and rear base. Namibia got involved because it is indebted to Angola. President Robert Mugabe of Zimbabwe, jealous of South Africa' new power in southern Africa, wanted to make himself the region' military leader. Others loiter in the background: North Korea has sent some 400 soldiers to help train Mr Kabila' fledgling army and tons of weapons, reportedly in exchange for future sales of copper, cobalt and uranium.

Many western diplomats and analysts, as well as most Congolese, suspect that America is secretly funding Rwanda and Uganda. State Department officials deny this, but it is hard to see how these poor countries can fight without outside resources. Their meagre defence budgets (Uganda' is allegedly $100m this year) cannot possibly sustain their operations in Congo.

Once in Congo, the interveners found commercial reasons to stay. The war has created huge business opportunities which have obscured its primary, political, cause. Hundreds of dodgy businessmen, mercenaries, arms dealers and security companies have come to the region. Diamonds are a big prize and the main source of foreign exchange for Mr Kabila. It is hardly surprising that the war ground to a halt around Mbuji-Mayi, the main diamond-producing area. Congo pays for Zimbabwe' presence with a diamond-mine concession. It has also formed a joint oil company with Angola.

Senior military officers from all the armies, as well as their political cronies back home, make money trading diamonds, gold, coffee and timber, and from contracts to feed and supply their troops. They have little interest in peace. Local and foreign businessmen often pay them to provide troops to guard a valuable mine or a farm. The Kilo Moto gold mine in Kivu has been taken over by freelance diggers, but the entrance is guarded by Ugandan soldiers who tax them. Kigali and Kampala are crawling with diamond dealers and others looking for Congo' rare minerals, such as tantalite and niobium. The loot is not confined to minerals. One Ugandan unit, returning from Congo, caused fury in both countries by having their newly acquired Congolese wives and girlfriends flown home with them at government expense. War booty, said chauvinistic Ugandan politicians. Rape and theft, said Congolese men.

THE KABILA DISASTER

When Laurent Kabila was catapulted to power by Uganda and Rwanda, everyone thought Congo would change. He could hardly do worse than Mobutu, they argued. Perhaps he would turn into one of the much-vaunted "new leaders" of Africa. He had few enemies. Everyone wanted to help him rebuild Congo. Sadly, he turned out to be little more than an outsize village chief, adept at staying in power, but with no vision and a deep distrust of competence. He has surrounded himself with relatives, friends and oddballs he scooped up on his march to Kinshasa. Mentally he is stuck in the cold war of the early 1960s, imagining global plots against Congo.

The formal economy is dead. Not far from the central bank in central Kinshasa, carefully tended cabbages have sprung from a small patch of waste ground by the roadside. Nearby, families have moved into the ruins of a half-built office block, hanging their washing over the abandoned concrete pillars and cooking on open fires on the floors of rooms designed for board meetings. Only about 20% of the city' 4m-5m people have jobs. Most of these pay, if at all, about $8 or $9 a month. The city has little fuel, so people get up before dawn to walk to work. Most eat nothing all day, then return on foot to the one daily meal of cassava porridge or bread. Less than 30% of the capital' children are in school, and few can afford medicine if they are ill.

Mr Kabila blames all this on the war. It has more to do with his old-fashioned statist policies and his arbitrary way of

handing out contracts and concessions and then cancelling them. That has frightened off foreign companies. So has his policy of locking up foreigners and demanding ransom. Heineken, a Dutch brewing company, recently paid $1m in cash to the finance minister to secure the release of its two senior executives in Kinshasa. Maurice Templesman, an American diamond dealer, also lost millions of dollars when his staff were seized and thrown out of the country. One foreign security company in Kinshasa says its best new business is negotiating the release of foreign nationals arrested by the government.

Mobutu played the country and its political elite like a chess master. Mr Kabila tries the same techniques; putting people in power or in prison and playing the ethnic card. But he is no expert. Long in exile, he barely understands Congo. There have been splits and mutinies in his fledgling army and his ministers are at each other' throats. Only in the south-east, his home territory, does he still have some support. The impoverished people of Kinshasa despise him, but will not demonstrate against him for fear of being accused of supporting the rebel movements—which they do not.

Mr Kabila is currently trying to get the Lusaka accord rewritten. He has blocked the deployment of UN military observers and humiliated and rejected Ketumile Masire, the former Botswanan president, who was appointed to organise a national dialogue. He even failed to turn up at meetings with his backers, Angola and Zimbabwe. President Eduardo dos Santos of Angola warned him in August that he had "had enough of his arrogance", and that the allies would withdraw from Congo if he continued to obstruct the peacemakers. But Mr dos Santos knows there is, as yet, no alternative to Mr Kabila and that there would be chaos if the allies withdrew now.

That is the crux of the problem. Mr Kabila has failed, but there is no one else who enjoys national support or looks remotely capable of pulling the country together. Mobutu ensured that every politician in Congo was smeared with his corruption. Nor do the rebel movements present an alternative. The Congolese Rally for Democracy (RCD) split apart, with one faction supported by Uganda and the other by Rwanda. Uganda then launched the MLC and, in June, the former allies fought a full-scale battle in Kisangani for six days, destroying much of the town' centre and killing 619 civilians. This engagement also destroyed the credibility of the two leaders, Mr Museveni and Rwanda' president, Paul Kagame, in Congo. America and western countries were furious with them and blocked Uganda' promised debt relief as punishment.

Both factions of the RCD are now deeply unpopular in their own areas. The clumsy intervention of Rwanda and Uganda in South and North Kivu has stirred up bitter ethnic rivalry. Much of this region suffers from the same Hutu-Tutsi divisions that exist in Rwanda and Burundi. The intervention has upset the fragile balance, and the region flares with massacre and counter-massacre.

Local communities have tried to defend themselves against all outsiders by forming self-defence militias, but many of these have degenerated into wandering gangs of mercenaries and bandits, the "negative forces" of the Lusaka accord. Some are linked to Rwandan Hutus, some fight against them. Mr Kabila is fanning the flames by sending them weapons across Lake Tanganyika. The Kivus are now a horrendous mess of wars and sub-wars that will burn on long after the national war is over.

In northern Congo, the picture is slightly better. Jean-Pierre Bemba, the young MLC leader and a businessman, is popular there because his Ugandan-run army is fairly disciplined and, in Mobutu' home area, he is seen as his successor. It is a label he vigorously rejects, since he knows it will kill support for him in other places.

WHAT HAPPENS NEXT

The present situation is deadlocked and unstable. The UN will not deploy its forces until it is convinced that all parties are serious about peace, but the "negative forces", Hutu militias, gangs and others have signed no ceasefire and have little interest in peace. That means the foreign forces cannot fulfill the Lusaka accord and leave. But their governments, even the oil-rich Angolans, are worried about the cost. They are all engaging in bilateral talks with each other; but that increases mistrust and suspicion.

The Rwandans, realising how unpopular they are in Congo, have given up hope of overthrowing Mr Kabila and instead have offered to withdraw their troops to the Kivus. Zimbabwe, hard-pressed by domestic problems, wants its 12,000 troops out as soon as there is a face-saving formula. Their departure could destabilise Mr Kabila. Maybe the Angolans, left holding the fort, will remove him. At present they seem to be trying to bring in Mr Bemba and a representative of the unarmed opposition to create a triumvirate with Mr Kabila. To achieve this, the Angolans have to trust Mr Bemba' backer, Uganda. They don't, because Uganda has been a conduit for arms to UNITA rebels in Angola. Besides, the Ugandan army and the MLC are still pushing westwards towards the strategic city of Mbandaka, garrisoned by Angolans.

And what of the Congolese people in all this? Impoverished, disregarded and oppressed, they still give one clear message almost unanimously in every conversation: they do not want Congo to break up. But the long decompositon of this vast country seems inevitable, whoever rules in Kinshasa.

This war could rumble on for years, if not decades. The Lusaka accord, concedes a senior UN representative, is not going to work; but no one has a better plan. The best he can suggest is that outsiders remain engaged, help the victims, try to understand what is happening—and not make it worse. Congo' experience of outsiders is, to put it mildly, discouraging.

Article 10   *Dollars and Sense,* May/June 1999

FREEDOM TO FARM—AND STARVE—IN KENYA

BY MARC BRESLOW

Marc Breslow is an economist and departing coeditor of Dollars and Sense.

It's a long bus ride from Kenya's capital of Nairobi to the main port, Mombasa. The distance is only 300 miles or so, but it takes eight hours or more because the highway is in such awful condition. It's a narrow two lanes, filled with large craters, and there are many stretches where the pavement disappears completely. Sometimes the bus drives on the small dirt shoulder, other times we detour onto a dirt track built off to the side. Often, while avoiding potholes, we drive precariously close to oncoming traffic. My friend Irene clutches her seat, fearful of a crash.

Terrible roads are one of the most obvious signs of the sad shape of Kenya's economy. The nation, a popular destination for affluent tourists planning to see large animals in the game preserves, has one of the world's most corrupt governments. President Daniel Arap Moi, in power more than 20 years, rules through a combination of dictatorial power, violence, and allowing his supporters to profit at the expense of the majority. The roads are not repaired because, the government claims, it has no money to do so.

I'm in Kenya for three weeks, visiting with Irene Danysh, a friend who teaches at a university in Nairobi, and trying to see a bit of what life is like for people here. Kenyans suffer at the hands of their own government, a class system like anywhere else, and the vagaries of global capitalism. Moi's government wastes much of the country's resources, through measures such as hiring thousands of do-nothing public employees and allowing businessmen to give bribes in order to avoid paying taxes. From 1980 to 1992 wages per person *fell* by 2.1% a year, and 37% of the population lives below Kenya's own poverty line, according to the World Bank and the United Nations Development Program.

Meanwhile, Kenya's majority still live on subsistence farms. In part due to pressures from the International Monetary Fund and World Bank, they have been subjected in recent years to an unbridled free market that makes it difficult to survive. Between 1970 and 1995 the daily supply of protein per person in Kenya *fell* by 17%.

RURAL KENYA

From Mombasa, Irene and I head back to Nairobi, and then to Western Province, the most densely populated part of the country. It is another full day's bus ride, this time on better-paved roads, to reach the town of Kakamega, not far from the Ugandan border. Along the way we pass large, well-maintained tea plantations, little of whose income seems to trickle down to the poor.

We stay overnight in Kakamega, a dusty, trash-strewn town dominated by a large outdoor marketplace. About two-thirds of Kenyans still live in rural areas, on small plots of land, eking out a living from subsistence and cash crops. For the poor majority, the basic diet consists largely of three items: ugali, a stiff corn meal porridge; sukuma wiki, a dish of sauteed kale; and tea. On occasion, there are bananas, root vegetables, eggs, and perhaps chicken.

We are traveling to the home of Luka Masinde and his extended family. They are friends of Helena Halperin, an American woman who lived in the area for a year. Halperin is writing a book on Kenyan women, and has arranged our visit. To get there we take a "matatu," one of the privately-run vans that dominate "public" transportation, perhaps 12 miles up the paved road, to an intersection called Kakunga. It is another eight miles or so by dirt road, and the only transportation is "boda bodas"—bicycle taxis. We find two, each fitted with a metal rack and large seat cushion over the rear wheel.

We arrive at the outdoor market near Luka's home. He happens to be there, and has no trouble spotting us—as few whites come here. Their family "compound" is a collection of mud huts spread among the farm fields, in which live Luka, several brothers and sons, and their families. Under the cultural rules

of the Luhya—the local ethnic group—the daughters all live elsewhere, with their husbands' families. It is beautiful here—pleasant cultivated land, trees, long views to hills in the distance.

To say they live in huts is inadequate—these are impressively constructed small homes. Built by layering mud over a frame of thin wooden posts, the walls are smooth enough that they could be mistaken for plaster or concrete. The roofs are made of thatched grass, which Luka tells us last for ten years, or longer if one builds a windbreak of trees around the hut. Rain runs off the roof into a trench dug around the house, which apparently stays dry even in heavy storms.

Inside, Luka's house is divided by a partial wall into a living room and bedroom. Cooking is done in a separate hut, the latrine is a third hut, and there is a separate washing area. If the latrine is built 20 feet deep, they tell us, it will also last for ten years.

The traditional gender roles here are obvious. As we talk with Luka and his brother Samuel Shiundu (who is a full generation younger—they have the same father but different mothers, as polygamy is common here), the women are nowhere in evidence. Samuel's wife, Evelyn, appears only in order to serve food. When we invite her to join us, she sits against the wall rather than at the table. We barely see Luka's wife, as his sons serve the food, and she seems to stay in the cooking hut.

THE CRISIS IN FARMING

For families in Western Province, growing enough food and getting enough money for their cash crops are the biggest worries. Some of this is due to rapid population growth, and consequent scarcity of farm land. But selling the crops is also a major difficulty. "During the rainy season, you cannot travel the roads," Luka tells us. "Nearly everywhere you have to carry your materials, or whatever cash crop you have harvested, on your bicycle or your wagon, which is hard." We can see why—the dirt roads near their home look more like dried-up stream beds, and it's a wonder that vehicles can travel them at all. Luka says the government used to come in with heavy equipment and grade the roads, but now says it can't afford to do so.

Besides, "The prices we get for our cash crops are low," Luka tells us, "but the prices for imports [of the same crops] are high." How can this be? At harvest times, local farmers must sell their crops for whatever price they can get, because the foods are perishable and they have no storage capacity. At other times of year, when local food supplies are short, people have no choice but to buy imported staples, even at higher prices.

Years ago there was a system designed to regulate the ups and downs of the farming year—with many similarities to the system developed by the U.S. government for farmers here—but that has disappeared. "When there was a lot of production, the government used to buy cereals from the farmers at a fair

HUMAN RIGHTS DENIED

Like most dictators, Moi has not shown great respect for human rights. Abuses take many forms, from unjust imprisonment, to torture, to theft of land from its legitimate owners. "Human rights defenders, prodemocracy activists and journalists were harassed, detained or ill-treated for nonviolent activities. Police officers routinely beat criminal suspects, apparently causing a number of deaths in custody, and violently attacked peaceful protesters and opposition party supporters," wrote Amnesty International in its 1998 report on Kenya.

Human Rights Watch said recently that Kenya's government has failed to carry out promised legal reforms that would allow more democracy. "1998 was marked both by deepening ethnic hatred and continuing violence, and a growing political crisis due to the government's unwillingness to allow any reform that would end the absolute executive power wielded by President Moi," commented the U.S.-based organization.

Kang'ethe Mungai, our guide at the Mathare slum, used to work for an organization called Release Political Prisoners, and now is with a new group, People Against Torture. Early in my visit, Kang'ethe introduced us to a woman whose son, Peter Muraya, was shot to death a week earlier while in jail, presumably by the police. He had been picked up for a minor offense, brewing illegal alcohol, and apparently had no other arrest record. According to Kang'ethe, while such killings are unusual, abuse of prisoners is common.

Struggles over land are a key issue. Recently the Karura Forest, the last untouched natural area within Nairobi itself, was "grabbed" by unknown people, presumably with government connections, who now have armed thugs guarding it. Professor Wangari Maathai, head of the Greenbelt Movement and a prominent environmental activist, has been leading protests against such land grabbing. "We are not dealing with a land shortage, we are dealing with greed and corruption," she says. Last January 8 Maathai led about 20 protesters to Karura, where she tried to plant seedlings at the gate. The guards attacked, beating people with whips, clubs, and stones. Maathai and several others were hospitalized.

price, store it, and then when supply was limited, they would sell it to the farmers at a fair price," says Peter, one of Luka's sons, who has studied agricultural engineering in college.

But now, under the urging of the World Bank and the International Monetary Fund (IMF), Kenya has "liberalized" agriculture—eliminating all efforts to control the free market, so the government no longer stores maize (corn), and it allows imports of food with few restrictions. Food production per person has fallen by 9% since 1980. "We are suffering from liberalization, because our economy has not grown, we have not improved our production techniques, so we cannot compete with our counterparts elsewhere," Peter argues. Another factor is that other countries subsidize domestic farming, allowing them to export cheaply to Kenya and elsewhere.

Later, in Nairobi, I talk to Sam Mwale, an agricultural economist who consults for development agencies, such as the U.S. Agency for International Development (USAID) and the

World Bank. Surprisingly, Mwale is openly critical about the effects of liberalization. "In the 1970s to about the mid-1980s, when Kenya was being touted as a success, we have a system that worked relatively well," he says. The government funded agricultural research; it ran an Agricultural Finance Corporation that provided credit to farmers; it bought crops at a guaranteed price; and sold fertilizer and certified seed to farmers at prices they could count on.

The system began to break down not from IMF-induced free-market reforms, but due to power-grabbing by President Moi. The national institutions supporting farmers, such as the Kenya Farmers Association and the National Cereals and Produce Board, were an alternative power center which Moi could not tolerate, so beginning in the 1980s he wrecked them—with no objection from the World Bank.

At that time the government still protected local farmers from international competition. But beginning in 1993 Kenya loosened controls on imports, in response to demands by the IMF for liberalization. Prices for farm products have fallen, Mwale tells me, and people are very bitter. Moreover, agricultural productivity—output per acre of land—has dropped during the 1990s.

Corruption is another factor making it difficult for domestic farmers to compete. Despite liberalization, there remain duties on imports, which should hinder them. But many people tell me that these duties can be evaded by people who have influence with the government. Then products such as sugar, perhaps the most important cash crop, come in from abroad at prices which undercut local farmers.

In January 1999 Kenyan newspapers reported that, although some poverty-stricken parts of the country faced starvation, heavy imports of maize meant plummeting prices, and local farmers feared selling their harvests at heavy losses. The National Cereals and Produce Board (NCPB) announced that it would spend 400 million shillings (about $6.5 million) to buy maize, in an effort to raise prices. But dissident members of parliament (MPs) said that at least ten times as much spending was needed, both to help farmers and to provide food for those in need. "A total ban should be slapped on maize and wheat imports," argued the three MPs.

Mwale believes that free-market liberalization could succeed if there was a government which effectively regulated the market. "Government should ensure that there is infrastructure, that there are rules of the game, but the government is not investing in making markets more competitive . . . We have moved from something that was at least a bit orderly, to something that does not work," he says.

The intelligentsia outside of Moi's circle are highly critical of the government's operations, including those in agriculture, but appear to have accepted liberalization as inevitable. Their views are expressed in *Our Problems, Our Solutions: An Economic and Public Policy Agenda for Kenya,* published in late 1998 by the Institute for Economic Affairs, a leading think-tank in Nairobi. "Before liberalisation of the grains subsector, the NCPB stabilised prices by buying and selling at government controlled prices . . . With liberalisation . . . Price instability, particularly of maize, leads to fluctuations in the availability of domestic supplies—thereby exacerbating food security problems in the country—with reduced incomes to producers and supplies for consumers." But while calling for greater price stability, *Our Problems, Our Solutions* does not suggest a return to greater regulation—probably because its authors so mistrust the government.

The World Bank and IMF have concentrated their attention on dissolving the system of agricultural regulation, including the marketing boards. But "reform as an anti-poverty strategy must involve land reform," argues Wachira Maina, a prominent constitutional lawyer and critic of the government. Most families face a shortage of land, which, along with population growth, results in its subdivision into efficient plots—while much of the land is held by a small number of wealthy owners, a result of corruption and the colonial legacy. "Politically connected and rich people have thousands of acres, which are too big even to use," says Wangari Maathai, the nation's leading environmental activist.

With farms failing to support them, many rural people operate some type of small business in addition to growing crops. Women are most often the entrepreneurs, either as individuals or as part of a small group. With Luka, we tour the "neighborhood"—farm fields and huts connected by dirt paths—and visit several such enterprises. At the market nearby, several women have open-air stalls at which they sell cheap consumer goods, vegetables, and dried fish. One family we visit has a sugar cane grinding mill, called a jaggery, from which they sell hardened cones of brown sugar that are used in brewing local beer. The local blacksmith, Simon, says that he makes hoes, ceremonial bells, and knives. Another family cuts and sells lumber, and there is an (illegal) alcohol brewer.

EDUCATION: EXPENSIVE AND RISKY

Luka and his family, although they are prominent in the local area, can no longer support everyone just from their own farm output. So, as with many families, they have gone to great lengths to send many of the brothers and sons to school. Flora Shiundu, the aged mother of Luka's younger brothers, tells us (in Luka's translation) that when her husband died she worked hard so all the brothers could go to school, that she went without a blanket in order to pay school fees.

Public education in Kenya is not free, and most families cannot afford to send their children beyond the primary grades. As of 1995, only 24% of secondary-age children were in school, and only 16% of total government spending went to education.

Yet in a nation with scarce jobs and absurdly low wages, getting an education is not enough. Luka's brother Samuel, an intelligent man who went to college to become an electronics technician, has been unable to find a permanent job. He has

---

CLINTON VERSUS JACKSON ON U.S. POLICY TOWARD AFRICA

Bill Clinton's vision for U.S. economic policy toward Africa is embodied in the "Africa Growth and Opportunity Act," dubbed "NAFTA-for-Africa" by its opponents. The administration claims that by reducing trade barriers between African countries and the United States, House of Representatives Bill 434 would aid African development.

But critics, including Public Citizen's Global Trade Watch, say that in order to get access to U.S. markets the bill would require African nations to impose harsh IMF-style changes to their economies, such as slashing spending on health and education, privatizing public enterprises and allowing foreign investors to buy them, and cutting corporate taxes. In addition, the trade benefits would be limited largely to textiles and clothing, and there would be lax standards for how workers are treated. NAFTA-for-Africa is backed by a corporate front, the Africa Growth and Opportunity Act Coalition, whose members include Chevron, Mobil, General Electric, and Kmart.

In February Chicago congressman Jesse Jackson Jr. and a list of cosponsors introduced an alternative, the HOPE for Africa Act, HR 772. It would require that companies exporting to the United States employ 80% African workers, have 60% African ownership, and respect internationally recognized labor rights. HR 772 would also establish a schedule to cancel Africa's external debts to the United States, international agencies, and the private sector, which currently stand at a crushing $230 billion. Besides Public Citizen and other U.S. groups, the bill has been endorsed by dozens of African organizations, including the Kenya National Farmers Union.

---

temporary work at the West Kenya Sugar factory, located about eight miles from the family compound. Samuel, like most Kenyans, works a six day week, but he makes only 135 shillings a day—barely more than $2. "Even if you have no family, that is not enough to live on, but you are forced to accept it, because there is no other employment," he says.

Another brother, Julius, tells us that he works at a sugar factory about 25 miles away, and comes home on weekends either by bicycle or matatu. Also educated, he works in the "audits" department, and says that the lowest-paid workers there get 3,200 shillings a month (about $52), but he has to spend 500 shillings a month on rent alone.

THE RICH AND POOR

Back in Nairobi the contrasts between rich and poor are extreme. With jobs scarce, and those that do exist paying barely enough to survive, crime is rampant. Westerners are told not to carry anything of value visibly while on the streets. My friend Irene rents a room in a house that's part of a compound seemingly typical of those used by the more affluent. It has high walls all around and a gate with 24-hour guards at the only entrance. Each house has bars on all the windows and from the ground to an extended roof outside the front and back doors.

A friend of Irene's, human rights activist Kang'ethe Mungai, takes us on a tour of what he says is the country's worst slum, the Mathare Valley in Nairobi. Mathare is indeed horrific. It is a dirt and rock hillside covered by hundreds, maybe thousands of one-room houses made from mud, scrap materials, and metal roofs. Entire families, some with many children, live in these shacks, with narrow lanes running between the rows of buildings. There is no water or sewage system, and sewage flows in small streams along the lanes. Surprisingly, the place does not smell foul.

Some people cook and sell food in front of their shacks. Cheap imported goods, such as clothes and toiletries, are sold at "stores" throughout the neighborhood. (Kenya used to manufacture clothing for its own use, but a few years ago liberalization caused a flood of cheap imports, both new and used, and domestic production collapsed.) Despite the conditions, the children run around, smile, and want their picture taken.

We talk to a committee of women who are fighting "redevelopment" of the slum. Wanjiku Muhia, the committee chair, speaks Kikuyu, her tribal (or ethnic) language, but Kang'ethe translates. In Kenya, most people's first language is a tribal tongue, while Kiswahili is spoken throughout the country. English is the official language, spoken by those who have had enough years of school.

The Amani Housing Trust, funded by the German government and run by the Catholic Church, is gradually tearing the shacks down, and replacing them with ten-foot square, one-room houses of unfired brick, that at least in terms of space don't seem any better than the shacks. People have to pay rent on the new buildings, 500 Kenyan shillings (about $8) a month, plus utilities—not much in western terms, but a lot for people who have little or no cash income. Kang'ethe tells us that these are supposed to be temporary structures, to be replaced by better ones—but in more than five years of redevelopment no "permanent" houses have yet been built.

CORRUPTION

Most people in Kenya believe that its incredibly corrupt government is the major source of their problems. For decades Moi has been using the country's government and economy largely as a tool for personal enrichment and to keep himself in power. Partially as a result, the government provides few of the services needed either by the general population or by private businesses, and little can be done by companies without paying off the government in some fashion.

Corruption takes various forms. There are huge numbers of people on the government payroll or those of the many state-owned enterprises, helping to ensure Moi's political support, but little money is available for carrying out their agencies' functions. "More than 80% of the government budget pays salaries, [of people] who do nothing, because they don't have

the tools to do their jobs," says Mbatao wa Ngai, an economics columnist with *The Daily Nation,* Kenya's leading newspaper.

Government contracts are often given in return for bribes, and the work may be done at higher cost than necessary, or in some cases no work is actually performed. Taxes of all types can be evaded through payoffs—one reason that the government is so short of funds. Perhaps most important, large tracts of the increasingly scarce arable land have been given out to Moi's backers, rather than to the millions of small farmers who need them.

Before the 1990s, the United States and its allied international agencies were fervent backers of Moi and his predecessor, Kenya's founding president, Jomo Kenyatta. Since achieving independence from the British in 1963, Kenya was a bulwark of anti-Communism, and the West was happy to overlook corruption, repression, and economic failures. But with the collapse of Communism in eastern Europe and the breakup of the Soviet Union, the capitalist powers became willing to criticize dictatorial regimes. Similarly, development agencies began demanding democratic reforms and less corrupt use of their funds—although the agencies' adherence to the free market remained unchanged.

As a result, the reform-minded Kenyan intelligentsia largely see the IMF, World Bank, and foreign lenders as having a positive role. Because Moi needs their loans, these institutions have more leverage on the government than anyone in Kenya itself. And whatever economic destruction their prescriptions may cause, these agencies have also pushed for democratization.

A NEW BEGINNING?

Under international pressure, Moi was forced to legalize political parties besides his own. He is scheduled to leave office in the year 2002, and a process is underway to write a new constitution by that time. While Kenya's founding constitution provided for democratic processes, over the years Moi managed to pass laws which have largely centralized power in his own office, leaving the parliament as a rubber stamp.

Despite his political dominance, the desperate shape of the economy has caused Moi to implement some reforms. After more than 20 years of the country's wealth being looted by the internal power structure, combined with global pressures felt throughout the third world, living standards in Kenya have been sliding downward, and Moi risks an explosion of popular discontent. The government also faced a severe budget crisis in 1998. One result was that it failed to honor a wage agreement with the National Association of Teachers, leading to a nationwide strike.

Many people have high hopes that the new constitution will bring both political and economic reform. But, despite pressures from outside the country, the outcome is in question. The first step in drafting a constitution, appointment of a 25-person drafting commission, is currently underway. Its members are being chosen by political parties, nongovernmental organizations, and church groups.

But most of these nominators are tied in to the existing political power structure, and are likely to choose members who will defend the status quo. Despite the commission's extensive plan to consult with the population, in the end the current parliament must approve the new constitution. And the parliament "represents the interests of the government, of the ruling party," the lawyer Wachira Maina told me. "If you want to reform a constitution in the context of an incumbency that is terrified, you will not get real change unless you have struck a bargain beforehand—such as amnesty, or other credible commitments. But in Kenya we have not done that. If I were the president, I would want to retain very tight control of the process," says Maina.

In a nation which has been exploited for so long by its own government, taking power away from that body, as the World Bank wants to do through privatizing most public enterprises, seems like the logical solution. It's difficult to make the case that the private sector is likely to treat people just as badly.

"At independence we had amazing faith in government," reports Maina. "Now, after thirty years, we have developed this amazing faith in the private sector, because the only institutions we see working are private ones—hospitals, schools, garbage collection . . . We are going to have a difficult process of recognizing the problems of private power, and seeing the role that government has in controlling private power."

Resources: Mama Anasema: Kenyan Women Talk About Their Lives and Hopes, Helena Halperin, forthcoming; *Our Problems, Our Solutions: An Economic and Public Policy Agenda for Kenya,* Wamuyu Gatheru and Robert Shaw, editors, Institute for Economic Affairs, Nairobi, 1998; *Human Development Report 1998,* United Nations Development Programme; Citizens Trade Watch web site, www.tradewatch.org.

Article 11   *Current History,* May 1999

Mauritius: Rethinking the Miracle

"Mauritius has faced globalization with a strong set of assets, including its creative private sector, solid democracy, and long-standing concern for social security. Mauritians themselves continually question their miracle, and it is this self-awareness, along with a remarkable adaptability, that will help bring the country successfully through the trials ahead."

DEBORAH BRÄUTIGAM

DEBORAH BRäUTIGAM, *an associate professor at American University's School of International Service, is a visiting Fulbright researcher at the University of Mauritius. She is the author of* Chinese Aid and African Development: Exporting Green Revolution *(New York: St. Martin's, 1998).*

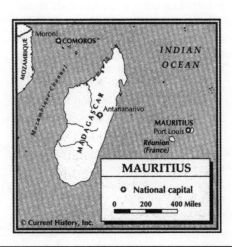

Mauritius is going through difficult times. Admired as Africa's only "tiger" economy because of its rapid, East Asian–style growth, this tiny island nation more than 800 miles off the East African coast has also been praised for an enduring record of democracy and social cohesion despite considerable ethnic fragmentation. Yet the past few years have raised questions about the robustness of the "Mauritian miracle."

Buffeted by inflation, shock waves from the Asian economic crisis, and a steep slide in the value of the country's currency, the rupee, Mauritians have grown angry over what they see as the government's inability to protect their hard-earned standard of living. Recent polls show deep pessimism about Mauritius's economic future. The new offshore services sector has been troubled by suspicion that it has become a financial haven used for money laundering. And the worst drought in 40 years is expected to significantly reduce the sugarcane harvest on which many Mauritians still depend for their livelihood.

Communal interests in multiethnic Mauritius remain delicately balanced and easily upset. The release of new currency notes last October led to widespread demonstrations by Mauritians of Tamil ancestry who were incensed that the positions of the Tamil and Hindi script on the notes had been reversed. But the worst blow to ethnic relations came at the end of this February when Afro-Creoles and Hindus clashed in three days of the most severe communal riots since 1968. Although the country has now returned to its normally calm state, the riots have damaged the country's prized reputation as an island of political stability. They have also made it impossible for Mauritians to ignore the fact that up to 20 percent of the population remains excluded from many of the benefits of two decades of growth.

THE MAURITIAN WAY

Although clearly inspired by East Asia's example, Mauritius differs in many ways from the East Asian model. Growth in Mauritius took off not long after the country established Africa's first export-processing zone in 1970. Yet unlike the authoritarian Asians, Mauritius built its export success on a democratic foundation that emphasized regular consultation with labor and a strong social security system.

Thirty years ago no one thought that Mauritius would ever be regarded as a model of development. Violent communal riots around the time of independence from Britain in 1968 left at least 25 people dead. Unemployment stood at about 20 percent, while the population was growing at an annual rate of 4 percent. Aside from a tiny industrial sector, Mauritians depended almost entirely on sugar for employment, export earnings, and government revenues.

The first postindependence coalition government recognized the importance of maintaining an investor-friendly regime, in part to retain the allegiance of economically powerful Franco-Mauritian minority coalition partners, but also to expand employment. At the same time the Labor Party, the largest member of the coalition, needed the support of labor and small-scale sugar farmers, and took care to secure benefits for them in its policy proposals. Yet when the labor movement began to look too strong, as in 1971 when the country was convulsed by a series of general strikes, the government clamped down. It imposed a state of emergency, jailed strike leaders, and canceled the 1972 elections. This brief authoritarian period was never repeated, and the 1976 elections were held as scheduled.

Over the next 10 years Mauritius underwent a dramatic structural transformation. By the late 1980s it ranked among the world's top three exporters of woolen knitwear. Today the country also exports flowers, optical goods, jewelry, and toys. Manufacturing makes up 24 percent of the economy (exports, primarily textiles and clothing, comprise 12 percent). Services, including tourism, the new offshore banking and nonbanking services sector, and the free port, comprise 66 percent of the economy, about the same as in Singapore. Agriculture (including sugarcane) accounts for barely 10 percent of the economy, compared with an average of 20 percent for the rest of Africa. At $3,685 in 1998, per capita income in Mauritius is almost equal to that in Malaysia, and well above the level of South Africa, putting Mauritius firmly in the upper middle income bracket. This growth has been accompanied by admirable social progress, with literacy, infant mortality, and life expectancy all approaching developed country standards.

The successful strategy rested on determined efforts to free the country from its dependence on sugar. Mauritius gambled by committing a large share of its sugar exports to Europe under a guaranteed quota made possible by the Lomé

Convention's 1975 sugar protocol (the Lomé Convention established quotas, prices, and duty-free access for products from former colonies of European Union member nations). The prices fixed annually under the sugar protocol are a function of the highly subsidized prices given to European farmers, and have historically been two to three times world market prices for sugar. The higher prices paid for Mauritian sugar helped underpin the social security system and also provided much of the private sector savings that are now invested in the export-processing zone (EPZ) and in upscale tourism.

Mauritians also decided against maintaining a standing army, which freed additional funds for social welfare. The government provided subsidized rice and flour and free health care, and gradually made education free up through the university level. Regular turnover of governments through elections, an independent judiciary, and a vigorously free press enforced considerable accountability of politicians.

These policies reaped rewards and gave Mauritius an enviable reputation. Over time, successive governments liberalized the economy while maintaining social protections. Local investment in the EPZ rose; at present, 73 percent of EPZ companies are Mauritian-owned or have substantial Mauritian participation. The 1997 World Economic Forum report on economic performance in Africa ranked Mauritius as the most competitive country in Africa.

What, then, is tarnishing the Mauritian model? Within a year after the current coalition government of Prime Minister Navin Ramgoolam took office following a landslide victory at the end of 1995, its approval rating plummeted from 66 percent to 25 percent as Mauritians expressed their disappointment with the new government's budget policies (substantially higher spending and taxes) and its highly visible infighting. Unemployment recently tripled from a record low of 2 percent in 1995 to almost 6 percent, while the Mauritian rupee slid from a fairly stable level of about Rs 15 to the United States dollar to almost Rs 25 to the dollar. By 1997, political quarreling had splintered the coalition government, leaving Ramgoolam's Labor Party with a bare majority.

The February 1999 riots crystallized growing concern about the state of affairs in Mauritius. Sparked by grief and rage over the suspicious death while in police custody of a popular Rastafarian "seggae" singer, Kaya, demonstrations turned violent as rioters attacked symbols of the state: police stations, traffic lights, and government-owned buses. The days that followed saw widespread looting, destruction of shops and some factories, and ultimately the ethnically targeted burning of dozens of homes and small businesses. At least three people were killed by police gunfire. For Mauritians, most of whom regard the 1968 riots as a distant historical event, the scale of the violence was shocking.

The riots were a sharp reminder that the dissatisfaction and pessimism reflected in recent opinion polls have roots in real challenges facing the country as it attempts to move beyond the economic strategy that brought such rapid and early success. Two of these challenges are especially vexing: maintaining the country's ability to compete successfully in export markets, and the malaise of exclusion. Progress in these areas will be essential if Mauritius hopes to maintain its model into the twenty-first century.

GLOBALIZATION'S CHALLENGES

"Globalization," commented Mauritian Minister of Economic Development Manou Bheenick last September, "is fantastic." More than most developing countries, Mauritius has made good use of its international linkages, but the world trading system that supported the country in its bid to become an "African tiger" is rapidly changing. The principal challenges are the threat to Mauritius's duty-free access to many markets, the rapidly rising cost of labor in export processing and a related drop in foreign

investment, and the continued high concentration of exports in just a few industries. The country is responding by further linking itself to the global economy: expanding its "economic space" into southern Africa; reducing its costs by importing labor from China; encouraging diversification of export products and markets; and positioning itself as a center for financial and business services and a major bridge between Asia and Africa.

While trade liberalization in the early 1990s reduced or removed duties on a large number of items, Mauritius's most important trade has for the most part not been "free" but based on quotas and special agreements. The Lomé Convention that has given it higher prices for its sugar exports has also given it preferential access for its clothing and other exports in Europe. But both of these are slowly being eroded. The preferential access enjoyed in Europe by African, Pacific, and Caribbean countries will come under increasingly stiff challenge, possibly from the United States, if the current "war" over Europe's preferential treatment of Caribbean bananas is a harbinger of the future. Special duty-free access for garments may disappear as soon as 2005, when the Multi-Fiber Agreement terminates, requiring Mauritius to compete with such low-cost producers as China and India.

Manufactured exports from Mauritius are concentrated in knitwear and other garments, a sector that relies heavily on low labor costs. Yet labor is no longer so cheap in Mauritius. Since the start of the EPZ boom in the early 1980s, labor costs have increased almost twice as fast as productivity. Average monthly earnings for EPZ employees in March 1998 were about $270, which is high when compared with most developing countries. Higher costs have led to several shakeouts in the EPZ. Many textile firms have now succeeded in upgrading to higher value-added production while moving lower-skill production to neighboring countries with cheaper labor. In addition, in a controversial move, the government has allowed firms to import

labor; at present, there are nearly 10,000 foreign workers in Mauritius, mainly young Chinese women. At the same time, the unemployment rate for Mauritian women has risen sharply and now stands above 10 percent.

Expanding the country's "economic space" into southern Africa is also an important part of the strategy for the future. Mauritius is a member of the Southern African Development Community and the Common Market for Eastern and Southern Africa (COMESA). Increased regional integration involves exports and investment. A recent study by Mauritian economist Rajen Dabee shows that Mauritian exports to Africa more than doubled over the past decade, but still made up only 5 percent of total exports in 1997. Trade between Mauritius and COMESA countries grew by almost 19 percent between 1996 and 1997, but most of this was related to inputs for Mauritian factories in Madagascar.

A third strategy has been to attempt to diversify exports and export markets. Mauritian exports are still highly concentrated: clothing accounts for almost 80 percent of EPZ exports, and almost half of EPZ exports go to just two countries, France and Britain. By allowing the market to decide what to produce and where to send it, successive governments in Mauritius failed to pave the way for diversification and for the necessary transitions ahead. Moreover, the skill base is weak. More than a third of Mauritian children still fail to graduate from primary school, and secondary school completion rates are well below 50 percent.

New efforts to diversify markets have been more successful, but here too Mauritius is facing problems. The United States market has been the prime target, and Mauritius has already been successful enough to prompt the United States to impose automatic quotas on imports of Mauritian garments. Mauritius and Kenya are the only sub-Saharan African countries so affected. The Africa Growth and Opportunity Bill that is before the United States House of Representatives would remove these quotas, and both the government and the Mauritius Export Processing Zone Association have lobbied hard for passage of the bill.

The fourth arm of the strategy for reinventing Mauritius is to position the country as a regional financial and business services center. Legislation passed in 1989 established an offshore banking sector, and nonbanking offshore services, such as registration for ships, were initiated in 1992. Estimates of the contribution of the offshore banking sector to the country's GDP range from 0.85 to 2.5 percent. This still lags behind tourism, which contributes 4.5 percent of GDP, and the EPZ, which contributes 12.2 percent. Growth in offshore nonbanking services has been strong, with more than 7,000 companies registered as of June 1998.

A free port has been in operation since 1994, with facilities near the airport and at the seaport of the capital, Port Louis. The free port is intended to promote Mauritius as an intercontinental distribution center offering logistical support for shipments between Asia and Africa.

Mauritius hopes to become a bridge between Asia and Africa. The island retains strong links with Asia and has a declared that it wants to "look east" for new business. Hong Kong, together with China, is the largest source of foreign investment in Mauritius. Both the government and the private sector have been promoting the offshore sector and the free port in Asia. Visiting delegations from China and Thailand have expressed interest in using the free port as a distribution center for their products and the offshore center as a base for investment in Southern Africa.

DEVELOPMENT FOR ALL

Compared with most developing countries. Mauritius has been remarkably inclusive in its development. Excellent human development indicators show that the free health and education system are reaching most people in the country. The Gini coefficient of income inequality (a scale where 0.0 represents perfect equality and 1.0 perfect inequality) was 0.42 in 1975 and had dropped to a respectable 0.38 in 1992, which also suggests that development in Mauritius has been very egalitarian, by most measures (South Africa's score was 0.58, Brazil's 0.60). Yet pockets of poverty remain serious problems in the country, as do often unexamined racism and casual discrimination. And inequality has recently been on the rise: the Gini coefficient for 1996–1997 was 0.39. The recent riots have brought these issues home again to Mauritians and ignited a national debate on what can be done about the approximately 20 percent of Mauritians who have not greatly benefited from the country's growth. Afro-Creoles, who are descended from freed slaves originally brought to the island to work the sugar plantations, and who today make up about a quarter of the population, are widely believed to be the most disadvantaged group, but there are also many poor among the majority Hindu population, especially those who still live and work in the sugar-producing areas.

Mauritius does not have an official poverty line, and statistics are not gathered on the basis of communal group or ethnicity. Studies indicate, however, that the poorer communities on the island tend to be those like the towns of Roche Bois, where the Afro-Creole population is concentrated, and Bambous, where many rural Hindus live. Infrastructure and schools in the disadvantaged communities are also measurably poorer than in the rest of the country, making it more difficult for youths from these areas to gain the skills and training they need to succeed. Research suggests that Afro-Creole communities have fewer representative organizations than other communities and thus less ability to lobby the government for services. There is no easy solution to the problem of exclusion, especially when it is combined with racism. Progress will require community mobilization, better government services, affirmative action, and better legal protections against discrimination.

MAURITIUS IN THE NEW MILLENNIUM

More than 30 years ago, Nobel laureate economist James Meade visited Mauritius and wrote pessimistically about the options available for the small island to escape its Malthusian trap of high population growth and unemployment. "The outlook for peaceful development is poor," he asserted. In recent years Mauritians have delighted in invoking this famous dismissal while pointing to their robust economy, social safety net, and generally harmonious ethnic relations.

But the recent wave of pessimism is requiring Mauritians to evaluate their development, often critically. "We must work harder to shake off the puffed-up image of a tiger," a recent newspaper article argued. "We are just a pussycat." Yet there is considerable evidence that the country will weather these storms and continue to reinvent itself. Although the riots, the drought, and a cyclone this March are expected to push the growth rate for 1999 below 5 percent, this will be an exception in a decades-long history of continual and rapid economic expansion. Compared with many emerging markets, Mauritius has faced globalization with a strong set of assets, including its creative private sector, solid democracy, and long-standing concern for social security. Mauritians themselves continually question their miracle, and it is this self-awareness, along with a remarkable adaptability, that will help bring the country successfully through the trials ahead.

Nigeria: The Politics of Marginalization

"Jostling for power by Nigeria's myriad ethnic groups has, for better and for worse, driven the country's political development since before independence from Britain in 1960. What is new is a rhetoric of the impossible: the marginalization of everyone."

Minabere Ibelema

After nearly 14 years of virtually uninterrupted military rule, Nigeria returned to electoral democracy in 1999. The restoration of democratic rule—made possible by the sudden death the previous year of the head of state, General Sani Abacha—engendered an optimism comparable only to the euphoria felt at the end of the civil war in January 1970. Yet it was short lived; the new government of President Olusegun Obassanjo was immediately beset by ethnic agitation and conflict. Grievances that had festered under military rule and had been suppressed with draconian measures suddenly found open expression with the democratic dispensation.

The recent institution or planned introduction of shariah (the Islamic penal code) by several Muslim-populated states in northern Nigeria has aggravated the already complex political atmosphere. Since October 1999, at least 5 northern states have passed laws in favor of implementing the code, and one—Zamfara—has signed it into law. Tension over imposing shariah climaxed in February in a bloody clash in the northern city of Kaduna between northern Muslims and southern Christians residing in the north. As many as 400 people were killed, most of them southerners. Reprisal killings of resident northerners soon followed in the southeastern city of Aba. The ensuing insecurity precipitated an exodus of southerners—especially members of the lgbo ethnic group, who are mainly Christian—from northern cities, and of northern Hausa-Fulani—who are mainly Muslim—from the south.

Following a February 29 meeting of the Council of States—attended by state governors and former heads of state—the federal government ordered the suspension of shariah as a criminal code. Its longstanding application to civil cases, which is acknowledged in the constitution, was allowed to continue. The responses of the affected states have been mixed. A few, such as Jigawa and Zamfara, seem intent on defying the federal government; Zamfara demonstrated its resolve in late March by amputating a convicted thief's right hand, as required under shariah. Other states, such as Niger and Yobe, have formally shelved the code, and Kwara has declared it will never implement it. Several states, including Kaduna and Plateau, appear ambivalent about their intent.

These ethnoreligious tensions are reminiscent of the events in 1966 and 1967 that precipitated Nigeria's civil war in which more than 1 million Nigerians died when the Igbos created the secessionist state of Biafra. Emeka Odumegwu Ojukwu, who led the 30-month secession, has been blamed by some northern leaders for fermenting this year's Kaduna crisis. Ojukwu has responded by calling the accusation a hallucination and by suggesting psychiatric examination for the accusers. But he has also said of the Igbos that "we have to get prepared, be on our toes and wait." Leaders used similar language directly preceding the declaration of secession in 1967.

That 36 smaller states rather than four powerful regions now constitute federal Nigeria would seem to militate against secession (Nigeria in 1966 was composed of the North, the East, the West, and the Midwest regions). Regional coordination among states has, however, created powerful alliances.

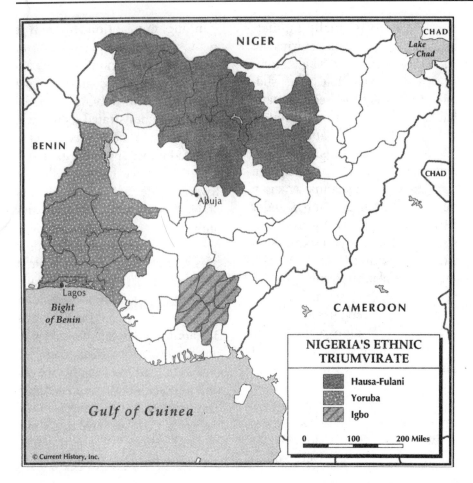

NIGER

CHAD

Lake
Chad

BENIN

Abuja

Lagos

*Bight
of Benin*

CAMEROON

Gulf of Guinea

© Current History, Inc.

NIGERIA'S ETHNIC TRIUMVIRATE

Hausa-Fulani

Yoruba

Igbo

| 0 | 100 | 200 Miles |

indicates that virtually all regions and nationalities in the country claim to be marginalized.

Ordinarily, marginalization entails the subordination of peripheral groups' interests by dominant groups in the formulation or execution of national policies. Accordingly, Nigerian minorities in all regions have historically complained of marginalization and domination. Usually, the complaint is directed at one or all of the numerically dominant groups that constitute the ethnic triumvirate of Nigerian politics: the Hausa-Fulanis in the north, the Yorubas in the west, and the Igbos in the east. But today these three groups claim, along with the minorities, to be marginalized.

Faced with this political Gordian knot, Nigeria would seem to have its Alexander the Great in Olusegun Obasanjo, the new president. At crucial moments in Nigeria's history, Obasanjo has emerged to play pivotal but often uncelebrated roles. As an army commander during the civil war, he helped create a unified front from the initially wary northern and western regions that eventually defeated the Biafran secession. In 1976 he became head of the country's military government and shepherded Nigeria's return to civilian rule in 1979. When the military once again stepped into power in 1984, he became an outspoken critic of the series of military leaders who were unwilling to follow Obasanjo's example and return Nigeria to democratic rule—an outspokenness that led to his imprisonment in 1995.

As president, Obasanjo has sought to reduce ethnic tension through meetings and exhortations, but with only moderate success. But for the most part, Obasanjo has been unable to abate Nigeria's myriad ethnic conflicts. His approach to the country's problems appears two-pronged: to grow the economy and alleviate hardship, and to make all groups feel included in the government. Ironically, the latter policy has had the effect of expanding the number of groups claiming to be marginalized.

Since the shariah crisis, political and religious leaders from northern, western, eastern, and southern minority states have met as discrete blocs to formulate unified positions or to discuss Nigeria's political future. Youths from the middle-belt states have also called for a separate leadership meeting of their states. Still, differences among the states within each bloc makes regional cohesion and secession unlikely.

As in 1967, claims have been made that some military personnel have supplied weapons to and otherwise aided civilians in the communal attacks. Unlike in 1967, however, the military is officially uninvolved, except in assisting the police when requested. In an address to his officers in the wake of the Kaduna riots, the chief of defense staff, Rear Admiral Ibrahim Ogohi, admonished them to eschew partisanship and to remain loyal to federal civilian authority. He pledged to defend Nigeria's nascent democracy.

Similar statements of commitment to a united and democratic Nigeria have been made by political and religious leaders on all sides. Yet these statements have been countered by others advocating confederation, dissolution, or even secession. Thus, the danger remains that Nigeria could splinter violently. Although the present crisis is veiled in religious differences, it is at root political. The causes of tension and instability in Nigeria remain the same as in the civil war: the fear of domination.

THE RHETORIC OF THE IMPOSSIBLE

Jostling for power by Nigeria's myriad ethnic groups has, for better and for worse, driven the country's political development since before independence from Britain in 1960. What is new is a rhetoric of the impossible: the marginalization of everyone. A perusal of Nigerian newspapers and magazines

Claims of marginalization center on four main issues: control of or participation in government, political appointments, leadership of government-owned and -affiliated industries, and budgetary allocations. At some point in Nigeria's recent history, each member of the country's ethnic triumvirate has enjoyed a disproportionate advantage in one or more of these areas. The loss of advantage has created an illusory or exaggerated sense of marginalization.

A major component in the claims is the apparent inequity in revenue sharing. This inequity, however, is inherent in a strong federal system in which a relatively small region of the country (the Niger Delta) accounts for a large proportion of the country's revenue (crude oil exports). The realities of lost privilege and inherent inequity are compounded by the country's economic decline in the past decade, a problem worsened by government graft. The resulting hardship has engendered finger-pointing and scapegoating among Nigeria's ethnic groups.

LOST PRIVILEGES . . .

In the case of the Igbos, the lasting impact of the civil war, along with the effects of the deteriorating economy, has been the main cause of their plight. The war saw an exodus of Igbos from the non-Igbo regions of Nigeria and from political and business positions that they have been unable to regain. With the creation of states in 1967, the Igbos also suffered diminished political and administrative clout in the Niger Delta and other minority areas in the east. Igbo frustration, which had been muted, is becoming increasingly shrill. Ojukwu probably spoke for many Igbos with his recent remark that the "problem is that we are in Nigeria and we are finding it extremely difficult to find accommodation in Nigeria."

The claim of marginalization by ethnic groups in what Nigerians call the core north, led by the Hausa-Fulanis, is an anomaly in the country's politics. Although the north has historically lagged in educational and industrial development, the Hausa-Fulanis have exercised political leadership through much of Nigeria's postcolonial history. The election of Obasanjo, a Yoruba, was itself a concession by the Hausa-Fulanis to southern pressure for a change from northern leadership. The concession reflects an apparent realization by the Hausa-Fulani leadership that Nigerian politics would continue to be haunted by the nullification of the 1993 presidential election if it were not redressed. (The results of the election, which appeared to make Yoruba businessman Moshood Abiola the winner, were canceled by the Hausa-Fulani-led military government, provoking a protracted political crisis.)

The People's Democratic Party (PDP), which nominated Obasanjo for the presidency, was sponsored or backed by several former northern leaders, both civilian and military. The party won substantial votes in the north as well as in the east. Ironically, the only region in which Obasanjo and the PDP lost was in the west, among the Yorubas. In effect, Obasanjo became the first Nigerian to be elected to the presidency without the support of his own ethnic group.

Having given its support to Obasanjo, the core north apparently expected a quid pro quo. But Obasanjo has pursued policies that emphasize inclusiveness and equity rather than patronage.

Of particular significance was Obasanjo's decision, soon after his inauguration in May 1999, to retire hundreds of senior officers in an attempt to rid the military of personnel who had become accustomed to the perquisites of political power. The Hausa-Fulanis believe that they were disproportionately affected because of the preponderance of Hausa-Fulanis in top military positions who were forcibly retired. This complaint was repeated after the Kaduna riots in a pro-shariah pamphlet distributed there by a group that identified itself as "Concerned Muslims."

The shariah crisis has made explicit the extent of some northerners' resentment of Obasanjo's policies. The grievances in the pamphlet are one indication; even more ominous are the utterances of former Nigerian heads of state Shehu Shagari and General Muhammadu Buhari. That the two former leaders, who are both northerners, took public positions against federal suspension of shariah suggests the political tenor of the crisis.

. . . AND UNREALIZED PRIVILEGES

The Yorubas have benefited enormously because they are the ethnic group native to the southwestern city of Lagos, which until recently was Nigeria's political capital and continues to be the hub of national industry and commerce. Their enviable representation in Nigeria's professional and managerial class is testimony to that privilege. They also gained more than any other ethnic group from the short-lived secession of Igbos in 1967. As the only ethnic group large enough to be a counterweight to the Hausa-Fulanis, the Yorubas rose in political stature during the war. And with their relatively high levels of education, they took advantage of positions abandoned by Igbos and other easterners.

But the failure of a Yoruba to reach the pinnacle of Nigerian politics—the prime ministership or the presidency—left many Yorubas feeling cheated. The election of Obasanjo, a Yoruba, should have rectified this. But a majority of Yoruba voters stunned Obasanjo's candidacy and party, still remembering Obasanjo's ambivalence toward the military's nullification of the 1993 election that would have made Moshood Abiola Nigeria's first Yoruba president. Yoruba fears that Obasanjo's political would be ultimately dictated from the north have also continued to color their relationship with the government and the rest of the Nigerian polity.[1] Thus, most Yorubas are still unsure of him. On the one hand, he is one of them; on the other, he is not.

Like the Yoruba, Nigeria's marginalized minority groups also believe they have been deprived of full participation in Nigeria's civil order. Although the problem of minority marginalization seemed solved in 1967 when Yakuba Gowon's administration created states out of the country's four regions, separating minorities from their dominant ethnic neighbors, it left unsolved the issue of revenue sharing among the country's minority groups.

An appropriate formula for revenue allocation is especially important for the minority peoples of the Niger Delta, the site of much of Nigeria's crude oil production. What proportion of the country's revenue should be allocated by the criteria of population and how much based on the amount of revenues derived from each region? Successive governments have failed to address this issue satisfactorily.

Because Nigeria's three major ethnic groups would be threatened by any derivation-weighted formula—with those in the north being particularly vulnerable—the criteria remained a minor part of the revenue-sharing equation. Yet if derivation had been applied, a small percentage of the oil revenue would have sufficed for the development of oil-producing communities such as those of the Ijaws, Ogonis, and Ibibios in the Niger Delta. Successive governments failed to do this, though, and the resulting years of frustration have bred radicalization and communal strife among the groups bearing the brunt of oil production, including land and river pollution from spillage. The resulting militancy led to the murder of four Ogoni chiefs in 1994 by youths who believed they had become too close to the Abacha government.

This was followed by the execution in 1995 of the Ogoni activist Ken Saro-Wiwa and nine colleagues, whom the government held responsible for the murders.

The Obasanjo administration has thus inherited radicalized minority groups, some of whom have made unrealistic demands. The Movement for the Survival of Ogoni People, for example, once demanded up to 13 percent of Nigeria's oil revenue and $10 billion in royalties and compensation. Given that oil sales accounted for about 80 percent of government revenue, the Ogonis were in effect asking for 10.4 percent of government revenues. For a group numbering about half a million in a country of more than 100 million people, that was improbable. (Of course, the government should clean up the Ogonis' polluted land and water, but that is a different matter from the issue of regular budgetary allocation.)

In oil-producing communities were compensated according to their contribution to government revenues, Nigeria would become a patchwork of Kuwaits and Haitis. An allocation formula that accounts for population, derivation, and needs would instead be the logical solution. Yet a formula that pleases most—let alone all—of the people has proved elusive.

The grievances of the country's ethnic communities would have been muted or mitigated if the country's resources had been managed competently and conscientiously. But Nigeria's governments—both military and civilian—

have looted or failed to prevent the looting of the country's treasury, reducing the pool of funds for distribution. This attitude may have changed, however. Since Abacha's death in 1998, the government has uncovered billions of dollars of looted funds Abacha and his aides had stashed in foreign banks.

PROSPECTS

Nigeria's political well-being lies in finding accommodation among its diverse peoples. The most pressing challenge is in dealing with the claims of marginalization, whether real or illusory. A de-escalation of the rhetoric that has accompanied these claims would be a strong start.

The realities and perception of marginalization cannot be redressed or assuaged overnight. Although Obasanjo has taken steps to improve inclusiveness, not all of Nigeria's more than 250 ethnic groups will ever feel adequately represented at the national level. It is improbable that any administration or policy can end the perception of marginalization. But equitable policies—especially with regard to revenue allocation—and realistic expectations hold out the best potential. Ultimately, the specter of another military coup and even civil war should work in favor of amicable solutions and accommodation.

MINABERE IBELEMA *is an assistant professor in the department of communication studies at the University of Alabama at Birmingham.*

Article 13   *The Christian Science Monitor,* Thursday, December 23, 1999

Faith's unbreakable force

As Sierra Leone takes courageous steps in peacemaking after almost a decade of civil war, the country's religious leaders have united to help end the conflict and lay a foundation for national reconstruction.

By Jane Lampman

Staff writer of The Christian Science Monitor

Amman, Jordan

West Africa, some outsiders have asserted, is a region collapsing in chaos and thuggery. Indeed, two nations—Sierra Leone and Liberia—have endured years of the "most brutal warfare in the modern world," in the words of Ahmad Tejan Kabbah, Sierra Leone's democratically elected president. Atrocities by bands of rebels have left thousands killed, maimed, and homeless. Hundreds of children have been kidnapped and turned into soldiers or sex slaves.

But like the diamonds gleaming out of the dark precincts of that country's mines, faith has shown itself to be an unbreakable force. "Sierra Leone has survived as a nation through faith—faith in God and in the principle of democracy," President Kabbah says, although "that faith has been aggressively challenged."

That faith took concrete form when Christian and Muslim leaders joined together in the Interreligious Council (IRC) of Sierra Leone, not only to console their flocks and help those who had been harmed, but to take courageous steps in peacemaking. Their example illustrates the impact religious leaders can have by voicing shared moral concerns and acting on their values in times of crisis. It's a story being played out, too, by the Interfaith Task Force in Liberia, and in other African countries.

Kabbah and IRC members shared their experience in shaping a fragile peace in their war-scarred country at last month's assembly of the World Conference on Religion and Peace (WCRP) held in Amman, Jordan. The IRC is a "national chapter" of WCRP, a global organization that promotes collaboration across faith traditions to solve common problems. WCRP is actively engaged in conflict resolution and peacebuilding in the Balkans and Indonesia as well as in Africa.

"We have been able to do what we have done because of religious tolerance," says the Rev. Alimamy Koroma, co-secretary of Sierra Leone's IRC.

"Tolerance is part of our culture down to the village level," says Roman Catholic Archbishop Joseph Ganda. "Extended families include members of different faiths." Kabbah himself, for example, is Muslim and his wife Catholic. "We have gold and diamonds, but we are proud we have this other national resource, religious tolerance," Kabbah says.

> "We have gold and diamonds, but we are proud we have this other national resource, religious tolerance."
>
> —Ahmad Tejan Kabbah, president of Sierra Leone

The IRC was created in April 1997 to strengthen citizenship in the brand new democracy, under threat from rebels in the countryside. But one month later, a military coup overthrew the year-old Kabbah government and the junta joined forces with the rebels.

"We informed the coup leadership that the IRC called for the government to be restored," says Haja Mahdi, leader of the Council of Muslim Women. "The military leaders tried to coerce us to conduct a religious service with them," Mrs. Mahdi adds. "We declined." It was a bold step at a time that hostilities were causing a mass exodus of people to neighboring countries.

Despite threats, 'we chose to stay'

"There was good reason for us to leave the country because of threats and harassment," says Mr. Koroma. "But we chose to stay and to try to inspire hope among our people."

"We learned that being willing to take risks is very important," Mahdi says. Since then, IRC members have taken risks under highly volatile circumstances. Archbishop Ganda was taken hostage at one point, but managed to escape.

Armed forces marshalled by the Economic Community of West African States (ECOWAS) restored the Kabbah government, but rebel troops continued to terrorize the countryside. And in January 1999, the rebels invaded Freetown, carrying out a savage reign of terror in the capital. In addition to ministering to a traumatized populace and providing aid to the injured and those displaced from their homes, the IRC sought to open lines of communication with all parties.

"They did an outstanding job," Kabbah says. "They went into the bush and sat on the ground with rebel forces."

Women members went too, hoping to win the freedom of child soldiers. "I talked to the rebels as a mother," says Mrs. Saimihafu Kassim, IRC treasurer. Some of the rebels, she adds, asked her to pray for them. In a goodwill gesture in response to IRC efforts, the Revolutionary United Front (RUF) released 53 children.

RUF leader Foday Sankoh urged the IRC to take the process further, to facilitate discussions between rebel factions in the bush as well as with the United Nations.

Meanwhile, the international community was urging Kabbah to take the "extraordinarily painful" step of negotiating with the rebels. "The Sierra Leone society was divided on the need for a cease-fire," says Francis Okelo, the UN secretary-general's special representative. Some wanted ECOMOG (ECOWAS forces) to keep fighting the RUF until a victory, he says, "but we felt a military victory was not possible."

"The IRC enjoys a unique position within the society, they have the respect and confidence of the people," Mr. Okelo adds, "so it was important to work closely with them right from the beginning of the peace process."

IRC members began communicating with all those who had a stake in the situation, including trips to neighboring countries to talk with religious counterparts and heads of state such as Charles Taylor of Liberia, a rebel backer.

"The IRC made it possible for the rebels to talk with the government," according to Kadi Sesay, head of Sierra Leone's human rights commission.

A cease-fire was reached in May, and when the rebels and government sat down at the peace table, both sides requested that the IRC be formally seated at the negotiations. There it continued the role as a go-between, convening parties when trouble developed, and serving as procedural guarantor of the talks (maintaining its independence on the agreement itself).

TOM BROWN—STAFF

"The talks were quite tense at times," Okelo says. "The RUF had demands so drastic the whole structure of the society and government would change if they were accepted. . . . I needed to use the IRC members constantly in dealing with the RUF and the government."

"The IRC raises the concerns of the average Sierra Leonean," says US Ambassador Joseph Melrose, in Freetown. "When things looked bad in the negotiations, they kept the dialogue going."

While the RUF did compromise, the peace agreement gave the rebels amnesty, and established a process for disarmament, demobilization, and reintegration of some 45,000 fighters back into society, to be carried out under ECOMOG and UN forces. It requires the first democratically elected government in 20 years to include top leaders of its enemies in a national unity government, something mature democracies would find difficult to do.

"I'm convinced I made the right decision to go that far," Kabbah says, "but only history will tell if I was right." Still, the issues of justice for the horrible wrongs committed are crucial ones the country will have to sort out along the way.

"With the peace agreement, there is a herculean task ahead of us," says Koroma. The religious institutions have the most highly developed social infrastructure in the country, and the IRC is now defining its roles, along with secular organizations, in consolidating the peace and working toward long-term social reconstruction.

"This is a treacherous stage in the peace where the process could unravel," says WCRP Secretary-General William Vendley. "There are issues among the rebel factions—some are frightened of being cut off and killed," and are not eager to give up arms. Dr. Vendley may play a third-party role with some rebel factions.

And along with disarmament, there is the resettlement of displaced people and repatriation of refugees. WCRP helps local chapters inventory their moral and social assets—their social capital, Vendley says, to see how they can best use their resources and to help them find financial support. Given the devastation over eight years, the needs are immense.

"We have begun sensitizing our various communities on the need to accept the peace and to work to live together again as one nation," Koroma says. "This will mean some aspect of forgiveness and reconciliation, but it will not be easy because our communities have been deeply hurt." A truth and reconciliation commission is planned, but it will take time to prepare both sides for that stage, he says.

Feeding soldiers to protect villagers

Public education on the agreement has taken place on TV, in villages, and among rebel camps. Perhaps the most controversial of IRC actions has been sending food to some rebel camps to keep hungry soldiers from making attacks on villages. Not everyone has appreciated such actions. But IRC members say ending the fighting is the first necessity. Only then can people have hope and reconstruction begin.

To that end, Koroma stresses, the roles of the international community are essential. "This war has gone on for eight years—for eight years we have been on our own—and I'm sure there are actors out there who could have stopped it. We need to ensure that we become a gun-free nation, as the guns have been silenced in the Gulf and Kosovo."

The disarmament process has gotten under way slowly. Some 3,000 ex-combatants, less than 10 percent, Okelo says, have entered demobilization centers.

"Please assist us in consolidating this peace, including with your prayers," urges Sheik Tejan Sillah. "We believe that prayers are the key to peace."

Article 14   Washington Post National Weekly Edition, December 20–27, 1999

Signs of Hope in Africa

World donors have ignored Somaliland as it slowly rebuilds

By Karen DeYoung
Washington Post Staff Writer

HARGEYSA, Somaliland

Perched atop the Horn of Africa, the farthest outpost in a forgotten place, Somaliland is trying to get the world's attention. It has been nearly five years since civil war ended here and traditional clan leaders made good on their decisions to declare independence from Somalia—the land to the south that has been synonymous this decade with wasted international aid, vicious warlords and dead American soldiers. Even as fighting in Somalia continues, peaceful Somaliland has a representative, functioning local government and an eager capitalist outlook.

Amid the dull brown rubble left by decades of war and neglect in this capital city are flashes of vitality as bright as the riotously colored scarves local women wrap themselves in. A downtown morning market thrives. A new restaurant, built by returning exiles, is surrounded by a carefully watered papaya grove. Microwave towers stretch above makeshift shacks, offering $1 a minute telephone calls to anywhere in the world.

In an earlier decade, Somaliland might have been welcomed as an up-by-its-bootstraps place where Western governments were eager to provide money and expertise for the kind of help this arid land now needs most: for housing, for textbooks and medicine, and for training to harness its entrepreneurial energy for rebuilding. But today, both the funds and the will of First World development programs, international banks and multinational private investors are in short supply.

The plight of Somaliland, and the larger tragedy of Somalia, illustrate some of the realities of foreign aid in the post-Cold War world. Even as the amount of money the world's richest countries are prepared to spend on aid has dropped precipitously, an ever-smaller share has gone to the world's poorest. And as many of those poor countries—particularly in Africa—remain sunken in seemingly senseless internal wars like Somalia's, fatigued and exasperated donors have gradually lost interest in funding programs of the kind that might help Somaliland.

AMONG THE WORLD'S LARGEST DONOR countries—the members of the Organization for Economic Cooperation and Development—aid to Africa fell by 22 percent between 1990 and 1996, decreasing by 18 percent to sub-Saharan countries between 1994 and 1996 alone. Contributors to United Nations aid and development programs have provided slightly more than half of the $800 million requested this year for African countries suffering from "complex emergencies"—the term applied when war and failed institutions, often combined with a natural disaster, leave vast numbers of people homeless and starving. Specific programs for some particularly problematic areas, such as the Great Lakes region of Central Africa including the two Congos, Rwanda and Burundi, have fared even less well.

Steven G. Wisecarver, the Nairobi-based deputy regional director of the U.S. Agency for International Development (AID), said after a visit to Somaliland in September that he would try to pitch Washington a development program to help consolidate Somaliland's "fragile process during a very critical time."

"They have a stable environment that it's important to support," Wisecarver said. "We have the good will of the people there, and have to realize that the government has no resources. Peace is their outstanding achievement, but it's not going to last forever."

Asked later whether a proposed development program for Somaliland was likely to fly, a senior AID official in Washington laughed ruefully and said, "Not any time soon."

The aid-averse Republican Congress in recent years has kept a tight lid on foreign assistance. But the United States long ago began moving away from all but emergency relief except in a handful of strategically significant countries. Nowhere is that decline more noticeable than in Africa, and nowhere are the reasons for it clearer than in Somalia.

In some ways, Somalia is unique among Africa's problem countries, the extreme example of how bad things can be.

Cobbled together as a country by departing European colonialists in 1960, embroiled in war with Ethiopia through much of the 1970s and '80s, and ruled by a military despot who was overthrown in 1991, it has been at war with itself ever since. Somalia has no national government, no central bank, no representation in international institutions, no embassies.

LAST SPRING, THE U.N. SECURITY COUNCIL expressed alarm over Somalia, largely out of concern that it was becoming a haven for arms and drug smugglers, a base of terrorist operations for Osama bin Laden and others, and a surrogate battlefield for combatants in other African wars. It ordered Secretary General Kofi Annan to investigate.

The lengthy document Annan delivered in August described a place convulsed by waves of violence, where life has regressed into an atavistic past in which "most children receive no health care . . . two generations have had no access to formal education," and life expectancy, at 43 years, is the lowest in the world.

"Virtually all the infrastructure of government—from buildings and communications facilities to furniture and office equipment—has been looted," Annan reported. "In most of the country, there are no police, judiciary or civil service. Communications . . . is nonexistent. Electricity is not available on a public basis . . . there is no postal service." At least a quarter-million Somalis live in refugee camps in neighboring countries.

In the southern two-thirds of the country, where the capital, Mogadishu, is located and nearly three-quarters of the population lives, little has changed since the departure in 1995 of UNOSOM, the multinational military force that for more than two years tried, and ultimately failed, to separate clan-based armies while it delivered food to their victims. Today, roving armed bands trade control over huge swaths of territory, answering to local warlords when they are paid, and resorting to banditry and kidnapping for ransom when they are not.

Although most aid agencies moved their Somali headquarters to neighboring Kenya after the departure of UNOSOM, aid programs continued. Twelve U.N. organizations with 170 foreign employees, the European Union, AID and its Danish equivalent, the Red Cross and Red Crescent and as many as 60 other non-governmental agencies such as CARE operate in Somalia, delivering food and medical care when security permits.

But as the situation has shown little improvement, money has become increasingly scarce. Continuing trends over the past several years, donors pledged this year to spend $70.1 million in Somalia, down from $95 million last year. The United Nations requested $64 million for emergency programs in fiscal 1999, but by late October only about 55 percent of the total had been funded by donor nations.

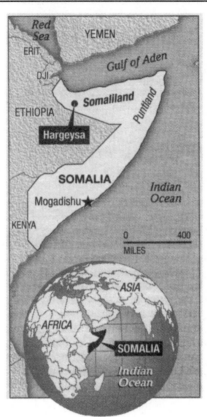

THE WASHINGTON POST

The United States, whose 1999 bilateral contribution was programmed at $22 million, initially responded to budget restraints this year by proposing to "zero out" Somalia as a hopeless case for all but emergency food relief in fiscal 2000. The European Union is at a similar crossroads in funding under the Lome Convention, its international aid and trade agreement with the developing world. The current 10-year convention was agreed to in 1990, when Somalia had a government. With negotiations underway for the next Lome agreement, there is no one in Mogadishu to talk to.

"We're an international organization, and we need at least a government," says Joao Duarte de Cavalho, the head of the European Commission's Nairobi-based Somalia Unit.

Yet even as the future seems bleakest, one player in the Somalia drama has stuck its head above the parapet and issued a challenge to itself and others. Rather than winding down, the United Nations has proposed more than doubling its efforts, with a fiscal 2000 appeal totaling $124 million.

Singling out Somalia as a test case for whether the world has learned anything about how to deal with collapsing states, the new U.N. appeal proposes abandoning, for the moment at least, the idea of reestablishing Somalia as a functioning entity. Instead, it hopes to rebuild pieces of it one by one, with small, targeted projects and a lot of cooperation from local people. When there are enough places where aid has been used to build local schools and health clinics, help plant crops and vaccinate livestock, when local economies and governmental institutions are in place, then the Somalis may want to talk about putting their country back together.

Saturday morning market in downtown Hargeysa is a whirlwind of dust, confusion and commerce. Thousands of people—many returned from years in refugee camps in Ethiopia, others more recently arrived on the run from fighting in southern Somalia—jostle along unpaved streets lined with tables piled high with second-hand shoes and T-shirts. Rows of money-changers sit on upturned boxes behind stacks of Somaliland currency offered for the dollars, marks and pounds sent to relatives by Somalis living abroad.

Goats and donkey-pulled water carts scramble out of the way of trucks and Land Rovers, and even the odd automobile, careening around potholes and people. Horns are honking, children are shouting, people are smiling.

In a drab, bullet-pocked building above the cacophony, an unarmed policeman stretches his leg across a narrow stairway, trying to keep out a horde of petitioners seeking entry to city hall. Behind a heavy door at the top of the stairs sits a former political prisoner and refugee, Abdiraham Ismail Hussein, 51, the mayor of Hargeysa.

"It's not easy to understand the real situation in my town," says Hussein, his gold teeth winking. "If you came here five years ago, you would have seen 10 percent of the town standing and the rest destroyed. There were no institutions, no police, no municipality. Nothing. We started from scratch, from zero."

NEARLY ALL OF WHAT SOMALILAND'S PEOPLE HAVE achieved thus far has been accomplished without much foreign help. Some residents believe that has been "a sort of a blessing," says Mohamed Fadal, a Somalilander and researcher for the War Torn Societies Project, a foreign-funded program helping to build Somaliland institutions. "Aid corrupts. People fight over it."

But now, Somaliland fears its stability is endangered unless it can show citizens that peace offers tangible benefits.

"My resources are very small, says Hussein. "Water is short, sanitation is poor—there is no garbage collection. But people are coming by the thousands." A good portion of those on the streets, he says, are beggars from the refugee camps.

Many of the estimated 350,000 residents of this capital—out of a population estimated at 1 million to 2 million people—live in stick and trash-bag huts strewn across the vast emptiness surrounding the city. Hundreds are camped in the bombed-out shell of the palatial British statehouse, once the seat of colonial rule, or in shacks scattered through its long-untended gardens.

In the city's 13 schools—about one-third of Hargeysa's children attend—students are packed 85 to 100 to a class. Health care is minimal. An estimated $500 million in annual remittances from Somalilanders living abroad and sales of nomad-raised livestock to the Arabian peninsula are the only outside sources of money. Somaliland's flat, semi-desert expanses grow little food, and most must be imported. Former militia fighters roam the streets or sit in demobilization camps, waiting for the life they have been promised in exchange for their guns.

"We need to start building the administration, the courts of law . . . and what we used to call in the old days the nomadic police force—which used to keep the peace among the tribes of the area," Somaliland President Mohamed Egal said in an interview last spring with Africa News Service. If the former militia members "who we promised we would put in vocational training schools . . . are disappointed and feel they should go back to . . . living by the Kalashnikov, well, then all the things we have built up here will go down the drain.

The road to a peaceful, functioning society has not always been smooth.

The Ogaden war with Ethiopia left Somalia's northern and western borders lined with mines. After he lost the war, Somali President Mohamed Siad Barre took out his frustration here, killing thousands and mining the interior of the country. In 1991, when Barre was overthrown, Somalilanders started fighting with each other, following the pattern that continues in the south.

Although clan elders declared independence that year, civil war among Somaliland's three main clans lasted until 1995. That was when the elders decided to try to make peace stick in their would-be country. So far, they have succeeded, and militias in the rest of Somalia fight their own wars.

Somaliland still disputes a border with Puntland, a Somali region just to the east. People there resent Somaliland's claim of independence—even though the claim is recognized by no country in the world.

Work on a new constitution and legal code by the Somaliland parliament is behind schedule, as are promised elections. Egal is under sporadic fire from the remnant militia leadership and public opinion for suspected flirtation with foreign proponents of a quickly reunited Somalia, who tempt him with the possibility that he could lead it all.

On the plus side, Somaliland has a long coastline, a good port and a belief that oil lies under the sea. There is a lively daily newspaper that freely criticizes the government and everyone else. Local entrepreneurs, most of them returning exiles, have brought a frontier vitality, investing money saved abroad in things like the five microwave telephone systems in Hargeysa.

One of the entrepreneurs is Abdi Hakin Saeed, 38, who returned here with his family last year after 13 years in the United States.

"People really believe in this place," Saeed says. "I was at the point of deciding to stay in America for good, to become an American, buy a house, and be like everybody else."

Instead, Saeed and his wife, Deqa Arab Essa, 32, like him a U.S.-trained accountant whose family fled Somalia in the late 1980s, decided to come home

and raise their American-born daughter in Somaliland. They have invested their savings in a furniture store and, on Hargeysa's main street, a "dollar store" selling U.S.-made sundries.

But the Saeeds, living in relative comfort behind heavy concrete walls, ask every day if they have made the right decision in returning to a place where their child cannot play outside and few have money to buy the goods they sell in their stores.

LITTLE HAS BEEN BUILT HERE SINCE THE DECADES of war, and much of what existed before lies in ruins. Mines blanket much of the countryside and roads and surround water sources, and unexploded bombs and grenades are scattered through virtually every town. Government regulation, taxation and banking systems are embryonic. Somalia was long ago written off by international lenders such as the World Bank or the International Monetary Fund, and no foreign company wants to risk putting money in a place that appears on no international map.

Although there are small development projects and an incipient mine removal program funded through international or non-governmental organizations, no country has a bilateral aid relationship with Somaliland and U.N. programs are limited by the need to spend scarce resources on emergency programs in the south.

"We are very grateful for the crumbs we are given here," says Egal. "But "nobody asks us what we need or how we want to be helped."

That is precisely what the United Nations is proposing that donors now do in Somaliland. Nearly $60 million of the U.N. 2000 request for Somalia is designated for economic and infrastructure development, much of it in the north, and reestablishing the refugee population.

But first, acknowledges David Stephen, the secretary general's representative for Somalia, "we have to convince them it's not money down the drain." Donors can continue to "write Somalia off," he says, "as long as it's a basket case."

Credits

Sources for Statistical Reports

U.S. State Department, *Background Notes* (2000).

C.I.A. *World Factbook* (2000).

World Bank, *World Development Report* (2000/2001).

UN *Population and Vital Statistics Report* (January 2001).

World Statistics in Brief (2000).

The Statesman's Yearbook (2000).

Population Reference Bureau, *World Population Data Sheet* (2000).

The World Almanac (2001).

The Economist Intelligence Unit (1999).

Glossary of Terms and Abbreviations

Acquired Immune Deficiency Syndrome (AIDS) A disease of immune system dysfunction widely believed to be caused by the human immunodeficiency virus (HIV), which allows opportunistic infections to take over the body.

African Development Bank Founded in 1963 under the auspices of the United Nations Economic Commission on Africa, the bank, located in Côte d'Ivoire, makes loans to African countries, although other nations can apply.

African National Congress (ANC) Founded in 1912, the group's goal is to achieve equal rights for blacks in South Africa through nonviolent action. "Spear of the Nation," the ANC wing dedicated to armed struggle, was organized after the Sharpeville massacre in 1960.

African Party for the Independence of Guinea-Bissau and Cape Verde (PAICG) An independence movement that fought during the 1960s and 1970s for the liberation of present-day Guinea-Bissau and Cape Verde from Portuguese rule. The two territories were ruled separately by a united PAIGC until a 1981 coup in Guinea-Bissau caused the party to split along national lines. In 1981 the Cape Verdean PAIGC formally renounced its Guinea links and became the PAICV.

African Socialism A term applied to a variety of ideas (including those of Nkrumah and Senghor) about communal and shared production in Africa's past and present. The concept of African socialism was especially popular in the early 1960s. Adherence to it has not meant governments' exclusion of private-capitalist ventures.

Afrikaners South Africans of European descent who speak Afrikaans and are often referred to as *Boers* (Afrikaans for "farmers").

Algiers Agreement The 1979 peace agreement when Mauritania made peace with the Polisario and abandoned claims to Western Sahara.

Amnesty International A London-based human-rights organization whose members "adopt" political prisoners or prisoners of conscience in many nations of the world. The organization generates political pressure and puts out a well-publicized annual report of human-rights conditions in each country of the world.

Aouzou Strip A barren strip of land between Libya and Chad contested by both countries.

Apartheid Literally, "separatehood," a South African policy that segregated the races socially, legally, and politically.

Arusha Declaration A document issued in 1967 by Tanzanian President Julius Nyerere, committing the country to socialism based on peasant farming, democracy under one party, and self-reliance.

Assimilado The Portuguese term for Africans who became "assimilated" to Western ways. Assimilados enjoyed equal rights under Portuguese law.

Azanian People's Organization (AZAPO) Founded in 1978 at the time of the Black Consciousness Movement and revitalized in the 1980s, the movement works to develop chapters and bring together black organizations in a national forum.

Bantu A major linguistic classification for many Central, Southern, and East African languages.

Bantustans Areas, or "homelands," to which black South Africans were assigned "citizenship" as part of the policy of apartheid.

Basarawa Peoples of Botswana who have historically been hunters and gatherers.

Berber The collective term for the indigenous languages and peoples of North Africa.

Bicameral A government made up of two legislative branches.

Black Consciousness Movement A South African student movement founded by Steve Biko and others in the 1970s to promote pride and empowerment of blacks.

Boers See *Afrikaners*.

Brotherhoods Islamic organizations based on specific religious beliefs and practices. In many areas, brotherhood leaders and their spiritual followers gain political influence.

Cabinda A small, oil-rich portion of Angola separated from the main body of that country by a coastal strip of the Democratic Republic of the Congo.

Caisse de Stabilization A marketing board that stabilizes the uncertain returns to producers of cash crops by offering them less than market prices in good harvest years while assuring them of a steady income in bad years. Funds from these boards are used to develop infrastructure, to promote social welfare, or to maintain a particular regime in power.

Caliphate The office or dominion of a caliph, the spiritual head of Islam.

Cassava A tropical plant with a fleshy, edible rootstock; one of the staples of the African diet. Also known as manioc.

Chimurenga A Shona term meaning "fighting in which everyone joins," used to refer to Zimbabwe's fight for independence.

Committee for the Struggle against Drought in the Sahel (CILSS) A grouping of eight West African countries, formed to fight the effects of drought in the region.

Commonwealth of Nations An association of nations and dependencies loosely joined by the common tie of having been part of the British Empire.

Congress of South African Trade Unions (COSATU) Established in 1985 to form a coalition of trade unions to press for workers' rights and an end to apartheid.

Copperbelt A section of Zambia with a high concentration of copper-mining concessions.

Creole A person or language of mixed African and European descent.

Dergue From the Amheric word for "committee," the ruling body of Ethiopia following the Revolution in 1974 to the 1991 Revolution (it was overthrown by the Ethiopian People's Revolutionary Democratic Front).

East African Community (EAC) Established in 1967, this organization grew out of the East African Common Services Organization begun under British rule. The EAC included Kenya, Tanzania, and Uganda in a customs union and involved common currency and development of infrastructure. It was disbanded in 1977, and the final division of assets was completed in 1983.

Economic Commission for Africa (ECA) Founded in 1958 by the Economic and Social Committee of the United Nations to aid African development through regional centers, field agents, and the encouragement of regional efforts, food self-sufficiency, transport, and communications development.

Economic Community of Central African States (CEEAC, also known as ECCA) An organization of all of the Central African states, as well as Rwanda and Burundi, whose goal is to promote economic and social cooperation among its members.

Economic Community of West Africa (CEAO) An economic organization of former French colonies that was formed to promote trade and regional economic cooperation.

Economic Organization of West African States (ECOWAS) Established in 1975 by the Treaty of Lagos, the organization includes all of the West African states except Western Sahara. The organization's goals are to promote trade, cooperation, and self-reliance among its members.

Enclave Industry An industry run by a foreign company that uses imported technology and machinery and exports the product to industrialized countries; often described as a "state within a state."

Eritrean People's Liberation Front (EPLF) The major group fighting the Ethiopian government for the independence of Eritrea.

European Community See *European Union*.

European Union (EU) Known as the European Community until 1994, this is the collective designation of three organizations with common membership—the European Economic Community, the European Coal and Steel Community, and the European Atomic Energy Community. Sometimes also referred to as the Common Market.

Evolués A term used in colonial Zaire (the Democratic Republic of the Congo) to refer to Western-educated Congolese.

Fokonolas Indigenous village management bodies.

Food and Agricultural Organization of the United Nations (FAO) Established in 1945 to oversee good nutrition and agricultural development.

Franc Zone (Commonly known as the CFA [*le franc des Colonies Françaises d'Afrique*] franc zone.) This organization includes members of the West African Monetary Union and the monetary organizations of Central Africa that have currencies linked to the French franc. Reserves are managed by the French treasury and guaranteed by the French franc.

Free French Conference A 1944 conference of French-speaking territories, which proposed a union of all the territories in which Africans would be represented and their development furthered.

Freedom Charter Established in 1955, this charter proclaimed equal rights for all South Africans and has been a foundation for almost all groups in the resistance against apartheid.

Frelimo See *Mozambique Liberation Front*.

French Equatorial Africa (FEA) The French colonial federation that included present-day Democratic Republic of the Congo, Central African Republic, Chad, and Gabon.

French West Africa The administrative division of the former French colonial empire that included the current independent countries of Senegal, Côte d'Ivoire, Guinea, Mali, Niger, Burkina Faso, Benin, and Mauritania.

Frontline States A caucus supported by the Organization of African Unity (consisting of Tanzania, Zambia, Mozambique, Botswana, Zimbabwe, and Angola) whose goal is to achieve black majority rule in all of Southern Africa.

Green Revolution Use of Western technology and agricultural practices to increase food production and agricultural yields.

Griots Professional bards of West Africa, some of whom tell history and are accompanied by the playing of the kora or harp-lute.

Gross Domestic Product (GDP) The value of production attributable to the factors of production in a given country regardless of their ownership. GDP equals GNP minus the product of a country's residents originating in the rest of the world.

Gross National Product (GNP) The sum of the values of all goods and services produced by a country's residents at home and abroad in any given year, less income earned by foreign residents and remitted abroad.

Guerrilla A member of a small force of irregular soldiers. Generally, guerrilla forces are made up of volunteers who make surprise raids against the incumbent military or political force.

Harmattan In West Africa, the dry wind that blows in from the Sahara Desert during January and February, which now reaches many parts of the West African coast. Its dust and haze are a sign of the new year and of new agricultural problems.

Homelands See *Bantustans*.

Horn of Africa A section of northeastern Africa including the countries of Djibouti, Ethiopia, Somalia, and the Sudan.

Hut Tax Instituted by the colonial governments in Africa, this measure required families to pay taxes on each building in the village.

International Monetary Fund (IMF) Established in 1945 to promote international monetary cooperation.

Irredentism   An effort to unite certain people and territory in one state with another, on the grounds that they belong together.

Islam   A religious faith started in Arabia during the seventh century A.D. by the Prophet Muhammad and spread in Africa through African Muslim leaders, migrations, and wars.

Jihad   A struggle, or "holy war," waged as a religious duty on behalf of Islam to rid the world of disbelief and error.

Koran   Writings accepted by Muslims as the word of God, as revealed to the Prophet Mohammed.

Lagos Plan of Action   Adopted by the Organization of African Unity in 1980, this agreement calls for self-reliance, regional economic cooperation, and the creation of a pan-African economic community and common market by the year 2000.

League of Nations   Established at the Paris Peace Conference in 1919, this forerunner of the modern-day United Nations had 52 member nations at its peak (the United States never joined the organization) and mediated in international affairs. The league was dissolved in 1945 after the creation of the United Nations.

Least Developed Countries (LDCs)   A term used to refer to the poorest countries of the world, including many African countries.

Maghrib   An Arabic term, meaning "land of the setting sun," that is often used to refer to the former French colonies of Morocco, Algeria, and Tunisia.

Mahdi   The expected messiah of Islamic tradition; or a Muslim leader who plays a messianic role.

Malinke (Mandinka, or Mandinga)   One of the major groups of people speaking Mande languages. The original homeland of the Malinke was Mali, but the people are now found in Mali, Guinea-Bissau, The Gambia, and other areas, where they are sometimes called Mandingoes. Some trading groups are called Dyoula.

Marabout   A dervish Muslim in Africa believed to have supernatural power.

Marxist-Leninism   Sometimes called "scientific socialism," this doctrine derived from the ideas of Karl Marx as modified by Vladimir Lenin; it was the ideology of the Communist Party of the Soviet Union and has been modified in many ways by other persons and groups who still use the term. In Africa, some political parties or movements have claimed to be Marxist-Leninist but have often followed policies that conflict in practice with the ideology; these governments have usually not stressed Marx's philosophy of class struggle.

Mfecane   The movement of people in the nineteenth century in the eastern areas of present-day South Africa to the west and north as the result of wars led by the Zulus.

Movement for the Liberation of Angola (MPLA)   A major Angolan liberation movement that has its strongest following among assimilados and Kimbundu speakers, who are predominant in Luanda, the capital, and the interior to the west of the city.

Mozambique Liberation Front (Frelimo)   Mozambique's single ruling party following a 10-year struggle against Portuguese colonial rule, which ended in 1974.

Mozambique National Resistance   See *Renamo*.

Muslim   A follower of the Islamic faith.

Naam   A traditional work cooperative in Burkina Faso.

National Front for the Liberation of Angola (FNLA)   One of the major Angolan liberation movements; its original focus was limited to the northern Kongo-speaking population.

National Union for the Total Independence of Angola (UNITA)   One of three groups that fought the Portuguese during the colonial period in Angola, later backed by South Africa and the U.S. CIA in fighting the independent government of Angola.

National Youth Service   Service to the state required of youth after completing education, a common practice in many African countries.

Nkomati Accords   An agreement signed in 1984 between South Africa and Mozambique, pledging that both sides would no longer support opponents of the other.

Nonaligned Movement (NAM)   A group of nations that chose not to be politically or militarily associated with either the West or the former communist bloc.

Nongovernmental Organizations (NGO)   A private voluntary organization or agency working in relief and development programs.

Organization for the Development of the Senegal River (OMVS)   A regional grouping of countries bordering the Senegal River that sponsors joint research and projects.

Organization of African Unity (OAU)   An association of all the independent states of Africa (except South Africa) whose goal is to promote peace and security as well as economic and social development.

Organization of Petroleum Exporting Countries (OPEC)   Established in 1960, this association of some of the world's major oil-producing countries seeks to coordinate the petroleum policies of its members.

Pan Africanist Congress (PAC)   A liberation organization of black South Africans that broke away from the ANC in the 1950s.

Parastatals   Agencies for production or public service that are established by law and that are, in some measure, government organized and controlled. Private enterprise may be involved, and the management of the parastatal may be in private hands.

Pastoralist   A person, usually a nomad, who raises livestock for a living.

Polisario Front   Originally a liberation group in Western Sahara seeking independence from Spanish rule. Today, it is battling Morocco, which claims control over the Western Sahara. See *Saharawi Arab Democratic Republic (SADR)*.

Popular Movement for the Liberation of Angola (MPLA)   A Marxist liberation movement in Angola during the resistance to Portuguese rule; now the governing party in Angola.

Renamo   A South African-backed rebel movement that attacked civilians in an attampt to overthrow the government of Mozambique.

Rinderpest   A cattle disease that periodically decimates herds in savanna regions.

Saharawi Arab Democratic Republic (SADR)   The Polisario Front name for Western Sahara, declared in 1976 in the struggle for independence from Morocco.

Sahel   In West Africa, the borderlands between savanna and desert.

Sanctions   Coercive measures, usually economic, adopted by nations acting together against a nation violating international law.

Savanna   Tropical or subtropical grassland with scattered trees and undergrowth.

Sharia   The Islamic code of law.

Sharpeville Massacre   The 1960 demonstration in South Africa in which 60 people were killed when police fired into the crowd; it became a rallying point for many antiapartheid forces.

Sorghum   A tropical grain that is a traditional staple in the savanna regions.

Southern African Development Community (SADC) (Formerly the Southern African Development Coordination Conference. Its name was changed in 1992.) An organization of nine African states (Angola, Zambia, Malawi, Mozambique, Zimbabwe, Lesotho, Botswana, Swaziland, and Tanzania) whose goal is to free themselves from dependence on South Africa and to cooperate on projects of economic development.

South-West Africa People's Organization (SWAPO) Angola-based freedom fighters who had been waging guerrilla warfare against the presence of South Africa in Namibia since the 1960s. The United Nations and the Organization of African Unity now recognize SWAPO as the only authentic representative of the Namibian people.

Structural Adjustment Program (SAP)   Economic reforms encouraged by the International Monetary Fund, which include devaluation of currency, cutting government subsidies on commodities, and reducing government expenditures.

Swahili   A trade and government Bantu language that covers much of East Africa and Congo region.

Tsetse Fly   An insect that transmits sleeping sickness to cattle and humans. It is usually found in the scrub-tree and forest regions of Central Africa.

Ujaama   In Swahili, "familyhood"; government-sponsored cooperative villages in Tanzania.

Unicameral   A political structure with a single legislative branch.

Unilateral Declaration of Independence (UDI)   A declaration of white minority settlers in Rhodesia, claiming independence from the United Kingdom in 1965.

United Democratic Front (UDF)   A multiracial, black-led group in South Africa that gained prominence during the 1983 campaign to defeat the government's Constitution, which gave only limited political rights to Asians and Coloureds.

United Nations (UN)   An international organization established on June 26, 1945, through official approval of the charter by delegates of 50 nations at a conference in San Francisco, California. The charter went into effect on October 24, 1945.

United Nations Development Program (UNDP)   Established to create local organizations for increasing wealth through better use of human and natural resources.

United Nations Educational, Scientific, and Cultural Organization (UNESCO)   Established on November 4, 1946, to promote international collaboration in education, science, and culture.

United Nations High Commission for Refugees (UNHCR)   Established in 1951 to provide international protection for people with refugee status.

Villagization   A policy whereby a government relocates rural dwellers to create newer, more concentrated communities.

West African Monetary Union (WAMU)   A regional association of member countries in West Africa (Benin, Burkina Faso, Côte d'Ivoire, Mali, Niger, Senegal, and Togo) that have vested authority to conduct monetary policy in a common central bank.

World Bank   A closely integrated group of international institutions providing financial and technical assistance to developing countries.

World Health Organization (WHO)   Established by the United Nations in 1948, this organization promotes the highest possible state of health in countries throughout the world.

Bibliography

RESOURCE CENTERS

African Studies Centers provide special services for schools, libraries, and community groups. Contact the center nearest you for further information about resources available.

African Studies Center
   Boston University
   270 Bay State Road
   Boston, MA 02215

African Studies Program
   Indiana University
   Woodburn Hall 221
   Bloomington, IN 47405

African Studies Educational Resource Center
   100 International Center
   Michigan State University
   East Lansing, MI 49923

African Studies Program
   630 Dartmouth
   Northwestern University
   Evanston, IL 60201

Africa Project
   Lou Henry Hoover Room 223
   Stanford University
   Stanford, CA 94305

African Studies Center
   University of California
   Los Angeles, CA 90024

Center for African Studies
   470 Grinter Hall
   University of Florida
   Gainesville, FL 32611

African Studies Program
   University of Illinois
   1208 W. California, Room 101
   Urbana, IL 61801

African Studies Program
   1450 Van Hise Hall
   University of Wisconsin
   Madison, WI 53706

Council on African Studies
   Yale University
   New Haven, CT 06520

Foreign Area Studies
   The American University
   5010 Wisconsin Avenue, NW
   Washington, DC 20016

African Studies Program
   Center for Strategic and International Studies
   Georgetown University
   1800 K Street, NW
   Washington, DC 20006

REFERENCE WORKS, BIBLIOGRAPHIES, AND OTHER SOURCES

Africa Research Bulletin (Political Series), Africa Research Ltd., Exeter, Devon, England (monthly).
   Political updates on current issues and events in Africa.

Africa South of the Sahara (updated yearly) (Detroit: Gale Research).

Africa Today: An Atlas of Reproductible Pages, rev. ed. (Wellesley: World Eagle, 1990).

Rosalid Baucham, *African-American Organizations:*
   A Selective Bibliography (Organizations and Institutional Groups) (New York: Garland, 1997)

Chris Cook and David Killingray, *African Political Facts Since 1945* (New York: Facts on File, 1990).
   Chronology of events; chapters on heads of state, ministers, parliaments, parties, armies, trade unions, population, biographies.

David E. Gardinier, *Africana Journal* notes, Volume xvii.
   A Bibliographic Library Guide and Review Forum, New York: Holmes & Meier, 1997)

Colin Legum, ed., *Africa Contemporary Record* (New York: Holmes & Meier) (annual).
   Contains information on each country for the reporting year.

Scarecrow Press, Metuchen, NJ, publishes *The African Historical Dictionaries*, a series edited by Jon Woronoff.
   There are more than 40 dictionaries, each under a specialist editor. They are short works with introductory essays and are useful guides for the beginner, especially for countries on which little has been published in English.

MAGAZINES AND PERIODICALS

Africa News, P.O. Box 3851, Durham, NC 27702.
   A weekly with short articles that are impartially written and full of information.

Africa Now, 212 Fifth Avenue, Suite 1409, New York, NY 10010.
   A monthly publication that gives current coverage and includes sections on art, culture, and business, as well as a special series of interviews.

Africa Recovery, DPI, Room S-1061, United Nations, New York, NY 10017.

Africa Today, 64 Washburn Ave., Wellesley, MA 02181.

African Arts, University of California, Los Angeles, CA.
   Beautifully illustrated articles review Africa's artistic heritage and current creative efforts.

African Concord, 5–15 Cromer Street, London WCIH 8LS, England.

The Economist, 122 E. 42nd St., 14th Floor, New York, NY 10168.
   A weekly that gives attention to African issues.

Newswatch, 62 Oregun Rd., P.M.B. 21499, Ikeja, Nigeria.

The UNESCO Courier, 31, Rue François Bonvin, 75732, Paris CEDEX 15, France.

This periodical includes short and clear articles on Africa, often by African authors, within the framework of the topic to which the monthly issues are devoted.

The Weekly Review, P.O. Box 42271, Nairobi, Kenya.

West Africa, Graybourne House, 52/54 Gray Inn Rd., London WCIX 8LT, England.

This weekly is the best source for West Africa, including countries as far south as Angola and Namibia. Continent-wide issues are also discussed.

NOVELS AND AUTOBIOGRAPHICAL WRITINGS

Chinua Achebe, *Things Fall Apart* (Portsmouth: Heinemann, 1965).

This is the story of the life and values of residents of a traditional Igbo village in the nineteenth century and of its first contacts with the West.

___, *No Longer at Ease* (Portsmouth: Heinemann, 1963).

The grandson of the major character of *Things Fall Apart* lives an entirely different life in the modern city of Lagos and faces new problems while remaining committed to some of the traditional ways.

Buchi Emecheta, *The Joys of Motherhood* (New York: G. Braziller, 1979).

The story of a Nigerian woman who overcomes great obstacles to raise a large family and then finds that the meaning of motherhood has changed.

Nadine Gordimer, *July's People* (New York: Viking, 1981).

This is a troubling and believable scenario of future revolutionary times in South Africa.

___, *A Soldier's Embrace* (New York: Viking, 1982).

These short stories treat the effects of apartheid on people's relations with each other. Films made from some of these stories are available at the University of Illinois Film Library, Urbana-Champaign, IL and the Boston University Film Library, Boston, MA.

Cheik Amadou Kane, *Ambiguous Adventure* (Portsmouth: Heinemann, 1972).

This autobiographical novel of a young man coming of age in Senegal, in a Muslim society, and, later, in a French school, illuminates changes that have taken place in Africa and raises many questions.

Alex LaGuma, *Time of the Butcherbird* (Portsmouth: Heinemann, 1979).

The people of a long-standing black community in South Africa's countryside are to be removed to a Bantustan.

Camara Laye, *The Dark Child* (Farrar Straus and Giroux, 1954).

This autobiographical novel gives a loving and nostalgic picture of a Malinke family of Guinea.

Okot p'Bitek, *Song of Lawino* (Portsmouth: Heinemann, 1983).

A traditional Ugandan wife comments on the practices of her Western-educated husband and reveals her own life-style and values.

Ousmane Sembene, *God's Bits of Wood* (Portsmouth: Heinemann, 1970).

The railroad workers' strike of 1947 provides the setting for a novel about the changing consciousness and life of African men and women in Senegal.

Joyce Sikakane, *A Window on Soweto* (London: International Defense and Aid Fund, 1977).

Wole Soyinka, *Ake: The Years of Childhood* (New York: Random House, 1983).

Soyinka's account of his first 11 years is full of the sights, tastes, smells, sounds, and personal encounters of a headmaster's home and a busy Yoruba town.

Ngugi wa Thiong'o, *A Grain of Wheat* (Portsmouth: Heinemann, 1968).

A story of how the Mau-Mau movement and the coming of independence affected several individuals after independence as well as during the struggle that preceded it.

INTRODUCTORY BOOKS

A. E. Afigbo, E. A. Ayandele, R. J. Gavin, J. D. Omer-Cooper, and R. Palmer, *The Making of Modern Africa,* vol. II, *The Twentieth Century,* 2nd ed. (London: Longman, 1986).

An introductory political history of Africa in the twentieth century.

Philip G. Altbach, *Muse of Modernity: Essays on Culture as Development in Africa,* (Lawrenceville, NJ: Africa World, 1997).

Fredoline O. Anunobi, *International Dimensions of Africa Political Economy: Trends, Challenges, and Realities* (Landham, MD: University Press of America, 1994).

Tony Binns, *People and Environment in Africa* (New York: Wiley, 1995).

Raymond Bonner, *At the Hand of Man: Peril and Hope for Africa's Wildlife* (New York: Random House, 1994).

Reviews the status of Africa's wildlife conservation.

Lynn C. Bowling, *Go Ye into . . . Africa* (Lafayette, LA: Prescott Press, 1993).

Gwendolen Carter and Patrick O'Meara, eds., *African Independence: The First Twenty-Five Years* (Midland Books, 1986).

Collected essays surrounding issues such as political structures, military rule, and economics.

Naomi Chazan et al., *Politics and Society in Contemporary Africa* (Boulder: L. Rienner Publishers, 1992).

John Chiasson, *African Journey* (Upland, CT: Bradbury Press, 1987).

An examination into Africa's social life and customs.

Basil Davidson, *Africa in History* (Macmillan, 1991).

A fine discussion of African history.

___, *The African Genius* (Boston: Little, Brown, 1979). Also published as *The Africans.*

Davidson discusses the complex political, social, and economic systems of traditional African societies, translating scholarly works into a popular mode without distorting complex material.

___, *The Black Man's Burden: Africa and the Curse of the Nation State* (New York: Random House, 1992).
A discussion on Africa's government and the status of the nation state.

___, *A History of Africa,* 2nd ed. (Unwin Hyman, 1989).
A comprehensive look at the historical evolution of Africa.

___, *Let Freedom Come* (Boston: Little, Brown, 1978).
A lively and interesting history of Africa in the twentieth century.

Clementine M. Faik-Nzuji, *Tracing Memory: Glossary of Graphic Signs & Symbols in African Art & Culture* (Seattle, WA: University of Washington Press, 1997).

Bill Freund, *The Making of Contemporary Africa: The Development of African Society since 1800* (Bloomington: Indiana University Press, 1984).
Recent African history from an economic history point of view, with emphasis on forces of production.

Joseph E. Harris, *Africans and Their History* (New York: Dutton 1998).

Adrian Hastings, *A History of African Christianity, 1950–1975* (Cambridge: Cambridge University Press, 1979).
A good introduction to the impact of Christianity on Africa in recent years.

Goren Hyden, *No Shortcut to Progress: African Development Management in Perspective* (Berkeley: University of California, 1983).
An assessment of development in relation to obstacles, prospects, and progress.

Timothy J. Keegan, *Colonial South Africa & the Origins of the Racial Order* (Charlottesville, VA: University Press of Virginia, 1997).

Omari H. Kohole, *Dimensions of Africa's International Relations* (Delmar, NY: Caravan Books, 1993).

Phyllis Martin and Patrick O'Meara, eds., *Africa*, 2nd ed. (Boomington: Indiana University Press, 1986).
This collection of essays covers history, culture, politics, and the economy.

John Mbiti, *African Religions and Philosophy* (Portsmouth: Heinemann, 1982).
This work by a Ugandan scholar is the standard introduction to the rich variety of religious beliefs and rituals of African peoples.

E. Jefferson Murphy, *African Mythology: Old and New* (Storrs, CT: I N Thut World Education Center, 1973).

Joseph M. Murphy, *Working the Spirit: Ceremonies of the African Diaspora* (Boston: Beacon Press, 1994).

J. H. Kwabena Nketia, *The Music of Africa* (New York: Norton, 1974).
The author, a Ghanaian by birth, is Africa's best-known ethnomusicologist.

Gladson I. Nwanna, *Do's & Don'ts around the World: A Country Guide to Cultural & Social Taboos & Etiquette in Africa,* (Baltimore: World Travel Institute, 1998).

Keith R. Richburg, *Out of Africa: A Black Man Confronts Africa* (New York: Basic Books, 1997).

Robert Ruly, *History of the African People* (New York: Macmillan, 1986).

Chris Searle, *We're Building the New School: Diary of a Teacher in Mozambique* (London: Zed Press, 1981; distributed in the United States by Laurence Hill & Co., Westport).
A lively book that shows that the lives of students and teachers in the nation of Mozambique are both exciting and difficult.

Timothy Shaw and Adebayo Adedeji, *Economic Crisis in Africa: African Perspectives on Development Problems and Potentials* (Boulder: L. Rienner, 1985).

James D. Traver, *The Demography of Africa* (New York: Praeger, 1996).

J. B. Webster, A. A. Boahen, and M. Tidy, *The Revolutionary Years: West Africa since 1800* (London: Longman, 1980).
An interesting, enjoyable, and competent introductory history to the West African region.

Frank Willett, *African Art* (New York: Oxford University Press, 1971).
A work to read for both reference and pleasure, by one of the authorities on Nigeria's early art.

Crawford Young, *The African Colonial State in Comparative Perspective* (New Haven, CT: Yale University Press, 1997).

COUNTRY AND REGIONAL STUDIES

Howard Adelman and John Sorenson, eds., *African Refugees* (Boulder: Westview, 1993).

Tony Avirgan and Martha Honey, *War in Uganda: The Legacy of Idi Amin* (Westport: Laurence Hill & Co., 1982).

John E. Bardill and James H. Cobbe, *Lesotho: Dilemmas of Dependence in Southern Africa* (Boulder: Westview Press, 1985).

Gerald Bender, *Angola under the Portuguese: The Myth and the Reality* (Berkeley: University of California Press, 1978).

William Bigelow, *Strangers in Their Own Country* (a curriculum on South Africa), 2nd ed. (Trenton: Africa World Press, 1989).

Allan R. Booth, *Swaziland: Tradition and Change in a Southern African Kingdom* (Boulder: Westview Press, 1984).

Thomas Borstelmann, *Apartheid, Colonialism, and the Cold War: The United States and Southern Africa* (New York: Oxford University Press, 1993).

Louis Brenner, ed., *Muslim Identity and Social Change in Sub-Saharan Africa* (Bloomington: Indiana University Press, 1993).

Mike Brogden and Clifford Shearing, *Policing for a New South Africa* (New York: Routledge, 1993).

Marcia M. Burdette, *Zambia: Between Two Worlds* (Boulder: Westview Press, 1988).

Thomas Callaghy and John Ravenhill, eds., *Hemmed In: Global Responses to Africa's Economic Decline* (New York: Columbia University Press, 1994).

Chazen et al., *Politics and Society in Contemporary Africa* (Boulder: Lynne Rienner, 1992).

T. Terry Childs, ed., *Society, Culture, and Technology in Africa* (Philadelphia: MASCA, University of Pennsylvania, 1994).

Christopher Clapham, *Transformation and Continuity in Revolutionary Ethiopia* (Cambridge: Cambridge University Press, 1988).

Robin Cohen and Harry Goulbourne, eds., *Democracy and Socialism in Africa* (Boulder: Westview Press, 1991).

Maureen Covell, *Madagascar: Politics, Economy, and Society* (London and New York: F. Pinter, 1987).

Toyin Falola and Julius Ihonvbere, *The Rise and Fall of Nigeria's Second Republic, 1979–1984* (London: Zed Press, 1985).

Robert Fatton, *The Making of a Liberal Democracy: Senegal's Passive Revolution, 1975–85* (Boulder: L. Rienner, 1987).

Foreign Area Studies (Washington, DC: Government Printing Office). Includes country study handbooks with chapters on history, politics, culture, and economics, with maps, charts, and bibliographies. There are more than 20 in the series, with new ones added and revised periodically.

Marcus Franda, *The Seychelles: Unquiet Islands* (Boulder: Westview Press, 1982).

Sheldon Gellar, *Senegal: An African Nation between Islam and the West* (Boulder: Westview Press, 1982).

April A. Gordon and Donald L. Gordon, *Understanding Contemporary Africa* (Boulder: L. Rienner Publishers, 1996).

Joseph Hanlon, *Mozambique: The Revolution under Fire* (London: Zed Press, 1984).

Tony Hodges, *Western Sahara: The Roots of a Desert War* (Westport: Laurence Hill & Co., 1983).

Allan and Barbara Isaacman, *Mozambique from Colonialism to Revolution, 1900–1982* (Boulder: Westview Press, 1983).

Richard Joseph, *Democracy and Prebendel Politics in Nigeria: The Rise and Fall of the Second Republic* (Cambridge: Cambridge University Press, 1987).

Michael P. Kelley, *A State in Disarray: Conditions of Chad's Survival* (Boulder: Westview Press, 1986).

Gaim Kibreab, *Refugees and Development in Africa: The Case of Eritrea* (Trenton: Red Sea Press, 1987).

Gerhard Kraus, *Human Development from an African Ancestry* (London: Karnak House, 1990).

David D. Laitin and Said S. Samatar, *Somalia: Nation in Search of a State* (Boulder: Westview Press, 1987).

J. Gus Liebenow, *Liberia: Quest for Democracy* (Bloomington: Indiana University Press, 1987).

David Martin and Phyllis Johnson, *The Struggle for Zimbabwe: The Chimurenga War* (Boston: Faber & Faber, 1981).

Norman N. Miller, *Kenya: The Quest for Prosperity* (Boulder: Westview Press, 1984).

Malyn Newitt, *The Comoro Islands: Struggle against Dependency in the Indian Ocean* (Boulder: Westview Press, 1984).

Roland Anthony Oliver, *The African Experience* (London: Weidenfeld & Nicholson, 1991).

Adebayo O. Olukoshi and Liisa Laakso, *Challenges to the Nation-State in Africa* (Uppsala: Nordiska Afrikainstitutet, in cooperation with Institute of Development Studies, University of Helsinki, 1996).

Thomas O'Toole, *The Central African Republic: The Continent's Hidden Heart* (Boulder: Westview Press, 1986).

Jack Parson, *Botswana: Liberal Democracy and the Labor Resource in Southern Africa* (Boulder: Westview Press, 1984).

Deborah Pellow and Naomi Chazan, *Ghana: Coping with Uncertainty* (Boulder: Westview Press, 1986).

F. Jeffress Ramsay, Barry Morton, and Themba Mgadla, *Building a Nation: A History of Botswana* (Gaborne: Longman Botswana, 1996).

Richard Sandbrook, *The Politics of Africa's Economic Recovery* (Cambridge: Cambridge University Press, 1993).

Alexander Sarris, *Ghana under Structural Adjustment* (New York: New York University Press, 1991).

Bereket Habte Selassie, *Conflict and Intervention in the Horn of Africa* (New York: Monthly Review Press, 1980).

Study Commission on U.S. Policy toward Southern Africa, *South Africa: Time Running Out* (Berkeley and Los Angeles: University of California Press, 1981).

Christopher C. Taylor, *Milk, Honey, and Money: Changing Concepts in Rwandan Healing* (Washington: Smithsonian Institution Press, 1992).

Time-Life Books, ed., *Africa's Glorious Legacy* (Alexandria, VA: Time-Life Books, 1994).

Rachid Tlemcani, *State and Revolution in Algeria* (Boulder: Westview Press, 1987).

Jan Vansina, *Habitat, Economy, and Society in the Central African Rainforest* (Providence: Berg Publishers, 1992).

Margaret A. Vogt, ed., *The Liberian Crisis and ECOMOG, a Bold Attempt at Regional Peacekeeping* (Lagos, Nigeria: Gabumo Publishing Co., 1992).

C. W. Wigwe, *Language, Culture, and Society in West Africa* (Elms Court, UK: Arthur H. Stockwell, 1990).

Michael Wolfers and Jane Bergerol, *Angola in the Frontline* (London: Zed Press, 1983).

Rodger Yeager, *Tanzania: An African Experiment* (Boulder: Westview Press, 1983).